ISBN 978-1-333-53281-9
PIBN 10516398

NOTICE.

H. S. NICHOLS, Ltd., respectfully beg to call the attention of purchasers to the fact that all Books issued by them are intended to be sold at the net advertised prices without deduction, and that they are supplied to Booksellers on terms which will not allow of any discount being given by them to the public.

THE LIBRARY EDITION

OF

The Arabian Nights' Entertainments

ILLUSTRATED

VOLUME VIII

No. 54.

Ma'aruf the Cobbler and his Wife Fatimah.

"Now while he sat weeping, behold, the wall clave and there came forth to him therefrom one of tall stature, whose aspect caused his body-pile to bristle and his flesh to creep."

TRANSLATED FROM THE ARABIC BY

CAPTAIN SIR R. F. BURTON

K.C.M.G. F.R.G.S. &c. &c. &c.

REPRINTED FROM THE ORIGINAL EDITION AND EDITED BY

LEONARD C. SMITHERS

ILLUSTRATED BY A SERIES OF SEVENTY-ONE ORIGINAL ILLUSTRATIONS REPRODUCED FROM THE ORIGINAL PICTURES IN OILS SPECIALLY PAINTED BY

ALBERT LETCHFORD

IN TWELVE VOLUMES—VOLUME VIII

H. S. NICHOLS LTD.

39 CHARING CROSS ROAD LONDON W.C.

MDCCCXCVII

PRINTED BY H. S. NICHOLS, LTD., 39 CHARING CROSS ROAD, LONDON, W.C.

VOLUME X.

PLAIN AND LITERAL TRANSLATION OF

ARABIAN NIGHTS' ENTERTAINMENTS, N

TITULED

THE BOOK OF THE

ousand Nights and a Nig

H INTRODUCTION EXPLANATORY NOTES ON

NNERS AND CUSTOMS OF MOSLEM MEN AND

MINAL ESSAY UPON THE HISTORY OF TH

GHTS

BY

RICHARD F. BURTON

TO

HIS EXCELLENCY YACOUB ARTIN PASHA,

MINISTER OF INSTRUCTION, ETC. ETC. ETC. CAIRO.

MY DEAR PASHA,

During the last dozen years, since we first met at Cairo, you have done much for Egyptian folk-lore and you can do much more. This volume is inscribed to you with a double purpose; first it is intended as a public expression of gratitude for your friendly assistance; and, secondly, as a memento that the samples which you have given us imply a promise of further gift. With this lively sense of favours to come I subscribe myself

Ever your friend and fellow worker,

RICHARD F. BURTON.

LONDON, *July* 12, 1886.

LIST OF ILLUSTRATIONS TO THE EIGHTH VOLUME.

(*LIBRARY EDITION.*)

PAGE

No. 54. MA'ARUF THE COBBLER AND HIS WIFE FATIMAH.

"Now while he sat weeping, behold, the wall clave and there came forth to him therefrom one of tall stature, whose aspect caused his body-pile to bristle and his flesh to creep" . . *(frontispiece)* 6

" 55. MA'ARUF THE COBBLER AND HIS WIFE FATIMAH.

"Then they entered the Cathedral-mosque and prayed the noon-prayers, and what was left him of the thousand gold pieces he scattered on the heads of the worshippers" 12

" 56. MA'ARUF THE COBBLER AND HIS WIFE FATIMAH.

"So the Jinni signed with his hand to the ground, which clave asunder . . . presently, there came forth young boys full of grace and fair of face, bearing golden baskets filled with gold" . 28

" 57. MA'ARUF THE COBBLER AND HIS WIFE FATIMAH.

"She dealt him a kick, her foot striking him full in the stomach, and he fell over on his back senseless; whereupon she cried out to her attendants, who came to her in haste" 42

CONTENTS OF THE EIGHTH VOLUME.

PA

170. MA'ARUF THE COBBLER AND HIS WIFE FATIMAH . .

(Lane—Vol. III. The Story of Maaroof: pp. 671-732.*)*

CONCLUSION . . . .

TERMINAL ESSAY.

PRELIMINARY . . . .

§I. THE ORIGIN OF THE NIGHTS—

A. The Birthplace . . . .

B. The Date . . . .

C. The Authors . . . .

§II. THE NIGHTS IN EUROPE— . . . .

§III. THE MATTER AND THE MANNER OF THE NIGHTS—

A. The Matter I

B. The Manner . . . .

§IV. SOCIAL CONDITION—

A. Al-Islam 1

B. Woman 1

C. Pornography 1

D. Pederasty 1

Contents.

PAGE

§V. OF THE PROSE RHYME AND THE POETRY OF THE NIGHTS—

A. The Saj'a 188

B. The Verse 190

Essay on Arabic Prosody, by Dr Steingass 202

L'ENVOI 228

ENDIX I.—

CONTRIBUTIONS TO THE BIBLIOGRAPHY OF THE THOUSAND AND ONE NIGHTS AND THEIR IMITATIONS, BY W. F. KIRBY 233

ENDIX II.—

I. TABLE OF CONTENTS OF THE VARIOUS ARABIC TEXTS—

A. The Unfinished Calcutta Edition (1814-1818) 308

B. The Breslau Text 310

C. The MacNaghten Text and the Bulak Edition 316

D. The same with Mr. Lane's and my Version 322

II. INDEX TO THE TALES AND PROPER NAMES 323

III. ALPHABETICAL TABLE OF THE NOTES (ANTHROPOLOGICAL, &c.) . 334

MA'ARUF THE COBBLER AND HIS WIFE FATIMAH.

THERE dwelt once upon a time in the God-guarded city of Cairo a cobbler who lived by patching old shoes.[1] His name was Ma'aruf[2] and he had a wife called Fatimah, whom the folk had nicknamed "The Dung[3]"; for that she was a whorish, worthless wretch, scanty of shame and mickle of mischief. She ruled her spouse and used to abuse him and curse him a thousand times a day; and he feared her malice and dreaded her misdoings; for that he was a sensible man and careful of his repute, but poor-conditioned. When he earned much he spent it on her, and when he gained little, she revenged herself on his body that night, leaving him no peace and making his night black as her book[4]; for she was even as of one like her saith the poet —

How manifold nights have I passed with my wife * In the saddest plight with all misery rife:
Would Heaven when first I went in to her * With a cup of cold poison I'd ta'en her life.

Amongst other afflictions which befell him from her, one day she said to him, "O Ma'aruf, I wish thee to bring me this night a vermicelli-cake dressed with bees' honey.[5]" He replied, "So Allah Almighty aid me to its price, I will bring it thee. By Allah, I

1 Arab. "Zarábín" (pl. of zarbún), lit. slaves' shoes or sandals, the chaussure worn by Mamelukes. Here the word is used in its modern sense of stout shoes or walking boots.

2 The popular word means goodness, etc., *e.g.* "A'mil al-Ma'arúf" = have the kindness; do me the favour.

3 Dozy translates "'Urrah" = Une Mégère: Lane terms it a "vulgar word signifying a wicked, mischievous shrew." But it is the fem. form of 'Urr = dung; not a bad name for a daughter of Billingsgate; and reminds us of the term "Dung-beardlings," applied by the amiable Hallgerda to her enemy's sons. (The Story of Burnt Njal, ii. 47.)

4 *i.e.* black like the book of her actions, which would be shown to her on Doomsday. (See night dccclxxi.) The ungodly hold it in the left hand, the right being bound behind their backs, and they appear in ten foul forms, apes, swine, etc., for which see Sale, sect. iv.

5 The "Kunáfah" (vermicelli-cake) is a favourite dish of wheaten flour, worked somewhat finer than our vermicelli, fried with samn (butter melted and clarified) and sweetened with honey or sugar. See Lane, M. E. chapt. v. Bees' honey is opposed to various syrups which are used as sweeteners. See night cccclxxxiv.

have no dirhams to-day, but our Lord will make things easy.[1]" Rejoined she,——And Shahrazad perceived the dawn of day and ceased to say her permitted say.

Now when it was the Nine Hundred and Ninetieth Night,

She resumed, It hath reached me, O auspicious King, that Ma'aruf the Cobbler said to his spouse, "If Allah aid me to its price, I will bring it to thee this night. By Allah, I have no dirhams to-day, but our Lord will make things easy to me!" She rejoined, "I wot naught of these words; whether He aid thee or aid thee not, look thou come not to me save with the vermicelli and bees' honey; and if thou come without it I will make thy night black as thy fortune whenas thou marriedst me and fellest into my hand." Quoth he, "Allah is bountiful!" and going out with grief scattering itself from his body, prayed the dawn-prayer and opened his shop, saying, "I beseech thee, O Lord, to vouchsafe me the price of the Kunafah and ward off from me the mischief of yonder wicked woman this night!" After which he sat in the shop till noon, but no work came to him and his fear of his wife redoubled. Then he arose and locking his shop, went out perplexed as to how he should do in the matter of the vermicelli-cake, seeing he had not even the wherewithal to buy bread. Presently he came up to the shop of the Kunafah-seller and stood before it distraught, whilst his eyes brimmed with tears. The pastry-cook glanced at him and said, "O Master Ma'aruf, why dost thou weep? Tell me what hath befallen thee.' So he acquainted him with his case, saying, "My wife is a shrew, a virago who would have me bring her a Kunafah: but I have sat in my shop till past mid-day and have not gained even the price of bread; wherefore I am in fear of her." The cook laughed and said, "No harm shall come to thee. How many pounds wilt thou have?" "Five pounds," answered Ma'aruf. So the man weighed him out five pounds of vermicelli-cake and said to him, "I have clarified butter, but no bees' honey. Here is drip-honey,[2] however, which is better than bees' honey; and what harm will there be if it be with drip-honey?" Ma'aruf was ashamed to object, because the pastry-cook was to have patience with him for the price, and

1 *i.e.* will send us aid. The Shrew's rejoinder is highly impious in Moslem opinion.

2 Arab "Asal Katr"; "a fine kind of black honey, treacle," says Lane; but it is afterwards called cane-honey ('Asal Kasab) I have never heard it applied to "the syrup which exudes from ripe dates when hung up."

said, "Give it me with drip-honey." So he fried a vermicelli-cake for him with butter and drenched it with drip-honey, till it was fit to present to Kings. Then he asked him, "Dost thou want bread[1] and cheese?" and Ma'aruf answered, "Yes." So he gave him four half-dirhams' worth of bread and one of cheese, and the vermicelli was ten nusfs. Then said he, "Know, O Ma'aruf, that thou owest me fifteen nusfs, so go to thy wife and make merry and take this nusf for the Hammam; and thou shalt have credit for a day or two or three till Allah provide thee with thy daily bread. And straiten not thy wife, for I will have patience with thee till such time as thou shalt have dirhams to spare." So Ma'aruf took the vermicelli-cake and bread and cheese and went away, with a heart at ease, blessing the pastry-cook and saying, "Extolled be Thy perfection, O my Lord! How bountiful art Thou!" When he came home, his wife enquired of him, "Hast thou brought the vermicelli-cake?" and replying "Yes," he set it before her. She looked at it and seeing that it was dressed with cane-honey,[2] said to him, "Did I not bid thee bring it with bees' honey? Wilt thou contrary my wish and have it dressed with cane-honey?" He excused himself to her, saying, "I bought it not save on credit"; but said she, "This talk is idle; I will not eat Kunafah save with bees' honey." And she was wroth with it and threw it in his face, saying, "Begone, thou pimp, and bring me other than this!" Then she dealt him a buffet on the cheek and knocked out one of his teeth. The blood ran down upon his breast and for stress of anger he smote her on the head a single blow and a slight; whereupon she clutched his beard and fell to shouting out and saying, "Help, O Moslems!" So the neighbours came in and freed his beard from her grip; then they reproved and reproached her, saying, "We are all content to eat Kunafah with cane-honey. Why, then, wilt thou oppress this poor man thus? Verily, this is disgraceful in thee!" And they went on to soothe her till they made peace between her and him. But, when the folk were gone, she sware that she would not eat of the vermicelli, and Ma'aruf, burning with hunger, said in himself, "She sweareth that she will not eat; so I will e'en eat." Then he ate, and when she saw him eating, she said, "Inshallah, may

---

1 Arab. "'Aysh," lit. = that on which man lives: "Khubz" being the more popular term. "Hubz and Joobn" is well-known at Malta.

2 Arab. "Asal Kasab," *i.e.* sugar, possibly made from sorgho-stalks (*Holcus sorghum*), of which I made syrup in Central Africa.

the eating of it be poison to destroy the far one's body.[1]" Quoth he, "It shall not be at thy bidding"; and went on eating, laughing and saying, "Thou swarest that thou wouldst not eat of this; but Allah is bountiful, and to-morrow night, an the Lord decree, I will bring thee Kunafah dressed with bees' honey, and thou shalt eat it alone." And he applied himself to appeasing her, whilst she called down curses upon him; and she ceased not to rail at him and revile him with gross abuse till the morning, when she bared her fore-arm to beat him. Quoth he, "Give me time and I will bring thee other vermicelli-cake." Then he went out to the mosque and prayed, after which he betook himself to his shop and opening it, sat down; but hardly had he done this when up came two runners from the Kazi's court and said to him, "Up with thee, speak with the Kazi, for thy wife hath complained of thee to him and her favour is thus and thus." He recognised her by their description; and saying, "May Allah Almighty torment her!" walked with them till he came to the Kazi's presence, where he found Fatimah standing with her arm bound up and her face-veil besmeared with blood; and she was weeping and wiping away her tears. Quoth the Kazi, "Ho man, hast thou no fear of Allah the Most High? Why hast thou beaten this good woman and broken her fore-arm and knocked out her tooth and entreated her thus?" And quoth Ma'aruf, "If I beat her or put out her tooth, sentence me to what thou wilt; but in truth the case was thus and thus, and the neighbours made peace between me and her." And he told him the story from first to last. Now this Kazi was a benevolent man; so he brought out to him a quarter dinar, saying, "O man, take this and get her Kunafah with bees' honey and do ye make peace, thou and she." Quoth Ma'aruf, "Give it to her." So she took it and the Kazi made peace between them, saying, "O wife, obey thy husband; and thou, O man, deal kindly with her.[2]" Then they left the court, reconciled at the Kazi's hands, and the woman went one way, whilst her husband returned by another way to his shop and sat there, when, behold, the runners came up to him and said, "Give us our fee." Quoth he, "The Kazi took not of me aught; on the contrary, he gave me a quarter dinar." But quoth they, "'Tis no concern of ours whether the Kazi took of thee or gave to thee, and if thou give us not our fee, we will exact

1 For this unpleasant euphemy see vol. iii. night cccxx.

2 This is a true picture of the leniency with which women were treated in the Kasi's court at Cairo.

it in spite of thee." And they fell to dragging him about the market; so he sold his tools and gave them half a dinar, whereupon they let him go and went away, whilst he put his hand to his cheek and sat sorrowful, for that he had no tools wherewith to work. Presently, up came two ill-favoured fellows and said to him, "Come, O man, and speak with the Kazi; for thy wife hath complained of thee to him." Said he, "He made peace between us just now." But said they, "We come from another Kazi, and thy wife hath complained of thee to our Kazi." So he arose and went with them to their Kazi, calling on Allah for aid against her; and when he saw her, he said to her, "Did we not make peace, good woman?" Whereupon she cried, "There abideth no peace between me and thee." Accordingly he came forward and told the Kasi his story, adding, "And indeed the Kazi Such-an-one made peace between us this very hour." Whereupon the Kazi said to her, "O strumpet, since ye two have made peace each with other, why comest thou to me complaining?" Quoth she, "He beat me after that"; but quoth the Kazi, "Make peace each with other, and beat her not again, and she will cross thee no more." So they made peace and the Kazi said to Ma'aruf, "Give the runners their fee." So he gave them their fee and going back to his shop, opened it and sat down, as he were a drunken man for excess of the chagrin which befell him. Presently, while he was still sitting, behold, a man came up to him and said, "O Ma'aruf, rise and hide thyself, for thy wife hath complained of thee to the High Court[1] and Abú Tabak[2] is after thee." So he shut his shop and fled towards the Gate of Victory.[3] He had five Nusfs of silver left of the price of the lasts and gear; and therewith he bought four worth of bread and one of cheese as he fled from her. Now it was the winter season and the hour of mid-afternoon prayer; so, when he came out among the rubbish-mounds the rain descended upon him, like water from the mouths of water-skins, and his clothes were drenched. He therefore entered the 'Ádiliyah,[4]

---

1 Arab. "Báb al-Áli" = the high gate or Sublime Porte; here used of the Chief Kazi's court: the phrase is a descendant of the Coptic "Per-ao" whence "Pharaoh."

2 "Abú Tabak," in Cairene slang is an officer who arrests by order of the Kazi, and means "Father of whipping" (= tabaka, a low word for beating, thrashing, whopping), because he does his duty with all possible violence *in terrorem*.

3 Bab al-Nasr, the Eastern or Desert Gate: see night dcxv.

4 This is a mosque outside the great gate built by Al-Malik al-'Ádil Tuman Bey in A.H. 906 (= 1501). The date is *not* worthy of much remark, for these names are often inserted by the scribe—for which see Terminal Essay.

where he saw a ruined place and therein a deserted cell without a door; and in it he took refuge and found shelter from the rain. The tears streamed from his eyelids, and he fell to complaining of what had betided him, and saying, "Whither shall I flee from this whore? I beseech Thee, O Lord, to vouchsafe me one who shall conduct me to a far country, where she shall not know the way to me!" Now while he sat weeping, behold, the wall clave and there came forth to him therefrom one of tall stature, whose aspect caused his body-pile to bristle and his flesh to creep, and said to him, "O man, what aileth thee that thou disturbest me this night? These two hundred years have I dwelt here and have never seen any enter this place and do as thou dost. Tell me what thou wishest and I will accomplish thy need, as ruth for thee hath got hold upon my heart." Quoth Ma'aruf, "Who and what art thou?" and quoth he, "I am the Haunter[1] of this place." So Ma'aruf told him all that had befallen him with his wife and he said, "Wilt thou have me convey thee to a country where thy wife shall know no way to thee?" "Yes," said Ma'aruf; and the other, "Then mount my back." So he mounted on his back and he flew with him from after supper-tide till daybreak, when he set him down on the top of a high mountain,——And Shahrazad perceived the dawn of day and ceased saying her permitted say.

Now when it was the Nine Hundred and Ninety-first Night,

She said, It hath reached me, O auspicious King, that the Marid having taken up Ma'aruf the Cobbler, flew off with him, and set him down upon a high mountain, and said to him, "O mortal, descend this mountain and thou wilt see the gate of a city. Enter it, for therein thy wife cannot come at thee." He then left him and went his way, whilst Ma'aruf abode in amazement and perplexity till the sun rose, when he said to himself, "I will up with me and go down into the city; indeed, there is no profit in my abiding upon this highland." So he descended to the mountain-foot and saw a city girt by towering walls, full of lofty palaces and gold-adorned buildings which was a delight to beholders. He entered in at the gate and found it a place such as lightened the grieving heart; but as he walked

1 Arab. "'Ámir" lit.=one who inhabiteth, a peopler: here used in technical sense. As has been seen, ruins and impure places such as privies and Hammám-baths are the favourite homes of the Jinn. The fire-drake in the text was summoned by the Cobbler's exclamation, and even Marids at times do a kindly action.

through the streets the towns-folk stared at him as a curiosity, and gathered about him, marvelling at his dress, for it was unlike theirs. Presently, one of them said to him, "O man, art thou a stranger?" "Yes." "What countryman art thou?" "I am from the city of Cairo the Auspicious." "And when didst thou leave Cairo?" "I left it yesterday at the hour of afternoon-prayer." Whereupon the man laughed at him, and cried out, saying, "Come look, O folk, at this man and hear what he saith!" Quoth they, "What doth he say?" and quoth the townsman, "He pretendeth that he cometh from Cairo and left it yesterday at the hour of afternoon-prayer!" At this they all laughed, and gathering round Ma'aruf, said to him, "O man, art thou mad to talk thus? How canst thou pretend that thou leftest Cairo at mid-afternoon yesterday and foundedst thyself this morning here, when the truth is that between our city and Cairo lieth a full year's journey?" Quoth he, "None is mad but you. As for me, I speak sooth, for here is bread which I brought with me from Cairo, and see 'tis yet new." Then he showed them the bread, and they stared at it, for it was unlike their country bread. So the crowd increased about him, and they said one to another, "This is Cairo bread: look at it"; and he became a gazing-stock in the city, and some believed him, whilst others gave him the lie and made mock of him. Whilst this was going on, behold, up came a merchant, riding on a she-mule and followed by two black slaves, and brake a way through the people, saying, "O folk, are ye not ashamed to mob this stranger and make mock of him and scoff at him?" And he went on to rate them till he drave them away from Ma'aruf, and none could make him any answer. Then he said to the stranger, "Come, O my brother, no harm shall betide thee from these folk. Verily they have no shame.[1]" So he took him, and carrying him to a spacious and richly-adorned house, seated him in a speak-room fit for a King, whilst he gave an order to his slaves, who opened a chest and brought out to him a dress such as might be worn by a merchant, worth a thousand.[2] He clad him therewith, and Ma'aruf, being a seemly man, became as he were consul of the merchants. Then his host called for food, and they set before them a tray of all manner exquisite viands. The twain ate and drank, and the merchant said to Ma'aruf, "O my brother, what is thy name?" "My name is Ma'aruf, and I am a cobbler by trade and patch old

1 The style is modern Cairene jargon.
2 Purses or gold pieces, see night dccccl xxxi.

shoes." "What countryman art thou?" "I am from Cairo." "What quarter?" "Dost thou know Cairo?" "I am of its children.[1]" "I come from the Red Street.[2]" "And whom dost thou know in the Red Street?" "I know Such-an-one and Such-an-one," answered Ma'aruf, and named several people to him. Quoth the other, "Knowest thou Shaykh Ahmad the druggist[3]?" "He was my next neighbour, wall to wall." "Is he well?" "Yes." "How many sons hath he?" "Three: Mustafà, Mohammed, and Ali." "And what hath Allah done with them?" "As for Mustafà, he is well, and he is a learned man, a professor[4]; Mohammed is a druggist, and opened him a shop beside that of his father, after he had married, and his wife hath borne him a son named Hasan." "Allah gladden thee with good news!" said the merchant; and Ma'aruf continued, "As for Ali, he was my friend when we were boys, and we always played together, I and he. We used to go in the guise of the children of the Nazarenes, and enter the church and steal the books of the Christians and sell them and buy food with the price. It chanced once that the Nazarenes caught us with a book; whereupon they complained of us to our folk and said to Ali's father:—An thou hinder not thy son from troubling us, we will complain of thee to the King. So he appeased them and gave Ali a thrashing; wherefore he ran away none knew whither, and he hath now been absent twenty years and no man hath brought news of him." Quoth the host, "I am that very Ali, son of Shaykh Ahmad the druggist, and thou art my playmate Ma'aruf.[5]" So they saluted each other, and after the salam Ali said, "Tell me why, O Ma'aruf, thou camest from Cairo to this city." Then he told him all that had befallen him of ill-doing with his wife Fatimah the Dung, and said, "So, when her annoy waxed on me, I fled from her towards the Gate of Victory and went forth the city. Presently, the rain fell heavy on me; so I entered a ruined cell in the Adiliyah, and sat there, weeping; whereupon there came forth to me the Haunter of the place, which was an Ifrit of the Jinn, and questioned me. I acquainted

---

1 *i.e.* I am a Cairene.

2 Ara . "Darb al-Ahmar," a street still existing near to and outside the noble Bab Zuwaylah, for which see vol. i. night xxv.

3 Arab. "'Attár," perfume-seller and druggist; the word is connected with our "Ottar" ('Atr).

4 Arab. "Mudarris" lit.=one who gives lessons or lectures (dars), and pop. applied to a professor in a collegiate mosque like Al-Azhar of Cairo.

5 This thoroughly dramatic scene is told with a charming naïveté. No wonder that The Nights has been made the basis of a national theatre amongst the Turks.

him with my case and he took me on his back and flew with me all night between heaven and earth, till he set me down on yonder mountain and gave me to know of this city. So I came down from the mountain and entered the city, when the people crowded about me and questioned me. I told them that I had left Cairo yesterday, but they believed me not, and presently thou camest up and, driving the folk away from me, carriedst me to this house. Such, then, is the cause of my quitting Cairo; and thou, what object brought thee hither?" Quoth Ali, "The giddiness[1] of folly turned my head when I was seven years old, from which time I wandered from land to land and city to city, till I came to this city, the name whereof is Ikhtiyán al-Khatan.[2] I found its people an hospitable folk and a kindly, compassionate for the poor man and selling to him on credit and believing all he said. So quoth I to them:—I am a merchant aud have preceded my packs, and I need a place wherein to bestow my baggage. And they believed me and assigned me a lodging. Then quoth I to them:—Is there any of you will lend me a thousand dinars till my loads arrive, when I will repay it to him; for I am in want of certain things before my goods come? They gave me what I asked, and I went to the merchants' bazar, where, seeing goods, I bought them and sold them next day at a profit of fifty gold pieces and bought others.[3] And I consorted with the folk and entreated them liberally, so that they loved me, and I continued to sell and buy, till I grew rich. Know, O my brother, that the proverb saith, The world is show and trickery: and the land where none wotteth thee, there do whatso liketh thee. Thou too, an thou say to all who ask thee, I'm a cobbler by trade and poor withal, and I fled from my wife and left Cairo yesterday, they will not believe thee and thou wilt be a laughing-stock among them as long as thou abidest in the city; whilst, an thou tell them, An Ifrit brought me hither, they will take fright at thee

---

1 Arab. "Taysh" lit. = vertigo, swimming of head.

2 Here Trébutien (iii. 265) reads "la ville de Khaïtan (so the Mac. Edit. iv. 708) capital du royaume de Sohatan." Ikhtiyán Lane suggests to be fictitious: Khatan is a district of Tartary east of Káshgar, so called by Sádik al-Isfaháni, p. 24.

3 This is a true picture of the tact and *savoir faire* of the Cairenes. It was a study to see how, under the late Khedive, they managed to take precedence of Europeans who found themselves in the background before they knew it. For instance, every Bey, whose degree is that of a Colonel, was made an "Excellency," and ranked accordingly at Court, whilst his father, some poor Fellah, was ploughing the ground. Tanfik Pasha began his ill-omened rule by always placing natives close to him in the place of honour, addressing them first, and otherwise snubbing Europeans who, when English, were often too obtuse to notice the petty insults lavished upon them.

and none will come near thee; for they will say, This man is possessed of an Ifrit and harm will betide whoso approacheth him. And such public report will be dishonouring both to thee and to me, because they ken I come from Cairo." Ma'aruf asked:— "How, then, shall I do?" and Ali answered, "I will tell thee how thou shalt do, Inshallah! To-morrow I will give thee a thousand dinars and a she-mule to ride and a black slave, who shall walk before thee and guide thee to the gate of the merchants' bazar; and do thou go into them. I will be there sitting amongst them, and when I see thee, I will rise to thee and salute thee with the salam and kiss thy hand and make a great man of thee. Whenever I ask thee of any kind of stuff, saying, Hast thou brought with thee aught of such a kind? do thou answer, 'Plenty.'[1] And if they question me of thee, I will praise thee and magnify thee in their eyes and say to them, Get him a store-house and a shop. I also will give thee out for a man of great wealth and generosity; and if a beggar come to thee, bestow upon him what thou mayst; so will they put faith in what I say, and believe in thy greatness and generosity and love thee. Then will I invite thee to my house and invite all the merchants on thy account and bring together thee and them, so that all may know thee and thou know them,"—And Shahrazad perceived the dawn of day and ceased to say her permitted say.

Now when it was the Nine Hundred and Ninety-second Night,

She continued, It hath reached me, O auspicious King, that the merchant Ali said to Ma'aruf, "I will invite thee to my house and invite all the merchants on thy account and bring together thee and them, so that all may know thee and thou know them, whereby thou shalt sell and buy and take and give with them; nor will it be long ere thou become a man of money." Accordingly, on the morrow he gave him a thousand dinars and a suit of clothes and a black slave, and mounting him on a she-mule, said to him, "Allah give thee quittance of responsibility for all this,[2] inasmuch as thou art my friend and it behoveth me to deal generously with thee. Have no care; but put away from thee the thought of thy wife's mis-ways and name her not to any." "Allah requite thee with good!" replied Ma'aruf, and rode on, preceded by his blackamoor

1 Arab. "Kathir" (pron. Katir) = much: here used in its slang sense, "no end."

2 *i.e.* "May the Lord soon make thee able to repay me; but meanwhile I give it to thee for thy own free use."

till the slave brought him to the gate of the merchants' bazar, where they were all seated, and amongst them Ali, who when he saw him rose and threw himself upon him, crying, "A blessed day, O Merchant Ma'aruf, O man of good works and kindness[1]!" And he kissed his hand before the merchants and said to them, "Our brothers, ye are honoured by knowing[2] the merchant Ma'aruf." So they saluted him, and Ali signed to them to make much of him, wherefore he was magnified in their eyes. Then Ali helped him to dismount from his she-mule and saluted him with the salam; after which he took the merchants apart, one after other, and vaunted Ma'aruf to them. They asked, "Is this man a merchant?" and he answered, "Yes; and indeed he is the chiefest of merchants, there liveth not a wealthier than he; for his wealth and the riches of his father and forefathers are famous among the merchants of Cairo. He hath partners in Hind and Sind and Al-Yaman, and is high in repute for generosity. So know ye his rank and exalt ye his degree and do him service, and wot also that his coming to your city is not for the sake of traffic, and none other save to divert himself with the sight of folk's countries: indeed, he hath no need of strangerhood for the sake of gain and profit, having wealth that fires cannot consume, and I am one of his servants," and he ceased not to extol him, till they set him above their heads and began to tell one another of his qualities. Then they gathered round him and offered him junkets[3] and sherbets, and even the Consul of the Merchants came to him and saluted him; whilst Ali proceeded to ask him, in the presence of the traders, "O my lord, haply thou hast brought with thee somewhat of such and such a stuff?" and Ma'aruf answered, "Plenty." Now Ali had that day shown him various kinds of costly clothes and had taught him the names of the different stuffs, dear and cheap. Then said one of the merchants, "O my lord, hast thou brought with thee yellow broad cloth?" and Ma'aruf said, "Plenty!" Quoth another, "And gazelles' blood red[4]?" and quoth the cobbler, "Plenty"; and as often as he asked him of aught, he made him the same answer. So the other said, "O Merchant Ali, had thy countryman a mind to transport a thousand

---

1 Punning upon his name. Much might be written upon the significance of names as ominous of good and evil; but the subject is far too extensive for a footnote.

2 Lane translates "Ánisa-kum" by "he hath delighted you by his arrival"; Mr. Payne, "I commend him to you."

3 Arab. "Fatúrát" = light food for the early breakfast, of which the "Fatirah"-cake was a favourite item. See vol. i. night xxix.

4 A dark red dye (Lane).

loads of costly stuffs, he could do so"; and Ali said, "He would take them from a single one of his store-houses, and miss naught thereof." Now whilst they were sitting, behold, up came a beggar and went the round of the merchants. One gave him a half-dirham and another a copper,[1] but most of them gave him nothing, till he came to Ma'aruf, who pulled out a handful of gold and gave it to him, whereupon he blessed him and went his ways. The merchants marvelled at this and said, "Verily, this is a King's bestowal, for he gave the beggar gold without count, and were he not a man of vast wealth and money without end, he had not given a beggar a handful of gold." After a while, there came to him a poor woman and he gave her a handful of gold; whereupon she went away, blessing him, and told the other beggars, who came to him, one after other, and he gave them each a handful of gold, till he disbursed the thousand dinars. Then he struck hand upon hand and said, "Allah is our sufficient aid and excellent is the Agent!" Quoth the Consul, "What aileth thee, O Merchant Ma'aruf?" and quoth he, "It seemeth that the most part of the people of this city are poor and needy; had I known their misery I would have brought with me a large sum of money in my saddle-bags and given largesse thereof to the poor. I fear me I may be long abroad[2] and 'tis not in my nature to baulk a beggar; and I have no gold left: so if a pauper come to me, what shall I say to him?" Quoth the Consul, "Say, Allah will send thee thy daily bread[3]!" but Ma'aruf replied, "That is not my practice, and I am care-ridden because of this. Would I had other thousand dinars wherewith to give alms till my baggage come!" "Have no care for that," quoth the Consul and sending one of his dependants for a thousand dinars, handed them to Ma'aruf, who went on giving them to every beggar who passed, till the call to noon-prayer. Then they entered the Cathedral-mosque and prayed the noon-prayers, and what was left him of the thousand gold pieces he scattered on the heads of the worshippers. This drew the people's attention to him and they blessed him, whilst the merchants marvelled at the abundance of his generosity and open-handedness. Then he turned to another trader, and borrowing of him other thousand ducats, gave these also away, whilst Merchant Ali looked on at what he did, but could not speak. He ceased not to do thus till the call to mid-afternoon prayer, when

1 Arab. "Jadid," see night dccccxxi.

2 Both the texts read thus, but the reading has little sense. Ma'aruf probably would say, "I fear that my loads will be long coming."

3 One of the many formulas of polite refusal.

No. 55.

Ma'aruf the Cobbler and his Wife Fatimah.

" Then they entered the Cathedral-mosque and prayed the noon-prayers, and what was left him of the thousand gold pieces he scattered on the heads of the worshippers."

he entered the mosque and prayed and distributed the rest of the money. On this wise, by the time they locked the doors of the bazar[1] he had borrowed five thousand sequins and given them away, saying to every one of whom he took aught, "Wait till my baggage come when, if thou desire gold I will give thee gold, and if thou desire stuffs, thou shalt have stuffs; for I have no end of them." At eventide Merchant Ali invited Ma'aruf and the rest of the traders to an entertainment and seated him in the upper end, the place of honour, where he talked of nothing but cloths and jewels, and whenever they made mention to him of aught, he said, "I have plenty of it." Next day he again repaired to the market-street, where he showed a friendly bias towards the merchants and borrowed of them more money, which he distributed to the poor: nor did he leave doing thus twenty days, till he had borrowed threescore thousand dinars, and still there came no baggage, no, nor a burning plague.[2] At last folk began to clamour for their money, and say, "The merchant Ma'aruf's baggage cometh not. How long will he take people's moneys and give them to the poor?" And quoth one of them, "My rede is that we speak to Merchant Ali." So they went to him and said, "O Merchant Ali, Merchant Ma'aruf's baggage cometh not." Said he, "Have patience, it cannot fail to come soon." Then he took Ma'aruf aside and said to him, "O Ma'aruf, what fashion is this? Did I bid thee brown[3] the bread or burn it? The merchants clamour for their coin and tell me that thou owest them sixty thousand dinars, which thou hast borrowed and given away to the poor. How wilt thou satisfy the folk, seeing that thou neither sellest nor buyest?" Said Ma'aruf, "What matters it[4]; and what are threescore thousand dinars? When my baggage shall come I will pay them in stuffs, or in gold and silver, as they will." Quoth Merchant Ali, "Allah is Most Great! Hast thou, then, any baggage?" and he said, "Plenty." Cried the other, "Allah and the Hallows[5] requite thee thine impudence! Did I teach thee this saying, that thou shouldst

1 Each bazar, in a large city like Damascus, has its tall and heavy wooden doors, which are locked every evening and opened in the morning by the Ghafir or guard. The "silver key," however, always lets one in.

2 Arab. "Wa lá Kabbata hámiyah," a Cairene vulgarism meaning, "There came nothing to profit him nor to rid the people of him."

3 Arab. "Kammir," *i.e.* brown it before the fire, toast it.

4 It is insinuated that he had lied till he himself believed the lie to be truth—not an uncommon process, I may remark.

5 Arab. "Rijál" = the Men, equivalent to the Walis, Saints, or Santons; with perhaps an allusion to the Rijál al-Ghayb, the Invisible Controls, concerning whom I have quoted Herklots in vol. ii. night lxxxiv.

repeat it to me? But I will acquaint the folk with thee." Ma'aruf rejoined, "Begone and prate no more! Am I a poor man? I have endless wealth in my baggage, and as soon as it cometh they shall have their money's worth, two for one. I have no need of them." At this Merchant Ali waxed wroth and said, "Unmannerly wight that thou art, I will teach thee to lie to me and be not ashamed!" Said Ma'aruf, "E'en work the worst thy hand can do! They must wait till my baggage come, when they shall have their due and more." So Ali left him and went away, saying in himself, "I praised him whilome and if I blame him now, I make myself out a liar and become of those of whom it is said:—Whoso praiseth and then blameth lieth twice.[1]" And he knew not what to do. Presently, the traders came to him and said, "O Merchant Ali, hast thou spoken to him?" Said he, "O folk, I am ashamed and, though he owe me a thousand dinars, I cannot speak to him. When ye lent him your money ye consulted me not; so ye have no claim on me. Dun him yourselves, and if he pay you not, complain of him to the King of the city, saying:—He is an impostor who hath imposed upon us. And he will deliver you from the plague of him." Accordingly, they repaired to the King and told him what had passed, saying, "O King of the Age, we are perplexed anent this merchant, whose generosity is excessive; for he doeth thus and thus, and all he borroweth he giveth away to the poor by handsful. Were he a man of naught, his sense would not suffer him to lavish gold on this wise; and were he a man of wealth, his good faith had been made manifest to us by the coming of his baggage; but we see none of his luggage, although he avoucheth that he hath a baggage-train and hath preceded it. Now some time hath past, but there appeareth no sign of his baggage-train, and he oweth us sixty thousand gold pieces, all of which he hath given away in alms." And they went on to praise him and extol his generosity. Now this King was a very covetous man, a more covetous than Ash'ab[2]; and when he heard tell of Ma'aruf's generosity and

---

1 A saying attributed to Al-Hariri (Lane). It is good enough to be his: the Persians say, "Cut not down the tree thou plantedst," and the idea is universal throughout the East.

2 A quotation from Al-Hariri (Ass. of the Badawin). Ash'ab (ob. A.H. 54), a Madinite servant of Caliph Osman, was proverbial for greed and sanguine, Micawber-like, expectation of "windfalls." The Scholiast Al-Sharishi (of Xeres) describes him in Theophrastic style. He never saw a man put hand to pocket without expecting a present, or a funeral go by without hoping for a legacy, or a bridal procession without preparing his own house, hoping they might bring the bride to him by mistake. . . . When asked if

open-handedness, greed of gain got the better of him and he said to his Wazir, "Were not this merchant a man of immense wealth, he had not shown all this munificence. His baggage-train will assuredly come, whereupon these merchants will flock to him and he will scatter amongst them riches galore. Now I have more right to this money than they; wherefore I have a mind to make friends with him and profess affection for him, so that, when his baggage cometh, whatso the merchants would have had I shall get of him; and I will give him my daughter to wife and join his wealth to my wealth." Replied the Wazir, "O King of the Age, methinks he is naught but an impostor, and 'tis the impostor who ruineth the house of the covetous";——And Shahrazad perceived the dawn of day and ceased saying her permitted say.

Now when it was the Nine Hundred and Ninety-third Night,

She pursued, It hath reached me, O auspicious King, that when the Wazir said to the King, "Methinks he is naught but an impostor, and 'tis the impostor who ruineth the house of the covetous"; the King said, "O Wazir, I will prove him and soon know if he be an impostor or a true man and whether he be a rearling of Fortune or not." The Wazir asked, "And how wilt thou prove him?" and the King answered, "I will send for him to the presence and entreat him with honour and give him a jewel which I have. An he know it and wot its price, he is a man of worth and wealth; but an he know it not, he is an impostor and an upstart, and I will do him die by the foulest fashion of deaths." So he sent for Ma'aruf, who came and saluted him. The King returned his salam and seating him beside himself, said to him, "Art thou the merchant Ma'aruf?" and said he, "Yes." Quoth the King, "The merchants declare that thou owest them sixty thousand ducats. Is this true?" "Yes," quoth he. Asked the King, "Then why dost thou not give them their money?" and he answered, "Let them wait till my baggage come and I will repay them twofold. An they wish for gold, they shall have gold; and should they wish for silver, they shall have silver; or an they prefer for merchandise, I will give them merchandise; and to whom I owe a thousand I will give two thousand in requital of that

---

he knew aught greedier than himself, he said, "Yes; a sheep I once kept upon my terrace-roof seeing a rainbow mistook it for a rope of hay, and jumping to seize it, broke its neck!" Hence "Ash'ab's sheep" became a by-word. (Preston tells the tale in full, p. 288.)

wherewith he hath veiled my face before the poor; for I have plenty." Then said the King, "O merchant, take this and look what is its kind and value." And he gave him a jewel the bigness of a hazel-nut, which he had bought for a thousand sequins, and not having its fellow, prized it highly. Ma'aruf took it and pressing it between his thumb and forefinger brake it, for it was brittle and would not brook the squeeze. Quoth the King, "Why hast thou broken the jewel?" and Ma'aruf laughed and said, "O King of the Age, this is no jewel. This is but a bittock of mineral worth a thousand dinars; why dost thou style it a jewel? A jewel I call such as is worth threescore and ten thousand gold pieces, and this is called but a piece of stone. A jewel that is not of the bigness of a walnut hath no worth in my eyes, and I take no account thereof. How cometh it, then, that thou, who art King, stylest this thing a jewel, when 'tis but a bit of mineral worth a thousand dinars? But ye are excusable, for that ye are poor folk and have not in your possession things of price." The King asked, "O merchant, hast thou jewels such as those whereof thou speakest?" and he answered, "Plenty." Whereupon avarice overcame the King, and he said, "Wilt thou give me real jewels?" Said Ma'aruf, "When my baggage-train shall come I will give thee no end of jewels; and all that thou canst desire I have in plenty and will give thee, without price." At this the King rejoiced, and said to the traders, "Wend your ways and have patience with him till his baggage arrive, when do ye come to me and receive your moneys from me." So they fared forth, and the King turned to his Wazir and said to him, "Pay court to Merchant Ma'aruf and take and give with him in talk and bespeak him of my daughter, Princess Dunyá, that he may wed her and so we gain these riches he hath." Said the Wazir, "O King of the Age, this man's fashion misliketh me, and methinks he is an impostor and a liar: so leave this whereof thou speakest lest thou lose thy daughter for naught." Now this Minister had sued the King aforetime to give him his daughter to wife and he was willing to do so, but when she heard of it she consented not to marry him. Accordingly, the King said to him, "O traitor, thou desirest no good for me, because in past time thou soughtest my daughter in wedlock, but she would none of thee; so now thou wouldst cut off the way of her marriage, and would have the Princess lie fallow, that thou mayst take her, but hear from me one word. Thou hast no concern in this matter. How can he be an impostor and a liar, seeing that he knew the price of the jewel, even that for which I bought it, and brake it because it pleased him not? He hath jewels in plenty, and when he goeth in to my daughter and seeth her to be beautiful, she will captivate his reason, and he will love her and give her jewels and things of price; but as for thee, thou wouldst forbid my daughter and myself these good things." So the Minister was silent, for fear of the King's anger, and said to himself, "Set the curs on the cattle[1]!" Then with show of friendly bias he betook himself to Ma'aruf, and said to him, "His highness the King loveth thee and hath a daughter, a winsome lady and a lovesome, to whom he is minded to marry thee. What sayst thou?" Said he, "No harm in that, but let him wait till my baggage come, for marriage-settlements on Kings' daughters are large, and their rank demandeth that they be not endowed save with a dowry befitting their degree. At this present I have no money with me till the coming of my baggage, for I have wealth in plenty and needs must I make her marriage-portion five thousand purses. Then I shall need a thousand purses to distribute amongst the poor and needy on my wedding-night, and other thousand to give to those who walk in the bridal procession, and yet other thousand wherewith to provide provaunt for the troops and others[2]; and I shall want an hundred jewels to give to the Princess on the wedding-morning,[3] and other hundred gems to distribute among the slave-girls and eunuchs, for I must give each of them a jewel in honour of the bride; and I need wherewithal to clothe a thousand naked paupers, and alms, too, needs must be given. All this cannot be done till my baggage come: but I have plenty, and once it is here I shall make no account of all this outlay." The Wazir returned to the King and told him what Ma'aruf said, whereupon quoth he, "Since this is his wish, how canst thou style him impostor and liar?" Replied the Minister, "And I cease not to say this." But the King chid him angrily and threatened him, saying, "By the life of my head, an thou cease not this talk, I will slay thee! Go back to him and fetch him to me and I will manage matters with him myself." So the Wazir returned to Ma'aruf and said to him, "Come and speak with the King." "I hear and I obey," said Ma'aruf, and went in to the King, who said to him, "Thou shalt not put me off with these excuses, for my treasury is full; so take the keys and spend all thou needest, and give what thou wilt and clothe the poor and do thy desire, and have no care for the girl and the handmaids. When the baggage shall come,

---

1 *i.e.* "Show a miser money and hold him back, if you can."
2 He wants £40,000 to begin with.
3 *i.e.* Arab. "Sabihat al-'urs," the morning after the wedding.

do what thou wilt with thy wife, by way of generosity, and we will have patience with thee anent the marriage-portion till then, for there is no manner of difference betwixt me and thee; none at all." Then he sent for the Shaykh al-Islam[1] and bade him write out the marriage-contract between his daughter and Merchant Ma'aruf, and he did so; after which the King gave the signal for beginning the wedding festivities and bade decorate the city. The kettle-drums beat and the tables were spread with meats of all kinds, and there came performers who paraded their tricks. Merchant Ma'aruf sat upon a throne in a parlour and the players and gymnasts and effeminates[2] and dancing-men of wondrous movements and posture-makers of marvellous cunning came before him, whilst he called out to the treasurer and said to him, "Bring gold and silver." So he brought gold and silver, and Ma'aruf went round among the spectators and largessed each performer by the handful; and he gave alms to the poor and needy and clothes to the naked, and it was a clamorous festival and a right merry. The treasurer could not bring money fast enough from the treasury, and the Wazir's heart was like to burst for rage; but he dared not say a word, whilst Merchant Ali marvelled at this waste of wealth, and said to Merchant Ma'aruf, "Allah and the Hallows visit this upon thy head-sides[3]! Doth it not suffice thee to squander the traders' money, but thou must squander that of the King to boot?" Replied Ma'aruf, "'Tis none of thy concern: whenas my baggage shall come, I will requite the King manifold." And he went on lavishing money and saying in himself, "A burning plague! What will happen will happen, and there is no flying from that which is fore-ordained." The festivities ceased not for the space of forty days, and on the one-and-fortieth day they made the bride's cortège and all the Emirs and troops walked before her. When they brought her in before Ma'aruf, he began scattering gold on the people's heads, and they made her a mighty fine procession, whilst Ma'aruf expended in her honour vast sums of money. Then they

---

1 Another sign of modern composition, as in Kamar al-Zaman II.

2 Arab. "Al-Jink" (from Turk.) are boys and youths, mostly Jews, Armenians, Greeks, and Turks, who dress in woman's dress with long hair braided. Lane (M.E. chapts. xix. and xxv.) gives some account of the customs of the "Gink" (as the Egyptians call them) but cannot enter into details concerning these catamites. Respectable Moslems often employ them to dance at festivals in preference to the Ghawázi-women, a freak of Mohammedan decorum. When they grow old they often preserve their costume, and a glance at them makes a European's blood run cold.

3 Lane translates this, "May Allah and the Rijal retaliate upon thy temple!"

brought him in to Princess Dunya and he sat down on the high diwan; after which they let fall the curtains and shut the doors and withdrew, leaving him alone with his bride; whereupon he smote hand upon hand and sat awhile sorrowful and saying, "There is no Majesty and there is no Might save in Allah, the Glorious, the Great!" Quoth the Princess, "O my lord, Allah preserve thee! What aileth thee that thou art troubled?" Quoth he, "And how should I be other than troubled, seeing that thy father hath embarrassed me and done with me a deed which is like the burning of green corn?" She asked, "And what hath my father done with thee? Tell me!" and he answered, "He hath brought me in to thee before the coming of my baggage, and I want at very least an hundred jewels to distribute among thy handmaids, to each a jewel, so she might rejoice therein and say:—My lord gave me a jewel on the night of his going in to my lady. This good deed would I have done in honour of thy station and for the increase of thy dignity; and I have no need to stint myself in lavishing jewels, for I have of them great plenty." Rejoined she, "Be not concerned for that. As for me, trouble not thyself about me, for I will have patience with thee till thy baggage shall come; and as for my women, have no care for them. Rise, doff thy clothes, and take thy pleasure; and when the baggage cometh we shall get the jewels and the rest." So he arose and putting off his clothes sat down on the bed and sought love-liesse and they fell to toying with each other. He laid his hand on her knee and she sat down in his lap and thrust her lip like a tit-bit of meat into his mouth, and that hour was such as maketh a man to forget his father and his mother. So he clasped her in his arms and strained her fast to his breast and sucked her lip, till the honey-dew ran out into his mouth; and he laid his hand under her left-armpit, whereupon his vitals and her vitals yearned; so there befell the mystery[1] concerning which there is no enquiry; and she cried the cry that needs must be cried.——And Shahrazad perceived the dawn of day and ceased to say her permitted say.

---

1 A mystery to the Author of Proverbs (xxx. 18-19):

There be three things which are too wondrous for me,
The way of an eagle in the air;
The way of a snake upon a rock;
And the way of a man with a maid.

Now when it was the Nine Hundred and Ninety-fourth Night,

She resumed, It hath reached me, O auspicious King, that while the Princess Dunya cried the cry which must be cried, Merchant Ma'aruf abated her virginity and that night was one not to be counted among lives for that which it comprised of the enjoyment of the fair, clipping and dallying till the dawn of day, when he arose and entered the Hammam whence, after donning a suit for sovrans suitable, he betook himself to the King's Diwan. All who were there rose to him and received him with honour and worship, giving him joy and invoking blessings upon him; and he sat down by the King's side and asked, "Where is the treasurer?" They answered, "Here he is, before thee"; and he said to him, "Bring robes of honour for all the Wazirs and Emirs and Dignitaries and clothe them therewith." The treasurer brought him all he sought, and he sat giving to all who came to him and lavishing largesse upon every man according to his station. On this wise he abode twenty days, whilst no baggage appeared for him nor aught else, till the treasurer was straitened by him to the uttermost and going in to the King, as he sat alone with the Wazir in Ma'aruf's absence, kissed ground between his hands and said, "O King of the Age, I must tell thee somewhat, lest haply thou blame me for not acquainting thee therewith. Know that the treasury is being exhausted; there is none but a little money left in it, and in ten days more we shall shut it upon emptiness." Quoth the King, "O Wazir, verily my son-in-law's baggage-train tarrieth long and there appeareth no news thereof." The Minister laughed and said, "Allah be gracious to thee, O King of the Age! Thou art none other but heedless with respect to this impostor, this liar. As thy head liveth, there is no baggage for him, no, nor a burning plague to rid us of him! Nay, he hath but imposed on thee without surcease, so that he hath wasted thy treasures and married thy daughter for naught. How long, therefore, wilt thou be heedless of this liar?" Then quoth the King, "O Wazir, how shall we do to learn the truth of his case?" and quoth the Wazir, "O King of the Age, none may come at a man's secret but his wife; so send for thy daughter and let her come behind the curtain, that I may question her of the truth of his estate, to the intent that she make question of him and acquaint us with his case." Cried the King, "There is no harm in that; and as my head liveth, if it be proved that he is a liar and an impostor, I will verily do him die by the foulest of deaths!" Then he carried the Wazir into the sitting-chamber and sent for his daughter, who came behind the curtain, her husband being absent, and said, "What wouldst thou, O my father?" Said he, "Speak with the Wazir." So she asked, "Ho thou the Wazir, what is thy will?" and he answered, "O my lady, thou must know that thy husband hath squandered thy father's substance and married thee without a dower; and he ceaseth not to promise us and break his promises, nor cometh there any tidings of his baggage; in short, we would have thee inform us concerning him." Quoth she, "Indeed his words be many, and he still cometh and promiseth me jewels and treasures and costly stuffs; but I see nothing." Quoth the Wazir, "O my lady, canst thou this night take and give with him in talk and whisper to him:—Say me sooth and fear from me naught, for thou art become my husband and I will not transgress against thee. So tell me the truth of the matter and I will devise thee a device whereby thou shalt be set at rest. And do thou play near and far[1] with him in words and profess love to him and win him to confess and after tell us the facts of his case." And she answered, "O my papa, I know how I will make proof of him." Then she went away and after supper her husband came in to her, according to his wont, whereupon Princess Dunya rose to him and took him under the armpit and wheedled him with winsomest wheedling (and all-sufficient[2] are woman's wiles whenas she would aught of men); and she ceased not to caress him and beguile him with speech sweeter than the honey till she stole his reason; and when she saw that he altogether inclined to her, she said to him, "O my beloved, O coolth of my eyes and fruit of my vitals, Allah never desolate me by loss of thee nor Time sunder us twain me and thee! Indeed, the love of thee hath homed in my heart and the fire of passion hath consumed my liver, nor will I ever forsake thee or transgress against thee. But I would have thee tell me the truth, for that the sleights of falsehood profit not, nor do they secure credit at all seasons. How long wilt thou impose upon my father and lie to him? I fear lest thine affair be discovered to him, ere we can devise some device and he lay violent hands upon thee? So acquaint me with the facts of the case, for naught shall befall thee save that which shall begladden thee; and, when thou shalt have

---

1 As we should say, "play fast and loose."

2 Arab. "Náhi-ka" lit. = thy prohibition, but idiomatically used = let it suffice thee.

spoken sooth, fear not harm shall betide thee. How often wilt thou declare that thou art a merchant and a man of money and hast a luggage-train? This long while past thou sayest, My baggage! my baggage! but there appeareth no sign of thy baggage, and visible in thy face is anxiety on this account. So an there be no worth in thy words, tell me and I will contrive thee a contrivance whereby thou shalt come off safe, Inshallah!" He replied, "I will tell thee the truth, and then do thou whatso thou wilt." Rejoined she, "Speak and look thou speak soothly; for sooth is the ark of safety, and beware of lying, for it dishonoureth the liar, and God-gifted is he who said:—

'Ware that truth thou speak, albe sooth when said * Shall cause thee in threatenèd fire to fall:
And seek Allah's approof, for most foolish he * Who shall anger his Lord to make friends with thrall.

He said, "Know, then, O my lady, that I am no merchant and have no baggage, no, nor a burning plague; nay, I was but a cobbler in my own country and had a wife called Fatimah the Dung, with whom there befell me this and that." And he told her his story from beginning to end; whereat she laughed and said, "Verily, thou art clever in the practice of lying and imposture!" Whereto he answered, "O my lady, may Allah Almighty preserve thee to veil sins and countervail chagrins!" Rejoined she, "Know that thou imposedst upon my sire and deceivedst him by dint of thy deluding vaunts, so that of his greed for gain he married me to thee. Then thou squanderedst his wealth and the Wazir beareth thee a grudge for this. How many a time hath he spoken against thee to my father, saying, Indeed, he is an impostor, a liar! But my sire hearkened not to his say, for that he had sought me in wedlock and I consented not that he be baron and I femme. However, the time grew longsome upon my sire and he became straitened and said to me, Make him confess. So I have made thee confess, and that which was covered is discovered. Now my father purposeth thee a mischief because of this; but thou art become my husband and I will never transgress against thee. An I told my father what I have learnt from thee, he would be certified of thy falsehood and imposture and that thou imposest upon Kings' daughters and squanderest royal wealth: so would thine offence find with him no pardon and he would slay thee sans a doubt: wherefore it would be bruited among the folk that I married a man who was a liar, an impostor, and this would smirch mine honour. Furthermore, an he kill thee, most like he will require me to wed another, and to such thing I will never consent; no, not though I die[1]! So rise now and don a Mameluke's dress and take these fifty thousand dinars of my moneys, and mount a swift steed and get thee to a land whither the rule of my father doth not reach. Then make thee a merchant and send me a letter by a courier who shall bring it privily to me, that I may know in what land thou art, so I may send thee all my hand can attain. Thus shall thy wealth wax great, and if my father die I will send for thee, and thou shalt return in respect and honour; and if we die, thou or I and go to the mercy of God the Most Great, the Resurrection shall unite us. This, then, is the rede that is right: and while we both abide alive and well, I will not cease to send thee letters and moneys. Arise ere the day wax bright and thou be in perplexed plight and perdition upon thy head alight!" Quoth he, "O my lady, I beseech thee of thy favour to bid me farewell with thine embracement"; and quoth she, "No harm in that.[2]" So he embraced her and had knowledge of her; after which he made the Ghusl-ablution; then, donning the dress of a white slave, he bade the syces saddle him a thoroughbred steed. Accordingly, they saddled him a courser and he mounted, and farewelling his wife, rode forth the city at the last of the night, whilst all who saw him deemed him one of the Mamelukes of the Sultan going abroad on some business. Next morning, the King and his Wazir repaired to the sitting-chamber and sent for Princess Dunya, who came behind the curtain; and her father said to her, "O my daughter, what sayst thou?" Said she, "I say, Allah blacken thy Wazir's face, because he would have blackened my face in my husband's eyes!" Asked the King, "How so?" and she answered, "He came in to me yesterday; but, before I could name the matter to him, behold, in walked Faraj the Chief Eunuch, letter in hand, and said:—Ten white slaves stand under the palace window and have given me this letter, saying:—Kiss for us the hands of our lord, Merchant Ma'aruf, and give him this letter, for we are of his Mamelukes with the baggage, and it hath reached us that he hath wedded the King's daughter, so we are come to acquaint him with that which befell us by the way. Accordingly, I took the letter and read as follows:—From the five hundred Mamelukes to his

1 A character-sketch like that of Princess Dunya makes ample amends for a book full of abuse of women. And yet the superficial say that none of the characters has much personal individuality.

2 This is indeed one of the touches of nature which makes all the world kin.

highness our lord Merchant Ma'aruf. But further. We give thee to know that, after thou quittedst us, the Arabs[1] came out upon us and attacked us. They were two thousand horse and we five hundred mounted slaves, and there befell a mighty sore fight between us and them. They hindered us from the road thirty days doing battle with them and this is the cause of our tarrying from thee."——And Shahrazad perceived the dawn of day and ceased saying her permitted say.

Now when it was the Nine Hundred and Ninety-fifth Night,

She said, It hath reached me, O auspicious King, that Princess Dunya said to her sire, "My husband received a letter from his dependants ending with:—The Arabs hindered us from the road thirty days, which is the cause of our being behind time. They also took from us of the luggage two hundred loads of cloth and slew of us fifty Mamelukes. When the news reached my husband, he cried, Allah disappoint them! What ailed them to wage war with the Arabs for the sake of two hundred loads of merchandise? What are two hundred loads? It behoved them not to tarry on that account, for verily the value of the two hundred loads is only some seven thousand dinars. But needs must I go to them and hasten them. As for that which the Arabs have taken, 'twill not be missed from the baggage, nor doth it weigh with me a whit, for I reckon it as if I had given it to them by way of an alms. Then he went down from me, laughing and taking no concern for the wastage of his wealth nor the slaughter of his slaves. As soon as he was gone, I looked out from the lattice and saw the ten Mamelukes who had brought him the letter, as they were moons, each clad in a suit of clothes worth two thousand dinars, there is not with my father a chattel to match one of them. He went forth with them to bring up his baggage and hallowed be Allah who hindered me from saying to him aught of that thou badest me, for he would have made mock of me and thee, and haply he would have eyed me with the eye of disparagement and hated me. But the fault is all with thy Wazir,[2] who speaketh against my husband

---

1 As we are in Tartary, "Arabs" here means plundering nomades, like the Persian "Iliyát" and other shepherd races.

2 The very cruelty of love which hates nothing so much as a rejected lover. The Princess, be it noted, is not supposed to be merely romancing but speaking with the second sight, the clairvoyance of perfect affection. Men seem to know very little upon this subject, though every one has at times been more or less startled by the abnormal introvision and divination of things hidden which are the property and prerogative of perfect love

words that besit him not." Replied the King, "O my daughter, thy husband's wealth is indeed endless and he recketh not of it; for, from the day he entered our city, he hath done naught but give alms to the poor. Inshallah, he will speedily return with the baggage, and good in plenty shall betide us from him." And he went on to appease her and menace the Wazir, being duped by her device. So fared it with the King; but as regards Merchant Ma'aruf he rode on into waste lands, perplexed and knowing not to what quarter he should betake him; and for the anguish of parting he lamented and in the pangs of passion and love-longing he recited these couplets:—

Time falsed our Union and divided who were one in tway; * And the sore tyranny of Time doth melt my heart away:
Mine eyes ne'er cease to drop the tear for parting with my dear; * When shall Disunion come to end and dawn the Union-day?
O favour like the full moon's face of sheen, indeed I'm he * Whom thou didst leave with vitals torn when faring on thy way.
Would I had never seen thy sight, or met thee for an hour; * Since after sweetest taste of thee to bitters I'm a prey.
Ma'aruf will never cease to be enthralled by Dunyá's[1] charms * And long live she albe he die whom love and longing slay.
O brilliance, like resplendent sun of noontide, deign them heal * His heart for kindness[2] and the fire of longing love allay!
Would Heaven I wot an e'er the days shall deign conjoin our lots, * Join us in pleasant talk o' nights, in Union glad and gay:
Shall my love's palace hold two hearts that savour joy, and I * Strain to my breast the branch I saw upon the sand-hill[3] sway?
O favour of full moon in sheen, never may sun o' thee * Surcease to rise from Eastern rim with all-enlightening ray!
I'm well content with passion-pine and all its bane and bate * For luck in love is evermore the butt of jealous Fate.

And when he ended his verses, he wept with sore weeping, for indeed the ways were walled up before his face, and death seemed to him better than dreeing life, and he walked on like a drunken man, for stress of distraction, and stayed not till noontide, when he came to a little town and saw a plougher hard by, ploughing with a yoke of bulls. Now hunger was sore upon him; and he went up to the ploughman and said to him, "Peace be with thee!"

---

1 The name of the Princess meaning "The World," not unusual amongst Moslem women.

2 Another pun upon his name, "Ma'aruf."

3 Arab. "Naká," the mound of pure sand which delights the eye of the Badawi leaving a town. See vol. i. night xxii, for the lines and explanation in night cmlxiv.

and he returned his salam and said to him, "Welcome, O my lord! Art thou one of the Sultan's Mamelukes?" Quoth Ma'aruf, "Yes": and the other said, "Alight with me for a guest-meal." Whereupon Ma'aruf knew him to be of the liberal and said to him, "O my brother, I see with thee naught with which thou mayst feed me: how is it, then, that thou invitest me?" Answered the husbandman, "O my lord, weal is well nigh.[1] Dismount thee here: the town is near hand and I will go and fetch thee dinner aud fodder for thy stallion." Rejoined Ma'aruf, "Since the town is near at hand, I can go thither as quickly as thou canst and buy me what I have a mind to in the bazar and eat." The peasant replied, "O my lord, the place is but a little village[2] and there is no bazar there, neither selling nor buying. So I conjure thee by Allah, alight here with me and hearten my heart, and I will run thither and return to thee in haste." Accordingly, he dismounted and the Fellah left him and went off to the village to fetch dinner for him, whilst Ma'aruf sat awaiting him. Presently he said in himself, "I have taken this poor man away from his work; but I will arise and plough in his stead till he come back, to make up for having hindered him from his work.[3]" Then he took the plough and starting the bulls, ploughed a little, till the share struck against something and the beasts stopped. He goaded them on, but they could not move the plough: so he looked at the share and finding it caught in a ring of gold, cleared away the soil and saw that it was set centre-most a slab of alabaster, the size of the nether millstone. He strave at the stone till he pulled it from its place, when there appeared beneath it a souterrain with a stair. Presently he descended the flight of steps and came to a place like a Hammam, with four daïses; the first full of gold from floor to roof; the second full of emeralds and pearls and coral also from ground to ceiling; the third of jacinths and rubies and turquoises; and the fourth of diamonds and all manner other preciousest stones. At the upper end of the place stood a coffer of clearest crystal, full of union-gems each the size of a walnut, and upon the coffer lay a casket of gold, the bigness of a lemon. When he saw this, he marvelled and rejoiced with joy exceeding and said to himself, "I wonder what is in this casket?" So he opened it and

---

1 Euphemistic: "I will soon fetch thee food." To say this bluntly might have brought misfortune.

2 Arab. "Kafr" = a village in Egypt and Syria, *e.g.* Capernaum (Kafr Nahum).

3 He has all the bonhomie of the Cairene and will do a kindness whenever he can.

found therein a seal-ring of gold, whereon were graven names and talismans, as they were the tracks of creeping ants. He rubbed the ring and behold, a voice said, "Adsum! Here am I, at thy service, O my lord! Ask and it shall be given unto thee. Wilt thou raise a city, or ruin a capital, or kill a king, or dig a river-channel, or aught of the kind? Whatso thou seekest, it shall come to pass, by leave of the King of All-might, Creator of day and night." Ma'aruf asked, "O creature of my lord, who and what art thou?" and the other answered, "I am the slave of this seal-ring, standing in the service of him who possesseth it. Whatsoever he seeketh, that I accomplish for him, and I have no excuse in neglecting that he biddeth me do; because I am Sultan over two-and-seventy tribes of the Jinn, each two-and-seventy thousand in number, every one of which thousand ruleth over a thousand Marids, each Marid over a thousand Ifrits, each Ifrit over a thousand Satans, and each Satan over a thousand Jinn: and they are all under command of me and may not gainsay me. As for me, I am spelled to this seal-ring and may not thwart whoso holdeth it. Lo! thou hast gotten hold of it and I am become thy slave; so ask what thou wilt, for I hearken to thy word and obey thy bidding; and if thou have need of me at any time, by land or by sea, rub the signet-ring and thou wilt find me with thee. But beware of rubbing it twice in succession, or thou wilt consume me with the fire of the names graven thereon; and thus wouldst thou lose me and afterwards regret me. Now I have acquainted thee with my case and—the Peace!"——And Shahrazad perceived the dawn of day and ceased to say her permitted say.

Now when it was the Nine Hundred and Ninety-sixth Night,

She continued, It hath reached me, O auspicious King, that when the Slave of the Signet-ring acquainted Ma'aruf with his case, the Merchant asked him, "What is thy name?" and the Jinni answered, "My name is Abú al-Sa'ádát.[1]" Quoth Ma'aruf, "O Abu al-Sa'adat, what is this place and who enchanted thee in this casket?" and quoth he, "O my lord, this is a treasure called the Hoard of Shaddád son of Ad, him who the base of Many-columned Iram laid, the like of which in the lands was never made.[2] I was his slave in his lifetime and this is his Seal-ring,

1 *i.e.* the Father of Prosperities: pron. Aboosa'ádát; as in the Tale of Hasan of Bassorah.

2 Koran, lxxxix. "The Daybreak," which also mentions Thamud and Pharaoh.

which he laid up in his treasure; but it hath fallen to thy lot." Ma'aruf enquired, "Canst thou transport that which is in this hoard to the surface of the earth?" and the Jinni replied, "Yes! Nothing were easier." Said Ma'aruf, "Bring it forth and leave naught." So the Jinni signed with his hand to the ground, which clave asunder, and he sank and was absent a little while. Presently, there came forth young boys full of grace and fair of face bearing golden baskets filled with gold, which they emptied out and going away, returned with more; nor did they cease to transport the gold and jewels, till ere an hour had sped they said, "Naught is left in the hoard." Thereupon out came Abu al-Sa'adat and said to Ma'aruf, "O my lord, thou seest that we have brought forth all that was in the hoard." Ma'aruf asked, "Who be these beautiful boys?" and the Jinni answered, "They are my sons. This matter merited not that I should muster for it the Marids, wherefore my sons have done thy desire and are honoured by such service. So ask what thou wilt beside this." Quoth Ma'aruf, "Canst thou bring me he-mules and chests and fill the chests with the treasure and load them on the mules?" Quoth Abu al-Sa'adat, "Nothing easier," and cried a great cry; whereupon his sons presented themselves before him, to the number of eight hundred, and he said to them, "Let some of you take the semblance of he-mules and others of muleteers and handsome Mamelukes, the like of the least of whom is not found with any of the Kings; and others of you be transmewed to muleteers, and the rest to menials." So seven hundred of them changed themselves into bât-mules and other hundred took the shape of slaves. Then Abu al-Sa'adat called upon his Marids, who presented themselves between his hands and he commanded some of them to assume the aspect of horses saddled with saddles of gold crusted with jewels. And when Ma'aruf saw them do as he bade, he cried, "Where be the chests?" They brought them before him and he said, "Pack the gold and the stones, each sort by itself." So they packed them and loaded three hundred he-mules with them. Then asked Ma'aruf, "O Abu al-Sa'adat, canst thou bring me some loads of costly stuffs?" and the Jinni answered, "Wilt thou have Egyptian stuffs or Syrian or Persian or Indian or Greek?" Ma'aruf said, "Bring me an hundred loads of each kind, on five hundred mules"; and Abu al-Sa'adat, "O my lord, accord me delay that I may dispose my Marids for this and send a company of them to each country to fetch an hundred loads of its stuffs and then take the form of he-mules and return, carrying the stuffs." Ma'aruf enquired, "What time dost thou want?" and Abu al-Sa'adat

No. 56.

Ma'aruf the Cobbler and his Wife Fatimah.

"So the Jinni signed with his hand to the ground, which clave asunder . . . presently, there came forth young boys full of grace and fair of face, bearing golden baskets filled with gold."

replied, "The time of the blackness of the night, and day shall not dawn ere thou have all thou desirest." Said Ma'aruf, "I grant thee this time," and bade him pitch him a pavilion. So they pitched it and he sat down therein and they brought him a table of food. Then said Abu al-Sa'adat to him, "O my lord, tarry thou in this tent and these my sons shall guard thee: so fear thou nothing; for I go to muster my Marids and despatch them to do thy desire." So saying he departed, leaving Ma'aruf seated in the pavilion, with the table before him and the Jinni's sons attending upon him, in the guise of slaves and servants and suite. And while he sat in this state behold, up came the husbandman, with a great porringer of lentils[1] and a nose-bag full of barley, and seeing the pavilion pitched and the Mamelukes standing hands upon breast, thought that the Sultan was come and had halted on that stead. So he stood open-mouthed and said in himself, "Would I had killed a couple of chickens and fried them red with clarified cow-butter for the Sultan!" And he would have turned back to kill the chickens as a regale for the Sultan; but Ma'aruf saw him and cried out to him and said to the Mamelukes, "Bring him hither." So they brought him and his porringer of lentils before Ma'aruf, who said to him, "What is this?" Said the peasant, "This is thy dinner and thy horse's fodder! Excuse me, for I thought not that the Sultan would come hither; and had I known that, I would have killed a couple of chickens and entertained him in goodly guise." Quoth Ma'aruf, "The Sultan is not come. I am his son-in-law and I was vexed with him. However, he hath sent his officers to make his peace with me, and now I am minded to return to city. But thou hast made me this guest-meal without knowing me, and I accept it from thee, lentils though it be, and will not eat save of thy cheer." Accordingly, he bade him set the porringer a-middlemost the table and ate of it his sufficiency, whilst the Fellah filled his belly with those rich meats. Then Ma'aruf washed his hands and gave the Mamelukes leave to eat; so they fell upon the remains of the meal and ate; and when the porringer was empty he filled it with gold and gave it to the peasant, saying, "Carry this to thy dwelling and come to me in the city, and I will entreat thee with honour." Thereupon the peasant took the porringer full of gold and returned to the village, driving the bulls before him and deeming himself akin to the

1 In Egypt the cheapest and poorest of food, never seen at a hotel table d'hôte.

King. Meanwhile, they brought Ma'aruf girls of the Brides of the Treasure,[1] who smote on instruments of music and danced before him, and he passed that night in joyance and delight, a night not to be reckoned among lives. Hardly had dawned the day when there arose a great cloud of dust which presently lifting, discovered seven hundred mules laden with stuffs and attended by muleteers and baggage-tenders and cresset-bearers. With them came Abu al-Sa'adat, riding on a she-mule, in the guise of a caravan-leader, and before him was a travelling litter, with four corner-terminals[2] of glittering red gold, set with gems. When Abu al-Sa'adat came up to the tent, he dismounted and kissing earth, said to Ma'aruf, "O my lord, thy desire hath been done to the uttermost and in the litter is a treasure-suit which hath not its match among Kings' raiment: so don it and mount the litter and bid us do what thou wilt." Quoth Ma'aruf, "O Abu al-Sa'adat, I wish thee to go to the city of Ikhtiyan al-Khutan and present thyself to my father-in-law the King; and go thou not in to him but in the guise of a mortal courier"; and quoth he, "To hear is to obey." So Ma'aruf wrote a letter to the Sultan and sealed it, and Abu al-Sa'adat took it and set out with it; and when he arrived, he found the King saying, "O Wazir, indeed my heart is concerned for my son-in-law and I fear lest the Arabs slay him. Would Heaven I wot whither he was bound, that I might have followed him with the troops! Would he had told me his destination!" Said the Wazir, "Allah be merciful to thee for this thy heedlessness! As thy head liveth, the wight saw that we were awake to him and feared dishonour and fled, for he is nothing but an impostor, a liar." And behold, at this moment in came the courier and, kissing ground before the King, wished him permanent glory and prosperity and length of life. Asked the King, "Who art thou and what is thy business?" "I am a courier," answered the Jinni, "and thy son-in-law, who is come with the baggage, sendeth me to thee with a letter, and here it is! So he took the letter and read therein these words: "After salutations galore to our uncle,[3] the glorious King! Know that I am at hand with the baggage-train:

---

1 The beautiful girls who guard ensorcelled hoards: see night dlxxiv.

2 Arab. "Asákir," the ornaments of litters, which are either plain balls of metal or tapering cones based on crescents or on balls and crescents. See in Lane (M. E. chapt. xxiv.) the sketch of the Mahmal.

3 Arab. "Amm" = father's brother, courteously used for "father-in-law," which suggests having slept with his daughter, and which is indecent in writing. Thus by a pleasant fiction the husband represents himself as having married his first cousin.

so come thou forth to meet me with the troops." Cried the King, "Allah blacken thy brow, O Wazir! How often wilt thou defame my son-in-law's name and call him liar and impostor? Behold, he is come with the baggage-train and thou art naught but a traitor." The Minister hung his head groundwards in shame and confusion and replied, "O King of the Age, I said not this save because of the long delay of the baggage and because I feared the loss of the wealth he hath wasted." The King exclaimed, "O traitor, what are my riches! Now that his baggage is come he will give me great plenty in their stead." Then he bade decorate the city and going in to his daughter, said to her, "Good news for thee! Thy husband will be here anon with his baggage; for he hath sent me a letter to that effect and here am I now going forth to meet him." The Princess Dunya marvelled at this and said in herself, "This is a wondrous thing! Was he laughing at me and making mock of me, or had he a mind to try me, when he told me that he was a pauper? But Alhamdolillah—Glory to God!—for that I failed not of my duty to him!" On this wise fared it in the Palace; but as regards Merchant Ali, the Cairene, when he saw the decoration of the city and asked the cause thereof, they said to him, "The baggage-train of Merchant Ma'aruf, the King's son-in-law, is come." Said he, "Allah is Almighty! What a calamity is this man[1]! He came to me, fleeing from his wife, and he was a poor man. Whence, then, should he get a baggage-train? But haply this is a device which the King's daughter hath contrived for him, fearing his disgrace, and Kings are not unable to do anything. May Allah the Most High veil his fame and not bring him to public shame!"——And Shahrazad perceived the dawn of day and ceased saying her permitted say.

Now when it was the Nine Hundred and Ninety-seventh Night,

She pursued, It hath reached me, O auspicious King, that when Merchant Ali asked the cause of the decorations, they told him the truth of the case; so he blessed Merchant Ma'aruf and cried, "May Allah Almighty veil his fame and not bring him to public shame!" And all the merchants rejoiced and were glad for that they would get their moneys. Then the King assembled his troops and rode forth, whilst Abu al-Sa'adat returned to Ma'aruf and acquainted him with the delivering of the letter. Quoth Ma'aruf, "Bind on the loads"; and when they had done so, he

1 *i.e.* a calamity to the enemy: see vol. i. night xlvi. and *passim*.

donned the treasure-suit, and mounting the litter, became a thousand times greater and more majestic than the King. Then he set forward; but, when he had gone half-way, behold, the King met him with the troops, and seeing him riding in the Takhtrawan and clad in the dress aforesaid, threw himself upon him and saluted him, and giving him joy of his safety, greeted him with the greeting of peace. Then all the Lords of the land saluted him, and it was made manifest that he had spoken the truth and that in him there was no lie. Presently he entered the city in such state procession as would have caused the gall-bladder of the lion to burst[1] for envy, and the traders pressed up to him and kissed his hands, whilst Merchant Ali said to him, "Thou hast played off this trick and it hath prospered to thy hand, O Shaykh of Impostors! But thou deservest it and may Allah the Most High increase thee of His bounty!" whereupon Ma'aruf laughed. Then he entered the palace and sitting down on the throne, said, "Carry the loads of gold into the treasury of my uncle the King and bring me the bales of cloth." So they brought them to him and opened them before him, bale after bale, till they had unpacked the seven hundred loads, whereof he chose out the best and said, "Bear these to Princess Dunya that she may distribute them among her slave-girls; and carry her also this coffer of jewels that she may divide them among her handmaids and eunuchs." Then he proceeded to make over to the merchants in whose debt he was, stuffs by way of payment for their arrears, giving him whose due was a thousand, stuffs worth two thousand or more; after which he fell to distributing to the poor and needy, whilst the King looked on with greedy eyes and could not hinder him; nor did he cease largesse till he had made an end of the seven hundred loads, when he turned to the troops and proceeded to apportion amongst them emeralds and rubies, and pearls and coral, and other jewels by handsful, without count, till the King said to him, "Enough of this giving, O my son! There is but little left of the baggage." But he said, "I have plenty." Then indeed, his good faith was become manifest, and none could give him the lie; and he had come to reck not of giving, for that the Slave of the Seal-ring brought him whatsoever he sought. Presently, the treasurer came in to the King and said, "O King of the Age, the treasury is full indeed, and will not hold the rest of the loads. Where shall we lay that which is left of the gold and jewels?"

---

1 Both texts read "Asad" (lion) and Lane accepts it: there is no reason to change it for "Hásid" (Envier), the Lion being the Sultan of the Beasts and the most majestic.

And he assigned to him another place. As for the Princess Dunya, when she saw this her joy redoubled, and she marvelled and said in herself, "Would I wot how came he by all this wealth!" In like manner the traders rejoiced in that which he had given them and blessed him; whilst Merchant Ali marvelled and said to himself, "I wonder how he hath lied and swindled, that he hath gotten him all these treasures[1]? Had they come from the King's daughter, he had not wasted them on this wise! But how excellent is his saying who said:—

When the Kings' King giveth, in reverence pause * And venture not to enquire the cause:
Allah gives His gifts unto whom He will, * So respect and abide by His Holy Laws!"

So far concerning him; but as regards the King, he also marvelled with passing marvel at that which he saw of Ma'aruf's generosity and open-handedness in the largesse of wealth. Then the Merchant went in to his wife, who met him, smiling and laughing-lipped and kissed his hand, saying, "Didst thou mock me or hadst thou a mind to prove me with thy saying:—I am a poor man and a fugitive from my wife? Praised be Allah for that I failed not of my duty to thee! For thou art my beloved, and there is none dearer to me than thou, whether thou be rich or poor. But I would have thee tell me what didst thou design by these words." Said Ma'aruf, "I wished to prove thee and see whether thy love were sincere or for the sake of wealth and the greed of worldly good. But now 'tis become manifest to me that thine affection is sincere, and as thou art a true woman, so welcome to thee! I know thy worth." Then he went apart into a place by himself and rubbed the seal-ring, whereupon Abu al-Sa'adat presented himself and said to him, "Adsum, at thy service! Ask what thou wilt." Quoth Ma'aruf, "I want a treasure-suit and treasure-trinkets for my wife, including a necklace of forty unique jewels." Quoth the Jinni, "To hear is to obey," and brought him what he sought, whereupon Ma'aruf dismissed him, and carrying the dress and ornaments in to his wife, laid them before her and said, "Take these and put them on and welcome!" When she saw this her wits fled for joy, and she found among the ornaments a pair of anklets of gold set with jewels of the handiwork of the magicians, and bracelets and earrings and a belt[2] such as no money could

1 The Cairene knew his fellow Cairene and was not to be taken in by him.

2 Arab. "Hizám": Lane reads "Khizám" = a nose-ring, for which see appendix to Lane's M. E. The untrained European eye dislikes these

buy. So she donned the dress and ornaments and said to Ma'aruf, "O my lord, I will treasure these up for holidays and festivals." But he answered, "Wear them always, for I have others in plenty." And when she put them on and her women beheld her, they rejoiced and bussed his hands. Then he left them, and going apart by himself, rubbed the seal-ring, whereupon its slave appeared, and he said to him, "Bring me an hundred suits of apparel, with their ornaments of gold." "Hearing and obeying," answered Abu al-Sa'adat, and brought him the hundred suits, each with its ornaments wrapped up within it. Ma'aruf took them and called aloud to the slave-girls, who came to him and he gave them each a suit; so they donned them and became like the black-eyed girls of Paradise, whilst the Princess Dunya shone amongst them as the moon among the stars. One of the handmaids told the King of this, and he came in to his daughter and saw her and her women dazzling all who beheld them; whereat he wondered with passing wonderment. Then he went out, and calling his Wazir, said to him, "O Wazir, such and such things have happened; what sayst thou now of this affair?" Said he, "O King of the Age, this be no merchant's fashion; for a merchant keepeth a piece of linen by him for years, and selleth it not but at a profit. How should a merchant have generosity such as this generosity, and whence should he get the like of these moneys and jewels of which but a slight matter is found with the Kings? So how should loads thereof be found with merchants? Needs must there be a cause for this; but, an thou wilt hearken to me, I will make the truth of the case manifest to thee." Answered the King, "O Wazir, I will do thy bidding." Rejoined the Minister, "Do thou forgather with thy son-in-law and make a show of affect to him and talk with him and say:—O my son-in-law, I have a mind to go, I and thou and the Wazir, but no more, to a flower-garden, that we may take our pleasure there. When we come to the garden we will set on the table wine, and I will ply him therewith and compel him to drink; for when he shall have drunken he will lose his reason and his judgment will forsake him. Then we will question him of the truth of his case and he will discover to us his secrets, for wine is a traitor and Allah-gifted is he who said:—

When we drank the wine, and it crept its way * To the place of
Secrets, I cried, "O stay!"

---

decorations and there is certainly no beauty in the hoops which Hindu women insert through the nostrils, camel-fashion, as if to receive the cord acting bridle. But a drop-pearl hanging to the septum is at least as pretty as the heavy pendants by which some European women lengthen their ears.

In my fear lest its influence stint my wits * And my friends spy matters that hidden lay.

When he hath told us the truth we shall ken his case and may deal with him as we will; because I fear for thee the consequences of this his present fashion: haply he will covet the kingship and win over the troops by generosity and lavishing money and so depose thee and take the kingdom from thee." "True," answered the King.——And Shahrazad perceived the dawn of day and ceased to say her permitted say.

Now when it was the Nine Hundred and Ninety-eighth Night,

She resumed, It hath reached me, O auspicious King, that when the Wazir devised this device the King said to him, "Thou hast spoken sooth!" and they passed the night on this agreement. And when morning morrowed the King went forth and sat in the guest-chamber, when lo and behold! the grooms and serving-men came in to him in dismay. Quoth he, "What hath befallen you?" and quoth they, "O King of the Age, the Syces curried the horses and foddered them and the he-mules which brought the baggage; but, when we arose in the morning, we found that thy son-in-law's Mamelukes had stolen the horses and mules. We searched the stables, but found neither horse nor mule; so we entered the lodging of the Mamelukes and found none there, nor know we how they fled." The King marvelled at this, unknowing that the horses and Mamelukes were all Ifrits, the subjects of the Slave of the Spell, and asked the grooms, "O accursed, how could a thousand beasts and five hundred slaves and servants flee without your knowledge?" Answered they, "We know not how it happened"; and he cried, "Go, and when your lord cometh forth of the Harim, tell him the case." So they went out from before the King and sat down bewildered, till Ma'aruf came out, and seeing them chagrined, enquired of them, "What may be the matter?" They told him all that had happened and he said, "What is their worth that ye should be concerned for them? Wend your ways." And he sat laughing and was neither angry nor grieved concerning the case; whereupon the King looked in the Wazir's face and said to him, "What manner of man is this, with whom wealth is of no worth? Needs must there be a reason for this?" Then they talked with him awhile and the King said to him, "O my son-in-law, I have a mind to go, I, thou and the Wazir, to a garden, where we may divert ourselves." "No harm in that," said Ma'aruf. So they went forth to a flower-garden. wherein every sort of fruit was of kinds twain and its waters were flowing and its trees towering and its birds carolling. There they entered a pavilion, whose sight did away sorrow from the soul, and sat talking, whilst the Minister entertained them with rare tales and quoted merry quips and mirth-provoking sayings and Ma'aruf attentively listened, till the time of dinner came, when they set on a tray of meats and a flagon of wine. When they had eaten and washed hands, the Wazir filled the cup and gave it to the King, who drank it off; then he filled a second and handed it to Ma'aruf, saying, "Take the cup of the drink to which Reason boweth neck in reverence." Quoth Ma'aruf, "What is this, O Wazir?" and quoth he, "This is the grizzled[1] virgin and the old maid long kept at home,[2] the giver of joy to hearts, whereof saith the poet:—

The feet of sturdy Miscreants[3] went trampling heavy tread, * And she
hath ta'en a vengeance dire on every Arab's head.
A Káfir youth like fullest moon in darkness hands her round * Whose
eyne are strongest cause of sin by him inspiritèd.

And Allah-gifted is he who said:—

'Tis as if wine and he who bears the bowl, * Rising tô show her charms
for man to see,[4]
Were dancing undurn-Sun whose face the moon * Of night adorned
with stars of Gemini.
So subtle is her essence it would seem * Through every limb like course
of soul runs she.

And how excellent is the saying of the poet:—

Slept in mine arms full Moon of brightest blee * Nor did that sun eclipse
in goblet see:
I nighted spying fire whereto bow down * Magians, which bowed from
ewer's lip to me.

And that of another:—

It runs through every joint of them as runs * The surge of health
returning to the sick.

---

1 Arab. "Shamtá," one of the many names of wine, the "speckled" alluding to the bubbles which dance upon the freshly filled cup.

2 *i.e.* in the cask. These "merry quips" strongly suggest the dismal toasts of our not remote ancestors.

3 Arab. "A'láj" plur. of "'Ilj," and rendered by Lane "the stout foreign infidels." The next line alludes to the cupbearer, who was generally a slave and a non-Moslem.

4 As if it were a bride. See night dccxvi. The stars of Jauzá (Gemini) are the cupbearer's eyes

And yet another :—

I marvel at its pressers, how they died * And left us *aqua vitæ*—lymph of life!

And yet goodlier is the saying of Abu Nowas :—

Cease then to blame me, for thy blame doth anger bring * And with the draught that madded me come med'cining:
A yellow girl[1] whose court cures every carking care; * Did a stone touch it would with joy and glee upspring:
She riseth in her ewer during darkest night * The house with brightest sheeniest light illumining:
And going round of youths to whom the world inclines[2] * Ne'er, save in whatso way they please, their hearts shall wring.
From hand of cup-dight[3] lass begarbed like handsome lad,[4] * Wencher and Tribe of Lot alike enamouring,
She comes: and say to him who dares claim lore of love * Something hast learnt but still there's many another thing.

But best of all is the saying of Ibn al-Mu'tazz[5]:—

On the shaded woody island[6] His showers Allah deign * Shed on Convent hight Abdún[7] drop and drip of railing rain:
Oft the breezes of the morning have awakened me therein * When the Dawn shows her blaze,[8] ere the bird of flight was fain;
And the voices of the monks that with chants awoke the walls, * Black-frocked shavelings ever wont the cup a-morn to drain.[9]
'Mid the throng how many fair with langour-kohl'd eyes[10] * And lids enfolding lovely orbs where black on white was lain,

---

1 *i.e.* light-coloured wine.

2 The usual homage to youth and beauty.

3 Alluding to the wine-bowl.

4 Here Abu Nowas alluded to the "Ghulámiyah," or girl dressed like boy to act cupbearer.

5 Abdallah ibn al-Mu'tazz, son of Al-Mu'tazz bi 'llah, the 13th Abbaside, and great-great-grandson of Harun al-Rashid. He was one of the most renowned poets of the third century (A.H.) and died A.D. 908, strangled by the partisans of his nephew, Al-Muktadir bi 'llah, 18th Abbaside.

6 Jazirat ibn Omar, an island and town on the Tigris, north of Mosul. "Some versions of the poem, from which these verses are quoted, substitute El-Mutireh, a village near Samara (a town on the Tigris, 60 miles north of Baghdad), for El-Jezireh, *i.e.* Jeziret ibn Omar." (Payne.)

7 The Convent of Abdun on the east bank of the Tigris opposite the Jazirah was so called from a statesman who caused it to be built. For a variant of these lines see Ibn Khallikan, vol. ii. 42; here we miss the shady groves of Al-Matírah."

8 Arab. "Ghurrah," the white blaze on a horse's brow. In Ibn Khallikan the bird is the lark.

9 Arab. "Táy'i" = thirsty, used with Jáy'i = hungry.

10 Lit. "Kohl'd with Ghunj," for which we have no better word than "coquetry." But see night ccclxxxvii. It corresponds with the Latin crissare for women and œvere for men.

In secret came to see me by shirt of night disguised • In terror and in caution a-hurrying amain !
Then I rose and spread my cheek like a carpet on his path • In homage, and with skirts wiped his trail from off the plain.
But threatening disgrace rose the Crescent in the sky • Like the paring of a nail yet the light would never wane:
Then happened whatso happened: I disdain to kiss and tell, • So deem of us thy best and with queries never mell.

And gifteth of God is he who saith:—

In the morn I am richest of men • And in joy at good news I start up.
For I look on the liquid gold[1] • And I measure it out by the cup.

And how goodly is the saying of the poet:—

By Allah, this is th' only alchemy, • All said of other science false we see!
Carat of wine on hundredweight of woe • Transmuteth gloomiest grief to joy and glee.

And that of another:—

The glasses are heavy when empty brought • Till we charge them all with unmixèd wine.
Then so light are they that to fly they're fain • As bodies lightened by soul divine.

And yet another:—

Wine-cup and ruby-wine high worship claim; • Dishonour 'twere to see their honour waste:
Bury me, when I'm dead, by side of vine • Whose veins shall moisten bones in clay misplaced;
Nor bury me in wold and wild, for I • Dread only after death no wine to taste.[2]"

And he ceased not to egg him on to the drink, naming to him such of the virtues of wine as he thought well and reciting to him what occurred to him of poetry and pleasantries on the subject, till Ma'aruf addressed himself to sucking the cup-lips and cared

---

1 *i.e.* gold-coloured wine, as the Vino d'Oro.

2 Compare the charming song of Abu Miján translated from the German of Dr. Weil in Bohn's Edit of Ockley (p 149):—

When the Death-angel cometh mine eyes to close,
Dig my grave 'mid the vines on the hill's fair side;
For though deep in earth may my bones repose,
The juice of the grape shall their food provide.
Ah, bury me not in a barren land,
Or Death will appear to me dread and drear!
While fearless I'll wait what he hath in hand
An the scent of the vineyard my spirit cheer.

The glorious old drinker!

no longer for aught else. The Wazir ceased not to fill for him and he to drink and enjoy himself and make merry, till his wits wandered and he could not distinguish right from wrong. When the Minister saw that drunkenness had attained in him to utterest and the bounds transgressed, he said to him, "By Allah, O Merchant Ma'aruf, I admire whence thou gottest these jewels whose like the Kings of the Chosroës possess not! In all our lives never saw we a merchant that had heaped up riches like unto thine or more generous than thou, for thy doings are the doings of Kings and not merchants' doings. Wherefore, Allah upon thee, do thou acquaint me with this, that I may know thy rank and condition." And he went on to test him with questions and cajole him, till Ma'aruf, being reft of reason, said to him, "I'm neither merchant nor King," and told him his whole story from first to last. Then said the Wazir, "I conjure thee by Allah, O my Lord Ma'aruf, show us the ring, that we may see its make." So in his drunkenness he pulled off the ring and said, "Take it and look upon it." The Minister took it and turning it over, said, "If I rub it, will its slave appear?" Replied Ma'aruf, "Yes. Rub it and he will appear to thee, and do thou divert thyself with the sight of him." Thereupon the Wazir rubbed the ring, and behold, forthright appeared the Jinni and said, "Adsum, at thy service, O my lord! Ask and it shall be given to thee. Wilt thou ruin a city or raise a capital or kill a king? Whatso thou seekest I will do for thee, sans fail." The Wazir pointed to Ma'aruf and said, "Take up yonder wretch and cast him down in the most desolate of desert lands, where he shall find nothing to eat nor drink, so he may die of hunger and perish miserably, and none know of him." Accordingly, the Jinni snatched him up and flew with him betwixt heaven and earth, which when Ma'aruf saw, he made sure of destruction and wept and said, "O Abu al-Sa'adat, whither goest thou with me?" Replied the Jinni, "I go to cast thee down in the Desert Quarter,[1] O ill-bred wight of gross wits. Shall one have the like of this talisman and give it to the folk to gaze at? Verily, thou deservest that which hath befallen thee; and but that I fear Allah, I would let thee fall from a height of a thousand fathoms, nor shouldst thou reach the earth till the winds had

1 Arab. "Rub'a al-Kharáb," in Ibn al-Wardi Central Africa south of the Nile-sources, one of the richest regions in the world. Here it prob. alludes to the Rub'a al-Kháli or Great Arabian Desert, for which see night dclxxiv. In rhetoric it is opposed to the "Rub'a Maskún," or populated fourth of the world, the rest being held to be ocean.

torn thee to shreds." Ma'aruf was silent[1] and did not again bespeak him till he reached the Desert Quarter and casting him down there, went away and left him in that horrible place.—— And Shahrazad perceived the dawn of day and ceased saying her permitted say.

Now when it was the Nine Hundred and Ninety-ninth Night,

She said, It hath reached me, O auspicious King, that the Slave of the Seal-ring took up Ma'aruf and cast him down in the Desert Quarter, where he left him and went his ways. So much concerning him; but returning to the Wazir who was now in possession of the talisman, he said to the King, "How deemest thou now? Did I not tell thee that this fellow was a liar, an imposter, but thou wouldst not credit me?" Replied the King, "Thou wast in the right, O my Wazir, Allah grant thee weal! But give me the ring that I may solace myself with the sight." The Minister looked at him angrily and spat in his face, saying, "O lack-wits, how shall I give it to thee and abide thy servant, after I am become thy master? But I will spare thee no more on life." Then he rubbed the Seal-ring and said to the Slave, "Take up this ill-mannered churl and cast him down by his son-in-law the swindler-man." So the Jinni took him up and flew off with him, whereupon quoth the King to him, "O creature of my Lord, what is my crime?" Abu al-Sa'adat replied, "That wot I not, but my master hath commanded me and I cannot cross whoso hath compassed the enchanted ring." Then he flew on with him till he came to the Desert Quarter and, casting him down where he had cast Ma'aruf, left him and returned. The King hearing Ma'aruf weeping, went up to him and acquainted him with his case; and they sat weeping over that which had befallen them and found neither meat nor drink. Meanwhile the Minister, after driving father-in-law and son-in-law from the country, went forth from the garden, and summoning all the troops, held a Diwan, and told them what he had done with the King and Ma'aruf, and acquainted them with the affair of the talisman, adding, "Unless ye make me Sultan over you, I will bid the Slave of the Seal-ring take you up one and all and cast you down in the Desert Quarter, where you shall die of hunger and thirst." They replied, "Do us no damage, for we accept thee as Sultan over us and will not anywise gainsay thy bidding."

---

1 This is the noble resignation of the Moslem What a dialogue there would have been in a European book between man and devil!

So they agreed, in their own despite, to his being Sultan over them, and he bestowed on them robes of honour, seeking all he had a mind to of Abu al-Sa'adat, who brought it to him forthwith. Then he sat down on the throne and the troops did homage to him; and he sent to Princess Dunya, the King's daughter, saying, "Make thee ready, for I mean to come in unto thee this night, because I long for thee with love." When she heard this she wept, for the case of her husband and father was grievous to her, and sent to him saying, "Have patience with me till my period of widowhood[1] be ended: then draw up thy contract of marriage with me and go in to me according to law." But he sent back to say to her, "I know neither period of widowhood nor to delay have I a mood; and I need not a contract nor know I lawful from unlawful; but needs must I go in unto thee this night." She answered him, saying, "So be it, then, and welcome to thee!" but this was a trick on her part. When the answer reached the Wazir he rejoiced and his breast was broadened, for that he was passionately in love with her. He bade set food before all the folk, saying, "Eat; this is my bride-feast; for I purpose to go in to the Princess Dunya this night." Quoth the Shaykh al-Islam, "It is not lawful for thee to go in unto her till her days of widowhood be ended and thou have drawn up thy contract of marriage with her." But he answered, "I know neither days of widowhood nor other period; so multiply not words on me." The Shaykh al-Islam was silent,[2] fearing his mischief, and said to the troops, "Verily, this man is a Kafir, a Miscreant, and hath neither creed nor religious conduct." As soon as it was evenfall, he went in to her and found her robed in her richest raiment and decked with her goodliest adornments. When she saw him she came to meet him, laughing, and said, "A blessed night! But hadst thou slain my father and my husband, it had been more to my mind." And he said, "There is no help but I slay them." Then she made him sit down and began to jest with him and make show of love, caressing him and smiling in his face so that his reason fled; but she cajoled him with her coaxing and cunning only that she might get possession

1 Arab. "Al-'iddah," the period of four months and ten days which must elapse before she could legally marry again. But this was a palpable wile: she was not sure of her husband's death and he had not divorced her; so that although a "grass widow," a "Strohwitwe" as the Germans say, she could not wed again either with or without interval.

2 Here the silence is of cowardice, and the passage is a fling at the "time-serving" of the Olema, a favourite theme, like "banging the bishops" amongst certain Westerns.

of the ring and change his joy into calamity on the mother of his forehead[1]: nor did she deal thus with him but after the rede of him who said[2]:—

> I attained by my wits • What no sword had obtained,
> And return wi' the spoils • Whose sweet pluckings I gained.

When he saw her caress him and smile upon him, desire surged up in him and he besought her of carnal knowledge; but when he approached her she drew away from him and burst into tears, saying, "O my lord, seest thou not the man looking at us? I conjure thee by Allah, screen me from his eyes! How canst thou know me what while he looketh on us? When he heard this, he was angry and asked, "Where is the man?" and answered she, "There he is, in the bezel of the ring! putting out his head and staring at us." He thought that the Jinni was looking at them and said, laughing, "Fear not; this is the slave of the Seal-ring, and he is subject to me." Quoth she, "I am afraid of Ifrits; pull it off and throw it afar from me." So he plucked it off and laying it on the cushion, drew near to her, but she dealt him a kick, her foot striking him full in the stomach,[3] and he fell over on his back senseless; whereupon she cried out to her attendants, who came to her in haste, and said to them, "Seize him!" So forty slave-girls laid hold on him, whilst she hurriedly snatched up the ring from the cushion and rubbed it; whereupon Abu al-Sa'adat presented himself, saying, "Adsum, at thy service, O my mistress." Cried she, "Take up yonder Infidel and clap him in jail and shackle him heavily." So he took him and throwing him into the Prison of Wrath[4] returned and reported, "I have laid him in limbo." Quoth she, "Whither wentest thou with my father and my husband?" and quoth he, "I cast them down in the Desert Quarter." Then cried she, "I command thee to fetch them to me forthwith." He replied, "I hear and I obey," and taking flight at once, stayed not till he reached the Desert Quarter, where he lighted down upon them and found them sitting weeping

---

1 Arab. "Umm al-raas," the poll, crown of the head, here the place where a calamity coming down from heaven would first alight.

2 From Al-Hariri (Lane): the lines are excellent.

3 When the charming Princess is so ready at the *voie de faits*, the reader will understand how common is such energetic action among women of lower degree. The "fair sex" in Egypt has a horrible way of murdering men, especially husbands, by tying them down and tearing out the testes. See Lane, M. E., chapt. xiii.

4 Arab. "Sijn al-Ghazab," the dungeons appropriated to the worst of criminals, where they suffer penalties far worse than hanging or guillotining.

No. 57.

Ma'aruf the Cobbler and his Wife Fatimah.

"She dealt him a kick, her foot striking him full in the stomach, and he fell over on his back senseless; whereupon she cried out to her attendants, who came to her in haste."

and complaining each to other. Quoth he, "Fear not, for relief is come to you"; and he told them what the Wazir had done, adding, "Indeed I imprisoned him with my own hands in obedience to her, and she hath bidden me bear you back." And they rejoiced in his news. Then he took them both up and flew home with them; nor was it more than an hour before he brought them in to Princess Dunya, who rose and saluted sire and spouse. Then she made them sit down and brought them food and sweetmeats, and they passed the rest of the night with her. On the next day she clad them in rich clothing and said to the King, "O my papa, sit thou upon thy throne and be King as before and make my husband thy Wazir of the Right and tell thy troops that which hath happened. Then send for the Minister out of prison and do him die, and after burn him, for that he is a Miscreant, and would have gone in unto me in the way of lewdness, without the rites of wedlock, and he hath testified against himself that he is an Infidel and believeth in no religion. And do tenderly by thy son-in-law, whom thou makest thy Wazir of the Right." He replied, "Hearing and obeying, O my daughter. But do thou give me the ring or give it to thy husband." Quoth she, "It behoveth not that either thou or he have the ring. I will keep the ring myself, and belike I shall be more careful of it than you. Whatso ye wish seek it of me and I will demand it for you of the Slave of the Seal-ring. So fear no harm so long as I live, and after my death do what ye twain will with the ring." Quoth the King, "This is the right rede, O my daughter," and taking his son-in-law, went forth to the Diwan. Now the troops had passed the night in sore chagrin for Princess Dunya and that which the Wazir had done with her, in going in to her after the way of lewdness, without marriage-rites, and for his ill-usage of the King and Ma'aruf, and they feared lest the law of Al-Islam be dishonoured, because it was manifest to them that he was a Kafir. So they assembled in the Diwan and fell to reproaching the Shaykh al-Islam, saying, "Why didst thou not forbid him from going in to the Princess in the way of lewdness?" Said he, "O folk, the man is a Miscreant and hath gotten possession of the ring, and I and you may not prevail against him. But Almighty Allah will requite him his deed, and be ye silent lest he slay you." And as the host was thus engaged in talk, behold the King and Ma'aruf entered the Diwan.——And Shahrazad perceived the dawn of day and ceased to say her permitted say.

Now when it was the One Thousandth Night,

She continued, It hath reached me, O auspicious King, that when the troops sorely chagrined sat in the Diwan talking over the ill-deeds done by the Wazir to their Sovran, his son-in-law and his daughter, behold, the King and Ma'aruf entered. Then the King bade decorate the city and sent to fetch the Wazir from the place of duresse. So they brought him, and as he passed by the troops, they cursed him and abused him and menaced him, till he came to the King, who commanded to do him dead by the vilest of deaths. Accordingly, they slew him and after burned his body, and he went to Hell after the foulest of plights; and right well quoth one of him:—

The Compassionate show no ruth to the tomb where his bones shall lie • And Munkar and eke Nakir[1] ne'er cease to abide thereby!

The King made Ma'aruf his Wazir of the Right and the times were pleasant to them and their joys were untroubled. They abode thus five years till, in the sixth year, the King died and the Princess Dunya made Ma'aruf Sultan in her father's stead, but she gave him not the Seal-ring. During this time she had conceived by him and had borne him a boy of passing loveliness, excelling in beauty and perfection, who ceased not to be reared in the laps of nurses till he reached the age of five, when his mother fell sick of a deadly sickness and calling her husband to her, said to him, "I am ill." Quoth he, "Allah preserve thee, O dearling of my heart!" But quoth she, "Haply I shall die and thou needest not that I commend to thy care thy son: wherefore I charge thee but be careful of the ring, for thine own sake and for the sake of this thy boy." And he answered, "No harm shall befall him whom Allah preserveth!" Then she pulled off the ring and gave it to him, and on the morrow she was admitted to the mercy of Allah the Most High,[2] whilst Ma'aruf abode in possession of the kingship and applied himself to the business of governing. Now it chanced that one day, as he shook the

---

1 According to some modern Moslems Munkar and Nakir visit the graves of Infidels (non-Moslems) and Bashshir and Mubashshir ("Givers of glad tidings") those of Mohammedans. Petis de la Croix (Les Mille et un Jours, vol. iii. 258) speaks of the "Zoubanya," black angels who torture the damned under their chief Dabilah.

2 Very simple and pathetic is this short sketch of the noble-minded Princess's death.

handkerchief[1] and the troops withdrew to their places that he betook himself to the sitting-chamber, where he sat till the day departed and the night advanced with murks bedight. Then came in to him his cup-companions of the notables according to their custom, and sat with him by way of solace and diversion till midnight, when they craved permission to withdraw. He gave them leave and they retired to their houses; after which there came in to him a slave-girl affected to the service of his bed, who spread him the mattrass and doffing his apparel, clad him in his sleeping-gown. Then he lay down and she kneaded his feet till sleep overpowered him; whereupon she withdrew to her own chamber and slept. But suddenly he felt something beside him in the bed and awaking started up in alarm and cried, "I seek refuge with Allah from Satan the Stoned!" Then he opened his eyes and seeing by his side a woman foul of favour, said to her. "Who art thou?" Said she, "Fear not, I am thy wife Fatimah al-Urrah." Whereupon he looked in her face and knew her by her loathly form and the length of her dog-teeth: so he asked her, "Whence camest thou in to me and who brought thee to this country?" "In what country art thou at this present?" "In the city of Ikhtiyan al-Khutan. But thou, when didst thou leave Cairo?" "But now." "How can that be?" "Know," said she, "that, when I fell out with thee and Satan prompted me to do thee a damage, I complained of thee to the magistrates, who sought for thee and the Kazis enquired of thee, but found thee not. When two days were past, repentance gat hold upon me and I knew that the fault was with me; but penitence availed me not, and I abode for some days weeping for thy loss, till what was in my hand failed and I was obliged to beg my bread. So I fell to begging of all, from the courted rich to the contemned poor, and since thou leftest me, I have eaten of the bitterness of beggary and have been in the sorriest of conditions. Every night I sat beweeping our separation and that which I suffered, since thy departure, of humiliation and ignominy, of abjection and misery." And she went on to tell him what had befallen her, whilst he stared at her in amazement, till she said, "Yesterday, I went about begging all day but none gave me aught; and as often as I accosted any one and craved of him a crust of bread, he reviled me and gave me naught. When night came, I went to bed supperless, and hunger

1 In sign of dismissal (vol. iii. night cclx.). I have noted that "throwing the kerchief" is not an Eastern practice: the idea probably arose from the Oriental practice of sending presents in richly embroidered napkins and kerchiefs.

burned me and sore on me was that which I suffered: and I sat weeping when behold, one appeared to me and said, O woman, why weepest thou? Said I, Erst I had an husband who used to provide for me and fulfil my wishes; but he is lost to me and I know not whither he went and have been in sore straits since he left me. Asked he, What is thy husband's name? and I answered, His name is Ma'aruf. Quoth he, I ken him. Know that thy husband is now Sultan in a certain city, and if thou wilt I will carry thee to him. Cried I, I am under thy protection: of thy bounty bring me to him! So he took me up and flew with me between heaven and earth, till he brought me to this pavilion and said to me:—Enter yonder chamber and thou shalt see thy husband asleep on the couch. Accordingly I entered, and found thee in this state of lordship. Indeed, I had not thought thou wouldst forsake me, who am thy mate, and praised be Allah who hath united thee with me!" Quoth Ma'aruf, "Did I forsake thee or thou me? Thou complainedst of me from Kazi to Kazi, and endedst by denouncing me to the High Court and bringing down on me Abú Tabak from the Citadel: so I fled in mine own despite." And he went on to tell her all that had befallen him, and how he was become Sultan and had married the King's daughter, and how his beloved Dunya had died, leaving him a son who was then seven years old. She rejoined, "That which happened was fore-ordained of Allah; but I repent me and I place myself under thy protection, beseeching thee not to abandon me, but suffer me eat bread with thee by way of an alms." And she ceased not to humble herself to him and to supplicate him till his heart relented towards her and he said, "Repent from mischief and abide with me, and naught shall betide thee save what shall pleasure thee: but, an thou work any wickedness I will slay thee nor fear any one. And fancy not that thou canst complain of me to the High Court, and that Abu Tabak will come down on me from the Citadel; for I am become Sultan and the folk dread me: but I fear none save Allah Almighty, because I have a talismanic ring which when I rub, the Slave of the Signet appeareth to me. His name is Abu al-Sa'adat, and whatsoever I demand of him he bringeth to me. So, an thou desire to return to thine own country, I will give thee what shall suffice thee all thy life long and will send thee thither speedily; but, an thou desire to abide with me, I will clear for thee a palace and furnish it with the choicest of silks and appoint thee twenty slave-girls to serve thee and provide thee with dainty dishes and sumptuous suits, and thou shalt be a Queen and live in all delight till thou die or I die. What sayest thou of this?" "I wish to abide with thee," she answered, and kissed his hand and vowed repentance from frowardness. Accordingly, he set apart a palace for her sole use and gave her slave-girls and eunuchs, and she became a Queen. The young Prince used to visit her as he visited his sire; but she hated him for that he was not her son; and when the boy saw that she looked on him with the eye of aversion and anger, he shunned her and took a dislike to her. As for Ma'aruf, he occupied himself with the love of fair handmaidens and bethought him not of his wife Fatimah the Dung, for that she was grown a grizzled old fright, foul-favoured to the sight, a bald-headed blight, loathlier than the snake speckled black and white; the more that she had beyond measure evil entreated him aforetime; and as saith the adage, "Ill-usage the root of desire disparts and sows hate in the soil of hearts"; and God-gifted is he who saith:—

Beware of losing hearts of men by thine injurious deed; * For when
Aversion takes his place none may dear Love restore:
Hearts, when affection flies from them, are likest unto glass * Which
broken, cannot whole be made,—'tis breached for evermore.

And indeed Ma'aruf had not given her shelter by reason of any praiseworthy quality in her, but he dealt with her thus generously only of desire for the approval of Allah Almighty.—Here Dunyazad interrupted her sister Shahrazad, saying, "How winsome are these words of thine which win hold of the heart more forcibly than enchanters' eyne; and how beautiful are these wondrous books thou hast cited, and the marvellous and singular tales thou hast recited!" Quoth Shahrazad, "And where is all this compared with what I shall relate to thee on the coming night, an I live and the King deign spare my days?" So when morning morrowed and the day brake in its sheen and shone, the King arose from his couch with breast broadened and in high expectation for the rest of the tale, and saying, "By Allah, I will not slay her till I hear the last of her story"; repaired to his Darbár, while the Wazir, as was his wont, presented himself at the Palace, shroud under arm. Shahryar tarried abroad all that day, bidding and forbidding between man and man; after which he returned to his Harim, and according to his custom, went in to his wife Shahrazad.[1]

1 Curious to say, both Lane and Payne omit this passage which appears in both texts (Mac. and Bul.). The object is evidently to prepare the reader for the ending by reverting to the beginning of the tale; and its prolixity has its

Now when it was the One Thousand and First Night,

Dunyazad said to her sister, "Do thou finish for us the History of Ma'aruf!" She replied, "With love and goodly gree, an my lord deign permit me recount it." Quoth the King, "I permit thee; for that I am fain of hearing it." So she said:—It hath reached me, O auspicious King, that Ma'aruf would have naught to do with his wife by way of conjugal duty. Now when she saw that he held aloof from her bed and occupied himself with other women, she hated him and jealousy gat the mastery of her and Iblis prompted her to take the Seal-ring from him and slay him and make herself Queen in his stead. So she went forth one night from her pavilion, intending for that in which was her husband King Ma'aruf: and it chanced by decree of the Decreer and His written destiny, that Ma'aruf lay that night with one of his concubines; a damsel endowed with beauty and loveliness, symmetry, and a stature all grace. And it was his wont, of the excellence of his piety, that, when he was minded to have to lie with a woman, he would doff the enchanted Seal-ring from his finger, in reverence to the Holy Names graven thereon, and lay it on the pillow, nor would he don it again till he had purified himself by the Ghusl-ablution. Moreover, when he had lain with a woman, he was used to order her go forth from him before daybreak, of his fear for the Seal-ring; and when he went to the Hammam he locked the door of the pavilion till his return, when he put on the ring, and after this, all were free to enter according to custom. His wife Fatimah the Dung knew of all this and went not forth from her place till she had certified herself of the case. So she sallied out when the night was dark, purposing to go in to him whilst he was drowned in sleep, and steal the ring, unseen of him. Now it chanced at this time that the King's son had gone out, without light, to the Chapel of Ease for an occasion, and sat down over the marble slab[1] of the jakes in the dark, leaving the door open. Presently, he saw Fatimah come forth of her pavilion and make stealthily for that of his father, and said in himself, "What aileth this witch to leave her lodging in the dead of the night and make for my father's pavilion? Needs must there be some reason for this": so he went out after

effect as in the old Romances of Chivalry from Amadis of Gaul to the Seven Champions of Christendom. If it provokes impatience it also heightens expectation; "it is like the long elm-avenues of our forefathers: we wish ourselves at the end, but we know that at the end there is something great."

1 Arab. "alá malákay bayti 'l-ráhah"; on the two slabs. See vol. i., night xxii.

her and followed in her steps unseen of her. Now he had a short sword of watered steel, which he held so dear that he went not to his father's Diwan except he were girt therewith; and his father used to laugh at him and exclaim, "Mahallah[1]! This is a mighty fine sword of thine, O my son! But thou hast not gone down with it to battle nor cut off a head therewith." Whereupon the boy would reply, "I will not fail to cut off with it some head which deserveth[2] cutting." And Ma'aruf would laugh at his words. Now when treading in her track, he drew the sword from its sheath and he followed her till she came to his father's pavilion and entered, whilst he stood and watched her from the door. He saw her searching about, and heard her say to herself, "Where hath he laid the Seal-ring?" whereby he knew that she was looking for the ring and he waited till she found it and said, "Here it is." Then she picked it up and turned to go out; but he hid behind the door. As she came forth, she looked at the ring and turned it about in her grasp. But when she was about to rub it, he raised his hand with the sword and smote her on the neck; and she cried a single cry and fell down dead. With this Ma'aruf awoke and seeing his wife strown on the ground, with her blood flowing, and his son standing with the drawn sword in his hand, said to him, "What is this, O my son?" He replied, "O my father, how often hast thou said to me:—Thou hast a mighty fine sword; but thou hast not gone down with it to battle nor cut off a head. And I have answered thee, saying, I will not fail to cut off with it a head which deserveth cutting. And now, behold, I have therewith cut off for thee a head well worth the cutting!" And he told him what had passed. Ma'aruf sought for the Seal-ring, but found it not; so he searched the dead woman's body till he saw her hand closed upon it; whereupon he took it from her grasp and said to the boy, "Thou art indeed my very son, without doubt or dispute; Allah ease thee in this world and the next, even as thou hast eased me of this vile woman! Her attempt led only to her own destruction, and Allah-gifted is he who said:—

When forwards Allah's aid a man's intent, • His wish in every case shall find consent:

---

1 Here the exclamation wards off the Evil Eye from the Sword and the wearer: Mr. Payne notes, "The old English exclamation 'Cock's 'ill!' (*i.e.* God's will, thus corrupted for the purpose of evading the statute of 3 Jac. i. against profane swearing) exactly corresponds to the Arabic"—with a difference, I add.

2 Arab. "Mustahakk"=deserving (Lane) or worth (Payne) the cutting.

But an that aid of Allah be refused • His first attempt shall do him damagement.

Then King Ma'aruf called aloud to some of his attendants, who came in haste, and he told them what his wife Fatimah the Dung had done, and bade them to take her and lay her in a place till the morning. They did his bidding, and next day he gave her in charge to a number of eunuchs, who washed her and shrouded her and made her a tomb[1] and buried her. Thus her coming from Cairo was but to her grave, and Allah-gifted is he who said[2]:—

We trod the steps appointed for us: and he whose steps are appointed must tread them.
He whose death is decreed to take place in our land shall not die in any land but that.

And how excellent is the saying of the poet:—

I wot not, whenas to a land I fare, • Good luck pursuing, what my lot shall be.
Whether the fortune I perforce pursue • Or the misfortune which pursueth me.

After this, King Ma'aruf sent for the husbandman, whose guest he had been when he was a fugitive, and made him his Wazir of the Right and his Chief Counsellor.[3] Then, learning that he had a daughter of passing beauty and loveliness, of qualities nature-ennobled at birth and exalted of worth, he took her to wife; and in due time he married his son. So they abode awhile in all solace of life and its delights, and their days were serene and their joys untroubled, till there came to them the Destroyer of delights and the Sunderer of societies, the Depopulator of populous places and the Orphaner of sons and daughters. And glory be to the Living who dieth not and in whose hand are the Keys of the Seen and the Unseen!

---

1 Arab. "Mashhad" the same as "Sháhid" = the upright stones at the head and foot of the grave. Lane mistranslates, "Make for her a funeral procession."

2 These lines have occurred before. I quote Lane.

3 There is nothing strange in such sudden elevations amongst Moslems and even in Europe we still see them occasionally. The family in the East, however humble, is a model and miniature of the state, and learning is not always necessary to wisdom.

Conclusion.

Now during this time Shahrazad had borne the King three boy children : so, when she had made an end of the story of Ma'aruf, she rose to her feet and kissing ground before him, said, "O King of the time and unique one[1] of the age and the tide, I am thine handmaid and these thousand nights and a night have I entertained thee with stories of folk gone before and admonitory instances of the men of yore. May I then make bold to crave a boon of Thy Highness?" He replied, "Ask, O Shahrazad, and it shall be granted to thee.[2]" Whereupon she cried out to the nurses and the eunuchs, saying, "Bring me my children." So they brought them to her in haste, and they were three boy children, one walking, one crawling and one sucking. She took them and setting them before the King, again kissed ground and said, "O King of the Age, these are thy children and I crave that thou release me from the doom of death, as a dole to these infants; for, an thou kill me, they will become motherless and will find none among women to rear them as they should be reared." When the King heard this, he wept and straining the boys to his bosom, said, "By Allah, O Shahrazad, I pardoned thee before the coming of these children, for that I found thee chaste, pure, ingenuous and pious! Allah bless thee and thy father and thy mother and thy root and thy branch! I take the Almighty to witness against me that I exempt thee from aught that can harm thee." So she kissed his hands and feet and rejoiced with exceeding joy, saying, "The Lord make thy life long and increase thee in dignity and majesty[3]!" presently adding, "Thou marvelledst at that which befell thee on the part of women; yet there betided the Kings of the Chosroës before thee greater mishaps and more grievous than that which hath befallen thee, and indeed I have set forth unto thee that which happened to Caliphs and Kings and others with their women, but the relation is longsome, and hearkening groweth tedious, and in this is all-sufficient warning for the man of wits and admonishment for the

1 Arab. "Fárid," which may also mean "union-pearl."

2 Trébutien (iii. 497) cannot deny himself the pleasure of a French touch, making the King reply, "C'est assez ; qu'on lui coupe la tête, car ces dernières histoires surtout m'ont causé un ennui mortel." This reading is found in some of the MSS

3 After this I borrow from the Bresl. Edit. inserting passages from the Mac. Edit.

wise." Then she ceased to speak, and when King Shahryar heard her speech and profited by that which she said, he summoned up his reasoning powers and cleansed his heart and caused his understanding revert, and turned to Allah Almighty and said to himself, "Since there befell the Kings of the Chosroës more than that which hath befallen me, never whilst I live shall I cease to blame myself for the past. As for this Shahrazad, her like is not found in the lands; so praise be to Him Who appointed her a means for delivering His creatures from oppression and slaughter!" Then he arose from his séance and kissed her head, whereat she rejoiced, she and her sister Dunyazad, with exceeding joy. When the morning morrowed the King went forth, and sitting down on the throne of the Kingship, summoned the Lords of his land; whereupon the Chamberlains and Nabobs and Captains of the host went in to him and kissed ground before him. He distinguished the Wazir, Shahrazad's sire, with special favour and bestowed on him a costly and splendid robe of honour, and entreated him with the utmost kindness, and said to him, "Allah protect thee for that thou gavest me to wife thy noble daughter, who hath been the means of my repentance from slaying the daughters of folk. Indeed, I have found her pure and pious, chaste and ingenuous, and Allah hath vouchsafed me by her three boy children; wherefore praised be He for His passing favour." Then he bestowed robes of honour upon his Wazirs and Emirs and Chief Officers and he set forth to them briefly that which had betided him with Shahrazad, and how he had turned from his former ways and repented him of what he had done, and purposed to take the Wazir's daughter Shahrazad to wife, and let draw up the marriage-contract with her. When those who were present heard this, they kissed ground before him and blessed him and his betrothed[1] Shahrazad, and the Wazir thanked her. Then Shahryar made an end of his sitting in all weal, whereupon the folk dispersed to their dwelling-places, and the news was bruited abroad that the King purposed to marry the Wazir's daughter, Shahrazad. Then he proceeded to make ready the wedding gear, and presently he sent after his brother, King Shah Zaman, who came, and King Shahryar went forth to meet him with the troops. Furthermore, they decorated the city after the goodliest fashion and diffused scents from censers and burnt aloes-wood and other perfumes in all the markets and thoroughfares and rubbed themselves with saffron,[2] what while the drums

1 *i.e.* whom he intended to marry with regal ceremony.

2 The use of coloured powders in sign of holiday-making is not obsolete in India. See Herklots for the use of "Huldee" (Haldí) or turmeric-powder, pp. 64-65.

beat and the flutes and pipes sounded and mimes and mountebanks played and plied their arts, and the King lavished on them gifts and largesse, and in very deed it was a notable day. When they came to the palace, King Shahryar commanded to spread the tables with beasts roasted whole, and sweetmeats, and all manner of viands, and bade the crier cry to the folk that they should come up to the Diwan and eat and drink, and that this should be a means of reconciliation between him and them. So high and low, great and small, came up unto him, and they abode on that wise, eating and drinking, seven days with their nights. Then the King shut himself up with his brother, and related to him that which had betided him with the Wazir's daughter Shahrazad during the past three years, and told him what he had heard from her of proverbs and parables, chronicles and pleasantries, quips and jests, stories and anecdotes, dialogues and histories, and elegies and other verses; whereat King Shah Zaman marvelled with the utmost marvel and said, "Fain would I take her younger sister to wife, so we may be two brothers-german to two sisters-german, and they on like wise be sisters to us; for that the calamity which befell me was the cause of our discovering that which befell thee, and all this time of three years past I have taken no delight in woman, save that I lie each night with a damsel of my kingdom, and every morning I do her to death; but now I desire to marry thy wife's sister Dunyazad." When King Shahryar heard his brother's words, he rejoiced with joy exceeding, and arising forthright, went in to his wife Shahrazad and acquainted her with that which his brother purposed, namely, that he sought her sister Dunyazad in wedlock; whereupon she answered, "O King of the Age, we seek of him one condition, to wit, that he take up his abode with us, for that I cannot brook to be parted from my sister an hour, because we were brought up together, and may not endure separation each from other.[1] If he accept this pact, she is his handmaid." King Shahriyar returned to his brother and acquainted him with that which Shahrazad had said; and he replied, "Indeed, this is what was in my mind, for that I desire nevermore to be parted from thee one hour. As for the kingdom, Allah the Most High shall send to it whomso He chooseth, for that I have no longer a desire for the kingship." When King Shahryar heard his brother's words, he rejoiced

1 Many Moslem families insist upon this before giving their girls in marriage, and the practice is still popular amongst many Mediterranean peoples.

exceedingly and said, "Verily, this is what I wished, O my brother. So Alhamdolillah—Praised be Allah!—who hath brought about union between us." Then he sent after the Kazis and Olema, Captains and Notables, and they married the two brothers to the two sisters. The contracts were written out, and the two Kings bestowed robes of honour of silk and satin on those who were present, whilst the city was decorated and the rejoicings were renewed. The King commanded each Emir and Wazir and Chamberlain and Nabob to decorate his palace, and the folk of the city were gladdened by the presage of happiness and contentment. King Shahryar also bade slaughter sheep, and set up kitchens and made bride-feasts and fed all comers, high and low: and he gave alms to the poor and needy and extended his bounty to great and small. Then the eunuchs went forth that they might perfume the Hammam for the brides; so they scented it with rose water and willow-flower water and pods of musk, and fumigated it with Kákilí[1] eagle-wood and ambergris. Then Shahrazad entered, she and her sister Dunyazad, and they cleansed their heads and clipped their hair. When they came forth of the Hammam-bath, they donned raiment and ornaments, such as men were wont prepare for the Kings of the Chosröes; and among Shahrazad's apparel was a dress purfled with red gold and wrought with counterfeit presentments of birds and beasts. And the two sisters encircled their necks with necklaces of jewels of price, in the like whereof Iskander[2] rejoiced not, for therein were great jewels such as amazed the wit and dazzled the eye; and the imagination was bewildered at their charms, for indeed each of them was brighter than the sun and the moon. Before them they lighted brilliant flambeaux of wax in candelabra of gold, but their faces outshone the flambeaux, for that they had eyes sharper than unsheathed swords and the lashes of their eyelids bewitched all hearts. Their cheeks were rosy red, and their necks and shapes gracefully swayed, and their eyes wantoned like the gazelle's; and the slave-girls came to meet them with instruments of music. Then the two Kings entered the Hammam-bath, and when they came forth they sat down on a couch set with pearls and gems, whereupon the two sisters came up to them and stood between their hands, as they were moons, bending and leaning from side to side in their beauty and loveliness. Presently they brought forward Shahrazad and displayed her, for the first dress,

---

1 *i.e.* Sumatran.

2 *i.e.* Alexander, according to the Arabs; see night cccclxiv.

in a red suit; whereupon King Shahryar rose to look upon her and the wits of all present, men and women, were bewitched for that she was even as saith of her one of her describers[1]:—

A sun on wand in knoll of sand she showed, * Clad in her cramoisy-hued chemisette:
Of her lips' honey-dew she gave me drink * And with her rosy cheeks quencht fire she set.

Then they attired Dunyazad in a dress of blue brocade, and she became as she were the full moon when it shineth forth. So they displayed her in this, for the first dress, before King Shah Zaman, who rejoiced in her and well-nigh swooned away for love-longing and amorous desire; yea, he was distraught with passion for her, whenas he saw her, because she was as saith of her one of her describers in these couplets[2]:—

She comes apparelled in an azure vest * Ultramarine as skies are deckt and dight:
I view'd th' unparallel'd sight, which showed my eyes * A Summer-moon upon a Winter-night.

Then they returned to Shahrazad and displayed her in the second dress, a suit of surpassing goodliness, and veiled her face with her hair like a chin-veil.[3] Moreover, they let down her side-locks, and she was even as saith of her one of her describers in these couplets:—

O hail to him whose locks his cheeks o'ershade, * Who slew my life by cruel hard despight:
Said I, "Hast veiled the Morn in Night?" He said, * "Nay, I but veil Moon in hue of Night."

Then they displayed Dunyazad in a second and a third and a fourth dress, and she paced forward like the rising sun, and swayed to and fro in the insolence of beauty; and she was even as saith the poet of her in these couplets[4]:—

The sun of beauty she to all appears * And, lovely coy, she mocks all loveliness:
And when he fronts her favour and her smile * A-morn, the sun of day in clouds must dress.

Then they displayed Shahrazad in the third dress and the fourth

---

1 These lines are in vol. i. night xxii.

2 I repeat the lines from vol. i. night xxii.

3 All these coquetries require as much inventiveness as a cotillon; the text alludes to fastening the bride's tresses across her mouth, giving her the semblance of beard and mustachioes.

4 Repeated from vol. i. night xxii.

and the fifth, and she became as she were a Bán-branch snell or a thirsting gazelle, lovely of face and perfect in attributes of grace, even as saith of her one in these couplets[1]:—

She comes like fullest moon on happy night, * Taper of waist with shape of magic might:
She hath an eye whose glances quell mankind, * And ruby on her cheeks reflects his light:
Enveils her hips the blackness of her hair; * Beware of curls that bite with viper-bite!
Her sides are silken-soft, what while the heart * Mere rock behind that surface 'scapes our sight:
From the fringed curtains of her eyne she shoots * Shafts that at furthest range on mark alight.

Then they returned to Dunyazad and displayed her in the fifth dress and in the sixth, which was green, when she surpassed with her loveliness the fair of the four quarters of the world, and outvied, with the brightness of her countenance, the full moon at rising tide; for she was even as saith of her the poet in these couplets[2]:—

A damsel 't was the tirer's art had decked with snare and sleight, * And robed with rays as though the sun from her had borrowed light:
She came before us wondrous clad in chemisette of green, * As veilèd by his leafy screen Pomegranate hides from sight:
And when he said, " How callest thou the fashion of thy dress ? " * She answered us in pleasant way, with double meaning dight,
"We call this garment *crève-cœur;* and rightly is it hight, * For many a heart wi' this we brake and harried many a sprite."

Then they displayed Shahrazad in the sixth and seventh dresses and clad her in youth's clothing, whereupon she came forward swaying from side to side, and coquettishly moving, and indeed she ravished wits and hearts and ensorcelled all eyes with her glances. She shook her sides and swayed her haunches, then put her hair on sword-hilt and went up to King Shahryar, who embraced her as hospitable host embraceth guest, and threatened her in her ear with the taking of the sword; and she was even as saith of her the poet in these words:—

Were not the Murk[3] of gender male, * Than feminines surpassing fair,
Tire-women they had grudged the bride, * Who made her beard and whiskers wear!

---

1 Repeated from vol. i. night xxii.
2 See vol. i night xxii.
3 Arab " Sawád = the blackness of the hair.

Thus also they did with her sister Dunyazad; and when they had made an end of the display, the King bestowed robes of honour on all who were present, and sent the brides to their own apartments. Then Shahrazad went in to King Shahryar and Dunyazad to King Shah Zaman, and each of them solaced himself with the company of his beloved consort, and the hearts of the folk were comforted. When morning morrowed, the Wazir came in to the two Kings and kissed ground before them; wherefore they thanked him and were large of bounty to him. Presently they went forth and sat down upon couches of Kingship, whilst all the Wazirs and Emirs and Grandees and Lords of the land presented themselves and kissed ground. King Shahryar ordered them dresses of honour and largesse, and they prayed for the permanence and prosperity of the King and his brother. Then the two Sovrans appointed their sire-in-law the Wazir to be Viceroy in Samarcand, and assigned him five of the Chief Emirs to accompany him, charging them attend him and do him service. The Minister kissed ground and prayed that they might be vouchsafed length of life: then he went in to his daughters, whilst the Eunuchs and Ushers walked before him, and saluted them and farewelled them. They kissed his hands and gave him joy of the kingship and bestowed on him immense treasures; after which he took leave of them, and setting out, fared days and nights, till he came near Samarcand, where the townspeople met him at a distance of three marches and rejoiced in him with exceeding joy. So he entered the city, and they decorated the houses and it was a notable day. He sat down on the throne of his kingship, and the Wazirs did him homage and the Grandees and Emirs of Samarcand and all prayed that he might be vouchsafed justice and victory and length of continuance. So he bestowed on them robes of honour and entreated them with distinction, and they made him Sultan over them. As soon as his father-in-law had departed for Samarcand, King Shahryar summoned the Grandees of his realm and made them a stupendous banquet of all manner of delicious meats and exquisite sweetmeats. He also bestowed on them robes of honour and guerdoned them, and divided the kingdoms between himself and his brother in their presence, whereat the folk rejoiced. Then the two Kings abode, each ruling a day in turn, and they were ever in harmony each with other, while on similar wise their wives continued in the love of Allah Almighty and in thanksgiving to Him; and the peoples and the provinces were at peace, and the preachers prayed for them from the pulpits, and their report was bruited abroad and the travellers bore tidings of them to all lands. In due time King Shahryar summoned chroniclers and copyists, and bade them write all that had betided him with his wife, first and last; so they wrote this and named it "The Stories of the Thousand Nights and A Night." The book came to thirty volumes and these the King laid up in his treasury. And the two brothers abode with their wives in all pleasance and solace of life and its delights, for that indeed Allah the Most High had changed their annoy into joy; and on this wise they continued till there took them the Destroyer of delights and the Severer of societies, the Desolator of dwelling-places, and Garnerer of grave-yards, and they were translated to the ruth of Almighty Allah; their houses fell waste and their palaces lay in ruins,[1] and the Kings inherited their riches. Then there reigned after them a wise ruler, who was just, keen-witted and accomplished, and loved tales and legends, especially those which chronicle the doings of Sovrans and Sultans, and he found in the treasury these marvellous stories and wondrous histories, contained in the thirty volumes aforesaid. So he read in them a first book and a second and a third and so on to the last of them, and each book astounded and delighted him more than that which preceded it, till he came to the end of them. Then he admired whatso he had read therein of description and discourse and rare traits and anecdotes and moral instances and reminiscences, and bade the folk copy them and dispread them over all lands and climes; wherefore their report was bruited abroad and the people named them "The marvels and wonders of the Thousand Nights and A Night." This is all that hath come down to us of the origin of this book, and Allah is All-knowing.[2] So Glory be to Him Whom the shifts of Time waste not away, nor doth aught of chance or change affect His sway: Whom one case diverteth not from other case, and Who is sole in the attributes of perfect grace. And prayer and the Peace be upon the Lord's Pontiff and Chosen One among His creatures, our Lord MOHAMMED the Prince of mankind through whom we supplicate Him for a goodly and a godly

FINIS.

1 Because Easterns build, but never repair.
2 *i.e.* God only knows if it be true or not.

والسلام

Terminal Essay.

PRELIMINARY.

THE reader who has reached this terminal stage will hardly require my assurance that he has seen the mediæval Arab at his best and, perhaps, at his worst. In glancing over the myriad pictures of this panorama, those who can discern the soul of goodness in things evil will note the true nobility of the Moslem's mind in the Moyen Age, and the cleanliness of his life from cradle to grave. As a child he is devoted to his parents, fond of his comrades, and respectful to his "pastors and masters," even schoolmasters. As a lad he prepares for man-hood with a will, and this training occupies him throughout youth-tide: he is a gentleman in manners without awkwardness, vulgar astonishment, or mauvaise-honte. As a man he is high-spirited and energetic, always ready to fight for his Sultan, his country and, especially, his Faith: courteous and affable, rarely failing in temperance of mind and self-respect, self-control, and self-command; hospitable to the stranger, attached to his fellow-citizens, submissive to superiors, and kindly to inferiors—if such classes exist: Eastern despotisms have arrived nearer the idea of equality and fraternity than any republic yet invented. As a friend he proves a model to the Damons and Pythiases: as a lover an exemplar to Don Quijote without the noble old Caballero's touch of eccentricity. As a knight he is the mirror of chivalry, doing battle for the weak and debelling the strong, while ever "defending the honour of women." As a husband his patriarchal position causes him to be loved and fondly loved by more than one wife: as a father, affection for his children rules his life: he is domestic in the highest degree, and he finds few pleasures beyond the bosom of his family. Lastly, his death is simple, pathetic and edifying as the life which led to it.

Considered in a higher phase, the mediæval Moslem mind displays, like the ancient Egyptian, a most exalted moral idea, the deepest reverence for all things connected with his religion, and a sublime conception of the Unity and Omnipotence of the Deity. Noteworthy, too, is a proud resignation to the decrees of Fate and Fortune (Kazá wa Kadar), of Destiny and Predestination—a feature which ennobles the low aspect of Al-Islam even in these her days of comparative degeneration and local decay. Hence his moderation in prosperity, his fortitude in adversity, his dignity, his perfect self-dominance and, lastly, his lofty quietism which sounds the true heroic ring. This, again, is softened and tempered by a simple faith in the supremacy of Love over Fear, an unbounded humanity, and charity for the poor and helpless; an unconditional forgiveness of the direst injuries ("which is the note of the noble"); a generosity and liberality which at times seem impossible, and an enthusiasm for universal benevolence and beneficence which, exalting kindly deeds done to man above every form of holiness, constitute the root and base of Oriental, nay, of all, courtesy. And the whole is crowned by pure trust and natural confidence in the progress and perfectability of human nature, which he exalts instead of degrading; this he holds to be the foundation-stone of society, and indeed the very purpose of its existence. His Pessimism resembles far more the Optimism which the so-called Books of Moses borrowed from the Ancient Copt than the mournful and melancholy creed of the true Pessimist, as Solomon the Hebrew, the Indian Buddhist, and the esoteric European imitators of Buddhism. He cannot but sigh when contemplating the sin and sorrow, the pathos and bathos of the world; and feel the pity of it, with its shifts and changes ending in nothingness, its scanty happiness and its copious misery. But his melancholy is expressed in—

> "A voice divinely sweet, a voice no less
> Divinely sad."

Nor does he mourn as they mourn who have no hope: he has an absolute conviction in future compensation; and mean.

while, his lively poetic impulse, the poetry of ideas, not of formal verse, and his radiant innate idealism breathe a soul into the merest matter of squalid work-a-day life, and awaken the sweetest harmonies of Nature epitomised in Humanity.

Such was the Moslem at a time when "the dark clouds of ignorance and superstition hung so thick on the intellectual horizon of Europe as to exclude every ray of learning that darted from the East, and when all that was polite or elegant in literature was classed among the *Studia Arabum*.[1]"

Nor is the shady side of the picture less notable. Our Arab at his worst is a mere barbarian who has not forgotten the savage. He is a model mixture of childishness and astuteness, of simplicity and cunning, concealing levity of mind under solemnity of aspect. His stolid instinctive conservatism grovels before the tyrant rule of routine, despite that turbulent and licentious independence which ever suggests revolt against the ruler: his mental torpidity, founded upon physical indolence, renders immediate action and all manner of exertion distasteful: his conscious weakness shows itself in overweening arrogance and intolerance. His crass and self-satisfied ignorance makes him glorify the most ignoble superstitions, while acts of revolting savagery are the natural results of a malignant fanaticism and a furious hatred of every creed beyond the pale of Al-Islam.

It must be confessed that these contrasts make a curious and interesting tout ensemble.

---

1 Ouseley's Orient. Collect. 1, vii.

§ I.

THE ORIGIN OF THE NIGHTS.

A.—The Birthplace.

Here occur the questions, Where and When was written and to Whom do we owe a prose-poem which, like the dramatic epos of Herodotus, has no equal?

I proceed to lay before the reader a procès-verbal of the sundry pleadings already in court, as concisely as is compatible with intelligibility, furnishing him with references to original authorities, and warning him that a fully-detailed account would fill a volume. Even my own reasons for decidedly taking one side and rejecting the other must be stated briefly. And before entering upon this subject I would distribute the prose-matter of our Recueil of Folk-lore under three heads.

1. The Apologue or Beast-fable proper, a theme which may be of any age, as it is found in the hieroglyphs and in the cuneiforms.

2. The Fairy-tale, as for brevity we may term the stories based upon supernatural agency; this was a favourite with olden Persia; and Mohammed, most austere and puritanical of the "Prophets," strongly objected to it because preferred by the more sensible of his converts to the dry legends of the Talmud and the Koran, quite as fabulous without the halo and glamour of fancy.

3. The Histories and historical anecdotes, analects, and acroamata, in which the names, when not used achronistically by the editor or copier, give unerring data for the earliest date à quo and which, by the mode of treatment, suggest the latest.

Each of these constituents will require further notice when the subject-matter of the book is discussed. The metrical portion of The Nights may also be divided into three categories, viz.:—

1. The oldest and classical poetry of the Arabs, *e.g.* the various quotations from the "Suspended Poems."

2. The mediæval, beginning with the laureates of Al-Rashid's court, such as Al-Asma'i and Abú Nowás; and ending with Al-Hariri A.H. 446-516 = 1030-1100.

3. The modern quotations and the *pièces de circonstance* by the editors or copyists of the compilation.[1]

Upon the metrical portion also further notices must be offered at the end of this Essay.

In considering the unde derivatur of The Nights we must carefully separate subject-matter from language-manner. The neglect of such essential difference has caused the remark, "It is not a little curious that the origin of a work which has been known to Europe and has been studied by many during nearly two centuries, should still be so mysterious, and that students have failed in all attempts to detect the secret." Hence also

---

1 This three-fold distribution occurred to me many years ago, and when far beyond reach of literary authorities; I was, therefore, much pleased to find the subjoined three-fold classification, with minor details, made by Baron von Hammer-Purgstall (Preface to Contes Inédits, etc. of G. S. Trébutien, Paris, mdcccxxviii.). (1) The older stories, which serve as a base to the collection, such as the Ten Wazirs ("Malice of Women") and Voyages of Sindbad (?) which may date from the days of Mahommed. These are distributed into two sub-classes; *(a)* the marvellous and purely imaginative (*e.g.* Jamasp and the Serpent Queen), and *(b)* the realistic mixed with instructive fables and moral instances. (2) The stories and anecdotes peculiarly Arab, relating to the Caliphs and especially to Al-Rashid; and (3) The tales of Egyptian provenance, which mostly date from the times of the puissant "Aaron the Orthodox." Mr. John Payne (Villon Translation, vol. ix. pp. 367-73) distributes the stories roughly under five chief heads, as follows: (1) Histories or long Romances, as King Omar bin Al-Nu'man. (2) Anecdotes or short stories dealing with historical personages and with incidents and adventures belonging to the every-day life of the period to which they refer: *e.g.* those concerning Al-Rashid and Hátim of Tayy. (3) Romances and romantic fictions comprising three different kinds of tales; *(a)* purely romantic and supernatural; *(b)* fictions and *nouvelles* with or without a basis and back-ground of historical fact and *(c)* Contes fantastiques. (4) Fables and Apologues; and (5) Tales proper, as that of Tawaddud.

the chief authorities at once branched off into two directions. One held the work to be practically Persian: the other as persistently declared it to be purely Arab.

Professor Galland, in his Epistle Dedicatory to the Marquise d'O, daughter of his patron M. de Guillerague, showed his literary acumen and unfailing sagacity by deriving The Nights from India viâ *Persia;* and held that they had been reduced to their present shape by an *Auteur Arabe inconnu.* This reference to India, also learnedly advocated by M. Langlès, was inevitable in those days: it had not then been proved that India owed all her literature to far older civilisations, and even that her alphabet the Nágari, erroneously called Devanágari, was derived through Phœnicia and Himyar-land from Ancient Egypt. So Europe was contented to compare The Nights with the Fables of Pilpay for upwards of a century. At last the Pehlevi or old Iranian origin of the work found an able and strenuous advocate in Baron von Hammer Purgstall[1] who worthily continued what Galland had begun: although a most inexact writer, he was extensively read in Oriental history and poetry. His contention was that the book is an Arabisation of the Persian Hazár Afsánah or Thousand Tales, and he proved his point.

Von Hammer began by summoning into Court the "Herodotus of the Arabs" (Ali Abú al-Hasan) Al-Mas'údi who, in A.H. 333 (=944) about one generation before the founding of Cairo, published at Bassorah the first edition of his far-famed Murúj al-Dahab wa Ma'ádin al-Jauhar, Meads of Gold and Mines of Gems. The Styrian Orientalist[2] quotes with sundry misprints[3] an ampler version of a passage in Chapter lxviii., which is abbreviated in the French translation of M. C. Barbier de Meynard.[4]

"And, indeed, many men well acquainted with their (Arab)

---

1 Journal Asiatique (Paris, Dondey-Dupré, 1826) "Sur l'origine des Mille et une Nuits."

2 Baron von Hammer-Purgstall's château is near Styrian Graz; and, when I last saw his library, it had been left as it was at his death.

3 At least, in Trébutien's Preface, pp. xxx.-xxxi., reprinted from the journ Asiat. August, 1839: for corrections see De Sacy's "Mémoire," p. 39.

4 Vol. iv. pp. 89-90, Paris, mdccclxv. Trébutien quotes chapt. lii. (for lxviii.), one of Von Hammer's manifold inaccuracies.

histories[1] opine that the stories above mentioned and other trifles were strung together by men who commended themselves to the Kings by relating them, and who found favour with their contemporaries by committing them to memory and by reciting them. Of such fashion is the fashion of the books which have come down to us translated from the Persian (Fárasiyah),[2] the Indian (Hindiyah),[3] and the Græco-Roman (Rúmíyah)[4]: we have noted the judgment which should be passed upon compositions of this nature. *Such is the book entituled Hazár Afsánah or The Thousand Tales, which word in Arabic signifies Khuráfah (Facetiæ): it is known to the public under the name of The Book of a Thousand Nights and a Night (Kitab Alf Laylah wa Laylah).*[5] This is an history of a King and his Wazir, the minister's daughter and a slave-girl (járiyah) who are named Shírzád (lion-born) and Dínár-zád (ducat-born).[6] Such also is the Tale of Farzah[7] (alii Firza), and Simás, containing details concerning the Kings and Wazirs of Hind: the Book of Al-Sindibád[8] and others of a similar stamp."

---

1 Alluding to Iram the Many-Columned, etc.

2 In Trébutien "Sihá," for which the Editor of the Journ. Asiat. and De Sacy rightly read "Sabil-há."

3 For this some MSS. have "Fahlawíyah" = Pehlevi.

4 *i.e.* Lower Roman, Grecian, of Asia Minor, etc., the word is still applied throughout Marocco, Algiers, and Northern Africa to Europeans in general.

5 De Sacy (Dissertation prefixed to the Bourdin Edition) notices the "thousand and one," and in his Mémoire "a thousand": Von Hammer's M.S. reads a thousand, and the French translation a thousand and one. Evidently no stress can be laid upon the numerals.

6 These names are noticed by me in nights i. and xxxiv. According to De Sacy some MSS. read "History of the Wazir and his Daughters."

7 Lane (iii. 735) has Wizreh or Wardeh which guide us to Wird Khan, the hero of the tale. Von Hammer's MS. prefers Djilkand (Jilkand), whence probably the Isegil or Isegild of Langlès (1814), and the Tséqyl of De Sacy (1833). The mention of "Simás" (Lane's Shemmas) identifies it with "King Jalí'ád of Hind," etc. (Night dcccxcix.) Writing in A.D. 961 Hamzah Isfaháni couples with the libri Sindbad and Schimas, the libri Baruc and Barsinas, four nouvelles out of nearly seventy. See also Al-Makri'zi's Khitat or Topography (ii. 485) for a notice of the Thousand or Thousand and One Nights.

8 Alluding to the "Seven Wazirs," alias "The Malice of Women" (night dlxxviii.), which Von Hammer and many others have carelessly confounded with Sindbad the Seaman. We find that two tales once separate have now been incorporated with The Nights, and this suggests the manner of its composition by accretion.

Von Hammer adds, quoting chapt. cxvi. of Al-Mas'údi, that Al-Mansúr (second Abbaside A.H. 136-158=754-775, and grandfather of Al-Rashíd) caused many translations of Greek and Latin, Syriac and Persian (Pehlevi) works to be made into Arabic, specifying the "Kalílah wa Damnah,[1]" the Fables of Bidpái (Pilpay), the Logic of Aristotle, the Geography of Ptolemy and the Elements of Euclid. Hence he concludes "L'original des Mille et une Nuits * * * selon toute vraisemblance, a été traduit au temps du Khalife Mansur, c'est-à-dire trente ans avant le règne du Khalife Haroun al-Raschid, qui, par la suite, devait lui-même jouer un si grand rôle dans ces histoires." He also notes that, about a century after Al-Mas'udi had mentioned the Hazár Afsánah, it was versified and probably remodelled by one "Rásti," the Takhallus or nom de plume of a bard at the Court of Mahmúd, the Ghaznevite Sultan who, after a reign of thirty-three years, ob. A.D. 1030.[2]

Von Hammer some twelve years afterwards (Journ. Asiat. August, 1839) brought forward, in his "Note sur l'origine Persane des Mille et une Nuits," a second and an even more important witness: this was the famous Kitab al-Fihrist,[3] or Index List of (Arabic) works, written (in A.H. 387=987) by Mohammed bin Is'hák al-Nadím (cup-companion or equerry), "popularly known as Ebou Yacoub el-Werrek.[4]" The following is an extract (p. 304)

---

1 Arabised by a most "elegant" stylist, Abdullah ibn al-Mukaffá (the shrivelled), a Persian Guebre named Roz-bih (Day good), who Islamised and was barbarously put to death in A.H. 158 (=775) by command of the Caliph al-Mansur (Al-Siyuti, p. 277). "He also translated from Pehlevi the book entitled *Sekiserán*, containing the annals of Isfandiyar, the death of Rustam, and other episodes of old Persic history," says Al-Mas'udi, chapt. xxi. See also Ibn Khallikan (i. 43), who dates the murder in A.H. 142 (=759-60).

2 "Notice sur Le Schah-namah de Firdoussi," a posthumous publication of M. de Wallenbourg, Vienna, 1810, by M. A. de Bianchi. In sect. iii. I shall quote another passage of Al-Mas'udi (viii. 175) in which I find a distinct allusion to the "Gaboriau-detective tales" of The Nights.

3 Here Von Hammer shows his customary inexactitude. As we learn from Ibn Khallikan (Fr. Tr. i. 630), the author's name was Abu al-Faraj Mohammed ibn Is'hak, pop. known as Ibn Ali Ya'kúb al-Warrák, the bibliographe, librarian, copyist. It was published (vol. i., Leipzig, 1871) under the editorship of G. Fluegel, J. Roediger, and A. Müller.

4 See also the Journ. Asiat., August, 1839, and Lane, iii. 736-37.

from the Eighth Discourse, which consists of three arts (funún).[1] "The first section on the history of the confabulatores nocturni (tellers of night tales) and the relaters of fanciful adventures, together with the names of books treating upon such subjects. Mohammed ibn Is'hák saith:—The first who indited themes of imagination and made books of them, consigning these works to the libraries, and who ordered some of them as though related by the tongues of brute beasts, were the palæo-Persians (and the Kings of the First Dynasty). The Ashkanian Kings of the Third Dynasty appended others to them, and they were augmented and amplified in the days of the Sassanides (the fourth and last royal house). The Arabs also translated them into Arabic, and the loquent and eloquent polished and embellished them and wrote others resembling them. The first work of such kind was entituled "The Book of Hazár Afsán," signifying Alf Khuráfah, the argument whereof was as follows. A King of their Kings was wont, when he wedded a woman and had lain one night with her, to slay her on the next morning. Presently he espoused a damsel of the daughters of the Kings, Shahrázád[2] hight, one endowed with intellect and erudition and, whenas she lay with him, she fell to telling him tales of fancy; moreover, she used to connect the story at the end of the night with that which might induce the King to preserve her alive and to ask her of its ending on the next night until a thousand nights had passed over her. Meanwhile, he cohabited with her till she was blest by boon of child of him, when she acquainted him with the device she had wrought upon him; wherefore he admired her intelligence and inclined to her and preserved her life. That King had also a Kahramánah (nurse and duenna, not *entremetteuse*), hight Dinárzád (Dunyázád?), who aided the wife in this (artifice). It is also said that this book was composed for (or, by) Humái daughter of Bahman[3] and in it were included other matters.

1 Called "Afsánah" by Al-Mas'udi, both words having the same sense = tale, story, parable, "facetiæ." Moslem fanaticism renders it by the Arab. "Khuráfah" = silly fables, and in Hindostan it = a jest:—"Bát-ki bát; khurafát-ki khurafát (a word for a word, a joke for a joke).

2 Al-Mas'údi (chapt. xxi.) makes this a name of the Mother of Queen Humái or Humáyah, for whom see below.

3 The preface of a copy of the Shah-nameh (by Firdausi, ob. A.D. 1021), collated in A.H. 829 by command of Bayisunghur Bahadur Khán (Atkinson,

Mohammed bin Is'hak adds:—And the truth is, Inshallah,[1] that the first that solaced himself with hearing night-tales was Al-Iskandar (he of Macedon), and he had a number of men who used to relate to him imaginary stories and provoke him to laughter: he, however, designed not therein merely to please himself, but that he might thereby become the more cautious and alert. After him the Kings in like fashion made use of the book entitled 'Hazár Afsán.' It containeth a thousand nights, but less than two hundred night-stories, for a single history often occupied several nights. I have seen it complete sundry times; and it is, in truth, a corrupted book of cold tales.[2]"

A writer in *The Athenæum*,[3] objecting to Lane's modern date for The Nights, adduces evidence to prove the greater antiquity of the work. (Abu al-Hasan) Ibn Sa'id (bin Musa al-Gharnáti = of Granada) born in A.H. 615 = 1218 and ob. Tunis A.H. 685 = 1286, left his native city and arrived at Cairo in A.H. 639 = 1241. This Spanish poet and historian wrote Al-Muhallá bi al-Ash'ár (The Adorned with Verses), a Topography of Egypt and Africa, which is now apparently lost. In this he quotes from Al-Kurtubi, the Cordovan[4]; and he in his turn is quoted by the Arab historian of Spain, Abú al-Abbás Ahmad bin Mohammed al-Makkári, in the "Windwafts of Perfume from the Branches of Andalusia the Blooming[5]" (A.D. 1628-29). Mr.

---

p. x.), informs us that the Hazar Afsanah was composed for or by Queen Humái whose name is Arabised to Humáyah. This Persian Marguerite de Navarre was daughter and wife to (Ardashir) Bahman, sixth Kayanian and surnamed Diraz-dast (Artaxerxes Longimanus), Abu Sásán from his son, the Eponymus of the Sassanides who followed the Kayanians when these were extinguished by Alexander of Macedon. Humai succeeded her husband as seventh Queen, reigned thirty-two years, and left the crown to her son Dárá or Dáráb 1st = Darius Codomanus. She is better known to Europe (through Herodotus) as Parysatis = Peri-zádeh, or the Fairy-born.

1 *i.e.* if Allah allow me to say sooth.

2 *i.e.* of silly anecdotes: here speaks the good Moslem!

3 No. 622 Sept. 29,'39; a review of Torrens which appeared shortly after Lane's vol. i. The author quotes from a MS. in the British Museum, No. 7334. fol. 136.

4 There are many Spaniards of this name: Mr. Payne (ix. 302) proposes Abu ja'afar ibn Abd al-Hakk al-Khazraji, author of a History of the Caliphs about the middle of the twelfth century.

5 The well-known Rauzah or Garden-island, of old Al-Saná'ah for Dár al-Saná'ah, the Darsana, the Arsenal (Ibn Khall. iii 573; Al-Mas'udi chapt xxxi), which is more than once noticed in The Nights. The name of the pavilion Al-Haudaj = a camel-litter, was probably intended to flatter the Badawi girl.

Payne (x. 301) thus translates from Dr. Dozy's published text:—

"Ibn Said (may God have mercy upon him!) sets forth in his book, El Muhella bi-l-ashar, quoting from El Curtubi the story of the building of the Houdej in the Garden of Cairo, the which was of the magnificent pleasaunces of the Fatimite Khalifs, the rare of ordinance and surpassing, to wit that the Khalif El Aamir bi-ahkam-illah[1] let build it for a Bedouin woman, the love of whom had gotten the mastery of him, in the neighbourhood of the 'Chosen Garden[2]' and used to resort often thereto and was slain as he went thither; and it ceased not to be a pleasuring-place for the Khalifs after him. The folk abound in stories of the Bedouin girl and Ibn Meyyah[3] of the sons of her uncle (cousin?) and what hangs thereby of the mention of El-Aamir, so that the tales told of them on this account became like unto the story of El Bettál[4] and the *Thousand Nights and a Night* and what resembleth them."

The same passage from Ibn Sa'id, corresponding in three MSS., occurs in the famous Khitat attributed to Al-Makrizi (ob. A.D. 1444) and was thus translated from a MS. in the British Museum by Mr. John Payne (ix. 303).

"The Khalif El-Aamir bi-ahkam-illah set apart, in the neighbourhood of the Chosen Garden, a place for his beloved the Bedouin maid (Aaliyah)[6] which he named El Houdej. Quoth Ibn Said, in the book El-Muhella bi-l-ashar, from the History of El Curtubi, concerning the traditions of the folk of the story

---

1 He was the Seventh Fatimite Caliph of Egypt: regn. A.H. 495-524 (=1101—1129),

2 Suggesting a private pleasaunce in Al-Rauzah which has ever been and still is a succession of gardens.

3 The writer in *The Athenæum* calls him Ibn Miyyah, and adds that the Badawiyah wrote to her cousin certain verses complaining of her thraldom, which the youth answered, abusing the Caliph. Al-'Ámir found the correspondence and ordered Ibn Miyyah's tongue to be cut out, but he saved himself by a timely flight.

4 In Night dccclxxxv. we have the passage, "He was a wily thief; none could avail against his craft as he were Abu Mohammed Al-Battál!" the word etymologically means The Bad; but see *infra*.

5 Amongst other losses which Orientalists have sustained by the death of Rogers Bey, I may mention his proposed translation of Al-Makrízí's great topographical work.

6 The name appears only in a later passage.

of the Bedouin maid and Ibn Menah (Meyyah) of the sons of her uncle and what hangs thereby of the mention of the Khalif El Aamír bi-ahkam-illah, so that their traditions (or tales) upon the garden became like unto El Bettál[1] and the *Thousand Nights* and what resembleth them."

This evidently means either that The Nights existed in the days of Al-'Ámir (xii^th^ cent.) or that the author compared them with a work popular in his own age. Mr. Payne attaches much importance to the discrepancy of titles, which appears to me a minor detail. The change of names is easily explained. Amongst the Arabs, as amongst the wild Irish, there is divinity (the proverb says luck) in odd numbers and consequently the others are inauspicious. Hence as Sir Wm. Ouseley says (Travels, ii. 21), the number Thousand and One is a favourite in the East (Olivier, Voyages vi. 385, Paris, 1807), and quotes the Cistern of the "Thousand and One Columns" at Constantinople. Kaempfer (Amœn, Exot. p. 38) notes of the Takiyahs or Dervishes' convents and the Mazárs or Santons' tombs near Koníah (Iconium), "Multa seges sepulchralium quæ virorum ex omni ævo doctissimorum exuvias condunt, mille et unum recenset auctor Libri qui inscribitur Hassaaer we jek mesaar (Hazár ve yek Mezár), *i.e.* mille et unum mausolea." A book, The Hazar o yek Rúz (= 1001 Days), was composed in the mid-xviith century by the famous Darwaysh Mukhlis, Chief Sufi of Isfahan: it was translated into French by Petis de la Croix, with a preface by Cazotte, and was Englished by Ambrose Phillips. Lastly, in India and throughout Asia where Indian influence extends, the number of cyphers not followed by a significant number is indefinite: for instance, to determine hundreds the Hindus affix the required figure to the end and for 100 write 101; for 1000, 1001. But the grand fact of the Hazár Afsánah is its being the archetype of The Nights, unquestionably proving that the Arab work borrows from the Persian bodily its cadre or frame-work, the principal characteristic; its exordium and its

1 Mr. Payne notes (viii. 137) "apparently some famous brigand of the time" (of Charlemagne). But the title may signify The Brave as well as the Bad, and the tale may be much older.

dénoûment, whilst the two heroines still bear the old Persic names.

Baron Silvestre de Sacy[1]—clarum et venerabile nomen—is the chief authority for the Arab provenance of The Nights. Apparently founding his observations upon Galland,[2] he is of opinion that the work, as now known, was originally composed in Syria[3] and written in the vulgar dialect; that it was never completed by the author, whether he was prevented by death or by other cause; and that imitators endeavoured to finish the work by inserting romances which were already known but which formed no part of the original recueil, such as the Travels of Sindbad the Seaman, the Book of the Seven Wazirs, and others. He accepts the Persian scheme and cadre of the work, but no more. He contends that no considerable body of præ-Mohammedan or non-Arabic fiction appears in the actual texts[4]; and that all the tales, even those dealing with events localised in Persia, India, China, and other Infidel lands, and dated from ante-Islamitic ages, mostly with the naïvest anachronism, confine themselves to depicting the people, manners, and customs of Baghdad and Mosul, Damascus and Cairo, during the Abbaside epoch; and he makes a point of the whole being impregnated with the strongest and most zealous spirit of Mohammedanism. He points out that the language is the popular or vulgar dialect, differing widely from the classical and literary; that it contains many words in common modern use, and that generally it

---

1 In his "Mémoire sur l'origine du Recueil des Contes intitulé Les Mille et une Nuits" (Mém. d'Hist. et de Littér. Orientale, extrait des tomes ix. et x. des Mémoires de l'Inst. Royal Acad. des Inscriptions et Belles Lettres, Paris, Imprimerie Royale, 1833). He read the Memoir before the Royal Academy on July 31, 1829. See also his Dissertation "Sur les Mille et une Nuits" (pp. i.-viii.) prefixed to the Bourdin Edit. When the first Arabist in Europe landed at Alexandria he could not exchange a word with the people: the same is told of Golius the lexicographer at Tunis.

2 Lane, Nights ii. 218.

3 This origin had been advocated a decade of years before by Shaykh Ahmad al-Shirawání; Editor of the Calc. text (1814-18): his Persian preface opines that the author was an Arabic-speaking Syrian who designedly wrote in a modern and conversational style, none of the purest withal, in order to instruct non-Arabists. Here we find the genus "Professor" pure and simple.

4 Such an assertion makes us enquire, Did De Sacy ever read through The Nights in Arabic?

suggests the decadence of Arabian literature. Of one tale he remarks: — The History of the loves of Camaralzaman and Budour, Princess of China, is no more Indian or Persian than the others. The prince's father has Moslems for subjects, his mother is named Fatimah, and when imprisoned he solaces himself with reading the Koran. The Genii who interpose in these adventures are, again, those who had dealings with Solomon. In fine, all that we here find of the City of the Magians, as well as of the fire-worshippers, suffices to show that one should not expect to discover in it anything save the production of a Moslem writer.

All this, with due deference to so high an authority, is very superficial. Granted, which nobody denies, that the archetypal Hazár Afsánah was translated from Persic into Arabic nearly a thousand years ago, it had ample time and verge enough to assume another and a foreign dress, the corpus, however, remaining untouched. Under the hands of a host of editors, scribes and copyists, who have no scruples anent changing words, names and dates, abridging descriptions and attaching their own decorations, the florid and rhetorical Persian would readily be converted into the straightforward, businesslike, matter of fact Arabic. And what easier than to Islamise the old Zoroasterism, to transform Ahrimán into Iblis the Shaytán, Ján bin Ján into Father Adam, and the Divs and Peris of Kayomars and the olden Guebre Kings into the Jinns and Jinniyahs of Sulayman? Volumes are spoken by the fact that the Arab adapter did not venture to change the Persic names of the two heroines and of the royal brothers, or to transfer the mise-en-scène any whither from Khorasan or outer Persia. Where the story has not been too much worked by the literato's pen, for instance the "Ten Wazirs" (in the Bresl. Edit. vi. 191-343) which is the Guebre Bakhtiyár-námah, the names and incidents are old Iranian and with few exceptions distinctly Persian. And at times we can detect the process of transition, *e.g.* when the Mázin of Khorásán[1] of the Wortley Montagu MS. becomes the Hasan of Bassorah of the Turner Macan MS. (Mac. Edit.).

1 Dr. Jonathan Scott's "translation," vi. 283.

Evidently the learned Baron had not studied such works as the Totá-kaháni or Parrot-chat which, notably translated by Nakhshabi from the Sanskrit Suka-Saptati,[1] has now become as orthoxdoically Moslem as The Nights. The old Hindu Rajah becomes Ahmad Sultan of Balkh, the Prince is Maymún and his wife Khujisteh. Another instance of such radical change is the later Syriac version of Kalílah wa Dimnah,[2] old "Pilpay" converted to Christianity. We find precisely the same process in European folk-lore; for instance, the Gesta Romanorum, wherein, after five hundred years, the life, manners and customs of the classical Romans lapse into the knightly and chivalrous, the Christian and ecclesiastical developments of mediæval Europe. Here, therefore, I hold that the Austrian Arabist has proved his point whilst the Frenchman has failed.

Mr. Lane, during his three years' labour of translation, first accepted Von Hammer's view and then came round to that of De Sacy; differing, however, in minor details, especially concerning the native country of The Nights. Syria had been chosen because then the most familiar to Europeans: the "Wife of Bath" had made three pilgrimages to Jerusalem; but few cared to visit the barbarous and dangerous Nile-Valley. Mr. Lane, however, was an enthusiast for Egypt or rather for Cairo, the only part of it he knew; and when he pronounces The Nights to be of purely "Arab," that is, of Nilotic origin, his opinion is entitled to no more deference than his deriving the sub-African and negroid Fellah from Arabia, the land per excellentiam of pure and noble blood. Other authors have wandered still further afield. Some finding Mosul idioms in the Recueil, propose "Middlegates" for its birth-place and Mr. W. G. P. Palgrave boldly says, "The original of this entertaining work appears to have been composed in Baghdad about the eleventh century; another less popular

1 For a note on this world-wide Tale see vol. i. night v.

2 In the annotated translation by Mr. I. G. N. Keith-Falconer, Cambridge University Press. I regret to see the wretched production called the 'Fables of Pilpay" in the "Chandos Classics" (London, F. Warne). The words are so mutilated that few will recognize them, *e.g.* Carchenas for Kár-shinás, Chaschmanah for Chashmey-e-Máh (Fountain of the Moon), etc.

but very spirited version is probably of Tunisian authorship and somewhat later.[1]"

B.—THE DATE.

The next point to consider is the date of The Nights in its present form; and here opinions range between the tenth and the sixteenth centuries. Professor Galland began by placing it arbitrarily in the middle of the thirteenth. De Sacy, who abstained from detailing reasons and who, forgetting the number of editors and scribes through whose hands it must have passed, argued only from the nature of the language and the peculiarities of style, proposed as its latest date le milieu du neuvième siècle de l'hégire (= A.D. 1445-6). Mr. Hole, who knew The Nights only through Galland's version, had already advocated in his "Remarks" the close of the fifteenth century; and M. Caussin de Perceval (vol. viii., p. viii.), upon the authority of a MS. note in Galland's MS.[2] (vol. iii. fol. 20, verso), declares the compiler to have been living in the seizième siècle, A.D. 1548 and 1565. Mr. Lane says "Not begun earlier than the last fourth of the fifteenth century nor ended before the first fourth of the sixteenth," *i.e.* soon after Egypt was conquered by Selim, Sultan of the Osmanli Turks in A.D. 1517. Lastly, the learned Dr. Weil says in his far too scanty Vorwort (p. ix. 2nd Edit.):—"Das wahrscheinlichste dürfte also sein, das im 15. Jahrhundert ein Egyptier nach altern Vorbilde Erzählungen

---

1 Article Arabia in Encyclop. Brit., 9th Edit., p. 263, col. 2. I do not quite understand Mr Palgrave, but presume that his "other version" is the Bresl. Edit., the manuscript of which was brought from Tunis; see its Vorwort (vol. i. p. 3).

2 There are three distinct notes according to De Sacy (Mém., p. 50). The first (in MS 1508) says, "This blessed book was read by the weak slave, etc. Wahabah son of Rizkallah the Kátib (secretary, scribe) of Tarábulus al-Shám (Syrian Tripoli), who prayeth long life for its owner (li máliki-h). This tenth day of the month First Rabi'a A.H. 955 (=1548)." A similar note by the same Wahabah occurs at the end of vol. ii. (MS. 1507) dated A.H. 973 (=1565) and a third (MS. 1506) is undated. Evidently M. Caussin has given undue weight to such evidence. For further information see "Tales of the East," to which is prefixed an Introductory Dissertation (vol. i. pp. 24-26, note) by Henry Weber, Esq., Edinburgh, 1812, in 3 vols. M. Zotenberg has also pointed out to me the earliest inscription by Rizkallah b. Yohanná b. Shaykh al-Nájj, father of Wahabah, dated Jamádá ii. A. H. 943=1537-8: it is in four lines at the end of vol. ii. There is also a fifth, and the latest, by Mohammed ibn Mahmúd, A.H. 1030=A.D. 1592.

für 1001 Nächte theils erdichtete, thiels nach mündlichen Sagen, oder frühern schriftlichen Aufzeichnungen, bearbeitete, dass er aber entweder sein Werk nicht vollendete, oder dass ein Theil desselben verloren ging, so dass das Fehlende von Andern bis ins 16. Jahrhundert hinein durch neue Erzählungen ergänzt wurde."

But, as justly observed by Mr. Payne, the first step when enquiring into the original date of The Nights is to determine the nucleus of the Repertory by a comparison of the four printed texts and the dozen MSS. which have been collated by scholars.[1] This process makes it evident that the tales common to all are the following thirteen:—

1. The Introduction (with a single incidental story, "The Bull and the Ass").
2. The Trader and the Jinni (with three incidentals).
3. The Fisherman and the Jinni (with four).
4. The Porter and the Three Ladies of Baghdad.
5. The Tale of the Three Apples.
6. The Tale of Núr al-Din Ali and his son Badr al-Din Hasan.
7. The Hunchback's Tale (with eleven).
8. Nur al-Dín and Anis al-Jalis.
9. Tale of Ghánim bin 'Ayyúb (with two).
10. Alí bin Bakkár and Shams al-Nahár (with two).
11. Tale of Kamar al-Zamán.
12. The Ebony Horse; and
13. Julnár the Seaborn.

These forty-two tales, occcupying one hundred and twenty Nights, form less than a fifth part of the whole collection which in the Mac. Edit.[2] contains a total of two hundred and sixty-four. Hence Dr. Patrick Russell,[3] the Natural Historian of

---

1 "Notice sur les douze manuscrits connus des Milles et une Nuits, que existent en Europe." Von Hammer in Trébutien, Notice, vol. i.

2 Printed from the MS. of Major Turner Macan, Editor of the Shah-namah: he bought it from the heirs of Mr. Salt, the historic Consul-General of England in Egypt, and after Macan's death it became the property of the now extinct Allens, then of Leadenhall Street (Torrens, Preface, i.). I have vainly enquired of the present house about its later adventures.

3 The short paper by "P. R." in the *Gentleman's Magazine* (Feb. 19th 1799, vol. lxíx. p. 61) tells us that MSS. of The Nights were scarce at Aleppo and that he found only 2 vols. (280 nights) which he had great difficulty in

Aleppo,[1] whose valuable monograph amply deserves study even in this our day, believed that the original Nights did not outnumber two hundred, to which subsequent writers added till the total of a thousand and one was made up. Dr. Jonathan Scott,[2] who quotes Russell, "held it highly probable that the tales of the original Arabian Nights did not run through more than two hundred and eighty Nights, if so many." To this suggestion I may subjoin, "Habent sua fata libelli." Galland, who preserves in his "Mille et une Nuit" only about one fourth of The Nights, ends them in No. cclxiv[3] with the seventh voyage of Sindbad: after that he intentionally omits the dialogue between the sisters and the reckoning of time, to proceed uninterruptedly with the tales. And so his imitator, Petis de la Croix,[4] in his "Mille et un Jours," reduces the thousand to two hundred and thirty-two.

The internal chronological evidence offered by the Collection is useful only in enabling us to determine that the tales were not written *after* a certain epoch: the actual dates and, consequently, all deductions from them, are vitiated by the habits of the scribes. For instance, we find the Tale of the Fisherman and the Jinni (vol. i. night iii.) placed in A.H. 169 = A.D. 785,[5] which is hardly possible. The immortal Barber in the "Tailor's Tale" (vol. i. night xxix.) places his adventure with the unfortunate lover on Safar 10, A.H. 653 (= March 25th, 1255) and 7,320 years of the era of Alexander.[6] This is supported in his Tale of Him-

---

obtaining leave to copy. He also noticed (in 1771) a MS., said to be complete, in the Vatican, and another in the "King's Library" (Bibliothèque Nationale), Paris.

1 Aleppo has been happy in finding such monographers as Russell and Maundrell, while poor Damascus fell into the hands of Mr. Missionary Porter, and suffered accordingly.

2 Vol. vi. Appendix, p. 452.

3 The numbers, however, vary with the Editions of Galland: some end the formula with night cxcvii.; others with the ccxxxvi.: I adopt that of the De Sacy Edition.

4 Contes Persans; suivis des Contes Turcs. Paris: Béchet Ainé, 1826.

5 In the old translation we have "eighteen hundred years since the prophet Solomon died" (B.C. 975) = A.D. 825.

6 Meaning the era of the Seleucides. Dr. Jonathan Scott shows (vol. ii. 324) that A.H. 653 and A.D. 1255 would correspond with 1557 of that epoch; so that the scribe has here made a little mistake of 5,763 years. Ex uno disce.

self (vol. i. nights xxxi. to xxxiv.), where he dates his banishment from Baghdad during the reign of the penultimate Abbaside, Al-Mustansir bi 'llah (A.H. 623-640 = 1225-1242), and his return to Baghdad after the accession of another Caliph who can be no other but Al-Muntasim bi 'llah (A.H. 640-656 = A.D. 1242-1258). Again at the end of the tale (vol. i. night xxxiv.) he is described as "an ancient man, past his ninetieth year" and "a very old man" in the days of Al-Mustansir (vol. i. night xxxi.); so that the Hunchback's adventure can hardly be placed earlier than A.D. 1265 or seven years after the storming of Baghdad by Huláku Khan, successor of Janghíz Khan, a terrible catastrophe which resounded throughout the civilised world. Yet there is no allusion to this crucial epoch and the total silence suffices to invalidate the date.[1] Could we assume it as true, by adding to A.D. 1265 half a century for the composition of the Hunchback's story and its incidentals, we should place the earliest date in A.D. 1315.

As little can we learn from inferences which have been drawn from the body of the book: at most they point to its several editions or redactions. In the Tale of the "Ensorcelled Prince" (vol. i. night viii.) Mr. Lane (i. 135) conjectured that the four colours of the fishes were suggested by the sumptuary laws of the Mameluke Soldan, Mohammed ibn Kala'un, "subsequently to the commencement of the eighth century of the Flight, or fourteenth of our era." But he forgets that the same distinction of dress was enforced by the Caliph Omar after the capture of Jerusalem in A.D. 636; that it was revived by Harun al-Rashid, a contemporary of Carolus Magnus, and that it was noticed as a long standing grievance by the so-called Maundeville in A.D. 1322. In the Tale of the Porter and the Ladies of Baghdad the "Sultáni oranges" (vol. i. night ix.) have been connected with Sultáníyah city in Persian Irák, which was founded about the middle of the thirteenth century: but "Sultáni" may simply mean "royal," a

---

1 In the Galland MS. and the Bresl. Edit. (ii. 253), we find the Barber saying that the Caliph (Al-Mustansir) was *at that time* (yaumaizin) in Baghdad; and this has been held to imply that the Caliphate had fallen. But such conjecture is evidently based upon insufficient grounds.

superior growth. The same story makes mention (vol. i. night x.) of Kalandars or religious mendicants, a term popularly corrupted, even in writing, to Karandal.[1] Here again "Kalandar" may be due only to the scribes as the Bresl. Edit. reads Sa'alúk = asker, beggar. The Khan al-Masrúr in the Nazarene Broker's story (vol. i. night xxv.) was a ruin during the early ninth century A.H. = A.D. 1420; but the Báb Zuwaylah (vol. i. night xxv.) dates from A.D. 1087. In the same tale occurs the Darb al-Munkari (or Munakkari) which is probably the Darb al-Munkadi of Al-Makrizi's careful topography, the Khitat (ii. 40). Here we learn that in his time (about A.D. 1430) the name had become obsolete, and the highway was known as Darb al-Amír Baktamír al-Ustaddar from one of two high officials who both died in the fourteenth century (circ. A.D. 1350). And lastly we have the Khan al-Jáwali built about A.D. 1320. In Badr al-Din Hasan (vol. i. nlght xxiii.) "Sáhib" is given as a Wazirial title and it dates only from the end of the fourteenth century.[2] In Sindbad the Seaman, there is an allusion (vol. iv. nights dxliv. and dlxii.) to the great Hindu Kingdom, Vijayanagar of the Narasimha,[3] the great power of the Deccan; but this may be due to editors or scribes as the despotism was founded only in the fourteenth century (A.D. 1320). The Ebony Horse (night ccclvii.) apparently dates before Chaucer; and "The Sleeper and The Waker" (Bresl. Edit. iv. 134-189; and my vol. ix. pp. 1-28) may precede Shakespeare's "Taming of the Shrew"; no stress, however, can be laid upon such resemblances, the nouvelles being world-wide. But when we come to the last stories, especially to Kamar al-Zaman II. and the tale of Ma'arúf, we are apparently in the fifteenth and sixteenth centuries. The first contains (night cmlxxii.) the word Láwandiyah = Levantine, the mention of a

---

1 De Sacy makes the "Kalandar" order originate in A.D. 1150; but the Shaykh Sharif bú Ali Kalandar died in A.D. 1323-24. In Sind the first Kalandar, Osmán-i-Marwándi surnamed Lál Sháhbáz, the Red Goshawk, from one of his miracles, died and was buried at Sehwán in A.D. 1274: see my "History of Sindh" chapt. viii. for details. The dates therefore run wild.

2 In this same tale H. H. Wilson observes that the title of Sultan of Egypt was not assumed before the middle of the xiith century.

3 Popularly called Vidyanagar of the Narsingha.

watch = Sá'ah in the next night[1]; and, further on (cmlxxvi.), the "Shaykh Al-Islam," an officer invented by Mohammed II. after the capture of Stambul in A.D. 1453. In Ma'aruf the 'Ádiliyah is named; the mosque founded outside the Bab al-Nasr by Al-Malik al-'Ádil, Túmán Bey in A.H. 906—A.D. 1501. But, I repeat, all these names may be mere interpolations.

On the other hand, a study of the vie intime in Al-Islam and of the manners and customs of the people proves that the body of the work, as it now stands, must have been written before A.D. 1400. The Arabs use wines, ciders and barley-beer, not distilled spirits; they have neither coffee nor tobacco and, while familiar with small-pox (judri), they ignore syphilis. The battles in The Nights are fought with bows and javelins, swords, spears (for infantry), and lances (for cavalry); and, whenever fire-arms are mentioned, we must suspect the scribe. This consideration would determine the work to have been written before the fourteenth century. We ignore the invention-date and the inventor of gunpowder, as of all old discoveries which have affected mankind at large: all we know is that the popular ideas betray great ignorance and we are led to suspect that an explosive compound, having been discovered in the earliest ages of human society, was utilised by steps so gradual that history has neglected to trace the series. Accord-

1 Time-measurers are of very ancient date. The Greeks had clepsydræ and the Romans gnomons, portable and ring-shaped, besides large standing town-dials as at Aquileja and San Sabba near Trieste. The "Saracens" were the perfecters of the clepsydra: Bosseret (p. 16) and the Chronicon Turense (Beckmann, ii. 340 *et seq.*) describe the water-clock sent by Al-Rashid to Karl the Great as a kind of "cuckoo-clock." Twelve doors in the dial opened successively and little balls dropping on brazen bells told the hour: at noon a dozen mounted knights paraded the face and closed the portals. Trithonius mentions an horologium presented in A.D. 1232 by Al-Malik al-Kámil, the Ayyubite Soldan, to the Emperor Frederick II.: like the Strasbourg and Padua clocks it struck the hours, told the day, month, and year, showed the phases of the moon, and registered the position of the sun and the planets. Towards the end of the fifteenth century Gaspar Visconti mentions in a sonnet the watch proper (certi orologii piccioli e portativi); and the "animated eggs" of Nurembourg became famous. The earliest English watch (Sir Ashton Lever's) dates from 1541: and in 1544 the portable chronometer became common in France.

ing to Demmin,[1] bullets for stuffing with some incendiary composition, in fact bombs, were discovered by Dr. Keller in the Palafites or Crannogs of Switzerland; and the Hindu's Agni-Astar ("fire-weapon"), Agni-bán ("fire-arrow" and Shatagni ("hundred-killer") like the Roman Phalarica, and the Greek fire of Byzantium, suggest explosives. Indeed, Dr. Oppert[2] accepts the statement of Flavius Philostratus that when Appolonius of Tyana, that grand semi-mythical figure was travelling in India, he learned the reason why Alexander of Macedon desisted from attacking the Oxydracæ who live between the Ganges and the Hyphasis (Satadru or Sutledge) :—"These holy men, beloved by the gods, overthrow their enemies with tempests and thunderbolts shot from their walls." Passing over the Arab sieges of Constantinople (A.D. 668) and Meccah (A.D. 690) and the disputed passage in Firishtah touching the Tufang or musket during the reign of Mahmúd the Ghaznevite[3] (ob. A.D. 1030), we come to the days of Alphonso the Valiant, whose long and short guns, used at the Siege of Madrid in A.D. 1084, are preserved in the Armeria Real. Viardot has noted that the African Arabs first employed cannon in A.D. 1200, and that the Maghribis defended Algeciras near Gibraltar with great guns in A.D. 1247, and utilised them to besiege Seville in A.D. 1342. This last feat of arms introduced the cannon into barbarous Northern Europe, and it must have been known to civilised Asia for many a decade before that date.

The mention of wine in The Nights, especially the Nabíz or fermented infusion of raisins well-known to the præ-Mohammedan Badawin, perpetually recurs. As a rule, except only in the case of holy personages and mostly of the Caliph Al-Rashid, the "service of wine" appears immediately after the hands are washed; and women, as well as men, drink, like true Orientals,

---

1 An illustrated History of Arms and Armour etc. (p. 59); London: Bell and Sons, 1877. The best edition is the Guide des Amateurs d'Armes; Paris: Renouard, 1889.

2 Chapt. iv. Dr. Gustav Oppert, "On the Weapons, etc., of the Ancient Hindus"; London: Trübner and Co., 1880.

3 I have given other details on this subject in pp. 631-637 of "Camoens, his Life and his Lusiads"

for the honest purpose of getting drunk—la recherche de l'idéal, as the process has been called. Yet distillation became well known in the fourteenth century. Amongst the Greeks and Romans it was confined to manufacturing aromatic waters, and Nicander the poet (B.C. 140) used for a still the term *ἄμβιξ*, like the Irish "pot" and its produce "poteen." The simple art of converting salt water into fresh, by boiling the former and passing the steam through a cooled pipe into a recipient, would not have escaped the students of the Philosopher's "stone"; and thus we find throughout Europe the Arabic modifications of Greek terms, Alchemy, Alembic (Al-*ἄμβιξ*), Chemistry and Elixir; while "Alcohol" (Al-Kohl), originally meaning "extreme tenuity or impalpable state of pulverulent substances," clearly shows the origin of the article. Avicenna, who died in A.H. 428=1036, nearly two hundred years before we read of distillation in Europe, compared the human body with an alembic, the belly being the cucurbit and the head the capital:—he forgot one important difference but n'importe. Spirits of wine were first noticed in the xiii[th] century, when the Arabs had over-run the Western Mediterranean, by Arnaldus de Villa Nova, who dubs the new invention a universal panacea; and his pupil, Raymond Lully (nat. Majorca, A.D. 1236), declared this essence of wine to be a boon from the Deity. Now The Nights, even in the latest adjuncts, never alludes to the "white coffee" of the "respectable" Moslem, the Ráki (raisin-brandy) or Ma-hayát (aqua vitæ) of the modern Mohammedan: the drinkers confine themselves to wine like our contemporary Dalmatians, one of the healthiest and the most vigorous of seafaring races in Europe.

Syphilis also, which at the end of the xv[th] century began to infect Europe, is ignored by the Nights. I do not say it actually began: diseases do not begin except with the dawn of humanity; and their history, as far as we know, is simple enough. They are at first sporadic and comparatively non-lethal: at certain epochs which we can determine, and for reasons which as yet we cannot, they break out into epidemics raging with frightful violence: they then subside into the endemic state, and lastly, they return to the milder sporadic form. For instance, "English cholera" was known of old: in 1831 (Oct. 26) the

Asiatic type took its place, and now, after sundry violent epidemics, the disease is becoming endemic on the Northern seaboard of the Mediterranean, notably in Spain and Italy. So small-pox (Al-judrí, vol. i. night xxv.) passed over from Central Africa to Arabia in the year of Mohammed's birth (A.D. 570) and thence overspread the civilised world, as an epidemic, an endemic, and a sporadic successively. The "Greater Pox" has appeared in human bones of pre-historic graves, and Moses seems to mention gonorrhœa (Levit. xv. 12). The scientific "syphilis" dates from Fracastori's poem (A.D. 1521) in which Syphilus the Shepherd is struck like Job, for abusing the sun.

The Nights, I have said, belongs to the days before coffee (A.D. 1550) and tobacco (A.D. 1650) had overspread the East. The former, which derives its name from the Káfá or Káffá province, lying south of Abyssinia proper and peopled by the Sidáma Gallas, was introduced to Mokha of Al-Yaman in A.D. 1429-30 by the Shaykh al-Shâzili who lies buried there, and found a congenial name in the Arabic Kahwah=old wine.[1] In the Nights (Mac. Edit.) it is mentioned twelve times[2]; but never in the earlier tales: except in the case of Kamar al-Zaman II. it evidently does not belong to the epoch and we may fairly suspect the scribe. In the xvi^th century coffee began to take the place of wine in the nearer East; and the barbarous gradually ousted the classical drink from daily life and from folk-tales.

It is the same with tobacco, which is mentioned only once by The Nights (night cmxxxi.), in conjunction with meat, vegetables and fruit, and where it is called "Tábah." Lane (iii. 615) holds it

---

1 For another account of the transplanter and the casuistical questions to which coffee gave rise, see my "First Footsteps in East Africa" (p. 76).

2 The first mention of coffee proper (not of Kahwah or old wine in vol. ii night c.) is in night cdxxvi., where the coffee-maker is called Kahwah-jiyyah, a mongrel term showing the modern date of the passage in Ali the Cairene. As the work advances notices become thicker, *e.g.* in night dccclxvi. where Ali Nur al-Din and the Frank King's daughter seems to be a modernisation of the story "Ala al-Din Abu al-Shámát" (vol. iii. night ccxlix); and in Abu Kir and Abu Sir (nights cmxxx. and cmxxxvi.) where coffee is drunk with sherbet after present fashion. The use culminates in Kamar al-Zaman II., where it is mentioned six times (nights cmlxvi., cmlxx., cmlxxi. twice; cmlxxiv. and cmlxxvii.), as being drunk after the dawn-breakfast and following the meal as a matter of course. The last notices are in Abdullah bin Fazil, nights cmlxxviii. and cmlxxix.

to be the work of a copyist; but in the same tale of Abu Kir and Abu Sir, sherbet and coffee appear to have become en vogue, in fact to have gained the ground they now hold. The result of Lord Macartney's Mission to China was a suggestion that smoking might have originated spontaneously in the Old World.[1] This is undoubtedly true. The Bushmen and other wild tribes of Southern Africa threw their Dakhá *(cannabis indica)* on the fire and sat round it inhaling the intoxicating fumes. Smoking without tobacco was easy enough. The North American Indians of the Great Red Pipe Stone Quarry and those who lived above the line where nicotiana grew, used the kinni-kinik or bark of the red willow and some seven other succedanea.[2] But tobacco proper, which soon superseded all materials except hemp and opium, was first adopted by the Spaniards of Santo Domingo in A.D. 1496 and reached England in 1565. Hence the word, which, amongst the so-called Red Men, denoted the pipe, the container, not the contained, spread over the Old World as a generic term with additions, like "Tutun,[3]" for especial varieties. The change in English manners brought about by the cigar after dinner has already been noticed; and much of the modified sobriety of the present day may be attributed to the influence of the Holy Herb en cigarette. Such, we know from history, was its effect amongst Moslems; and the normal wine-parties of The Nights suggest that the pipe was unknown even when the latest tales were written.

C.

We know absolutely nothing of the author or authors who produced our marvellous Recueil. Galland justly observes (Epist. Dedic.), "probably this great work is not by a single hand; for how can we suppose that one man alone could own a fancy fertile enough to invent so many ingenious fictions?" Mr. Lane, and

---

1 It has been suggested that Japanese tobacco is an indigenous growth, and sundry modern travellers in China contend that the potato and the maize, both white and yellow, have there been cultivated from time immemorial.

2 For these see my "City of the Saints," p. 136.

3 Lit. meaning smoke: hence the Arabic "Dukhán," with the same signification.

Mr. Lane alone, opined that the work was written in Egypt by one person or at most by two, one ending what the other had begun, and that he or they had re-written the tales and completed the collection by new matter composed or arranged for the purpose. It is hard to see how the distinguished Arabist came to such a conclusion: at most it can be true only of the editors and scribes of MSS. evidently copied from each other, such as the Mac. and the Bul. texts. As the Reviewer (Forbes Falconer?) in the "Asiatic Journal" (vol. xxx., 1839) says, "Every step we have taken in the collation of these agreeable fictions has confirmed us in the belief that the work called the *Arabian Nights* is rather a vehicle for stories, partly fixed and partly arbitrary, than a colleetion fairly deserving, from its constant identity with itself, the name of a distinct work, and the reputation of having wholly emanated from the same inventive mind. To say nothing of the improbability of supposing that one individual, with every license to build upon the foundation of popular stories, a work which had once received a definite form from a single writer, would have been multiplied by the copyist with some regard at least to his arrangement of words as well as matter. But the various copies we have seen bear about as much mutual resemblance as if they had passed through the famous process recommended for disguising a plagiarism: 'Translate your English author into French and again into English.'"

Moreover, the style of the several Tales, which will be considered in a future page (§ iii.), so far from being homogeneous, is heterogeneous in the extreme. Different nationalities show themselves; West Africa, Egypt, and Syria are all represented, and while some authors are intimately familiar with Baghdad, Damascus and Cairo, others are equally ignorant. All copies, written and printed, absolutely differ in the last tales, and a measure of the divergence can be obtained by comparing the Bresl. Edit. with the Mac. text: indeed, it is my conviction that the MSS. preserved in Europe would add sundry volumes full of tales to those hitherto translated; and here the Wortley-Montagu copy can be taken as a test. We may, I believe, safely compare the history of The Nights with the so-called Homeric poems, the Iliad and the Odyssey, a collection of immortal ballads and old Epic formulæ and verses traditionally handed down from rhapsode to rhapsode, incorporated in a slowly-increasing body of poetry and finally welded together about the age of Pericles.

To conclude. From the data above given I hold myself justified in drawing the following deductions:—

1. The framework of the book is purely Persian perfunctorily Arabised; the archetype being the Hazár Afsánah.[1]

2. The oldest tales, such as Sindibad (the Seven Wazirs) and King Jali'ád, may date from the reign of Al-Mansur, eighth century A.D.

3. The thirteen tales mentioned above (p. 75) as the nucleus of the Repertory, together with "Dalilah the Crafty,[2]" may be placed in our tenth century.

4. The most modern tales, notably Kamar al-Zaman the Second, and Ma'aruf the Cobbler, are as late as the sixteenth century.

5. The work assumed its present form in the thirteenth century.[3]

6. The author is unknown for the best reason; there never was one: for information touching the editors and copyists we must await the fortunate discovery of some MSS.

---

1 Unhappily the book is known only by name: for years I have vainly troubled friends and correspondents to hunt for a copy. Yet I am sanguine enough to think that some day we shall succeed: Mr. Sydney Churchill of Teheran, is ever on the look-out.

2 In § 3 I shall suggest that this tale also is mentioned by Al-Mas'udi.

3 The learned M. H. Zotenberg attributes to the second half of the xivth century the three remaining volumes of the Arab. MS. used by Galland for his translation. It is thus the most ancient known in Europe, and certain of its *lacunæ* are filled up by additions of the xviith and xviiith centuries.

§ II.

THE NIGHTS IN EUROPE.

The history of The Nights in Europe is one of slow and gradual development. The process was begun (1704-17) by Galland, a Frenchman, continued (1823) by Von Hammer, an Austro-German, and finished by Mr. John Payne (1882-84) an Englishman. But we must not forget that it is wholly and solely to the genius of the Gaul that Europe owes The "Arabian Nights' Entertainments" over which Western childhood and youth have spent so many spelling hours. Antoine Galland was the first to discover the marvellous fund of material for the Story-teller buried in the Oriental mine; and he had in a high degree that art of telling a tale which is far more captivating than culture or scholarship. Hence his delightful version (or perversion) became one of the world's classics and at once made "Sheherazade" and "Dinarzarde," "Haroun Alraschid," the "Calendars" and a host of other personages as familiar to the home reader as Prospero, Robinson Crusoe, Lemuel Gulliver and Dr. Primrose. Without the name and fame won for the work by the brilliant paraphrase of the learned and single-minded Frenchman, Lane's curious hash and Latinized English, at once turgid and emasculated, would have found few readers. Mr. Payne's admirable version appeals to the Orientalist and the "stylist," not to the many-headed; and mine to the anthropologist and student of Eastern manners and customs. Galland did it and alone he did it; his fine literary *flaire*, his pleasing style, his polished taste, and perfect tact at once made his work take high rank in the republic of letters, nor will the immortal fragment ever be superseded in the infallible judgment of childhood. As the Encyclopædia Britannica has been pleased to ignore this excellent man and admirable Orientalist, numismatologist and littérateur, the reader may not be unwilling to see a short sketch of his biography.[1]

Antoine Galland was born in A.D. 1646 of peasant parents, "poor and honest," at Rollot (not "Rollo" as Weber has it), a little bourg in Picardy some two leagues from Montdidier. He was a seventh child and his mother, left a widow in early life and compelled to earn her livelihood, saw scant chance of educating the boy, who was but four years old when the kindly assistance of a Canon of the Cathedral and President of the Collége de Noyon relieved her difficulties. In this establishment Galland studied Latin, Greek, and Hebrew, for nine or ten years, after which he lost his patrons, and the "strait thing at home" apprenticed him at the age of 13 or 14 to a trade. But he was made for letters; he hated manual labour and after a twelvemonth of purgatory he removed *en cachette* to Paris, where he knew only an ancient kinswoman. She introduced him to a priestly relative of the Canon of Noyon, who in turn recommended him to the "Sous-principal" of the Collége Du Plessis. Here he made such notable progress in Oriental studies, that M. Petitpied, a "Doctor of Sorbonne," struck by his abilities, enabled him to study at the Collége Royal and eventually to catalogue the Eastern MSS. in the great ecclesiastical Society. Thence he passed to the Collége Mazarin, where a Professor, M. Godouin, was making an experiment which might be revived to advantage in our present schools. He collected a class of boys, aged about four, the Duc de Meilleraye amongst the number, and proposed to teach them Latin speedily and easily by making them converse in the classical language as well as read and write it.[2] Galland, his assistant, had not time to register success or failure before he was appointed

---

1 I have extracted it from many books, especially from Hoeffer's Biographie Générale, Paris, Firmin Didot, mdccclvii.; Biographie Universelle, Paris, Didot, 1816, etc., etc. All are taken from the work of M. de Boze, his "Bozzy," the Secrétaire Perpétual de l'Acad. des Inscriptions, etc.

2 As learning a language is an affair of pure memory, almost without other exercise of the mental faculties, it should be assisted by the ear and the tongue as well as the eyes. I would invariably make pupils talk, during lessons, Latin and Greek, no matter how badly at first; but unfortunately I should have to begin with teaching the pedants who, as a class are far more unwilling and unready to learn than are those they teach.

attaché-secretary to the Marquis de Nointel, antiquary and masterful diplomatist, named in 1670 Ambassadeur de France for Constantinople. His special province was to study the dogmas and doctrines, and to obtain official attestations concerning the articles of the Orthodox (or Greek) Christianity, especially their doctrine of the Eucharist, which had then been a subject of lively discussion amongst certain Catholics, especially Arnauld (Antoine) and Claude the Minister, and which even in our day occasionally crops up amongst "Protestants.[1]" Galland, by frequenting the cafés and listening to the tale-teller, soon mastered Romaic and grappled with the religious question, under the tuition of a deposed Patriarch and of sundry Matráns or Metropolitans, whom the persecutions of the Pashas had driven for refuge to the Palais de France. M. de Nointel, after settling certain knotty points in the Capitulations, visited the harbour-towns of the Levant and the "Holy Places," including Jerusalem, where Galland copied epigraphs, sketched monuments, and collected medals and other antiques, such as the marbles in the Baudelot Gallery of which Père Dom Bernard de Montfaucon presently published specimens in his "Palæographia Græca," etc. (Parisiis, 1708).

In Syria Galland was unable to buy a copy of the Nights, or as he always calls them, "des Mille et une Nuit": he expressly states in his Epistle Dedicatory to the Marquis d'O, *il a fallu le faire venir de Syrie.* But he prepared himself for translating it by studying the manners and customs, the religion and superstitions, of the people; and in 1676, leaving his chief, who was ordered to Stambul, he returned to France. In Paris his numismatic fame recommended him to MM. Vaillant, Carcary and Giraud, who strongly urged a second visit (1679) to the Levant, for the purpose of collecting, and he set out without delay. In 1679 he made a third journey, travelling at the expense of the Compagnie des Indes-Orientales, with the main object of making purchases for the Library and Museum of Colbert the Magnificent. The commission ended eighteen months afterwards with

1 The late Dean Stanley was notably trapped by the wily Greek who had only political purposes in view. In religions as a rule the minimum of difference breeds the maximum of disputation, dislike, and disgust.

the changes of the Company, when Colbert and the Marquis de Louvois caused him to be created "Antiquary to the King," Louis le Grand, and charged him with collecting coins and medals for the royal cabinet. As he was about to leave Smyrna, he had a narrow escape from the earthquake and subsequent fire, which destroyed some fifteen thousand of the inhabitants: he was buried in the ruins; but his kitchen being cold as becomes a philosopher's, he was dug out unburnt.[1]

Galland again returned to Paris, where his familiarity with Arabic and Hebrew, Persian and Turkish, recommended him to M. Thevenot, who employed him in the Royal Library till his death in 1692, and to Dr. Bignon. This first President of the Grand Council acknowledged his services by the gift of a farm and a pension. He also became a favourite with D'Herbelot, whose Bibliothèque Orientale, left unfinished, and but half-printed at his death, he had the honour of completing and prefacing.[2] He also furnished materials for the first volume of the "Ménagiana," and sundry translations from Turkish and other Eastern tongues. President Bignon died within the twelvemonth, which made Galland attach himself in 1697 to M. Foucault, Councillor of State and Intendant (governor) of Caen in Lower Normandy, then famous for its academy. In his new patron's fine library and numismatic collection he found materials for a long succession of works, including a version of the Koran.[3] They recommended him strongly to the literary world, and in 1701, when it was re-established, he was made a member of the Académie des Inscriptions et Belles Lettres.

At Caen Galland issued in 1704,[4] six volumes, the first part of his Mille et une Nuit, Contes Arabes traduits en François,

---

1 See in Trébutien (Avertissement iii.) how Baron von Hammer escaped drowning by the blessing of The Nights.

2 He signs his name to the Discours pour servir de Préface.

3 I need not trouble the reader with their titles, which fill up nearly a column and a half in M. Hoeffer. His collection of maxims from Arabic, Persian, and Turkish authors appeared in English in 1695.

4 Galland's version was published in 1704-1717 in 12 vols. 12mo. (Hoeffer's Biographie; Graesse's Trésor de Livres rares, and Encyclop. Britannica, ixth Edit.).

which at once became famous as "The Arabian Nights' Entertainments." Abridged to one-fourth, mutilated, fragmentary, and paraphrastic though the tales were, the glamour of imagination, the marvel of the miracles, and the gorgeousness and magnificence of the scenery at once secured an exceptional success: it was a revelation in romance, and the public recognised that it stood in presence of a monumental literary work. France was a-fire with delight at a something so new, so unconventional, so entirely without purpose, religious, moral or philosophical; the Oriental wanderer in his stately robes was a startling surprise to the easy-going and utterly corrupt Europe of the *ancien régime* with its indecently tight garments and perfectly loose morals. "Ils produisirent," said Charles Nodier, a genius in his way, "dès le moment de leur publication, cet effet qui assure aux productions de l'esprit une vogue populaire, quoiqu'ils appartinssent à une littérature peu connue en France; et que ce genre de composition admit ou plutôt exigeât des détails de moeurs, de caractère, de costume et de localités absolument étrangers à toutes les idées établies dans nos contes et nos romans. On fut étonné du charme que résultait de leur lecture. C'est que la vérité des sentimens, la nouveauté des tableaux, une imagination féconde en prodiges, un coloris plein de chaleur, l'attrait d'une sensibilité sans prétention, et le sel d'un comique sans caricature, c'est que l'esprit et le naturel enfin plaisent partout, et plaisent à tout le monde.[1]"

The Contes Arabes at once made Galland's name, and a popular tale is told of them and him known to all reviewers who, however, mostly mangle it. In the Biographie Universelle of Michaud[2] we find:—Dans les deux premiers volumes de ces contes l'exorde était toujours, "Ma chère sœur, si vous ne dormez pas, faites-nous un de ces contes que vous savez." Quelques jeunes gens, ennuyés de cette plate uniformité, allèrent une nuit qu'il faisait très-grand froid, frapper à la porte de l'auteur, qui courut en chemise à sa fenêtre. Après

1 See also Leigh Hunt, "The Book of a Thousand Nights and One Night," etc., etc. London and Westminster Review, Art. iii., No lxiv mentioned in Lane, iii. 746.

2 Edition of 1856, vol. xv.

l'avoir fait morfondre quelque temps par diverses questions insignificantes, ils terminèrent en lui disant, "Ah, Monsieur Galland, si vous ne dormez pas, faites-nous un de ces beaux contes que vous savez si bien." Galland profita de la leçon, et supprima dans les volumes suivants le préambule qui lui avait attiré la plaisanterie. This legend has the merit of explaining why the Professor so soon gave up the Arab framework which he had deliberately adopted.

England at once annexed The Nights from France,[1] though when, where, and by whom the work was done, no authority seems to know. In Lowndes' "Bibliographer's Manual" the English Editio Princeps is thus noticed: "Arabian Nights' Entertainments, translated from the French, London, 1724, 12mo., 6 vols.," and a footnote states that this translation, very inaccurate and vulgar in its diction, was often reprinted. In 1712 Addison introduced into the Spectator (No. 535, Nov. 13) the Story of Alnaschar (=Al-Nashshár, the Sawyer) and says that his remarks on Hope "may serve as a moral to an Arabian tale which I find translated into French by Monsieur Galland." His version appears, from the tone and style, to have been made by himself, and yet in that year, a second English edition had appeared. The nearest approach to the Edit. Princeps in the British Museum[2] is a set of six

1 To France England also owes her first translation of the Koran, a poor and mean version by Andrew Ross of that made from the Arabic (No iv.) by André du Reyer, Consul de France for Egypt. It kept the field till ousted in 1734 by the learned lawyer, George Sale, whose conscientious work, including Preliminary Discourse and Notes (4to. London), a mine of reference for all subsequent writers, brought him the ill-fame of having "turned Turk."

2 Catalogue of Printed Books, 1884, p 159, col. i. I am ashamed to state this default in the British Museum, concerning which Englishmen are apt to boast, and which so carefully mulcts modern authors in unpaid copies. But it is only a slight specimen of the sad state of art and literature in England, neglected equally by Conservatives, Liberals and Radicals. What has been done for the endowment of research? What is our equivalent for the Prix de Rome? Since the death of Dr. Birch, who can fairly deal with a Demotic papyrus? Contrast the Société Anthropologique and its palace and professors in Paris with our "Institute" *au second* in a corner of Hanover Square and its skulls in the cellar! In speaking thus of the British Museum, I would by no means reflect upon any of the officials, to whose kindness and attention I am greatly indebted, and notably to Mr. Ellis, M.A., Assistant in the Dep. of Printed Books, who lent me valuable assistance in finding Hindi versions of The Nights.

volumes bound in three and corresponding with Galland's first half dozen (decade ?). Tomes i. and ii. are from the fourth edition of 1713, Nos. iii. and iv. are from the second of 1712, and v. and vi. are from the third of 1715. It is conjectured that the first two volumes were reprinted several times, apart from their subsequents, as was the fashion of the day; but all is mystery. We (my friends and I) have turned over scores of books in the British Museum, the University Library, and the Advocates' Libraries of Edinburgh and Glasgow: I have been permitted to put the question in "Notes and Queries" and in the "Antiquary"; but all our researches hitherto have been in vain.

The popularity of The Nights in England must have rivalled their vogue in France, judging from the fact that in 1713, or nine years after Galland's Edit. Prin. appeared, they had already reached a fourth issue. Even the ignoble national jealousy which prompted Sir William Jones grossly to abuse that valiant scholar, Auquetil du Perron, could not mar their popularity. But as there are men who cannot read Pickwick, so they were not wanting who spoke of "Dreams of the distempered fancy of the East.[1]" When the work first appeared in England," says Henry Weber,[2] "it seems to have made a considerable impression upon the public." Pope in 1720 sent two volumes (French? or English?) to Bishop Atterbury, without making any remarks on it; but from his very silence, it may be presumed that he was not displeased with the perusal. The bishop, who does not appear to have joined a relish for the flights of imagination to his other estimable qualities, expressed his dislike of these tales pretty strongly, and stated it to be his opinion, founded on the frequent descriptions of female dress, that they were the work of some Frenchman (*i.e.* Petis de la Croix, a mistake afterwards corrected

1 A t. vii. pp. 139-168. "On the Arabian Nights and translators, Weil, Torrens, and Lane (vol. i.) with the Essai of A. Loisseleur Deslongchamps." The Foreign Quarterly Review, vol. xxiv., Oct., 1839—Jan., 1840. London, Black and Armstrong, 1840.

2 Introduction to his Collection "Tales of the East," 3 vols., Edinburgh, 1812. He was the first to point out the resemblance between the introductory adventures of Shahryar and Shah Zaman and those of Astolfo and Giacondo in the Orlando Furioso (canto xxviii.). M. E. Lévêque in Les Mythes et les Légendes de l'Inde et la Perse (Paris, 1880), gives French versions of the Arabian and Italian narratives, side by side in p. 543 ff. (Clouston).

by Warburton). The *Arabian Nights*, however, quickly made their way to public favour. We have been informed of a singular instance of the effect they produced soon after their first appearance. Sir James Stewart, Lord Advocate for Scotland, having one Saturday evening found his daughters employed in reading these volumes, he seized them, with a rebuke for spending the evening before the sabbath in such worldly amusements; but the grave advocate became himself a prey to the fascination of these tales, being found on the morning of the sabbath itself employed in their perusal, from which he had not risen the whole of the night." As late as 1780 Dr. Beattie professed himself uncertain whether they were translated or fabricated by M. Galland; and, while Dr. Pusey wrote of them, "Noctes Mille et Una dictæ, quæ in omnium firmè populorum cultiorum linguas conversæ, in deliciis omnium habentur, manibusque omnium terentur,[1]" the author of "Thalaba" declared, "The Arabian Tales have lost their metaphorical rubbish in passing through the filter of a French translation." And the amiable Carlyle, in the gospel according to Saint Froude, characteristically termed them "downright lies" and forbade the house to such "unwholesome literature." What a sketch of character in two words!

The only fault found in France with the Contes Arabes was that their style is *peu correcte;* in fact they want classicism. Yet all Gallic imitators, Trébutien included, have carefully copied their leader, and Charles Nodier remarks:—"Il me semble que l'on n'a pas rendu assez de justice au style de Galland. Abondant sans être prolixe, naturel et familier sans être lâche ni trivial, il ne manque jamais de cette elegance qui résulte de la facilité, et qui présente je ne sais quel mélange de la naïveté de Perrault et de la bonhomie de La Fontaine."

Our Professor, with a name now thoroughly established, returned in 1706 to Paris, where he was an assiduous and efficient member of the Société Numismatique and corresponded largely

1 Notitiæ Codicis MI. Noctium. Dr. Pusey studied Arabic to familiarise himself with Hebrew, and was very different from his predecessor at Oxford in my day, who, when applied to for instruction in Arabic, refused to lecture except to a class.

with foreign Orientalists. Three years afterwards he was made Professor of Arabic at the Collége Royal, succeeding Pierre Dippy (Díbí) of Aleppo, who professed Arabic and Syriac[1]; and during the next half decade he devoted himself to publishing his valuable studies. Then the end came. In his last illness, an attack of asthma complicated with pectoral mischief, he sent to Noyon for his nephew Julien Galland[2] to assist him in ordering his MSS. and in making his will after the simplest military fashion; he bequeathed his writings to the Bibliothèque du Roi, his Numismatic Dictionary to the Academy, and his Alcoran to the Abbé Bignon. He died, aged sixty-nine, on February 17, 1715, leaving his second part of The Nights, also in six volumes, unpublished.[3]

Professor Galland was a French littérateur of the good old school, which is rapidly becoming extinct. Homme vrai dans les moindres choses (as his Éloge stated); simple in life and manners and single-hearted in his devotion to letters, he was almost childish in worldly matters, while notable for penetration and acumen in his studies. He would have been as happy, one of his biographers remarks, in teaching children the elements of education as he was in acquiring his immense erudition. Briefly, truth and honesty, exactitude and indefatigable industry, characterised his most honourable career.

Galland informs us (Epist. Ded.) that his MS. consisted of four volumes, only three of which are extant,[4] bringing the work

---

1 And of whom De Sacy (Chrest. iii. 131) tells an unpleasant tale of fraud.

2 This nephew was the author of "Recueil des Rits et Cérémonies du Pélérinage de La Mecque," etc, etc. Paris and Amsterdam, 1754, in 12mo.

3 The concluding part did not appear, I have said, till 1717: his "Contes et Fables Indiennes de Bidpai et de Lokman," were first printed in 1724, 2 vols. in 12mo. Hence, I presume, Lowndes' mistake.

4 M. Caussin (de Perceval), Professor of Arabic at the Imperial Library, who edited Galland in 1806, tells us that he found there only two MSS., both imperfect. The first (Galland's) is in three small vols. 4to., each of about pp. 140. The stories are more detailed, and the style, more correct than that of other MSS., is hardly intelligible to many Arabs, whence he presumes that it contains the original (an early?) text which has been altered and vitiated. The date is supposed to be circa A.D. 1600 The second Parisian copy is a single folio of some 800 pages, and is divided into 29 sections and cmv. nights, the last two sections being reversed. The MS. is very imperfect, the 12th, 15th, 16th, 18th, 20th, 21st-23rd, 25th, and 27th parts are wanting; the sections

down to night cclxxxii., or about the beginning of "Camar-alzaman." The missing portion, if it contained like the other volumes, 140 pages, would end that tale together with the Stories of Ghánim and the Enchanted (Ebony) Horse; and such is the disposition in the Bresl. Edit., which mostly favours in its ordinance the text used by the first translator. But this would hardly have filled more than two-thirds of his volumes: for the other third he interpolated, or is supposed to have interpolated, the ten[1] following tales:—

1. Histoire du Prince Zeyn Al-asnam et du Roi des Génies.[2]
2. „ de Codadad et de ses frères (including *La Princesse de Deryabar*).
3. „ de la Lampe merveilleuse (Aladdin).

---

which follow the 17th contain sundry stories repeated, there are anecdotes from Bidpai, the Ten Wazirs, and other popular works, and *lacunæ* everywhere abound. Galland's Arab. copy of The Nights in the Bibliothèque Nationale (Cat. MSS. Bibl. Reg., Tome i. 258) is attributed by the learned M. Hermann Zotenberg *to the xivth century*. It is inversely numbered in the catal; for instance, "MDVI. Codex bombycinus, olim Gallandianus, quo continetur fabula romanensis inscripta Noctes Mille et Una; incipit a centesima sexagesima septima," is vol. iii.; "MDVII." is vol. ii., and "MDVIII." is vol. i. The first volume proper (70 feuillets, date of registering Jan. 22, 1876) contains 25 lines to the page (19 centimètres x 12); white paper with 15 yellow leaves at the end; titles in red ink: no vowel-points; marginal corrections in rare places; a few notes (Latin and French) and scribblings at the beginning, not at the end (suggesting that it was originally the first half of what is now vol. ii.). This tome ends with half-night lxvii. The second volume (76 feuillets, Jan. 22, 1876) is the largest, the edges having been less trimmed (yet cuttings show in verso, p. 64); 25 lines to page and 26 to first page (20 cent. x 12); yellow paper; only 18 leaves white; few marginal corrections (a long one in p. 30), and inscription of Rizkallah, four lines, in p. 60, with erasure and hiatus between it and p. 61; scribblings on pp. 64, 65. Begins by ending night lxvii. and ends night clxvi. all but two lines. The third volume, 81 feuillets, Jan. 22, 1876) same format as vol. i. (page 19 cent x 12); edges much cut; of total 81 leaves, 34 are yellow and the rest white; few marginal corrections, vowel-points as everywhere omitted, long inscription p. 20; ends night cclxxxii. and begins the next; colophon reads, "Here endeth the third Juz (= section) of the wondrous and marvellous Tales of a Thousand Nights and a Night, and Allah is the Aider,"—proving a defective codex.

1 Mr. Payne (ix. 264) makes eleven, including the Histoire du Dormeur éveillé = The Sleeper and the Waker, which he afterwards translated from the Bresl. Edit. in his "Tales from the Arabic" (vol. i. 5, etc.).

2 Mr. E. J. W. Gibb has come upon this tale in a Turkish story-book, from which he drew his "Jewád"; and his version is printed in vol. ix. *post*.

4. Histoire de l'Aveugle Baba Abdalla.
5. „ de Sidi Nouman.
6. „ de Cogia Hassan Alhabbal.
7. „ d'Ali Baba, et de Quarante Voleurs exterminés par une Esclave.
8. „ d'Ali Cogia, Marchand de Bagdad.
9. „ du Prince Ahmed et de la fée Peri-Banou.
10. „ de deux Sœurs jalouses de leur Cadette.[1]

Concerning these interpolations (?), which contain two of the best and most widely known stories in the work, Alaeddin[2] and the Forty Thieves, conjectures have been manifold, but they mostly ran upon three lines. De Sacy held that they were found by Galland in the public libraries of Paris. Mr. Chenery, whose acquaintance with Arabic grammar was ample, suggested that the Professor had borrowed them from the recitations of the Rawis, rhapsodists, or professional story-tellers in the bazars of Smyrna and other ports of the Levant. The late Mr. Henry Charles Coote (in the "Folk-Lore Record," vol. iii. part ii., p. 178 *et seq.*), "On the source of some of M. Galland's Tales," quotes from popular Italian, Sicilian, and Romaic stories incidents identical with those in Prince Ahmad, Alaeddin, Ali Baba, and the Envious Sisters, suggesting that the Frenchman had heard these *paramythia* in Levantine coffee-houses, and had inserted them into his unequalled *corpus fabularum.* Mr. Payne (ix. 268) conjectures the probability "of their having been composed at a comparatively recent period by an inhabitant of Baghdad, in imitation of the legends of Haroun er Rashid and other well-known tales of the original work"; and adds, "It is possible that an exhaustive examination of the various MS. copies of the Thousand and One Nights known to exist in the public libraries of Europe might yet cast some light upon the question of the origin of the interpolated

---

1. A littérateur lately assured me that Nos. ix. and x. have been found in the Bibliothèque Nationale (du Roi) Paris; but two friends were kind enough to enquire, and ascertained that it was a mistake. Such Persianisms as Codadad (Khudadad), Baba Cogia (Khwájah) and Peri (fairy) suggest a Persic MS.

2. I shall prefer this form when translating the Tale, even to M. De Sacy's "Ala-eddin."

Tales." I quite agree with him, taking "The Sleeper and the Waker" and "Zeyn Al-asnam" as cases in point; but I should expect, for reasons before given, to find the stories in a Persic rather than an Arabic MS. And I feel convinced that all will be recovered: Galland was not the man to commit a literary forgery.

As regards Alaeddin, the most popular tale of the whole work, I am convinced that it is genuine, although my unfortunate friend, the late Professor Palmer, doubted its being an Eastern story. It is laid down upon all the lines of Oriental fiction. The mise-en-scène is China, "where they drink a certain warm liquor" (tea); the hero's father is a poor tailor; and, as in "Judar and his Brethren," the Maghribi Magician presently makes his appearance, introducing the Wonderful Lamp and the Magical Ring. Even the Sorcerer's cry, "New lamps for old lamps!"—a prime point—is paralleled in the Tale of the Fisherman's son,[1] where the Jew asks in exchange only old rings, and the Princess, recollecting that her husband keeps a shabby, well-worn ring in his writing-stand, and he being asleep, takes it out and sends it to the man. In either tale the palace is transported to a distance, and both end with the death of the wicked magician and the hero and heroine living happily together ever after.[2]

All Arabists have remarked the sins of omission and commission, of abridgment, amplification, and substitution, and the audacious distortion of fact and phrase in which Galland freely indulged, whilst his knowledge of Eastern languages proves that he knew better. But literary license was the order of his

1 Vol. vi. p. 212, "The Arabian Nights' Entertainments (London: Longmans, 1811) by Jonathan Scott, with the Collection of New Tales from the Wortley-Montagu MS. in the Bodleian." I regret to see that Messieurs Nimmo in reprinting Scott have omitted his sixth volume. The Rev. George F. Townsend, M.A., "The Arabian Nights' Entertainments," (London: Warne, 1866 and 1869) has followed in his so-called "Revised Edition" Dr. Scott's text, "as being at once more accurate (!) than that of M. Galland; less diffuse and verbose than that of Forster; less elevated (!), difficult (! !) and abstruse (! ! !) than that of Lane." (Pref.)

2 Since this was written, M. Hermann Zotenberg, the well-known translator of Tabari, bought for the Bibliothèque Nationale, Paris, two Arabic folios containing Zayn al-Asnam and Alaeddin. The learned Arabist kindly lent me his transcript for my translation (vol. x. *post*), and is printing the text in Paris.

day, and at that time French, always the most bégueule of European languages, was bound by a rigorisme of the narrowest and the straightest of lines, from which the least écart condemned a man as a barbarian and a *tudesque*. If we consider Galland fairly we shall find that he errs mostly for a purpose, that of popularising his work; and his success has indeed justified his means. He has been derided (by scholars) for "Hé Monsieur!" and "Ah Madame!" but he could not write "O mon sieur" and "O ma dame"; although we can borrow from Biblical and Shakespearean English, "O my lord!" and "O my lady!" "Bon Dieu! ma sœur" (which our translators English by "O heavens," night xx.) is good French for Wa 'lláhi —by Allah; and "cinquante cavaliers bien faits" ("fifty handsome gentlemen on horseback") is a more familiar picture than fifty knights. "L'officieuse Dinarzade" (night lxi.), and "Cette plaisante querelle des deux frères" (night lxxii.) become ridiculous only in translation—"the officious Dinarzade" and "this pleasant quarrel"; while "ce qu'il y de remarquable" (night lxxiii.) would relieve the Gallic mind from the mortification of "Destiny decreed." "Plusieurs sortes de fruits et de bouteilles de vin" (night ccxxxi. etc.) Europeanises flasks and flagons; and the violent convulsions in which the girl dies (night cliv., her head having been cut off by her sister) is mere Gallic squeamishness: France laughs at "le shoking" in England, but she has only to look at home, especially during the reign of Galland's contemporary—Roi Soleil. The terrible "Old man" (Shaykh) "of the Sea" (-board) is badly described by "l'incommode vieillard" ("the ill-natured old fellow"): "Brave Maimune" and "Agréable Maimune" are hardly what a Jinni would say to a Jinniyah (ccxiii.); but they are good Parisian. The same may be noted of "Plier les voiles pour marque qu'il se rendait" (night ccxxxv.), a European practice; and of the false note struck in two passages. "Je m'estimais heureuse d'avoir fait une si belle conquête" (night lxvii.) gives a Gaulòis turn; and, "Je ne puis voir sans horreur cet abominable barbier que voilà: quoiqu'il soit né dans un pays où tout le monde est blanc, il ne laisse pas à resembler à un Éthiopien; mais il a l'âme encore plus noire et horrible que le visage" (night clvii.), is a mere affectation of

Orientalism. Lastly, "Une vieille dame de leur connaissance" (night clviii.) puts French polish upon the matter-of-fact Arab's "old woman."

The list of absolute mistakes, not including violent liberties, can hardly be held excessive. Professor Weil and Mr. Payne (ix. 271) justly charge Galland with making the Trader (night i.) throw away the *shells (écorces)* of the date which has only a pellicle, as Galland certainly knew; but dates were not seen every day in France, while almonds and walnuts were of the quatre mendiants. He preserves the écorces, which later issues have changed to noyaux, probably in allusion to the jerking practice called Inwá. Again in the "First Shaykh's Story" (vol. i. night i.) the "maillet" is mentioned as the means of slaughtering cattle, because familiar to European readers: at the end of the tale it becomes "le couteau funeste." In Badr al-Din a "tarte à la crême," so well known to the West, displaces, naturally enough, the outlandish "mess of pomegranate-seeds." Though the text especially tells us the hero removed his bag-trousers (not only "son habit") and placed them under the pillow, a crucial fact in the history, our Professor sends him to bed fully dressed, apparently for the purpose of informing his readers in a foot-note that Easterns "se couchent en caleçon" (night lxxx). It was mere ignorance to confound the arbalète or cross-bow with the stone-bow (night xxxviii.), but this has universally been done, even by Lane, who ought to have known better: and it was an unpardonable carelessness or something worse to turn Nár (fire) and Dún (in lieu of) into "le faux dieu Nardoun" (night lxv.): as this has been untouched by De Sacy, I cannot but conclude that he never read the text with the translation. Nearly as bad also to make the Jewish physician remark, when the youth gave him the left wrist (night cl.), "voilà une grande ignorance de ne savoir pas que l'on presente la main droite à un médecin et non pas la gauche"—whose exclusive use all travellers in the East must know. I have noticed the incuriousness which translates "along the Nile-shore" by "up towards Ethiopia" (night cli.), and the "Islands of the *Children* of Khaledan" (night ccxi.) instead of the Khálidatáni or Khálidát, the Fortunate Islands. It was by no means "des petits soufflets" ("some tips from time to time with her fingers") which the sprightly dame administered to the Barber's second brother (night clxxi.), but sound and heavy "cuffs" on the nape; and the sixth brother (night clxxx.) was not "aux lèvres fendues" ("he of the hare-lips"), for they had been cut off by the Badawi jealous of his fair wife. Abu al-Hasan would not greet his beloved by saluting "le tapis à ses pieds": he would kiss her hands and feet. Haratalnefous (Hayat al-Nufús, night ccxxvi.) would not "throw cold water in the Princess's face": she would sprinkle it with eau-de-rose. "Camaralzaman" I. addresses his two abominable wives in language purely European (ccxxx.), "et de la vie il ne s'approche d'elles," missing one of the fine touches of the tale which shows its hero a weak and violent man, hasty and lacking the pundonor. "La belle Persienne," in the Tale of Nur al-Din, was no Persian; nor would her master address her, "Venez çà, impertinente!" ("come hither, impertinence." In the story of Badr, one of the Comoro Islands becomes "L'île de la Lune." "Dog" and "dog-son" are not "injures atroces et indignes d'un grand roi": the greatest Eastern kings allow themselves far more energetic and significant language. Fitnah[1] is by no means "Force de cœurs": our author misread "Kút al-Kulúb" (Food of Hearts) and made it "Kuwwal al-Kulúb"= Force of Hearts. Lastly, the *dénoûment* of The Nights is widely different in French and in Arabic; but that is not Galland's fault, as he never saw the original, and indeed he deserves high praise for having invented so pleasant and sympathetic a close, inferior only to the Oriental device.[2]

1 Dr. Scott, who uses Fitnah (iv. 42), makes it worse by adding "Alcolom (Al-Kulúb?) signifying Ravisher of Hearts," and his names for the six slave-girls (vol. iv. 37) such as "Zohorob Bostan" (Zahr al-Bústán), which Galland rightly renders by "Fleur du Jardin," serve only to heap blunder upon blunder. Indeed the Anglo-French translations are below criticism: it would be waste of time to notice them. The characteristic is a servile suit paid to the original, *e.g.* rendering hair, "accomodé en boucles" by "hair festooned in buckles" (night ccxiv.), and Île d'Ébène (Jazirat al-Abnús, night xliii.) by "the Isle of Ebene." A certain surly old littérateur tells me that he prefers these wretched versions to Mr. Payne's. Padrone! as the Italians say: I cannot envy his taste or his temper.

2 De Sacy (Mémoire, p. 52) notes that in some MSS., the Sultan, ennuyé by the last tales of Shahrázad, proposes to put her to death, when she produces her three children and all ends merrily without marriage-bells. Von Hammer prefers this version as the more dramatic, the Frenchman rejects it on account of the difficulties of the *accouchements*. He strains at the gnat--a common process.

Galland's fragment has a strange effect upon the Orientalist, and those who take the scholastic view, be it wide or narrow. De Sacy does not hesitate to say that the work owes much to his fellow-countryman's hand; but I judge otherwise: it is necessary to dissociate the two works and to regard Galland's paraphrase, which contains only a quarter of The Thousand Nights and a Night, as a wholly different book. Its attempts to amplify beauties and to correct or conceal the defects and the grotesqueness of the original, absolutely suppress much of the local colour, clothing the bare body in the best of Parisian suits. It ignores the rhymed prose and excludes the verse, rarely and very rarely rendering a few lines in a balanced style. It generally rejects the proverbs, epigrams, and moral reflections which form the pith and marrow of the book; and, worse still, it disdains those finer touches of character which are often Shakespearean in their depth and delicacy, and which, applied to a race of familiar ways and thoughts, manners and customs, would have been the wonder and delight of Europe. It shows only a single side of the gem that has so many facets. By deference to public taste it was compelled to expunge the often repulsive simplicity, the childish indecencies, and the wild orgies of the original, contrasting with the gorgeous tints, the elevated morality, and the religious tone of passages which crowd upon them. We miss the odeur du sang which taints the parfums du harem; also the humouristic tale and the Rabelaisian outbreak which relieve and throw out into strong relief the splendour of Empire and the havoc of Time. Considered in this light it is a caput mortuum, a magnificent texture seen on the wrong side; and it speaks volumes for the genius of the man who could recommend it in such blurred and caricatured condition to readers throughout the civilised world. But those who look only at Galland's picture, his effort to "transplant into European gardens the magic flowers of Eastern fancy," still compare his tales with the sudden prospect of magnificent mountains seen after a long desert-march: they arouse strange longings and indescribable desires; their marvellous imaginativeness produces an insensible brightening of mind and an increase of fancy-power, making one dream that behind them lies the new and unseen, the strange and unexpected—in fact, all the glamour of the unknown.

The Nights has been translated into every far-extending Eastern tongue, Persian, Turkish and Hindostani. The latter entitles them Hikáyát al-Jalilah or Noble Tales, and the translation was made by Munshi Shams al-Din Ahmad for the use of the College of Fort George in A.H. 1252=1836.[1] All these versions are direct from the Arabic: my search for a translation of Galland into any Eastern tongue has hitherto been fruitless.[2]

I was assured by the late Bertholdy Seemann that the "Language of Hoffmann and Heine" contained a literal and complete translation of The Nights; but personal enquiries at Liepzig and elsewhere convinced me that the work still remains to be done. The first attempt to improve upon Galland and to show the world what the work really is was made by Dr. Max Habicht and was printed at Breslau (1824-25), in fifteen small square volumes.[3] Thus it appeared before the "Tunis Manuscript[4]" of which it purports to be a translation. The German version is, if possible, more condemnable than the Arabic original. It lacks every charm of style; it conscientiously shirks every difficulty; it abounds in the most extraordinary blunders, and it is utterly useless as a picture of manners or a book of reference. We can explain its lâches only by the theory that the eminent Professor left the labour to his collaborateurs and did not take the trouble to revise their careless work.

---

1 See Journ. Asiatique, iii. série, vol. viii. Paris, 1839.

2 Since this was written I have found no fewer than three in Hindostani alone; and these will be noticed in vol x. *post.*

3 "Tausend und Eine Nacht: Arabische Erzählungen. Zum ersten mal aus einer Tunesischen Handschrift ergänzt und vollständig übersetzt," Von Max Habicht, F H. Von der Hagen und Karl Schall (the offenders?).

4 Dr. Habicht informs us (Vorwort, iii. vol. ix 7) that he obtained his MS. with other valuable works from Tunis, through a personal acquaintance, a learned Arab, Herr M. Annagar (Mohammed Al-Najjár?) and was aided by Baron de Sacy, Langlès, and other savants in filling up the *lacunæ* by means of sundry MSS. The editing was a prodigy of negligence: the corrigenda (of which brief lists are given) would fill a volume; and as before noticed, the indices of the first four tomes were printed in the fifth, as if the necessity of a list of tales had just struck the dense editor. After Habicht's death in 1839 his work was completed in four vols. (ix-xii) by the well-known Prof H. L. Fleischer, who had shown some tartness in his "Dissertatio Critica de Glossis Habichtianis." He carefully imitated all the shortcomings of his predecessor, and even omitted the Verzeichniss, etc, the Varianten, and the Glossary of Arabic words not found in Golius, which formed the only useful part of the first eight volumes.

The next German translation was by Aulic Councillor J. von Hammer-Purgstall[1] who, during his short stay at Cairo and Constantinople, turned into French the tales neglected by Galland. After some difference with M. Caussin (de Perceval) in 1810, the Styrian Orientalist entrusted his MS. to Herr Cotta, the publisher of Tubingen. Thus a German version appeared, the translation of a translation, at the hand of Professor Zinserling,[1] while the French version was unaccountably lost en route to London. Finally the "Contes inédits," etc., appeared in a French translation by G. S. Trébutien (Paris, mdcccxxviii.). Von Hammer took liberties with the text which can compare only with those of Lane: he abridged and retrenched till the likeness in places entirely disappeared; he shirked some difficult passages, and he mis-explained others. In fact the work did no honour to the amiable and laborious historian of the Turks.

The only good German translation of The Nights is due to Dr. Gustav Weil who, born on April 24, 1808, is still (1886) professing at Heidelburg.[2] His originals (he tells us) were the Breslau Edition, the Bulak text of Abd al-Rahman al-Safati, and a MS. in the library of Saxe Gotha. The venerable savant, who has rendered such service to Arabism, informs me that Aug. Lewald's "Vorhalle" (pp. i.-xv.)[3] was written without his knowledge. Dr. Weil neglects the division of days, which enables him to introduce any number of tales: for instance,

1 Der Tausend und Eine Nacht noch nicht übersetzte Märchen, Erzählungen und Anekdoten. zum erstenmal aus dem Arabischen in's Französische übersetzt von J. von Hammer, und aus dem Französischen in's Deutsche von Aug. E. Zinserling, Professor. Stuttgart und Tübingen, 1823. Drei Bände 8°. Trébutien's, therefore, is the translation of a translation of a translation.

2 Tausend und Eine Nacht Arabische Erzählungen. Zum erstenmale aus dem Urtexte vollständig und treu uebersetzt von Dr. Gustav Weil. He began his work on return from Egypt in 1836, and completed his first version of the Arabische Meisterwerk in 1838-42 (3 vols. roy. oct.). I have the Zweiter Abdruck der dritten Auflage (2nd reprint of 3rd) in 4 vols. 8vo., Stuttgart, 1872. It has more than a hundred woodcuts, all of that art fashionable in Europe till Lane taught what Eastern illustrations should be.

3 My learned friend Dr. Wilhelm Storck, to whose admirable translations of Camoens I have often borne witness, also notes that this Vorhalle, or Porch to the first edition, a rhetorical introduction addressed to the general public, is held in Germany to be valueless, and that it was noticed only for the Bemerkung concerning the offensive passages which Professor Weil had toned down in his translation. In the Vorwort of the succeeding editions (Stuttgart) it is wholly omitted.

Galland's decade occupies a large part of vol. iii. The Vorwort wants development; the notes, confined to a few words, are inadequate and verse is everywhere rendered by prose, the Saj'a or assonance being wholly ignored. On the other hand, the scholar shows himself by a correct translation, contrasting strongly with those which preceded him, and by a strictly literal version, save where the treatment required to be modified in a book intended for the public. Under such circumstances it cannot well be other than longsome and monotonous reading.

Although Spain and Italy have produced many and remarkable Orientalists, I cannot find that they have taken the trouble to translate The Nights for themselves: cheap and gaudy versions of Galland seem to have satisfied the public.[1] Notes on the Romaic, Icelandic, Russian (?) and other versions, will be found in Appendix No. I. *infra*.

Professor Galland has never been forgotten in France where, amongst a host of editions, four have claims to distinction[2]; and his success did not fail to create a host of imitators and to attract what De Sacy justly terms "une prodigieuse importation de marchandise de contrabande." As early as 1823 Von Hammer numbered seven in France (Trébutien, Préface xviii) and during later years they have grown prodigiously. Mr. William F. Kirby, who has made a special study of the subject, has favoured me with detailed bibliographical notes on Galland's imitators, which are printed in Appendix No. I.

---

1 The older are "Novelle Arabe divise in Mille ed una Notte, tradotte dall' idioma Francese nel volgare Italiano": in Bingen, mdccxxiii., per Sebastiano Coleti (12 vols 8vo); and "Le Mille ed una Notte: Novelle Arabe; Milano presso la Libraria Ferrario Editria. The most popular are now "Mille ed una Notte Novelle Arabe." Napoli, 1867, 8vo, illustrated, 4 francs; the "Mille ed una Notte. Novelle Arabe, versione italiana nuovamente emendata e corredata di note"; 4 vols. in-32 (dateless) Milano, 8vo., 4 francs; and Prof Pietro Malan's so-called "translation" (Persur, Perino, 1882). It is not a little curious that the illustrations are almost the same in Weil De Sacy, Malan and Mr. W. F. Kirby's 'New Arabian Nights"; and I may add that nothing could be more grotesque—Orientalism drawn from the depths of European self-consciousness.

2 These are (1) by M. Caussin (de Perceval), Paris, 1806, 9 vols. 12mo, now exceedingly rare and expensive; (2) Edouard Gauttier, Paris, 1822-24, 7 vols 8vo., valued for its hideous illustrations, yet I procured a good copy for 15 francs; (3) M. Destain, Paris, 1823-25, 6 vols. 8vo; and (4) Baron de Sacy, Paris, 1838 (?) 3 vols. large 8vo., illustrated (and vilely illustrated).

§ III.

THE MATTER AND THE MANNER OF THE NIGHTS.

A.—The Matter.

Returning to my threefold distribution of this Prose Poem (§ i) into Fable, Fairy Tale, and Historical Anecdote,[1] let me proceed to consider these sections more carefully.

The Apologue or Beast-fable, which apparently antedates all other subjects in The Nights, has been called "One of the earliest creations of the awakening consciousness of mankind." I should regard it despite a monumental antiquity, as the offspring of a comparatively civilised age, when a jealous despotism or a powerful oligarchy threw difficulties and dangers in the way of speaking "plain truths" A hint can be given and a friend or foe can be lauded or abused as Belins the sheep or Isengrim the wolf, when the author is debarred the higher enjoyment of praising him or dispraising him by name. And, as the purposes of fables are twofold—

> Duplex libelli dos est: quod risum movet,
> Et quod prudenti vitam consilio monet—

The speaking of brute beasts would give a piquancy and a pleasantry to moral design as well as to social and political satire.

The literary origin of the fable is not Buddhistic: we must especially shun that "Indo-Germanic" school which goes to India for its origins, when Pythagoras, Solon, Herodotus, Plato, Aristotle, and possibly Homer, sat for instruction at the feet of the Hir-seshtha, the learned grammarians of the Pharaohnic court. Nor was it

---

1 The number of fables and anecdotes varies in the different texts, but may be assumed to be upwards of four hundred, about half of which were translated or abridged by Lane.

Æsopic, evidently Æsop inherited the boarded wealth of ages. As Professor Lepsius taught us, "In the olden times within the memory of man, we know only of *one* advanced culture; of only *one* mode of writing, and of only *one* literary development, viz. those of Egypt." The invention of an alphabet, as opposed to a syllabary, unknown to Babylonia, to Assyria, and to that extreme bourne of their civilising influences, China, would for ever fix their literature—poetry, history and criticism,[1] the apologue, and the anecdote. To mention no others, the Lion and the Mouse appears in a Leyden papyrus dating from B.C. 1200-1166, the days of Rameses III. (Rhampsinitus) or Hak On, not as a rude and early attempt, but in a finished form, postulating an ancient origin and illustrious ancestry. The dialogue also is brought to perfection in the discourse between the Jackal Koufi and the Ethiopian Cat (Revue Égyptologique, ivme. année, Parti.). Africa, therefore, was the home of the Beast-fable not, as Professor Mahaffy thinks, because it was the chosen land of animal worship, where

Oppida tota canem venerantur nemo Dianam[2];

but simply because the Nile-land originated every form of literature from Fabliau and Epos.

From Kemi the Black-land it was but a step to Phœnicia, Judæa,[3] Phrygia and Asia Minor, whence a ferry led over to Greece.

1 I have noticed these points more fully in the beginning of chapt. iii. "The Book of the Sword."

2 A notable instance of Roman superficiality, incuriousness, and ignorance. Every old Egyptian city had its idols (images of metal, stone or wood), in which the Deity became incarnate as in the Catholic host; besides its own symbolic animal used as a Kiblah or prayer-direction (Jerusalem or Meccah), the visible means of fixing and concentrating the thoughts of the vulgar, like the crystal of the hypnotist or the disk of the electro-biologist. And goddess Diana was in no way better than goddess Pasht. For the true view of idolatry see Koran, xxxix. 4. I am deeply grateful to Mr. P. le Page Renouf (Soc. of Biblic. Archæology, April 6, 1886) for identifying the Manibogh, Michabo, or Great Hare of the American indigenes with Osiris Unnefer ("Hare God") These are the lines upon which scientific investigation should run. And of late years there is a notable improvement of tone in treating of symbolism or idolatry: the Lingam and the Yoni are now described as "mystical representations, and perhaps the best possible impersonal representatives, of the abstract expressions paternity and maternity" (Prof. Monier Williams in "Folk-lore Record," vol. iii. part i. p. 118).

3 See Jotham's fable of the Trees and King Bramble (Judges ix. 8) and Nathan's parable of the Poor Man and his little ewe Lamb (2 Sam. xii. 1).

Here the Apologue found its populariser in Αἴσωπος, Æsop, whose name, involved in myth, possibly connects with Αιθίοψ:—"Æsopus et Aithiops idem sonant" says the sages. This would show that the Hellenes preserved a legend of the land where the Beast-fable arose, and we may accept the fabulist's æra as contemporary with Crœsus and Solon (B.C. 570), about a century after Psammeticus (Psamethik 1st) threw Egypt open to the restless Greek.[1] From Africa, too, the Fable would in early ages migrate eastwards and make for itself a new home in the second great focus of civilisation formed by the Tigris-Euphrates Valley. The late Mr. George Smith found amongst the cuneiforms fragmentary Beast-fables, such as dialogues between the Ox and the Horse, the Eagle and the Sun. In after centuries, when the conquests of Macedonian Alexander completed what Sesostris and Semiramis had begun, and mingled the manifold families of mankind by joining the eastern to the western world, the Orient became formally Hellenised. Under the Seleucidæ and during the life of the independent Bactrian kingdom (B.C. 255-125), Grecian art and science, literature and even language over-ran the old Iranic reign and extended eastwards throughout northern India. Porus sent two embassies to Augustus in B.C. 19, and in one of them the herald Zarmanochagas (Shramanácharya) of Bargosa, the modern Baroch in Gujarat, bore an epistle upon vellum written in Greek (Strabo xv. 1 § 78). "Videtis gentes populosque mutasse sedes," says Seneca (De Cons. ad Helv. c. vi.). Quid sibi volunt in mediis barbarorum regionibus Græcæ artes? Quid inter Indos Persasque Macedonicus sermo? Atheniensis in Asia turba est." Upper India, in the Macedonian days would have been mainly Buddhistic, possessing a rude alphabet borrowed from Egypt through Arabia and Phœnicia, but still in a low and barbarous condition: her buildings were wooden, and she lacked, as far as we know, stone-architecture—the main test of social development. But the Bactrian Kingdom gave an impulse to her civilisation and the

1 Herodotus (ii. c. 134) notes that "Æsop the fable-writer (ὁ λογόποιος) was one of her (Rhodopis) fellow slaves." Aristophanes (Vespæ, 1446) refers to his murder by the Delphians and his fable beginning, "Once upon a time there was a fight"; while the Scholiast finds an allusion to The Serpent and the Crab, in Pax 1084; and others in Vespæ 1401, and Aves 651.

result was classical opposed to vedic Sanskrit. From Persia Greek letters, extending southwards to Arabia, would find indigenous imitators, and there Æsop would be represented by the sundry sages who share the name Lokman.[1] One of these was of servile condition, tailor, carpenter, or shepherd ; and a "Habashi" (Æthiopian) meaning a negro slave with blubber lips and splay feet, so far showing a superficial likeness to the Æsop of authentic history.

The Æsopic fable, carried by the Hellenes to India, might have fallen in with some rude and fantastic barbarian of Buddhistic "persuasion" and indigenous origin: so Reynard the Fox has its analogue amongst the Kafirs and the Vái tribe of Mandengan negroes in Liberia[2] amongst whom one Doalu invented or rather

1 There are three distinct Lokmans who are carefully confounded in Sale (Koran, chapt. xxxi) and in Smith's Dict. of Biography etc., art. Æsopus. The first or eldest Lokman, entitled Al-Hakim (the Sage) and the hero of the Koranic chapter which bears his name, was son of Bá'úrá of the Children of Azar, sister's son to Job or son of Job's maternal aunt ; be witnessed David's miracles of mail-making, and when the tribe of 'Ád was destroyed, he became King of the country. The second, also called the Sage, was a slave, an Abyssinian negro, sold to the Israelites during the reign of David or Solomon, synchronous with the Persian Kay Káús and Kay Khusrau, also with Pythagoras the Greek (!). His physique is alluded to in the saying, "Thou resemblest Lokman (in black ugliness) but not in wisdom" (Ibn Khallikan, i. 145). This negro or negroid, after a godly and edifying life, left a volume of "Amsál," proverbs, and exempla (not fables or apologues) ; and Easterns still say, "One should not pretend to teach Lokman"—in Persian, "Hikmat ba Lokman ámokhtan." Three of his apothegms dwell in the public memory : "The heart and the tongue are the best and worst parts of the human body." "I learned wisdom from the blind, who make sure of things by touching them" (as did St. Thomas) ; and, when he ate the colocynth offered by his owner, "I have received from thee so many a sweet that 'twould be surprising if I refused this one bitter." He was buried (says the Tárikh Muntakháb) at Ramlah, in Judæa, with the seventy Prophets stoned in one day by the Jews. The youngest Lokman "of the vultures" was a prince of the tribe of 'Ad who lived 3,500 years, the age of seven vultures (Tabari). He could dig a well with his nails ; hence the saying, "Stronger than Lokman" (A. P. i. 701) ; and he loved the arrow-game, hence "More gambling than Lokman" (ibid., ii. 938). "More voracious than Lokman" (ibid , i. 134) alludes to his eating one camel for breakfast and another for supper. His wife Barákish also appears in proverb, *e.g.* "Camel us and camel thyself" (ibid., i. 295) *i.e.* give us camel flesh to eat, said when her son by a former husband brought her a fine joint which she and her husband relished. Also, "Barákish hath sinned against her kin" (ibid., ii. 89). More of this in Chenery's Al-Hariri, p. 422 ; but the three Lokmans are there reduced to two.

2 I have noticed them in vol. ii. pp. 47-49 of "To the Gold Coast for Gold."

borrowed a syllabarium. The modern Gypsies are said also to have Beast-fables which have never been traced to a foreign source (Leland). But I cannot accept the refinement of difference which Professor Benfey, followed by Mr. Keith-Falconer, discovers between the Æsopic and the Hindu apologue:—"In the former animals are allowed to act as animals: the Oriental makes them act as men in the form of animals." The essence of the beast-fable is a reminiscence of Homo primigenius with erected ears and hairy hide, and its expression is to make the brother brute behave, think, and talk like him with the superadded experience of ages. To early man, the "lower animals," which are born, live and die like himself, showing all the same affects and disaffects, loves and hates, passions, prepossessions, and prejudices, must have seemed quite human enough and on an equal level to become his substitutes. The savage when he began to reflect would regard the carnivor and the serpent with awe, wonder and dread; and would soon suspect the same mysterious potency in the brute as in himself: so the Malays still look upon the Uran-utan, or Wood-man, as the possessor of superhuman wisdom. The hunter and the herdsman, who had few other companions, would presently explain the peculiar relations of animals to themselves by material metamorphosis, the bodily transformation of man to brute giving increased powers of working him weal and wóe. A more advanced stage would find the step easy to metempsychosis, the beast containing the Ego (*alias* soul) of the human: such instinctive belief explains much in Hindu literature, but it was not wanted at first by the Apologue.

This blending of blood, this racial baptism, would produce a fine robust progeny; and, after our second century, Ægypto-Græco-Indian stories over-ran the civilised globe between Rome and China. Tales have wings and fly farther than the jade hatchets of proto-historic days. And the rèsult was a book which has had more readers than any other except the Bible. Its original is unknown.[1] The volume, which in Pehlevi became the Jávidán Khirad ("Wisdom of Ages"), or the Testament of Hoshang, that ancient Guebre King, and in Sanskrit the

1 I can hardly accept the dictum that the Katha Sarit Sagara, of which more presently, is the "earliest representation of the first collection."

Panchatantra ("Five Chapters"), is a recueil of apologues and anecdotes related by the learned Brahman, Vishnu Sharmá for the benefit of his pupils the sons of an Indian Rajah. The Hindu original has been adapted and translated under a host of names into a number of languages; Arabic, Hebrew and Syraic, Greek and Latin, Persian and Turkish.[1] Voltaire[2] wisely remarks of this venerable production:—Quand on fait réflexion que presque toute la terre a été enfatuée de pareils contes, et qu'ils ont fait l'éducation du genre humain, on trouve les fables de Pilpay, de Lokman,[3] d'Ésope, bien raisonnables. But methinks the sage of Ferney might have said far more. These fables speak with the large utterance of early man; they have also their own especial beauty—the charms of well-preserved and time-honoured old age. There is in their wisdom a perfume of the past, homely and ancient-fashioned like a whiff of *pot pourri*, wondrous soothing withal to olfactories agitated by the patchoulis and jockey clubs of modern pretenders and petit-maitres, with their grey young heads and pert intelligence, the motto of whose ignorance is "Connu!" Were a dose of its antique, mature experience adhibited to the Western before he visits the East, those few who could digest it might escape the normal lot of being twisted round the fingers of every rogue they meet from Dragoman to Rajah. And a quotation from them tells at once: it shows the quoter to be a man of education, not a "Jangali," a sylvan, or savage, as the Anglo-Indian official is habitually termed by his more civilised "fellow-subject."

The main difference between the classical apologue and the

---

1 The Pehlevi version of the days of King Anushirwan (A.D. 531-72) became the Humáyun-námeh ("August Book") turned into Persian for Bahram Shah the Ghaznavite: the Hitopadesa ("Friendship-boon") of Prakrit, avowedly compiled from the "Panchatantra," became the Hindu Panchopakhyan, the Hindostani Akblák-i-Hindi ("Moralities of Ind") and in Persia and Turkey the Anvar-i-Suhayli ("Lights of Canopus"). Arabic, Hebrew and Syriac writers entitle their version Kalílah wa Damnah, or Kalilaj wa Damnaj, from the name of the two jackal-heroes, and Europe knows the recueil as the Fables of Pilpay or Bidpay (Bidyá-pati, Lord of learning?) a learned Brahman reported to have been Premier at the Court of the Indian King Dabishlim.

2 Diet. Philosoph. S. V. Apocryphes.

3 The older Arab writers, I repeat, do not ascribe fables or Beast-apologues to Lokman; they record only "dictes" and proverbial sayings.

fable in The Nights is that while Æsop and Gabrias write laconic tales with a single event and a simple moral, the Arabian fables are often "long-continued novelle involving a variety of events, each characterised by some social or political aspect, forming a narrative highly interesting in itself, often exhibiting the most exquisite moral, and yet preserving, with rare ingenuity, the peculiar characteristics of the actors.[1]" And the distinction between the ancient and the mediæval apologue, including the modern, which, since "Reineke Fuchs," is mainly German, appears equally pronounced. The latter is humorous enough and rich in the wit which results from superficial incongruity; but it ignores the deep underlying bond which connects man with beast. Again, the main secret of its success is the strain of pungent satire, especially in the Renardine Cycle, which the people could apply to all unpopular "lordes and prelates, gostly and worldly."

Our Recueil contains two distinct sets of apologues.[2] The first (vol. ii.) consists of eleven, alternating with five anecdotes (nights cxlvi.-cliii.), following the lengthy and knightly romance of King Omar bin al Nu'uman and followed by the melancholy love tale of Ali bin Bakkár. The second series in vol. vii., consisting of eight fables, not including ten anecdotes (nights cmi.-cmxxiv.), is injected into the romance of King Jali'ad and Shimas mentioned by Al-Mas'udi as independent of The Nights. In both places the Beast-fables are introduced with some art and add variety to the subject-matter, obviating monotony—the deadly sin of such works—and giving repose to the hearer or reader after a climax of excitement such as the murder of the Wazirs. And even these are not allowed to pall upon the mental palate, being mingled with anecdotes and short tales, such as the Hermits (ii. 348), with biographical or literary episodes, acroamata, table-talk, and analects where humorous Rabelaisian anecdote finds a place; in fact the fabliau or novella. This style of composition

1 Professor Taylor Lewis: Preface to Pilpay.

2 In the Katha Sarit Sagara the beast-apologues are more numerous, but they can be reduced to two great nuclei; the first in chapter lx. (Lib. x.) and the second in the same book, Chapters lxii.-lxv. Here, too, they are mixed up with anecdotes and acroamata after the fashion of The Nights, suggesting great antiquity for this style of composition.

may be as ancient as the apologues. We know that it dates as far back as Rameses III., from the history of the Two Brothers in the Orbigny papyrus,[1] the prototype of Yusuf and Zulaykha, the Koranic Joseph and Potiphar's wife. It is told with a charming naïveté and such sharp touches of local colour as, "Come, let us make merry an hour and lie together. *Let down thy hair!*"

Some of the apologues in The Nights are pointless enough, rien moin qu'amusants; but in the best specimens, such as the Wolf and the Fox[2] (the wicked man and the wily man), both characters are carefully kept distinct, and neither action nor dialogue ever flags. Again the Flea and the Mouse (ii. 37), of a type familiar to students of the Pilpay cycle, must strike the home-reader as peculiarly quaint.

Next in date to the Apologue comes the Fairy Tale proper, where the natural universe is supplemented by one of purely imaginative existence. "As the active world is inferior to the rational soul," says Bacon, with his normal sound sense, "so Fiction gives to Mankind what History denies and in some measure satisfies the Mind with Shadows when it cannot enjoy the Substance. And as real History gives us not the success of

1 Brugsch, History of Egypt, vol. i. 266, *et seq.* This fabliau is interesting in more ways than one. Anepu the elder (Potiphar) understands the language of cattle, an idea ever cropping up in Folk-lore; and Bata (Joseph), his "little brother," who becomes a "panther of the South (Nubia) for rage" at the wife's impudique proposal, takes the form of a bull—metamorphosis full blown. It is not, as some have called it, the "oldest book in the world"; that name was given by M. Chabas to a MS. of Proverbs, dating from B.C. 2200. See also the "Story of Saneha," a novel earlier than the popular date of Moses, in the Contes Populaires d'Égypte.

2 The fox and the jackal are confounded by the Arabic dialects not by the Persian, whose "Rubáh" can never be mistaken for "Shaghál" "Sa'lab" among the Semites is locally applied to either beast, and we can distinguish the two only by the fox being solitary and rapacious, and the jackal gregarious and a carrion-eater. In all Hindu tales the jackal seems to be an awkward substitute for the Grecian and classical fox, the Giddar or Kolá *(Canis aureus)* being by no means sly and wily as the Lomri *(Vulpes vulgaris)*. This is remarked by Weber (Indishche Studien) and Prof. Benfey's retort about "King Nobel" the lion, is by no means to the point. See Katha Sarit Sagara, ii. 28. I may add that in Northern Africa jackal's gall, like jackal's grape (*Solanum nigrum*=black nightshade), ass's milk and melted camel-hump, is used aphrodisiacally as an unguent by both sexes. See p. 239, etc. of Le Jardin parfumé du Cheikh Nefzaoui, of whom more presently.

things according to the deserts of vice and virtue, Fiction corrects it and presents us with the fates and fortunes of persons rewarded and punished according to merit." But I would say still more. History paints or attempts to paint life as it is, a mighty maze with or without a plan: Fiction shows or would show us life as it should be, wisely ordered and laid down on fixed lines. Thus Fiction is not the mere handmaid of History: she has a household of her own, and she claims to be the triumph of Art which, as Goëthe remarked, is "Art because it is not Nature." Fancy, *la folle du logis*, is "that kind and gentle portress who holds the gate of Hope wide open, in opposition to Reason, the surly and scrupulous guard.[1]" As Palmerin of England says and says well, "For that the report of noble deeds doth urge the courageous mind to equal those who bear most commendation of their approved valiancy; this is the fair fruit of Imagination and of ancient histories." And last, but not least, the faculty of Fancy takes count of the cravings of man's nature for the marvellous, the impossible, and of his higher aspirations for the Ideal, the Perfect: she realises the wild dreams and visions of his generous youth, and pourtrays for him a portion of that "other and better world," with whose expectation he would console his age.

The imaginative varnish of The Nights serves admirably as a foil to the absolute realism of the picture in general. We enjoy being carried away from trivial and commonplace characters, scenes and incidents; from the matter of fact surroundings of a work-a-day world, a life of eating and drinking, sleeping and waking, fighting and loving, into a society and a mise-en-scène which we suspect can exist and which we know do not. Every man at some turn or term of his life has longed for supernatural powers and a glimpse of Wonderland. Here he is in the midst of it. Here he sees mighty spirits summoned to work the human mite's will, however whimsical, who can transport him in an eye-twinkling whithersoever he wishes; who can ruin cities and build palaces of gold and silver, gems and jacinths; who can serve up delicate viands and delicious drinks in priceless chargers and impossible cups and bring the choicest fruits from farthest Orient:

1 Rambler, No. lxvii.

here he finds magas and magicians who can make kings of his friends, slay armies of his foes, and bring any number of beloveds to his arms. And from this outraging probability and out-stripping possibility arises not a little of that strange fascination exercised for nearly two centuries upon the life and literature of Europe by The Nights, even in their mutilated and garbled form. The reader surrenders himself to the spell, feeling almost inclined to enquire, "And why may it not be true[1]?" His brain is dazed and dazzled by the splendours which flash before it, by the sudden procession of Jinns and Jinniyahs, demons and fairies, some hideous, others preternaturally beautiful; by good wizards and evil sorcerers, whose powers are unlimited for weal and for woe; by mermen and mermaids, flying horses, talking animals, and reasoning elephants; by magic rings and their slaves, and by talismanic couches which rival the carpet of Solomon. Hence, as one remarks, these Fairy Tales have pleased and still continue to please almost all ages, all ranks, and all different capacities.

Dr. Hawkesworth[2] observes that these Fairy Tales find favour "because even their machinery, wild and wonderful as it is, has its laws; and the magicians and enchanters perform nothing but what was naturally to be expected from such beings, after we had once granted them existence." Mr. Heron "rather supposes the very contrary is the truth of the fact. It is surely the strangeness, the unknown nature, the anomalous character of the supernatural agents here employed, that makes them to operate so powerfully on our hopes, fears, curiosities, sympathies, and, in short, on all the feelings of our hearts. We see men and women, who possess qualities to recommend them to our favour, subjected to the influence of beings, whose good or ill will, power or weakness, attention or neglect, are regulated by motives and circumstances which we cannot comprehend: and hence, we naturally tremble for their fate with the same anxious concern as we should for a friend wandering in a dark night amidst torrents and pre-

---

1 Some years ago I was asked by my old landlady if ever in the course of my travels I had come across Captain Gulliver.

2 In "The Adventurer" quoted by Mr. Heron, "Translator's Preface to the Arabian Tales of Chaves and Cazotte."

cipices; or preparing to land on a strange island, while he knew not whether he should be received on the shore by cannibals waiting to tear him piecemeal and devour him, or by gentle beings disposed to cherish him with fond hospitality." Both writers have expressed themselves well, but meseems each has secured, as often happens, a fragment of the truth and holds it to be the whole Truth. Granted that such spiritual creatures as Jinns walk the earth, we are pleased to find them so very human, as wise and as foolish in word and deed as ourselves: similarly we admire in a landscape natural forms like those of Staffa or the Palisades which favour the works of architecture. Again, supposing such preternaturalisms to be around and amongst us, the wilder and more capricious they prove, the more our attention is excited and our forecasts are baffled to be set right in the end. But this is not all. The grand source of pleasure in Fairy Tales is the natural desire to learn more of the Wonderland which is known to many as a word and nothing more, like Central Africa before the last half century: thus the interest is that of the "Personal Narrative" of a grand exploration to one who delights in travels. The pleasure must be greatest where faith is strongest; for instance, amongst imaginative races like the Kelts and especially Orientals, who imbibe supernaturalism with their mothers' milk. "I am persuaded," writes Mr. Bayle St. John,[1] "that the great scheme of preternatural energy, so fully developed in The Thousand and One Nights, is believed in by the majority of the inhabitants of all the religious professions both in Syria and Egypt." He might have added "by every reasoning being from prince to peasant, from Mullah to Badawi, between Marocco and Outer Ind."

The Fairy Tale in The Nights is wholly and purely Persian. The gifted Iranian race, physically the noblest and the most beautiful of all known to me, has exercised upon the world-history an amount of influence which has not yet been fully recognised. It repeated for Babylonian art and literature what

---

1 "Life in a Levantine Family," chapt. xi. Since the able author found his "family" firmly believing in The Nights, much has been changed in Alexandria; but the faith in Jinn and Ifrit, ghost and vampire is lively as ever.

Greece had done for Egyptian, whose dominant idea was that of working for eternity a κτῆμα εἰς ἀεί. Hellas and Iran instinctively chose as their characteristic the idea of Beauty, rejecting all that was exaggerated and grotesque; and they made the sphere of Art and Fancy as real as the world of Nature and Fact, and this innovation was hailed by the Hebrews. The so-called Books of Moses deliberately and ostentatiously ignored the future state of rewards and punishments, the other world which ruled the life of the Egyptian in this world: the law-giver, whoever he may have been, Osarsiph or Moshe, apparently held the tenet to be unworthy of a race whose career he was directing to conquest and isolation in dominion. But the Jews, removed to Mesopotamia, the second cradle of the creeds, presently caught the infection of their Asiatic media; superadded Babylonian legend to Egyptian myth; stultified the Law by supplementing it with the "absurdities of foreign fable" and ended, as the Talmud proves, with becoming the most wildly superstitious and "other-worldly" of mankind.

The same change befell Al-Islam. The whole of its supernaturalism is borrowed bodily from Persia, which had "imparadised Earth by making it the abode of angels." Mohammed, a great and commanding genius, blighted and narrowed by surroundings and circumstance to something little higher than a Covenanter or a Puritan, declared to his followers,

> "I am sent to 'stablish the manners and customs";

and his deficiency of imagination made him dislike everything but "women, perfumes, and prayers," with an especial aversion to music and poetry, plastic art and fiction. Yet his system, unlike that of Moses, demanded thaumaturgy and metaphysical entities, and these he perforce borrowed from the Jews who had borrowed them from the Babylonians: his soul and spirit, his angels and devils, his cosmogony, his heavens and hells, even the Bridge over the Great Depth, are all either Talmudic or Iranian. But there he stopped and would have stopped others. His enemies among the Koraysh were in the habit of reciting certain Persian fabliaux and of extolling them as superior to the silly and equally fictitious stories of the "Glorious Koran." The leader of these scoffers was one Nazr Ibn Háris who, taken prisoner after the Battle of Bedr, was incontinently decapitated, by apostolic command, for what appears to be a natural and sensible preference. It was the same furious fanaticism and one-idea'd intolerance which made Caliph Omar destroy all he could find of the Alexandrian Library, and prescribe burning for the Holy Books of the Persian Guebres. And the taint still lingers in Al-Islam: it will be said of a pious man, "He always studies the Koran, the Traditions, and other books of Law and Religion; and he never reads poems nor listens to music or to stories."

Mohammed left a dispensation or rather a reformation so arid, jejune, and material, that it promised little more than the "Law of Moses" before this was vivified and racially baptised by Mesopotamian and Persic influences. But human nature was stronger than the Prophet, and thus outraged, took speedy and absolute revenge. Before the first century had elapsed, orthodox Al-Islam was startled by the rise of Tasawwuf or Sufyism[1] a revival of classic Platonism and Christian Gnosticism, with a mingling of modern Hylozoism; which, quickened by the glowing imagination of the East, speedily formed itself into a creed the most poetical and impractical, the most spiritual and the most transcendental, ever invented; satisfying all man's hunger for "belief" which, if placed upon a solid basis of fact and proof, would forthright cease to be belief.

I will take from The Nights, as a specimen of the true Persian romance, "The Queen of the Serpents" (vol. iv.) the subject of Lane's Carlylean denunciation. The first gorgeous picture is the Session of the Snakes which, like their Indian congeners the Nága kings and queens, have human heads and reptile bodies, an Egyptian myth that engendered the "old serpent" of Genesis. The Sultánah welcomes Hásib Karím al-Dín, the hapless lad who had been left in a cavern to die by the greedy woodcutters; and, in order to tell him her tale, introduces the "Adventures of Bulúkiyá": the latter is an Israelite converted by editor and scribe to Mohammedanism; but we can detect under his assumed faith the older creed. Solomon is not buried by authentic his-

1 The name dates from the second century A.H., or before A.D. 815.

tory "beyond the Seven (mystic) Seas," but at Jerusalem or Tiberias; and his seal-ring suggests the Jám-i-Jam, the crystal cup of the great King Jamshid. The descent of the Archangel Gabriel, so familiar to Al-Islam, is the manifestation of Bahman, the First Intelligence, the mightiest of the Angels who enabled Zarathustra-Zoroaster to walk like Bulukiya over the Dálati or Caspian Sea.[1] Amongst the sights shown to Bulukiya, as he traverses the Seven Oceans, is a battle royal between the believing and the unbelieving Jinns, true Magian dualism, the eternal duello of the Two Roots or antagonistic Principles, Good and Evil, Hormuzd and Ahriman, which Milton has debased into a common-place modern combat fought also with cannon. Sakhr the Jinni is Eshem chief of the Divs, and Kaf, the encircling mountain, is a later edition of Persian Alborz. So in the Mantak al-Tayr (Colloquy of the Flyers) the Birds, emblems of souls, seeking the presence of the gigantic feathered biped Simurgh, their god, traverse seven Seas (according to others seven Wadys) of Search, of Love, of Knowledge, of Competence, of Unity, of Stupefaction, and of Altruism (*i.e.* annihilation of self), the several stages of contemplative life. At last, standing upon the mysterious island of the Simurgh, and "casting a clandestine glance at him they saw thirty birds[2] in him; and when they turned their eyes to themselves the thirty birds seemed one Simurgh: they saw in themselves the entire Simurgh; they saw in the Simurgh the thirty birds entirely." Therefore they arrived at the solution of the problem "*We* and *Thou*"; that is, the identity of God and Man; they were for ever annihilated in the Simurgh, and the shade vanished in the sun (Ibid. iii., 250). The wild ideas concerning Khalit and Malit (night ccccxciii.) are again Guebre. "From the seed of Kayomars (the androgyne, like pre-Adamite man) sprang a tree shaped like two human beings and thence proceeded Meshia and Meshinah, first man and woman, progenitors of mankind"; who, though created for "Shídistán, Lightland," were seduced by Ahriman. This "two-man-tree" is evidently

---

1 Dabistan, i. 231, etc.

2 Because Si=thirty and Murgh=bird. In McClenachan's Addendum to Mackay's Encyclopædia of Freemasonry we find the following definition: "Simorgh. A monstrous griffin, guardian of the Persian mysteries."

the duality of Physis and Anti-physis, Nature and her counterpart, the battle between Mihr, Izad or Mithra with his Surush and Feristeh (Seraphs and Angels) against the Divs who are the children of Time led by the arch-demon Esham. Thus when Hormuzd created the planets, the dog, and all useful animals and plants, Ahriman produced the comets, the wolf, noxious beasts and poisonous growths. The Hindus represent the same metaphysical idea by Bramhá the Creator and Visvakarma, the Anti-creator,[1] miscalled by Europeans Vulcan: the former fashions a horse and a bull and the latter caricatures them with an ass and a buffalo,—"evolution" turned topsy turvy. After seeing nine angels and obtaining an explanation of the Seven Stages of Earth which is supported by the Gáv-i-Zamín, the energy, symbolised by a bull, implanted by the Creator in the mundane sphere, Bulukiya meets the four Archangels, to wit Gabriel, who is the Persian Rawánbakhsh or Life-giver; Michael or Beshter, Raphael or Isráfil alias Ardibihisht, and Azazel or Azrail who is Dumá or Mordád, the Death-giver; and the four are about to attack the Dragon, that is, the demons hostile to mankind who were driven behind Alborz-Káf by Tahmuras the ancient Persian king. Bulukiya then recites an episode within an episode, the "Story of Jánsháh," itself a Persian name and accompanied by two others (night ccccxcix.), the *mise-en-scène* being Kabul, and the King of Khorasan appearing in the proem. Janshah, the young Prince, no sooner comes to man's estate than he loses himself out hunting and falls in with cannibals whose bodies divide longitudinally, each moiety going its own way: these are the Shikk (split ones) which the Arabs borrowed from the Persian Ním-chihrah or Half-faces. They escape to the Ape-island whose denizens are human in intelligence and speak articulately, as the universal East believes they can: these Simiads are at chronic war with the Ants, alluding to some obscure myth which gave rise to the gold-diggers of Herodotus and other

1 For a poor and inadequate description of the festivals commemorating this "Architect of the Gods," see vol. iii. p. 177., "View of the History, etc., of the Hindus" by the learned Dr. Ward, who could see in them only the "low and sordid nature of idolatry." But we can hardly expect better things from a missionary in 1822, when no one took the trouble to understand what "idolatry" means.

classics, "emmets in size somewhat less than dogs but bigger than foxes.[1]" The episode then falls into the banalities of Oriental folk-lore. Janshah, passing the Sabbation river and reaching the Jews' city, is persuaded to be sewn up in a skin and is carried in the normal way to the top of the Mountain of Gems, where he makes acquaintance with Shaykh Nasr, Lord of the Birds: he enters the usual forbidden room; falls in love with the pattern Swan-maiden; wins her by the popular process; loses her and recovers her through the Monk Yaghmús, whose name, like that of King Teghmús, is a burlesque of the Greek; and, finally, when she is killed by a shark, determines to mourn her loss till the end of his days. Having heard this story Bulukiya quits him; and, resolving to regain his natal land, falls in with Khizr; and the Green Prophet, who was Wazir to Kay Kobad (vi^th^ century B.C.) and was connected with Macedonian Alexander (!) enables him to win his wish. The rest of the tale calls for no comment.

Thirdly and lastly we have the histories, historical stories and the "Ana" of great men in which Easterns as well as Westerns delight: the gravest writers do not disdain to relieve the dullness of chronicles and annals by means of such discussions, humorous or pathetic, moral or grossly indecent. The dates must greatly vary; some of the anecdotes relating to the early Caliphs appear almost contemporary; others, like Ali of Cairo and Abu al-Shámát, may be as late as the Ottoman Conquest of Egypt (sixteenth century). All are distinctly Sunnite and show fierce animus against the Shi'ah heretics, suggesting that they were written after the destruction of the Fatimite dynasty (twelfth century) by Salah al-Din (Saladin the Kurd) one of the latest historical personages and the last king named in The Nights.[2] These anecdotes are so

---

1 Rawlinson (ii. 491) on Herod. iii. c. 102. Nearchus saw the skins of these formicæ Indicæ, by some rationalists explained as "jackals" whose stature corresponds with the text, and by others as "pangolins" or ant-eaters *(manis pentedactyla)*. The learned Sanskritist, Horace H. Wilson, quotes the name Pippilika = ant-gold, given by the people of Little Thibet to the precious dust thrown up in the emmet heaps.

2 A writer in the *Edinburgh Review* (July, '86), of whom more presently, suggests that The Nights assumed essentially their present shape during the

often connected with what a learned Frenchman terms the "regne féerique de Haroun er-Réschid,[1]" that the Great Caliph becomes the hero of this portion of The Nights. Aaron the Orthodox was the central figure of the most splendid empire the world had seen, the Viceregent of Allah combining the powers of Cæsar and Pope, and wielding them right worthily according to the general voice of historians. To quote a few: Ali bin Talib al-Khorásáni described him, in A.D. 934, a century and-a-half after his death when flattery would be tongue-tied, as, "one devoted to war and pilgrimage, whose bounty embraced the folk at large." Sa'adi (ob. A.D. 1291) tells a tale highly favourable to him in the "Gulistan" (lib. i. 36). Fakhr al-Din[2] (xiv[th] century) lauds his merits, eloquence, science and generosity, and Al-Siyuti (nat. A.D. 1445) asserts, "He was one of the most distinguished of Caliphs and the most illustrious of the Princes of the Earth" (p. 290). The Shaykh al-Nafzáwi[3] (sixteenth century) in his Rauz al-'Átir fí Nazáh al-Khátir = the Scented Garden Man's heart to gladden, calls Harun (chapt. vii.) the "Master of munificence and bounty, the best of the generous." And even the latest writers have not ceased to

---

general revival of letters, arts, and requirements which accompanied the Kurdish and Tartar irruptions into the Nile Valley, a golden age which embraced the whole of the thirteenth, fourteenth, and fifteenth centuries, and ended with the Ottoman Conquest in A.D. 1527.

1 Let us humbly hope not again to hear of the golden prime of

"The good (fellow?) Haroun Alrasch'id,"

a mispronunciation which suggests only a rasher of bacon. Why will not poets mind their quantities, in lieu of stultifying their lines by childish ignorance? What can be more painful than Byron's

"They laid his dust in Ar'qua (for Arqua') where he died"?

2 See De Sacy's Chrestomathie Arabe (Paris, 1826), vol. i.

3 See Le Jardin Parfumé du Cheikh Nefzaoui, Manuel d'Érotologie Arabe, Traduction revue et corrigée, Édition privée, imprimé à deux cent vingt exemplaires pour Isidore Liseux et ses Amis, Paris, 1886. The editor has forgotten to note that the celebrated Sidi Mohammed copied some of the tales from The Nights and borrowed others (I am assured by a friend) from Tunisian MSS. of the same work. The book has not been fairly edited: the notes abound in mistakes, the volume lacks an index, etc., etc. Since this was written the Jardin Parfumé has been twice translated into English as "The Perfumed Garden of the Cheikh Nefzaoui, a Manual of Arabian Erotology (sixteenth century). Revised and corrected translation, Cosmopoli; mdccclxxxvi.: for the Kama Shastra Society of London and Benares and for private circulation only."

praise him. Says Alí Aziz Efendi the Cretan, in the Story of Jewád[1] (p. 81), "Harun was the most bounteous, illustrious and upright of the Abbaside Caliphs."

The fifth Abbaside was fair and handsome, of noble and majestic presence, a sportsman and an athlete who delighted in polo and archery. He showed sound sense and true wisdom in his speech to the grammarian-poet Al-Asma'i, who had undertaken to teach him:—"Ne m'enseignez jamais en public, et ne vous empressez pas trop de me donner des avis en particulier. Attendez ordinairement que je vous interroge, et contentez-vous de me donner une réponse précise à ce que je vous demanderai, sans y rien ajouter de superflu. Gardez vous surtout de vouloir me préoccuper pour vous attirer ma créance, et pour vous donner de l'autorité. Ne vous étendez jamais trop en long sur les histoires et les traditions que vous me raconterez, si je ne vous en donne la permission. Lorsque vous verrai que je m'eloignerai de l'équité dans mes jugements, ramenez-moi avec douceur, sans user de paroles fâcheuses ni de réprimandes. Enseignez-moi principalement les choses qui sont les plus nécessaires pour les discours que je dois faire en public, dans les mosquées et ailleurs; et ne parlez point en termes obscurs, ou mystérieux, ni avec des paroles trop recherchées.[2]"

He became well read in science and letters, especially history and tradition, for "his understanding was as the understanding of the learned"; and, like all educated Arabs of his day, he was a connoisseur of poetry which at times he improvised with success.[3]" He made the pilgrimage every alternate year and sometimes on foot, while "his military expeditions almost equalled his pilgrimages." Day after day during his Caliphate he prayed a hundred "bows," never neglecting them, save for some especial reason, till his death; and he used to give from his privy purse alms to the extent of an hundred dirhams per diem.

1 Translated by a well-known Turkish scholar, Mr. E. J. W. Gibb. (Glasgow, Wilson and McCormick, 1884)

2 D'Herbelot (s. v. "Asmai"): I am reproached by a dabbler in Orientalism for using this admirable writer who, despite occasional carelessness—he did not live to revise his work—shows more knowledge in one page than my critic ever did in a whole volume.

3 For specimens see Al-Siyuti, pp 301 and 304: and the Shaykh al-Nafzawi, pp 134-35

He delighted in panegyry and liberally rewarded its experts, one of whom, Abd al-Sammák the Preacher, fairly said of him, "Thy humility in thy greatness is nobler than thy greatness." "No Caliph," says Al-Niftawayh, "had been so profusely liberal to poets, lawyers and divines, although as the years advanced he wept over his extravagance amongst other sins." There was vigorous manliness in his answer to the Grecian Emperor who had sent him an insulting missive:—"In the name of Allah! From the Commander of the Faithful, Harun al-Rashid, to Nicephorus the Roman dog. I have read thy writ, O son of a miscreant mother! Thou shalt not hear, thou shalt see my reply." Nor did he cease to make the Byzantine feel the weight of his arm till he "nakh'd[1]" his camel in the imperial Court-yard; and this was only one instance of his indomitable energy and hatred of the Infidel. Yet, if the West is to be believed, he forgot his fanaticism in his diplomatic dealings and courteous intercourse with Carolus Magnus.[2] Finally, his civilised and well-regulated rule contrasted as strongly with the barbarity and turbulence of occidental Christendom, as the splendid Court and the luxurious life of Baghdad and its carpets and hangings devanced the quasi-savagery of London and Paris, whose palatial halls were spread with rushes.

The great Caliph ruled twenty-three years and a few months (A.H. 170-193=A.D. 786-808); and, as his youth was chequered and his reign was glorious, so was his end obscure.[3] After a

---

1 The word "nakh" (to make a camel kneel) has been explained in night lv.

2 The present of the famous horologium-clepsydra-cuckoo clock, the dog Becerillo and the elephant Abu Lubábah sent by Harun to Charlemagne is not mentioned by Eastern authorities and consequently no reference to it will be found in my late friend Professor Palmer's little volume, "Haroun Alraschid," London, Marcus Ward, 1881. We have allusions to many presents, the clock and elephant, tent and linen hangings, silken dresses, perfumes, and candelabra of auricalch brought by the Legati (Abdalla, Georgius Abba et Felix) of Aaron Amiralmumminim Regis Persarum who entered the Port of Pisa (A.D. 801) in (vol. v. 178) Recueil des Hist. des Gaules et de la France, etc., par Dom Martin Bouquet, Paris, mdccxliv. The author also quotes the lines:—

Persarum Princeps illi devinctus amore
Præcipuo fuerat, nomen habens Aaron.
Gratia cui Caroli præ cunctis Regibus atque
Illis Principibus tempora cara fuit.

3 Many have remarked that the actual date of the decease is unknown.

vision foreshadowing his death,[1] which happened, as becomes a good Moslem, during a military expedition to Khorasan, he ordered his grave to be dug and himself to be carried to it in a covered litter: when sighting the fosse he exclaimed, "O son of man, thou art come to this!" Then he commanded himself to be set down and a perlection of the Koran to be made over him in the litter on the edge of the grave. He was buried (æt. forty-five) at Sanábád, a village near Tús.

Aaron the Orthodox appears in The Nights as a headstrong and violent autocrat, a right royal figure according to the Moslem ideas of his day. But his career shows that he was not more tyrannical nor more sanguinary than the normal despot of the East, or the contemporary Kings of the West: in most points, indeed, he was far superior to the historic misrulers who have afflicted the world from Spain to furthest China. But a single great crime, a tragedy whose details are almost incredibly horrible, marks his reign with the stain of infamy, with a blot of blood never to be washed away. This tale, "full of the waters of the eye," as Firdausi sings, is the massacre of the Barmecides; a story which has often been told and which cannot here be passed over in silence. The ancient and noble Iranian house, belonging to the "Ebná" or Arabised Persians, had long served the Ommiades till, early in our eighth century, Khálid bin Bermek,[2] the chief, entered the service of the first Abbaside and became Wazir and Intendant of Finance to Al-Saffáh. The most remarkable and distinguished of the family, he was in office when Al-Mansur transferred the capital from Damascus, the head-quarters of the hated Ommiades, to Baghdad, built ad hoc. After securing the highest character in history by his personal gifts and public services, he was succeeded by his son and heir Yáhyá (John), a statesman famed from early youth for prudence and profound intelligence, liberality and nobility of soul.[3] He was charged by the Caliph Al-Mahdi with

---

1 See Al-Siyuti (p 305) and Dr. Jonathan Scott's "Tales, Anecdotes, and Letters" (p. 296).

2 I have given (vol. i. night xix.) the vulgar derivation of the name; and D'Herbelot (*s v.* Barmakian) quotes some Persian lines alluding to the "supping up." Al-Mas'udi's account of the family's early history is unfortunately lost. This Khálid succeeded Abu Salámah, first entitled "Wazir" under Al-Saffah (Ibn Khallikan, i. 468).

3 For his poetry see Ibn Khallikan, iv. 103.

the education of his son Harun, hence the latter was accustomed to call him father; and until the assassination of the fantastic tyrant Al-Hádi, who proposed to make his own child Caliph, he had no little difficulty in preserving the youth from death in prison. The Orthodox, once seated firmly on the throne, appointed Yahya his Grand Wazir. This great administrator had four sons, Al-Fazl, Ja'afar, Mohammed, and Musa,[1] in whose time the house of Bermek rose to that height from which decline and fall are, in the East, well-nigh certain and imminent. Al-Fazl was a foster-brother of Harun, an exchange of suckling infants having taken place between the two mothers for the usual object, a tightening of the ties of intimacy: he was a man of exceptional mind, but he lacked the charm of temper and manner which characterised Ja'afar. The poets and rhetoricians have been profuse in their praises of the cadet who appears in The Nights as an adviser of calm sound sense, an intercessor and a peace-maker, and even more remarkable than the rest of his family for an almost incredible magnanimity and generosity—une générosité effrayante. Mohammed was famed for exalted views and nobility of sentiment, and Musa for bravery and energy: of both it was justly said, "They did good and harmed not.[2]"

For ten years (not including an interval of seven) from the time of Al-Rashid's accession (A.D. 786) to the date of their fall (A.D. 803), Yahya and his sons, Al-Fazl and Ja'afar, were virtually rulers of the great heterogeneous empire, which extended from Mauritania to Tartary, and they did notable service in arresting its disruption. Their downfall came sudden and terrible, like "a thunderbolt from the blue." As the Caliph and Ja'afar were halting in Al-'Umr (the convent) near Anbár-town on the Euphrates, after a convivial evening spent in different pavilions, Harun during the dead of the night called up his page Yásir al-Rikhlah,[3] and bade him bring Ja'afar's head. The messenger

---

1 Their flatterers compare them with the four elements.

2 Al-Mas'udi, chapt. cxii.

3 Ibn Khallikan (i. 310) says the eunuch Abú Háshim Masrúr, the Sworder of Vengeance, who is so pleasantly associated with Ja'afar in many nightly disguises; but the Eunuch survived the Caliph. Fakhr al-Din (p. 27) adds that Masrur was an enemy of Ja'afar; and gives further details concerning the execution.

found Ja'afar still carousing with the blind poet Abú Zakkár and the Christian physician Gabriel ibn Bakhtiashú, and was persuaded to return to the Caliph and report his death; the Wazir adding, "An he express regret I shall owe thee my life; and, if not, whatso Allah will be done." Ja'afar followed to listen, and heard only the Caliph exclaim, "O slave, if thou answer me another word, I will send thee before him!" whereupon he at once bandaged his own eyes and received the fatal blow. Al-Asma'í, who was summoned to the presence shortly after, recounts that when the head was brought to Harun he gazed at it, and summoning two witnesses commanded them to decapitate Yasir, crying, "I cannot bear to look upon the slayer of Ja'afar!" His vengeance did not cease with the death: he ordered the head to be gibbetted at one end and the trunk at the other abutment of the Tigris bridge, where the corpses of the vilest malefactors used to be exposed; and, some months afterwards, he insulted the remains by having them burned—the last and worst indignity which can be offered to a Moslem. There are indeed pity and terror in the difference between two such items in the Treasury-accounts as these: "Four hundred thousand dinars (£200,000) to a robe of honour for the Wazir Ja'afar bin Yahya"; and, "Ten kirát, (5 shill.) to naphtha and reeds for burning the body of Ja'afar the Barmecide."

Meanwhile Yahya and Al-Fazl, seized by the Caliph Harun's command at Baghdad, were significantly cast into the prison "Habs al-Zanádikah"—of the Guebres—and their immense wealth which, some opine, hastened their downfall, was confiscated. According to the historian Tabari, (vol. iv. 468) who, however, is not supported by all the annalists, the whole Barmecide family, men, women, and children numbering over a thousand, were slaughtered, with only three exceptions; Yahya, his brother Mohammed, and his son Al-Fazl. The Caliph's foster-father, who lived to the age of seventy-four, was allowed to die in jail (A.D. 805) after two years' imprisonment at Rakkah. Al-Fazl, after having been tortured with two hundred blows in order to make him produce concealed property, survived his father three years and died in Nov. A.D. 808, some four months before his terrible foster-brother. A pathetic tale is told of the son warming water for the old man's use by pressing the copper ewer to his own stomach.

The motives of this terrible massacre are variously recounted, but no sufficient explanation has yet been, or possibly ever will be, given. The popular idea is embodied in The Nights.[1] Harun, wishing Ja'afar to be his companion even in the Harem, had wedded him, pro formâ, to his eldest sister Abbásah, "the loveliest woman of her day," and brilliant in mind as in body; but he had expressly said, "I will marry thee to her, that it may be lawful for thee to look upon her but thou shalt not touch her." Ja'afar bound himself by a solemn oath; but his mother Attábah was mad enough to deceive him in his cups, and the result was a boy (Ibn Khallikan) or, according to others, twins. The issue was sent, under the charge of a confidential eunuch and a slave-girl, to Meccah for concealment; but the secret was divulged to Zubaydah, who had her own reasons for hating husband and wife, and who cherished an especial grievance against Yahya.[2] Thence it soon found its way to head-quarters. Harun's treatment of Abbásah supports the general conviction: according to the most credible accounts she and her child were buried alive in a pit under the floor of her apartment.

But, possibly, Ja'afar's perjury was only "the last straw." Already Al-Fazl bin Rabí'a, the deadliest enemy of the Barmecides, had been entrusted (A.D. 786) with the Wazirate, which he kept seven years. Ja'afar had also acted generously but imprudently in abetting the escape of Yahya bin Abdillah, Sayyid and Alide, for whom the Caliph had commanded confinement in a close dark dungeon: when charged with disobedience the Wazir had made full confession and Harun had (they say) exclaimed, "Thou hast done well!" but was heard to mutter, "Allah slay me an I slay thee not.[3]" The great house seems at times to have

1 Bresl. Edit., night dlxvii. vol. vii. pp. 258-260; translated in Mr. Payne's "Tales from the Arabic," vol. i. 189, and headed, "Al-Rashid and the Barmecides." See vol. ix. p. 115, post. It is far less lively and dramatic than the account of the same event given by Al-Mas'udi (chapt. cxii.), by Ibn Khallikan, by Tabari, and by Fakhr al-Din.

2 Al-Mas'udi, chapt. cxi.

3 See Dr. Jonathan Scott's extracts from Major Ouseley's "Tarikh-i-Barmaki."

abused its powers by being too peremptory with Harun and Zubaydah, especially in money matters[1]; and its very greatness would have created for it many and powerful enemies and detractors who plied the Caliph with anonymous verse and prose. Nor was it forgotten that, before the spread of Al-Islam, they had presided over the Naubehár or Pyræthrum of Balkh; and Harun is said to have remarked anent Yahya, "The zeal for Magianism, rooted in his heart, induces him to save all the monuments connected with his faith.[2]" Hence the charge that they were "Zanádikah," a term properly applied to those who study the Zend scripture, but popularly meaning Mundanists, Positivists, Reprobates, Agnostics (Know-nothings), Atheists; and it may be noted that immediately after Al-Rashid's death violent religious troubles broke out in Baghdad. Ibn Khallikan[3] quotes Sa'id ibn Sálim, a well-known grammarian and traditionist, who philosophically remarked, "Of a truth the Barmecides did nothing to deserve Al-Rashid's severity, but the day (of their power and prosperity) had been long and whatso endureth long waxeth longsome." Fakhr al-Din says (p. 27), "On attribue encore leur ruine aux manières fières et orgueilleuses de Djafar (Ja'afar) et de Fadhl (Al-Fazl), manières que les rois ne sauroient supporter." According to Ibn Badrún, the poet, when the Caliph's sister 'Olayyah[4] asked him, "O my lord, I have not seen thee enjoy one happy day since putting Ja'afar to death: wherefore didst thou slay him?" he answered, "My dear life, an I thought that my shirt knew the reason I would tare it in tatters!" I therefore hold with Al-Mas'udi, "As regards the intimate cause (of the catastrophe) it is unknown and Allah is Omniscient."

Aaron the Orthodox appears sincerely to have repented his enormous crime. From that date he never enjoyed refreshing

1 Al-Mas'udi, chapt. cxii. For the liberties Ja'afar took, see Ibn Khallikan, i. 303.

2 Ibid. chapt. xxiv. In vol. i. night xxxvii. of The Nights, I find signs of Ja'afar's suspected heresy. For Al-Rashid's hatred of the Zindiks, see Al-Siyuti, pp. 292, 301; and as regards the religious troubles, Ibid. p. 362 and *passim*.

3 Biogr. Dict., i. 309

4 This accomplished princess had a practice that suggests the Dame aux Camélias.

sleep: he would have given his whole realm to recall Ja'afar to life; and, if any spoke slightingly of the Barmecides in his presence, he would exclaim, "Allah damn your fathers! Cease to blame them or fill the void they have left." And he had ample reason to mourn the loss. After the extermination of the wise and enlightened family, the affairs of the Caliphate never prospered: Fazl bin Rabí'a, though a man of intelligence and devoted to letters, proved a poor substitute for Yahya and Ja'afar; and the Caliph is reported to have applied to him the couplet:—

No sire to your sire,[1] I bid you spare * Your calumnies or their place replace.

His unwise elevation of his two rival sons filled him with fear of poison, and, lastly, the violence and recklessness of the popular mourning for the Barmecides,[2] whose echo has not yet died away, must have added poignancy to his tardy penitence. The crime still "sticks fiery off" from the rest of Harun's career: it stands out in ghastly prominence as one of the most terrible tragedies recorded by history, and its horrible details make men write passionately on the subject to this our day.[3]

As of Harun so of Zubaydah, it may be said that she was far superior in most things to contemporary royalties, and she was not worse at her worst than the normal despot-queen of the Morning-land. We must not take seriously the tales of her jealousy in The Nights, which mostly end in her selling off or burying alive her rivals; but, even were all true, she acted after the recognised fashion of her exalted sisterhood. The secret history of Cairo during the last generation, tells of many a viceregal dame who committed all the crimes, without any of the virtues which characterised Harun's cousin-spouse. And

---

1 *i.e.* Perdition to your fathers, Allah's curse on your ancestors

2 See vol. iii. night ccxcix., "Ja'afar and the Bean-seller"; where the great Wazir is said to have been "crucified"; and vol. iii. night cccv. Also Roebuck's Persian Proverbs, i. 2, 346, "This also is through the munificence of the Barmecides."

3 I especially allude to my friend Mr. Payne's admirably written account of it in his concluding Essay (vol. ix.). From his iews of the Great Caliph and the Lady Zubaydah I must differ in every point except the destruction of the Barmecides.

the difference between the manners of the Caliphate and the "respectability" of the nineteenth century may be measured by the Tale called "Al-Maamun and Zubaydah.[1]" The lady, having won a game of forfeits from her husband and being vexed with him for imposing unseemly conditions when he had been the winner, condemned him to lie with the foulest and filthiest kitchen-wench in the palace; and thus was begotten the Caliph who succeeded and destroyed her son.

Zubaydah was the grand-daughter of the second Abbaside Al-Mansur, by his son Ja'afar, whom The Nights persistently term Al-Kasim; her name was Amat al-Aziz or Handmaid of the Almighty; her cognomen was Umm Ja'afar as her husband's was Abú Ja'afar; and her popular name "Creamkin" derives from Zubdah,[2] cream or fresh butter, on account of her plumpness and freshness. She was as majestic and munificent as her husband; and the hum of prayer was never hushed in her palace. Al-Mas'udi[3] makes a historian say to the dangerous Caliph Al-Káhir, "The nobleness and generosity of this Princess, in serious matters as in her diversions, place her in the highest rank"; and he proceeds to give ample proof. Al-Siyuti relates how she once filled a poet's mouth with jewels, which he sold for twenty thousand dinars. Ibn Khallikan (i. 523) affirms of her, "Her charity was ample, her conduct virtuous, and the history of her pilgrimage to Meccah and of what she undertook to execute on the way is so well-known that it were useless to repeat it." I have noted (Pilgrimage, iii. 2) how the Darb al-Sharki or Eastern road from Meccah to Al-Madinah was due to the piety of Zubaydah who dug wells from Baghdad to the Prophet's burial place and built not only cisterns and caravanserais, but even a wall to direct pilgrims over the shifting sands. She also supplied Meccah, which suffered severely from want of water, with the chief requisite for public hygiene by connecting it, through

1 Bresl Edit., vol. vii. 261-62.

2 Mr. Grattan Geary, in a work previously noticed, informs us (i. 212), "The Sitt al-Zobeide, or the Lady Zobeide, was so named from the great Zobeide tribe of Arabs occupying the country East and West of the Euphrates near the Hindi'ah Canal; she was the daughter of a powerful Sheik of that tribe." Can this explain the "Kásim"?

3 Vol. viii. 296.

levelled hills and hewn rocks, with the Ayn al-Mushásh in the Arafat sub-range; and the fine aqueduct, some ten miles long, was erected at a cost of 1,700,000 to 2,000,000 of gold pieces.[1] We cannot wonder that her name is still famous among the Badawin and the "Sons of the Holy Cities." She died at Baghdad, after a protracted widowhood, in A.H. 216, and her tomb, which still exists, was long visited by the friends and dependants who mourned the loss of a devout and most liberal woman.

The reader will bear with me while I run through the tales and add a few remarks to the notices given in the notes: the glance must necessarily be brief, however extensive be the theme. The admirable introduction follows, in all the texts and MSS. known to me, the same main lines, but differs greatly in minor details as will be seen by comparing Mr. Payne's translation with Lane's and mine. In the Tale of the Sage Dúbán appears the speaking head which is found in the Kámil, in Mirkhond and in the Kitáb al-Uyún: M. C. Barbier de Meynard (v. 503) traces it back to an abbreviated text of Al-Mas'udi. I would especially recommend to students The Porter and the Three Ladies of Baghdad (vol i.), whose mighty orgie ends so innocently in general marriage. Lane (iii. 746) blames it "because it represents Arab *ladies* as acting like Arab *courtesans*"; but he must have known that during his day the indecent frolic was quite possible in some of the highest circles of his beloved Cairo. To judge by the style and changes of person, some of the most "archaic" expressions suggest the hand of the Ráwi or professional tale-teller; yet as they are in all the texts they cannot be omitted in a loyal translation. The following story of the Three Apples perfectly justifies my notes concerning which certain carpers complain. What Englishman would be jealous enough to kill his cousin-wife because a blackamoor in the streets boasted of her favours? But after reading what is annotated in vol. i. and purposely placed there to give the key-note of the book, he will understand the reasonable nature of the suspicion; and I may add that the same cause has commended these "skunks of the human race" to debauched women in England.

1 Burckhardt, "Travels in Arabia," vol. i. 185.

The next tale, sometimes called "The Two Wazirs,' is notable for its regular and genuine drama-intrigue which, however, appears still more elaborate and perfected in other pieces. The richness of this Oriental plot-invention constrasts strongly with all European literatures except the Spaniard's, whose taste for the theatre determined his direction, and the Italian's, which in Boccaccio's day had borrowed freely through Sicily from the East. And the remarkable deficiency lasted till the romantic movement dawned in France, when Victor Hugo and Alexander Dumas showed their marvellous powers of faultless fancy, boundless imagination, and scenic luxuriance, "raising French poetry from the dead and *not* mortally wounding French prose.[1]" The Two Wazirs is followed by the gem of the volume, The Adventure of the Hunchback-jester (vol. i.), also containing an admirable surprise and a fine development of character, while its "wild but natural simplicity" and its humour are so abounding that it has echoed through the world to the farthest West. It gave to Addison the Story of Alnaschar[2] and to Europe the term "Barmecide Feast," from the "Tale of Shacabac" (vol. i.). The adventures of the corpse were known to the Occident long before Galland, as shown by three fabliaux in Barbazan. I have noticed that the Barber's Tale of Himself (vol. i.) is historical, and I may add that it is told in detail by Al-Mas'udi (chapt. cxiv.).

Follows the tale of Núr al-Dín Alí, and what Galland miscalls "The Fair Persian" (vol. i.), a brightly written historiette with not a few touches of true humour. Noteworthy are the Slaver's address, the fine description of the Baghdad

1 The reverse has been remarked by more than one writer; and contemporary French opinion seems to be that Victor Hugo's influence on French prose was, on the whole, not beneficial.

2 Mr. W. A. Clouston informs me the first to adapt this witty anecdote was jacques de Vitry, the crusading bishop of Accon (Acre) who died at Rome in 1240, after setting the example of "Exempla" or instances in his sermons. He had probably heard it in Syria, and he changed the day-dreamer into a Milk-maid and her Milk-pail to suit his "flock." It then appears as an "Exemplum" in the Liber de Donis or de Septem Donis (or De Dono Timoris from Fear the first gift) of Stephanus de Borbone, the Dominican, ob. Lyons, 1261: the book treated of the gifts of the Holy Spirit (Isaiah xi. 2, 3). Timor, Pietas, Scientia, Fortitudo, Consilium, Intellectus et Sapientia; and was plentifully garnished with narratives for the use of preachers.

garden, the drinking-party, the Caliph's frolic, and the happy end of the hero's misfortunes. Its brightness is tempered by the gloomy tone of the tale which succeeds, and which has variants in the Bágh o Bahár, a Hindustani version of the Persian "Tale of the Four Darwayshes", and in the Turkish Kirk Vezir, or "Book of the Forty Vezirs." Its dismal péripéties are relieved only by the witty indecency of Eunuch Bukhayt and the admirable humour of Eunuch Káfur, whose "half-lie" is known throughout the East. Here also the lover's agonies are piled upon him for the purpose of unpiling at last: the Oriental tale-teller knows by experience that, as a rule, doleful endings "don't pay."

The next is the long romance of chivalry, "King Omar bin al-Nu'uman" etc., which occupies an eighth of the whole repertory and the best part of two volumes. Mr. Lane omits it because "obscene and tedious," showing the license with which he translated; and he was set right by a learned reviewer,[1] who truly declared that "the omission of half-a-dozen passages out of four hundred pages would fit it for printing in any language and the charge of tediousness could hardly have been applied more unhappily." The tale is interesting as a picture of mediæval Arab chivalry and has many other notable points; for instance, the lines (night cxlii.), beginning "Allah holds the kingship!" are a lesson to the Manichæanism of Christian Europe. It relates the doings of three royal generations, and has all the characteristics of Eastern art: it is a phantasmagoria of Holy Places, palaces and Harems; convents, castles and caverns, here restful with gentle landscapes and there bristling with furious battle-pictures and tales of princely prowess and knightly derring-do. The characters stand out well. King Nu'uman is an old lecher who deserves his death; the ancient dame Zát al-Dawáhí merits her title Lady of Calamities (to her foes); Princess Abrízah appears as a charming Amazon, doomed to a miserable and pathetic end; Zau al-Makán is a wise and pious royalty; Nuzhat al-Zamán, though a longsome talker, is a model sister; the Wazir Dandán,

---

1 The Asiatic Journal and Monthly Register (new series, vol. xxx. Sept.-Dec. 1830; London, Allens, 1839); p. 69, Review of the Arabian Nights, the Mac. Edit. vol. i., and H. Torrens.

a sage and sagacious counsellor, contrasts with the Chamberlain, an ambitious miscreant; Kánmakán is the typical Arab knight, gentle and brave:—

> Now managing the mouthes of stubborne steedes
> Now practising the proof of warlike deedes;

And the kind-hearted, simple-minded Stoker serves as a foil to the villains, the kidnapping Badawi, and Ghazbán the detestable negre. The fortunes of the family are interrupted by two episodes, both equally remarkable. Táj al-Mulúk is the model lover whom no difficulties or dangers can daunt. In Aziz and Azizah (vol. ii.) we have the beau idéal of a loving maiden: the writer's object was to represent a "softy" who had the luck to win the love of a beautiful and clever cousin and the mad folly to break her heart. The poetical justice which he receives at the hands of women of quite another stamp leaves nothing to be desired. Finally, the plot of "King Omar" is well worked out; and the gathering of all the actors upon the stage before the curtain drops may be improbable but it is highly artistic.

The long Crusading Romance is relieved by a sequence of sixteen fabliaux, partly historiettes of men and beasts, and partly apologues proper—a subject already noticed. We have then (night cliii.) the saddening and dreary love-tale of Ali bin Bakkár, a Persian youth, and the Caliph's concubine Shams al-Nahár. Here the end is made doleful enough by the deaths of the "two martyrs," who are killed off, like Romeo and Juliet,[1] a lesson that the course of true Love is sometimes troubled, and that men as well as women *can* die of the so-called "tender passion." It is followed (night clxx.) by the long tale of Kamar al-Zamán, or Moon of the Age, the first of that name, the "Camaralzaman" whom Galland introduced into the best European society. Like "The Ebony Horse," it seems to have been derived from a common source with "Peter of Provençe" and "Cleomades and Claremond"; and we can hardly wonder at its wide diffusion: the tale is brimful of life, change, movement;

---

1 I have lately found these lovers at Schloss Sternstein near Cilli in Styria, the property of my excellent colleague, Mr. Consul Faber, of Fiume, dating from A.D. 1300 when Jobst of Reichenegg and Agnes of Sternstein were aided and abetted by a Capuchin of Seitzkloster.

containing as much character and incident as would fill a modern three-volumer and the Supernatural pleasantly jostles the Natural; Dahnash the Jinn and Maymúnah, daughter of Al-Dimiryát, a renowned King of the Jann, being as human in their jealousy about the virtue of their lovers as any children of Adam, and so their metamorphosis to fleas has all the effect of a surprise. The *troupe* is again drawn with a broad firm touch. Prince Charming, the hero, is weak and wilful, shifty and immoral, hasty and violent: his two spouses are rivals in abominations as his sons, Amjad and As'ad, are examples of a fraternal affection rarely found in half-brothers by sister-wives. There is at least one fine melodramatic situation (night clxxix.); and marvellous feats of indecency, a practical joke which would occur only to the canopic mind, emphasise the recovery of her husband by that remarkable "blackguard," the Lady Budúr. The interpolated tale of Ni'amah and Naomi (night ccxxxvii.), a simple and pleasing narrative of youthful amours, contrasts well with the boiling passions of the incestuous and murderous Queens, and serves as a pause before the grand *dénoûment* when the departed meet, the lost are found, the unwedded are wedded, and all ends merrily as a xix^th^ century society novel.

The long tale of Alá al-Dín, our old friend "Aladdin," is wholly out of place in its present position (night ccxlix.): it is a counterpart of Ali Núr al-Dín and Miriam the Girdle-Girl (night dccclxiii.); and the mention of the Shahbandar or Harbour-master, the Kunsúl or Consul, the Kaptán (Capitano), the use of cannon at sea, and the choice of Genoa-city prove that it belongs to the xv^th^ or xvi^th^ century and should accompany Kamar al-Zamán II. and Ma'aruf at the end of The Nights. Despite the lutist Zubaydah being carried off by the Jinn, the Magic Couch, a modification of Solomon's carpet, and the murder of the King who refused to Islamize, it is evidently a European tale, and I believe with Dr. Bacher that it is founded upon the legend of "Charlemagne's" daughter Emma and his secretary Eginhardt, as has been noted in the counterpart (Ali Núr al-Dín).

This quasi-historical fiction is followed by a succession of fabliaux, novelle and historiettes till we reach the terminal story, The Queen of the Serpents (night ccccIxxxii.) It appears to me that most of them are historical and could easily be traced. Not a few are in Al-Mas'udi; for instance, the grim Tale of Hatim of Tayy (night cclxix.) is given bodily in "Meads of Gold" (iii. 327); and the two adventures of Ibrahim al-Mahdi with the barber-surgeon (night cclxxiii.) and the Merchant's sister (night cccxlvi.) are also in his pages (vol. vii. pp. 68 and 18). The City of Labtayt (night cclxxii.) embodies the legend of Don Rodrigo, last of the Goths, and may have reached the ears of Washington Irving: Many-Columned Iram (night cclxxvi.) is held by all Moslems to be factual, and sundry writers have recorded the tricks played by Al-Maamun with the Pyramids of Jízah, which still show his handiwork.[1] The germ of Isaac of Mosul (night cclxxx.) is found in Al-Mas'udi who (vii. 65) names "Burán" the poetess (Ibn Khall. i. 268); and The Tale of Harun al-Rashid and the Slave-girl (night ccxcvi.) is told by a host of writers. Ali the Persian is a rollicking bit of fun from some Iranian jest-book: Abu Mohammed hight Lazybones belongs to the cycle of "Sindbad the Seaman," with a touch of Whittington and his Cat; and Zumurrud ("Smaragdine") in Ali Shar (night cccviii.) shows at her sale the impudence of Miriam the Girdle-girl, and in bed the fescennine device of the Lady Budur. The "Ruined Man who became Rich," etc. (night cccli.) is historical, and Al-Mas'udi (vol. vii. 281) relates the coquetry of Mahbúbah the concubine (night ccclii.): the historian also quotes four couplets, two identical with Nos. 1 and 2 in the Nights (night ccclii.), and adding :—

Then see the slave who lords it o'er her lord * In lover privacy and public site:
Behold these eyes that one like Ja'afar saw: * Allah on Ja'afar reign boons infinite!

---

1 Omitted by Lane for some reason unaccountable as usual. A correspondent sends me his version of the lines which occur in The Nights (vol. iv. night cccxcviii) :—

Behold the Pyramids and hear them teach
What they can tell of Future and of Past:
They would declare, had they the gift of speech,
The deeds that Time hath wrought from first to last.

* * * *

My friends, and is there aught beneath the sky
Can with th' Egyptian Pyramids compare?
In fear of them strong Time hath passèd by;
And everything dreads Time in earth and air.

Uns al-Wújúd (vol. iv., p. 1) is a love-tale which has been translated into a host of Eastern languages; and The Lovers of the Banu Ozrah belong to Al-Mas'udí's "Martyrs of Love" (vii. 355), with the "Ozrite love" of Ibn Khallikan (iv. 537). "Harun and the Three Poets" (night ccclxxxvi.) has given to Cairo a proverb which Burckhardt renders "The day obliterates the word or promise of the Night," for

The promise of night is effaced by day.

It suggests Congreve's Doris:—

For who o'er night obtain'd her grace,
She can next day disown, etc.

"Harun and the three Slave-girls" (night ccclxxxvii.) smacks of Gargantua (lib. i. c. 11): "It belongs to me, said one: 'Tis mine, said another"; and so forth. The Simpleton and the Sharper (night ccclxxxviii.) like the Foolish Dominie (night cccciii.) is an old Joe Miller in Hindu as well as Moslem folk-lore. "Kisra Anushirwán" (night ccclxxxix.) is "The King, the Owl and the Villages" of Al-Mas'údi (iii. 171), who also notices the Persian monarch's four seals of office (ii. 204); and "Masrur the Eunuch and Ibn Al-Káribi" (night cccc.) is from the same source as Ibn al-Magházili the Reciter, and a Eunuch belonging to the Caliph Al-Mu'tazad (viii. 161). In the Tale of Tawaddud (night ccccxxxvi.) we have the fullest development of the disputation and displays of learning then so common in Europe, teste the "Admirable Crichton"; and these were affected not only by Eastern tale-tellers but even by sober historians. To us it is much like "padding" when Nuzhat al-Zamán (night lx.) fags her hapless hearers with a discourse covering sixteen mortal pages; when the Wazir Dandan (night lxxix.) reports at length the cold speeches of the five high-bosomed maids and the Lady of Calamities; and when Wird Khan, in presence of his papa (nights cmxiv-xvi.) discharges his patristic exercitations and heterogeneous knowledge. Yet Al-Mas'udi also relates, at dreary extension (vol. vi. 369) the disputation of the twelve sages in presence of Barmecide Yahya upon the origin, the essence, the accidents and the omnes res of Love; and in another place (vii. 181) shows Honayn, author of the Book of Natural Questions, undergoing a long examination before the Caliph

Al-Wásik (Vathek) and describing, amongst other things, the human teeth. See also the dialogue or catechism of Al-Hajjáj and Ibn Al-Kirríya in Ibn Khallikan (vol. i. 238-240).

These disjecta membra of tales and annals are pleasantly relieved by the seven voyages of Sindbad the Seaman (vol. iv.). The "Arabian Odyssey" may, like its Greek brother, descend from a noble family, the "Shipwrecked Mariner," a Coptic travel-tale of the twelfth dynasty (B.C. 3500) preserved on a papyrus at St. Petersburg. In its actual condition "Sindbad" is a fanciful compilation, like De Foe's "Captain Singleton," borrowed from travellers' tales of an immense variety, and extracts from Al-Idrisi, Al-Kazwíni and Ibn al-Wardi. Here we find the Polyphemus, the Pygmies, and the cranes of Homer and Herodotus; the escape of Aristomenes; the Plinian monsters well known in Persia; the magnetic mountain of Saint Brennan (Brandanus); the aeronautics of "Duke Ernest of Bavaria[1]" and sundry cuttings from Moslem writers dating between our ninth and fourteenth centuries.[2] The "Shaykh of the Seaboard," the true reading of the "Old Man of the Sea," appears in the Persian romance of Kámarupa translated by Francklin, all the particulars absolutely corresponding. The "Odyssey" is valuable because it shows how far Eastward the mediæval Arab had extended: already in The Ignorance he had reached China, and had formed a centre of trade at Canton. But the higher merit of the cento is to produce one of the most charming books of travel ever written, like Robinson Crusoe the delight of children and the admiration of all ages.

The hearty life and realism of Sindbad are made to stand out in strong relief by the deep melancholy which pervades "The City of Brass" (vol. v. p. 1) a dreadful book for a dreary day. It is curious to compare the doleful verses (nights dlxxii. and dlxxiii.)

1 A rhyming Romance by Henry of Waldeck (flor. A.D. 1160) with a Latin poem on the same subject by Odo and a prose version still popular in Germany. (Lane's Nights, iii. 81, and Weber's "Northern Romances.")

2 *e.g.* 'Ajáib al-Hind (=Marvels of Ind) ninth century, translated by J. Marcel Devic, Paris, 1878; and about the same date the Two Mohammedan Travellers, translated by Renaudot. In the eleventh century we have the famous Sayyid al-Idrisi; in the thirteenth the 'Ajáib al-Makhlúkát of Al-Kazwini (see De Sacy, vol. iii.); and in the fourteenth the Kharídat al-Ajáib of Ibn al-Wardi. Lane *(in loco)* traces most of Sindbad to the two latter sources.

with those spoken to Caliph Al-Mutawakkil by Abu al-Hasan Ali (Al-Mas'udi, vii. 246). We then enter upon the venerable Sindibad-nameh, the Malice of Women (vol. v.), of which, according to the Kitab al-Fihrist (vol. i. 305) there were two editions, a Sinzibád al-Kabir and a lesser Sinzibád al-Saghír, the latter being probably an epitome of the former. This bundle of legends, I have shown, was incorporated with The Nights as an editor's addition; and as an independent work it has made the round of the world. Space forbids any detailed notice of this choice collection of anecdotes for which a volume would be required. I may, however, note that the "Wife's Device" (night dlxxxiv.) has its analogues in the Kathá (chapt. xiii.) in the Gesta Romanorum (No. xxviii.) and in Boccaccio (Day iii. 6, and Day vi. 8), modified by La Fontaine to Richard Minutolo (Contes, lib. i. tale 2): it is quoted almost in the words of The Nights by the Shaykh al-Nafzáwi (p. 207). That most witty and indecent tale, The Three Wishes (night dxcvi.), has forced its way disguised as a babe into our nurseries. Another form of it is found in the Arab proverb, "More luckless than Basús" (Kamus), a fair Israelite who persuaded her husband, also a Jew, to wish that she might become the loveliest of women. Allah granted it, spitefully as Jupiter; the consequence was that her contumacious treatment of her mate made him pray that the beauty might be turned into a bitch; and the third wish restored her to her original state.

The Story of Júdar (night dcvii.) is Egyptian, to judge from its local knowledge (nights dcviii. and dcxxiii.) together with its ignorance of Marocco (night dcxi.). It shows a contrast, in which Arabs delight, of an almost angelical goodness and forgiveness with a well-nigh diabolical malignity, and we find the same extremes in Abú Sír the noble-minded Barber and the hideously inhuman Abú Kír (night cmxxx.). The excursion to Mauritania is artfully managed and gives a novelty to the *mise-en-scène*. Gharíb and Ajíb (night dcxxiv.) belongs to the cycle of Antar and King Omar bin al-Nu'uman: its exaggerations make it a fine type of Oriental Chauvinism, pitting the superhuman virtues, valour, nobility, and success of all that is Moslem, against the scum of the earth which is non-Moslem. Like the exploits of Friar John of the Chopping-knives (Rabelais, i. c. 27) it suggests ridicule cast on impossible battles and tales of giants, paynims and paladins. The long romance is followed by thirteen historiettes all apparently historical: compare "Hind, daughter of Al-Nu'uman" (night dclxxxi.) and "Isaac of Mosul and the Devil" (night dxcv.) with Al-Mas'udi, v. 365 and vi. 340. They end in two long detective-tales like those which M. Gaboriau has popularised, the Rogueries of Dalilah and the Adventures of Mercury Ali, being based upon the principle, "One thief wots another." The former, who has appeared before (night cxxiii.) seems to have been a noted character. Al-Mas'udi says (viii. 175), "In a word this Shaykh (Al-'Ukáb) outrivalled in his rogueries and the ingenuities of his wiles *Dállah* (Dalilah?) the *Crafty* and other tricksters and coney-catchers, ancient and modern."

The Tale of Ardashir (night dccxix.) lacks originality. We are now entering upon a series of pictures which are replicas of those preceding. This is not the case with that charming Undine, Julnár the Sea-born (night dccxxxviii.), which, like Abdullah of the Land and Abdullah of the Sea (vol. vii. night cmxl.), describes the vie intime of mermen and merwomen. Somewhat resembling Swift's inimitable creations, the Houyhnhnms, for instance, they prove, amongst other things, that those who dwell in a denser element can justly blame and severely criticise the contradictory and unreasonable prejudices and predilections of mankind. Sayf al-Mulúk (night dcclviii.), the romantic tale of two lovers, shows by its introduction that it was originally an independent work, and it is known to have existed in Persia during the eleventh century: this novella has found its way into every Moslem language of the East, even into Sindi, which calls the hero "Sayfal." Here we again meet the "Old Man of the Sea," or rather the Shaykh of the Seaboard and make acquaintance with a Jinni whose soul is outside his body: thus he resembles Hermotimos of Klazamunæ in Apollonius, whose spirit left his mortal frame à discrétion. The author, philanthropically remarking (night dcclxxviii.), "Knowest thou not that a single mortal is better in Allah's sight than a thousand Jinn?" brings the wooing to a happy end, which leaves a pleasant savour upon the mental palate.

Hasan of Bassorah (vol. vi. night dcclxxviii.) is a Master Shoetie on a large scale like Sindbad, but his voyages and travels extend into the supernatural and fantastic rather than the natural world. Though long, the tale is by no means wearisome, and the characters are drawn with a fine, firm hand. The hero with his hen-like persistency of purpose, his weeping, fainting, and versifying, is interesting enough, and proves that "Love can find out the way." The charming adopted sister, the model of what the feminine friend should be; the silly little wife who never knows that she is happy till she loses happiness; the violent and hard-hearted queen with all the cruelty of a good woman; and the manners and customs of Amazon-land are outlined with a life-like vivacity. Khalifah, the next tale (vol. vi.) is valuable as a study of Eastern life, showing how the fisherman emerges from the squalor of his surroundings and becomes one of the Caliph's favourite cup-companions. Ali Nur al-Din (vol. vii. p. 1) and King Jali'ad (vol. vii. night dcccxcix.) have been noticed elsewhere, and there is little to say of the concluding stories, which bear the evident impress of a more modern date.

Dr. Johnson thus sums up his notice of The Tempest. "Whatever might have been the intention of their author, these tales are made instrumental to the production of many characters diversified with boundless invention, and preserved with profound skill in nature, extensive knowledge of opinions, and accurate observation of life. Here are exhibited princes, courtiers, and sailors, all speaking in their real characters. There is the agency of airy spirits and of earthy goblins, the operations of magic, the tumults of a storm, the adventures on a desert island, the native effusion of untaught affection, the punishment of guilt, and the final happiness of those for whom our passions and reason are equally interested."

We can fairly say this much and far more for our Tales. Viewed as a tout ensemble in full and complete form, they are a drama of Eastern life, and a Dance of Death made sublime by faith and the highest emotions, by the certainty of expiation and the fulness of atoning equity, where virtue is victorious, vice is vanquished, and the ways of Allah are justified to man. They are a panorama which remains ken-speckle upon the mental retina. They form a phantasmagoria in which archangels and angels, devils and goblins, men of air, of fire, of water, naturally mingle with men of earth; where flying horses and talking fishes are utterly realistic: where King and Prince meet fisherman and pauper, lamia and cannibal; where citizen jostles Badawi, eunuch meets knight; the Kazi hob-nobs with the thief; the pure and pious sit down to the same tray with the pander and the procuress; where the professional religionist, the learned Koranist, and the strictest moralist consort with the wicked magician, the scoffer, and the debauchee-poet like Abu Nowas; where the courtier jests with the boor, and where the sweep is bedded with the noble lady. And the characters are "finished and quickened by a few touches swift and sure as the glance of sunbeams." The work is a kaleidoscope where everything falls into picture; gorgeous palaces and pavilions; grisly underground caves and deadly wolds; gardens fairer than those of the Hesperid; seas dashing with clashing billows upon enchanted mountains; valleys of the Shadow of Death; air-voyages and promenades in the abysses of ocean; the duello, the battle and the siege; the wooing of maidens and the marriage-rite. All the splendour and squalor, the beauty and baseness, the glamour and grotesqueness, the magic and the mournfulness, the bravery and the baseness of Oriental life are here: its pictures of the three great Arab passions, love, war and fancy, entitle it to be called "Blood, Musk and Hashish.[1]" And still more, the genius of the story-teller quickens the dry bones of history, and by adding Fiction to Fact revives the dead past: the Caliphs and the Caliphate return to Baghdad and Cairo, whilst Asmodeus kindly removes the terrace-roof of every tenement and allows our curious glances to take in the whole interior. This is, perhaps, the best proof of their power. Finally, the picture-gallery opens with a series of weird and striking adventures and shows as a tail-piece, an idyllic scene of love and wedlock in halls before reeking with lust and blood.

I have noticed in my Foreword that the two main characteristics of The Nights are Pathos and Humour, alternating with highly artistic contrast, and carefully calculated to pro-

1 So Hector France proposed to name his admirably realistic volume "Sous le Burnous" (Paris, Charpentier, 1886).

voke tears and smiles in the coffee-house audience which paid for them. The sentimental portion mostly breathes a tender passion and a simple sadness: such are the Badawi's dying farewell (vol. i. night viii.); the lady's broken heart on account of her lover's hand being cut off (vol. i. night xxvi.); the Wazir's death, the mourner's song and the "tongue of the case" (vol. i. night xxxv.); the murder of Princess Abrízah with the babe sucking its dead mother's breast (vol. ii. night lii.); and, generally, the last moments of good Moslems (*e.g.* night ccccxxv.), which are described with inimitable terseness and naïveté. The sad and the gay mingle in the character of the good Hammam-stoker who becomes Roi Crotte; and the melancholy deepens in the Tale of the Mad Lover (night ccccxi.); the Blacksmith who could handle fire without hurt (night cccclxxi.); the Devotee Prince (night cccci.) and the whole Tale of Azízah (vol. ii.), whose angelic love is set off by the sensuality and selfishness of her more fortunate rivals. A new note of absolutely tragic dignity seems to be struck in the Sweep and the Noble Lady (night cclxxxii.), showing the piquancy of sentiment which can be evolved from the common and the unclean. The pretty conceit of the Lute (night cccclxi.) is afterwards carried out in the Song (night dccclxvii.), which is a masterpiece of originality[1] and (in the Arabic) of exquisite tenderness and poetic melancholy, the wail over the past, and the vain longing for reunion. And the very depths of melancholy, of majestic pathos, and of true sublimity are reached in Many-Columned Iram (night cclxxvi.) and the City of Brass (vol. v. p. 1): the metrical part of the latter shows a luxury of woe; it is one long wail of despair which echoes long and loud in the hearer's heart.

In my Foreword I have compared the humorous vein of the comic tales with our northern "wut," chiefly for the dryness and slyness which pervade it. But it differs in degree as much as the pathos varies. The staple article is Cairene "chaff," a peculiar banter possibly inherited from their pagan forefathers: instances of this are found in the Cock and Dog (vol. i. Intro.), the Eunuch's

1 I mean in European literature, not in Arabic where it is a lieu commun. See three several forms of it in one page (505) of Ibn Kallikan, vol. iii.

address to the Cook (vol. i. night xxiv.), the Wazir's exclamation, "Too little pepper!" (vol. i., night xxiv.), the self-communing of Judar (night dcix.), the Hashish-eater in Ali Shár (night cccxx.), the scene between the brother-Wazirs (vol. i. night xx.), the treatment of the Gobbo (vol. i. nights xxii and xxiii.), the Water of Zemzem (vol. i. night xxvii.), and the Eunuchs Bukhayt and Kafur[1] (vol. i. night xxxix.). At times it becomes a masterpiece of fun, of rollicking Rabelaisian humour underlaid by the caustic mother-wit of Sancho Panza, as in the orgie of the Ladies of Baghdad (vol. i. night ix.); the Holy Ointment applied to the beard of Luka the Knight—"unxerunt regem Salomonem" (vol. ii. night lxxxix); and Ja'afar and the Old Badawi (night cccxcv.), with its reminiscence of "chaffy" King Amasis. This reaches its acme in the description of ugly old age (night ccclvii.); in The Three Wishes, the wickedest of satires on the alter sexus (night dxcvi.); in Ali the Persian (night ccxcv.); in the Lady and her Five Suitors (night dxciii.), which corresponds and contrasts with the dully told Story of Upakosa and her Four Lovers of the Kathá (p. 17); and in The Man of Al-Yaman (night cccxxxiv.) where we find the true Falstaffian touch. But there is sterling wit, sweet and bright, expressed without any artifice of words, in the immortal Barber's tales of his brothers, especially the second, the fifth, and the sixth (vol. i. nights xxxi.-xxxiii.). Finally, wherever the honest and independent old debauchee Abu Nowas makes his appearance, the fun becomes fescennine and Milesian.

B.—The Manner of The Nights.

And now, after considering the matter, I will glance at the language and style of The Nights. The first point to remark is the peculiarly happy framework of the Recueil, which I cannot but suspect set an example to the Decameron and its host of successors.[2] The admirable Introduction, which evidently gave rise

1 My attention has been called to the resemblance between the half-lie and Job (i 13-19), an author who seems to be growing more modern with every generation of commentators.

2 Boccaccio (ob Dec. 2, 1375), may easily have heard of The Thousand Nights and a Night or of its archetype the Hazár Afsánah. He was followed by the Piacevoli Notti of Giovan Francisco Straparola (A.D. 1550), translated

to the adventures of Astolfo and Giocondi (O. Furioso, canto viii.), a perfect mise-en-scène, gives the amplest raison d'être of the work, which thus has all the unity required for a great romantic cento. We perceive this when reading the contemporary Hindu work the Kathá Sarit Ságara,[1] which is at once so like and so unlike The Nights: here the preamble is insufficient; the whole is clumsy for want of a thread upon which the many

---

into almost all European languages but English: the original Italian is now rare. Then came the Heptameron ou Histoire des amans fortunez of Marguerite d'Angoulême, Reyne de Navarre and only sister of Francis I. She died in 1549 before the days were finished: in 1558 Pierre Boaistuan published the Histoire des amans fortunez and in 1559 Claude Guiget the "Heptameron." Next is the Hexameron of A. de Torquemada, Rouen, 1610; and, lastly, the Pentamerone or El Cunto de li Cunte of Giambattista Basile (Naples, 1637), known by the meagre abstract of J. E. Taylor and the caricatures of George Cruikshank (London, 1847-50). I propose to translate this Pentamerone direct from the Neapolitan, and have already finished half the work. [This translation has since been published.—L. C. S.]

1 Translated and well annotated by Prof. Tawney, who, however, affects asterisks and has considerably bowdlerised sundry of the tales, *e.g.* the Monkey who picked out the Wedge (vol. ii. 28). This tale, by-the-by, is found in the Khirad Afroz (i. 128) and in the Anwar-i-Suhayli (chapt. i) and gave rise to the Persian proverb, "What has a monkey to do with carpentering?" It is curious to compare the Hindu with the Arabic work, whose resemblances are as remarkable as their differences, while even more notable is their correspondence in impressionising the reader. The Thaumaturgy of both is the same: the Indian is profuse in demonology and witchcraft; in transformation and restoration; in monsters as wind-men, fire-men, and water-men; in air-going elephants and flying horses (i. 541-43); in the wishing cow, divine goats, and laughing fishes (i. 24); and in the speciosa miracula of magic weapons. He delights in fearful battles (i. 400) fought with the same weapons as the Moslem, and rewards his heroes with a "turband of honour" (i. 266) in lieu of a robe. There is a quaint family likeness arising from similar stages and states of society: the city is adorned for gladness; men carry money in a robe-corner and exclaim "Ha! good!" (for "Good, by Allah!"): lovers die with exemplary facility; the "soft-sided" ladies drink spirits (i. 61), and princesses get drunk (i. 476); whilst the Eunuch, the Hetaira, and the bawd (Kuttini) play the same preponderating parts as in The Nights. Our Brahman is strong in love-making: he complains of the pains of separation in this phenomenal universe; he revels in youth, "twin-brother to mirth," and beauty which has illuminating powers; he foully reviles old age, and he alternately praises and abuses the sex, concerning which more presently. He delights in truisms, the fashion of contemporary Europe (see Palmerin of England, chapt. vii.), such as, "It is the fashion of the heart to receive pleasure from those things which ought to give it," etc., etc. "What is there the wise cannot understand?" and so forth. He is liberal in trite reflections and frigid conceits (i. 19, 55, 97, 103, 107, in fact everywhere): and his puns run through whole lines; this in fine Sanskrit style is inevitable. Yet some of

independent tales and fables should be strung[1]; and the consequent disorder and confusion tell upon the reader, who cannot remember the sequence without taking notes.

As was said in my Foreword, "without the Nights no Arabian Nights!" and now, so far from holding the pauses "an intolerable interruption to the narrative," I attach additional importance to these pleasant and restful breaks introduced into long and intricate stories. Indeed beginning again I should adopt the plan of the Cal. Edit., opening and ending every division with a dialogue between the sisters. Upon this point, however,

---

his expressions are admirably terse and telling, *e.g.* Ascending the swing of Doubt: Bound together (lovers) by the leash of gazing: Two babes looking like Misery and Poverty; Old Age seized me by the chin: (A lake) first assay of the Creator's skill: (A vow) difficult as standing on a sword-edge: My vital spirits boiled with the fire of woe: Transparent as a good man's heart: There was a certain convent full of fools: Dazed with scripture-reading: The stones could not help laughing at him: The Moon kissed the laughing forehead of the East: She was like a wave of the Sea of Love's insolence (ii. 127), a wave of the Sea of Beauty tossed up by the breeze of Youth: The King played dice, he loved slave-girls, he told lies, he sat up o' nights, he waxed wroth without reason, he took wealth wrongously, he despised the good and honoured the bad (i. 562); with many choice bits of the same kind. Like the Arab, the Indian is profuse in personification; but the doctrine of pre-existence, of incarnation and emanation and an excessive spiritualism, ever aiming at the infinite, makes his imagery run mad. Thus we have Immoral Conduct embodied; the God of Death; Science; the Svarga-heaven; Evening; Untimeliness; and the Earth-bride, while the Ace and Deuce of dice are turned into a brace of Demons. There is also that grotesqueness which the French detect even in Shakespeare, *e.g.* She drank in his ambrosial form with thirsty eyes like partridges (i. 476) and it often results from the comparison of incompatibles, *e.g.* a row of birds likened to a garden of nymphs; and from forced allegories, the favourite figure of contemporary Europe. Again, the rhetorical Hindu style differs greatly from the sobriety, directness, and simplicity of the Arab, whose motto is Brevity combined with precision, except where the latter falls into "fine writing." And, finally, there is a something in the atmosphere of these Tales which is unfamiliar to the West, and which makes them, as more than one have remarked to me, very hard reading.

1 The Introduction (i. 1-5) leads to the Curse of Pushpadenta and Mályaván who live on Earth as Vararúchi and Gunádhya and this runs through lib. i. Lib. ii. begins with the Story of Udáyana, to whom we must be truly grateful as our only guide: he and his son Naraváhanadatta fill up the rest and end with lib. xviii. Thus the want of the clue or plot compels a division into books, which begin, for instance, with "We worship the elephantine proboscis of Ganesha" (lib x. 1), a reverend and awful object to a Hindu, but to Englishmen mainly suggesting the "Zoo." The "Bismillah" of The Nights is much more satisfactory.

opinions will differ and the critic will remind me that the concensus of the MSS. would be wanting. The Bres. Edit. in many places merely interjects the number of the night without interrupting the tale; and Galland ceases to use the division after the ccxxxvith Night and in some editions after the cxcviith.[1] A fragmentary MS., according to Scott, whose friend J. Anderson found it in Bengal, breaks away after night xxix.; and in the Wortley Montagu, the Sultan relents at an early opportunity, the stories, as in Galland, continuing only as an amusement. I have been careful to preserve the balanced sentences with which the tales open; the tautology and the prose-rhyme serving to attract attention, *e.g.*, "In days of yore and in times long gone before there was a King," etc.; in England where we strive not to waste words this becomes, "Once upon a time." The closings also are artfully calculated, by striking a minor chord after the rush and hurry of the incidents, to suggest repose: "And they led the most pleasurable of lives and the most delectable, till there came to them the Destroyer of delights and the Severer of societies and they became as though they had never been." Place this by the side of Boccaccio's favourite formulæ:—Egli conquistò poi la Scozia, e funne re coronato (ii. 3); Et onorevolmente visse infino àlla fine (ii. 4); Molte volte goderono del loro amore: Iddio faccia noi goder del nostro (iii. 6): E cosi nella sua grossezza si rimase e ancor vi si sta (vi. 8). We have further docked this tail into: "And they lived happily ever after."

I cannot take up the Nights, in their present condition, without feeling that the work has been written down from the Ráwi or Nakkál,[2] the conteur or professional story-teller, also called Kassás and Maddáh, corresponding with the Hindu Bhat

1 See pp. 5-6, Avertissement des Éditeurs, Le Cabinet des Fées, vol. xxxviii.: Geneva, 1788. Galland's Edit. of mdccxxvi. ends with night ccxxxiv. and the English translations with ccxxxvi. and cxcvii. See *retro*, p. 76.

2 There is a shade of difference in the words; the former is also used for Reciters of Traditions—a serious subject. But in the case of Hammád surnamed Al-Ráwiyah (the Rhapsode) attached to the Court of Al-Walid, it means simply a conteur. So the Greeks had Homeristæ = reciters of Homer, as opposed to the Homeridæ or School of Homer.

or Bard. To these men my learned friend Baron A. von Kremer would attribute the Mu'allakát vulgarly called the Suspended Poems, as being "indited from the relation of the Ráwi." Hence in our text the frequent interruption of the formula Kál' al-Ráwi = quotes the reciter; *dice Turpino*. Moreover, The Nights read in many places like a hand-book or guide for the professional, who would learn them by heart; here and there introducing his "gag" and "patter." To this "business" possibly we may attribute much of the ribaldry which starts up in unexpected places: it was meant simply to provoke a laugh. How old the custom is and how unchangeable is Eastern life is shown, a correspondent suggests, by the Book of Esther which might form part of the Alf Laylah. "On that night (we read in chap. vi. 1) could not the King sleep, and he commanded to bring the book of records of the chronicles; and they were read before the King." The Ráwi would declaim the recitative somewhat in conversational style; he would intone the Saj'a or prose-rhyme and he would chant to the twanging of the Rabáb, a one-stringed viol, the poetical parts. Dr. Scott[1] borrows from the historian of Aleppo a life-like picture of the Story-teller. "He recites walking to and fro in the middle of the coffee-room, stopping only now and then, when the expression requires some emphatical attitude. He is commonly heard with great attention; and not unfrequently in the midst of some interesting adventure, when the expectation of the audience is raised to the highest pitch, he breaks off abruptly and makes his escape, leaving both his hero or heroine and his audience in the utmost embarrassment. Those who happen to be near the door endeavour to detain him, insisting upon the story being finished before he departs; but he always makes his retreat good[2]; and the auditors suspending their curiosity are induced to return at the same time next day to hear the sequel. He has no sooner made his exit than the

1 Vol. i. Preface, p. v. He notes that Mr. Dallaway ("Constantinople, Ancient and Modern") describes the same scene at Stambul, where the Story-teller was used, like the modern "Organs of Government" in newspaper shape, for "reconciling the people to any recent measure of the Sultan and Vizier." There are women Ráwiyahs for the Harems, and some have become famous like the Mother of Hasan al-Basri (Ibn Khall. i. 370).

2 Hence the Persian proverb, "Báki-e-dastán fardá = the rest of the tale to-morrow, said to askers of silly questions.

company in separate parties fall to disputing about the characters of the drama or the event of an unfinished adventure. The controversy by degrees becomes serious and opposite opinions are maintained with no less warmth than if the fall of the city depended upon the decision."

At Tangier, where a murder in a "coffee-house" had closed these hovels, pending a sufficient payment to the Pasha; and where, during the hard winter of 1885-86, the poorer classes were compelled to puff their Kayf (Bhang, *cannabis indica*) and sip their black coffee in the muddy streets under a rainy sky, I found the Ráwi active on Sundays and Thursdays, the market-days. The favourite place was the "Soko de barra," or large bazar, outside the town, whose condition is that of Suez and Bayrut half a century ago. It is a foul slope; now slippery with viscous mud, then powdery with fetid dust, dotted with graves and decaying tombs, unclean booths, gargottes and tattered tents, and frequented by women, mere bundles of unclean rags, and by men wearing the haik or burnús, a Franciscan frock, tending their squatting camels and chaffering over cattle for Gibraltar beef-eaters. Here the market-people form ring about the reciter, a stalwart man affecting little raiment besides a broad waist-belt into which his lower chiffons are tucked, and noticeable only for his shock hair, wild eyes, broad grin, and generally disreputable aspect. He usually handles a short stick; and, when drummer and piper are absent, he carries a tiny tom-tom shaped like an hour-glass, upon which he taps the periods. This Scealuidhe, as the Irish call him, opens the drama with extempore prayer, proving that he and the audience are good Moslems: he speaks slowly and with emphasis, varying the diction with breaks of animation, abundant action, and the most comical grimace: he advances, retires, and wheels about, illustrating every point with pantomine; and his features, voice, and gestures are so expressive that even Europeans who cannot understand a word of Arabic divine the meaning of his tale. The audience stands breathless and motionless, surprising strangers[1] by the ingenuousness and

1 The scene is excellently described in "Morocco: Its People and Places," by Edmondo de Amicis (London: Cassell, 1882), a most refreshing volume after the enforced platitudes and commonplaces of English travellers.

freshness of feeling hidden under their hard and savage exterior. The performance usually ends with the embryo actor going round for alms and flourishing in air every silver bit, the usual honorarium being a few "f'lús," that marvellous money of Barbary, big coppers worth one-twelfth of a penny. All the tales I heard were purely local, but Fakhri Bey, a young Osmanli domiciled for some time in Fez and Mequinez, assured me that The Nights are still recited there.

Many travellers, including Dr. Russell, have complained that they failed to find a complete MS. copy of The Nights. Evidently they never heard of the popular superstition which declares that no one can read through them without dying—it is only fair that my patrons should know this. Yacoub Artin Pasha declares that the superstition dates from the fourteenth and fifteenth centuries, and he explains it in two ways. Firstly, it is a facetious exaggeration, meaning that no one has leisure or patience to wade through the long repertory. Secondly, the work is condemned as futile. When Egypt produced savants and legists like Ibn al-Hajar, Al-'Ayni, and Al-Kastallání, to mention no others, the taste of the country inclined to dry factual studies and positive science; nor, indeed, has this taste wholly died out: there are not a few who, like Khayri Pasha, contend that the mathematic is more useful even for legal studies than history and geography, and at Cairo the chief of the Educational Department has always been an engineer, *i.e.*, a mathematician. The Olema declared war against all "futilities," in which they included not only stories but also what is politely entitled Authentic History. From this to the fatal effect of such lecture is only a step. Society, however, cannot rest without light literature; so the novel-reading class was thrown back upon writings which had all the indelicacy and few of the merits of The Nights.

Turkey is the only Moslem country which has dared to produce a regular drama,[1] and to arouse the energies of such brilliant

---

1 It began, however, in Persia, where the celebrated Darwaysh Mukhlis, Chief Sufi of Isfahan in the xvii[th] century, translated into Persian tales certain Hindu plays of which a MS. entitled Alfaraga Badal-Schidda (Al-Faraj ba'd al-Shiddah = Joy after annoy) exists in the Bibliothèque Nationale, Paris. But to give an original air to his work, he entitled it "Hazár o yek Ruz" =

writers as Muníf Pasha, statesman and scholar; Ekrem Bey, literato and professor; Kemál Bey held by some to be the greatest writer in modern Osmanli-land and Abd al-Hakk Hamid Bey, first Secretary of the London Embassy. The theatre began in its ruder form by taking subjects bodily from The Nights; then it annexed its plays as we do—the Novel having ousted the Drama—from the French; and lastly it took courage to be original. Many years ago I saw Harun al-Rashid and the Three Kalandars, with deer-skins and all their properties de rigueur, in the court-yard of Government House, Damascus, declaiming to the extreme astonishment and delight of the audience. It requires only to glance at The Nights for seeing how much histrionic matter they contain.

In considering the style of The Nights we must bear in mind that the work has never been edited according to our ideas of the process. Consequently there is no just reason for translating the whole verbatim et literatim, as has been done by Torrens, Lane and Payne in his "Tales from the Arabic.[1]" This conscientious treatment is required for versions of an author like Camoens whose works were carefully corrected and arranged by a competent littérateur, but it is not merited by The Nights as they now are. The Macnaghten, the Bulak and the Bayrut texts,

---

Thousand and One Days, and in 1675 he allowed his friend Petis de la Croix, who happened to be at Isfahan, to copy it. Le Sage (of Gil Blas) is said to have converted many of the tales of Mukhlis into comic operas, which were performed at the Théâtre Italien. I still hope to see The Nights at the Lyceum.

1 This author, however, when hazarding a change of style which is, I think, regretable, has shown abundant art by filling up the frequent deficiencies of the text after the fashion of Baron McGuckin de Slane in Ibn Khallikan. As regards the tout ensemble of his work, a noble piece of English, my opinion will ever be that expressed in my Foreword. A carping critic has remarked that the translator, "As may be seen in every page, is no Arabic scholar." If I be a judge, the reverse is the case: the brilliant and beautiful version thus ignobly traduced is almost entirely free from the blemishes and carelessness which disfigure Lane's, and thus it is far more faithful to the original. But it is no secret that on the staff of that journal the translator of Villon has sundry enemies, *vrais diables enjuponés*, who take every opportunity of girding at him because he does not belong to the clique and because he does good work when theirs is mostly sham. The sole fault I find with Mr. Payne is that his severe grace of style treats an unclassical work as a classic, when the romantic and irregular would have been a more appropriate garb. But this is a mere matter of private judgment.

though printed from MSS. identical in order, often differ in minor matters. Many friends have asked me to undertake the work: but, even if lightened by the aid of Shaykhs, Munshis, and copyists, the labour would be severe, tedious, and thankless: better leave the holes open than patch them with fancy work or with heterogeneous matter. The learned, indeed, as Lane tells us (i. 74; iii. 740), being thoroughly dissatisfied with the plain and popular, the ordinary and "vulgar" note of the language, have attempted to refine and improve it and have more than once threatened to remodel it, that is, to make it odious. This would be to dress up Robert Burns in plumes borrowed from Dryden and Pope.

The first defect of the texts is in the distribution and arrangement of the matter, as I have noticed in the case of Sindbad the Seaman (vol. iv.). Moreover, many of the earlier Nights are overlong and not a few of the others are overshort; this, however, has the prime recommendation of variety. Even the vagaries of editor and scribe will not account for all the incoherences, disorder, and inconsequence, and for the vain iterations which suggest that the author has forgotten what he said. In places there are dead allusions to persons and tales which are left dark, *e.g.* vol. i. nights iii., v., vi., etc. The digressions are abrupt and useless, leading nowhere, whilst sundry pages are wearisome for excess of prolixity or hardly intelligible for extreme conciseness. The perpetual recurrence of mean colloquialisms and of words and idioms peculiar to Egypt and Syria[1] also takes from the

1 Here I offer a few, but very few, instances from the Breslau text, which is the greatest sinner in this respect. Mas. for fem., vol. i. p. 9, and three times in seven pages. Ahná and nahná for nabnú (iv. 370, 372); Aná ba-ashtari = I will buy (iii. 109); and Aná 'Ámil = I will do (v. 367). Alayki for Alayki (i 18), Anti for Anti (iii. 66) and generally long ī for short ĭ. 'Ammál (from 'amala = he did) tahlam = certainly thou dreamest, and 'Ammálin yaakulú = they were about to eat (ix. 315); Aywá, a time-honoured corruption for Ay wa'lláhi = yes, by Allah *(passim)*. Bitá' = belonging to, *e.g.* Sára bitá'k = it is become thine (ix. 352) and Matá' with the same sense (iii. 80). Dá 'l-khurj = this saddle-bag (ix. 336) and Dí (for hazah) = this woman (iii. 79) or this time (ii. 162). Fayn as ráha fayn = whither is he gone? (iv. 323); Kamá badri = he rose early (ix. 318); Kamán = also, a word known to every European (ii. 43); Katt = never (ii. 172); Kawám (pronounced 'awám) = fast, at once (iv. 385) and Rih ásif kawi (pron. 'awí) = a wind, strong very.

pleasure of the perusal. Yet we cannot deny that it has its use: this unadorned language of familiar conversation in its day, adapted for the understanding of the people, is best fitted for the Rawi's craft in the camp and caravan, the Harem, the bazar, and the coffee-house. Moreover, as has been well said, The Nights is the only written half-way house between the literary and colloquial Arabic which is accessible to readers, and thus it becomes necessary to the students who would qualify themselves for service in Moslem lands from Mauritania to Mesopotamia. It freely uses Turkish words like "Khátún" and Persian terms as "Sháhbandar," thus requiring for translation not only a somewhat archaic touch, but also a vocabulary borrowed from various sources: otherwise the effect would not be reproduced. In places, however, the style rises to the highly ornate approaching the pompous; *e.g.* the Wazirial addresses in the tale of King Jali'ad. The battle-scenes, mostly admirable (night dxix.), are told with the conciseness of a despatch and the vividness of an artist; the two combining to form perfect "word-pictures." Of the Badi'a or euphuistic style, "parleying euphuism," and of Al-Saj'a, the prose rhyme, I shall speak in a future page.

The characteristics of the whole are naïveté and simplicity, clearness, and a singular concision. The gorgeousness is in the imagery not in the language; the words are weak, while the sense, as in the classical Scandinavian books, is strong; and here the

---

Laysh, *e.g* bi-tasalní laysh (ix. 324) = why do you ask me? a favourite form for li ayya shayyin, also an old form; so Máfish = má fihi shayyun (there is no thing) in which Herr Landberg (p. 425) makes "Sha, le présent de pouvoir." Min ajalí = for my sake; and Li-ajal al-taudí'a = for the sake of taking leave (Mac. Edit., i. 384). Rijál nautiyah = men sailors when the latter word would suffice; Shuwayh (dim. of Shayy) = a small thing, a little (iv. 309) like Moyyah (dim. of Má) a little water; Waddúní = they carried me (ii. 172); and lastly the abominable Wáhid gharíb = one (for) stranger. These few must suffice; the tale of Judar and his brethren, which in style is mostly Egyptian, will supply a number of others. It must not, however, be supposed, as many have done, that vulgar and colloquial Arabic is of modern date: we find it in the first century of Al-Islam, as is proved by the tale of Al-Hajjáj and Al-Shabi (Ibn Khallikan, ii. 6). The former asked "Kam ataa-k?" (= how much is thy pay?) to which the latter answered, "Alfayn!" (= two thousand!). "Tut," cried the Governor, "Kam atau-ka?" to which the poet replied as correctly and classically, "Alfáni."

Arabic differs diametrically from the florid exuberance and turgid amplifications of the Persian story-teller, which sound so hollow and unreal by the side of a chaster model. It abounds in formulæ such as repetitions of religious phrases which are unchangeable. There are certain stock comparisons, as Lokman's wisdom, Joseph's beauty, Jacob's grief, Job's patience, David's music, and Maryam the Virgin's chastity. The eyebrow is a Nún: the eye a Sád, the mouth a Mím. A hero is more prudent than the crow, a better guide than the Katá-grouse, more generous than the cock, warier than the crane, braver than the lion, more aggressive than the panther, finer-sighted than the horse, craftier than the fox, greedier than the gazelle, more vigilant than the dog, and thriftier than the ant. The cup-boy is a sun rising from the dark under-world symbolised by his collar; his cheek-mole is a crumb of ambergris, his nose is a scymitar grided at the curve; his lower lip is a jujube; his teeth are the Pleiades, or hail-stones; his brow-locks are scorpions; his young hair on the upper lip is an emerald; his side beard is a swarm of ants or a Lám (l-letter) enclosing the roses or anemones of his cheek. The cup-girl is a moon who rivals the sheen of the sun; her forehead is a pearl set off by the jet of her "idiot-fringe"; her eyelashes scorn the sharp sword; and her glances are arrows shot from the bow of the eyebrows. A mistress necessarily belongs, though living in the next street, to the Wady Liwá in Al-Naja, the Arabian Arcadia; also to a hostile clan of Badawin whose blades are ever thirsting for the lover's blood and whose malignant tongues aim only at the "defilement of separation." Youth is upright as an Alif, or slender and bending as a branch of the Bán-tree, which we should call a willow-wand,[1] while Age, crabbed and crooked, stoops groundwards vainly seeking in the dust his lost juvenility. As Baron de Slane says of these stock comparisons (Ibn Khall. i. xxxvi.), "The figurative language of Moslem poets

---

1 In Russian folk-songs a young girl is often compared with this tree, *e.g.*—

Ivooshka, ivooshka zelonaia moia
(O Willow, O green Willow mine!)

is often difficult to be understood. The *narcissus* is the eye; the *feeble* stem of that plant bends *languidly* under its flower, and thus recalls to mind the languor of the eyes. *Pearls* signify both *tears* and *teeth;* the latter are sometimes called *hailstones*, from their whiteness and moisture; the *lips* are *cornelians* or *rubies;* the *gums*, a *pomegranate flower;* the dark *foliage* of the *myrtle* is synonymous with the *black hair* of the beloved, or with the first down on the cheeks of puberty. The *down* itself is called the *izâr* or head-stall of the bridle, and the curve of the izar is compared to the letters lâm (ل) and nûn (ن).[1] Ringlets trace on the cheek or neck the letter Wâw (و); they are called *Scorpions* (as the Greek σκορπίος), either from their dark colour or their agitated movements; the *eye* is a *sword;* the *eyelids*, *scabbards;* the *whiteness* of the complexion, *camphor;* and a *mole* or *beauty-spot*, *musk*, which term denotes also *dark hair*. A *mole* is sometimes compared also to an *ant* creeping on the cheek towards the *honey* of the mouth; a *handsome face* is both a *full moon* and *day; black hair* is *night;* the *waist* is a *willow-branch* or a *lance;* the *water of the face*[2] is *self-respect:* a poet *sells the water of his face* when he bestows mercenary praises on a rich patron."

This does not sound promising: yet, as has been said of Arab music, the persistent repetition of the same notes in the minor key is by no means monotonous, and ends with haunting the ear, occupying the thought, and touching the soul. Like the distant frog-concert and chirp of the cicada, the creak of the water-wheel, and the stroke of hammers upon the anvil from afar, the murmur of the fountain, the sough of the wind and the plash of the wavelet, they occupy the sensorium with a soothing effect, forming a barbaric music full of soothing sweetness and peaceful pleasure.

---

1 So in Hector France ("La vache enragée") "Le sourcil en accent circonflexe et l'œil en point d'interrogation."

2 In Persian "Áb-i-rú," by Indians pronounced Ábrú.

§ IV.

SOCIAL CONDITION.

I HERE propose to treat of the Social Condition which The Nights discloses, of Al-Islam at the earlier period of its development, concerning the position of women, and about the pornology of the great Saga-book.

A.—AL-ISLAM.

A splendid and glorious life was that of Baghdad in the days of the mighty Caliph,[1] when the capital had towered to the zenith of grandeur and was already trembling and tottering to the fall. The centre of human civilisation, which was then confined to Greece and Arabia, and the metropolis of an Empire exceeding in extent the widest limits of Rome, it was essentially a city of pleasure, a Paris of the ixth century. The "Palace of Peace" (Dár al-Salám), worthy successor of Babylon and Nineveh, which had outrivalled Damascus, the "Smile of the Prophet," and Kufah, the successor of Hira and the magnificent creation of Caliph Omar, possessed unrivalled advantages of site and climate. The Tigris-Euphrates Valley, where the fabled Garden of Eden has been placed, in early ages succeeded the Nile-Valley as a great centre of human development; and the prerogative of a central and commanding position still promises it, even in the present state of decay and desolation under the unspeakable Turk, a magnificent future,[2] when railways and

1 For further praises of his poetry and eloquence see the extracts from Fakhr al-Din of Rayy (an annalist of the xivth century A.D.) in De Sacy's Chrestomathie Arabe, vol. i.

2 After this had been written I received "Babylonien, das reichste Land in der Vorzeit und das lohnendste Kolonisationsfeld für die Gegenwart," by my earned friend Dr. Aloys Sprenger, Heidelberg, 1886.

canals shall connect it with Europe. The city of palaces and government offices, hotels and pavilions, mosques and colleges, kiosks and squares, bazars and markets, pleasure grounds and orchards, adorned with all the graceful charms which Saracenic architecture had borrowed from the Byzantines, lay couched upon the banks of the Dijlah-Hiddekel under a sky of marvellous purity and in a climate which makes mere life a "Kayf"—the luxury of tranquil enjoyment. It was surrounded by far-extending suburbs, like Rusáfah (the Dyke) on the Eastern side and villages like Baturanjah, dear to the votaries of pleasure; and with the roar of a gigantic capital mingled the hum of prayer, the trilling of birds, the thrilling of harp and lute, the shrilling of pipes, the ministrel's lay, and the witching strains of the professional Almah.

The population of Baghdad must have been enormous when the smallest number of her sons who fell victims to Hulâku Khan in 1258 was estimated at eight hundred thousand, while other authorities more than double the terrible "butcher's bill." Her policy and polity were unique. A well-regulated routine of tribute and taxation, personally inspected by the Caliph; a network of waterways, canaux d'arrosage; a noble system of highways, provided with viaducts, bridges, and caravanserais, and a postal service of mounted couriers enabled it to collect as in a reservoir the wealth of the outer world. The facilities for education were upon the most extended scale; large sums, from private as well as public sources, were allotted to Mosques, each of which, by the admirable rule of Al-Islam, was expected to contain a school; these establishments were richly endowed and stocked with professors collected from every land between Khorasan and Marocco[1]; and immense libraries[2] attracted the learned of all nations. It was a golden age for poets and

---

1 The first school for Arabic literature was opened by Ibn Abbas, who lectured to multitudes in a valley near Meccah, this rude beginning being followed by public teaching in the great Mosque of Damascus. For the rise of the "Madrasah," Academy, or College, see Introd. to Ibn. Khallikan, pp. xxvii.-xxxii.

2 When Ibn Abbád the Sáhib (Wazir) was invited to visit one of the Samanides, he refused, one reason being that he would require 400 camels to carry only his books.

panegyrists, Koranists and literati, preachers and rhetoricians, physicians and scientists who, besides receiving high salaries and fabulous presents, were treated with all the honours of Chinese Mandarins; and, like these, the humblest Moslem—fisherman or artizan—could aspire through knowledge or savoir faire to the highest offices of the Empire. The effect was a grafting of Egyptian, and old Mesopotamian, of Persian and Græco-Latin fruits, by long Time deteriorated, upon the strong young stock of Arab genius; and the result, as usual after such imping, was a shoot of exceptional luxuriance and vitality. The educational establishments devoted themselves to the three main objects recognised by the Moslem world, Theology, Civil Law, and Belles Lettres; and a multitude of trained Councillors enabled the ruling powers to establish and enlarge that complicated machinery of government, at once concentrated and decentralised, a despotism often fatal to the wealthy great but never neglecting the interests of the humbler lieges, which forms the beau idéal of Oriental administration. Under the Chancellors of the empire the Kazis administered law and order, justice and equity; and from their decisions the poorest subject, Moslem or miscreant, could claim with the general approval of the lieges, access and appeal to the Caliph, who, as Imám or Antistes of the Faith, was High President of a Court of Cassation.

Under wise administration, Agriculture and Commerce, the twin pillars of national prosperity, necessarily flourished. A scientific canalisation, with irrigation-works inherited from the ancients, made the Mesopotamian Valley a rival of Kemi the Black Land, and rendered cultivation a certainty of profit, not a mere speculation as it must ever be to those who perforce rely upon the fickle rains of Heaven. The remains of extensive mines prove that this source of public wealth was not neglected; navigation laws encouraged transit and traffic; and ordinances for the fisheries aimed at developing a branch of industry which is still backward even during the xix[th] century. Most substantial encouragement was given to trade and commerce, to manufacturers and handicrafts, by the flood of gold which poured in from all parts of earth; by the presence of a splendid and luxurious court, and by the call for new arts and industries which such a civilisation would necessitate. The crafts were distributed into guilds and syndicates under their respective chiefs, whom the government did not "govern too much"; these Shahbandars, Mukaddams and Nakíbs regulated the several trades, rewarded the industrious, punished the fraudulent, and were personally answerable, as we still see at Cairo, for the conduct of their constituents. Public order, the sine quâ non of stability and progress, was preserved first, by the satisfaction of the lieges, who, despite their characteristic turbulence, had few if any grievances; and, secondly, by a well-directed and efficient police, an engine of statecraft which in the West seems most difficult to perfect. In the East, however, the Wali or Chief Commissioner can reckon more or less on the unsalaried assistance of society: the cities are divided into quarters shut off one from other by night, and every Moslem is expected, by his law and religion, to keep watch upon his neighbours, to report their delinquencies, and, if necessary, himself to carry out the penal code. But in difficult cases the guardians of the peace were assisted by a body of private detectives, women as well as men. These were called Tawwábún = the Penitents, because, like our Bow-street runners, they had given up an even less respectable calling. Their adventures still delight the vulgar, as did the Newgate Calendar of past generations; and to this class we owe the Tales of Calamity Ahmad, Dalilah the Wily One, Al-Malik al-Nasir with the three Chiefs of Police (night cccxliii.), and Al-Malik al-Záhir with the Sixteen Constables (vol ix. p. 247, *infra;* Bresl. Edit., xi. pp. 321-99). Here and in many other places we also see the origin of that "picaresque" literature which arose in Spain and over-ran Europe; and which begat Le Moyen de Parvenir.[1]

I need say no more on this heading, the civilisation of Baghdad contrasting with the barbarism of Europe then Germanic, The Nights itself being the best expositor. On the other hand, the action of the State-religion upon the

---

1 This "Salmagondis" by François Beroalde de Verville was afterwards worked by Tabarin, the pseudo-Bruscambille d'Aubigné and Sorel.

state, the condition of Al-Islam during the reign of Al-Rashid, its declension from the primitive creed and its relation to Christianity and Christendom, require a somewhat extended notice. In offering the following observations it is only fair to declare my standpoints.

1. All forms of "faith," that is, belief in things unseen, not subject to the senses and therefore unknown and (in our present stage of development) unknowable, are temporary and transitory: no religion hitherto promulgated amongst men shows any prospect of being final or otherwise than finite.

2. Religious ideas, which are necessarily limited, may all be traced home to the old seat of science and art, creeds and polity in the Nile-valley, and to this day they retain the clearest signs of their origin.

3. All so-called "revealed" religions consist mainly of three portions, a cosmogony more or less mythical, a history more or less falsified, and a moral code more or less pure.

Al-Islam, it has been said, is essentially a fighting faith, and never shows to full advantage save in the field. The exceeding luxury of a wealthy capital, the debauchery and variety of vices which would spring up therein, naturally as weeds in a rich fallow, and the cosmopolitan views which suggest themselves in a meeting-place of nations, were sore trials to the primitive simplicity of the "Religion of Resignation"—the saving faith. Harun and his cousin-wife, as has been shown, were orthodox and even fanatical; but the Barmecides were strongly suspected of heretical leanings; and while the many-headed showed itself, as usual, violent, and ready to do battle about an Azan-call, the learned, who sooner or later leaven the masses, were profoundly dissatisfied with the dryness and barrenness of Mohammed's creed, so acceptable to the vulgar, and were devising a series of schisms and innovations.

In the Tale of Tawaddud (night ccccxxxvi. *et seq.*) the reader has seen a fairly extended catechism of the Creed (Dín), the ceremonial observances (Mazhab) and the apostolic practices (Sunnat) of the Shafi'í school, which with minor modifications applies to the other three orthodox. Europe has by this time clean forgotten some tricks of her former bigotry, such as "Mawmet" (an idol!)

and "Mahommerie" (mummery[1]), a place of Moslem worship: educated men no longer speak with Ockley of the "great impostor Mahomet," nor believe with the learned and violent Dr. Prideaux, that he was foolish and wicked enough to dispossess "certain poor orphans, the sons of an inferior artificer" (the Banú Najjár!). A host of books has attempted, though hardly with success, to enlighten popular ignorance upon a crucial point; namely, that the Founder of Al-Islam, like the Founder of Christianity, never pretended to establish a new religion. His claims, indeed, were limited to purging the "School of Galilee" of the dross of ages and of the manifold abuses wherewith long use had infected its early constitution: hence, to the unprejudiced observer, his reformation seems to have brought it nearer the primitive and original doctrine than any subsequent attempts, especially the Judaizing tendencies of the so-called neo-"Protestant" churches. The Meccan Apostle preached that the Hanafíyyah or orthodox belief, which he subsequently named Al-Islam, was first taught by Allah in all its purity and perfection to Adam, and consigned to certain inspired volumes now lost; and that this primal Holy Writ received additions in the days of his descendants Shís (Seth) and Idrís (Enoch?), the founder of the Sabian (not "Sabæan") faith. Here, therefore, Al-Islam at once avoided the deplorable assumption of the Hebrews and the Christians—an error which has been so injurious to their science and their progress—of placing their "first man" in circa B.C. 4000 or somewhat subsequent to the building of the Pyramids: the Pre-Adamite[2] races and dynasties of the Moslems remove a great stumbling-block, and square with

1 I prefer this derivation to Strutt's, adopted by the popular, "*mumm* is said to be derived from the Danish word *mumme*, or *momme* in Dutch (Germ. = lava) and signifies disguise in a mask, hence a mummer." In the Promptorium Parvulorum we have "Mummynge, mussacio, vel mussatus": it was a pantomime in dumb show, *e.g.*, "I mumme in a mummynge"; "Let us go mumme (mummer) to nyghte in women's apparayle." "Mask" and "Mascarade," for persona, larva or vizard, also derive, I have noticed, from an Arabic word—Maskharah.

2 The Pre-Adamite doctrine has been preached but with scant success in Christendom. Peyrère, a French Calvinist, published (A.D. 1655) his "Præadamitæ, sive exercitatio supra versibus 12, 13, 14 cap. v. Epist. Paul ad Romanos," contending that Adam was called the first man because with him the law began. It brewed a storm of wrath, and the author was fortunate to escape with only imprisonment for belief in "Adam Kadmon."

the anthropological views of the present day. In process of time, when the Adamite religion demanded a restoration and a supplement, its pristine virtue was revived, restored, and further developed by the books communicated to Abraham, whose dispensation thus takes the place of the Hebrew Noah and his Noachidæ. In due time the Torah, or Pentateuch, superseded and abrogated the Abrahamic dispensation; the "Zabúr" of David (a book not confined to the Psalms) reformed the Torah; the Injil or Evangel reformed the Zabur and was itself purified, quickened, and perfected by the Koran which means κατ' ἐξοχήν, the Reading or the Recital. Hence Locke, with many others, held Moslems to be unorthodox, that is anti-Trinitarian Christians who believe in the immaculate Conception, in the Ascension and in the divine mission of Jesus; and when Priestley affirmed "that Jesus was sent from God," all Moslems do the same. Thus they are, in the main point of doctrine connected with the Deity, simply Arians as opposed to Athanasians. History proves that the former was the earlier faith which, though formally condemned in A.D. 325 by Constantine's Council of Nice,[1] overspread the Orient beginning with Eastern Europe, where Ulphilas converted the Goths; which extended into Africa with the Vandals, claimed a victim or martyr as late as in the sixteenth century[2] and has by no means died out in this our day.

The Talmud had been completed a full century before Mohammed's time, and the Evangel had been translated into Arabic; moreover, travel and converse with his Jewish and Christian friends and companions must have convinced the Meccan apostle that Christianity was calling as loudly for reform as Judaism had done.[3] An exaggerated Trinitarianism or rather

---

1 According to Socrates the verdict was followed by a free fight of the Bishop-voters over the word "consubstantiality."

2 Servetus, burnt (in A.D. 1553 for publishing his Arian tractate) by Calvin, whom half-educated Roman Catholics in England firmly believe to have been a pederast. This arose, I suppose, from his meddling with Rabelais, who, in return for the good joke Rabie læsus, presented a better anagram, "Jan (a pimp or cuckold) Cul" (Calvinus)

3 There is no more immoral work than the "Old Testament." Its deity is an ancient Hebrew of the worst type, who condones, permits, or commands every sin in the Decalogue to a Jewish patriarch, *quâ* patriarch. He orders Abraham to murder his son and allows Jacob to swindle his brother; Moses

Tritheism, a "Fourth Person," and Saint-worship, had virtually dethroned the Deity; whilst Mariolatry had made the faith a religio muliebris, and superstition had drawn from its horrid fecundity an incredible number of heresies and monstrous absurdities. Even ecclesiastic writers draw the gloomiest pictures of the Christian Church in the fourth and seventh centuries, and one declares that the "Kingdom of Heaven had become a Hell." Egypt, distracted by the blood-thirsty religious wars of Copt and Greek, had been covered with hermitages by a gens æterna of semi-maniacal superstition. Syria, ever "feracious of heresies,' had allowed many of her finest tracts to be monopolised by monkeries and nunneries.[1] After many a tentative measure Mohammed seems to have built his edifice upon two bases, the unity of the Godhead and the priesthood of the pater-familias. He abolished for ever the "sacerdos alter Christus" whose existence, as someone acutely said, is the best proof of Christianity, and whom all know to be its weakest point. The Moslem family, however humble, was to be the model in miniature of the State, and every father in Al-Islam was made priest and pontiff in his own house, able unaided to marry himself, to circumcise (to baptise as it were) his children, to instruct them in the law

to slaughter an Egyptian, and the Jews to plunder and spoil a whole people, after inflicting upon them a series of plagues which would be the height of atrocity if the tale were true. The nations of Canaan are then extirpated. Ehud, for treacherously disembowelling King Eglon, is made judge over Israel. Jael is blessed above women (Joshua v. 24) for vilely murdering a sleeping guest; the horrid deeds of Judith and Esther are made examples to mankind; and David, after an adultery and a homicide which deserved ignominious death, is suffered to massacre a host of his enemies, cutting some in two with saws and axes and putting others into brick-kilns. For obscenity and impurity we have the tales of Onan and Tamar, Lot and his daughters, Amnon and his fair sister (2 Sam. xiii), Absalom and his father's concubines, the "wife of whoredoms" of Hosea, and, capping all, the Song of Solomon. For the horrors forbidden to the Jews, who, therefore, must have practised them, see Levit viii. 24; xi. 5; xvii. 7; xviii. 7, 9, 10, 12, 15, 17, 21, 23, and xx. 3. For mere filth what can be fouler than 2nd Kings xviii. 27; Tobias ii. 11; Esther ii. 2; Isaiah xxxvi. 12; Jeremiah iv. 5, and Ezekiel iv. 12-15. Ce qui excuse Dieu, said Henry Beyle, c'est qu'il n'existe pas,—I add, as man has made him.

1 It was the same in England before the "Reformation," and in France where, during our days, a returned priesthood collected in a few years "Peter-pence" to the tune of five hundred millions of francs. And these men wonder at being turned out!

and canonically to bury himself (night dcclxxxiv.). Ritual, properly so called, there was none; congregational prayers were merely those of the individual en masse, and the only admitted approach to a sacerdotal order were the Olema or scholars learned in the legistic and the Mullah or schoolmaster. By thus abolishing the priesthood Mohammed reconciled ancient with modern wisdom. "Scito dominum," said Cato, "pro totâ familiâ rem divinam facere": "No priest at a birth, no priest at a marriage, no priest at a death," is the aspiration of the present Rationalistic School.

The Meccan apostle wisely retained the compulsory sacrament of circumcision and the ceremonial ablutions of the Mosaic law; and the five daily prayers not only diverted man's thoughts from the world but tended to keep his body pure. These two institutions had been practised throughout life by the Founder of Christianity; but the followers who had never even seen him abolished them for purposes evidently political and propagandist. By ignoring the truth that cleanliness is next to godliness they paved the way for such saints as Simon Stylites and Sabba who, like the lowest Hindu orders of ascetics, made filth a concomitant and an evidence of piety: even now English Catholic girls are at times forbidden by Italian priests a frequent use of the bath as a sign-post to the sin of "luxury." Mohammed would have accepted the morals contained in the Sermon on the Mount much more readily than did the Jews from whom its matter was borrowed.[1] He did something to abolish the use of wine, which in the East means only its abuse; and he denounced games of chance, well knowing that the excitable races of sub-tropical climates cannot play with patience, fairness, or moderation. He set aside certain sums for charity to be paid by every Believer, and he was the first to establish a poor-rate (Zakát): thus he avoided the shame and scandal of mendicancy which, beginning in the Catholic countries of Southern Europe, extends to Syria and as far East as Christianity is found. By these and other measures of the same import he made the ideal Moslem's life physically clean, moderate, and temperate.

But Mohammed the "master mind of the age," had, we must own, a "genuine prophetic power, a sinking of self in the Divine,

1 Deutsch on the Talmud: Quarterly Review, 1867.

not distinguishable in kind from the inspiration of the Hebrew prophets," especially in that puritanical and pharisaic narrowness which, with characteristic simplicity, can see no good outside its own petty pale. He had insight as well as outsight, and the two taught him that personal and external reformation were mean matters compared with elevating the inner man. In the "purer Faith," which he was commissioned to abrogate and to quicken, he found two vital defects equally fatal to its energy and to its longevity. These were (and are) its egoism and its degradation of humanity. Thus it cannot be a "pleroma": it needs a Higher Law.[1] As Judaism promised the good Jew all manner of temporal blessings, issue, riches, wealth, honour, power, length of days, so Christianity offered the good Christian, as a bribe to lead a godly life, personal salvation and a future state of happiness, in fact, the Kingdom of Heaven, with an alternative threat of Hell. It never rose to the height of the Hindu Brahmans and Lao-Tse (the "Ancient Teacher"); of Zeno the Stoic and his disciples the noble Pharisees[2] who believed and preached that Virtue is its own reward. It never dared to say, "Do good for Good's sake[3]"; even now it does not declare with Cicero, "The sum of all is that what is right should be sought for its own sake,

1 Evidently. Its cogmography is a myth read literally: its history is, for the most part, a highly immoral distortion, and its ethics are those of the Tamudic Hebrews. It has done good work in its time; but now it shows only decay and decrepitude in the place of vigour and progress. It is dying hard, but it is dying of the slow poison of science.

2 These Hebrew Stoics would justly charge the Founder of Christianity with preaching a more popular and practical doctrine, but a degradation from their own far higher and more ideal standard

3 Dr. Theodore Christlieb ("Modern Doubt and Christian Belief," Edinburgh: Clark, 1874) can even now write:—"So then the 'full age' to which humanity is at present supposed to have attained, consists in man's doing good purely for goodness' sake! Who sees not the hollowness of this bombastic talk? *That* man has yet to be born whose practice will be regulated by this insipid theory *(dieser grauen Theorie)*. What is the idea of goodness per se? * * * The abstract idea of goodness is not an effectual motive for well-doing" (p. 104). My only comment is *c'est ignoble!* His reverence acts the part of Satan in Holy Writ, "Does Job serve God for naught?" Compare this selfish, irreligious, and immoral view with Philo Judæus (On the Allegory of the Sacred Laws, cap. lviii.), to measure the extent of the fall from Pharisaism to Christianity. And the latter is still infected with the "bribe-and-threat doctrine"; I once immensely scandalised a Consular Chaplain by quoting the noble belief of the ancients, and it was some days before he could recover mental equanimity. The degradation is now inbred.

because it is right, and not because it is enacted." It does not even now venture to say with Philo Judæus, "The good man seeks the day for the sake of the day, and the light for the light's sake; and he labours to acquire what is good for the sake of the good itself, and not of anything else." It does not even say with the Moslem Súfí, "We have no bargaining with Thee, and we do not adore Thee with the view of thereby gaining Heaven or escaping Hell." So far for the egotism, naïve and unconscious, of Christianity, whose burden is, "Do good to escape Hell and gain Heaven."

A no less defect in the "School of Galilee" is its low view of human nature. Adopting as sober and authentic history an Osirian-Hebrew myth which Philo and a host of Rabbis explain away, each after his own fashion, Christianity dwells, lovingly as it were, upon the "Fall" of man[1] and seems to revel in the contemptible condition to which "original sin" condemned him; thus grovelling before God ad majorem Dei gloriam. To such a point was and is this carried that the Synod of Dort declared, Infantes infidelium morientes in infantiâ reprobatos esse statuimus; nay, many of the orthodox still hold a Christian babe dying unbaptised to be unfit for a higher existence, and some have even created a "limbo" expressly to domicile the innocents "of whom is the kingdom of Heaven." Here, if anywhere, the cloven foot shows itself and teaches us that the only solid stratum underlying priestcraft is one composed of £ s. d.

And I never can now believe it, my Lord! (Bishop) we come to this earth
Ready damned, with the seeds of evil sown quite so thick at our birth,

sings Edwin Arnold.[2] We ask, can infatuation or hypocrisy—for it must be the one or the other—go farther? But the Adamical myth is opposed to all our modern studies. The deeper we dig into the Earth's "crust," the lower are the specimens of human remains which occur; and hitherto not a single "find" has come to revive the faded glories of

Adam the goodliest man of men since born (!)
His sons, the fairest of her daughters Eve.

---

1 Of the doctrine of the Fall the heretic Marcion wrote: "The Deity must either be deficient in goodness if He willed, in prescience if He did not foresee, or in power if He did not prevent it."

2 In his charming book, "India Revisited."

Thus Christianity, admitting, like Judaism, its own saints and santons, utterly ignores the progress of humanity, perhaps the only belief in which the wise man can take unmingled satisfaction. Both have proposed an originally perfect being with hyacinthine locks, from whose type all the subsequent humans are degradations physical and moral. We on the other hand hold, from the evidence of our senses, that early man was a savage very little superior to the brute; that during man's millions of years upon earth there has been a gradual advance towards perfection, at times irregular and even retrograde, but in the main progressive; and that a comparison of man in the xixth century with the cave-man[1] affords us the means of measuring past progress and of calculating the future of humanity.

Mohammed was far from rising to the moral heights of the ancient sages: he did nothing to abate the egotism of Christianity; he even exaggerated the pleasures of its Heaven and the horrors of its Hell. On the other hand, he did much to exalt human nature. He passed over the "Fall" with a light hand; he made man superior to the angels: he encouraged his fellow-creatures to be great and good by dwelling upon their nobler not their meaner side; he acknowledged, even in this world, the perfectability of mankind, including womankind, and in proposing the loftiest ideal he acted unconsciously upon the grand dictum of chivalry—Honneur oblige.[2] His prophets were mostly faultless men; and if the "Pure of Allah" sinned, he "sinned against himself." Lastly, he made Allah predetermine the career and fortunes, not only of empires but of every created being; thus inculcating sympathy and tolerance of others, which is true humanity, and a proud resignation to evil as to good fortune. This is the doctrine which teaches the vulgar Moslem a dignity observed even by the "blind traveller," and which enables him to display a moderation, a fortitude, and a self-command rare enough amongst the followers of the "purer creed."

Christian historians explain variously the portentous rise of

1 This is the answer to those who contend with much truth that the moderns are by no means superior to the ancients of Europe; they look at the results of only 3000 years instead of 30,000 or 300,000.

2 As a maxim the saying is attributed to the Duc de Lévis, but it is much older.

Al-Islam and its marvellous spread over vast regions, not only of pagans and idolaters but of Christians. Prideaux disingenuously suggests that it "seems to have been purposely raised up by God to be a scourge to the Christian Church for not living in accordance with their most holy religion." The popular excuse is by the free use of the sword; this, however, is mere ignorance: in Mohammed's day and in early Al-Islam only actual fighters were slain[1]: the rest were allowed to pay the Jizyah, or capitation-tax, and to become tributaries, enjoying almost all the privileges of Moslems. But even had forcible conversions been most systematically practised, it would have afforded an insufficient explanation of the phenomenal rise of an empire which covered more ground in eighty years than Rome had gained in eight hundred. During so short a time the grand revival of Christian Monotheism had consolidated into a mighty nation, despite their eternal blood-feuds, the scattered Arab tribes; a six-years' campaign had conquered Syria, and a lustre or two utterly overthrew Persia, humbled the Græco-Roman, subdued Egypt, and extended the Faith along northern Africa as far as the Atlantic. Within three generations the Copts of Nile-land had formally cast out Christianity, and the same was the case with Syria, the cradle of the Nazarene, and Mesopotamia, one of his strongholds, although both were backed by all the remaining power of the Byzantine empire. North-western Africa, which had rejected the idolatro-philosophic system of pagan and imperial Rome, and had accepted, after lukewarm fashion, the Arian Christianity imported by the Vandals, and the "Nicene mystery of the Trinity," hailed with enthusiasm the doctrines of the Koran, and has never ceased to be most zealous in its Islam. And while Mohammedanism speedily reduced the limits of Christendom by one-third, while throughout the Arabian, Saracenic, and Turkish invasions whole Christian peoples embraced the monotheistic faith, there are hardly any instances of defec-

1 There are a few, but only a few, frightful exceptions to this rule, especially in the case of Khálid bin Walid, the sword of Allah, and his ferocious friend, Darár ibn al-Azwar. But their cruel excesses were loudly blamed by the Moslems, and Caliph Omar only obeyed the popular voice in superseding the fierce and furious Khalid by the mild and merciful Abú Obaydah.

tion from the new creed and, with the exception of Spain and Sicily, it has never been suppressed in any land where once it took root. Even now, when Mohammedanism no longer wields the sword, it is spreading over wide regions in China, in the Indian Archipelago, and especially in Western and Central Africa, propagated only by self-educated individuals, trading travellers, while Christianity makes no progress and cannot exist on the Dark Continent without strong support from Government. Nor can we explain this honourable reception by the "licentiousness" ignorantly attributed to Al-Islam, one of the most severely moral of institutions; or by the allurements of polygamy and concubinage, slavery,[1] and a "wholly sensual Paradise" devoted to eating, drinking[2] and the pleasures of the sixth sense. The true and simple explanation is that this grand Reformation of Christianity was urgently wanted when it appeared, that it suited the people better than the creed which it superseded, and that it has not ceased to be sufficient for their requirements, social, sexual, and vital. As the practical Orientalist, Dr. Leitner, well observes from his own experience, "The Mohammedan religion can adapt itself better than any other, and has adapted itself to circumstances and to the needs of the various races which profess it, in accordance with the spirit of the age.[3]" Hence, I add, its wide diffusion and its impregnable position. "The dead hand, stiff and motionless" is a forcible simile for the present condition of Al-Islam; but it results from limited and

---

1 This, too, when St. Paul sends the Christian slave Onesimus back to his unbelieving (?) master, Philemon; which in Al-Islam would have created a scandal.

2 This, too, when the Founder of Christianity talks of "Eating and drinking at his table!" (Luke xxii. 29). My notes have often touched upon this inveterate prejudice, the result, like the soul-less woman of Al-Islam, of ad captandum, pious fraud. "No soul knoweth what joy of the eyes is reserved for the good in recompense for their works" (Koran xxxii. 17) is surely as "spiritual" as St. Paul (1 Cor. ii. 9). Some lies, however, are very long-lived, especially those begotten by self-interest.

3 I have elsewhere noted its strict conservatism which, however, it shares with all Eastern faiths in the East. But progress, not quietism, is the principle which governs humanity, and it is favoured by events of most different nature. In Egypt the rule of Mohammed Ali the Great, and in Syria the Massacre of Damascus (1860) have greatly modified the constitution of Al-Islam throughout the nearer East.

imperfect observation, and it fails in the sine quâ non of similes and metaphors, a foundation of fact.

I cannot quit this subject without a passing reference to an admirably written passage in Mr. Palgrave's travels[1] which is essentially unfair to Al-Islam. The author has had ample opportunities of comparing creeds: of Jewish blood and born a Protestant, he became a Catholic and a Jesuit (Père Michel Cohen)[2] in a Syrian convent; he crossed Arabia as a good Moslem and he finally returned to his premier amour, Anglicanism. But his picturesque depreciation of Mohammedanism, which has found due appreciation in more than one popular volume,[3] is a notable specimen of special pleading, of the ad captandum in its modern and least honest form. The writer begins by assuming the arid and barren Wahhabi-ism, which he had personally studied, as a fair expression of the Saving Faith. What should we say to a Moslem traveller who would make the Calvinism of the sourest Covenanter, model, genuine and ancient Christianity? What would sensible Moslems say to these propositions of Professor Maccovius and the Synod of Dort:—Good works are an obstacle to salvation. God does by no means will the salvation of all men: He does will sin and He destines men to sin, as sin? What would they think of the Inadmissible Grace, the Perseverance of the Elect, the Supralapsarian and the Sublapsarian and, finally, of a Deity the author of man's existence, temptation and fall, who deliberately pre-ordains sin and ruin? "Father Cohen" carries out into the regions of the extreme his strictures on the one grand vitalising idea of Al-Islam, "There is no god but God[4]"; and his deduction concerning the Pantheism of force sounds unreal and

---

1 Chapt. viii. "Narrative of a Year's Journey through Central and Eastern Arabia" (London: Macmillan, 1865).

2 The Soc. Jesu has, I believe, a traditional conviction that converts of Israelitic blood bring only misfortune to the Order.

3 I especially allude to an able but most superficial book, the "Ten Great Religions" by James F. Clarke (Boston, Osgood, 1876), which caricatures and exaggerates the false portraiture of Mr. Palgrave. The writer's admission that "Something is always gained by learning what the believers in a system have to say in its behalf," clearly shows us the man we have to deal with and the "depths of his self-consciousness."

4 But how could the Arabist write such hideous grammar as "La Ilāh illa Allāh" for "Lá iláha (accus.) ill' Allah?"

unsound compared with the sensible remarks upon the same subject by Dr. Badger[1] who sees the abstruseness of the doctrine and does not care to include it in hard and fast lines or to subject it to mere logical analysis. Upon the subject of "Predestination" Mr. Palgrave quotes, not from the Koran, but from the Ahádís, or Traditional Sayings of the Apostle; but what importance, however, attaches to a legend in the Mischnah, or Oral Law, of the Hebrews utterly ignored by the Written Law? He joins the many in complaining that even the mention of "the love of God" is absent from Mohammed's theology, burking the fact that it never occurs in the Jewish scriptures, and that the genius of Arabic, like Hebrew, does not admit the expression: worse still, he keeps from his reader such Koranic passages as, to quote no other, "Allah loveth you and will forgive your sins" (iii. 29). He pities Allah for having "no son, companion or counsellor" and, of course, he must equally commiserate Jehovah. Finally his views of the lifelessness of Al-Islam are directly opposed to the opinions of Dr. Leitner and the experience of all who have lived in Moslem lands. Such are the ingenious but not ingenuous distortions of fact, the fine instances of the pathetic fallacy, and the noteworthy illustrations of the falsehood of extremes, which have engendered "Mohammedanism a Relapse: the worst form of Monotheism,[2]"

1 p. 996 "Muhammad" in vol. iii. Dictionary of Christian Biography See also the Illustration of the Mohammedan Creed, etc., from Al-Ghazáli introduced (pp. 72-77) into Bell and Sons' "History of the Saracens" by Simon Ockley, B.D. (London, 1878). I regret that some Orientalist did not correct the proofs; everybody will not detect "Al-Lauh al-Mahfúz" (the Guarded Tablet) in "Allauh ho'hnehphoud" (p. 171); and this but a pinch out of a camel-load.

2 The word should have been Arianism. This "heresy" of the early Christians was much aided by the "Discipline of the Secret," supposed to be of apostolic origin, which concealed from neophytes, catechumens, and penitents all the higher mysteries, like the Trinity, the Incarnation, the Metastoicheiosis (transubstantiation), the Real Presence, the Eucharist, and the Seven Sacraments; when Arnobius could ask, Quid Deo cum vino est? and when Justin, fearing the charge of Polytheism, could expressly declare the inferior nature of the Son to the Father. Hence the creed was appropriately called Symbol, *i.e.* Sign of the Secret. This "mental reservation" lasted till the Edict of Toleration, issued by Constantine in the fourth century, held Christianity secure when divulging her "mysteries"; and it allowed Arianism to become *the* popular creed.

and which have been eagerly seized upon and further deformed by the authors of popular books, that is, volumes written by those who know little, for those who know less.

In Al-Rashid's day a mighty change had passed over the primitive simplicity of Al-Islam, the change to which faiths and creeds, like races and empires and all things sublunary, are subject. The proximity of Persia and the close intercourse with the Græco-Romans had polished and greatly modified the physiognomy of the rugged old belief: all manner of metaphysical subtleties had cropped up, with the usual disintegrating effect, and some of these threatened even the unity of the Godhead. Musaylimah, Al-Aswad and Aywalah bin Ka'b had left traces of their handiwork; whilst Karmat was about to preach and the Mutazilites (separatists or secessors) actively propagated their doctrine of a created and temporal Koran. The Khárijí or Ibázi, who rejects and reviles Abú Turáb (Caliph Ali), contended passionately with the Shi'ah who reviles and rejects the other three "Successors"; and these sectarians, favoured by the learned, and by the Abbasides in their jealous hatred of the Ommiades, went to the extreme length of the Ali-Iláhi—The God-makers of Ali—whilst the Dahri and the Zindík, the Mundanist and the Agnostic, proposed to sweep away the whole edifice. The neo-Platonism and Gnosticism which had not essentially affected Christendom,[1] found in Al-Islam a rich fallow, and gained strength and luxuriance by the solid materialism and stolid conservatism of its basis. Such were a few of the distracting and resolving influences which Time had brought to bear upon the True Believer and which, after some half a dozen generations, had separated the several schisms by a wider breach than that which yawns between Orthodox, Romanist, and Lutheran. Nor was this scandal in Al-Islam abated until the Tartar sword applied to it the sharpest remedy.

---

1 The Gnostics played rather a fantastic rôle in Christianity with their Demiurge, their Æonogony, their Æons by syzygies or couples, their Maio and Sabscho and their beatified bride of Jesus, Sophia Achamoth; and some of them descended to absolute absurdities, *e.g.* the Tascodrugitæ and the Pattalorhinchitæ, who during prayers placed their fingers upon their noses or in their mouths, &c., reading literally Psalm cxli. 3.

B.—Woman.

The next point I propose to consider is the position of womanhood in The Nights, so curiously at variance with the stock ideas concerning the Moslem home and domestic polity still prevalent, not only in England, but throughout Europe. Many readers of these volumes have remarked to me with much astonishment that they find the female characters more remarkable for decision, action, and manliness than the male; and are wonderstruck by their masterful attitude and by the supreme influence they exercise upon public and private life.

I have glanced at the subject of the sex in Al-Islam to such an extent throughout my notes that little remains here to be added. Women, all the world over, are what men make them; and the main charm of Amazonian fiction is to see how they live and move and have their being without aid masculine. But it is the old ever-new fable

"Who drew the Lion vanquished? 'Twas a man!"

The books of the Ancients, written in that stage of civilisation when the sexes are at civil war, make women even more than in real life the creatures of their masters: hence from the dawn of literature to the present day the sex has been the subject of disappointed abuse and eulogy almost as unmerited. Ecclesiastes, perhaps the strangest specimen of an "inspired volume" the world has yet produced, boldly declares, "One (upright) man among a thousand I have found; but a woman among all have I not found" (vii. 28), thus confirming the pessimism of Petronius:—

Femina nulla bona est, et si bona contigit ulla
Nescio quo fato res mala facta bona est.

In the Psalms again we have the old sneer at the three insatiables, Hell, Earth and Feminine Concupiscence *(os vulvæ)*; and Rabbinical learning has embroidered these and other texts, producing a truly hideous caricature. A Hadis attributed to Mohammed runs, "They (women) lack wits and faith. When Eve was created Satan rejoiced saying:—Thou art half of my host, the trustee of my secret, and my shaft wherewith I shoot and miss not!" Another tells us, "I stood at the gate of Heaven, and lo! most of its inmates were poor, and I stood at the gate of Hell, and lo! most of its inmates were women.[1]" "Take care of the glass phials!" cried the Prophet to a camel-guide, singing with a sweet voice. Yet the Meccan apostle made, as has been seen, his own household produce two perfections. The blatant popular voice follows with such "dictes" as, "Women are made of nectar and poison"; "Women have long hair and short wits," and so forth. Nor are the Hindus behindhand. Woman has fickleness implanted in her by Nature like the flashings of lightning (Kathá s.s. i. 147); she is valueless as a straw to the heroic mind (169); she is hard as adamant in sin and soft as flour in fear (170), and, like the fly, she quits camphor to settle on compost (ii. 17). "What dependence is there in the crowing of a hen?" (women's opinions) says the Hindi proverb: also "A virgin with grey hairs!" (*i.e.* a monster); and "Wherever wendeth a fair face a devil wendeth with her." The same superficial view of holding woman to be lesser (and very inferior) man is taken generally by the classics; and Euripides distinguished himself by misogyny, although he drew the beautiful character of Alcestis. Simonides, more merciful than Ecclesiastes, after naming his swine-women, dog-women, cat-women, etc., ends the decade with the admirable bee-woman thus making ten per cent. honest. In mediæval or Germanic Europe the doctrine of the Virgin-mother gave the sex a status unknown to the ancients except in Egypt, where Isis was the help-mate and completion of Osiris, in modern parlance "The Woman clothed with the Sun." The kindly and courtly Palmerin of England, in whose pages "gentlemen may find their choice of sweet inventions and gentlewomen be satisfied with courtly expectations," suddenly blurts out, "But in truth women are never satisfied by reason, being governed by accident or appetite" (chapt. xlix.).

The Nights, as might be expected from the emotional East, exaggerates these views. Women are mostly "Sectaries of the god Wünsch"; beings of impulse, blown about by

---

1 "Kitáb al-'Unwán fi Makáid al-Niswán" = The Book of the Beginnings on the Wiles of Womankind (Lane i. 38).

every gust of passion; stable only in instability; constant only in inconstancy. The false ascetic, the perfidious and murderous crone, and the old hag-procuress who pimps like Umm Kulsum,[1] for mere pleasure in the luxury of sin, are drawn with an experienced and loving hand. Yet not the less do we meet with examples of the dutiful daughter, the model lover matronly in her affection, the devoted wife, the perfect mother, the saintly devotee, the learned preacher, Univira the chaste widow, and the self-sacrificing heroic woman. If we find (night clxxi.) the sex described as :—

An offal cast by kites where'er they list,

and the studied insults of night ccxxi., we also come upon admirable sketches of conjugal happiness and, to mention no other, Shahryar's attestation to Shahrazad's excellence in the charming last pages of the Nights.[2] It is the same with the Kathá, whose praise and dispraise are equally enthusiastic; *e.g.*, "Women of good family are guided by their own virtue, the sole efficient chamberlain; but the Lord Himself can hardly guard the unchaste. Who can stem a furious stream and a frantic woman?" (i. 328). "Excessive love in woman is your only hero for daring" (i. 339). "Thus fair ones, naturally feeble, bring about a series of evil actions which engender discontent and aversion to the world; but here and there you will find a virtuous woman who adorneth a glorious house as the streak of the moon arrayeth the breadth of the Heavens" (i. 346). "So you see, King, honourable matrons are devoted to their husbands and 'tis not the case that women are always bad" (ii. 624). And there is true wisdom in that even balance of feminine

1 This person was one of the Amsál or Exempla of Arabian history, and she lived a life of peculiar infamy. For her first thirty years she whored; during the next three decades she pimped for friend and foe; and during the last third of her life she was bedridden by age and infirmities. These proverbial models will be found quoted and explained by those who care to study the subject in the Arabum Proverbia, *Arabice et Latine*, Commentarii illustravit Freytag, 3 vols. Bonnæ, 1831-43.

2 And modern Moslem feeling upon the subject has apparently undergone a change. Ashraf Khan, the Afghan poet, sings :—

Since I, the parted one, have come the secrets of the world to ken,
Women in hosts therein I find, but few (and very few) of men.

And the Osmanli proverb is, "Of ten men nine are women!"

qualities advocated by our Hindu-Hindi class-book the Toti-námah or Parrot volume. The perfect woman has seven requisites. She must not always be merry (1), nor sad (2); she must not always be talking (3), nor silently musing (4); she must not always be adorning herself (5), nor neglecting her person (6); and (7) at all times she must be moderate and self-possessed.

The legal status of womankind in Al-Islam is exceptionally high, a fact of which Europe has often been assured, although the truth has not even yet penetrated into the popular brain. Nearly a century ago one Mirza Abú Tálib Khán, an Amildár or revenue collector, after living two years in London, wrote an "apology" for, or rather a vindication of, his countrywomen which is still worth reading and quoting.[1] Nations are but superficial judges of one another: where customs differ they often remark only the salient distinctive points which, when examined, prove to be of minor importance. Europeans seeing and hearing that women in the East are "cloistered" as the Grecian matron was wont *ἔνδον μένειν* and *οἰκουρεῖν*; that wives may not walk out with their husbands and cannot accompany them to "balls and parties"; moreover, that they are always liable, like the ancient Hebrew, to the mortification of the "sister-wife," have most ignorantly determined that they are mere serviles and that their lives are not worth living. Indeed, a learned lady, Miss Martineau, once visiting a Harem went into ecstasies of pity and sorrow because the poor things knew nothing of—say trigonometry and the use of the globes. Sonnini thought otherwise, and my experience, like that of all old dwellers in the East, is directly opposed to this conclusion.

I have noted (night cmlxii.) that Mohammed, in the fifth year of his reign,[2] after his ill-advised and scandalous

---

1 His Persian paper "On the Vindication of the Liberties of the Asiatic Women" was translated and printed in the Asiatic Annual Register for 1801 (pp. 100-107); it is quoted by Dr. Jon. Scott (Introd. vol. i. p. xxxiv. *et seq.*) and by a host of writers. He also wrote a book of Travels, translated by Prof. Charles Stewart in 1810 and re-issued (3 vols. 8vo.) in 1814.

2 The beginning of which I date from the Hijrah, lit. = the separation, popularly "The Flight." Stating the case broadly, it has become the practice of modern writers to look upon Mohammed as an honest enthusiast at Meccah and an unscrupulous despot at Al-Madinah, a view which appears to me eminently unsound and unfair. In a private station the Meccan Prophet was

marriage[1] with his foster-daughter Zaynab, established the Hijáb or veiling of women: probably an exaggeration of local usage: a modified separation of the sexes, which extended and still extends even to the Badawi, must long have been customary in Arabián cities, and its object was to deliver the sexes from temptation, as the Koran says (xxxiii. 53), "purer will this (practice) be for your hearts and their hearts.[2]" The women, who all the world over delight in restrictions which tend to their honour, accepted it willingly and still affect it; they do not desire a liberty or rather a license which they have learned to regard as inconsistent with their time-honoured notions of feminine decorum and delicacy; and they would think very meanly of a husband who permitted them to be exposed, like hetairæ, to the public gaze.[3] As Zubayr Pasha, exiled to Gibraltar for another's treason, said to my friend, General Buckle, after visiting quarters evidently laid out by a jealous husband, "We Arabs think that when a man has a precious jewel, 'tis wiser to lock it up in a box than to leave it about for

---

famed as a good citizen, *teste* his title Al-Amín = the Trusty. But when driven from his home by the pagan faction he became de facto as de jure a king: nay, a royal pontiff; and the preacher was merged in the Conqueror of his foes and the Commander of the Faithful. His rule, like that of all Eastern rulers, was stained with blood; but, assuming as true all the crimes and cruelties with which Christians charge him and which Moslems confess, they were mere blots upon a glorious and enthusiastic life, ending in a most exemplary death, compared with the tissue of horrors and havock which the Law and the Prophets attribute to Moses, to Joshua, to Samuel, and to the patriarchs and prophets, by express commandment of Jehovah.

1 It was not, however, incestuous: the scandal came from its ignoring the Arab "pundonor."

2 The "opportunism" of Mohammed has been made a matter of obloquy by many who have not reflected and discovered that time-serving is the very essence of "Revelation." Says the Rev. W. Smith ("Pentateuch," chapt. xiii), "As the journey (Exodus) proceeds, so laws originate from the accidents of the way"; and he applies this to successive decrees (Numbers xxvi. 32-36; xxvii. 8-11 and xxxvi. 1-9) holding it indirect internal evidence of Mosaic authorship (?). Another tone, however, is used in the case of Al-Islam. "And now, that he might not stand in awe of his wives any longer, *down comes a revelation*" says Ockley, in his bluff and homely style, which admits such phrases as "the impostor has the impudence to say." But why, in common honesty, refuse to the Koran the concessions freely made to the Torah? It is a mere petitio principii to argue that the latter is "inspired" while the former is not; moreover, although we may be called upon to believe things *beyond* Reason, it is hardly fair to require our behalf in things *contrary* to Reason.

3 This is noticed in my wife's volume on The Inner Life of Syria, vol. i. chapt. xii. 155.

anyone to take." The Eastern adopts the instinctive, the Western prefers the rational, method. The former jealously guards the treasure, surrounds it with all precautions, fends off from it all risks, and if the treasure go astray, kills it. The latter, after placing it *en evidence* upon an eminence in ball dress with back and bosom bare to the gaze of society, a bundle of charms exposed to every possible seduction, allows it to take its own way, and if it be misled, he kills or tries to kill the misleader. It is a fiery trial; and the few who safely pass through it may claim a higher standpoint in the moral world than those who have never been sorely tried. But the crucial question is whether Christian Europe has done wisely in offering such temptations.

The second and main objection to Moslem custom is the marriage-system, which begins with a girl being wedded to a man whom she knows only by hearsay. This was the habit of our forbears not many generations ago, and it still prevails amongst noble houses in Southern Europe, where a lengthened study of it leaves me doubtful whether the "love-marriage," as it is called, or wedlock with an utter stranger, evidently the two extremes, is likely to prove the happier. The "sister-wife" is or would be a sore trial to monogamic races like those of Northern Europe, where Caia, all but the equal of Caius in most points mental and physical, and superior in some, not unfrequently proves herself the "man of the family," the "only man in the boat." But in the East, where the sex is far more delicate, where a girl is brought up in polygamy, where religious reasons separate her from her husband, during pregnancy and lactation, for three successive years; and where often enough like the Mormon damsel she would hesitate to "nigger it with a one-wife-man," the case assumes a very different aspect, and the load, if burden it be, falls comparatively light. Lastly, the "patriarchal household" is mostly confined to the grandee and the richard, whilst Holy Law and public opinion, neither of which can openly be disregarded, assign command of the household to the *equal* or first wife, and jealously guard the rights and privileges of the others.

Mirza Abu Talib, "the Persian Prince,[1]" offers six reasons

1 Mirza preceding the name means Mister, and following it Prince. Addison's "Vision of Mirza" (Spectator No. 159) is therefore "The Vision of Mister."

why "the liberty of the Asiatic women appears less than that of the Europeans," ending with,

> I'll fondly place on either eye
> The man that can to this reply.

He then lays down eight points in which the Moslem wife has greatly the advantage over her Christian sisterhood; and we may take his first as a specimen. Custom, not contrary to law, invests the Mohammedan mother with despotic government of the homestead, slaves, servants and children, especially the latter; she alone directs their early education, their choice of faith, their marriage, and their establishment in life; and in case of divorce she takes the daughters, the sons going to the sire. She has also liberty to leave her home, not only for one or two nights, but for a week or a fortnight, without consulting her husband; and whilst she visits a strange household, the master and all males above fifteen are forbidden the Harem. But the main point in favour of the Moslem wife is her being a "legal sharer": inheritance is secured to her by Koranic law; she must be dowered by the bridegroom to legalise marriage, and all she gains is secured to her; whereas in England a "Married Woman's Property Act" was completed only in 1882 after many centuries of the grossest abuses.

Lastly, Moslems and Easterns in general study and intelligently study the art and mystery of satisfying the physical woman. In my Foreword I have noticed among barbarians the system of "making men,[1]" that is, of teaching lads first arrived at puberty the nice conduct of the instrumentum paratum plantandis civibus; a branch of the knowledge-tree which our modern education grossly neglects, thereby entailing untold miseries upon individuals, families, and generations.[2] The mock virtue, the most

---

1 And women. The course of instruction lasts from a few days to a year, and the period of puberty is fêted by magical rites and often by some form of mutilation. It is described by Waitz, Réclus and Schoolcraft, Péchuel-Loecksa, Collins, Dawson, Thomas, Brough Smyth, Reverends Bulmer and Taplin, Carlo Wilhelmi Wood, A. W. Howitt, C. Z. Muhas (Mem. de la Soc. Anthrop. Allemande, 1882, p. 265) and by Professor Mantegazza (chapt. i.) for whom see *infra*.

2 "There is one word I might like to offer for thought and consideration in both a religious and moral point of view. It is difficult to say it, because it cuts two ways, and I am bound to say that this question never struck me at

immodest modesty of England and of the United States in the xixth century, pronounces the subject foul and fulsome: "Society" sickens at all details; and hence it is said abroad that the English have the finest women in Europe and least know how to use them. Throughout the East such studies are aided by a long series of volumes, many of them written by learned physiologists, by men of social standing, and by religious dignitaries high in office. The Egyptians especially delight in aphrodisiac literature treating, as the Turks say, de la partie au-dessous de la taille; and from fifteen hundred to two thousand copies of a new work, usually lithographed in cheap form, readily sell off. The pudibund Lane makes allusion to and quotes (A. N. 1. 216) one of the most outspoken, a 4to. of 464 pages, called the Halbat al-Kumayt or "Race-Course of the Bay Horse," a poetical and horsey term for

---

all till I came to live in England after my husband's death, because abroad it does not exist, it is an English growth. I think innocence and ignorance are too much confounded, and yet they have no connection—no relation to each other. I believe that half the crime, and misery, and ruined bodies and souls, and the fall of families proceeds from *ignorance*, not *from knowledge*. Are there not wise and good educated moral people who could obviate this? Is there *no* way of having a little physiological instruction, at once religious and scientific, with which parents, or guardians, or pastors could open the eyes of a boy of ten, and a girl of thirteen, to show them the straight path? I see so many parents utterly unfit to have children, and to bring them up. *They* will cry out "Fie! for shame; what! *take the bloom off the peach?* if the world is horrid, we would so much rather our dear children did not find it out as long as possible, not till they are grown up men and women and married." Then all I have got to say is, one day the beautiful bloom on the skin of the peach that is cut open will show you the whole inside *rotten to the core*. You cannot keep your darling under a glass case and lock it up in a room, and if you did Evil would come down the chimney. There are bad companions, there are public schools, there are dictionaries, there are infamous nurses; and now-a-days there is cheap indecent literature [leaflets telling the young people where to buy it are inserted in their newspapers] and prints, and some suggestive plays. Nature begins to speak, but the child does not understand its language, and when it *does* know, it is *too late*. A religious man may shut his eyes, and contemplate the final scene on the death bed, when the poor soul would say, 'Oh, my God! in what a condition am I to appear before you; I have misused *all* the gifts of my body *my whole life long*, but I did not know. My father and mother, what did they do? They told me not to go too near the fire, lest my pinafore should catch; they told me not to eat the nightshade from the hedges, because it would poison me; they told me not to play with *strange* dogs lest they should bite me: they told me not to play with the dirty little boys in the streets lest I should become vulgar, and so on *ad infinitum*. *But* they never told me the most important thing: I was never allowed to know for

grape wine. Attributed by D'Herbelot to the Kazi Shams al-Din Mohammed, it is wholly upon the subject of wassail and women till the last few pages, when his reverence exclaims:—"This much, O reader, I have recounted, the better thou mayst know what to avoid"; and so forth, ending with condemning all he had praised.[1] Even the divine and historian Jalál al-Dín al-Siyuti is credited with having written, though the authorship is much disputed, a work entitled "Kitáb al-Ízáh fi 'ilm al-Nikah = The Book of Exposition in the Science of Coition: my copy, a lithograph of 33 pages, undated, but evidently Cairene, begins with exclaiming, "Alhamdolillah—Laud to the Lord who adorned the virginal bosom with breasts!" To the same amiable theologian are also ascribed the "Kitáb Nawázir al-Ayk fi al-Nayk" = Green Splendours of the Copse in Copulation, an abstract of the "Kitáb

---

what my body was made, what I *could* do with it and *must* not do with it, or what were the consequences of one course, and what of the other,—that was too "shocking"—until I was *well lost*, and, *then too late*, I understood. I have lost the blessings of paternity (or maternity, according to sex), I am a mass of disease, and, my God! they say You are *just*, and yet *I* am to be lost eternally, whilst these parents who deserve my curse, are to go to Heaven.' This is to *my* eyes how *that* matter stands; let parents and guardians look to it for themselves. I know a father who, as each son's tenth birthday was kept, took him into his study and told him everything, and explained the consequences of well doing, and the consequences of evil doing; and he finished up, 'Never tell a lie, never break a promise, never betray a secret, owe no man sixpence, and fight when you ought to.' There were four boys, and they all turned out moral men and gentlemen. The purest woman I have ever known was told everything by a bad companion at eight years old; the mother was one of those who '*preserve the bloom*.' The child was observed to pine and dwindle away, but nobody could account for it. The father being called away one night the child slept with the mother, who heard the little thing sobbing at various intervals of the night. Taking it in her arms, she said, 'Child! you are breaking my heart, what is it?' The child throwing her arms round her mother's neck, said, 'Oh mother, mother, is it true?' and gradually it all came out. 'Yesi child,' she answered, 'It is perfectly true, and God made it, it is a law of Nature. Never think of it again, and never mention it to your sisters or anybody else.' The child's mind was perfectly settled, she grew quite well and happy, and she has often told me since that the subject never crossed her mind after, and, as I have said, she is the purest woman I know, and the best of wives. If these matters came in a proper, natural way, in a course of religious and scientific instruction, would it not do away with all these moral sores?"—LADY BURTON in *The Humanitarian*, Novr. 1894.

1 Similarly certain Australian tribes act scenes of rape and pederasty, saying to the young, If you do this you will be killed.

al-Wisháh fí fawáid al-Nikáh" = Book of the Zone on Coition-boon. Of the abundance of pornographic literature we may judge from a list of the following seven works, given in the second page of the "Kitáb Rujú'a al-Shaykh ila Sabáh fi 'l-Kuwwat 'alà 'l Báh[1]" = Book of Age-rejuvenescence in the power of Concupiscence: it is the work of Ahmad bin Sulayman, surnamed Ibn Kamál Pasha.

1. Kitáb al-Báh by Al-Nahli.
2. Kitáb al-'Ars wa al-'Aráis (Book of the Bridal and the Brides) by Al-Jáhiz.
3. Kitáb al-Kiyán (Maiden's Book) by Ibn Hájib al-Nu'mán.
4. Kitáb al-Ízáh fí asrár al-Nikáh (Book of the Exposition on the Mysteries of Married Fruition).
5. Kitáb Jámi' al-Lizzah (The Compendium of Pleasure) by Ibn Samsamáni.
6. Kitáb Barján (Yarján ?) wa Janáhib[2] (? ?).
7. Kitáb al-Munákahah wa al-Mufátahah fí Asnáf al-Jimá' wa Álátih, by Aziz al-Din al-Masihi.[3]

To these I may add the Lizzat al-Nisá (Pleasures of Women), a text-book in Arabic, Persian and Hindostani; it is a translation and a very poor attempt, omitting much from, and adding naught to, the famous Sanskrit work Ananga-Ranga (Stage of the Bodiless One, *i.e.* Cupido) or Hindu Art of Love (Ars Amoris

---

1 "Báh" is the popular term for the amatory appetite; hence such works are called Kutub al-Báh, lit. = Books of Lust.

2 I can make nothing of this title, nor can those whom I have consulted: my only explanation is that they may be fanciful names proper.

3 Amongst the Greeks we find erotic specialists (1) Aristides of the Libri Milesi; (2) Astyanassa, the follower of Helen who wrote on androgynisation; (3) Cyrene the artist of amatory Tabellæ or ex-votos offered to Priapus; (4) Elephantis the poetess who wrote on Varia concubitis genera; (5) Evemerus whose Sacra Historia, preserved in a fragment of Q. Ennius, was collected by Hieronymus Columna; (6) Hemitheon of the Sybaritic books; (7) Musæus the lyrist; (8) Niko the Samian girl; (9) Philænis, the poetess of Amatory Pleasures, in Athen viii 13, attributed to Polycrates the Sophist; (10) Protagorides, Amatory Conversations; (11) Sotades the Mantinæan who, says Suidas, wrote the poem "Cinædica"; (12) Sphodrias the Cynic, his Art of love; and (13) Trepsicles, Amatory Pleasures. Amongst the Romans we have Aedituus, Annianus (in Ausonius), Anser, Bassus Eubius, Helvius Cinna, Lævius (of Io and the Erotopægnion), Memmius, Cicero (to Cerellia), Pliny the Younger, Sabellus (de modo coeundi); Sisenna, the pathic Poet and translator of Milesian Fables, and Sulpitia the modest erotist. For these see the Dictionnaire Érotique of Blondeau, pp ix. and x (Paris, Liseux, 1885).

Indica).[1] I have copies of it in Sanskrit and Maráthi, Guzrati and Hindostani: the latter is an unpaged 8vo. of 66 pages, including eight pages of most grotesque illustrations showing the various Ásan (the Figuræ Veneris), which seem to be the triumphs of contortionists. These pamphlets lithographed in Bombay are broad cast over the land.[2]

It must not be supposed that such literature is purely and simply aphrodisiacal. The learned Sprenger, a physician as well as an Arabist, says (Al-Mas'údi, p. 384) of a tractate by the celebrated Rhazes in the Leyden Library, "The number of curious observations, the correct and practical ideas, and the novelty of the notions of Eastern nations on these subjects, which are contained in this book, render it one of the most important productions of the medical literature of the Arabs." I can conscientiously recommend to the Anthropologist a study of the "Kutub al-Báh." Moreover, the conscientious study would be useful to humanity by teaching the use and unteaching the abuse of the Malthusian system, whereby the family is duly limited to the necessities of society.

C.—Pornography.

Here it will be advisable to supplement what was said in my Foreword (p. xxiv.) concerning the *turpiloquium* of The Nights. Readers who have perused the ten[3] volumes will probably agree with me that the naïve indecencies of the text are rather *gaudisserie* than prurience; and, when delivered with mirth and humour, they are rather the "excrements of wit" than designed for debauching the mind. Crude and indelicate with infantile plainness; even gross and, at "times" nasty, in their terrible frankness, they

1 It has been translated from the Sanskrit and annotated by A. F. F. and B. F. R. Reprint: Cosmopoli: mdccclxxxv.: for the Kamashastra Society, London and Benares, and for private circulation only. The first print has been exhausted and a reprint will presently appear.

2 The local press has often proposed to abate this nuisance of erotic publication, which is most debasing to public morals already perverted enough. But the "Empire of opinion" cares very little for such matters and, in the matter of the "native press," generally seems to seek only a quiet life. In England if erotic literature were not forbidden by law, few would care to sell or to buy it, and only the legal pains and penalties keep up the phenomenally high prices.

3 [In this edition, eight.]

cannot be accused of corrupting suggestiveness or subtle insinuation of vicious sentiment. Theirs is a coarseness of language, not of idea; they are indecent, not depraved; and the pure and perfect naturalness of their nudity seems almost to purify it, showing that the matter is rather of manners than of morals. Such throughout the East is the language of every man, woman and child, from prince to peasant, from matron to prostitute: all are as the naïve French traveller said of the Japanese: "si grossiers qu'ils ne sçavent nommer les choses que par leur nom." This primitive stage of language sufficed to draw from Lane and Burckhardt strictures upon the "most immodest freedom of conversation in Egypt," where, as all the world over, there are three several stages for names of things and acts sensual. First we have the *mot cru*, the popular term, soon followed by the technical and scientific, and, lastly, the literary or figurative nomenclature, which is often much more immoral because more attractive, suggestive, and seductive than the "raw word." And let me observe that the highest civilisation is now returning to the language of nature. In La Glu of M. J. Richepin, a triumph of the realistic school, we find such "archaic" expressions as la petée, putain, foutue à la six-quatre-dix; un facétieuse pétarade; tu t'es foutue de, etc. Eh vilain bougre! and so forth.[1] To those critics who complain of these raw vulgarisms and puerile indecencies in The Nights, I can reply only by quoting the words said to have been said by Dr. Johnson to the lady who complained of the naughty words in his dictionary:—"You must have been looking for them, Madam!"

But I repeat (p. xxv.) there is another element in The Nights, and that is one of absolute obscenity utterly repugnant to English readers, even the least prudish. It is chiefly connected with what our neighbours call *Le vice contre nature.*[2] Upon this subject I must offer details, as it does not enter into my plan to ignore any theme which is interesting to the Orientalist and the Anthro-

---

1 The Spectator (No. 119) complains of an "infamous piece of good breeding," because "men of the town, and particularly those who have been polished in France, make use of the most coarse and uncivilised words in our language, and utter themselves often in such a manner as a clown would blush to hear."

2 Among the wiser ancients, sinning contra naturam was not marrying and begetting children.

pologist. And they, methinks, do abundant harm who, for shame or disgust, would suppress the very mention of such matters: in order to combat a great and growing evil deadly to the birth-rate —the mainstay of national prosperity—the first requisite is careful study. As Albert Bollstoedt, Bishop of Ratisbon, rightly says:— Quia malum non evitatum nisi cognitum, ideo necesse est cognoscere immundiciem coitus et multa alia quæ docentur in isto libro. Equally true are Professor Mantegazza's words[1]: Cacher les plaies du cœur humain au nom de la pudeur, ce n'est au contraire qu'hypocrisie ou peur. The late Mr. Grote had reason to lament that when describing such institutions as the far-famed ιέρὸς λόχος of Thebes, the Sacred Band annihilated at Chaeroneia, he was compelled to a reticence which permitted him to touch only the surface of the subject. This was inevitable under the present rule of Cant[2] in a book intended for the public: but the same does not apply to my version of The Nights, and now I proceed to discuss the matter sérieusement, honnêtement, historiquement; to show it in decent nudity not in suggestive fig-leaf or *feuille de vigne*.

D.—PEDERASTY.

[It has been deemed necessary to omit from this volume the Article on Pederasty.]

The pederasty of The Nights may briefly be distributed into three categories. The first is the funny form, as the unseemly practical joke of masterful Queen Budúr and the not less hardi jest of the slave-princess Zumurrud. The second is in the grimmest and most earnest phase of the perversion, for instance where Abu Nowas[3] debauches the three youths; whilst in the

---

1 Avis au Lecteur, "L'Amour dans l'Humanité," par P. Mantegazza, traduit par Emilien Chesneau, Paris, Fetscherin et Chuit, 1886.

2 See "H. B." (Henry Beyle, French Consul at Civita Vecchia) par un des Quarante (Prosper Mérimée), Elutheropolis, An mdccclxiv. De l'Imposture du Nazaréen.

3 Of this peculiar character Ibn Khallikan remarks (ii. 43), "There were four poets whose works clearly contraried their character. Abu al-Atahíyah wrote pious poems, himself being an atheist; Abú Hukayma's verses proved his impotence, yet he was more salacious than a he-goat; Mohammed ibn

third form it is wisely and learnedly discussed, to be severely blamed, by the Shaykhah or Reverend Woman (night ccccxxiii.).

To conclude this part of my subject, the éclaircissement des obscénités. Many readers will regret the absence from The Nights of that modesty which distinguishes "Amadis de Gaul"; whose author when leaving a man and a maid together says, "And nothing shall be here related; for these and such-like things which are conformable neither to good conscience nor nature, man ought in reason lightly to pass over, holding them in slight esteem as they deserve." Nor have we less respect for Palmerin of England who, after a risqué scene, declares, "Herein is no offence offered to the wise by wanton speeches, or encouragement to the loose by lascivious matter." But these are not Oriental ideas and we must e'en take the Eastern as we find him. He still holds "Naturalia non sunt turpia," together with "Mundis omnia munda"; and, as Bacon assures us the mixture of a lie doth add to pleasure, so the Arab enjoys the startling and lively contrast of extreme virtue and horrible vice placed in juxtaposition.

Those who have read through these ten volumes will agree with me that the proportion of offensive matter bears a very small ratio to the mass of the work. In an age saturated with cant and hypocrisy, here and there a venal pen will mourn over the "Pornography" of The Nights, dwell upon the "Ethics of Dirt" and the "Garbage of the Brothel"; and will lament the "wanton dissemination (!) of ancient and filthy fiction." This self-constituted Censor morum reads Aristophanes and Plato, Horace and Virgil, perhaps even Martial and Petronius, because "veiled in the decent obscurity of a learned language"; he allows men Latinè loqui; but he is scandalised at stumbling-blocks much less important in plain English. To be consistent he must begin by bowdlerising not only the classics, with which boys' and youths' minds and memories are soaked and saturated at schools and colleges, but also Boccaccio and Chaucer, Shakespeare and Rabelais; Burton, Sterne, Swift, and a long list of works which

---

Házim praised contentment, yet he was greedier than a dog; and Abú Nowás hymned the joys of pederasty, yet he was more passionate for women than a baboon."

are yearly reprinted and republished without a word of protest. Lastly, why does not this inconsistent puritan purge the Old Testament of its hosts of indecent and obscene allusions and passages? But this he will not do, the whited sepulchre! To the interested critic of the Edinburgh Review (No. 335 of July, 1886), I return my warmest thanks for his direct and deliberate falsehoods:—lies are one-legged and short-lived, and venom evaporates.[1] It appears to me that when I show to such men, so "respectable" and so impure, a landscape of magnificent prospects whose vistas are adorned with every charm of nature and art, they point their unclean noses at a little heap of muck here and there lying in a field-corner.

---

1 A virulently and unjustly abusive critique never yet injured its object: in fact it is generally the greatest favour an author's unfriends can bestow upon him. But to notice in a popular Review books which have been printed but not published is hardly in accordance with the established courtesies of literature. At the end of my work I propose to write a paper, "The Reviewer Reviewed," which will, amongst other things, explain the motif of the writer of the critique and the editor of the Edinburgh.

§ V.

ON THE PROSE-RHYME AND THE POETRY OF THE NIGHTS.

A.—The Saj'a.

According to promise in my Foreword (p. xxiv.), I here proceed to offer a few observations concerning the Saj'a or rhymed prose, and the Sh'ir, or measured sentence, that is, the verse of The Nights. The former has in composition, metrical or unmetrical, three distinct forms. Saj'a mutawázi (parallel), the most common, is when the ending words of sentences agree in measure, assonance, and final letter, in fact our full rhyme: next is Saj'a mutarraf (the affluent), when the periods, hemistichs or couplets end in words whose terminal letters correspond, although differing in measure and number; and thirdly, Saj'a muwázanah (equilibrium) is applied to the balance which affects words corresponding in measure but differing in final letters.[1]

Al-Saj'a, the fine style or style fleuri, also termed Al-Badí'a, or euphuism, is the basis of all Arabic euphony. The whole of the Koran is written in it; and the same is the case with the Makámát of Al-Hariri and the prime master-pieces of rhetorical composition: without it no translation of the Holy Book can be satisfactory or final, and where it is not the Assemblies become the prose of prose. Thus universally used, the assonance has necessarily been abused, and its excess has given rise to the saying "Al-Saj'a faj'a"—prose rhyme's a pest. English translators have, unwisely I think, agreed in rejecting it, while Germans have not. Mr. Preston assures us that "rhyming prose is extremely ungraceful in English and introduces an air

---

1 For detailed examples and specimens see p. 10 of Gladwin's "Dissertations on Rhetoric," etc., Calcutta, 1801.

of flippancy": this was certainly not the case with Friedrich Rückert's version of the great original, and I see no reason why it should be so or become so in our tongue. Torrens (Pref. p. vii.) declares that "the effect of the irregular sentence with the iteration of a jingling rhyme is not pleasant in our language": he therefore systematically neglects it and gives his style the semblance of being "scamped" with the object of saving study and trouble. Mr. Payne (ix. 379) deems it an "excrescence born of the excessive facilities for rhyme afforded by the language," and of, Eastern delight in antithesis of all kinds whether of sound or of thought; and, aiming elaborately at grace of style, he omits it wholly, even in the proverbs.

The weight of authority was against me, but my plan compelled me to disregard it. The dilemma was simply either to use the Saj'a or to follow Mr. Payne's method and "arrange the disjecta membra of the original in their natural order"; that is to remodel the text. Intending to produce a faithful copy of the Arabic, I was compelled to adopt the former and still hold it to be the better alternative. Moreover, I question Mr. Payne's dictum (ix. 383) that "the Seja-form is utterly foreign to the genius of English prose, and its preservation would be fatal to all vigour and harmony of style." The English translator of Palmerin of England, Anthony Munday, attempted it in places with great success as I have before noted (night dccxcvii); and my late friend Edward Eastwick made artistic use of it in his Gulistán. Had I rejected the "Cadence of the cooing-dove" because un-English, I should have adopted the balanced periods of the Anglican marriage service[1] or the essentially English system of alliteration, requiring some such artful aid to distinguish from the vulgar recitative style the elevated and classical tirades in The Nights. My attempt has found with reviewers more favour than I

1 For instance: I, M. | take thee N. | to my wedded wife, | to have and to hold | from this day forward, | for better for worse, | for richer for poorer, | in sickness and in health, | to love and to cherish, | till death do us part, etc. Here it becomes mere blank verse which is, of course, a defect in prose style. In that delightful old French the Saj'a frequently appeared when attention was solicited for the titles of books, *e.g.* Le Romant de la Rose, où tout l'art d'amours est enclose.

expected; and a kindly critic writes of it, "These melodious fragments, these little eddies of song set like gems in the prose, have a charming effect on the ear. They come as dulcet surprises and mostly recur in highly-wrought situations, or they are used to convey a vivid sense of something exquisite in nature or art. Their introduction seems due to whim or caprice, but really it arises from a profound study of the situation, as if the Tale-teller felt suddenly compelled to break into the rhythmic strain."

B.—The Verse.

The Shi'r or metrical part of The Nights is considerable, amounting to not fewer than ten thousand lines, and these I could not but render in rhyme or rather in mono-rhyme. This portion has been a bugbear to translators. De Sacy noticed the difficulty of the task (p. 283). Lane held the poetry untranslatable because abounding in the figure Tajnís, our paronomasia or paragram, of which there are seven distinct varieties,[1] not to speak of other rhetorical flourishes. He therefore omitted the greater part of the verse as tedious and, through the loss of measure and rhyme, "generally intolerable to the reader." He proved his position by the bald literalism of the passages which he rendered in truly prosaic prose, and succeeded in changing the facies and present-ment of the work. For the Shi'r, like the Saj'a, is not introduced arbitrarily; and its unequal distribution throughout The Nights may be accounted for by rule of art. Some tales, like Omar bin al-Nu'uman and Tawaddud, contain very little, because the theme is historical or realistic; whilst in stories of love and courtship, as that of Rose-in-hood, the proportion may rise to one-fifth of the whole. And this is true to nature. Love, as Addison said, makes even the mechanic (the British mechanic!) poetical, and Joe Hume of material memory once fought a duel about a fair object of dispute.

Before discussing the verse of The Nights it may be advisable to enlarge a little upon the prosody of the Arabs. We know

1 See Gladwin, *loc. cit.* p. 8. Tajnis also is=alliteration (Ibn Khall. ii. 316).

nothing of the origin of their poetry, which is lost in the depths of antiquity, and the oldest bards of whom we have any remains belong to the famous epoch of the war Al-Basús, which would place them about A.D. 500. Moreover, when the Muse of Arabia first shows, she is not only fully developed and mature, she has lost all her first youth, her beauté du diable, and she is assuming the characteristics of an age beyond "middle age." No one can study the earliest poetry without perceiving that it results from the cultivation of centuries, and that it has already assumed that artificial type and conventional process of treatment which presages inevitable decay. Its noblest period is included in the century preceding the Apostolate of Mohammed and the oldest of that epoch is the prince of Arab songsters, Imr al-Kays, "The Wandering King." The Christian Fathers characteristically termed poetry Vinum Dæmonorum. The stricter Moslems called their bards "enemies of Allah"; and when the Prophet, who hated verse and could not even quote it correctly, was asked who was the best poet of the Peninsula, he answered that the "Man of Al-Kays," *i.e.* the worshipper of the Priapus-idol, would usher them all into Hell. Here he only echoed the general verdict of his countrymen who loved poetry and, as a rule, despised poets. The earliest complete pieces of any volume and substance saved from the wreck of old Arabic literature and familiar in our day are the seven Kasídahs (purpose-odes or tendence-elegies) which are popularly known as the Gilded or the Suspended Poems; and in all of these we find, with an elaboration of material and formal art which can go no further, a subject-matter of trite imagery and stock ideas which suggest a long ascending line of model ancestors and predecessors. Scholars are agreed upon the fact that many of the earliest and best Arab poets were, as Mohammed boasted himself, unalphabetic[1] or rather could neither read nor write. They addressed

---

1 He called himself "Nabiyun ummi" = illiterate prophet; but only his most ignorant followers believe that he was unable to read and write. His last words, accepted by all traditionists, were "Aatíní dawáta wa kalam" (bring me ink-case and pen); upon which the Shi'ah or Persian sectaries base, not without probability, a theory that Mohammed intended to write down the name of Ali as his Caliph or successor, when Omar, suspecting the intention, exclaimed, "The Prophet is delirious; have we not the Koran?" thus impiously

the ear and the mind, not the eye. They "spoke verse," learning it by rote, and dictating it to the Ráwi, and this reciter again transmitted it to the musician whose pipe or zither accompanied the minstrel's song. In fact the general practice of writing began only at the end of the first century after The Flight.

The rude and primitive measure of Arab song, upon which the most complicated system of metres subsequently arose, was called Al-Rajaz, literally "the trembling," because it reminded the highly imaginative hearer of a pregnant she-camel's weak and tottering steps. This was the carol of the camel-driver, the lover's lay, and the warrior's chaunt of the heroic ages; and its simple, unconstrained flow adapted it well for extempore effusions. Its merits and demerits have been extensively discussed amongst Arab grammarians and many, noticing that it was not originally divided into hemistichs, make an essential difference between the Shá'ir who speaks poetry and the Rájiz who speaks Rajaz. It consisted, to describe it technically, of iambic dipodia (⏑ - ⏑ -), the first three syllables being optionally long or short. It can generally be read like our iambs and, being familiar, is pleasant to the English ear. The dipodia are repeated either twice or thrice; in the former case Rajaz is held by some authorities, as Al-Akhfash (Sa'íd ibn Másadah), to be mere prose. Although Labid and Antar composed in iambics, the first Kasídah or regular poem in Rajaz was by Al-Aghlab al-Ajibi, temp. Mohammed: the Alfíyah-grammar of Ibn Málik is in Rajaz Muzdawij, the hemistichs rhyming and the assonance being confined to the couplet. Al-Hariri also affects Rajaz in the third and fifth assemblies. So far Arabic metre is true to Nature: in impassioned speech the movement of language is iambic: we say "I *will*, I *will*," not "I will."

For many generations the Sons of the Desert were satisfied with Nature's teaching; the fine perceptions and the nicely trained ear of the bard needing no aid from art. But in time came the inevitable prosodist under the formidable name of Abu Abd al-

preventing the precaution. However that may be, the legend proves that Mohammed could read and write even when not "under inspiration." The vulgar idea would arise from a pious intent to add miracle to the miraculous style of the Koran.

Rahmán al-Khalíl, i. Ahmad, i. Amrú, i. Tamím al-Faráhidi (of the Faráhid sept), al-Azdi (of the Azd clan), al-Yahmadi (of the Yahmad tribe), popularly known as Al-Khalíl ibn Ahmad al-Basri, of Bassorah, where he died æt. 68 (scanning verses they say), in A.H. 170 (=786-87). Ibn Khallikán relates (i. 493) on the authority of Hamzah al-Isfaháni how this "father of Arabic grammar and discoverer of the rules of prosody" invented the science as he walked past a coppersmith's shop on hearing the strokes of a hammer upon a metal basin: "two objects devoid of any quality which could serve as a proof and an illustration of anything else than their own form and shape, and incapable of leading to any other knowledge than that of their own nature.[1]" According to others he was passing through the Fullers' Bazar at Basrah when his ear was struck by the Dak-dak (دق دق) and the Dakak-dakak (دقق دقق) of the workmen. In these two onomapoetics we trace the expression which characterises the Arab tongue: all syllables are composed of consonant and vowel, the latter long or short as Bā and Bă; or of a vowelled consonant followed by a consonant as Bal, Bau (بو).

The grammarian, true to the traditions of his craft which looks for all poetry to the Badawi,[2] adopted for metrical details

---

1 I cannot but vehemently suspect that this legend was bodily taken from much older traditions. We have Jubal, the semi-mythical, who, "by the different falls of his hammer on the anvil, discovered by ear the first rude music that pleased the antediluvian fathers." Then came Pythagoras, of whom Macrobius (lib. ii.) relates how this Græco-Egyptian philosopher, passing by a smithy, observed that the sounds were grave or acute according to the weights of the hammers; and he ascertained by experiment that such was the case when different weights were hung by strings of the same size. The next discovery was that two strings of the same substance and tension, the one being double the length of the other, gave the diapason-interval or an eighth; and the same was effected from two strings of similar length and size, the one having four times the tension of the other. Belonging to the same cycle of invention-anecdotes are Galileo's discovery of the pendulum by the lustre of the Pisan Duomo; and the kettle-lid, the falling apple, and the copper hook which inspired Watt, Newton, and Galvani. Compare the legend of Handel's "Harmonious Blacksmith," a motif (very simple, with variations) which he heard a blacksmith singing in his forge, where he took refuge during rain.

2 To what an absurd point this has been carried we may learn from Ibn Khallikan (i. 114). A poet addressing a single individual does not say, "My friend!" or "My friends!" but "My two friends!" (in the dual) *because* a Badawi required a pair of companions, one to tend the sheep and the other pasture the camels.

the language of the Desert. The distich, which amongst Arabs is looked upon as one line, he named "Bayt," nighting-place, tent or house; and the hemistich Misrá'ah, the one leaf of a folding door. To this "scenic" simile all the parts of the verse were more or less adapted. The metres, our feet, were called "Arkán," the stakes and stays of the tent; the syllables were "Usúl" or roots divided into three kinds: the first or "Sabab" (the tent-rope) is composed of two letters, a vowelled and a quiescent consonant as "Lam.[1]" "The Watad" or tent-peg of three letters is of two varieties; the Majmú', or united, a foot (iamb) in which the first two consonants are moved by vowels, and the last is jazmated or made quiescent by apocope as "Lakad"; and the Mafrúk, or disunited, when the two moved consonants are separated by one jazmated, as "Kabla." And lastly the "Fásilah" or intervening space, applied to the main pole of the tent, consists of four letters.

The metres were called Buhúr or "seas" (plur. of Báhr), also meaning the space within the tent-walls, the equivoque alluding to pearls and other treasures of the deep. Al-Khalil, the systematiser, found in general use only five Dáirah (circles, classes, or groups of metre); and he characterised the harmonious and stately measures, all built upon the original Rajaz, as Al-Tawil (the long),[2] Al-Kámil (the complete), Al-Wáfir (the copious), Al-Basit (the extended), and Al-Khafif (the light).[3] These embrace all the Mu'allakát and the Hamásah, the great Anthology of Abú Tammám; but the crave for variety and the extension of foreign intercourse had multiplied wants and Al-Khalil deduced, from the original five Dáirah, fifteen, to which Al-Akhfash (ob. A.D. 830) added a sixteenth, Al-Khabab. The Persians extended the number to nineteen: the first four were peculiarly Arab; the fourteenth, the fifteenth and seventeenth peculiarly Persian, and all the rest were Arab and Persian.[4]

1 For further details concerning the Sabab, Watad and Fasilah, see at the end of this Essay the learned remarks of Dr. Steingass.

2 *e.g.* the Mu'allakats of "Amriolkais," Tarafah and Zubayr compared by Mr. Lyall (Introduction to Translations) with the metre of Abt Vogler, *e.g.*:

Ye know why the forms are fair, ye hear how the tale is told.

3 *e.g.* the Poem of Hareth which often echoes the hexameter.

4 Gladwin, p. 80.

Arabic metre so far resembles that of Greece and Rome that the value of syllables depends upon the "quantity" or position of their consonants, not upon accent, as in English and the Neo-Latin tongues. Al-Khalil was doubtless familiar with the classic prosody of Europe, but he rejected it as unsuited to the genius of Arabic and like a true Eastern Gelehrte he adopted a process devised by himself. Instead of scansion by pyrrhics and spondees, iambs and trochees, anapæsts, and similar simplifications, he invented a system of weights ("wuzún"). Of these there are nine[1] memorial words used as quantitive signs, all built upon the root "fa'l," which has rendered such notable service to Arabic and Hebrew[2] grammar and varying from the simple "fa'ál," in Persian "fa'úl," (⏑ –) to the complicated "Mutafá'ilun" (⏑⏑ - ⏑ -), anapæst + iamb. Thus the prosodist would scan the Shahnámeh of Firdausi as

Fa'úlun, fa'úlun, fa'úlun, fa'úl.

⏑ - - ⏑ - - ⏑ - - ⏑ -

These weights also show another peculiarity of Arabic verse. In English we have few if any spondees: the Arabic contains about three longs to one short; hence its gravity, stateliness, and dignity. But these longs again are peculiar, and sometimes strike the European ear as shorts, thus adding a difficulty for those who would represent Oriental metres by western feet, ictus and accent. German Arabists can register an occasional success in such attempts: Englishmen none. My late friend Professor Palmer of Cambridge tried the tour de force of dancing on one leg instead of two, and notably failed: Mr. Lyall also strove to imitate Arabic metre and produced only prose bewitched.[3] Mr.

1 Gladwin (p. 77) gives only eight, omitting Fă'ūl which he, or his author, probably considers the Muzáhaf, imperfect or apocopêd form of Fă'ūlūn, as Măfā'īl of Măfā'īlūn. For the infinite complications of Arabic prosody the Khafif (soft breathing) and Sahih (hard breathing); the Sadr and Arúz (first and last feet), the Ibtidá and Zarb (last foot of every line); the Hashw (cushion-stuffing) or body-part of verse; the 'Amúd al-Kasídah or Al-Musammat (the strong), and other details, I must refer readers to such specialists as Freytag and Sam. Clarke (Prosodia Arabica), and to Dr. Steingass's notes *infra*.

2 The Hebrew grammarians of the Middle Ages wisely copied their Arab. cousins by turning Fa'la into Pael and so forth.

3 Mr. Lyall, whose "Ancient Arabic Poetry" (Williams and Norgate, 1885) I reviewed in *The Academy* of Oct. 3, '85, did the absolute reverse of what

Payne appears to me to have wasted trouble in "observing the exterior form of the stanza, the movement of the rhyme, and (as far as possible) the identity in number of the syllables composing the beits." There is only one part of his admirable version concerning which I have heard competent readers complain; and that is the metrical, because here and there it sounds strange to their ears.

I have already stated my conviction that there are two and only two ways of translating Arabic poetry into English. One is to represent it by good heroic or lyric verse, as did Sir William Jones; the other is to render it after French fashion, by measured and balanced Prose, the little sister of Poetry. It is thus and thus only that we can preserve the peculiar *cachet* of the original. This old-world Oriental song is spirit-stirring as a "blast of that dread horn," albeit the words be thin. It is heady as the "Golden Wine" of Libanus, to the tongue water and brandy to the brain —the clean contrary of our nineteenth-century effusions. Technically speaking, it can be vehicled only by the verse of the old English ballad or by the prose of the Book of Job. And Badawi poetry is a perfect expositor of Badawi life, especially in the good and gladsome old Pagan days ere Al-Islam, like the creed which it abolished, overcast the minds of men with its dull grey pall of realistic superstition. They combined to form a marvellous picture—those contrasts of splendour and squalor amongst the sons of the sand. Under airs pure as æther, golden and ultramarine above and melting over the horizon into a diaphanous green which suggested a reflection of Kaf, that unseen mountain-wall of emerald, the so-called Desert changed face twice a year; now brown and dry as summer-dust; then green as Hope, beautified with infinite verdure and broad sheetings of rain-water. The vernal and autumnal shiftings of camp, disruptions of homesteads, and partings of kith and kin, friends and lovers, made the life,

---

is required: he preserved the metre and sacrificed the rhyme even when it naturally suggested itself. For instance, in the last four lines of No. xli. what would be easier than to write—

> Ah sweet and soft wi' thee her ways: bethink thee well! The day shall be
> When some one favoured as thyself shall find her fair and fain and free;
> And if she swear that parting ne'er shall break her word of constancy,
> When did rose-tinted finger-tip with pacts and pledges e'er agree?

many-sided as it was, vigorous and noble, the outcome of hardy frames, strong minds, and spirits breathing the very essence of liberty and independence. The day began with the dawn-drink, "generous wine bought with shining ore," poured into the crystal goblet from the leather bottle swinging before the cooling breeze. The rest was spent in the practice of weapons; in the favourite arrow-game known as Al-Maysar, gambling which at least had the merit of feeding the poor; in racing, for which the Badawin had a mania, and in the chase, the foray and the fray which formed the serious business of his life. And how picturesque the hunting scenes; the greyhound, like the mare, of purest blood; the falcon cast at francolin and coney; the gazelle standing at gaze; the desert ass scudding over the ground-waves; the wild cows or bovine antelopes browsing with their calves, and the ostrich-chickens flocking round the parent bird! The Musámarah or night-talk round the camp-fire was enlivened by the lute-girl and the glee-man, whom the austere Prophet described as "roving distraught in every vale," and whose motto in Horatian vein was, "To-day we shall drink, to-morrow be sober; wine this day, that day work." Regularly once a year, during the three peaceful months when war and even blood revenge were held sacrilegious, the tribes met at Ukádh (Ocaz) and other fair-steads, where they held high festival and the bards strave in song and prided themselves upon doing honour to women and to the successful warriors of their tribe. Brief, the object of Arab life was to *be*—to be free, to be brave, to be wise; while the endeavours of other peoples was and is to *have*—to have wealth, to have knowledge, to have a name; and while moderns make their "epitome of life" to be, to do, and to *suffer*. Lastly the Arab's end was honourable as his life was stirring: few Badawin had the crowning misfortune of dying "the straw-death."

The poetical forms in The Nights are as follows:—The Misrá'ah or hemistich is half the "Bayt" which, for want of a better word, I have rendered couplet: this, however, though formally separated in MSS. is looked upon as one line, one verse; hence a word can be divided, the former part pertaining to the first and the latter to the second moiety of the distich. As the Arabs ignore blank verse, when we come upon a rhymeless couplet we know that it is an extract from a longer composition in monorhyme. The Kit'ah is a fragment, either an occasional piece or more frequently a portion of a Ghazal (ode) or Kasídah (elegy), other than the Matlá, the initial Bayt with rhyming distichs. The Ghazal and Kasídah differ mainly in length: the former is popularly limited to eighteen couplets: the latter begins at fifteen and is of indefinite number. Both are built upon monorhyme, which appears twice in the first couplet and ends all the others, *e.g.*, aa + ba + ca, etc., nor may the same assonance be repeated, unless at least seven couplets intervene. In the best poets, as in the old classic verse of France, the sense must be completed in one couplet and not run on to a second; and, as the parts cohere very loosely, separate quotation can generally be made without injuring their proper effect. A favourite form is the Rubá'i or quatrain, made familiar to English ears by Mr. Fitzgerald's masterly adaptation of Omar-i-Khayyám: the movement is generally aa + ba; but it also appears as ab + cb, in which case it is a Kit'ah or fragment. The Murabbá, tetrastichs or four-fold song, occurs once only in The Nights (vol. i. p. 90); it is a succession of double Bayts or of four-lined stanzas rhyming aa + bc + dc + ec: in strict form the first three hemistichs rhyme with one another only, independently of the rest of the poem, and the fourth with that of every other stanza, *e.g.*, aa + ab + cb + db. The Mukhammas, cinquains or pentastichs (night cmlxiv.), represents a stanza of two distichs and a hemistich in monorhyme, the fifth line being the "bob" or burden: each succeeding stanza affects a new rhyme, except in the fifth line, *e.g.*, aaaab + ccccb + ddddb, and so forth. The Muwwál is a simple popular song in four to six lines; specimens of it are given in the Egyptian grammar of my friend the late Dr. Wilhelm Spitta.[1] The Muwashshah, or ornamented verse, has two main divisions: one applies to our acrostics in which the

---

1 See p 439. Grammatik des Arabischen Vulgär Dialekts von Ægyptien, by Dr. Wilhelm Spitta Bey, Leipzig, 1880. In pp. 489-493 he gives specimens of eleven Mawáwil varying in length from four to fifteen lines. The assonance mostly attempts monorhyme: in two tetrastichs it is aa + ba, and it does not disdain alternates, ab + ab + ab.

initials form a word or words; the other is a kind of Musaddas, or sextines, which occurs once only in The Nights (cmlxxxvii.). It consists of three couplets or six-line strophes: all the hemistichs of the first are in monorhyme; in the second and following stanzas the first three hemistichs take a new rhyme, but the fourth resumes the assonance of the first set and is followed by the third couplet of No. 1, serving as bob or refrain, *e.g.* aaaaaa + bbbaaa + cccaaa, and so forth. It is the most complicated of all the measures, and is held to be of Morisco or Hispano-Moorish origin.

Mr. Lane (Lex.) lays down, on the lines of Ibn Khallikan (i. 476, etc.) and other representative literati, as our sole authorities for pure Arabic, the precedence in following order. First of all ranks the Jáhili (Ignoramus) of The Ignorance, the Ἀραβίας ἄρειον ἔθνος: these pagans left hemistichs, couplets, pieces, and elegies which once composed a large corpus and which is now mostly forgotten. Hammád al-Ráwiyah, the Reciter, a man of Persian descent (ob. A.H. 160=777) who first collected the Mu'allakát, once recited by rote in a séance before Caliph Al-Walid two thousand poems of præ-Mohammedan bards.[1] After the Jáhili stands the Mukhadram or Muhadrim, the "Spurious," because half Pagan half Moslem, who flourished either immediately before or soon after the preaching of Mohammed. The Islámi or full-blooded Moslem at the end of the first century A.H. (=720) began the process of corruption in language; and lastly, he was followed by the Muwallad of the second century, who fused Arabic with non-Arabic, and in whom purity of diction disappeared.

I have noticed (1 § A.) that the versical portion of The Nights may be distributed into three categories. First are the olden poems which are held classical by all modern Arabs; then comes the mediæval poetry, the effusions of that brilliant throng which adorned the splendid Court of Harun al-Rashid and which ended with Al-Hariri (ob. A.H. 516); and, lastly, are the various *pièces de circonstance* suggested to editors or scribes by the occasion.

1 Al-Siyuti, p. 235, from Ibn Khallikan. Our knowledge of oldest Arab verse is drawn chiefly from the Kitáb al-Aghání (Song-book) of Abu al-Faraj the Isfaháni who flourished A.H. 284-356 (=897-969); it was printed at the Bulak Press in 1868.

It is not my object to enter upon the historical part of the subject: a mere sketch would have neither value nor interest, whilst a finished picture would lead too far: I must be contented to notice a few of the most famous names.

Of the præ-Islamites, we have Ádi bin Zayd al-Ibádi the "celebrated poet" of Ibn Khallikán (i. 188); Nábighat (the full-grown) al-Zubyáni who flourished at the Court of Al-Nu'man in A.D. 580-602, and whose poem is compared with the "Suspendeds,[1]" and Al-Mutalammis the "pertinacious" satirist, friend, and intimate with Tarafah of the "Prize Poem." About Mohammed's day we find Imr al-Kays "with whom poetry began," to end with Zú al-Rummah; Amrú bin Mádi Karab al-Zubaydi, Labid; Ka'b ibn Zubayr, the father one of the Mu'allakah-poets, and the son author of the Burdah or Mantle-poem (see night cclxxvii.) and Abbás bin Mirdás who lampooned the Prophet and had "his tongue cut out," *i.e.*, received a double share of booty from Ali. In the days of Caliph Omar we have Alkamah bin Olátha followed by Jamil bin Ma'mar of the Banu Ozrah (ob. A.H. 82), who loved Azzá. Then came Al-Kuthayyir (the dwarf, *ironicè*), the lover of Buthaynah, "who was so lean that birds might be cut to bits with her bones": the latter was also a poetess (Ibn Khall. i. 87), like Hind bint al-Nu'man who made herself so disagreeable to Al-Hajjáj (ob. A.H. 95). Jarir al-Khatafah, the noblest of the Islami poets in the first century, is noticed at full length by Ibn Khallikan (i. 294) together with his rival in poetry and debauchery, Abú Firás Hammám or Homaym bin Ghalib al-Farazdak, the Tamimi, the Ommiade poet "without whose verse half Arabic would be lost[2]": he exchanged satires with Jarir and died forty days before him (A.H. 110). Another contemporary, forming the poetical triumvirate of the period, was the debauched Christian poet Al-Akhtal al-Taghlibi. They were followed by Al-Ahwas al-Ansári, whose witty lampoons banished him to Dahlak Island in the Red Sea (ob. A.H. 179 = 795); by Bashshár ibn Burd and by Yúnus ibn Habib (ob. A.H. 182).

The well-known names of the Harun-cycle are Al-Asma'i,

---

1 See Lyall, *loc. cit.* p 97

2 His Diwán has been published with a French translation, par R. Boucher, Paris, Labitte, 1870.

rhetorician and poet, whose epic with Antar for hero is not forgotten (ob. A.H. 216); Isaac of Mosul (Ishak bin Ibrahim of Persian origin); Al-'Utbi "the Poet" (ob. A.H. 228); Abu al-Abbás al-Rakáshi; Abu al-Athiyah, the lover of Otbah; Muslim bin al-Walid al-Ansari; Abú Tammám of Tay, compiler of the Hamásah (ob. A.H. 230), "A Muwallad of the first class" (says Ibn Khallikan, i. 392); the famous or infamous Abu Nowás; Abu Mus'ab (Ahmad ibn Ali) who died in A.H. 242; the satirist Dibil al-Khuzái (ob. A.H. 246) and a host of others quos nunc perscribere longum est. They were followed by Al-Bohtori "the Poet" (ob. A.H. 286); the royal author Abdullah ibn al-Mu'tazz (ob. A.H. 315); Ibn Abbád the Sahib (ob. A.H. 334); Mansúr al-Halláj the martyred Sufi; the Sahib ibn Abbad; Abu Faras al-Hamdáni (ob. A.H. 357); Al-Námi (ob. A.H. 399) who had many encounters with that model Chauvinist Al-Mutanabbi, nicknamed Al-Mutanabbih (the "wide-awake"), killed A.H. 354; Al-Manázi of Manazjird (ob. A.H. 427); Al-Tughrai, author of the Lámiyat al-'Ajam (ob. A.H. 375); Al-Hariri, the model rhetorician (ob. A.H. 516); Al-Hájiri al-Irbili, of Arbela (ob. A.H. 632); Babá al-Din al-Sinjari (ob. A.H. 622); Al-Kátib or the Scribe (ob. A.H. 656); Abdun Al-Andalúsi the Spaniard (our xiith century) and about the same time Al Náwaji, author of the Halbat al-Kumayt, or "Race-course of the Bay-horse"—poetical slang for wine.[1]

---

1 I find also minor quotations from the Imám Abu al-Hasan al-Askari (of Sarra man raa) ob. A.D. 868; Ibn Makúla (murdered in A.D. 862?); Ibn Durayd (ob. A.D. 933); Al-Zahr the Poet (ob. A.D. 963); Abu Bakr al-Zubaydi (ob. A.D. 989); Kábús ibn Wushmaghır (murdered in A.D. 1012-13). Ibn Nabatah the Poet (ob. A.D. 1015); Ibn al-Sa'ati (ob. A.D. 1028); Ibn Zaydun al-Andalusi who died at Hums (Emessa, the Arab name for Seville) in A.D. 1071; Al-Mu'tasim ibn Sumadih (ob. A.D. 1091); Al-Murtaza ibn al-Shahrozuri the Sufi (ob. A.D. 1117); Ibn Sara al-Shantaráni (of Santarem) who sang of Hind, and died A.D. 1123; Ibn al-Kházin (ob. A.D. 1124); Ibn Kalakis (ob. A.D. 1172); Ibn al-Ta'wizi (ob. A.D. 1188); Ibn Zabádah (ob. A.D. 1198); Babá al-Dín Zuhayr (ob. A.D. 1249); Muwaffak al-Din Muzaffar ob. A.D. 1266, and sundry others. Notices of Al-Utayyah (vol. i. p. 9), of Ibn al-Sumám (vol. i. night ix), and of Ibn Sáhib al-Ishbíli, of Seville (vol. i. night x.), are deficient. The most notable point in Arabic verse is its savage satire, the language of excited "destructiveness" which characterises the Badawi: he is "keen for satire as a thirsty man for water," and half his poetry seems to consist of foul innuendo, of lampoons, and of gross personal abuse.

Of the third category, the pièces d'occasion, little need be said. I may refer readers to my notes on the doggrels in nights xxxvii., lxxi., lxxii., lxxv., c., ccclxxviii., dcccl., dcccli, &c., &c.

Having a mortal aversion to the details of Arabic prosody, I have persuaded my friend Dr. Steingass to undertake in the following pages the subject as far as concerns the poetry of The Nights. He has been kind enough to collaborate with me from the beginning, and to his minute lexicographical knowledge I am deeply indebted for discovering not a few blemishes which would have been "nuts to the critic." The learned Arabist's notes will be highly interesting to students: mine (§ V.) are intended to give a superficial and popular idea of the Arab's verse-mechanism.

The principle of Arabic Prosody (called 'Arúz, pattern standard, or 'Ilm al-'Arúz, science of the 'Arúz), in so far resembles that of classical poetry, as it chiefly rests on metrical weight, not on accent, or in other words a verse is measured by short and long quantities, while the accent only regulates its rhythm. In Greek and Latin, however, the quantity of the syllables depends on their vowels, which may be either naturally short or long, or become long by position, *i.e.* if followed by two or more consonants. We all remember from our school-days what a fine string of rules had to be committed to and kept in memory, before we were able to scan a Latin or Greek verse, without breaking its neck by tripping over false quantities. In Arabic, on the other hand, the answer to the question, what is metrically long or short, is exceedingly simple, and flows with stringent cogency from the nature of the Arabic Alphabet. This, strictly speaking, knows only consonants (Harf, pl. Hurúf). The vowels which are required, in order to articulate the consonants, were at first not represented in writing at all. They had to be supplied by the reader, and are not improperly called "motions" (Harakát), because they move or lead on as it were, one letter to another. They are three in number, a (Fathah), i (Kasrah), u (Zammah), originally sounded as the corresponding English vowels in bat, bit and butt respectively, but in certain cases modifying their pronunciation under the influence of a neighhouring consonant. When the necessity made itself felt to represent them in writing, especially for the sake of fixing the correct reading of the Koran, they were rendered by additional signs, placed above or beneath the consonant, after which they are pronounced, in a similar way as it is done in some systems of English shorthand. A consonant followed by a short vowel is called a "moved letter" (Muharrakah); a consonant without such vowel is called "resting" or "quiescent" (Sákinah), and can stand only at the end of a syllable or word.

And now we are able to formulate the *one* simple rule, which determines the prosodical quantity in Arabic: any moved letter, as ta, li, mu, is counted short; any moved letter followed by a quiescent one, as taf, lun, mus, *i.e.* any closed syllable beginning and terminating with a consonant and having a short vowel between, forms a long quantity. This is certainly a relief in comparison with the numerous rules of classical Prosody, proved by not a few exceptions, which for instance in Dr. Smith's elementary Latin Grammar fill eight closely-printed pages.

Before I proceed to show how from the prosodical unities, the moved and the quiescent letter, first the metrical elements, then the feet and lastly the metres are built up, it will be necessary to obviate a few misunderstandings, to which our mode of transliterating Arabic into the Roman character might give rise.

The line:—

"Love in my heart they lit and went their ways" (vol. i. night xxiii.),

runs in Arabic:—

"Akámú al-wajda fí kalbi wa sárú." (Mac. Ed. i. 179.)

Here, according to our ideas, the word akámú would begin with a short vowel a, and contain two long vowels á and ú; according to Arabic views neither is the case. The word begins with "Alif," and its second syllable ká closes in Alif after Fathah (a), in the same way, as the third syllable mú closes in the letter Wáw (w) after Zammah (u).

The question, therefore, arises, what is "Alif"? It is the first of the twenty-eight Arabic letters, and has through the medium of the Greek Alpha nominally entered into our alphabet, where it now plays rather a misleading part. Curiously enough, however, Greek itself has preserved for us the key to the real nature of the letter. In Ἀλφα the initial a is preceded by the so-called spiritus lenis ('), a sign which must be placed in front or at the top of any vowel beginning a Greek word, and which represents that slight aspiration or soft breathing almost involuntarily uttered, when we try to pronounce a vowel by itself. We need not go far to find how deeply rooted this tendency is and to what exaggerations it will sometimes lead, nay, how it will revenge itself by a curious counterpart or equipoise, the dropping of the rightful aspirate. We deeply sympathise with the terror of the good clergyman's wife, who, on enquiring, "What place is this?" received from the railway porter the terse rejoinder: "Hell, M'am" (Elmham). This spiritus lenis is the silent h of the French "homme" and the English "honour," corresponding exactly to the Arabic Hamzah, whose mere prop the Alif is, when it is moved by any of the three vowel-signs at the beginning or by Fathah in the middle and at the end of a word; a native Arabic Dictionary does not begin with Báb al-Alif (Gate or Chapter of the Alif), but with Báb al-Hamzah. What the Greeks call Alpha and have transmitted to us as a name for the vowel a, is in fact nothing else but the Arabic Hamzah-Alif (أ), moved by Fathah, *i.e.* bearing the sign (ـَ) for a at the top (أَ), just as it might have the sign *Zammah* (ـُ) superscribed to express u (أُ), or the sign Kasrah (ـِ) subjoined to represent i (إ). In each case the Hamzah-Alif, although scarcely audible to our ear, is the real letter and might fitly be rendered in transliteration by the above-mentioned silent h, wherever we make an Arabic word begin with a vowel not preceded by any other sign. This latter restriction refers to the sign ('), which in Sir Richard Burton's translation of The Nights, as frequently in books published in this country, is used to represent the Arabic letter ع in whose very name 'Ayn it occurs. The 'Ayn is "described as produced by a smart compression of the upper part of the windpipe and forcible emission of breath," imparting a guttural tinge to a following or preceding vowel-sound; but it is by no means a mere guttural vowel, as Professor Palmer styles it. For Europeans, who do not belong to the Israelitic dispensation, as well as for Turks and Persians, its exact pronunciation is most difficult, if not impossible to acquire.

In reading Arabic from transliteration for the purpose of scanning poetry, we have therefore in the first instance to keep in mind that no Arabic word or syllable can begin with a vowel. Where our mode of rendering Arabic in the Roman character would make this appear to be the case, either Hamzah (silent h), or 'Ayn (represented by the sign ') is the real initial, and the only element to be taken in account as a *letter*. It follows as a self-evident corollary that wherever a single consonant stands between two vowels, it never closes the previous syllable, but always opens the next one. Our word "Akámú," for instance, can only be divided into the syllables: A (properly Ha)-ká-mú, never into Ak-á-mú or Ak-ám-ú.

It has been stated above that the syllable ká is closed by the letter Alif after Fathah, in the same way as the syllable mú is closed by the letter Wáw, and I may add now, as the word fí is closed by the letter Yá (y). To make this perfectly clear, I must repeat that the Arabic Alphabet, as it was originally written, deals only with consonants. The signs for the short vowel-sounds were added later for a special purpose, and are generally not represented even in printed books, *e.g.* in the various editions of The Nights, where only quotations from the Koran or poetical passages are provided with the vowel-points. But among those consonants there are three, called weak letters (Hurúf al-'illah), which have a particular organic affinity to these vowel-sounds; the guttural Hamzah, which is akin to a; the palatal Yá, which is related to i; and the labial Wáw, which is homogeneous with u. Where any of the weak letters follows a vowel of its own class, either at the end of a word or being itself followed by another consonant, it draws out or lengthens the preceding vowel and is in this sense called a letter of prolongation (Harf al-Madd). Thus, bearing in mind that the Hamzah is in reality a silent h, the syllable ká might be written kah, similarly to the German word "sah," where the h is not pronounced either, but imparts a lengthened sound to the a. In like manner mú and fí are written in Arabic muw and fiy respectively, and form long quantities not because they contain a vowel long by nature, but because their initial "Muharrakah" is followed by a "Sákinah," exactly as in the previously mentioned syllables taf, lun, mus.[1] In the Roman

1 If the letter preceding Wáw or Yá is moved by Fathah, they produce the diphthongs au (aw), pronounced like ou in "bout," and ai, pronounced as i in "bite."

transliteration, Akámú forms a word of five letters, two of which are consonants, and three vowels; in Arabic it represents the combination H(a)k(a)hm(u)w, consisting also of five letters but all consonants, the intervening vowels being expressed in writing either merely by superadded external signs, or more frequently not at all. Metrically, it represents one short and two long quantities (⏑ - -), forming in Latin a trisyllabic foot, called Bacchius, and in Arabic a quinqueliteral "Rukn" (pillar) or "Juz" (part, portion), the technical designation for which we shall introduce presently.

There is one important remark more to be made with regard to the Hamzah: at the beginning of a word it is either conjunctive, Hamzat al-Wasl, or disjunctive, Hamzat al Kat'. The difference is best illustrated by reference to the French so-called aspirated h, as compared with the above-mentioned silent h. If the latter, as initial of a noun, is preceded by the article, the article loses its vowel, and, ignoring the silent h altogether, is read with the following noun almost as one word: le homme becomes l'homme (pronounced lomme), as le ami becomes l'ami. This resembles very closely the Arabic Hamzah Wasl. If, on the other hand, a French word begins with an aspirated h, as for instance héros, the article does not drop its vowel before the noun, nor is the h sounded as in the English word "hero," but the effect of the aspirate is simply to keep the two vowel sounds apart, so as to pronounce le éros with a slight hiatus between, and this is exactly what happens in the case of the Arabic Hamzah Kat'.

With regard to the Wasl, however, Arabic goes a step further than French. In the French example, quoted above, we have seen it is the silent h and the *preceding* vowel, which are eliminated; in Arabic both the Hamzah and its own Harakah, *i.e.* the short vowel *following* it, are supplanted by their antecedent. Another example will make this clear. The most common instance of the Hamzah Wasl is the article al (for h(a)l = the Hebrew hal), where it is moved by Fathah. But it has this sound only at the beginning of a sentence or speech, as in "Al-hamdu" at the head of the Fatihah, or in

"Alláhu" at the beginning of the third Surah. If the two words stand in grammatical connection, as in the sentence, "Praise be to God," we cannot say Al-Hamdu li-Alláhi," but the junction (Wasl) between the dative particle li and the noun which it governs must take place. According to the French principle, this junction would be effected at the cost of the preceding element and li Alláhi would become l'Alláhí; in Arabic, on the contrary, the kasrated l of the particle takes the place of the following fathated Hamzah and we read li 'lláhi instead. Proceeding in the Fatihah we meet with the verse, "Iyyáka na'budu wa iyyáka nasta'ínu," Thee do we worship and of Thee do we ask aid. Here the Hamzah of iyyáka (properly hiyyáka with silent h) is disjunctive, and therefore its pronunciation remains the same at the beginning and in the middle of the sentence, or to put it differently, instead of coalescing with the preceding wa into wa'yyáka, the two words are kept separate by the Hamzah, reading wa iyyáka, just as it was the case with the French Le héros.

If the conjunctive Hamzah is preceded by a quiescent letter, this takes generally Kasrah: "Tálat al-Laylah," the night was longsome, would become Tálati 'l-Laylah. If, however, the quiescent letter is one of prolongation, it mostly drops out altogether, and the Harakah of the next preceding letter becomes the connecting vowel between the two words, which in our parlance would mean, that the end-vowel of the first word is shortened before the elided initial of the second. Thus "fí al-bayti," in the house, which in Arabic is written f(i)y h(a)l-b(a)yt(i) and which we transliterate fí 'l-bayti, is in poetry read fil-bayti, where we must remember that the syllable fil, in spite of its short vowel, represents a long quantity, because it consists of a moved letter followed by a quiescent one. Fíl would be over-long and could, according to Arabic prosody, stand only in certain cases at the end of a verse, *i.e.* in pause, where a natural tendency prevails to prolong a sound.

The attentive reader will now be able to fix the prosodical value of the line quoted above with unerring security. For metrical purposes it syllabifies into: A-ká-mul-waj-da fí kal-bí wa sá-rú, containing three short and eight long quantities. The initial unaccented a is short, for the same reason why the syllables da and wa are so, that is, because it corresponds to an Arabic letter, the Hamzah or silent h, moved by Fathah. The syllables ká, fí, bi, sá, rú, are long for the same reason, why the syllables mul, waj, kal, are so, that is, because the accent in the transliteration corresponds to a quiescent Arabic letter, following a moved one. The same simple criterion applies to all the poetical pieces contained in the Mac. edition.

The prosodical unities, then, in Arabic are the moved and the quiescent letter, and we are now going to show how they combine into metrical elements, feet, and metres.

i. The metrical elements (Usúl) are:—

1. The Sabab,[1] which consists of *two* letters and is either khafif (like) or sakíl (heavy). A moved letter followed by a quiescent, *i.e.* a closed syllable, like the afore-mentioned taf, lun, mus, to which we may now add fá = fah, 'í = 'iy, 'ú = 'uw, from a Sabab khafif, corresponding to the classical long quantity (-). Two moved letters in succession, like muta, 'ala, constitute a Sabab sakíl, for which the classical name would be Pyrrhic (⏑ ⏑). As in Latin and Greek, they are equal in weight and can frequently interchange, that is to say, the Sabab khafíf can be evolved into a sakíl by moving its second Harf, or the latter contracted into the former, by making its second letter quiescent.

2. The Watad, consisting of *three* letters, one of which is quiescent. If the quiescent follows the two moved ones, the Watad is called majmú' (collected or joined), as fa'ú (= fa'uw), mafá (= mafah), 'ilun, and it corresponds to the classical Iambus (⏑ -). If, on the contrary, the quiescent intervenes or separates between the two moved letters, as in fá'i (= fah'i), látu (= lahtu), taf'i, the Watan is called mafrúk (separated), and has its classical equivalent in the Trochee (- ⏑).

3. The Fásilah,[2] containing *four* letters, *i.e.* three moved ones

---

1 For the explanation of this name and those of the following terms, see Terminal Essay, p. 194

2 This Fásilah is more accurately called sughrà, the smaller one; there is another Fásilah kubrà, the greater, consisting of four moved letters followed

followed by a quiescent, and which, in fact, is only a shorter name for a Sabab sakíl followed by a Sabab khafíf, as muta + fá, or 'ala + tun, both of the measure of the classical Anapaest, (⏑ ⏑ -).

ii. These three elements, the Sabab, Watad and Fásilah, combine further into feet Arkán, pl. of Rukn, or Ajzá, pl. of Juz, two words explained *supra*, p. 206. The technical terms by which the feet are named, are derivatives of the root fa'l, to do, which, as the student will remember, serves in Arabic Grammar to form the Auzán or weights, in accordance with which words are derived from roots. It consists of the three letters Fá (f), 'Ayn ('), Lám (l), and, like any other Arabic root, cannot strictly speaking be pronounced, for the introduction of any vowel-sound would make it cease to be a root and change it into an individual word. The above fa'l, for instance, where the initial Fá is moved by Fathah (a), is the Infinitive or verbal noun, "to do," "doing." If the 'Ayn also is moved by Fathah, we obtain fa'al, meaning in colloquial Arabic "he did" (the classical or literary form would be fa'ala). Pronouncing the first letter with Zammah (u), the second with Kasrah (i), *i.e.*, fu'il, we say "it was done" (classically fu'ila). Many more forms are derived by prefixing, inserting, or subjoining certain additional letters called Hurúf al-Ziyádah (letters of increase) to the original radicals: fá'il for instance, with an Alif of prolongation in the first syllable, means "doer"; maf'úl (=maf'uwl), where the quiescent Fá is preceded by a fathated Mím (m), and the zammated 'Ayn followed by a lengthening Waw, means "done"; Mufá'alah, where in addition to a prefixed and inserted letter, the feminine termination ah is subjoined after the Lám means "to do a thing reciprocally." Since these and similar changes are with unvarying regularity applicable to all roots, the grammarians use the derivations of Fa'l as model-forms for the corresponding derivations of any other root, whose letters are in this case called its Fá, 'Ayn and Lám. From a root, *e.g.* which has Káf (k) for its

---

by a quiescent, or of a Sabab sakíl followed by a Watad majmú'. But it occurs only as a variation of a normal foot, not as an integral element in its composition, and consequently no mention of it was needed in the text.

first letter or Fá, Tá (t) for its second letter or 'Ayn, and Bá (b) for its third letter or Lám,

fa'l would be katb = to write, writing;
fa'al would be katab = he wrote;
fu'il would be kutib = it was written;
fá'il would be kátib = writer, scribe;
maf'úl would be maktúb = written, letter;
mufá'alah would be mukátabah = to write reciprocally, correspondence.

The advantage of this system is evident. It enables the student, who has once grasped the original meaning of a root, to form scores of words himself, and in his readings to understand hundreds, nay thousands, of words, without recourse to the Dictionary, as soon as he has learned to distinguish their radical letters from the letters of increase, and recognises in them a familiar root. We cannot wonder, therefore, that the inventor of Arabic Prosody readily availed himself of the same plan for his own ends. The Taf'íl, as it is here called, that is the representation of the metrical feet by current derivatives of fa'l, has in this case, of course, nothing to do with the etymological meaning of those typical forms. But it proves none the less useful in another direction: in simply naming a particular foot it shows at the same time its prosodical measure and character, as will now be explained in detail.

We have seen *supra* p. 206 that the word Akámú consists of a short syllable followed by two long ones (⏑ - -), and consequently forms a foot, which the classics would call Bacchius. In Latin there is no connection between this name and the metrical value of the foot: we must learn both by heart. But if we are told that its Taf'íl in Arabic is Fa'úlun, we understand at once that it is composed of the Watad majmú' fa'ú (⏑ -) and the Sabab khafif lun (-), and as the Watad contains three, the Sabab two letters, it forms a quinqueliteral foot or Juz khamásí.

In combining into feet, the Watad has the precedence over the Sabab and the Fásilah, and again the Watad majmú' over the Watad mafrúk. Hence the Prosodists distinguish between Ajzá aslíyah or primary feet (from Asl, root), in which this precedence is observed, and Ajzá far'iyah or secondary feet (from Far'=branch), in which it is reversed. The former are four in number:—

1. Fa'ú.lun, consisting, as we have just seen, of a Watad majmú' followed by a Sabab khafíf,=the Latin Bacchíus (⏑ - -).

2. Mafá.'í.lun, *i.e.* Watad majmú, followed by two Sabab khafíf=the Latin Epitritus primus (⏑ - - -).

3. Mufá.'alatun, *i.e.* Watad majmú, followed by Fásilah=the Latin Iambus followed by Anapaest (⏑ - ⏑ ⏑ -).

4. Fá'i.lá.tun, *i.e.* Watad mafrúk followed by two Sabab khafíf=the Latin Epitritus secundus (- ⏑ - -).

The number of the secondary feet increases to six, for as Nos. 2 and 4 contain two Sabab, they "branch out" into two derived feet each, according to both Sabab or only one changing place with regard to the Watad. They are:—

5. Fá.'ilun, *i.e.* Sabab khafíf followed by Watad majmú'= the Latin Creticus (- ⏑ -). The primary Fa'ú.lun becomes by transposition Lun.fa'ú. To bring this into conformity with a current derivative of fa'l, the initial Sabab must be made to contain the first letter of the root, and the Watad the two remaining ones in their proper order. Fá is therefore substituted for lun, and 'ilun for fa'ú, forming together the above Fá.'ilun. By similar substitutions, which it would be tedious to specify in each separate case, Mafá.'í.lun becomes:—

6. Mus.taf.'ilun, for 'Í.lun.mafá. *i.e.* two Sabab khafíf, followed by Watad majmú' = the Latin Epitritus tertius (- - ⏑ -), or:

7. Fá.'ilá.tun, for Lun.mafá.'í, *i.e.* Watad majmú' between two Sabab khafif = the Latin Epitritus secundus (- ⏑ - -).

8. Mutafá.'ilun (for 'Alatun.mufá, the reversed Mufá.'alatun) *i.e.* Fásilah followed by Watad majmú'=the Latin Anapaest succeeded by Iambus (⏑ ⏑ - ⏑ -). The last two secondary feet are transpositions of No. 4, Fá.'ilá'.tun, namely:—

9. Maf.'ú.látu, for Lá.tun.fá'i, *i.e.* two Sabab khafíf, followed by Watad mafrúk=the Latin Epitritus quartus (- - - ⏑).

10. Mus.taf'i.lun, for Tun.fá'i.lá, *i.e.* Watad Mafrúk between two Sabab khafíf=the Latin Epitritus tertius (- - ⏑ -).[1]

---

1 It is important to keep in mind that the seemingly identical feet 10 and 6, 7 and 3, are distinguished by the relative positions of the constituting elements in either pair. For, as it will be seen that Sabab and Watad are subject to *different* kinds of alterations, it is evident that the effect of such alteration upon a foot will vary, if Sabab and Watad occupy *different* places with regard to each other.

The "branch"-foot Fá. 'ilun (No. 5), like its "root" Fa'úlun (No. 1), is quinqueliteral. All other feet, primary or secondary, consist necessarily of seven letters, as they contain a triliteral Watad (see *supra*, i. 2) with either two biliteral Sabab khafif (i. 1), or a quadriliteral Fásilah (i. 3). They are, therefore, called Sabá'í=seven lettered.

iii. The same principle of the Watad taking precedence over Sabab and Fásilah, rules the arrangement of the Arabic metres, which are divided into five circles (Dawáir, pl. of Dáirah) so called for reasons presently to be explained. The first is named:

A. Dáirat al-Mukhtalif, circle of "the varied" metre, because it is composed of feet of various length, the five-lettered Fa'úlun (*supra*, ii. 1) and the seven-lettered Mafá'ílun (ii. 2) with their secondaries Fá'ilun, Mustaf.'ilun and Fá.'ilátun (ii. 5-7), and it comprises three Buhúr or metres (pl. of Bahr, sea), the Tawíl, Madíd and Basit.

1. Al-Tawil, consisting of twice

Fa'ú.lun Mafá.'ílun Fa'ú.lun Mafá.'ilun,

the classical scheme for which would be

⏑ - - | ⏑ - - - | ⏑ - - | ⏑ - - - |

If we transfer the Watad Fa'ú from the beginning of the line to the end, it would read:—

Lun.mafá'í Lun.fa'ú Lun.mafá'í Lun.fa'ú which, after the substitutions indicated above (ii. 7 and 5), becomes:—

2. Al-Madid, consisting of twice

Fá.'ilátun Fá.'llun Fá.'ilatun Fá.'ilun,

which may be represented by the classical scheme

- ⏑ - - | - ⏑ - | - ⏑ - - | - ⏑ - |

If again, returning to the Tawíl, we make the break after the Watad of the second foot we obtain the line:—

'Ílun.fa'ú. Lun.mafá 'Ílun.fa'u Lun.mafá, and as metrically 'Ílun.fa'ú (two Sabab followed by Watad) and Lun.mafá (one Sabab followed by Watad) are = 'Ílun.mafá and Lun.fa'ú respectively, their Taf'il is effected by the same substitutions as in ii. 5 and 6, and they become:—

3. Basit, consisting of twice

Mustaf.'ilun Fá.'ilun Mustaf.'ilun Fá.'ilun,

in conformity with the classical scheme :—

- - ⏑ - | - ⏑ - | - - ⏑ - | - ⏑ - |

Thus one metre evolves from another by a kind of rotation, which suggested to the Prosodists an ingenious device of representing them by circles (hence the name Dáirah), round the circumference of which on the outside the complete Taf'íl of the original metre is written, while each moved letter is faced by a small loop, each quiescent by a small vertical stroke[1] inside the circle. Then, in the case of this present Dáirat al-Mukhtalif for instance, the loop corresponding to the initial f of the first Fa'úlun is marked as the beginning of the Tawil, that corresponding to its l (of the Sabab lun) as the beginning of the Madid, and that corresponding to the 'Ayn of the next Mafá'ílun as the beginning of the Basít. The same process applies to all the following circles, but our limited space compels us simply to enumerate them, together with their Buhúr, without further reference to the mode of their evolution.

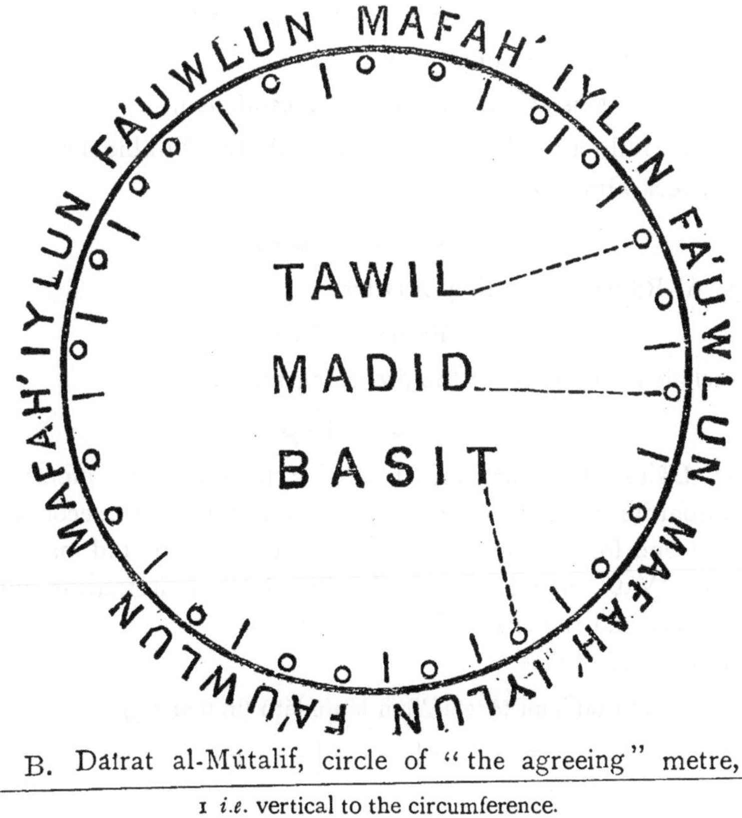

B. Dairat al-Mútalif, circle of "the agreeing" metre, so

1 *i.e.* vertical to the circumference.

called because all its feet agree in length, consisting of seven letters each. It contains:—

1. Al-Wáfir, composed of twice

Mufá.'alatun Mufá.'alatun Mufá.'alatun (ii. 3)

= ⏑ - ⏑ ⏑ - | ⏑ - ⏑ ⏑ - | ⏑ - ⏑ ⏑ - |

where the Iambus in each foot precedes the Anapaest, and its reversal:—

2. Al-Kámil, consisting of twice

Mutafá.'ilun Mutafá.'ilun Mutafá.'ilun (ii. 8)

= ⏑ ⏑ - ⏑ - | ⏑ ⏑ - ⏑ - | ⏑ ⏑ - ⏑ - |

where the Anapaest takes the first place in every foot.

C. Dáirat al-Mujtalab, circle of "the brought on" metre, so called because its seven-lettered feet are brought on from the first circle.

1. Al-Hazaj, consisting of twice

Mafá.'ílun Mafá.'ílun Mafá.'ílun (ii. 2)

= ⏑ - - - | ⏑ - - - | ⏑ - - - | ⏑ - - - |

2. Al-Rajaz, consisting of twice

Mustaf.'ilun Mustaf.'ilun Mustaf.'ilun,

and, in this full form, almost identical with the Iambic Trimeter of the Greek Drama:—

- - ⏑ - | - - ⏑ - | - - ⏑ - |

3. Al-Ramal, consisting of twice

Fá.'ilátun Fá.'ilátun Fá.'ilátun,

the trochaic counterpart of the preceding metre

= - ⏑ - - | - ⏑ - - | - ⏑ - - |

D. Dáirat al-Mushtabih, circle of "the intricate" metre, so called from its intricate nature, primary mingling with secondary feet, and one foot of the same verse containing a Watad majmú', another a Watad mafrúk, *i.e.* the Iambic rhythm alternating with the trochaic and *vice versa*. Its Buhúr are:—

1. Al-Sari', twice

Mustaf.'ilun Mustaf.'ilun Mafú.látu (ii. 6 and 9)

= - - ⏑ - | - - ⏑ - | - - - ⏑

2. Al-Munsarih, twice

Mustaf.'ilun Mafú.látu Mustaf.'ilun (ii. 6. 9. 6)

= - - ⏑ - | - - - ⏑ | - - ⏑ - |

3. Al-Khafíf, twice

Fá.'ilátun Mustaf'i.lun Fá.'ilátun (ii. 7. 10. 7)

= - ⏑ - - | - - ⏑ - | - ⏑ - - |

4. Al-Muzári', twice

Mafá.'ílun Fá'i.látun Mafá.'ílun (ii. 2. 4. 2)

= - - - | - ⏑ - - | ⏑ - - - |

5. Al-Muktazib, twice

Maf'ú.látu Mustaf.'ilun Maf'ú.látu (ii. 9. 6. 9)

= - - - ⏑ | - - ⏑ - | - - - ⏑ |

6. Al-Mujtass, twice

Mustaf'i.lun Fá.'ilátun Mustaf'i.lun (ii. 10. 7. 10)

= - - ⏑ - | - ⏑ - - | - - ⏑ - |

E. Dáirat al-Muttafik, circle of "the concordant" metre, so called for the same reason why circle B is called "the agreeing," *i.e.* because the feet all harmonise in length, being here, however, quinqueliteral, not seven-lettered as in the Mútalif. Al-Khalíl, the inventor of the 'Ilm al-'Arúz, assigns to it only one metre:—

1. Al-Mutakárib, twice

Fa'úlun Fa'úlun Fa'úlun Fa'úlun (ii. 1)

= ⏑ - - | ⏑ - - | ⏑ - - | ⏑ - - |

Later Prosodists added:—

2. Al-Mútadárak, twice

Fá'ilun Fá'ilun Fá'ilun Fá'ilun (ii. 5)

= - ⏑ - | - ⏑ - | - ⏑ - | - ⏑ - |

The feet and metres as given above are, however, to a certain extent merely theoretical; in practice the former admit of numerous licenses and the latter of variations brought about by modification or partial suppression of the feet final in a verse. An Arabic poem (Kasídah, or if numbering less than ten couplets, Ghazal, and if the first two lines are not rhyming, Kat'ah) consists of Bayts or couplets, bound together by a continuous rhyme, which connects the first two lines (except in a Kat'ah) and is repeated at the end of every second line throughout the poem. The *last* foot of every odd line is called 'Arúz (fem. in contradistinction of 'Arúz in the sense of Prosody which is masc.) pl. A'ariz, that of every even line is called Zarb, pl. Azrub, and the remaining feet may be termed Hashw (stuffing), although in stricter parlance a further distinction is made between the *first* foot of every odd and even line as well.

Now with regard to the Hashw on the one hand, and the 'Aruz and Zarb on the other, the changes which the normal feet undergo are of two kinds: Zuháf (deviation) and 'Illah (defect). Zuhaf applies, as a rule, occasionally and optionally to the second letter of a Sabab in those feet which compose the Hashw or body-part of a verse, making a long syllable short by suppressing its quiescent final, or contracting two short quantities in a long one, by rendering quiescent a moved letter which stands second in a Sabab sakíl. In Mustaf'ilun (ii. 6. = - - ᴗ -), for instance, the s of the first syllable, or the f of the second, or both may be dropped and it will become accordingly Mutaf'ilun, by substitution Mafá'ilun (ᴗ - ᴗ -), or Musta'ilun, by substitution, Mufta'ilun (- ᴗ ᴗ -), or Muta'ilun, by substitution Fa'ilatun[1] (ᴗ ᴗ ᴗ -). This means that wherever the foot Mustaf.'ilun occurs in the Hashw of a poem, we can represent it by the scheme ⏓ ⏓ ᴗ - *i.e.* the Epitritus tertius can, by poetical license change into Diiambus, Choriambus or Paeon quartus. In Mufá'alatun (ii. 3, = ᴗ - ᴗ ᴗ -) and Mutafá'ilun (ii. 8. = ᴗ ᴗ - ᴗ -), again, the Sabab 'ala and muta may become khafif by suppression of their final Harakah and thus turn into Mufá'altun. by substitution Mafá'ílun (ii. 2. = ᴗ - - -), and Mutfá'ilun, by substitution Mustaf'ilun (ii. 6 = - - ᴗ - as above). In other words the two feet correspond to the schemes ᴗ - ᴗ̄ᴗ - and ᴗ̄ᴗ - ᴗ -, where a Spondee can take the place of the Anapaest after or before the Iambus respectively.

'Illah, the second way of modifying the primitive or normal feet, applies to both Sahab and Watad, but only in the 'Aruz and Zarb of a couplet, being at the same time constant and obligatory. Besides the changes already mentioned, it consists in adding one or two letters to a Sabab or Watad, or curtailing them more or

[1] This would be a Fásilah kubrà spoken of in note 2, p. 208, ante.

less, even to cutting them off altogether. We cannot here exhaust this matter any more than those touched upon until now, but must be satisfied with an example or two, to show the proceeding in general and indicate its object.

We have seen that the metre Basit consists of the two lines:

Mustaf.'ilun Fá.'ilun Mustaf'ilun Fá'ilun
Mustaf ilun Fá'ilun Mustaf'ilun Fá'ilun.

This complete form, however, is not in use amongst Arab poets. If by the Zuháf Khabn, here acting as 'Illah, the Alif in the final Fá'ilun is suppressed, changing it into Fa'ilun (◡ ◡ -), it becomes the first 'Aruz, called makhbúnah, of the Basít, the first Zarb of which is obtained by submitting the final Fá'ilun of the second line to the same process. A second Zarb results, if in Fá'ilun the final n of the Watad 'ilun is *cut* off and the preceding l made quiescent by the 'Illah Kat', thus giving Fá'il and by substitution Fa'lun (- -). Thus the formula becomes:—

Mustaf'ilun Fá'ilun Mustaf'ilun Fa'ilun
Mustaf'ilun Fá'ilun Mustaf'ilun { Fa'ilun / Fa'lun }

As in the Hashw, *i.e.* the first three feet of each line, the Khabn can likewise be applied to the medial Fá'ilun, and for Mustaf'ilun the poetical licenses, explained above, may be introduced, this first 'Arúz or Class of the Basit with its two Zarb or subdivisions will be represented by the scheme

◡ ◡	◡	◡ ◡	
- - ◡ -	- ◡ -	- - ◡ -	◡ ◡ -
◡ ◡	◡	◡ ◡	{ ◡ ◡ -
- - ◡ -	- ◡ -	- - ◡ -	{ - -

that is to say in the first subdivision of this form of the Basit both lines of each couplet end with an Anapaest and every second line of the other subdivision terminates in a Spondee.

The Basít has four more A'áriz, three called majzúah, because each line is shortened by a Juz or foot, one called mashtúrah (halved), because the number of feet is reduced from four to two, and we may here notice that the former kind of lessening the number of feet is frequent with the hexametrical circles (B.C.D.), while the latter kind can naturally only occur in those circles whose couplet forms an octameter (A.E.). Besides being majzúah, the second 'Aruz is sahíhah (perfect), consisting of the normal foot Mustaf'ilun. It has three Azrub: 1. Mustaf'ilán (- - ⏑ ⏑́), with an overlong final syllable, see *supra*, p. 207), produced by the 'Illah Tazyíl, *i.e.* addition of a quiescent letter at the end (Mustaf'ilunn, by substitution Mustaf'ilán); 2. Mustaf'ilun, like the 'Aruz; 3. Maf'últun (- - -), produced by the 'Illah Kat' (see the preceding page; Mustaf'ilun, by dropping the final n and making the l quiescent becomes Mustaf'il and by substitution Maf'úlun). Hence the formula is:—

Mustaf'ilun Fá'ilun Mustaf'ilun

Mustaf'ilun Fà'ilun { Mustaf'ilán / Mustaf'ilun / Maf'úlun,

which, with its allowable licenses, may be represented by the scheme:—

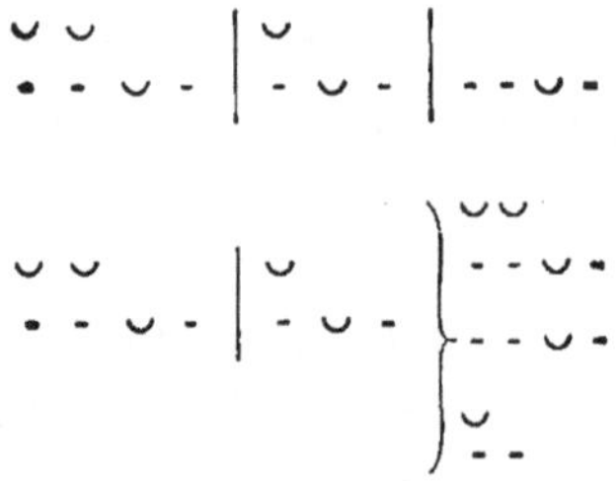

The above will suffice to illustrate the general method of the Prosodists, and we must refer the reader for the remaining classes and subdivisions of the Basit as well as the other metres to more special treatises on the subject, to which this Essay is intended merely as an introduction, with a view to facilitate the first steps of the student in an important, but I fear somewhat neglected, field of Arabic learning.

If we now turn to the poetical pieces contained in The Nights, we find that out of the fifteen metres, known to Al-Khalil, or the sixteen of later Prosodists, instances of thirteen occur in the Mac N. edition, but in vastly different proportions. The total number amounts to 1,385 pieces (some, however, repeated several times), out of which 1,128 belong to the first two circles, leaving only 257 for the remaining three. The same disproportionality obtains with regard to the metres of each circle. The Mukhtalif is represented by 331 instances of Tawil and 330 of Basít against

3 of Madíd; the Mutalif by 321 instances of Kámil against 143 of Wáfir; the Mujtalab by 32 instances of Ramal and 30 of Rajaz against 1 of Hazaj; the Mushtabih by 72 instances of Khafíf and 52 of Sarí' against 18 of Munsarih and 15 of Mújtass; and lastly, the Muttafik by 37 instances of Mutakárib. Neither the Mutadárak (E. 2), nor the Muzári' and Muktazib (D. 4. 5), are met with.

Finally, it remains for me to quote a couplet of each metre, showing how to scan them, and what relation they bear to the theoretical formulas exhibited on p. 212 to p. 215.

It is characteristic for the preponderance of the Tawil over all the other metres, that the first four lines, with which my alphabetical list begins, are written in it. One of these belongs to a poem which has for its author Bahá al-Dín Zuhayr (born A.D. 1186 at Mekkah or in its vicinity, ob. 1249 at Cairo), and is to be found in full in Professor Palmer's edition of his works, p. 164. Sir Richard Burton translates the first Bayt (vol. i. night xxviii.):

An I quit Cairo and her pleasances * Where can I hope to find so gladsome ways?

Professor Palmer renders it:

Must I leave Egypt where such joys abound?
What place can ever charm me so again.

In Arabic it scans:

⏑ - ⏑ | ⏑ - - - | ⏑ - ⏑ | ⏑ - ⏑ - |
A-arhalu 'an Misrin wa tibi na'ímihi[1]

⏑ - ⏑ | ⏑ - - - | ⏑ - ⏑ | ⏑ - ⏑ - |
Fa-ayyu makánin ba'dahá li-ya sháiku.

In referring to iii. A. 1. p. 212, it will be seen that in the Hashw Fa'úlun (⏑ - -) has become Fa'úlu (⏑ - ⏑) by a Zuháf called Kabz (suppression of the fifth letter of a foot if it is quiescent), and that in the 'Arúz and Zarb Mafá'ílun (⏑ - - -) has changed

1 In pause, that is at the end of a line, a short vowel counts either as long or is dropped, according to the exigencies of the metre. In the Hashw the u or i of the pronominal affix for the third person sing. masc., and the final u of the enlarged pronominal plural forms, humu and kumu may be either short or long, according to the same exigencies. The end-vowel of the pronoun of the first person aná, I, is generally read short, although it is written with Alif.

into Mafá'ilun (ᴗ - ᴗ -) by the same Zuháf acting as 'Illah. The latter alteration shows the couplet to be of the second Zarb of the first 'Arúz of the Tawil. If the second line did terminate in Mafá'ílun, as in the original scheme, it would be the first Zarb of the same 'Arúz; if it did end in Fa'úlun (ᴗ - -) or Mafá'íl (ᴗ - ´) it would represent the third or fourth subdivision of this first class respectively. The Tawil as one other 'Arúz, Fa'úlun, with a twofold Zarb, either Fa'úlun also, or Mafá'ilun.

The first instance of the Basit occurring in The Nights is the lines translated vol. i. night i.:

Containeth Time a twain of days, this of blessing, that of bane * And holdeth Life a twain of halves, this of pleasure, that of pain.

In Arabic (Mac N. i. 11):

- - ᴗ - | - ᴗ - | - - ᴗ - | ᴗ ᴗ - |
Al-Dabru yaumáni zá amnun wa zá hazaru

- - ᴗ - | - ᴗ - | - - ᴗ - | ᴗ ᴗ - |
Wa'l-'Ayshu shatráni zá safwun wa zá kadaru.

Turning back to p. 213, where the A'áríz and Azrub of the Basit are shown, the student will have no difficulty to recognise the Bayt as one belonging to the first Zarb of the first 'Arúz.

As an example of the Madid we quote the original of the lines (vol. iv. night ccccviii.):—

I had a heart, and with it lived my life * 'Twas seared with fire and burnt with loving-lowe.

They read in Arabic:—

- ᴗ - - | - ᴗ - | ᴗ ᴗ - |
Kána li kalbun a'íshu bihi

- ᴗ - - | - ᴗ - | ᴗ - |
Fa'ktawà bi'l-nári wa'htarak.

If we compare this with the formula (iii. A. 2 p. 212), we find that either line of the couplet is shortened by a foot; it is, therefore, majzú. The first 'Arúz of this abbreviated metre is Fá'ilátun (- ᴗ - -), and is called sahíhah (perfect) because it consists of the normal third foot. In the second 'Arúz Fá'ilátun loses its end syllable tun by the 'Illah Hafz (suppression of a final Sabab khafif), and becomes Fá'ilá (- ᴗ -), for which Fá'ilun is substituted. Shortening the first syllable of Fá'ilun, *i.e.* eliminating the Alif by Khabn, we obtain the third 'Arúz Fa'ilun (⏑ ⏑ -) as that of the present lines, which has two Azrub: Fa'ilun, like the 'Arúz, and Fa'lun (- -), here, again by Khabn, further reduced to Fa'al (⏑ -).

Ishak of Mosul, who improvises the piece, calls it "so difficult and so rare, that it went nigh to deaden the quick and to quicken the dead"; indeed, the native poets consider the metre Madid as the most difficult of all, and it is scarcely ever attempted by later writers. This accounts for its rare occurrence in The Nights, where only two more instances are to be found, Mac N. ii. 244 and iii. 404.

The second and third circle will best be spoken of together, as the Wáfir and Kámil have a natural affinity to the Hazaj and Rajaz. Let us revert to the line:—

⏑ - - - | ⏑ - - - | ⏑ - - |

Akámú 'l-wajda fí kalbi wa sárú.

Translated, as it were, into the language of the Prosodists it will be:—

Mafá'ílun[1] Mafá'ílun Fa'úlun,

and this, standing by itself, might *prima facie* be taken for a line of the Hazaj (iii. C. 1), with the third Mafá'ílun shortened by Hafz (see above) into Mafá'í for which Fa'úlun would be subsituated. We have seen (p. 216) that, and how the foot Mufá'alatun can change into Mafá'ílun, and if in any poem which otherwise would belong to the metre Hazaj, the former measure appears even in one foot only along with the latter, it is considered to be the original measure, and the poem counts no longer as Hazaj but as Wáfir. In the piece now under consideration, it is the second Bayt where the characteristic foot of the Wáfir first appears:—

⏑ - - - | ⏑ - ⏑ ⏑ - | ⏑ - - |

Naat 'anní'l-rubú'u wa sákiníhá

⏑ - ⏑ ⏑ - | ⏑ - ⏑ ⏑ - | ⏑ - - |

Wa kad ba'uda 'l-mazáru fa-lá mazáru.

---

1 On p. 206 the word akámú, as read by itself, was identified with the foot Fa'úlun. Here it must be read together with the following syllable as "akámulwaj," which is Mafá'ílun.

Anglicè (vol. iii. night ccxiv.):—

Far lies the camp and those who camp therein; • Far is her tent-shrine where I ne'er shall tent.

It must, however, be remarked that the Hazaj is not in use as a hexameter, but only with an 'Arúz majzúah or shortened by one foot. Hence it is only in the second 'Arúz of the Wáfir, which is likewise majzúah, that the ambiguity as to the real nature of the metre can arise[1]; and the isolated couplet:—

⏑ - - - | ⏑ - - - | ⏑ - - |
Yarídu 'l-mar-u an yu'tà munáhu
⏑ - - - | ⏑ - - - | ⏑ - - |
Wa yabà 'lláhu illá má yurídu

Man wills his wish to him accorded be • But Allah naught accords save what He wills (vol. iii. night ccxcviii.),

being hexametrical, forms undoubtedly part of a poem in Wáfir although it does not contain the foot Mufá'alatun at all. Thus the solitary instance of Hazaj in The Nights is Abú Nowás' abomination, beginning with:—

⏑ - - - | ⏑ - - - |
Fa-lá tas'au ilà ghayrî
⏑ - - - | ⏑ - - - |
Fa-'indi ma'dinu 'l-khayri (Mac N. ii. 377).

Steer ye your steps to none but me • Who have a mine of luxury (vol. iv. night ccclxxxi.)

If in the second 'Arúz of the Wáfir Maf'áïlun (⏑ - - -) is further shortened to Mafá'ilun (⏑ - ⏑ -), the metre resembles the second 'Arúz of Rajaz, where, as we have seen, the latter foot can, by license, take the place of the normal Mustaf'ilun (- - ⏑ -).

The Kámil bears a similar relation to the Rajaz, as the Wáfir bears to the Hazaj. By way of illustration we quote from Mac N. ii. 8 the first two Bayts of a little poem taken from the 23rd Assembly of Al-Hariri:—

---

1 Prof. Palmer, p. 328 of his Grammar, identifies this form of the Wafir, when every Mufá'alatun of the Hashw has become Mafá'ilun, with the second form of the Rajaz. It should be Hazaj. Professor Palmer was misled, it seems, by an evident misprint in one of his authorities, the Muhit al-Dairah by Dr. Van Dayk, p. 52.

- - ⏑ - | - - ⏑ - | ⏑ ⏑ - ⏑ - |

Yá khátiba 'l-dunyá 'l-daniyyati innahá

⏑ ⏑ - ⏑ - | ⏑ ⏑ - ⏑ - | - - - |

Sharaku 'l-radà wa karáratu 'l-akdári

- - ⏑ - | - - ⏑ - | - - ⏑ - |

Dárun matà má azhakat fí yaumihá

- - ⏑ - | - - ⏑ - | - - - |

Abkat ghadan bu'dan lahá min dári.

In Sir Richard Burton's translation (vol. iii. night ccxxii.) :—

O thou who woo'st a World unworthy, learn * 'Tis house of evils, 'tis Perdition's net :
house where whoso laughs this day, shall weep * The next ; then perish house of fume and fret.

The 'Arúz of the first couplet is Mutafá'ilun, assigning the piece to the first or perfect (sahíhah) class of the Kámil. In the Hashw of the opening line and in that of the whole second Bayt this normal Mutafá'ilun has, by license, become Mustaf'ilun, and the same change has taken place in the 'Arúz of the second couplet; for it is a peculiarity which this metre shares with a few others, to allow certain alterations of the kind Zuháf in the 'Arúz and Zarb as well as in the Hashw. This class has three subdivisions: the Zarb of the first is Mutafá'ilun, like the 'Arúz; the Zarb of the second is Fa'alátun (⏑ ⏑ - -), a substitution for Mutafá'il, which latter is obtained from Mutafá'ilun by suppressing the final *n* and rendering the *l* quiescent; the Zarb of the third is Fa'lun (- -) for Mútfá, derived from Mutafá'ilun by cutting off the Watad 'ilun and dropping the medial *a* of the remaining Mutafá.

If we make the 'Ayn of the second Zarb Fa'alátun also quiescent by the permitted Zuháf Izmár, it changes into Fa'látun, by substitution Maf'úlun (- - -) which terminates the rhyming lines of the foregoing quotation. Consequently the two couplets, taken together, belong to the second Zarb of the first 'Arúz of the Kámil, and the metre of the poem with its licenses may be represented by the scheme :—

 -        | - | - |
⏑ ⏑ - ⏑ - | ⏑ ⏑ - ⏑ - | ⏑ ⏑ - ⏑ - |

 -        | - | - |
⏑ ⏑ - ⏑ - | ⏑ ⏑ - ⏑ - | ⏑ ⏑ - - |

Taken isolated, on the other hand, the second Bayt might be of the metre Rajaz, whose first 'Arúz Mustaf'ilun has two Azrub: one equal to the 'Arúz, the other Maf'úlun as above, but here substituted for Mustaf'il after applying the 'Illah Kat' (see p. 217) to Mustaf'ilun. If this were the metre of the poem throughout, the scheme with the licenses peculiar to the Rajaz would be:—

```
⏑ ⏑      | ⏑ ⏑      | ⏑ ⏑      |
- - ⏑ -  | - - ⏑ -  | - - ⏑ -  |

⏑ ⏑      | ⏑ ⏑      | ⏑        |
- - ⏑ -  | - - ⏑ -  | - - -    |
```

The pith of Al-Hariri's Assembly is that the knight errant, not to say the arrant wight of the Romance, Abú Sayd of Sarúj, accuses before the Wáli of Baghdad his pretended pupil, in reality his son, of having appropriated a poem of his by lopping off two feet of every Bayt. If this is done in the quoted lines, they read:—

- - ⏑ - | - - ⏑ - |
Yá khátiba 'l-dunyá 'l-daniy.

⏑ ⏑ - ⏑ - | ⏑ ⏑ - ⏑ - |
Yati innahá sharaku 'l-radà

- - ⏑ - | - - ⏑ - |
Dárun matà má azhakat

- - ⏑ - | - - ⏑ - |
Fí yaumihá abkat ghadá,

with a different rhyme and of a different variation of metre. The amputated piece belongs to the fourth Zarb of the third 'Aruz of Kámil, and its second couplet tallies with the second sub-division of the second class of Rajaz.

The Rajaz, an iambic metre pure and simple, is the most popular, because the easiest, in which even the Prophet was caught napping sometimes, at the dangerous risk of following the perilous leadership of Imru 'l-Kays. It is the metre of improvisation, of ditties, and of numerous didactic poems. In the latter case, when the composition is called Urjúzah, the two lines of every Bayt rhyme, and each Bayt has a rhyme of its own. This is the form in which, for instance, Ibn Málik's

Alfíyah is written, as well as the remarkable grammatical work of the modern native scholar, Nasíf al-Yazijí, of which a notice will be found in Chenery's Introduction to his Translation of Al-Hariri.

While the Hazaj and Rajaz connect the third circle with the first and second, the Ramal forms the link between the third and fourth Dáirah. Its measure Fá'ilátun (- ᴗ - -) and the reversal of it, Maf'úlátu (- - - ᴗ), affect the trochaic rhythm, as opposed to the iambic of the two first-named metres. The Iambic movement has a ring of gladness about it, the trochaic a wail of sadness: the former resembles a nimble pedestrian, striding apace with an elastic step and a cheerful heart; the latter is like a man toiling along on the desert path, where his foot is ever and anon sliding back in the burning sand (Raml, whence probably the name of the metre). Both combined in regular alternation, impart an agitated character to the verse, admirably fit to express the conflicting emotions of a passion-stirred mind.

Examples of these more or less plaintive and pathetic metres are numerous in the Tale of Uns al-Wujúd and the Wazir's Daughter, which, being throughout a story of love, as has been noted, vol. iv. night ccclxxi., abounds in verse, and, in particular, contains ten out of the thirty-two instances of Ramal occurring in The Nights. We quote:—

Ramal, first Zarb of the first 'Arúz (Mac N. ii. 361):—

- ᴗ - - | ᴗ ᴗ - - | - ᴗ - |
Inna li 'l-bulbuli sautan fí 'l-sahar

- ᴗ - - | ᴗ ᴗ - - | - ᴗ - |
Ashghala 'l-'áshika 'an husni 'l-watar

The Bulbul's note, whenas dawn is nigh * Tells the lover from strains of strings to fly (vol. iv. night ccclxxvi.).

Sarí', second Zarb of the first 'Arúz (Mac N. ii. 359):—

ᴗ - ᴗ - | - - ᴗ - | - ᴗ - |
Wa fákhitin kad kála fí nauhihi

- - ᴗ - | - - ᴗ - | - ᴗ - |
Yá Dáiman shukran 'alà balwatí

I heard a ringdove chanting soft and plaintively, * "I thank Thee, O Eternal for this misery" (vol. iv. night ccclxxvi.).

Khafíf, full or perfect form (sahih), both in Zarb and Arúz (Mac N. ii. 356):—

- ⏑ - - | ⏑ - ⏑ - | - ⏑ - - |
Yá li-man ashtakí 'l-gharáma 'llazí bí

⏑ ⏑ - - | ⏑ - ⏑ - | - ⏑ - - |
Wa shujúní wa furkatí 'an habibi

O to whom now of my desiré complaining sore shall I • Bewail my parting from my fere compèlled thus to fly (vol. iv. night ccclxxv.).

Mujtass, the only 'Arúz (majzúah sahíhah, *i.e.* shortened by one foot and perfect) with equal Zarb (Mac N. ii. 367):—

- - ⏑ - | ⏑ ⏑ - - |
Ruddú 'alayya habibi

- - ⏑ - | - ⏑ - - |
Lá hajatan li bi-málin

To me restore my dear • I want not wealth untold (vol. iv. night ccclxxviii.).

As an instance of the Munsarih, I give the second occurring in The Nights, because it affords me an opportunity to show the student how useful a knowledge of the laws of Prosody frequently proves for ascertaining the correct reading of a text. Mac N. i. 33 we find the line:—

- ⏑ ⏑ - | - ⏑ ⏑ - | - ⏑ ⏑ - |
Arba'atun má 'jtama'at kattu izá.

This would be Rajaz with the license Mufta'ilun for Mustaf'ilun. But the following lines of the fragment evince that the metre is Munsarih; hence, a clerical error must lurk somewhere in the second foot. In fact, on page 833 of the same volume, we find the piece repeated, and here the first couplet reads

- ⏑ ⏑ - | - - ⏑ | - ⏑ ⏑ - |
Arba'atun má 'jtama'na kattu siwà

⏑ - ⏑ - | - ⏑ - ⏑ | - ⏑ ⏑ |
Alà azá mujhatí wa safki dami

Four things which ne'er conjoin unless it be • To storm my vitals and to shed my blood (vol. iii. night clxxxiii.).

The Mutakárib, the last of the metres employed in The Nights, has gained a truly historical importance by the part which it plays in Persian literature. In the form of trimetrical double-lines, with a several rhyme for each couplet, it has become the "Nibelungen-"stanza of the Persian epos: Firdausí's immortal "Book of Kings" and Nizámi's Iskander-námah are written in it, not to mention a host of Masnawis in which Sufic mysticism combats Mohammedan orthodoxy. On account of its warlike and heroical character, therefore, I choose for an example the knightly Jamrakán's challenge to the single fight in which he conquers his scarcely less valiant adversary Kaurajan (Mac N. iii. 296):—

⏑ – – | ⏑ – ⏑ | ⏑ – – | ⏑ – – |

Aná 'l-Jamrakánu kawiyyn 'l-janáni

⏑ – – | ⏑ – ⏑ | ⏑ – – | ⏑ – – |

Jamí'u 'l-fawárisi takhshà kitálí.

Here the third syllable of the second foot in each line is shortened by license, and the final Kasrah of the first line, standing in pause, is long, the metre being the full form of the Mutakárib as exhibited p. 215, iii. E. i. If we suppress the Kasrah of Al-Janáni, which is also allowable in pause, and make the second line to rhyme with the first, saying, for instance:—

⏑ – – | ⏑ – ⏑ | ⏑ – – | ⏑ –́

Aná 'l-Jamrakánu kawiyyu 'l-janán

⏑ – – | ⏑ – | ⏑ – – | ⏑ –́

La-yakshà kitálí shijá'u 'l-zamán,

we obtain the powerful and melodious metre in which the Sháh-námah sings of Rustam's lofty deeds, of the tender love of Rúdabah and the tragic downfall of Siyawush.

Shall I confess that in writing the foregoing pages it has been my ambition to become a conqueror, in a modest way, myself: to conquer, I mean, the prejudice frequently entertained, and shared even by my accomplished countryman, Rückert, that Arabic Prosody is a clumsy and repulsive doctrine. I have tried to show that it springs naturally from the character of the language, and, intimately connected, as it is, with the grammatical system of the Arabs, it appears to me quite worthy of the acumen of a people to whom, amongst other things, we owe the invention of Algebra, the stepping-stone of our whole modern system of Mathematics.

I cannot refrain, therefore, from concluding with a little anecdote anent Al-Khalíl, which Ibn Khallikán tells in the following words. His son went one day into the room where his father was, and on finding him scanning a piece of poetry by the rules of prosody, he ran out and told the people that his father had lost his wits. They went in immediately and related to Al-Khalil what they had heard, on which he addressed his son in these terms:

"Had you known what I was saying, you would have excused me, and had you known what you said, I should have blamed you. But you did not understand me, so you blamed me, and I knew that you were ignorant, so I pardoned you."

L'Envoi.

Here end, to my sorrow, the labours of a quarter-century and here I must perforce say with the "poets' Poet,"

> "Behold! I see the haven nigh at hand,
> To which I mean my wearie course to bend;
> Vere the main shete, and bear up with the land
> The which afore is fairly to be ken'd."

Nothing of importance now indeed remains for me but briefly to estimate the character of my work and to take cordial leave of my readers, thanking them for the interest they have accorded to these volumes and for enabling me thus successfully to complete the decade.

Without pudor malus or over-diffidence I would claim to have fulfilled the promise contained in my Foreword. The anthropological notes and notelets, which not only illustrate and read between the lines of the text, but assist the student of Moslem life and of Arabo-Egyptian manners, customs and language in a multitude of matters shunned by books, form a repertory of Eastern knowledge in its esoteric phase, sexual as well as social.

To assert that such lore is unnecessary is to state, as every traveller knows, an "absurdum." Few phenomena are more startling than the vision of a venerable infant, who has lived half his long life in the midst of the wildest anthropological vagaries and monstrosities, and yet who absolutely ignores all that India or Burmah enacts under his very eyes. This is crass ignorance, not the naïve innocence of Saint Francis who, seeing a man and a maid in a dark corner, raised his hands to Heaven and thanked the Lord that there was still in the world so much of Christian Charity.

Against such lack of knowledge my notes are a protest; and I may claim success despite the difficulty of the task. A traveller familiar with Syria and Palestine, Herr Landberg, writes, "La plume refuserait son service, la langue serait insuffisante, si celui qui connaît la vie de tous les jours des Orientaux, surtout des classes élevées, voulait la devoiler. L'Europe est bien loin d'en avoir la moindre idée."

In this matter I have done my best, at a time too when the hapless English traveller is expected to write like a young lady for young ladies, and never to notice what underlies the most superficial stratum. And I also maintain that the free treatment of topics usually taboo'd and held to be "alekta"—unknown and unfitted for publicity—will be a national benefit to an "Empire of Opinion," whose very basis and buttresses are a thorough knowledge by the rulers of the ruled. Men have been crowned with gold in the Capitol for lesser services rendered to the Respublica.

That the work contains errors, shortcomings and many a lapsus, I am the first and foremost to declare. Yet in justice to myself I must also notice that the maculæ are few and far between; even the most unfriendly and interested critics have failed to point out an abnormal number of slips. And before pronouncing the "Vos plaudite!" or, as the Easterns more politely say, "I implore that my poor name may be raised aloft on the tongue of praise," let me invoke the fair field and courteous favour which the Persian poet expected from his readers.

بپوش گر بخطای رسی و طعنه مزن
که هیچ بشر خالی از خطا نبود

(Veil it, an fault thou find, nor jibe nor jeer :—
None may be found of faults and failings clear!)

RICHARD F. BURTON.

ATHENÆUM CLUB, *September* 30, '86.

APPENDICES.

MEMORANDUM.

I MAKE no apology for the extent of bibliographical and other lists given in this Appendix: they may cumber the book, but they are necessary to complete my design. This has been to supply throughout the ten volumes the young Arabist and student of Orientalism and Anthropology with such assistance as I can render him; and it is my conviction that if with the aid of this version he will master the original text of the "Thousand Nights and a Night," he will find himself at home amongst educated men in Egypt and Syria, Najd and Mesopotamia, and be able to converse with them like a gentleman; not, as too often happens in Anglo-India, like a "Ghoráwálá" (groom). With this object he will learn by heart what instinct and inclination suggest of the proverbs and instances, the verses, the jeux d'esprit, and especially the Koranic citations scattered about the text; and my indices will enable him to hunt up the passage which he may require for quotation even when writing an ordinary letter to a "native" correspondent. Then he will be spared the wasted labour of wading through volumes in order to pick up a line.

The following is the list of Indices :—

APPENDIX I.

Contributions to the Bibliography of the Thousand and One Nights, and their Imitations, with a Table showing the contents of the principal Editions and Translations of the Nights. By W. F. Kirby, Author of "Ed-Dimiryaht, an Oriental Romance"; "The New Arabian Nights," &c.

APPENDIX II.

I. Tables of Contents of the various Arabic texts.
   A. The Unfinished Calcutta Edition (1814-18).
   B. The Breslau Text (1825-43) from Mr. Payne's Version.
   C. The Macnaghten or Turner-Macan Text (A.D. 1839-42), and Bulak Edition (A.H. 1251 = A.D. 1835-36), from Mr. Payne's Version.
   D. The same with Mr. Lane's and my Version.

II. Index to the Tales in the Ten Volumes.

III. Alphabetical Table of the Notes (Anthropological, etc.) prepared by F. Steingass, Ph.D.

Appendix I.

CONTRIBUTIONS TO THE BIBLIOGRAPHY OF THE THOUSAND AND ONE NIGHTS, AND THEIR IMITATIONS, WITH A TABLE SHOWING THE CONTENTS OF THE PRINCIPAL EDITIONS AND TRANSLATIONS OF THE NIGHTS.

BY W. F. KIRBY,

Author of "Ed-Dimiryaht: an Oriental Romance," "The New Arabian Nights," &c.

THE European editions of the Thousand and One Nights, even excluding the hundreds of popular editions which have nothing specially noticeable about them, are very numerous; and the following Notes must, I am fully aware, be incomplete, though they will, perhaps, be found useful to persons interested in the subject. Although I believe that editions of most of the English, French, and German versions of any importance have passed through my hands, I have not had an opportunity of comparing many in other languages, some of which at least may be independent editions not derived from Galland. The imitations and adaptations of The Nights are, perhaps, more numerous than the editions of The Nights themselves, if we exclude mere reprints of Galland; and many of them are even more difficult of access.

In the following Notes, I have sometimes referred to tales by their numbers in the Table.

GALLAND'S MS. AND TRANSLATION.

The first MS. of The Nights known in Europe was brought to Paris by Galland at the close of the 17th century; and his translation was published in Paris, in twelve small volumes, under the title of "Les Mille et une Nuit: Contes Arabes, traduits en François par M. Galland." These volumes appeared at intervals between 1704 and 1717. Galland himself died in 1715, and it is uncertain how far he was responsible for the latter part of the work. Only the first six of the twelve vols. are divided into nights, vol. 6 completing the story of Camaralzaman, and ending with Night 234. The Voyages of Sindbad are not found in Galland's MS., though he has intercalated them as Nights 69-90 between Nos. 3 and 4. It should be mentioned, however, that in some texts (Breslau, for instance) No. 133 is placed much earlier in the series than in others.

The stories in Galland's last six vols. may be divided into two classes, viz., those known to occur in genuine texts of The Nights, and those which do not. To the first category belong Nos. 7, 8, 59, 153, and 170; and some even of these are not found in Galland's own MS., but were derived by him from other sources. The remaining tales (Nos. 191-198) do not really belong to The Nights; and, strange to say, although they are certainly genuine Oriental tales, the actual originals have never been found. I am inclined to think that Galland may, perhaps, have written and adapted them from his recollection of stories which he himself heard related during his own residence in the East, especially as most of these tales appear to be derived rather from Persian or Turkish than from Arabian sources.

The following Preface appeared in vol. 9, which I translate from Talander's German edition, as the original is not before me:—

"The two stories with which the eighth volume concludes do not properly belong to the Thousand and One Nights. They were added and printed without the previous knowledge of the translator, who had not the slightest idea of the trick that had been played upon him until the eighth volume was actually on sale. The reader must not, therefore, be surprised that the story of the Sleeper Awakened, which commences vol. 9, is written as if Scheherazade had related it immediately after the story of Ganem, which forms the greater part of vol. 8. Care will be taken to omit these two stories in a new edition, as not belonging to the work."

It is, perhaps, not to be wondered at that when the new edition was actually published, subsequently to Galland's death, the condemned stories were retained, and the preface withdrawn, though No. 170 still reads as if it followed No. 8.

The information I have been able to collect respecting the disputed tales is very slight. I once saw a MS. advertised in an auction catalogue (I think that of the library of the late Prof. H. H. Wilson) as containing two of Galland's doubtful tales, but which they were was not stated. The fourth and last volume of the MS. used by Galland is lost; but it is almost certain that it did not contain any of these tales (compare Payne, ix. 265, note).

The story of Zeyn Alasnam (No. 191) is derived from the same source as that of the Fourth Durwesh, in the well-known Hindustani reading-book, the Bagh o Bahar. If it is based upon this, Galland has greatly altered and improved it, and has given it the whole colouring of a European moral fairy tale.

The story of Ali Baba (No. 195) is, I have been told, a Chinese tale. It occurs under the title of the Two Brothers and the Forty-nine Dragons in Geldart's Modern Greek Tales. It has also been stated that the late Prof. Palmer met with a very similar story among the Arabs of Sinai (Payne, ix. 266).

The story of Sidi Nouman (No. 194b) may have been based partly upon the Third Shaykh's Story (No. 1c), which Galland omits. The feast of the Ghools is, I believe, Greek or Turkish, rather than Arabic, in character, as vampires, personified plague, and similar horrors are much commoner in the folk-lore of the former peoples.

Many incidents of the doubtful, as well as of the genuine, tales, are common in European folk-lore (versions of Nos. 2 and 198, for instance, occur in Grimm's Kinder und Hausmärchen), and some of the doubtful tales have their analogues in Scott's MS., as will be noticed in due course.

I have not seen Galland's original edition in 12 vols.; but the Stadt-Bibliothek of Frankfort-on-Main contains a copy, published at La Haye, in 12 vols. (with frontispieces), made up of two or more editions, as follows:—

Vol. i. (ed. 6) 1729; vols. ii. iii. iv. (ed. 5) 1729; vols. v. vi. viii. (ed. 5) 1728; vol. vii. (ed. 6) 1731; vols. ix. to xi. (ed. not noted) 1730; and vol. xii. (ed. not noted) 1731.

The discrepancies in the dates of the various volumes looks (as Mr. Clouston has suggested) as if separate volumes were reprinted as required, independently of the others. This might account for vols. v. vi. and viii. of the fifth edition having been apparently reprinted before vols. ii. iii. and iv.

The oldest French version in the British Museum consists of the first eight vols., published at La Haye, and likewise made up of different editions, as follows:—

i. (ed. 5) 1714; ii. iii. iv. (ed. 4) 1714; v. vi. (ed. 5) 1728; vii. (ed. 5) 1719; viii. ("suivant la copie imprimée à Paris"), 1714.

Most French editions (old and new) contain Galland's Dedication, "À Madame, Madame la Marquise d'O., Dame du Palais de Madame la Duchesse de Bourgogne," followed by an "Avertissement." In addition to these, the La Haye copies have Fontenelle's Approbation prefixed to several volumes, but in slightly different words, and bearing different dates. December 27th, 1703 (vol. i.); April 14th, 1704 (vol. vi.); and October 4th, 1705 (vol. vii.). This is according to the British Museum copy; I did not examine the Frankfort copy with reference to the Approbation. The Approbation is translated in full in the old English version as follows: "I have read, by Order of my Lord Chancellor, this Manuscript, wherein I find nothing that ought to hinder its being Printed. And I am of opinion that the Publick will be very well pleased with the Perusal of these Oriental Stories. Paris, 27th December, 1705 [apparently a misprint for 1703] (Signed) FONTENELLE."

In the Paris edition of 1726 *(vide infrà)*, Galland says in his Dedication, "Il a fallu le faire venir de Syrie, et mettre en François, le premier volume que voici, de quatre seulement qui m'ont été envoyez." So, also, in a Paris edition (in eight vols. 12mo.) of 1832; but in the La Haye issue of 1714, we read not "quatre" but "six" volumes. The old German edition of Talander *(vide infrà)* does not contain Galland's Dedication (Epitre) or Avertissement.

The earliest French editions were generally in 12 vols., or six; I possess a copy of a six-volume edition, published at Paris in 1726. The title-page designates it as "nouvelle edition, corrigée."

Galland's work was speedily translated into various European languages, and even now forms the original of all the numerous popular editions. The earliest English editions appear to have been in six volumes, corresponding to the first six of Galland, and ending with the story of Camaralzaman Some of the earlier English editions do not extend further, though the last six volumes of Galland were certainly translated into English before the middle of the last century. The date of appearance of the first edition is unknown to bibliographers; Lowndes quotes an edition of 1724 as the oldest; but the British Museum contains a set of six vols., made up of portions of the second, third and fourth editions, as follows:—

Vols. i. ii. (ed. 4) 1713; vols. iii. iv. (ed. 2) 1712; and vols. v. vi. (ed. 3) 1715.

Here likewise the separate volumes seem to have been reprinted independently of each other; and it is not unlikely that the English translation may have closely followed the French publication, being issued volume by volume, as the French appeared, as far as vol. vi. The title-page of this old edition is very quaint:—

"Arabian Nights Entertainments, consisting of One thousand and one Stories, told by the Sultaness of the Indies to divert the Sultan from the Execution of a Bloody Vow he had made, to marry a Lady every day, and have her head cut off next Morning, to avenge himself for the Disloyalty of the first Sultaness, also containing a better account of the Customs, Manners and Religion of the Eastern Nations, viz., Tartars, Persians and Indians than is to be met with in any Author hitherto published. Translated into French from the Arabian MSS. by Mr. Galland of the Royal Academy, and now done into English. Printed for Andrew Bell at the Cross Keys and Bible, in Cornhill."

I have an English copy in 12 vols., corresponding to the French, published in London, 1753 and 1754, in which vols. 1-5 are ed. X.; vol. 6, ed. IX.; vol. 7, ed. VIII.; vols. 8-10, ed. not stated, and vols. 11 and 12 are ed. V.

The British Museum has an edition in 4to. published in 1772, in farthing numbers, every Monday, Wednesday and Friday. It extends to 79 numbers, forming five volumes ending with Camaralzaman.

The various editions of the old English version appear to be rare, and the set in the British Museum is very poor. I have seen an old edition called the 14th which includes the latter half of Galland's version, and was published in London in four volumes, in 1778. Curiously enough, the "13th edition," also containing the conclusion, was published at Edinburgh in three volumes in 1780. Perhaps it is a reprint of a London edition published before that of 1778. The Scotch appear to have been fond of The Nights, as there are many Scotch editions both of The Nights and the imitations.

Revised or annotated editions by Piguenit (4 vols., London, 1792) and Gough (4 vols., Edinburgh, 1798) may deserve a passing notice.

A new translation of Galland, by Rev. E. Forster, in five vols. 4to.

with engravings from pictures by Robert Smirke, R.A., appeared in 1802; and now commands a higher price than any other edition of Galland. A new edition in 8vo. appeared in 1810. Most of the recent popular English versions are based either upon Forster's or Scott's.

Another translation from Galland by G. S. Beaumont (four vols. 8vo.), appeared in 1811. (Lowndes writes *William* Beaumont.)

Among the various popular editions of later date we may mention an edition in two vols., 8vo., published at Liverpool (1813), and containing Cazotte's Continuation; an edition published by Griffin and Co., in 1866, to which Beckford's "Vathek" is appended; an edition "arranged for the perusal of youthful readers," by the Hon. Mrs. Sugden (Whittaker & Co., 1863); and "Five Favourite Tales from The Arabian Nights in words of one syllable, by A. & E. Warner" (Lewis, 1871).

Some of the English editions of Galland aim at originality by arranging the tales in a different order. The cheap edition published by Dicks in 1868 is one instance.

An English version of Galland was published at Lucknow, in four vols., 8vo., in 1880.

I should, perhaps, mention that I have not noticed De Sacy's "Mille et une Nuit," because it is simply a new edition of Galland; and I have not seen Cardonne's Continuation (mentioned in Cabinet des Fées, xxxvii. p. 83). As Cardonne died in 1784, his Continuation, if genuine, would be the earliest of all.

The oldest German version, by Talander, seems to have appeared in volumes, as the French was issued; and these volumes were certainly reprinted when required, without indication of separate editions; but in slightly varied style, and with alteration of dates. This old German version is said to be rarer than the French. It is in twelve parts—some, however, being double. The set before me is clearly made up of different reprints, and the first title-page is as follows: "Die Tausend und eine Nacht, worinnen seltzame Arabische Historien und wunderbare Begebenheiten, benebst artigen Liebes-Intriguen, auch Sitten und Gewohnheiten der Morgenländer, auf sehr anmuthige Weise erzehlet werden; Erstlich vom Hrn. Galland, der Königl. Academie Mitgliede aus der Arabischen Sprache in die Französische und aus selbiger anitzo ins Deutsche übersetzt: Erster und Anderer Theil. Mit der Vorrede Herrn Talanders. Leipzig: Verlegts Moritz Georg Weidmann Sr. Königl. Maj. in Pohlen und Churfürstl. Durchl. zu Sachsen Buchhändler, Anno 1730." Talander's Preface relates chiefly to the importance of the work as illustrative of Arabian manners and customs, etc. It is dated from "Liegnitz, den 7 Sept., Anno 1710," which fixes the approximate date of publication of the first part of this translation. Vols. i. and ii. of my set (double vol. with frontispiece) are dated 1730, and have Talander's preface; vols. iii. and iv. (divided, but consecutively paged, and with only one title-page and frontispiece and reprint of Talander's preface) are dated 1719; vols. v. and vi (same remarks, except that Talander's preface is here dated 1717) are dated 1737; vol. vii. (no frontispiece; preface dated 1710) is dated 1721; vol. 8 (no frontispiece nor preface, nor does Talander's name appear on the title-page) is dated 1729; vols. ix. and x. (divided, but consecutively paged, and with only one title-page and frontispiece; Talander's name and preface do not appear, but Galland's preface to vol. ix., already mentioned, is prefixed) are dated 1731; and vols. xi. and xii. (same remarks, but no preface) are dated 1732.

Galland's notes are translated, but not his preface and dedication.

There is a later German translation (6 vols. 8vo., Bremen, 1781-1785) by J. H. Voss, the author of the standard German translation of Homer.

The British Museum possesses a Portuguese translation of Galland, in 4 volumes: "As Mil e uma Noites, Contos Arabes," published by Ernesto Chardron, Editor, Porto e Braga, 1881.

There are two editions of a modern Greek work in the British Museum (1792 and 1804), published at Venice (Ενετιηριν) in three small volumes. The first volume contains Galland (Nos. 1-6 of the table) and vols. ii. and iii. chiefly contain the Thousand and One Days. It is, apparently, translated from some Italian work.

Several editions in Italian (Mille ed una Notte) have appeared at Naples and Milan; they are said by Sir R. F. Burton to be mere reprints of Galland.

There are, also, several in Dutch, one of which, by C. Van der Post, in 3 vols. 8vo., published at Utrecht in 1848, purports, I believe, to be a translation from the Arabic, and has been reprinted several times. The Dutch editions are usually entitled, "Arabische Vertellinge." A Danish edition appeared at Copenhagen in 1818, under the title of "Prindsesses Schehezerade. Fortällinger eller de saakatle Tusende og een Nat. Udgivna paa Dansk vid Heelegaan." Another, by Rasmassen, was commenced in 1824; and a third Danish work, probably founded on the Thousand and One Nights, and published in 1816, bears the title, "Digt og Eventyr fra Osterland, af arabiska og persischen utrykta kilder."

I have seen none of these Italian, Dutch or Danish editions; but there is little doubt that most, if not all, are derived from Galland's work.

The following is the title of a Javanese version, derived from one of the Dutch editions, and published at Leyden in 1865: "Eenige Vertel. llngen uit de Arabisch duizend en één Nacht Naar de Nederduitsche vertaling in het Javaansch vertaald, door Winter-Roorda."

Mr. A. G. Ellis has shown me an edition of Galland's Aladdin (No. 193) in Malay, by M. Van der Lawan (?) printed in Batavia, A.D. 1869.

CAZOTTE'S CONTINUATION, AND THE COMPOSITE EDITIONS OF THE ARABIAN NIGHTS.

We shall speak elsewhere of the Cabinet des Fées; but the last four volumes of this great collection (38 to 41) published at Geneva from 1788 to 1793, contain a work entitled, "Les Veillées du Sultan Schahriar avec la Sultane Scheherazade; histoires incroyables, amusantes et morales, traduites de l'arabe par M. Cazotte et D. Chavis. Faisant suite aux Mille et une Nuits" Some copies bear the abridged title of "La suite des Mille et une Nuits. Contes Arabes, traduits par Dom Chavis et M. Cazotte."

This collection of tales was pronounced to be spurious by many critics, and has even been styled "a bare-faced forgery" by a writer in the *Edinburgh Review* of July, 1886. It is, however, certain that the greater part, if not all, of these tales are founded on genuine Eastern sources, though very few have any real claim to be regarded as actually part of the Thousand and One Nights.

Translations of the originals of most of these tales have been published by Caussin de Perceval and Gauttier; and a comparison clearly shows the great extent to which Chavis and Cazotte have altered, amplified and (in a literary sense) improved their materials.

It is rather surprising that no recent edition of this work seems to have been issued, perhaps owing to the persistent doubts cast upon its authenticity, only a few of the tales, and those not the best, having appeared in different collections. My friend, Mr. A. G. Ellis, himself an Oriental scholar, has remarked to me that he considers these tales as good as the old "Arabian Nights;" and I quite agree with him that Chavis and Cazotte's Continuation is well worthy of re-publication in its entirety.

The following are the principal tales comprised in this collection, those included in our Table from later authors being indicated.

1. The Robber Caliph, or the Adventures of Haroun Alraschid with the Princess of Persia, and the beautiful Zutulbe. (No. 246.)
2. The Power of Destiny, being the History of the Journey of Giafar to Damas, containing the Adventures of Chebib and his Family. (No. 280.)
3. History of Halechalbe and the Unknown Lady. (No. 204c).
4. Story of Xailoun the Idiot.
5. The Adventures of Simoustapha and the Princess Ilsetilsone. (No. 247.)
6. History of Alibengiad, Sultan of Herak, and of the False Birds of Paradise.
7. History of Sinkarib and his Two Viziers. (No. 249.)
8. History of the Family of the Schebandad of Surat.
9. Story of Bohetzad and his Ten Viziers. (No. 174.)
10. Story of Habib and Dorathil-Goase. (No. 251.)
11. History of the Maugraby, or the Magician.

Of these, Nos. 4, 6, 8 and 11 only are not positively known in the original. No. 11 is interesting, as it is the seed from which Southey's "Thalaba the Destroyer" was derived.

On the word Maugraby, which means simply Moor, Cazotte has the following curious note: "Ce mot signifie barbare, barbaresque plus proprement. On jure encore par lui en Provençe, en Languedoc, et en Gascogne Maugraby; ou ailleurs en France Meugrebleu."

The Domdaniel, where Zatanai held his court with Maugraby and his pupil-magicians, is described as being under the sea near Tunis. In Weil's story of Joodar and Mahmood (No. 201) the magician Mahmood is always called the Moor of Tunis.

No. 3 (=our No. 204c) contains the additional incident of the door opened only once a year which occurs in our No. 9a, aa.

Moore probably took the name Namouna from Cazotte's No. 5, in which it occurs. In the same story we find a curious name of a Jinniyah, Setelpedour. Can it be a corruption of Sitt El Budoor?

For further remarks on Cazotte's Continuation, compare Russell's History of Aleppo, i. p. 385; and Russell and Scott, Ouseley's Oriental Collections, i. pp. 246, 247; ii. p. 25; and the "Gentleman's Magazine" for February, 1779.

An English version under the title "Arabian Tales, or a Continuation of the Arabian Nights' Entertainments," translated by Robert Heron, was published in Edinburgh in 1792 in 4 vols., and in London in 1794 in 3 vols. It was reprinted in Weber's "Tales of the East" (Edinburgh, 1812); and, as already mentioned, is included in an edition of the Arabian Nights published in Liverpool in 1813.

A German translation forms vols. 5 to 8 of the "Blaue Bibliothek," published in Gotha in 1790 and 1791; and the British Museum possesses vols. 3 and 4 of a Russian edition, published at Moscow in 1794 and 1795.

Respecting the work of Chavis and Cazotte, Sir R. F. Burton remarks, "Dom Dennis Chavis was a Syrian priest of the order of Saint Basil, who was invited to Paris by the learned minister, Baron Arteuil, and he was assisted by M. Cazotte, a French author, then well known, but wholly ignorant of Arabic. These tales are evidently derived from native sources; the story of Bohetzad (King Bakhtiyár) and his Ten Wazirs is taken bodily from the Bres. Edit. [not so; but the original Arabic had long been known in the French libraries]. As regards the style and treatment, it is sufficient to say that the authors out-Gallanded Galland, while Heron exaggerates every fault of his original."

The first enlarged edition of Galland in French was published by Caussin de Perceval at Paris in 9 vols., 8vo. (1806). In addition to Galland's version he added four tales (Nos. 21a, 22, 32 and 37), with which he had been furnished by Von Hammer. He also added a series of tales, derived from MSS. in the Parisian libraries, most of which correspond to those of Cazotte.

Les Mille et une Nuits, Contes Arabes, Traduits en François par Galland, Nouvelle édition revue sur les textes orientaux et augmentée de plusieurs nouvelles et contes traduites des langues orientaux, par M. Destains, précédée d'un notice historique sur Galland par M. Charles Nodier. Paris, 1822.

This edition is in 6 vols. 8vo, and proves to be of special interest. The first 5 vols. contain the ordinary version of Galland, and the 6th vol. contains a selection of tales translated from Scott's vol. 6, eked out with Chavis and Cazotte's Story of Habib. (No. 250 of our Table.)

The most important of the later French editions was published by E. Gauttier in 7 vols. in 1822; it contains much new matter. At the end the editor gives a list of all the tales which he includes, with arguments. He has rather oddly distributed his material so as to make only 568 nights. The full contents are given in our Table; the following points require more special notice. Vol. i. Gauttier omits the Third Shaykh's Story (No. 1c) on account of its indecency, although it is really no worse than any other story in The Nights. In the story of the Fisherman he has fallen into a very curious series of errors. He has misunderstood King Yunan's reference to King Sindibad (Burton, i. night v.) to refer to the Book of Sindibad (No. 135), and has confounded it with the story of the Forty Vazirs, which he says exists in Arabic as well as in Turkish. Of this latter, therefore, he gives an imperfect version, embedded in the story of King Yunan (No. 2a). Here it may be observed that another imperfect French version of the Forty Vazirs had previously been published by Petis de la Croix under the title of Turkish Tales. A complete German version by Dr. Walter F. A. Behrnauer was published at Leipzig in 1851, and an English version by Mr. E. J. W. Gibb was published by Redway in 1886.

Vol. ii. After No. 6 Gauttier places versions of Nos. 32 and 184 by Langlès. The Mock Caliph is here called Aly-Chah. The other three tales given by Caussin de Perceval from Von Hammer's MSS. are omitted by Gauttier. Vol. v. (after No. 198) concludes with two additional tales (Nos. 207h and 218) from Scott's version. But the titles are changed, No. 207h being called the Story of the Young Prince and the Green Bird, and No. 218 the Story of Mahmood, although there is another story of Mahmood in vol. i. (= No. 135 m) included as part of the Forty Vazirs.

Vol. vi. includes the Ten Vazirs (No. 174) derived, however, not from the Arabic, but from the Persian Bakhtiyár Nameh. Three of the subordinate tales in the Arabic version are wanting in Gauttier's, and another is transferred to his vol. vii., but he includes one, the King and Queen of Abyssinia (No. 252), which appears to be wanting in the Arabic. The remainder of the volume contains tales from Scott's version, the title of Mazin of Khorassaun (No. 215) being altered to the Story of Azem and the Queen of the Genii.

Vol. vii. contains a series of tales of which different versions of six only (Nos. 30, 174, 246, 248, 249 and 250) were previously published. Though these have no claim to be considered part of The Nights, they are of sufficient interest to receive a passing mention, especially as Gauttier's edition seems not to have been consulted by any later writer on The Nights, except Habicht, who based his own edition mainly upon it. Those peculiar to Gauttier's edition are therefore briefly noticed.

Princess Ameny (No. 253).—A princess who leaves home disguised as a man, and delivers another princess from a black slave. The episode (253b) is a story of enchantment similar to Nos. 1a-c.

Aly Djohary (No. 254).—Story of a young man's expedition in search of a magical remedy.

The Princes of Cochin China (No. 255).—The princes travel in search of their sister who is married to a Jinni, who is under the curse of Solomon. The second succeeds in breaking the spell, and thus rescues both his brother, his sister, and the Jinni by killing a bird to which the destiny of the last is attached. (This incident is common in fiction; we find it in the genuine Nights in Nos. 154a and 201.)

The Wife with Two Husbands (No. 256).—A well-known Eastern story; it may be found in Wells' "Mehemet the Kurd," pp. 121-127, taken from the Forty Vazirs. Compare Gibb, the 24th Vazir's Story, pp. 257-266.

The Favourite (No. 257).—One of the ordinary tales of a man smuggled into a royal harem in a chest (compare Nos. 6b and 166).

Youssouf and the Indian Merchant (No. 258).—Story of a ruined man travelling to regain his fortune.

Prince Benazir (No. 258).—Story of a Prince promised at his birth, and afterwards given up by his parents to an evil Jinni, whom he ultimately destroys. (Such promises, especially, as here, in cases of difficult labour, are extremely common in folk-tales; the idea probably originated in the dedication of a child to the Gods). Gauttier thinks that this story may have suggested that of Maugraby to Cazotte; but it appears to me rather doubtful whether it is quite elaborate enough for Cazotte to have used it in this manner.

Selim, Sultan of Egypt (No. 261).—This and its subordinate tales chiefly relate to unfaithful wives; that of Adileh (No. 261b) is curious; she is restored to life by Jesus (whom Gauttier, from motives of religious delicacy, turns into a Jinni!) to console her disconsolate husband, and immediately betrays the latter. These tales are apparently from the Forty Vazirs; cf. Gibb, the 10th Vazir's Story, pp. 122-129 (= our No. 261) and the Sixth Vazir's Story, pp. 32-84 (= No. 261b).

The bulk of the tales in Gauttier's vol. vii. are derived from posthumous MSS. of M. Langlès, and several have never been published in English. Gauttier's version of Heycar (No. 248) was contributed by M. Agoub.

The best-known modern German version (Tausend und Eine Nacht, Arabische Erzählungen, Deutsch von Max. Habicht, Fr. H. von der Hagen und Carl Schall. Breslau, 15 vols. 12mo.) is mainly based upon Gauttier's edition, but with extensive additions, chiefly derived from the Breslau text. An important feature of this version is that it includes translations of the prefaces of the various editions used by the editors, and therefore supplies a good deal of information not always easily accessible elsewhere. There are often brief notes at the end of the volumes.

The fifth edition of Habicht's version is before me, dated 1840; but the preface to vol. i. is dated 1824, which may be taken to represent the approximate date of its first publication. The following points in the various vols. may be specially noticed:—

Vol. i. commences with the preface of the German editor, setting forth the object and scope of his edition; and the prefaces of Gauttier and Galland follow. No. 1c, omitted by Gauttier, is inserted in its place. In vols. ii. and iii. (No. 133) notes, chiefly from Langlès, are appended to the Voyages of Sindbad; and the destinations of the first six are given as follows:—

I. Voyage to Sumatra.	IV. Voyage to the Sunda Islands.
II. Voyage to Ceylon.	V. Voyage to the Sunda Islands.
III. Voyage to Selahat.	VI. Voyage to Zeilan.

Vol. v. contains an unimportant notice from Galland, with additional remarks by the German editors, respecting the division of the work into Nights.

Vol vi. contains another unimportant preface respecting Nos. 191 and 192.

Vol. x.—Here the preface is of more importance, relating to the contents of the volume, and especially to the Ten Vazirs (No. 174).

Vol. xi. contains tales from Scott. The preface contains a full account of his MSS., and the tales published in his vol. vi. This preface is taken partly from Ouseley's Oriental Collections, and partly from Scott's own preface.

Vol. xii. contains tales from Gauttier, vol. vii. The preface gives the full contents of Clarke's and Von Hammer's MSS.

Vol. xiii. includes Caussin de Perceval's Preface, the remaining tales from Gauttier's vol. vii. (ending with night 568); and four tales from Caussin which Gauttier omits (Nos. 21a, 22, 37 and 202).

Vols. xiv. and xv. (extending from night 884 to night 1001) consist of tales from the Breslau edition, to which a short preface, signed by Dr. Max. Habicht, is prefixed. The first of these tales is a fragment of the important Romance of Saif Zul Yezn (so often referred to by Lane), which seems to have been mixed with Habicht's MS. of The Nights by mistake. (Compare Payne, Tales, iii. 243.)

In this fragment we have several incidents resembling The Nights; there is a statue which sounds an alarm when an enemy enters a city (cf. Nos. 59 and 137); Saif himself is converted to the faith of Abraham, and enters a city where a book written by Japhet is preserved. The text of this story has lately been published; and Sir R. F. Burton informs me that he thinks he has seen a complete version in some European language; but I have not succeeded in obtaining any particulars concerning it.

On account of the interest and importance of the work, I append to this section an English version of the fragment translated into German by Habicht. (From the extreme simplicity of the style, which I have preserved, I suspect that the translation is considerably abridged.)

There is an Icelandic version of The Nights (Þúsund og ein Nott. Arabiskar Sögur. Kaupmannahöfn, 1857, 4 vols. roy. 8vo.), which contains Galland's tales, and a selection of others, distributed into 1001 Nights, and apparently taken chiefly from Gauttier, but with the addition of two or three which seem to be borrowed from Lane (Nos. 9a, 163, 165, etc.). It is possibly derived immediately from some Danish edition.

There is one popular English version which may fairly be called a composite edition; but it is not based upon Gauttier. This is the "Select Library Edition. Arabian Nights' Entertainments, selected and revised for general use. To which are added other specimens of Eastern Romance. London: James Burns, 1847. 2 vols."

It contains the following tales from the Nights: Nos. 134, 3, 133, 162, 1, 2, 155, 191, 193, 192, 194, 194a, 194c, 21, 198, 170, 6.

No. 134 is called the City of Silence, instead of the City of Brass, and is certainly based partly upon Lane. In No. 155, Manar Al-Sanr is called Nur Al-Nissa. One story, "The Wicked Dervise," is taken from the latter part of that of Prince Fadlallah (1001 Days), cf. posteà, No. 4a, or from No. 251, j, of the Table, *post.* Another, "The Enchanters, or the Story of Misnar," is taken from the "Tales of the Genii." Four other tales, "Jalaladdeen of Bagdad," "The two Talismans," "The Story of Haschem," and "Jussof, the Merchant of Balsora," clearly German imitations, are said to be translated from the German of Grimm; and there are two others, "Abdullah and Balsora," and "The King and his Servant," the origin of which I do not recognise, although I think I have read the last before.

Grimm's story of Haschem concludes with the hero's promotion to the post of Grand Vizier to Haroun Al-Rashid, in consequence of the desire of the aged "Giafar" to end his days in peaceful retirement! The principal incident in Jalaladdeen is that of the Old Woman in the Chest, borrowed from the well-known story of the Merchant Abudah in the "Tales of the Genii," and it is thus an imitation of an imitation.

THE COMMENCEMENT OF THE STORY OF SAIF ZUL YEZN (ZU'L YAZAN) ACCORDING TO HABICHT'S GERMAN VERSION.

In very ancient times, long before the age of Mohammed, there lived a King of Yemen, named Zul Yezn. He was a Himyarite of the race of Fubbaa (Tabbá'), and had large armies and a great capital. His Minister was named Yottreb (Yathrab = Medinat), and was well skilled in the knowledge of the ancients. He once had a vision in which the name of the Prophet was revealed to him, with the announcement of his mission in later times; and he was also informed that he would be the last of the Prophets. In consequence of this vision he believed in the Prophet before his advent; but he concealed his faith. One day the King held a review of his troops, and was delighted with their number and handsome appearance. He said to the Wazir, "Is there any person on earth whose power can compare with mine?" "O yes," answered the Wazir, "there is King Baal-Beg, whose troops fill the deserts and the cultivated lands, the plains and the valleys." "I must make war upon him, then," exclaimed the King, "and destroy his power." He immediately ordered the army to prepare to march, and after a few days the drums and trumpets were heard. The King and his Wazir set forth in magnificent array, and after a rapid march they arrived before the holy city Medina [Mekka?], which may God keep in high renown! The Wazir then said to the King, "Here is the holy house of God, and the place of great ceremonies. No one should enter here who is not perfectly pure, and with head and feet bare. Pass around it with your companions, according to the custom of the Arabs." The King was so pleased with the place that he determined to destroy it, to carry the stones to his own country, and to rebuild it there, that the Arabs might come to him on pilgrimage, and that he might thus exalt himself above all Kings. He pondered over this plan all night, but next morning he found his body fearfully swollen. He immediately sent for his Wazir, and lamented over his misfortune. "This is a judgment sent upon you," replied the Wazir, "by the Lord of this house. If you alter your intention of destroying the temple, you will be healed at once." The King gave up his project, and soon found himself cured. Soon afterwards he said to himself, "This misfortune happened to me at night, and left me next day of its own accord; but I will certainly destroy the house." But next morning his face was so covered with open ulcers that he could no longer be recognised. The Wazir then approached him and said, "O King, renounce your intention, for it would be rebellion against the Lord of Heaven and Earth, Who can destroy every one who opposes Him." When the King heard this, he reflected awhile and said, "What would you wish me to do?" The Wazir replied, "Cover the house with carpets from Yemen." The King resolved to do this, and when night came he retired to rest. He then saw an apparition which ordered him not to march further into the country of King Baal-Beg, but to turn towards Abyssinia and Nigritia, adding, "Remain there, and choose it as thy residence, and assuredly one of thy race will arise through whom the threat of Noah shall be fulfilled." When the King awoke next morning he related this to the Wazir, who advised him to use his own judgment about it. The King immediately gave orders to march. The army set forth, and after ten days they arrived at a country the soil of which seemed to consist of chalk, for it appeared quite white. The Wazir Yottreb then went to the King and requested his permission to found a city here for his people. "Why so?" asked the King. "Because," replied the Wazir, "this will one day be the place of Refuge of the Prophet Mohammed, who will be sent at the end of time." The King then gave his consent, and Yottreb immediately summoned architects and surveyors, who dug out the ground, and reared the walls, and erected beautiful palaces. They did not desist from the work until the Wazir ordered a number of his people to remove to this city with their families. This was done, and their posterity inhabit the city to this day. He then gave them a scroll, and said, "He who comes to you as a fugitive to this house will be the ruler of this city." He then called the city Yottreb after his own name, and the scroll descended from father to son till the Apostle of God arrived as a fugitive from Mecca, when the inhabitants went out to meet him, and presented him with it. They afterwards became his auxiliaries and were known as the Ansar. But we must now return to King Zul Yezn. He marched several days towards Abyssinia, and at last arrived in a beautiful and fertile country where he informed his Wazir that he would like to build a city for his subjects. He gave the necessary orders, which were diligently executed; canals were dug and the surrounding country cultivated; and the city was named Medinat El-Hamra, the Red. At last the news reached the King of Abyssinia, whose name was Saif Ar-Raad (Thunder-sword), and whose capital was called Medinat ad-Durr (the Rich in Houses). Part of this city was built on solid land and the other was built in the sea. This Prince could bring an army of 600,000 men into the field, and his authority extended to the extremity of the then known world. When he was informed of the invasion of Zul Yezn, he summoned his two Wazirs, who were named Sikra Divas and Ar-Ryf. The latter was well versed in ancient books, in which he had discovered that God would one day send a Prophet who would be the last of the series. He believed this himself, but concealed it from the Abyssinians, who were still worshippers of Saturn. When the Wazirs came before the King, he said to them, "See how the Arabs are advancing against us; I must fight them." Sikra Divas opposed this design, fearing lest the threat of Noah should be fulfilled. "I would rather advise you," said he, "to make the King a present and to send with it the most beautiful maiden in your Palace. But give her poison secretly, and instruct her to poison the King when she is alone with him. If he is once dead, his army will retire without a battle." The King adopted this advice, and prepared rich presents, and summoned a beautiful girl, whose artfulness and malice were well known. Her name was Kamrya (Moonlight). The King said to her, "I have resolved to send you as a present, for a secret object. I will give you poison, and when you are alone with the Prince to whom I will send you, drop it into his cup, and let him take it. As soon as he is dead, his army will leave us in peace." "Very well, my master," replied the girl, "I will accomplish your wish." He then sent her with the other presents and a letter to the city of Zul Yezn. But the Wazir Ar-Ryf had scarcely left the King's presence when he wrote a letter, and commanded a slave to carry it to Zul Yezn. "If you can give it to him before the arrival of the slave-girl," added he, "I will give you your freedom." The slave made all possible haste to the Arab King, but yet the presents arrived before him. A chamberlain went to the King and informed him that a messenger had arrived at the gate with presents from the King of Abyssinia, and requested permission to enter. Zul Yezn immediately ordered that he should be admitted, and the presents and the maiden were at once delivered to him. When he saw her he was astonished at her beauty, and was greatly delighted. He immediately ordered her to be conveyed to his palace, and was very soon overcome with love for her. He was just about to dissolve the assembly to visit Kamrya, when the Wazir Yottreb detained him, saying, "Delay a while, O King, for I fear there is some treachery hidden behind this present. The Abyssinians hate the Arabs exceedingly, but are unwilling to make war with them, lest the threat of Noah should be fulfilled. It happened one day that Noah was sleeping when intoxicated with wine, and the wind uncovered him. His son Ham laughed, and did not cover him; but his other son Seth [*sic*] came forward and covered him up. When Noah awoke, he exclaimed to Ham, 'May God blacken thy face!' But to Seth he said, 'May God make the posterity of thy brother the servants of thine until the Day of Resurrection!' This is the threat which they dread as the posterity of Ham." While the King was still conversing with his Wazir, the Chamberlain announced the arrival of a messenger with a letter. He was immediately admitted, and delivered the letter, which was read by the Wazir Yottreb. Ar-Ryf had written, "Be on your guard against Kamrya, O King, for she hath poison with her, and is ordered to kill you when she is alone with you." The King now began loudly to praise the acuteness of his Wazir, and went immediately to Kamrya with his drawn sword. When he entered, she rose and kissed the ground, but he exclaimed, "You have come here to poison me!" She was confounded, and took out the poison and handed it to the King, full of artifice, and thinking, "If I tell him the truth, he will have a better opinion of me, and if he confides in me I can kill him in some other manner than with this poison." It fell out as she expected, for the King loved her, gave her authority over his palace and his female slaves, and found himself very happy in her possession But she herself found her life so pleasant that, although King Ar-Raad frequently sent to ask her why she had not fulfilled her commission, she always answered, "Wait a little; I am seeking an opportunity, for the King is very suspicious." Some time passed over, and at length she became pregnant. Six months afterwards Zul Yezn fell ill; and as his sickness increased, he assembled the chief men of his Court, informed them of the condition of Kamrya, and after commending her to their protection, he ordered that if she bore a son he should succeed him. They promised to fulfil his commands, and a few days afterwards Zul Yezn died. Kamrya now governed the country, till she brought forth a son. He was a child of uncommon beauty, and had a small mole on his cheek. When she saw the child she envied him, and said to herself, "What! shall he take away the Kingdom from me? No, it shall never be"; and from this time forward she determined to put him to death. After forty days, the people requested to see their King. She showed him to them, and seated him on the throne of the kingdom, whereupon they did homage to him and then dispersed. His mother took him back into the Palace, but her envy increased so much that she had already grasped a sword to kill him, when her nurse entered and asked what she was going to do? "I am about to kill him," answered she. "Have you not reflected?" said the nurse, "that if you kill him the people will revolt, and may kill you also?" "Let me kill him," persisted she, "for even should they kill me too, I should at least be released from my envy." "Do not act thus," warned the nurse, "or you may repent it when repentance cannot help you." "It must be done," said Kamrya. "Nay, then," said the nurse, "it it cannot be avoided, let him at least be cast into the desert, and if he lives, so much the better for him; but if he dies, you are rid of him for ever." She followed this advice, and set out on the way at night time with the child, and halted at a distance of four days' journey, when she sat down under a tree in the desert. She took him on her lap, and suckled him once more, and then laid him on a bed, putting a purse under his head, containing a thousand gold pieces and many jewels. "Whoever finds him," said she, "may use the money to bring him up"; and thus she left him.

It happened by the gracious decree of God that hunters who were chasing gazelles surprised a female with a fawn; the former took to flight, and the hunters carried off the little one. When the mother returned from the pasture and found her fawn gone, she traversed the desert in all directions in search of it, and at length the crying of the deserted child attracted her. She lay down by the child and the child sucked her. The gazelle left him again to go to graze, but always returned to the little one when she was satisfied. This went on till it pleased God that she should fall into the net of a hunter. But she became enraged, tore the net, and fled. The hunter pursued her, and overtook her when she reached the child, and was about to give him suck. But the arrival of the hunter compelled the gazelle to take flight, and the child began to cry because he was not yet satisfied. The hunter was astonished at the sight, and when he lifted the child up he saw the purse under his head, and a string of jewels round his neck. He immediately took the child with him, and went to a town belonging to an Abyssinian king named Afrakh, who was a dependent of King Saif Ar-Raad. He handed over the child to him, saying that he had found it in the lair of a gazelle. When the King took the child from the hunter, it smiled at him, and God awakened a feeling of love towards him in the King's heart; and he then noticed the mole on his cheek. But when his Wazir Sikar Diun, the brother of Sikar Divas, who was Wazir to King Saif Ar-Raad, entered and saw the child, God filled his heart with hate towards him. "Do not believe what this man told you," he said, when the King told him the wonderful story of the discovery, "it can only be the child of a mother who has come by it wrongly, and has abandoned it in the desert, and it would be better to kill it." "I cannot easily consent to this," said the King. But he had hardly spoken when the Palace was filled with sounds of rejoicing, and he was informed that his wife had just been safely delivered of a child. On this news he took the boy on his arm, and went to his wife, and found that the new-born child was a girl, and that she had a red mole on her cheek. He wondered when he saw this, and said to Sikar Diun, "See how beautiful they are!" But when the Wazir saw it, he slapped his face and cast his cap on the ground, exclaiming, "Should these two moles unite, I prophesy the downfall of Abyssinia, for they presage a great calamity. It would be better to kill either the boy or your daughter." "I will kill neither of them," replied the King, "for they have been guilty of no crime." He immediately provided nurses for the two children, naming his daughter Shama (Mole) and the boy Wakhs[1] El Fellat (Lonely One, or Desert); and he reared them in separate apartments that they might not see each other. When they were ten years old, Wakhs El Fellat grew very strong, and soon became a practised

---

1 Probably Wakksh al-Falák = Feral of the Wild.

horseman, and surpassed all his companions in this accomplishment and in feats of arms. But when he was fifteen, he was so superior to all others, that Sikar Diun threatened the King that he would warn King Saif Ar-Raad that he was nurturing his enemy in his house, if he did not immediately banish him from the country: and this threat caused King Afrakh great alarm. It happened that he had a general, who was called Gharag El Shaker (Tree-splitter), because he was accustomed to hurl his javelin at trees, and thus to cleave them asunder. He had a fortress three days' journey from the town; and the King said to him, "Take Wakhs El Fellat to your castle, and never let him return to this neighbourhood." He added privately, "Look well after him and preserve him from all injury, and have him instructed in all accomplishments." The general withdrew, and took the boy with him to his castle, and instructed him thoroughly in all accomplishments and sciences. One day he said to him, "One warlike exercise is still unknown to you." "What is that?" said Wakhs El Fellat. "Come and see for yourself," replied he. The general then took him to a place where several trees were growing, which were so thick that a man could not embrace the trunk. He took his javelin, hurled it at one of them, and split the trunk. Wakhs El Fellat then asked for the javelin, and performed the same feat to the astonishment of his instructor. "Woe to thee," exclaimed he, "for I perceive that you are the man through whom the threat of Noah will be fulfilled against us. Fly, and never let yourself be seen again in our country, or I will kill you." Wakhs El Fellat then left the town, not knowing where to go. He subsisted for three days on the plants of the earth, and at last he arrived at a town encircled with high walls, the gates of which were closed. The inhabitants were clothed in black, and uttered cries of lamentation. In the foreground he saw a bridal-tent and a tent of mourning. This was the city of King Afrakh who had reared him, and the cause of the mourning of the inhabitants was as follows. Sikar Diun was very angry that the King had refused to follow his advice, and put the boy to death, and had left the town to visit one of his friends, who was a magician, to whom he related the whole story. "What do you propose to do now?" asked the magician. "I will attempt to bring about a separation between him and his daughter," said the Wazir. "I will assist you," was the answer of the magician. He immediately made the necessary preparations, and summoned an evil Jinni named Mukhtatif (Ravisher) who enquired, "What do you require of me?" "Go quickly to the city of King Afrakh, and contrive that the inhabitants shall leave it." In that age men had intercourse with the more powerful Jinn, and each attained their ends by means of the other. The Jinn did not withdraw themselves till after the advent of the Prophet. The Magician continued, "When the inhabitants have left the city, they will ask you what you want. Then say, Bring me out Shama, the daughter of your King, adorned with all her jewels, and I will come to-morrow and carry her away. But if you refuse, I will destroy your city, and destroy you all together." When Mukhtatif heard the words of this priest of magic, he did as he was commanded, and rushed to the city. When Sikar Diun saw this, he returned to King Afrakh to see what would happen; but he had scarcely arrived when the voice of Mukhtatif resounded above the city. The inhabitants went to the King, and said, "You have heard what is commanded, and if you do not yield willingly you will be obliged to do so by force." The King then went weeping to the mother of the Princess, and informed her of the calamity. She could scarcely contain herself for despair, and all in the Palace wept at parting from the Princess. Meantime Shama was richly attired, torn from her parents, and hurried to the bridal tent before the town, to be carried away by the evil Jinni. The inhabitants were all assembled on the walls of the city, weeping. It was just at this moment that Wakhs El Fellat arrived from the desert, and entered the tent to see what was going on. When King Afrakh, who was also on the wall, saw him, he cried out to him, but he did not listen, and dismounted, fastened his horse to a tent-stake, and entered. Here he beheld a maiden of extraordinary beauty and perfection, but she was weeping. While he was completely bewildered by her beauty, she was no less struck by his appearance. "Who art thou?" said the maiden to him. "Tell me rather who art thou?" returned he. "I am Shama, the daughter of King Afrakh." "Thou art Shama?" he exclaimed, "and I am Wakhs El Fellat, who was reared by thy father." When they were thus acquainted, they sat down together to talk over their affairs, and she took this opportunity of telling him what had passed with the Jinni, and how he was coming to carry her away. "O you shall see how I will deal with him," answered he; but at this moment the evil Jinni approached, and his wings darkened the sun. The inhabitants uttered a terrible cry, and the Jinni darted upon the tent, and was about to raise it when he saw a man there, talking to the daughter of the King. "Woe to thee, O son of the earth!" he exclaimed; "What authority have you to sit by my betrothed?" When Wakhs El Fellat saw the terrible form of the Jinni, a shudder came over him, and he cried to God for aid. He immediately drew his sword, and struck at the Jinni, who had just extended his right hand to seize him, and the blow was so violent that it struck off the hand. "What! you would kill me?" exclaimed Mukhtatif, and he took up his hand, put it under his arm, and flew away. Upon this there was a loud cry of joy from the walls of the city The gates were thrown open, and King Afrakh approached, accompanied by a crowd of people with musical instruments, playing joyful music; and Wakhs El Fellat was invested with robes of honour: but when Sikar Diun saw it, it was gall to him. The King prepared an apartment expressly for Wakhs El Fellat, and while Shama returned to her Palace, he gave a great feast in honour of her deliverance from the fiend. After seven days had passed, Shama went to Wakhs El Fellat; and said to him, "Ask me of my father to-morrow, for you have rescued me, and he will not be able to refuse you." He consented very willingly, and went to the King early next morning. The King gave him a very favourable reception, and seated him with him on the throne: but Wakhs El Fellat had not courage to prefer his suit, and left him after a short interview. He had not long returned to his own room when Shama entered, saluted him, and asked, "Why did you not demand me?" "I was too bashful," he replied. "Lay this feeling aside," returned she, "and demand me." "Well, I will certainly do so to-morrow," answered he. Thereupon she left him and returned to her own apartment. Early next morning Wakhs El Fellat went again to the King, who gave him a friendly reception and made him sit with him. But he was still unable to prefer his suit, and returned to his own room. Soon after Shama came to him and said, "How long is this bashfulness to last? Take courage, and if not, request some one else to speak for you." She then left him, and next morning he repeated his visit to the King. "What is your request?" asked the latter. "I am come as a suitor," said Wakhs El Fellat, "and ask the hand of your noble daughter Shama." When Sikar Diun heard this, he slapped his face. "What is the matter with you?" asked the King. "This is what I have foreseen," answered he, "for if these two moles unite, the destruction of Abyssinia is accomplished." "How can I refuse him?" replied the King, "when he has just delivered her from the fiend." "Tell him," answered Sikar Diun, "that you must consult with your Wazir." The King then returned to Wakhs El Fellat, and said, "My son, your request is granted as far as I am concerned, but I leave my Wazir to arrange it with you, so you must consult him about it." Wakhs El Fellat immediately turned to the Wazir, and repeated his request to him. Sikar Diun answered him in a friendly manner. "The affair is as good as arranged, no one else is suited for the King's daughter, but you know that the daughters of the Kings require a dowry." "Ask what you please," returned Wakhs El Fellat. "We do not ask you for money or money's worth," said the Wazir, "but for the head of a man named Sudun, the Ethiopian." "Where can I find him?" said the Prince. The Wazir replied, "He is said to dwell in the fortress of Reg, three days' journey from here." "But what if I fail to bring the head of Sudun?" asked he. "Nay, you will have it," returned the Wazir; and after this understanding the audience ceased, and each returned to his dwelling.

Now this Sudun had built his fortress on the summit of a high hill. It was very secure, and he defended it with the edge of the sword. It was his usual resort, from whence he sallied forth on plundering expeditions, and rendered the roads unsafe. At length the news of him reached King Saif Ar-Raad, who sent against him three thousand men, but he routed and destroyed them all. Upon this the King sent a larger number against him, who experienced the same fate. He then despatched a third army, upon which Sudun fortified himself afresh, and reared the walls of his fortress so high that an eagle could scarcely pass them. We will now return to Shama, who went to Wakhs El Fellat, and reproached him with the conditions he had agreed to, and added, "It would be better for you to leave this place and take me with you, and we will put ourselves under the protection of some powerful king." "God forbid," replied he, "that I should take you with me in so dishonourable a manner." As he still positively refused to consent, she grew angry, and left him. Wakhs El Fellat lay down to rest, but he could not sleep. So he rose up, mounted his horse, and rode away at midnight; and in the morning he met a horseman who stationed himself in his path, but who was so completely armed that his face was concealed. When Wakhs El Fellat saw him, he cried to him, "Who are you, and where are you going?" But instead of replying, he pressed upon him, and aimed a blow which Wakhs El Fellat successfully parried. A fight then commenced between them, which lasted till nearly evening. At last the difference in their strength became perceptible, and Wakhs El Fellat struck his adversary so violent a blow with his javelin that his horse fell to the ground. He then dismounted, and was about to slay him, when the horseman cried to him, "Do not kill me, O brave warrior, or you will repent when repentance will no more avail you." "Tell me who you are?" returned Wakhs El Fellat. "I am Shama, the daughter of King Afrakh," replied the horseman. "Why have you acted thus?" asked he. "I wished to try whether you would be able to hold your own against Sudun's people," she replied. "I have tried you now, and found you so valiant that I fear no longer on your account. Take me with you, O hero." "God forbid that I should do so," he returned; "what would Sikar Diun and the others say? They would say that if Shama had not been with him he would never have been able to prevail against Sudun." She then raised her eyes to heaven, and said, "O God, permit him to fall into some danger from which I alone may deliver him!" Upon this Wakhs El Fellat pursued his journey without giving any attention to her words. On the third day he arrived at the valley where the fortress of Sudun was situated, when he began to work his way along behind the trees; and towards evening he arrived at the fortress itself, which he found to be surrounded with a moat; and the gates were closed. He was still undecided what course to take, when he heard the sound of an approaching caravan; and he hid himself in the fosse of the fortress to watch it. He then saw that it was driven forward by a large body of men, and that the merchants were bound on their mules. When they arrived at the castle, they knocked at the gate; and when the troop entered, Wakhs El Fellat entered with them; and they unloaded the goods and bound the prisoners without noticing him. When the armed men had finished their work, they ascended to the castle, but he remained below. After a time, he wished to follow them, but when he trod on the first step, it gave way under him, and a dagger flew out, which struck him in the groin. Upon this his eyes filled with tears, and he already looked upon his destruction as certain, when a form came towards him from the entrance of the castle to deliver him; and as it drew nearer, he perceived that it was Shama. He was filled with astonishment, and cried out, "God has heard your prayer! How did you come here?" "I followed your traces," she replied, "till you entered the castle, when I imitated your example and mingled with the troops. I have now saved your life, although you have refused to take me with you; but if you wish to advance further, do not neglect to try whether each step is fixed with the point of your sword." He now again began to ascend, feeling the way before him and Shama followed, till they arrived at the last stair, when they saw that the staircase ended in a revolving wheel. "Spring higher," advised Shama, "for I see a javelin which magic art has placed here." They sprang over it and pursued their way till they reached a large ante-room, lighted by a high cupola. They stopped here awhile, and examined everything carefully. At last they approached the door of a room, and on looking through the crevices they saw about an hundred armed negroes, among whom was a black slave who looked as savage as a lion. The room was lighted by wax candles, placed on gold and silver candlesticks. At this moment the black said, "Slaves, what have you done with the prisoners belonging to the caravan?" "We have chained them up in the prison below, and left them in the safest place," was the reply. But he continued, "If one of them was carelessly bound, he might be able to release himself and the others, and to gain possession of the stairs. Let one of you, therefore, go down, examine them carefully, and tighten their bonds." Upon this, one of them came out, and the two strangers hid themselves in the ante-room. When he had passed them, Wakhs El Fellat stepped forward and pierced him through with his sword; Shama dragged his body aside and they both remained quiet for a time. But as the slave remained away from his companions too long, Sudun exclaimed, "Go and see why he does not return, for I have been in great alarm ever since we entered the castle to-day." A second then rose and took his sword, and as he came into the ante-room, Wakhs El Fellat clove him in twain at one blow and Shama dragged his body also on one side. They again waited quietly for a time, when Sudun said, "It seems as if hunters are watching our slaves, and are killing them one after another." A third then hastened out, and Wakhs El Fellat struck him such a blow that he fell dead to the ground, and Shama dragged him also away. But as he likewise remained absent so long, Sudun himself stood up, and all the others with him, and he said, "Did I not warn and caution you? There is a singing in my ears and my heart trembles, for there must be people here who are watching our men." He himself now came out, and the others followed him with lights and holding their hands on their swords, when one of the foremost suddenly stopped. "Why do you not advance?" cried the others. "How shall I go forward," said he, "when he who has slain our friends stands before us." This answer was repeated to Sudun, when he reproached them in a voice of thunder for their hesitation. When he heard this, he forced his way through them till he perceived Wakhs El Fellat. "Who are you, Satan?" cried he, "and who brought you here?" "I came here," replied he, "to cut off your head, and destroy your memory." "Have you any blood-feud against me?" asked Sudun, "or any offence to revenge upon me?" "I have no enmity against you in my heart," said Wakhs El Fellat, "and you have never injured me; but I have asked Shama in marriage of her father, and he has demanded of me your head as a condition. Be on your guard, that you may not say I acted foully towards you." "Madman," cried Sudun, "I challenge you to a duel. Will you fight inside or outside the fortress?" "I leave that to you," returned Wakhs El Fellat. "Well, then, await me here," was the reply.

Sudun then went in, clothed himself in gilded armour, girt on a saw-like sword, and came out holding a shining club in his hand. He was so enraged that he knew not what to say, and at once attacked Wakhs El Fellat, who threw himself on his adversary like a raging lion, and they fought together like hungry wolves; but both despaired of victory. The swords spake a hard language on the shields, and each of the combatants wished that he had never been born. When this desperate fight had lasted a long time, Shama was greatly troubled lest Sudun should prove victorious. So she seized a dagger and struck at Sudun, wounding the nerves of his hand, so that he dropped his sword, while she exclaimed to Wakhs El Fellat, "Make an end of him." "No," replied Wakhs El Fellat, "I will make him my prisoner, for he is a brave and valiant man." "With whom are you speaking?" asked Sudun. "With Shama," answered he. "What," said Sudun, "did she come with you?" "Yes," replied he. "Then let her come before me." She came forward, and Sudun said, "Is the world too narrow for your father that he could demand nothing as your dowry but my head?" "This was his desire," answered she. Wakhs El Fellat then said, "Take your sword and defend yourself, for I will not fight with you now that it has fallen out of your hand." But Sudun replied, "I will not fight with you, for I am wounded, so take my head, and go in peace with your bride." He then sat down and bowed his head. "If you speak truly," said Wakhs El Fellat, "separate yourself from your people." "Why so?" "Because I fear lest they may surround me, and compel me to fight with them, and there is no need for me to shed their blood." Sudun then left the castle, bowed his head, and said, "Finish your work." But Wakhs El Fellat said, "If you speak truth, come with me across the fosse of the castle into the open ground." He did so, carefully barring the castle behind him, and said, "Now take my head."

When the slaves saw this, they mounted the walls, and wept and lamented. But Shama cried out, "Take his head, and let us hasten our return before morning dawns." "What!" said Wakhs El Fellat, "should I kill so brave a man in so treacherous a manner, when he is so noble and magnanimous?" He then went up to Sudun, kissed his head, and said, "Rise up, O warrior of the age, for you and your companions are safe from me." They now all embraced each other, and made an offensive and defensive compact. "Take me with you alive, O brave man," said Sudun, "and hand me over to the King as his daughter's dowry. If he consents, well; but if not, take my head, and demand your wife." "God forbid," said Wakhs El Fellat, "that I should act thus after your magnanimity. Rather return to the castle, and assure your companions of your safety." All this passed under the eyes of the other armed men. They rejoiced at the knightly conduct of both, and now came down, fell at the feet of Sudun, and embraced him. They then did the same to Wakhs El Fellat, whose hands they kissed and loaded him with praises. After this, they all returned to the castle, and agreed to set out presently. They took with them whatever treasures there were, and Wakhs El Fellat commanded them to release the prisoners and restore to them their goods. They now all mounted their horses and journeyed to the country of King Afrakh, greatly rejoiced at the mutual love of the warriors. When they approached the town, Shama parted from them, that nothing should be known of her presence with the Cavalcade. During this time King Afrakh and Sikar Diun had amused themselves with hunting, jesting, and sporting, and sent out scouts daily to look for Wakhs El Fellat. "What can have become of him?" said the King once to Sikar Diun. "Sudun has certainly killed him," replied the latter, "and you will never see him again." While they were thus talking, they observed a great cloud of dust, and as it drew nearer, they could see the armed men more distinctly. The company was led by a black knight, by whose side rode a younger white horseman. When the King saw this, he exclaimed, "Wakhs El Fellat has returned, in company with Sudun and his host." "Wait a little," replied Sikar Diun, "till we are certain of it." But when they drew nearer, and they could doubt no longer, Sikar Diun mounted his horse and fled, accompanied by the King and his followers, till they reached the town, and barred the gates. They then watched from the walls to see what would happen. When they saw that the strangers dismounted and pitched tents, the King thought it was a good sign. He therefore ordered the town to be decorated, and the gates to be opened, and rode out, attended by a considerable escort, and approached the tents. The other party now mounted their horses to go to meet them. When they approached each other, King Afrakh was about to dismount, but Wakhs El Fellat would not allow it, and the King embraced him, and congratulated him on his safety. He then saluted Sudun also, but the latter did not return his salutation. He invited him to enter the town, but he declined, as did Wakhs El Fellat likewise, who did not wish to part from his companions. The King returned accompanied only by his own people, and prepared the best reception for the new-comers. On the following morning the King held a general council, at which Sikar Diun appeared greatly depressed. "Did I not warn you before-hand," said he to the King, "what you now see for yourself of this evil-doer? Did we not send him to bring the head of Sudun, and he returns with him safe and sound, and on the best of terms, while our hearts are oppressed with anxiety?" "You may be right," replied the King, "but what are we to do now?"

This conversation was interrupted by a tumult caused by the arrival of Wakhs El Fellat and Sudun, who came to pay their respects to the King. The King invited them to sit down, but Sudun remained standing, and when he asked him again, he replied, "You craven, was the world too narrow for you that you desired my head as your daughter's dowry?" "Sit down," said the King, "for I know that you are angry." "How can I sit down," returned Sudun, "when you have ordered my death?" "God forbid that I should act so unjustly," said the King: "it was Sikar Diun." "What," said he, "do you accuse me of such an action in my presence?" "Did you not make this condition with Wakhs El Fellat," said the King: "and send him on his errand?" Sikar Diun then turned to Sudun, and said, "Sit down, brave warrior, for we only did so from love to you, that we might be able to make a treaty with you, and that you might join our company." After this answer Sudun concealed his anger, and sat down. Refreshments were now brought in, and after partaking of them, Wakhs El Fellat and Sudun returned to their tents. Several days passed in this manner, and at length Sudun said to Wakhs El Fellat, "O my master, it is time for you to demand Shama in marriage, now you have won her with the edge of the sword. You have fulfilled their conditions long since by bringing them my head, but you have made no further progress at present. Ask for her once more, and if they will not give her up, I will fall upon them with the sword, and we will carry Shama off, and then lay waste the city." "I will demand her as my wife again to-morrow," replied the other. When he went to the palace next day, he found the King and all the court assembled. When they saw him, they all rose from their seats, and when they sat down again he alone remained standing. "Why do you not sit down," said the King, "for all your wishes are now fulfilled?" "I have still to ask for Shama," he replied. "You know," returned the King, "that ever since her birth I have allowed Sikar Diun to make all arrangements for her." He now turned to Sikar Diun, who replied in a friendly tone, "She is yours, for you have fulfilled the conditions, and you have only now to give her ornaments." "What kind of ornaments?" asked he. "Instead of ornaments," replied the traitor, "we desire to receive a book containing the history of the Nile. If you bring it us, she is wholly yours; but if not, there is no marriage to be thought of." "Where is it to be found?" "I cannot tell you myself." "Well then," returned Wakhs El Fellat, "if I do not bring you the book, Shama is lost to me; all present ere witnesses to this." He went out with these words, pushing his way through the crowded assembly, and Sudun behind him, till they reached their tents. "Why did you promise that?" said Sudun, "let us rather overcome them with the sword, and take Shama from them." "Not so," replied Wakhs El Fellat, "I will only possess her honourably." "And yet you do not even know how to find the book," said Sudun, "rather listen to my advice, retire to my fortress, and leave me in their power." "I would never act thus," said Wakhs El Fellat, "though I should suffer death." After these and similar speeches, supper was brought in, and each retired to his sleeping apartment. But Wakhs El Fellat had scarcely entered his room when Shama came in. "What have you done," said she, "and what engagement have you undertaken? How can you fulfil this condition? Do you not see that their only object is to destroy you, or at least to get rid of you? I have come to warn you again, and I say to you once more, take me with you to Sudun's castle, where we can live at peace, and do not act as they tell you." "I will carry out my engagement," he replied; "I will not possess you like a coward, even though I should be cut to pieces with swords." Upon this, Shama was angry and left him, while he lay down to rest but could not sleep. He therefore rose up, saddled aud mounted his horse and rode away, without knowing where, abandoning himself wholly to the will of God. He wandered about thus for several days, until he reached a lonely tower. He knocked at the door, and a voice answered, "Welcome, O thou who hast separated thyself from thy companions; enter without fear, O brave

Saif, son of Zul Yezn." When he pushed the door it opened, and his eyes beheld a noble and venerable old man, from whose appearance it was at once obvious that he busied himself with the strictest life and fear of God. "Welcome," cried he again; "If you had travelled from east to west you would have found no one who could show you how to obtain the book you seek as well as I can, for I have dwelt here awaiting your arrival for sixty years." "But that was before I was born," said Wakhs El Fellat to himself. He then asked aloud, "By what name did you address me just now?" "O Saif," answered the old man, "that is your true name, for you are a sword (Saif) to the Abyssinians; but whom do you worship?" "O my master," was the reply, "the Abyssinians worship Saturn (Sukhal) but I am in perplexity, and know not whom to worship." "My son," replied the old man, "worship Him who has reared the heavens over us without pillars, and who has rested the earth on water; the only and eternal God, the Lord who is only and alone to be reverenced. I worship Him and none other beside Him, for I follow the religion of Abraham." "What is your name?" asked Wakhs El Fellat. "I am called Shaikh Gyat." "What declaration must I make," he asked the old man, "to embrace your religion?" "Say, 'There is no God but God, and Abraham is the Friend of God.' If you make this profession, you will be numbered among the believers." He at once repeated the formula, and Shaikh Gyat was much pleased, and devoted the night to teaching him the history of Abraham and his religion, and the forms of worship. Towards morning he said, "O my son, whenever you advance to battle, say, 'God is great, grant me victory, O God, and destroy the infidels,' and help will be near you. Now pursue your journey, but leave your horse here until your return. Enter the valley before you, under the protection of God, and after three days you will meet someone who will aid you." Wakhs El Fellat set out on that road, and after three days he met a horseman who saluted him, and exclaimed, "Welcome, Saif Zul Yezn, for you bring happiness to this neighbourhood." Saif returned his salutation, and asked, "How do you know me, and how do you know my name?" "I am not a brave or renowned warrior," was the answer, "but one of the maidens of this country and my mother taught me your name." "What is your name and that of your mother?" "My mother's name is Alka," answered she, "and I am called Taka." When he heard this he was greatly rejoiced, for he remembered that Shaikh Gyat had said to him, "O thou, whose destiny will be decided by Alka and Taka." "O noble virgin," said he, "where is your mother, Alka?" "Look round," she replied; and he saw a very large and lofty city at some distance. "Know," said she, "that 360 experienced philosophers dwell in that city. My mother Alka is their superior, and directs all their affairs and actions. She knew that you would come to this neighbourhood in search of a book concerning the Nile, which was written by Japhet, the son of Noah, and she wishes you to attain your end by her means. She also informed me of your coming, and promised me to you, saying, 'You shall have no other husband but him.' We expected you to-day, and she sent me to meet you, adding, 'Warn him not to enter the town by daylight, or it will be his destruction.' Wait here, therefore, till nightfall, and only approach the city after dark. Turn to the right along the wall, and stand still when you reach the third tower, where we will await you. As soon as we see you we will throw you a rope; bind it round your waist, and we will draw you up. The rest will be easy." "But why need you give yourselves all this trouble?" said Saif Zul Yezn. "Know," replied she, "that the inhabitants of this city have been informed of your approaching arrival by their books, and are aware that you are about to carry away their book, which they hold in superstitious reverence. On the first day of each month they repair to the building where it is preserved; and they adore it and seek counsel from it respecting their affairs. They have also a King whose name is Kamrun. When they knew that you were coming for the book they constructed a talisman against you. They have made a copper statue, and fixed a brazen horn in its hand, and have stationed it at the gate of the city. If you enter, the statue will sound the horn, and it will only do so upon your arrival. They would then seize you and put you to death. On this account we desire to baffle their wisdom by drawing you up to the walls of the city at another place." "May God reward you a thousand-fold," replied he; "but go now, and announce my arrival to your mother." She went away, and he approached the city in the darkness of night, and turned towards the third tower on the right, where he found Alka and Taka. When they recognised him, they immediately threw him the rope, which he fastened about him. When he was drawn up, they descended from the wall, and were about to proceed to Alka's house, when the talisman suddenly acted, and the statue blew the horn loudly. "Hasten to our house," cried Alka; and they succeeded in reaching it safely and barred the doors, when the noise increased. The whole population of the city rose up, and the streets were filled. "What is this disturbance about?" asked Saif. "This is all due," replied Alka, "to the alarm sounded by the statue, because you have entered the town. There will be a great meeting held to-morrow, where all the wise men will assemble to attempt to discover the whereabouts of the intruder; but by God's help, I will guide them wrong and confuse their counsels. Go to our neighbour the fisherman," added she to her daughter, "and see what he has caught." She went, and brought news that he had taken a large fish of the size of a man. "Take this piece of gold," said her mother, "and bring us the fish"; and when she did so, she told her to clean it, which was done. Food was then brought in, and they ate and talked. The night passed quietly, but on the following morning Alka ordered Saif Zul Yesn to undress, and to hide in the skin of the fish. She put her mouth to the mouth of the fish, and took a long rope, which she fastened under Saif's arm-pits. She then let him down in a deep well, and fastened him there, saying, "Remain here, till I come back." She then left him, and went to the great hall of the King, where the divan was already assembled, and the King had taken his seat, on the throne. All rose up when she entered, and when she had seated herself, the King said to her, "O mother, did you not hear the blast of the horn yesterday, and why did you not come out with us?" "I did hear it," she replied, "but I did not heed it." "But you know," said he, "that the sound can only be heard upon the arrival of the stranger who desires to take the book." "I know it, O King; but permit me to choose forty men from among those assembled here." She did so, and selected ten from among the forty again. She then said to them, "Take a Trakhtramml (sandboard on which the Arabs practice geomancy and notation) and look and search." They did so, but had scarcely finished when they looked at each other in amazement. They destroyed their calculation, and began a second, and confused this too, and began a third, upon which they became quite confounded. "What are you doing there?" asked the King at last. "You go on working and obliterating your work; what have you discovered?" "O King," replied they, "we find that the stranger has entered the town, but not by any gate. He appears to have passed in between heaven and earth, like a bird. After this, a fish swallowed him, and carried him down into some dark water." "Are you fools?" asked the King, angrily; and turning to Alka, continued, "Have you ever seen a man flying between heaven and earth, and afterwards swallowed by a fish, which descends with him into dark water?" "O King," replied she, "I always forbid the wise men to eat heavy food, for it disturbs their understanding and weakens their penetration; but they will not heed me." At this the King was angry. and immediately drove them from the hall. But Alka said, "It will be plain to-morrow what has happened." She left the hall, and when she reached home, she drew Saif Zul Yezn out of the well, and he dressed himself again. They sat down, and Alka said, "I have succeeded in confounding their deliberations to-day! and there will be a great assembly to-morrow, when I must hide you in a still more out-of-the way place." After this they supped and went to rest. Next morning Alka called her daughter, and said, "Bring me the gazelle." When it was brought her, she said, "Bring me the wings of an eagle." Taka gave them to her, and she bound them on the back of the gazelle. She then took a pair of compasses, which she fixed in the ceiling of the room. She next took two other pairs of compasses, and tied one between the fore feet, and the other between the hind feet, of the gazelle. She then tied a rope to the compasses in the roof, and the two ends to the other pairs. But she made Saif Zul Yezn lie down in such a position that his head was between the feet of the gazelle. She then said to him, "Remain here till I come back"; and went to the King; with whom she found a very numerous assemblage of the wise men. As soon as she entered, the King made her sit beside him on the throne. "O my mother Alka," he said, "I could not close an eye last night from anxiety concerning yesterday's events." "Have you no wise men," returned she, "who eat the bread of the divan?" She then turned to them, saying, "Select the wisest among you!" and they chose the wisest among them. She ordered them to take the sandboard again, but they became so confused that they were obliged to begin again three times from the beginning. "What do you discover?" said the King, angrily. "O our master," replied they, "he whom we seek has been carried away by a beast of the desert, which is flying with him between heaven and earth." "How is this?" said the King to Alka; "have you ever seen anything like it?" He seized his sword in a rage, and three fled, and he killed four of the others. When Alka went home she released Saif, and told him what had happened. Next morning Alka took the gazelle, and slaughtered it in a copper kettle. She then took a golden mortar, and reversed it over it, and said to Saif Zul Yezn, "Sit on this mortar till I come back. She then went to the divan, and chose out six wise men, who again took the sandboard, and began again three times over in confusion. "Alas," said the King, in anger, "what misfortune do you perceive?" "O our master," they exclaimed in consternation, "our understanding is confused, for we see him sitting on a golden mountain, which is in the midst of a sea of blood, surrounded by a copper wall." The King was enraged, and broke up the assembly, saying, "O Alka, I will now depend on you alone." "To-morrow I will attempt to show you the stranger," she replied. When she came home she related to Saif what had happened, and said, "I shall know by to-morrow what to tell the King to engage his attention, and prevent him from pursuing you." Next morning she found Taka speaking to Saif Zal Yezn alone; and she asked her, "What does he wish?" "Mother," replied Taka, "he wishes to go to the King's palace, to see him and the divan." "What you wish shall be done," said she to Saif, "but you must not speak." He assented to the condition, and she dressed him as her attendant, gave him a sandboard, and went with him to the King, who said to her, "I could not sleep at all last night, for thinking of the stranger for whom we are seeking." "Now that the affair is in my hands," returned she, "you will find me a sufficient protection against him." She immediately ordered Saif to give her the sandboard. She took it, and when she had made her calculations, she said joyfully to the King, "O my lord, I can give you the welcome news of the flight of the stranger, owing to his dread of you and your revenge." When the King heard this, he rent his clothes, slapped his face, and said, "He would not have departed without having taken the book." "I cannot see if he has taken anything," replied she. "This is the first of the month," said the King, "come and let us see if it is missing." He then went with a large company to the building where the book was kept. Alka turned away from the King for a moment to say to Saif, "Do not enter with us, for if you enter the case will open of itself, and the book will fall into your hands. This would at once betray you, and you would be seized and put to death, and all my labour would have been in vain." She then left him and rejoined the King. When they reached the building, the doors were opened, and when the King entered they found the book. They immediately paid it the customary honours, and protracted this species of worship, while Saif stood at the door, debating with himself whether to enter or not. At last his impatience overcame him, and he entered, and at the same instant the casket was broken to pieces, and the book fell out. The King then ordered all to stand up, and the book rolled to Saif Zul Yezn. Upon this all drew their swords and rushed upon him. Saif drew his sword also, and cried "God is great!" as Shaikh Gyat had taught him. He continued to fight and defend himself, and struggled to reach the door. The entire town arose in tumult to pursue him, when he stumbled over a dead body and was seized. "Let me not see his face," cried the King, "but throw him into the mine." This mine was eighty yards deep, and had not been opened for sixty years. It was closed by a heavy leaden cover, which they replaced, after they had loaded him with chains, and thrown him in. Saif sat there in the darkness, greatly troubled, and lamenting his condition to Him who never sleeps. Suddenly, the side wall of the mine opened, and a figure came forth which approached and called him by his name. "Who are you?" asked Saif. "I am a woman named Akissa, and inhabit the mountain where the Nile rises. We are a nation who hold the faith of Abraham. A very pious man lives below us in a beautiful palace. But an evil Jinni named Mukhtatif lived near us also, who loved me, and demanded me in marriage of my father. He consented from fear, but I was unwilling to marry an evil being who was a worshipper of fire. 'How can you promise me in marriage to an infidel?' said I to my father. 'I shall thereby escape his malice myself,' replied he. I went out and wept, and complained to the pious man about the affair. 'Do you know who will kill him?' said he to me, and I answered, 'No.' 'I will direct you to him who has cut off his hand,' said he. 'His name is Saif Zul Yezn, and he is now in the city of King Kamrun, in the mine.' Thereupon he brought me to you, and I come as you see me, to guide you to my country, that you may kill Mukhtatif, and free the earth from his wickedness." She then moved him, and shook him, and all his chains fell off. She lifted him on her shoulders, and carried him to the palace of the Shaikh, who was named Abbas Salam. Here he heard a voice crying, "Enter, Saif Zul Yezn." He did so, and found a grave and venerable old man, who gave him a very friendly reception, saying, "Wait till to-morrow, when Akissa will come to guide you to the castle of Mukhtatif." He remained with him for the night, and when Akissa arrived next morning, the old man told her to hasten that the world might be soon rid of the monster. They then left this venerable man, and when they had walked awhile, Akissa said to Saif, "Look before you." He did so, and perceived a black mass at some distance. "This is the castle of the evil-doer," said she, "but I cannot advance a step further than this." Saif therefore pursued his way alone, and when he came near the castle, he walked round it to look for the entrance. As he was noticing the extraordinary height of the castle, which was founded on the earth, but appeared to overtop the clouds, he saw a window open, and several people looked out, who pointed at him with their fingers, exclaiming, "That is he, that is he!" They threw him a rope, which they directed him to bind round him. They drew him up by it, when he found himself in the presence of three hundred and sixty damsels, who saluted him by his name.

* * * *

Here Habicht's fragment ends.

SCOTT'S MSS. AND TRANSLATIONS.

In 1800, Jonathan Scott, LL.D., published a volume of "Tales, Anecdotes, and Letters, translated from the Arabic and Persian," based upon a fragmentary MS., procured by J. Anderson in Bengal, which included the commencement of the work (Nos. 1-3) in 29 Nights; two tales not divided into Nights (Nos. 261 and 135) and No. 21.

Scott's work includes these two new tales (since republished by Kirby and Clouston), with the addition of various anecdotes, etc. derived from other sources. The "Story of the Labourer and the Chair" has points of resemblance to that of "Malek and the Princess Chirine" (Shirin ?) in the Thousand and One Days; and also to that of "Tuhfet El Culoub" (No. 183a) in the Breslau Edition. The additional tales in this MS. and vol. of translations are marked "A" under Scott in our Tables. Scott published the following specimens (text and translation) in Ouseley's Oriental Collections (1797 and following years) No. 135m (pp. 245-257) and Introduction (ii. pp. 160-172; 228-257). The contents are fully given in Ouseley, vol. ii. pp. 34, 35.

Scott afterwards acquired an approximately complete MS. in 7 vols, written in 1764, which was brought from Turkey by E. Wortley Montague. Scott published a table of contents (Ouseley, ii. pp. 25-34), in which, however, the titles of some few of the shorter tales, which he afterwards translated from it, are omitted, while the titles of others are differently translated. Thus "Greece" of the Table becomes "Yemen" in the translation; and "labourer" becomes "sharper." As a specimen, be subsequently printed the text and translation of No. 145 (Ouseley, ii. pp. 349-367).

This MS., which differs very much from all others known, is now in the Bodleian Library at Oxford.

In 1811, Scott published an edition of the Arabian Nights' Entertainments, in 6 vols., vol. 1 containing a long introduction, and vol. 6 including a series of new tales from the Oxford MS. (There is a small paper edition; and also a large paper edition, the latter with frontispieces and an Appendix including a Table of the Tales contained in the MS.). It had originally been Scott's intention to retranslate the MS.; but he appears to have found it beyond his powers. He therefore contented himself with re-editing Galland, altering little except the spelling of the names, and saying that Galland's version is in the main so correct that it would be useless repetition to go over the work afresh. Although he says that he found many of the tales both immoral and puerile, he translated most of those near the beginning, and omitted much more (including several harmless and interesting tales, such as No. 152) towards the end of his MS. than near the beginning. The greater part of Scott's additional tales, published in vol. 6, are included in the composite French and German editions of Gauttier and Habicht; but, except Nos. 208, 209, and 215, republished in my "New Arabian Nights," they have not been reprinted in England, being omitted in all the many popular versions which are professedly based upon

Scott, even in the edition in 4 vols., published in 1882, which reprints Scott's Preface.

The edition of 1882 was published about the same time as one of the latest re-issues of Lane's Thousand and One Nights; and the *Saturday Review* of Nov. 4, 1882 (p. 609) published an article on the Arabian Nights, containing the following amusing passage: "Then Jonathan Scott, LL.D. Oxon, assures the world that he intended to retranslate the tales given by Galland; but he found Galland so adequate on the whole that he gave up the idea, and now reprints Galland, with etchings[1] by M. Lalauze, giving a French view of Arab life. Why Jonathan Scott, LL.D., should have thought to better Galland, while Mr. Lane's version is in existence, and has just been reprinted, it is impossible to say."

The most interesting of Scott's additional tales, with reference to ordinary editions of The Nights, are as follows:—

No. 204b is a variant of No. 37.

No. 204c is a variant of 3e, in which the wife, instead of the husband, acts the part of a jealous tyrant. (Compare Cazotte's story of Halechalbe).

No. 204e. Here we have a reference to the Nesnás, which only appears once in the ordinary versions of The Nights (No. 132b; Burton, night di.).

No. 206b is a variant of No. 156.

No. 207c. This relates to a bird similar to that in the Jealous Sisters (No. 198), and includes a variant of 3ba.

No. 207h. Another story of enchanted birds. The prince who seeks them encounters an "Oone" under similar circumstances to those under which Princess Parizade (No. 198) encounters the old durwesh. The description is hardly that of a Marid, with which I imagine the Ons are wrongly identified.

No. 208 contains the nucleus of the famous story of Aladdin (No. 193).

No. 209 is similar to No. 162; but we have again the well incident of No. 3ba, and the exposure of the children as in No. 198.

No. 215. Very similar to Hassan of Bassorah (No. 155). As Sir R. F. Burton (night dccxcvi.), has called in question my identification of the Islands of Wák-Wák, with the Aru Islands near New Guinea, I will quote here the passages from Mr. A. R. Wallace's Malay Archipelago (chap. 31) on which I based it:—"The trees frequented by the birds are very lofty. . . . . One day I got under a tree where a number of the Great Paradise birds were assembled, but they were high up in the thickest of the foliage, and flying and jumping about so continually that I could get no good view of them. . . . . Their voice is most extraordinary. At early morn, before the sun has risen, we hear a cry of 'Wawk—wawk—wawk, wŏk—wŏk—wŏk,' which resounds through the forest, changing its direction continually. This is the Great Bird of Paradise going to seek his breakfast. . . . . The birds had now commenced what the

1 Only 19 of the 21 etchings by Lalauze were issued in this 1882 edition.

people here call their 'sacaleli,' or dancing-parties, in certain trees in the forest, which are not fruit-trees as I first imagined, but which have an immense head of spreading branches and large but scattered leaves, giving a clear space for the birds to play and exhibit their plumes. On one of these trees a dozen or twenty full-plumaged male birds assemble together, raise up their wings, stretch out their necks, and elevate their exquisite plumes, keeping them in a continual vibration. Between whiles they fly across from branch to branch in great excitement, so that the whole tree is filled with waving plumes in every variety of attitude and motion."

No. 216bc appears to be nearly the same as No. 42.

No. 225 is a variant of No. 135q.

WEIL'S TRANSLATION.

The only approximately complete orginal German translation is "Tausend und eine Nacht. Arabische Erzählungen. Zum Erstenmale aus dem Urtexte vollständig und treu übersetzt von Dr. Gustav Weil," four vols., Stuttgart. The first edition was in roy. 8vo., and was published at Stuttgart and Pforzheim in 1839-1842; the last volume I have not seen; it is wanting in the copy in the British Museum. This edition is divided into Nights, and includes No. 25b. In the later editions, which are in small square 8vo., but profusely illustrated, like the larger one, this story is omitted (except No. 135m, which the French editors include with it), though Galland's doubtful stories are retained; and there is no division into Nights. The work has been reprinted several times, and the edition quoted in our Table is described as "Zweiter Abdruck der dritten vollständig umgearbeiteten, mit Anmerkungen und mit einer Einleitung verschenen Auflage" (1872).

Weil has not stated from what sources he drew his work, except that No. 201 is taken from a MS. in the Ducal Library at Gotha. This is unfortunate, as his version of the great transformation scene in No. 3b (Burton, vol. i., night xiv.), agrees more closely with Galland than with any other original version. In other passages, as when speaking of the punishment of Aziz (No. 9a, aa), Weil seems to have borrowed an expression from Lane, who writes, "a cruel wound"; Weil saying, "a severe (schwere) wound."

Whereas Weil gives the only German version known to me of No. 9 (though considerably abridged) he omits many tales contained in Zinserling and Habicht, but whether because his own work was already too bulky, or because his original MSS. did not contain them, I do not know; probably the first supposition is correct, for in any case it was open to him to have translated them from the printed texts, to which he refers in his Preface.

Two important stories (Nos. 200 and 201) are not found in any other version; but as they are translated in my "New Arabian Nights," I need not discuss them here. I will, however, quote a passage from the story of Judar and Mahmood, which I omitted because it is not required by the context, and because I thought it a little out of place in a book published in a juvenile series. It is interesting from its analogy to the story of Semele.

When King Kashuk (a jinni) is about to marry the daughter of King Shamkoor, we read (New Arabian Nights, p. 182), "Shamkoor immediately summoned my father, and said, 'Take my daughter, for you have won her heart.' He immediately provided an outfit for his daughter, and when it was completed, my father and his bride rode away on horseback, while the trousseau of the Princess followed on three hundred camels." The passage proceeds (the narrator being Daruma, the offspring of the marriage), "When my father had returned home, and was desirous of celebrating his marriage (his Wazir) Kandarin said to him, 'Your wife will be destroyed if you touch her, for you are created of fire and she is created of earth, which the fire devours. You will then bewail her death when it is too late. To-morrow,' continued he, 'I will bring you an ointment with which you must rub both her and yourself; and you may then live long and happily together.' On the following day he brought him a white ointment, and my father anointed himself and his bride with it, and consummated his marriage without danger."

I may add that this is the only omission of the smallest consequence in my rendering of either story.

I have heard from more than one source that a complete German translation of The Nights was published, and suppressed; but I have not been able to discover the name of the author, the date, or any other particulars relating to the subject.

VON HAMMER'S MS., AND THE TRANSLATIONS DERIVED FROM IT.

Several complete copies of The Nights were obtained by Europeans about the close of the last or the beginning of the present century; and one of these (in 4 vols.) fell into the hands of the great German Orientalist, Joseph von Hammer. This MS. agrees closely with the printed Bul. and Mac. texts, as well as with Dr. Clarke's MS., though the names of the tales sometimes vary a little. One story, "The Two Wazirs," given in Von Hammer's list as inedited, no doubt by an oversight, is evidently No. 7, which bears a similar title in Torrens. One title, "Al Kavi," a story which Von Hammer says was published in "Mag. Encycl.," and in English (probably by Scott in Ouseley's Oriental Collections, vide anteà) puzzled me for some time; but from its position and the title, I think I have identified it as No. 145, and have entered it as such. No. 9a in this as well as in several other MSS., bears the title of the Two Lovers, or of the Lover and the Beloved.

Von Hammer made a French translation of the unpublished tales, which he lent to Caussin de Perceval, who extracted from it four tales only (Nos. 21a, 22, 32, and 37), and only acknowledged his obligations in a general way to a distinguished Orientalist, whose name he pointedly suppressed. Von Hammer, naturally indignant, reclaimed his MS., and had it translated into German by Zinserling. He then sent the French MS. to De Sacy, in whose hands it remained for some time, although he does not appear to have made any use of it, when it was despatched to England for publication; but the courier lost it on the journey, and it was never recovered.

Zinserling's translation was published under the title, "Der Tausend und einen Nacht noch nicht übersetzte Mährchen, Erzählungen und Anekdoten, zum erstenmale aus dem Arabischen in's Französische übersetzt von Joseph von Hammer, und aus dem Französischen in's Deutsche von Aug. E. Zinserling, Professor." (3 vols., Stuttgart and Tübingen, 1823.) The introductory matter is of considerable importance, and includes notices of 12 different MSS., and a list of contents of Von Hammer's MS. The tales begin with No. 23, Nos. 9-19 being omitted, because Von Hammer was informed that they were about to be published in France. (This possibly refers to Asselan Riche's "Scharkan," published in 1829.) The tales and anecdotes in this edition follow the order of the Nights. No. 163 is incomplete, Zinserling giving only the commencement; and two other tales (Nos. 132b and 168) are related in such a confused manner as to be unintelligible, the former from transpositions (perhaps in the sheets of the original MS.) and the latter from errors and omissions. On the other hand, some of the tales (No. 137 for instance) are comparatively full and accurate.

A selection from the longer tales was published in English in 3 vols. in 1826, under the title of "New Arabian Nights' Entertainments, selected from the original Oriental MS. by Jos. von Hammer, and now first translated into English by the Rev. George Lamb." I have only to remark that No. 132b is here detached from its connection with No. 132, and is given an independent existence.

A complete French re-translation of Zinserling's work, also in 3 vols., by G. S. Trébutien (Contes inédits des Mille et une Nuits) was published in Paris in 1828; but in this edition the long tales are placed first, and all the anecdotes are placed together last.

The various MSS. mentioned by Von Hammer are as follows:—

I. Galland's MS. in Paris.

II. Another Paris MS., containing 870 Nights. (No. 9 is specially noticed as occurring in it.) This seems to be the same as a MS. subsequently mentioned by Von Hammer as consulted by Habicht.

III. Scott's MS. (Wortley Montague).

IV. Scott's MS. (Anderson).

V. Dr. Russell's MS. from Aleppo (224 Nights).

VI. Sir W. Jones' MS., from which Richardson extracted No. 6ee for his grammar.

VII. A MS. at Vienna (200 Nights).

VIII. MS. in Italinski's collection.

IX. Clark's MS.

X. An Egyptian MS. at Marseilles.

XI. Von Hammer's MS.

XII. Habicht's MS. (=Bres. text).

XIII. Caussin's MS.

XV. One or more MSS. in the Vatican.

TRANSLATIONS OF THE PRINTED TEXTS.

These are noticed by Sir R. F. Burton in his "Foreword" (vol. 1, pp. xx.-xxii.) and consequently can be passed over with a brief mention here.

Torrens' edition (vol. 1) extends to the end of Night 50 (Burton, ii. 22).

Lane's translation originally appeared in monthly half-crown parts, from 1839 to 1841. It is obvious that he felt himself terribly restricted in space; for the third volume, although much thicker than the others, is not only almost destitute of notes towards the end, but the author is compelled to grasp at every excuse to omit tales, even excluding No. 168, which he himself considered "one of the most entertaining tales in the work" (chap. xxix., note 12) on account of its slight resemblance to Nos. 1b and 3d. Part of the matter in Lane's own earlier notes is apparently derived from No. 132a, which he probably did not at first intend to omit. Sir R. F. Burton has taken 5 vols. to cover the same ground which Lane has squeezed into his vol. 3. But it is only fair to Lane to remark that in such cases the publisher is usually far more to blame than the author.

In 1847 appeared a popular edition of Lane, entitled, "The Thousand and One Nights, or the Arabian Nights Entertainments, translated and arranged for family reading, with explanatory notes. Second edition." Here Galland's old spelling is restored, and the "explanatory notes," ostentatiously mentioned on the title page, are entirely omitted. This edition was in 3 vols. I have seen a copy dated 1850; and think I have heard of an issue in 1 vol.; and there is an American reprint in 2 vols. The English issue was ultimately withdrawn from circulation in consequence of Lane's protests. (Mr. S. L. Poole's Life of E. W. Lane, p. 95.) It contains the woodcut of the Flying Couch, which is wanting in the later editions of the genuine work; but not Galland's doubtful tales, as Poole asserts.

Several editions of the original work, edited by Messrs E. S. and S. L. Poole, have appeared at intervals from 1859 to the present time. They differ little from the original edition except in their slightly smaller size.

The short tales included in Lane's notes were published separately as one of Knight's Weekly Volumes, in 1845, under the title of "Arabian Tales and Anecdotes, being a selection from the notes to the new translation of the Thousand and One Nights, by E. W. Lane, Esq."

Finally, in 1883, Mr. Stanley Lane Poole published a classified and arranged edition of Lane's notes under the title of "Arabian Society in the Middle Ages."

Mr. John Payne's version of the Mac. edition was issued in 9 vols. by the Villon Society to subscribers only. It appeared from 1882 to 1884, and only 500 copies were printed. Judging from the original prospectus, it seems to have been the author's intention to have completed the work in 8 vols., and to have devoted vol. 9 to Galland's doubtful tales; but as they are omitted, he must have found that the work ran to a greater length than he had anticipated, and that space failed him. He published some preliminary papers on the Nights in the New Quarterly Magazine for January and April, 1879.

Mr. Payne subsequently issued "Tales from the Arabic of the Breslau and Calcutta (1814-18) editions of the Thousand Nights and One Night, not occurring in the other printed texts of the work." (Three vols., London, 1884.) Of this work, issued, like the other, by the Villon Society, to subscribers only, 750 copies were printed, besides 50 on large paper. The third volume includes indices of all the tales in the four principal printed texts. The substance of these 3 vols. is contained in the first 2 vols. of Burton's "Supplemental Nights." In 1889 Mr. Payne issued another volume, entitled, "Alaeddin and the Enchanted Lamp, Zeyn ul Asnam, and the King of the Jinn; two stories done into English from the recently-discovered Arabic text, by John Payne."

Finally, we have Sir R. F. Burton's translation now in its entirety before his subscribers. It was restricted to 1,000 copies. (Why not 1,001?) The six supplementary vols. include tales wanting in the Mac. edition, but found in other texts (printed and MS.), while the present edition will allow of the free circulation of Sir R. F. Burton's work among all classes of the reading public.

COLLECTIONS OF SELECTED TALES.

There are many volumes of selections derived from Galland, but these hardly require mention; the following may be noticed as derived from other sources:—

1. Caliphs and Sultans, being tales omitted in the usual editions of the Arabian Nights' Entertainments. Re-written and re-arranged by Sylvanus Hanley, F.L.S., etc., London, 1868; 2nd edition 1870.

Consists of portions of tales chiefly selected from Scott, Lamb, Chavis and Cazotte, Trébutien and Lane; much abridged, and frequently strung together, as follows:—

Nos. 246, 41, 32 (including Nos. 111, 21a, and 89); 9a (including 9 aa [which Hanley seems, by the way, to have borrowed from some version which I do not recognise], 22 and 248); 155, 156, 136, 162; Xailoun the Silly (from Cazotte); 132 and 132a; and 169 (including 134 and 135x).

2. Ilâm-en-Nâs. Historical tales and anecdotes of the time of the early Kalîfahs. Translated from the Arabic and annotated by Mrs. Godfrey Clerk, author of "The Antipodes and round the World." London, 1873.

Many of these anecdotes, as is candidly admitted by the authoress in her Preface, are found with variations in The Nights, though not translated by her from this source.

3. The New Arabian Nights. Select tales not included by Galland or Lane. By W. F. Kirby, London, 1882.

Includes the following tales, slightly abridged, from Weil and Scott: Nos. 200, 201, 264, 215, 209, and 208.

Several editions have appeared in England, besides reprints in America and Australia.

SEPARATE EDITIONS OF SINGLE OR COMPOSITE TALES.

6e (ee).—The Barber's Fifth Brother.

Mr. W A. Clouston (in litt.) calls attention to the version of this story by Addison in the "Spectator," No. 535, Nov. 13, 1712, after Galland. There is good reason to suppose that this is subsequent to the first English edition, which, however, Addison does not mention. There is also an English version in Faris' little Arabic Grammar (London, 1856), and likewise in Richardson's Arabic Grammar. The latter author extracted it from a MS. belonging to Sir W. Jones.

5.—Nur Al-Din and Badr Al-Din Hasan.

There are two Paris editions of the "Histoire de Chems-Eddine et de Nour-Eddine," edited by Prof. Cherbonneau. The first (1852) contains text and notes, and the second (1869) includes text, vocabulary and translations.

7.—Nur Al-Din and Anis Al-Jalis.

An edition by Kasimirski of "Enis el-Djelis, ou histoire de la belle Persane," appeared in Paris in 1867. It includes text, translation and notes.

9.—King Omar Bin Al-Nu'uman.

There is a French abridgment of this story entitled, "Scharkan, Conte Arabe, suivi de quelques anecdotes orientales ; traduit par M. Asselan Riche, Membre de la Société Asiatique de Paris (Paris and Marseilles, 12mo, 1829, pp. 240). The seven anecdotes appended are as follows: (1) the well-known story of Omar's prisoner and the glass of water ; (2) Elhedjadj and a young Arab; (3 = our No. 140; (4) Anecdote of Elhedjadj and a story-teller; (5) = our No. 86; (6) King Bahman and the Moubed's parable of the Owls; (7) = our No. 145.

133.—Sindbad the Seaman.

This is the proper place to call attention to a work specially relating to this story, "Remarks on the Arabian Nights' Entertainments; in which the origin of Sindbad's Voyages and other Oriental Fictions is particularly described. By Richard Hole, LL.D." (London, 1797, pp. iv. 259.)

It is an old book, but may still be consulted with advantage.

There are two important critical editions of No. 133, one in French and one in German.

1. Les Voyages de Sind-bâd le marin et la ruse des Femmes. Contes arabes. Traduction littérale, accompagnée du Texte et des Notes. Par L. Langlès (Paris, 1814).

The second story is our No. 184.

2. Die Beiden Sindbad oder Reiseabenteuer Sindbads des Seefahrers. Nach einer zum ersten Male in Europa bedruckten Ægyptischen Handschrift unmittelbar und wörtlich treu aus dem Arabischen übersetzt und

mit erklärenden Anmerkungen, nebst zwei sprachlichen Beilagen zum Gebrauch für abgehende Orientalisten herausgegeben von J. G. H. Reinsch (Breslau, 1826).

135.—The Craft and Maliee of Women.

The literature of this cluster of tales would require a volume in itself, and I cannot do better than refer to Mr. W. A. Clouston's "Book of Sindibad" (8vo., Glasgow, 1884) for further information. This book, though privately printed and limited to 300 copies, is not uncommon.

136.—Judar and his Brethren.

An edition of this story, entitled "Histoire de Djouder le Pécheur," edited by Prof. Houdas, was published in the Bibliothèque Algérienne, at Algiers, in 1865. It includes text and vocabulary.

174.—The Ten Vazirs.

This collection of tales has also been frequently reprinted separately. It is the Arabic version of the Persian Bakhtyar Nameh, of which Mr. Clouston issued a privately-printed edition in 1883.

The following versions have come under my notice:—

1. Nouveaux Contes Arabes, ou Supplement aux Mille et une Nuits suivies de Mélanges de Littérature orientale et de lettres, par l'Abbe*** (Paris, 1788, pp. 425).

This work consists chiefly of a series of tales selected and adapted from the Ten Vazirs. "Written in Europe by a European, and its interest is found in the Terminal Essay, on the Mythologia Æsopica" (Burton in litt.).

2. Historien om de ti Vezirer og hoorledes det gik dem med Kong Azád Bachts Sön, oversat af Arabisk ved R. Rask (8vo., Kobenhavn, 1829).

3. Habicht, x. p. vi., refers to the following:—Historia decem Vezirorum et filii regis Azad-Bacht insertis XIII. ahis narrationibus, in usum tironum Cahirensem, edid. G. Knós, Göttingen, 1807, 8vo.

He also states that Knös published the commencement in 1805, in his "Disquisitio de fide Herodoti, quo perhibet Phœnices Africam navibus circumvectos esse cum recentiorum super hac re sententiis excussis.—Adnexum est specimen sermonis Arabici vulgaris s. initium historiæ filii regis Azad-Bacht e Codice inedito."

4. Contes Arabes. Histoire des dix Vizirs (Bakhtyar Nameh) Traduite et annotée par René Basset, Professeur à l'école supérieure des lettres d'Algérie. Paris, 1883.

Chavis and Cazotte (anteà) included a version of the Ten Vazirs in their work; and others are referred to in our Table of Tales.

248.—The Wise Heycar.

Subsequently to the publication of Gauttier's edition of The Nights, Agoub republished his translation under the title of "Le Sage Heycar, conte Arabe" (Paris, 1824).

A few tales published by Scott in Ouseley's Oriental Collections have already been noticed.

TRANSLATIONS OF COGNATE ORIENTAL ROMANCES ILLUSTRATIVE OF THE NIGHTS.

I. Les Mille et un Jours. Contes Persanes.

"In imitation of the Arabian Nights, was composed a Persian collection entitled 'Hazár Yek Rúz (هزار يك روز) or the Thousand and One Days,' of which Petis de la Croix published a French rendering [in 1710], which was done into English [by Dr. King, and published in 2 vols. (with the Turkish Tales = Forty Vezirs) as early as 1714; and subsequently] by Ambrose Phillips" (in 1738), (Clouston, in litt). Here, and occasionally elsewhere, I have quoted from some MS. notes on The Nights by Mr. W. A. Clouston, which Sir R. F. Burton kindly permitted me to inspect. Mr. Clouston then quotes Cazotte's Preface (not in my edition of the Thousand and One Days), according to which the book was written by the celebrated Dervis Moelès (Mukhlis) chief of the Sofis (Sufis ?) of Ispahan, founded upon certain Indian comedies. Petis de la Croix was on friendly terms with Mukhli, who allowed him to take a copy of his work in 1675, during his residence in Ispahan. (I find these statements confirmed in the Cabinet des Fées, xxxvii. pp. 266, 274, 278, and in Weber's "Tales of the East," i. pp. xxxvi., xxxxii.) The only recent English translation was published by Justin Huntly M'Carthy in 1892, in 2 vols., with frontispieces.

The framework of the story is the same as Nos. 9a and 152: a Princess, who conceives an aversion to men from dreaming of the self-devotion of a doe, and the indifference and selfishness of a stag. Mr. Clouston refers to Nakhshabí's Túti Náma (No. 33 of Káderí's abridgment, and 39 of India Office MS. 2,573); whence he thinks it probable that Mukhlis may have taken the tale. But the tale itself is repeated over and over again in many Arabic, Persian, and Turkish collections: in fact, there are few of commoner occurrence.

The tales are told by the nurse in order to overcome the aversion of the Princess to men. They are as follows:

Introduction and Conclusion: Story of the Princess of Cashmir.

1. Story of Aboulcassem Bafry.
2. Story of King Ruzvanchad and the Princess Cheheristani.
    - *a.* Story of the young King of Thibet and the Princess of the Naimans.
    - *b.* Story of the Vazir Cavercha.
3. Story of Couloufe and the Beautiful Dilara.
4. Story of Prince Calaf and the Princess of China.
    - *a.* Story of Prince Fadlallah, son of Ben-Ortoc, King of Moussel. Nos. 184 and 251.
5. Story of King Bedreddin-Lolo, and his Vazir Atalmulk, surnamed the Sad Vazir.
    - *a.* Story of Atalmulk and the Princess Zelica Beghume.
    - *b.* Story of Prince Seyf-el-Molouk.

c. Story of Malek and the Princess Chirine.
d. Story of King Hormuz, surnamed the King without trouble.
da. Story of Avicenna.
e. Story of the fair Arouya. Cf. Nos. 135q, and 225.
f. Singular Adventures of Aboulfawaris, surnamed the Great Traveller (2 Voyages).
6. Story of the Two Brother Genii, Adis and Dahy.
7. Story of Nasiraddolé, King of Moussel, of Abderrahman, Merchant of Bagdad, and the Beautiful Zeineb.
8. Story of Repsima. No. 181r.

This work has many times been reprinted in France, where it holds a place only second to The Nights.

Sir R. F. Burton remarks, concerning the Persian and Turkish Tales of Petis de la Crois (the latter of which form part of the Forty Vazirs, No. 251). "Both are weak and servile imitations of Galland by an Orientalist who knew nothing of the East. In one passage in the story of Fadlallah, we read of 'Le Sacrifice du Mont Arafáte,' which seems to have become a fixture in the European brain. I found the work easy writing and exceedingly hard reading."

The following tales require a passing notice:—

1. *Story of Aboulcassem Bafry.*—A story of concealed treasure; it has also some resemblance to No. 31.

2. *Ruzvanchad and Cheheristani.*—Cheheristani is a jinniyah, who is pursued by the King, under the form of a white doe; marries him, and becomes the mother of Balkis, the Queen of Sheba. She exacts a promise from him never to rebuke her for any of her actions: he breaks it, and she leaves him for a time.

2a. *The Young King of Thibet.*—Two impostors obtain magic rings by which they can assume the shapes of other persons.

2a b. *The Vazir Cavercha.*—This is one of Scott's stories (No. 223 of our Table). It goes back at least as far as the Ring of Polycrates. It is the 8th Vezir's Story in Mr. Gibb's Forty Vezirs (pp. 200-205.)

4. *Prince Calaf.*—This story is well known, and is sometimes placed as a comedy. It was dramatised by Schiller, under the title of "Turandet, Princessin von China Ein tragikonissches Măhrchennach Gozzi." The Princess Turandot puts riddles to her suitors, and beheads them if they fail to answer.

5b. *Story of Prince Seyf-el-Molouk.*—This story is perhaps an older version than that which appears in The Nights (No. 154a). It is placed long after the time of Solomon; Saad is devoured by ants[1]; and when Seyf enters the palace of Malika (=Daulet Khatoon), the jinni surprises them, and is overpowered by Seyf's ring. He then informs him of the death of Saad; and that Bedy al-Jemal was one of the mistresses of Solomon; and has also long been dead.

5b. *Malek and Chirine.*—Resembles No. 264; Malek passes himself off as the Prophet Mohammed; burns his box (not chair) with fireworks on his wedding-day, and is thus prevented from ever returning to the Princess.

5f. *Adventures of Aboulfawaris.*—Romantic travels, resembling Nos. 132a and 133.

---

1. Weber (ii. 426) has substituted wild beasts!

2. *Antar.*—This is the most famous of the Badawi romances. It resembles No. 137 in several particulars, but is destitute of supernaturalism. An English abridgment in 4 vols., extending to Antar's marriage, was published in 1820; and the substance of vol. 1 had appeared, as a fragment, in the previous year, under the title of "Antar, a Bedoueen Romance translated from the Arabic by Terrick Hamilton, Esq., Oriental Secretary to the British Embassy at Constantinople." I have also seen vol. 1 of a French translation, published about 1862, and extending to the death of Shas.

Lane (Modern Egyptians, ch. 21-23) describes several other Arab romances, which have not yet been translated; viz. Aboo-Zeyd; Ez-Zahir, and Delhemeh.

3. GLAIVE-DES-COURONNES (Seif el-Tidjân) سيف التيجان Roman traduit de l'Arabe. Par M. le Dr. Perron (Paris, 1862).

A romantic story of Arab chivalry, less overloaded with supernaturalism than No. 137; but more supernatural than Antar. The hero marries (among other wives) two jinniyahs of the posterity of Iblis. In ch. 21 we have an account of a magical city much resembling the City of Brass (No. 134) and defended by similar talismans.

4. MEHEMET THE KURD, and other tales, from Eastern sources, by Charles Wells, Turkish Prizeman of King's College, London, and Member of the Royal Asiatic Society (London, 1865).

The first story, taken from an Arabic MS., is a narrative of a handsome simple-minded man, with whom Princesses fall in love, and who is raised to a mighty throne by their enchantments. Some of the early incidents are not unlike those in the well-known German story of Lucky Hans (Hans im Glück). In one place there is an enchanted garden, where Princesses disport themselves in feather dresses (as in No. 155, etc.), and where magic apples grow. (Note that apples are always held in extraordinary estimation in The Nights, cf Nos. 4 and 264.) Among the shorter stories we find No. 251h; a version of Nos. 9a and 152 (probably that referred to by Mr. Clouston as in the Tuti Nama); a story "The Prince Tailor," resembling No. 251; No. 256, and one or two other tales not connected with The Nights. (Most of Wells' shorter tales are evidently taken from the Forty Vezirs.)

5. RECUEIL DES CONTES POPULAIRES de la Kabylie du Djardjara, recueillis et traduits par J. Rivière (Paris, 1882). Includes short popular stories of no literary merit, but occasionally illustrative of the Nights.

6. THE STORY OF JEWAD, a Romance by 'Alī 'Aziz Efendi the Cretan. Translated from the Turkish by E. J. W. Gibb, M.R.A.S., &c. (Glasgow, 1884).

A modern Turkish work, written in A.H. 1211 (1796-7). It contains the following tales:—

THE STORY OF JEWAD.

1. The Story of Ebū-'Alī-Sinā.
2. The Story of Monia Emīn.
3. The Story of Ferah-Nāz, the daughter of the King of China.
    a. The Story of Khoja 'Abdu-llah.

4. The Story told by Jewād to Iklilu'l Mulk.
   a. The Story of Shābūr and Humā.
   c. The Story of Ghazanfer and Rāhila.
5. The Story of Qara Khan.

The following deserve notice from our present point of view:—

The Story of Jewād.—Here we have magical illusions, as in Nos. 247 and 251a. Such narratives are common in the East; (Lane, Nights, ch. i. note 15) is inclined to attribute such illusions to the influence of drugs; but the narratives seem rather to point to so-called electro-biology, or the Scotch Glamour (such influences, as is notorious, acting far more strongly upon Orientals than upon Europeans).

2. *The Story of Monia Emīn* corresponds to the Story of Naerdan and Guzulbec, in Caylus' Oriental Tales. A story of magical illusions.

3. *The Story of Ferah Nāz.*—Here again we have a variant of Nos. 9a and 152.

3a. *Khoja 'Abdu-llah.*—This is a version of the Story of Aboulcassem in the Thousand and One Days.

4a. *Shābūr and Humā.*—The commencement of this story might have suggested to Southey the adventures of Thalaba and Oneida in the Gardens of Aloadin; the remainder appears to be taken from the Story of the young King of Thibet, in the Thousand and One Days.

5. *Qara Khan.*—The principal part of this story is borrowed from the First Voyage of Aboulfawaris in the Thousand and One Days; it has some resemblance to the story of the Mountain of Loadstone in No. 3c.

7. Früchte des Asiatischen Geist, von A. T. Hartmann. 2 vols., 12mo. (Münster), 1803. A collection of anecdotes, etc., from various Eastern sources, Arabic, Indian, etc. I think it not impossible that this may be the work referred to by Von Hammer in the preface to Zinserling's "1001 Nacht" (p. xxvii. note) as "Asiatische Perleuschnur von Hartmann." At least I have not yet met with any work to which the scanty indication would apply better.

8. Tuti-Nama. I could hardly pass over the famous Persian and Turkish "Parrot-Book" quite without notice; but its tales have rarely any direct connection with those in The Nights, and I have not attempted to go into its very extensive bibliography.

DR. CLARKE'S MS.

Dr. Edward Daniel Clarke has given an account of an important MS. nearly agreeing with Bul. and Mac., which he purchased in Egypt, in his "Travels in various countries of Europe, Asia and Africa." Part ii. Greece, Egypt, and the Holy Land. Section i. (1812) App. iii., pp. 701-704. Unfortunately, this MS. was afterwards so damaged by water during a shipwreck that it was rendered totally illegible. The list of tales (as will be seen by the numbers in brackets, which correspond to our Table, as far as the identifications are safe) will show the approximate contents of the MS., but the list (which is translated into German by Habicht in the preface to his vol. 12) was evidently compiled carelessly by a person nearly ignorant of Arabic, perhaps with the aid of an interpreter, Maltese, or other, and seems to abound with the most absurd mistakes. The full text of Clarke's App. iii. is as follows: "List of One Hundred and Seventy-two Tales, contained in a manuscript copy of The 'Alif Lila va Lilin,' or 'Arabian Nights,' as it was procured by the Author in Egypt.

"N.B.—The Arabic words mentioned in this list are given as they appeared to be pronounced in English characters, and of course, therefore, adapted to English pronunciation.

"The number of tales amounts to 172, but one tale is supposed to occupy many nights in the recital, so that the whole number is divided into "*One Thousand and One Nights.*" It rarely happens that any two copies of the Alif Lila va Lilin resemble each other. This title is bestowed upon any collection of Eastern tales divided into the same number of parts. The compilation depends upon the taste, the caprice, and the opportunities of the scribe, or the commands of his employer. Certain popular stories are common to almost all copies of the Arabian Nights, but almost every collection contains some tales which are not found in every other. Much depends upon the locality of the scribe. The popular stories of Egypt will be found to differ materially from those of Constantinople. A nephew of the late Wortley Montague, living in Rosetta, had a copy of the Arabian Nights, and upon comparing the two manuscripts it appeared that out of the 172 tales here enumerated only 37 were found in his manuscript. In order to mark, therefore, the stories which were common to the two manuscripts, an asterisk has been prefixed to the thirty-seven tales which appeared in both copies."

1. The Bull and the Ass (a).
2. The Merchant and the Hobgoblin (1; Habicht translates Kobold!).
3. The Man and the Antelope (1a).
4. The Merchant and Two Dogs (1b).
5. The Old Man and the Mule (1c).
*6. The History of the Hunters (2).
7 & 8. The History of King Unam and the Philosopher Reinan (2a).
*9. History of King Sinbad and Elbase (2a, ab).
*10. History of the Porter (3).
*11. History of Karănduli.
12. Story of the Mirror.
13. Story of the Three Apples (4).
*14. Of Shensheddin Mohammed, and his Brother Noureddin (5).
*15. Of the Taylor, Little Hunchback, the Jew and the Christian (6).
16. The History of Noureddin Ali (7).
17. Ditto of Gaumayub, etc. (8).
*18. The History of King Omar and Oman and his Children. (This tale is extremely long, and occupies much of the manuscript) (9).
*19. Of the Lover and the Beloved (9a).
20. Story of the Peacock, the Goose, the Ass, the Horse, &c. (10).

21. Of the Pious Man (11).
22 Of the Pious Shepherd.
23. Of the Bird and the Turtle (12).
24. Of the Fox, the Hawk, &c. (13).
25. Of the Lord of the Beasts.
•26. Of the Mouse and the Partridge (14).
27. Of the Raven and the Cat (15).
28. Of the Raven, the Fox, the Mouse, the Flea, &c., &c. (16).
29. Story of the Thief (18).
•30. Of Aul Hassan and the Slave Shemsney Har (20).
•31. Of Kamrasaman, &c. (21).
32. Of Naam and Nameto la (21a).
•33. Of Aladin Abuskelmat (22).
34. Of Hallina Die (23).
35. Story of Maan Jaamnazida (24).
36. History of the Town Litta (26).
37. Story of Hassan Abdulmelac (27).
38. Of Ibrahim Elmachde, Brother of Haroun al-Raschid (28).
•39. History of the Famous Garden Ezem (Paradise) (29).
40. Of Isaac of Mossul (30).
41. Of Hasli Hasli.
42. Of Mohammed Eli Ali (32).
43. Of Ali the Persian (33).
44. History of the Raschid and his Judge (34).
45. Of Haled Immi Abdullah.
46. Of Jafaard the Barnasside (36).
47. Of Abokohammed Kurlan (37).
48. Of Haroun al-Raschid and Sala.
49. History of Mamoan (40).
50. Of Shar and the Slave Zemroud (41).
51. Of the Lady Bedoor *(literally Mrs. Moon-face)* and Mr. Victorious (42).
52. Of Mammon and Mohammed of Bassorah.
53. Of Haroun al-Raschid and his Slave (44).
54. Of the Merchant in Debt (45).
55. Of Hassoun Medin, the Governor (46).
56. Of King Nassir and his Three Children—the Governor of Cairo, the Governor of Bulac, and the Governor of Old Cairo (47).
57. History of the Banker and the Thief (48).
58. Of Aladin, Governor of Constantinople.
59. Of Mamoon and Ibrahim (50).
60. Of a certain King (51).
61. Of a Pious Man (52).
62. Of Abul Hassan Ezeada (53).
63. Of a Merchant (54).
64. Of a Man of Bagdad (55).
65. Of Modavikil (56).
•66. Of Virdan in the time of Hakim Veemrelack (N.B.—He built the Mosque in going from Cairo to Heliopolis) (57).

67. Of a Slave and an Ape (58).
*68. Story of the Horse of Ebony (59).
*69. Of Insilvujud (60).
70. Of Eban Vas (61).
71. Of an Inhabitant of Bassora (62).
72. History of a Man of the tribe of Arabs of Beucadda (63).
73. History of Benriddin, Vizir of Yemen (64).
74. Of a Boy and a Girl (63).
75. Of Mutĕlmis (66).
76. Of Haroun al-Raschid and the Lady Zebeda (67).
77. Of Mussa ab imni Zibir (69).
78. Of the Black Father.
79. Of Haroun al-Raschid.
80. Story of an Ass Keeper (74?).
81. Of Haroun al-Raschid and Eboo Yussuf (75).
82. Of Hakim, Builder of the Mosque (76).
83. Of Melikel Horrais.
84. Of a Gilder and his Wife (78).
85. Of Hashron, &c. (79).
86. Of Yackyar, &c., the Barmadride (80).
87. Of Mussa, &c.
88. Of Said, &c.
89. Of the Whore and the Good Woman.
90. Of Raschid and Jacob his Favourite.
91. Of Sherif Hussein.
92. Of Mamoon, son of Haroun al-Raschid (87).
93. Of the Repenting Thief (88).
94. Of Haroun al-Raschid (89).
95. Of a Divine, &c. 90).
96. Another Story of a Divine.
97. The Story of the Neighbours.
98. Of Kings (94).
99. Of Abdo Rackman (95).
100. Of Hind, daughter of Nackinan (96).
101. Of Tabal (97).
102. Of Isaac son of Abraham (98).
103. Of a Boy and a Girl.
104. Story of Chassim Imni Addi.
105. Of Abul Abass.
106. Of Ebubecker Ben Mohammed.
107. Of Ebi Evar.
108. Of Emmin, brother of Mamon (105).
109. Of Six Scheiks of Bagdad.
110. Of an Old Woman.
111 Of a Wild Girl.
112. Of Hasan Elgevire of Bagdad.
113. Of certain Kings.
114. Of a King of Israel (116)
115. Of Alexander (117).

116. Of King Nusharvian (118).
117. Of a Judge and his Wife (119).
118. Of an Emir.
119. Of Malek Imnidinar.
120. Of a Devout Man of the Children of Israel (122).
121. Of Hedjage Himni Yussuf (123).
122. Of a Blacksmith (124).
123. Of a Devout Man (125).
124. Of Omar Imnilchatab.
125. Of Ibrahim Elchaber.
126. Of a Prophet (128).
127. Of a Pious Man (129).
128. Of a Man of the Children of Israel (130).
129. Of Abul Hassan Duradge (131).
130. Of Sultana Hayaat.
*131. Of the Philosopher Daniel (132).
*132. Of Belukia (132A).
*133. The Travels of Sinbad—certain seven voyages, &c. (133).
134. Of the Town of Copper (134).
135. Of the Seven Virgins and the Slave (135).
*136. Story of Judais (136).
137. The Wonderful History.
138. Of Abdullah Imni Mohammi.
139. Of Hind Imni Haman (139).
140. Of Chazmimé Imni Bashés (140).
141. Of Jonas the Secretary (141).
142. Of Haroun al Raschid (142).
143. Of ditto.
144. Of Ebon Isaac Ibrahim (144).
145. Of Haroun al-Raschid, Misroor and the Poet.
146. Of the Caliph Moavia.
147. Of Haroun al-Raschid.
148. Of Isaac Imni Ibrahim (148).
149. Of Ebwi Amér.
*150. Of Achmet Ezenth and the old Female Pimp.
151. Of the Three Brothers.
152. Of Erdeshir and Hiaker, of Julmar El Bacharia (152).
153. Of Mahomet, &c.
154. Ditto (154?).
*155. Story of Safil Moluki (154A).
*156. Of Hassan, &c. (155).
*157. Of Caliph the Hunter (156).
*158. Of Mersir and his Mistress (157).
159. Of Noureddin and Mary (158).
160. Of a Bedouin and a Frank (159).
161. Of a Man of Baghdad and his Female Slave (160).
162. Of a King, his Son, and the Vizir Shemar (161).
*163. Of a Merchant and the Thieves.
*164. Of Abousir and Aboukir (162).

*165. Abdulak El Beri and Abdulak El Backari (163).
*166. Of Haroun al-Raschid.
167. Of the Merchant Abul Hassan al-Omani (164).
168. Of Imnil Echarib (168).
169. Of Moted Bila.
*170. Of Kamasi Zemuan (167).
*171. Of Abdulah Imni Fasil (168).
*172. The Story of Maroof (169).

IMITATIONS AND MISCELLANEOUS WORKS HAVING MORE OR LESS CONNECTION WITH THE NIGHTS.

The success of Galland's work led to the appearance of numerous works more or less resembling it, chiefly in England and France. Similar imitations, though now less numerous, have continued to appear down to the present day.

The most important of the older works of this class were published in French in the "Cabinet des Fées" (Amsterdam and Geneva, 1785-1793; 41 vols.); in English in "Tales of the East: comprising the most popular Romances of Oriental origin, and the best imitations by European authors, with new translations and additional tales never before published, to which is prefixed an introductory dissertation, containing an account of each work and of its author or translator. By Henry Weber, Esq." (Edinburgh, 1812, 3 vols.); and in German in "Tausand und ein Tag. Morgenländische Erzählungen aus dem Persisch, Turkisch und Arabisch, nach Petis de la Croix, Galland, Cardonne, Chavis und Cazotte, dem Grafen Caylus, und Anderer. Übersetzt von F. H. von der Hagen" (Prenzlau, 1827-1837, 11 vols.). In the "Cabinet des Fées" I find a reference to an older collection of tales (partly Oriental) called the Bibliothèque des Fées et des Génies," by the Abbé de la Porte, which I have not seen, but which is, in part, incorporated in the "Cabinet." It formed only 2 vols. 12mo., and was published in 1765.

The examination of these tales is difficult, for they comprise several classes, not always clearly defined:—

1. Satires on The Nights themselves (*e.g.* the Tales of the Count of Hamilton).

2. Satires in an Oriental garb (*e.g.* Beckford's Vathek).

3. Moral tales in an Oriental garb (*e.g.* Mrs. Sheridan's Nourjahad).

4. Fantastic tales with nothing Oriental about them but the name (*e.g.* Stevenson's New Arabian Nights).

5. Imitations pure and simple (*e.g.* G. Meredith's Shaving of Shagpat).

6. Imitations more or less founded on genuine Oriental sources (*e.g.* the Tales of the Comte de Caylus).

7. Genuine Oriental Tales (*e.g.* Mille et une Jours, translated by Petis de la Croix).

Most of the tales belonging to Class 7 and some of those belonging to Class 6 have been treated of in previous sections. The remaining tales and imitations will generally need only a very brief notice; sometimes only the title and the indication of the class to which they belong. We will begin with an enumeration of the Oriental contents of the Cabinet des Fées, adding W. i. ii. and iii. to show which are included in Weber's "Tales of the East":—

7-11. 1001 Nuits (W. 1).

12, 13. Les Aventures d'Abdalla (W. iii.).

14, 15. 1001 Jours (Persian Tales, W. ii.).

15. Histoire de la Sultane de Perse et des Visirs. Contes Turcs (Turkish tales, W. 3 = our 251).

16. Les Voyages de Zulma dans le pays des Fées.

17, 18. Contes de Bidpai.

19. Contes Chinois, ou les Aventures merveilleuses du Mandarin Fum-Hoam (W. iii.).

21, 22. Les Mille et un Quart d'Heures. Contes Tartares (W. iii.).

22, 23. Les Sultanes de Guzerath, ou les Songes des hommes eveillés. Contes Moguls (W. iii.).

25. Nouveaux Contes Orientaux, par le Comte de Caylus (W. ii.).

29, 30. Les Contes des Génies (W. iii.).

30. Les Aventures de Zeloide et d'Amanzarifdine.

32. Contes Indiens par M. de Moncrif.

33. Nourjahad (W. ii.).

34. Contes de M. Pajon.

38-41. Les Veillées du Sultan Schahriar, &c. (Chavis and Cazotte; cf. anteà; and W. i. ii.).

(Weber also includes, in his vol. ii. Nos. 21a, 22, 32, and 37, after Caussin de Perceval.)

12, 13. *The Adventures of Abdallah, the Son of Hanif* (Class 5 or 6).

Originally published in 1713; attributed to M. de Bignon, a young Abbé. A series of romantic travels, in which Eastern and Western fictions are more or less mixed.

16. *The Voyages of Zulma in Fairy Land* (Class 4).

European fairy tales, with nothing Oriental about them but the names of persons and places. The work is unfinished.

17, 18. *The Tales of Bidpai* (translated by Galland) are Indian, and therefore need no further notice here.

19-23. *Chinese, Tartarian and Mogul Tales* (Class 6).[1]

Published in 1723, and later by Thomas Simon Gueulette.

Concerning these tales, Mr. Clouston remarks (in litt.): "Much of the groundwork [of these clever imitations of the Arabian Nights has been, directly or indirectly, derived from Eastern sources; for instance, in the so-called Tartar tales, the adventures of the Young Calendar find parallels, (1) in the well-known Bidpai tale of the Bráhman, the Sharpers and the Goat (Kalila and Dimna, Pánchatantra, Hitopadesa, &c.) and (2) in the world-wide story of the Farmer who outwitted the Six Men (Indian Antiquary, vol. 3) of which there are many versions current in

1 [I have edited, and Messrs. H. S. Nichols & Co. have published, in 1893-94, a new edition of Gueulette's "Chinese Tales" and Tartarian Tales.—

Europe, such as the Norse tale of Big Peter and Little Peter, the Danish tale of Great Claus and Little Claus; the German tale (Grimm) of the Little Farmer; the Irish tale of Little Fairly (Samuel Lover's collection of Irish Fairy Legends and Stories); four Gaelic versions in Campbell's Popular Tales of the West Highlands; a Kaba'il version in Rivière's French collection (Contes populaires Kabylies); Uncle Capriano in Crane's recently published Italian Popular Tales; and a Latin mediæval version (written probably in the 11th century) in which the hero is called 'Unibos,' because he had only one cow."]

25. *Oriental Tales* (Class 6).

Mr. Clouston observes, "Appeared in 1749 and on the title page are said to have been translated from MSS. in the Royal French Library. The stories are, however, largely the composition of De Caylus himself, and those elements of them which are traceable to Asiatic sources have been considerably Frenchified."

Nevertheless, they are not without interest, and are nearly all of obviously Oriental origin. One of the stories is a fantastic account of the Birth of Mahomet, including romantic travels largely borrowed from No. 132a. Another story is a version of that of the Seven Sleepers. Other noteworthy tales are the story of the Dervish Abounader, which resembles Nos. 193 and 216d; and the story of Naerdan and Guzulbec, which is a tale of magical illusions similar to that of Monia Emīn, in the Turkish story of Jewad.

The Count de Caylus was the author of various European as well as Oriental fairy tales. Of his Oriental collection, Sir R. F. Burton remarks:—"The stories are not Eastern but Western fairy tales proper, with kings and queens, giants and dwarfs, and fairies, good and bad. 'Barbets' act as body guard and army. Written in good old style, and free language, such as, for instance, son pétenlaire, with here and there a touch of salt humour, as in Rosanie 'Charmante reine (car on n'a jamais parlé autrement à une reine, quel que laide qu'elle ait été).'"

29, 30. *Tales of the Genii* (Class 3).

Written in the middle of the last century by Rev. James Ridley, but purporting to be translated from the Persian of Horam, the son of Asmar, by Sir Charles Morell.

These tales have been reprinted many times; but it is very doubtful if they are based on any genuine Oriental sources. The amount of Oriental colouring may be guessed from the story of Urad, who having consented to become the bride of a Sultan on condition that he should dismiss all his concubines, and make her his sole queen (like Harald Harfagr on his marriage with Ragnhilda) is presented to his loving subjects as their Sultana!

30. *Adventures of Zeloide and Amanzarifdine.* Indian Tales, by M. de Moncrif (Class 4).

Ordinary European Fairy Tales, with the scene laid in the East.

33. *Nourjahad*, by Mrs. Sheridan (Class 3).

---

1 This is the date of the Paris edition. There was an earlier edition published at La Haye in 1734.

An unworthy favourite is reformed by a course of practical moral lessons conveyed by the Sultan through supposed supernatural agencies. Mr. Clouston regards it as "One of the very best of the imitations of Eastern fiction. The plot is ingeniously conceived and well wrought out, and the interest never flags throughout."

34. *Pajon's Oriental Tales* (Class 5). These demand no special notice.

In addition to the above, the following Oriental works are mentioned in the Cabinet des Fées, but not reprinted :—

1. Apologues orientaux, par l'abbé Blanchet.
2. Mélanges de littérature orientale, par Cardonne. (Paris, 2 vols. 1770).
3. Neraïr et Meloe, roman oriental, par H. B. Deblanes (1759).
4. Contes orientaux, par M. de la Dixmerie.
5. Les Cinq Cent Matinées et une demie, contes Syriens, par le chevalier de Duclos.
6. Abassâi, conte oriental, par Mademoiselle Fault (ou Fauques) : 1752.
7. Les Contes du Serail, par Mdlle. Fault (1753).
8. Kara Mustapha, conte oriental, par Fromaget (1745).
9. Zilia et Cénie, par Françoise d'Isembourg d'Hippincourt de Graffigny.
10. Salned et Garalde, conte oriental, par A. H. De la Motte.
11. Anecdotes orientales, par G. Mailhol (2 vols. 1752).
12. Alzahel, traduit d'un manuscrit arabe, par Mdlle. Raigné de Malfontaine (Mercure, 1773).
13. Mahmoud le Gasnevide, conte oriental, par J. F. Melon.
14. Contes Orientaux, ou les recits du Sage Caleb, voyageur persan, par Mme. Mouet.
15. Nadir, par A. G. de Montdorge
16. Lettres Persanes, de Montesquieu.
17. Les Amusements de Jour, ou recueil de petits contes, par Mme. de Mortemar.
18. Mirloh, conte oriental, par Martine de Morville (1769).
19. Ladila, anecdote turque (par la même) 1769.
20. Daira, histoire orientale, par A. J. J. de la Riche de la Poupelinière (1761).
21. Cara Mustapha, par de Preschat.
22. Des trois Nations, conte oriental, par Marianne Robert (1760).
23. Contes Orientaux, tirés des manuscrits de la Bibliothèque du Roi, 2 vols. 12mo. (1749).

This is the same as the Count de Caylus' Oriental Tales (vide anteà). Sir R. F. Burton has received the following memorandum, respecting a copy of an earlier edition of the same work: "Contes Orientaux, tirés des manuscrits de la Bibliothèque du Roy de France, ornés de figures en taille douce. À la Haye, 1743, 2 vols. 12mo, polished calf gilt, gilt edges, arms in gilt on the sides.

"The Preface says, 'M. Petit et M. Galland n'ont en aucune connaissance des manuscrits dont cet ouvrage est tiré.'

"The Tales are from the MSS. and translations sent by those despatched by the French Ministers to Constantinople to learn Arabic, &c., and so become fit to act as Dragomans and Interpreters to the French Embassy."

There is a copy of this work in the British Museum; it proves, as I expected, to be the series of tales subsequently attributed to the Count de Caylus.

In addition to the above, the following, of which I can only give the names, are mentioned in the Cabinet des Fées, but not reprinted:—

1. Alma-Moulin, conte oriental, 1779.
2. Gengiskan, histoire orientale, par M. de St. M.

From "les mercures."

3. Almanzor et Zelira, conte arabe, par M. Bret. (1772).
4. Almerine et Zelima, ou les Dangers de la Beauté, conte orientale, 1773.
5. Les Ames, conte arabe, par M. B——.
6. Balky, conte oriental, 1768.
7. Mirza, ou la necessité d'etre utile (1774).
8. Zaman, histoire orientale, par M. B.
9. Anecdotes Orientales, par Mayol, 1752. 12mo.
10. Contes très moguls.
11. Foka ou les Metamorphoses, conte chinois. Derobé à M. de V. 1777. 12mo.
12. Mahulem, histoire orientale. 12mo. 1776.
13. Mille et une heure, contes Peruviens. 4 vols. 12mo. 1733.
14. Histoire de Khedy. Hermite de Mont Ararat. Conte orientale, traduit de l'Anglais, 12mo., 1777, by — Mackenzie. The edition was published in Dublin in 1781; but there must have been an earlier one.
15. Zambeddin, histoire orientale. 12mo., 1768.
16. Zelmoille et Zulmis et Turlableu. Par M. l'Abbé de Voisem, 12mo., 1747.
17. Roman Oriental, Paris, 1753.

The remaining imitations, &c., known to me I shall place roughly in chronological order, premising that I fear the list must be very incomplete, and that I have met with very few except in English and French.

A.—French.

1. *Zadig, ou la Destinée*, par Voltaire[1] probably partakes of classes 2 and 6; said to be partly based on Gueulette's "Soirées Bretonnes," published in 1712. The latter is included in Cabinet des Fées, vol. 32.

2. *Vathek, an Arabian Tale*, by William Beckford. I include this book here because it was written and first published in French. Its popularity was once very great, and it contains some effective passages, though it belongs to Class 2, and is rather a parody than an imitation of Oriental fiction. The Caliph Vathek, after committing many crimes at the instance of his mother, the witch Carathis, in order to propitiate

1 There are two other Oriental romances by Voltaire; viz. Babouc, and the Princess of Babylon.

Eblis, finally starts on an expedition to Istakar. On the way he seduces Nouronihar, the beautiful daughter of the Emir Fakreddin, and carries her with him to the Palace of Eblis, where they are condemned to wander eternally, with their hearts surrounded with flames.

This idea (which is certainly not Oriental, so far as I know) took the fancy of Byron, who was a great admirer of Vathek, and he has mixed it with genuine Oriental features in a powerful passage in the Giaour, beginning:—

"But thou, false Infidel! shalt writhe
Beneath avenging Monkir's scythe;
And from its torment 'scape alone
To wander round lost Eblis' throne;
And fire unquenched, unquenchable,
Around, within thy heart shall dwell;
Nor ear can hear, nor tongue can tell
The tortures of that inward hell!"

How errors relative to Eastern matters are perpetuated is illustrated by the fact that I have seen these lines quoted in some modern philosophical work as descriptive of the hell in which the Mohammedans believe!

Southey, in Thalaba, b. 1. speaks of the Sarsar, "the Icy Wind of Death," an expression which he probably borrowed from Vathek.

3. *The Count of Hamilton's Fairy Tales.* Class I.—Written shortly after the first publication of Galland's work. There is an English translation among Bohn's Extra Volumes.

4. *Les Mille et un Fadaises,* par Cazotte. Class 1. I have not seen them.

5. La Mille et deuxième Nuit, par Theophile Gautier (Paris, 1880). Probably Class 1 or 2; I have not seen it.

B.—English.

1. *The Vision of Mirza* (Addison in the "Spectator") Class 3.

2. *The Story of Amurath.* Class 3. I do not know the author. I read it in a juvenile book published about the end of last century, entitled the Pleasing Instructor.

3. *The Persian Tales of Inatulla of Delhi.* Published in 1768, by Colonel Alexander Dow at Edinburgh. A French translation appeared at Amsterdam in two vols. and in Paris in one vol. (1769). Class 6. Chiefly founded on a well-known Persian work, of which a more correct, though still incomplete, version was published in 3 vols., by Jonathan Scott in 1799, under the title of Bahar Danush, or Garden of Knowledge.

5. *Rasselas,* by Samuel Johnson. Class 3. Too well-known to need comment.

6. *Almoran and Hamet,* by Dr. Hawkesworth. Class 3. Very popular at the beginning of the present century, but now forgotten.

7. *Oriental Fairy Tales* (London, 1853). Class 4. A series of very pretty fairy tales, by an anonymous author, in which the scene is laid in the East (especially Egypt).

8. *The Shaving of Shagpat*, by George Meredith. (London, 1855.) Class 5. I prefer this to most other imitations of an Oriental tale.

9. *The Thousand and One Humbugs.* Classes 1 and 2. Published in "Household Words," vol. xi. (1855) pp. 265-267, 289-292, 313-316 Parodies on Nos. 1, 195, 6d, and 6e, f.

10. *Eastern Tales, by many story-tellers.* Compiled and edited from ancient and modern authors by Mrs. Valentine, author of "Sea Fights and Land Battles," &c. (Chandos Classics).

In her preface, the authoress states that the tales "are gathered from both ancient and modern French, Italian and English sources."

Contains 14 tales, some genuine, others imitations. One "Alischar and Smaragdine," is a genuine story of The Nights (No. 41 of our Table), and is probably taken from Trébutien. Three tales, "Jalaladeen," "Haschem," and "Jussuf," are Grimm's imitations, taken probably from the composite English edition of 1847, and with the same illustrations. "The Seven Sleepers," and the "Four Talismans," are from the Count de Caylus' tales; "Halechalbe" and "Bohetzad" (our No. 174) are from Chavis and Cazotte; "The Enchanters," and "Urad," are from the "Tales of the Genii"; and "The Pantoufles" is the well-known story of the miser Casem and his slippers, but I know not where it first appeared. The remaining three tales are unknown to me, and as I have seen no volume of Italian Oriental tales, some, no doubt, are derived from the Italian sources of which the authoress spoke. They are the following: "The Prince and the Lions," "The City of the Demons" (a Jewish story purporting to have been written in England) and "Sadik Beg."

11. *New Arabian Nights*, by R. L. Stevenson. (London, 1882.)

12. *More New Arabian Nights. The Dynamiter.* By R. L. Stevenson and Vander Grift (London, 1882). Class 4.

Of these tales, Sir R. F. Burton observes, "The only visible connection with the old Nights is in the habit of seeking adventures under a disguise. The method is to make the main idea possible and the details extravagant. In another 'New Arabian Nights,' the joint production of MM. Brookfield, Besant and Pollock, the reverse treatment is affected, the leading idea being grotesque and impossible, and the details accurate and lifelike."

C.—German.

It is quite possible that there are many imitations in German, but I have not met with them. I can only mention one or two tales by Hauff (the Caliph turned Stork, and the Adventures of Said); a story called "Ali and Gulhindi," by what author I do not now remember; and some imitations said to be by Grimm, already mentioned in reference to the English composite edition of 1847. They are all European fairy tales, in an Eastern dress.

CONCLUSION.

Among books specially interesting to the student of The Nights, I may mention Weil's "Biblische Legenden der Muselmänner, aus arabischen Quellen zusammengetragen, und mit jüdischen Sagen verglichen"

(Frankfort-on-Main, 1845). An anonymous English translation appeared in 1846 under the title of "The Bible, the Koran, and the Talmud," and it also formed one of the sources from which the Rev. S. Baring-Gould compiled his "Legends of Old Testament Characters" (2 vols., 1871). The late Prof. Palmer's "Life of Haroun Al-Raschid" (London, 1881), is not much more than a brief popular sketch.

The references to The Nights in English and other European literatures are innumerable; but I cannot refrain from quoting Mark Twain's identification of Henry the Eighth with Shahryar (Hucklebury Finn, chap. xxiii.).

"My, you ought to see old Henry the Eighth when he was in bloom. He *was* a blossom. He used to marry a new wife every day, and chop off her head next morning. And he would do it just as indifferent as if he was ordering up eggs. "Fetch up Nell Gwynne," he says. They fetch her up. Next morning, "Chop off her head." And they chop it off. "Fetch up Jane Shore," he says; and up she comes. Next morning, "Chop off her head." And they chop it off. "Ring up Fair Rosamun." Fair Rosamun answers the bell. Next morning, "Chop off her head." And he made every one of them tell him a tale every night, and he kept that up till he had hogged a thousand and one tales that way, and then he put them all in a book, and called it Domesday Book—which was a good name, and stated the case. You don't know kings, Jim, but I know them, and this old rip of ourn is one of the cleanest I've struck in history. Well, Henry, he takes a notion he wants to get up some trouble with this country. How does he do it—give notice?—give the country a show? No. All of a sudden he heaves all the tea in Boston Harbour overboard, and whacks out a declaration of independence, and dares them to come on. That was *his* style—he never give anybody a chance. He had suspicions of his father, the Duke of Wellington. Well, what did he do?—ask him to show up? No—drowned him in a butt of mamsey, like a cat. Spose people left money laying around where he was—what did he do? He collared it. Spose he contracted to do a thing, and you paid him, and didn't set down there and see that he done it—what did he do? He always done the other thing. Spose he opened his mouth—what then? If he didn't shut it up powerful quick he'd lose a lie, every time. That's the kind of a bug Henry was."

COMPARATIVE TABLE OF THE TALES IN THE PRINCIPAL EDITIONS OF THE THOUSAND AND ONE NIGHTS, viz:—

1. Galland.
2. Caussin de Perceval.
3. Gauttier.
4. Scott's MS. (Wortley Montague).
5. Ditto (Anderson; marked A).
6. Scott's Arabian Nights.
7. Scott's Tales and Anecdotes (marked A).
8. Von Hammer's MS.
9. Zinserling.
10. Lamb.
11. Trébutien.
12. Bul. text.
13. Lane.
14. Bres. text.
15. Habicht.
16. Weil.
17. Mac. text.
18. Torrens.
19. Payne.
20. Payne's Tales from the Arabic (marked I. II. III.).
21. Calc.
22. Burton.

As nearly all editions of The Nights are in several volumes, the volumes are indicated throughout, except in the case of some of the texts. Only those tales in No. 5, not included in No. 4, are here indicated in the same column. All tales which there is good reason to believe do not belong to the genuine Nights are marked with an asterisk.

The blank column may be used to enter the contents of some other edition.

	Galland.	Caus in de Perceval.	Gauttier.	Scott's MS.	Scott.	Von Hammer's MS.	Zinserling.	Lamb.	Trébutien.	"Bul." Text.	Lane.	"Bres." Text.	Habicht.	Weil.	"Mac." Text.	Torrens.	Payne.	Calc.	Burton (Lady).	Burton (Sir R.F.).
Introduction	—	...	...	1	—	(Full contents from Introd. to No. 4 not given: 3*e* and 4 are apparently wanting.)	...	...	...	+	1	+	...	1	+	1	1	+	1	1
Story of King Shahryar and his Brother	1	1	1	1	1		...	...	...	+	1	+	1	1	+	1	1	+	1	1
a. Tale of the Bull and the Ass	1	1	1	A	1		...	...	...	+	1	+	1	1	+	1	1	+	1	1
1. Tale of the Trader and the Jinni	1	1	1	1	1		...	...	...	+	1	+	1	1	+	1	1	+	1	1
a. The First Shaykh's Story	1	1	1	1	1		...	...	...	+	1	+	1	1	+	1	1	+	1	1
b. The Second Shaykh's Story	1	1	1	1	1		...	...	...	+	1	+	1	1	+	1	1	+	1	1
c. The Third Shaykh's Story	—	—	...	1	—		...	...	...	+	1	+	1	1	+	1	1	—	1	1
2. The Fisherman and the Jinni	1	1	1	1	1		...	...	...	+	1	+	1	1	+	1	1	+	1	1
a. Tale of the Wazir and the Sage Duban	1	1	1	1	1		...	...	...	+	1	+	1	1	+	1	1	+	1	1
ab. Story of King Sindibad and his Falcon	—	—	...	?	—		...	...	...	+	—	—	—	1	+	1	1	—	1	1
ac. Tale of the Husband and the Parrot	1	1	1	?	1		...	...	...	—	1	+	1	1	—	—	—	+	1	1
ad. Tale of the Prince and the Ogress	1	1	1	?	1		...	...	...	+	1	+	1	1	+	1	1	+	1	1
b Tale of the Ensorcelled Prince	1	1	1	1	1		...	...	...	+	1	+	1	1	+	1	1	+	1	1
3. The Porter and the Three Ladies of Baghdad	1	1	1	1	1		...	...	...	+	1	+	2	1	+	1	1	+	1	1
a. The First Kalandar's Tale	2	1	1	1	1		...	...	...	+	1	+	2	1	+	1	1	+	1	1
b. The Second Kalandar's Tale	2	1	1	1	1		...	...	...	+	1	+	2	1	+	1	1	+	1	1
ba. Tale of the Envier and the Envied	2	1	1	?	1		...	...	...	—	1	+	2	1	+	1	1	+	1	1
c. The Third Kalandar's Tale	2	1	1	1	1		...	...	...	+	1	+	2	1	+	1	1	+	1	1
d. The Eldest Lady's Tale	2	2	1	1	1		...	...	...	+	1	+	2	1	+	1	1	+	1	1
e. Tale of the Portress	2	2	1	1	1		...	...	...	+	1	+	2	1	+	1	1	—	1	1
Conclusion of the Story of the Porter and Three Ladies	2	2	1	1	1		...	...	...	+	1	+	2	1	+	1	1	+	1	1
4 Tale of the Three Apples	3	2	2	...	2		...	...	...	+	1	+	3	1	+	1	1	+	1	1
5. Tale of Nur Al-Din and his Son Badr Al-Din Hasan	3, 4	2	2	...	2	1	...	...	...	+	1	+	3	1	+	1	1	+	1	1
6. The Hunchback's Tale	4	2	2	1	2	1	...	...	...	+	1	+	3	1	+	1	1	+	1	1

a. The Nazarene Broker's Story	4	2	2	1	2	1	...	...	...	+	1	+	3	1	+	1	1	+	1	1
b. The Reeve's Tale	4	2	2	1	2	1	...	...	...	+	1	+	3	1	+	1	1	+	1	1
c. Tale of the Jewish Doctor	4	3	2	?	2	1	...	...	...	+	1	+	3	1	+	1	1	+	1	1
d. Tale of the Tailor	4, 5	3	2	1	2	1	...	...	...	+	1	+	3	1	+	1	1	+	1	1
e. The Barber's Tale of Himself	5	3	2	1	2	1	...	...	...	+	1	+	4	1	+	1	1	+	1	1
ea. The Barber's Tale of his First Brother	5	3	2	1	2	1	...	...	...	+	1	+	4	1	+	1	1	+	1	1
eb. The Barber's Tale of his Second Brother	5	3	2	?	2	1	...	...	...	+	1	+	4	1	+	1	1	+	1	1
ec. The Barber's Tale of his Third Brother	5	3	2	1	2	1	...	...	...	+	1	+	4	1	+	1	1	+	1	1
ed. The Barber's Tale of his Fourth Brother	5	3	2	1	2	1	...	...	...	+	1	+	4	1	+	1	1	+	1	1
ee. The Barber's Tale of his Fifth Brother	5	3	2	1	2	1	...	...	...	+	1	+	4	1	+	1	1	+	1	1
ef. The Barber's Tale of his Sixth Brother	5	3	2	1	2	1	...	...	...	+	1	+	4	1	+	1	1	+	1	1
The End of the Tailor's Tale	5	3	2	1	2	1	...	...	...	+	1	+	4	1	+	1	1	+	1	1
7. Nur Al-Din Ali and the Damsel Anis Al-Jalis	7	4	3	1	3	1	...	...	...	+	1	+	5, 6	1	+	1	1	+	1	2
8. Tale of Ghanim Bin Ayyub, the Distraught, the Thrall o' Love	8	4, 5	4	...	4	1	...	...	...	+	1	+	8	2	+	1	1	...	1	2
a. Tale of the First Eunuch, Bukhayt	...	...	...	...	...	?	...	...	...	+	–	+	...	2	+	1	1	...	...	2
b. Tale of the Second Eunuch, Kafur	...	...	...	...	...	?	...	...	...	+	1	...	...	2	+	1	1	...	1	2
9. Tale of King Omar Bin Al-Nu'uman, and his sons Sharrkan and Zau Al-Makan	...	...	...	...	...	1	...	...	...	+	–	...	...	3	+	1(p)	2	...	1, 2	2, 3
a. Tale of Taj Al-Muluk and the Princess Dunya	...	...	...	...	...	1	...	...	...	+	1	...	...	3	+	...	2	...	2	2, 3
aa. Tale of Aziz and Azizah	...	...	...	...	...	1	...	...	...	+	1	...	...	3	+	...	2	...	2	2. 3
b. Tale of the Hashish-Eater	...	...	...	...	...	?	...	...	...	+	–	...	...	–	+	...	2	...	...	3
c. Tale of Hammad the Badawi	...	...	...	...	...	1	...	...	...	+	–	...	...	–	+	...	2	...	2	3
10. The Birds and Beasts and the Carpenter	...	...	...	...	...	Nos. 10-19 represented by 7 Fables.)	...	...	...	+	2	...	...	2	+	...	3	...	2	3
11. The Hermits	...	...	...	...	...		...	...	...	+	–	...	...	2	+	...	3	...	2	3
12. The Water-fowl and the Tortoise	...	...	...	...	...		...	...	...	+	–	...	...	...	+	...	3	...	2	3
13. The Wolf and the Fox	...	...	...	...	...		...	...	...	+	2	...	...	...	+	...	3	...	2	3
a. Tale of the Falcon and the Partridge	...	...	...	...	...		...	...	...	+	2	...	...	...	+	...	3	...	2	3
14. The Mouse and the Ichneumon	...	...	...	...	...		...	...	...	+	–	...	...	...	+	...	3	...	2	3
15. The Cat and the Crow	...	...	...	...	...		...	...	...	+	–	...	...	2	+	...	3	...	2	3
16. The Fox and the Crow	...	...	...	...	...		...	...	...	+	–	...	...	...	+	...	3	...	2	3
a. The Flea and the Mouse	...	...	...	...	...		...	...	...	+	–	...	...	...	+	...	3	...	2	3
b. The Saker and the Birds	...	...	...	...	...		...	...	...	+	–	...	...	...	+	...	3	...	2	3
c. The Sparrow and the Eagle	...	...	...	...	...		...	...	...	+	–	...	...	...	+	...	3	...	2	3

	Galland.	Caussin de Perceval.	Gauttier.	Scott's MS.	Scott.	Von Hammer's MS.	Zinserling.	Lamb.	Trébutien.	"Bul." Text.	Lane.	"Bres." Text.	Habicht.	Weil.	"Mac." Text.	Torrens.	Payne.	Calc.	Burton (Lady).	Burton (Sir R. F.)
17. The Hedgehog and the Wood Pigeons	...	...	...	...	...	...	...	...	...	+	–	...	...	...	+	...	3	...	2	3
a. The Merchant and the Two Sharpers	...	...	...	...	...	...	...	...	...	+	–	...	...	...	+	...	3	...	2	3
18. The Thief and his Monkey	...	...	...	...	...	...	...	...	...	+	–	...	...	...	+	...	3	...	2	3
a. The Foolish Weaver	...	...	...	...	...	...	...	...	...	+	–	...	...	...	+	...	3	...	2	3
19 The Sparrow and the Peacock	...	...	...	...	...	...	...	...	...	+	–	...	...	...	+	...	3	...	2	3
20. Ali Bin Bakkar and Shams Al-Nahar	5, 6	3	3	...	2, 3	1	...	...	...	+	2	+	4	1	+	...	3	+	2	3
21. Tale of Kamar Al-Zaman	6	3, 4	3	2	3	1, 2	...	...	...	+	2	+	5	1	+	...	3	...	2	3, 4
a. Ni'amah bin Al-Rabia and Naomi his Slave-girl	...	9	...	...	...	?	...	...	...	+	2	+	13	2	+	...	3	...	2	4
22. Ala Al-Din Abu Al-Shamat	...	9	...	...	...	2	...	...	...	+	2	+	13	2	+	...	3	...	2	4
23. Hatim of the Tribe of Tayy	...	...	...	...	...	2	1	...	3	+	2	+	...	2	+	...	3	...	2	4
24. Ma'an the son of Zaidah and the Three Girls	...	...	...	...	...	2	1	...	3	+	2	+	...	2	+	...	3	...	2	4
25. Ma'an son of Zaidah and the Badawi	...	...	...	...	...	2	1	...	3	+	2	+	...	2	+	...	3	...	2	4
26. The City of Labtayt	...	...	...	...	...	2	1	...	3	+	–	+	...	2	+	...	3	...	2	4
27. The Caliph Hisham and the Arab Youth	...	...	...	...	...	2	1	...	3	+	–	+	...	2	+	...	3	...	2	4
28. Ibrahim bin Al-Mahdi and the Barber-Surgeon	...	...	...	...	...	2	1	...	3	+	2	+	...	2	+	...	3	...	2	4
29. The City of Many-Columned Iram and Abdullah son of Abi Kalabah	...	...	...	...	...	2	1	...	3	+	2	+	...	2	+	...	3	...	2	4
30. Isaac of Mosul	...	...	7	...	...	2	1	...	3	+	2	+	13	2	+	...	3	+	3	4
31. The Sweep and the Noble Lady	...	...	...	...	...	2	1	...	3	+	–	...	...	4	+	...	3	...	...	4
32. The Mock Caliph	...	9	2	...	...	2	–	...	–	+	2	+	4	2	+	...	3	...	3	4
33. Ali the Persian	...	...	...	...	...	2	1	...	3	+	–	...	...	4	+	...	3	...	3	4
34. Harun Al-Rashid and the Slave-Girl and the Imam Abu Yusuf	...	...	...	...	...	–	–	...	–	+	–	+	...	2	+	...	4	...	3	4
35. The Lover who feigned himself a Thief	...	...	...	...	...	2	1	...	3	+	2	+	...	2	+	...	4	...	3	4
36. Ja'afar the Barmecide and the Bean-Seller	...	...	...	...	...	2	–	...	–	+	2	...	...	4	+	...	4	...	3	4

37. Abu Mohammed hight Lazybones	...	9	...	...	...	2	–	...	–	+	2	+	13	2	+	...	4	...	3	4
38. Generous dealing of Yahya bin Khalid the Barmecide with Mansur	...	...	...	...	...	?	–	...	–	+	2	...	..	...	+	...	4	...	3	4
39. Generous dealing of Yahya son of Khalid with a man who forged a letter in his name	...	...	...	...	...	?	–	...	–	+	2	+	...	...	+	...	4	...	3	4
40. Caliph Al-Maamun and the Strange Scholar . .	...	...	...	...	...	2	1	...	3	+	2	...	...	...	+	...	4	..	3	4
41. Ali Shar and Zumurrud	...	...	...	...	...	2	1	...	1	+	2	+	...	2	+	...	4	...	3	4
42. The Loves of Jubayr Bin Umayr and the Lady Budur	...	...	...	...	...	2	1	...	1	+	2	+	...	2	+	...	4	...	3	4
43. The Man of Al-Yaman and his six Slave-Girls . .	...	...	...	...	...	2	1	...	3	+	–	+	...	2	+	...	4	...	...	4
44. Harun al-Rashid and the Damsel and Abu Nowas .	...	...	...	...	...	2	1	...	3	+	–	+	...	2	+	...	4	...	...	4
45. The Man who stole the dish of gold whence the dog ate	...	...	...	...	...	2	1	...	3	+	2	+	...	4	+	...	4	...	3	4
46. The Sharper of Alexandria and the Chief of Police .	...	...	...	...	...	2	1	...	3	+	2	...	...	4	+	...	4	...	3	4
47. Al-Malik Al-Nasir and the three Chiefs of Police .	...	...	...	...	...	2	1	...	3	+	2	+	...	4	+	...	4	...	3	4
a. Story of the Chief of the New Cairo Police .	...	...	...	...	...	2	1	...	3	+	2	+	...	4	+	...	4	...	3	4
b. Story of the Chief of the Bulak Police . .	...	...	...	...	...	2	1	...	3	+	2	+	...	4	+	...	4	...	3	4
c. Story of the Chief of the Old Cairo Police .	...	...	...	...	...	2	1	...	3	+	2	+	...	4	+	...	4	...	3	4
48. The Thief and the Sharper	...	...	...	...	...	–	–	...	–	+	2	+	...	4	+	...	4	...	3	4
49. The Chief of the Kus Police and the Sharper . .	...	...	...	...	...	–	–	...	–	+	–	...	...	...	+	...	4	...	3	4
50. Ibrahim bin al-Mahdi and the Merchant's Sister .	...	...	...	...	...	2	1	...	3	+	2	+	...	...	+	...	4	...	3	4
51. The Woman whose hands were cut off for almsgiving	...	...	...	...	...	2	1	...	3	+	2	+	...	4	+	...	4	...	3	4
52. The devout Israelite	...	...	...	...	...	2	1	...	3	+	2	...	...	4	+	...	4	...	3	4
53. Abu Hassan Al-Ziyadi and the Khorasan Man . .	...	...	...	...	...	2	1	...	3	+	2	...	...	4	+	...	4	...	3	4
54. The Poor Man and his Friend in Need	...	...	...	...	...	–	–	...	–	+	2	+	...	4	+	...	4	...	3	4
55. The Ruined Man who became rich again through a dream	...	...	...	...	...	2	1	...	3	+	2	+	...	4	+	...	4	...	3	4
56. Caliph Al-Mutawakkil and his Concubine Mahbubah	...	...	...	...	...	2	1	...	3	+	2	...	...	4	+	...	4	...	3	4
57. Wardan the Butcher's Adventure with the Lady and the Bear	...	...	...	...	...	2	1	...	3	+	–	...	...	4	+	...	4	...	...	4
58. The King's Daughter and the Ape	...	...	...	...	...	2	1	...	3	+	–	...	...	...	+	...	4	...	...	4
59. The Ebony Horse	11	7	5	...	5	2	–	...	–	+	2	+	9	1	+	...	4	...	3	5
60. Uns Al-Wujud and the Wazir's Daughter Rose-in-Hood	...	...	6	4	6	2	1	...	1	+	2	+	11	2	+	...	4	...	3	5

	Galland.	Caussin de Perceval.	Gauttier.	Scott's MS.	Scott.	Von Hammer's MS.	Zinserling.	Lamb.	Trebutien.	"Bul." Text.	Lane.	"Bres." Text.	Habicht.	Weil.	"Mac." Text.	Tor rens.	Payne's.	Calc.	Burton (Lady).	Burton (Sir R. F.)
61. Abu Nowas with the Three Boys and the Caliph Harun Al-Rashid	...	...	...	...	...	2	1	...	–	–	–	+	...	...	+	...	4	...	...	5
62. Abdullah bin Ma'amar with the Man of Bassorah and his Slave-Girl	...	...	...	...	...	2	1	...	3	+	2	...	...	...	+	...	4	...	3	5
63. The Lovers of the Banu Ozrah	...	...	...	...	...	–	–	...	–	+	2	+	11	4	+	...	4	...	3	5
64. The Wazir of Al-Yaman and his young Brother	...	...	...	...	...	2	1	...	3	+	–	...	...	...	+	...	4	...	...	5
65. The Loves of the Boy and Girl at School	...	...	...	...	...	2	1	...	3	+	2	...	..	4	+	...	4	...	3	5
66. Al-Mutalammis and his Wife Umaymah	...	...	...	...	...	–	–	...	–	+	–	+	...	4	+	...	4	...	3	5
67. Caliph Harun Al-Rashid and Zubaydah in the Bath	...	...	...	...	...	2	1	...	3	+	–	+	...	...	+	...	4	...	..	5
68. Harun Al-Rashid and the Three Poets	...	...	...	...	...	2	1	...	3	+	–	+	...	2	+	...	4	...	...	5
69. Mus'ab bin Al-Zubayr and Ayishah his Wife	...	...	...	...	...	2	1	...	3	+	–	+	...	...	+	...	4	...	...	5
70. Abu Al-Aswad and his Slave-Girl	...	...	...	...	...	–	–	...	...	+	–	+	...	...	+	...	4	...	...	5
71. Harun Al-Rashid and the two Slave-Girls	...	...	...	...	...	2	1	...	3	+	–	+	...	...	+	...	4	...	...	5
72. Harun Al-Rashid and the Three Slave-Girls	...	...	...	...	...	–	–	...	...	+	–	+	...	...	+	...	4	...	...	5
73. The Miller and his Wife	...	...	...	...	...	2	1	...	3	+	2	...	...	...	+	...	4	...	3	5
74. The Simpleton and the Sharper	...	...	...	...	...	–	–	...	–	+	2	+	...	4	+	...	4	...	3	5
75. The Kazi Abu Yusuf with Harun Al-Rashid and Queen Zubaydah	...	...	...	A	A	–	–	...	–	+	–	+	...	...	+	...	4	...	3	5
76. The Caliph Al-Hakim and the Merchant	...	...	...	...	...	2	1	...	3	+	2	+	...	4	+	...	4	...	3	5
77. King Kisra Anushirwan and the Village Damsel	...	...	...	...	...	2	1	...	3	+	2	+	...	4	+	...	4	...	3	5
78. The Water-carrier and the Goldsmith's Wife	...	...	...	...	...	2	1	...	3	+	–	+	...	...	+	...	4	...	3	5
79. Khusrau and Shirin and the Fisherman	...	...	...	...	...	2	1	...	3	+	2	+	...	...	+	...	4	...	3	5
80. Yahya bin Khalid and the Poor Man	...	...	...	...	...	–	–	...	–	+	2	+	...	...	+	...	4	...	3	5
81. Mohammed al-Amin and the Slave-Girl	...	...	...	...	...	–	–	...	–	+	2	+	...	...	+	...	4	...	3	5
82. The Sons of Yahya bin Khalid and Said bin Salim	...	...	...	...	...	–	–	...	–	+	2	...	...	...	+	...	4	...	3	5
83. The Woman's Trick against her Husband	...	...	...	...	...	2	1	..	3	+	2	+	...	...	+	...	4	...	3	5

84. The Devout Woman and the Two Wicked Elders	...	...	...	...	...	2	1	...	3	+	−	+	...	4	+	...	4	...	3	5
85. Ja'afar the Barmecide and the old Badawi	...	...	...	...	...	2	1	...	3	+	−	+	...	4	+	...	4	...	3	5
86. Omar bin Al-Khattab and the Young Badawi	...	...	...	...	...	2	1	1	3	+	2	...	...	...	+	...	4	...	3	5
87. Al-Maamun and the Pyramids of Egypt	...	...	...	...	...	2	1	...	3	+	−	...	...	4	+	...	4	...	3	5
88. The Thief and the Merchant	...	...	...	...	...	2	1	...	3	+	2	+	...	4	+	...	4	...	3	5
89. Masrur the Eunuch and Ibn Al-Karibi	...	...	...	...	...	2	1	...	3	+	2	+	...	4	+	...	4	...	3	5
90. The Devotee Prince	...	...	...	...	...	2	1	3	3	+	2	+	...	4	+	...	4	...	3	5
91. The Schoolmaster who fell in Love by Report	...	...	...	...	...	2	1	...	3	+	−	+	...	4	+	...	4	...	3	5
92. The Foolish Dominie	...	...	...	...	...	−	−	...	...	+	−	+	...	...	+	...	4	...	3	5
93. The Illiterate who set up for a Schoolmaster	...	...	...	...	...	2	1	...	3	+	2	+	...	...	+	...	4	...	3	5
94. The King and the Virtuous Wife	...	...	...	...	...	2	1	...	3	+	−	...	...	4	+	...	4	...	...	5
95. Abd Al-Rahman the Maghribi's story of the Rukh	...	...	...	...	...	2	1	...	3	+	2	...	...	...	+	...	4	...	3	5
96. Adi bin Zayd and the Princess Hind	...	...	...	...	...	2	1	...	3	+	−	+	...	...	+	...	4	...	3	5
97. Di'ibil Al-Khuza'i with the Lady and Muslim bin Al Walid	...	...	...	...	...	2	1	...	3	+	−	+	...	...	+	...	4	...	3	5
98. Isaac of Mosul and the Merchant	...	...	...	...	...	2	1	...	3	+	−	+	...	...	+	...	4	...	3	5
99. The Three Unfortunate Lovers	...	...	...	...	...	2	1	...	3	+	−	+	...	...	+	...	4	...	3	5
101. The Lovers of the Banu Tayy	...	...	...	...	...	2	1	...	3	+	2	+	...	...	+	...	4	...	3	5
102. The Mad Lover	...	...	...	...	...	2	1	...	3	+	2	+	...	...	+	...	4	...	3	5
103. The Prior who became a Moslem	...	...	...	...	...	2	1	2	3	+	2	+	...	4	+	...	4	...	3	5
104. The Loves of Abu Isa and Kurrat Al-Ayn	...	...	...	...	...	2	1	...	3	+	2	+	...	...	+	...	4	...	3	5
105. Al-Amin and his Uncle Ibrahim bin Al-Mahdi	...	...	...	...	...	2	1	...	3	+	−	+	...	...	+	...	4	...	...	5
106. Al-Fath bin Khakan and Al-Mutawakkil	...	...	...	...	...	2	1	...	3	+	−	+	..	...	+	...	4	...	.	5
107. The Man's dispute with the Learned Woman concerning the relative excellence of male and female	...	...	...	...	...	2	1	...	3	+	−	+	...	...	+	...	4	...	..	5
108. Abu Suwayd and the pretty Old Woman	...	...	...	...	...	2	1	...	3	+	−	+	...	...	+	...	4	...	...	5
109. Ali bin Tahir and the girl Muunis	...	...	...	...	...	2	1	...	3	+	−	+	...	...	+	...	4	...	..	5
110. The Woman who had a Boy, and the other who had a Man to lover	...	...	...	...	...	2	1	...	3	+	−	+	...	...	+	...	4	...	...	5
111. Ali the Cairene and the Haunted House in Baghdad	...	...	...	...	...	2	1	...	1	+	2	+	...	4	+	...	4	...	3	5
112. The Pilgrim Man and the Old Woman	...	...	...	...	...	2	1	...	3	+	2	...	...	...	+	...	4	...	3	5
113. Abu Al-Husn and his Slave-girl Tawaddud	...	...	...	...	...	2	1	...	1	+	−	...	...	...	+	...	4	...	3	5
114. The Angel of Death with the Proud King and the Devout Man	...	...	...	...	...	2	1	...	3	+	−	...	...	4	+	...	5	...	3	5

	Galland.	Caussin de Perceval.	Gautier.	Scott's MS.	Scott.	Von Hammer's MS.	Zinserling.	Lamb.	Trébutien.	"Bul." Text.	Lane.	"Bres." Text.	Habicht.	Weil.	"Mac." Text.	Torrens.	Payne.	Calc.	Burton (Lady).	Burton (Sir R.F.)
115. The Angel of Death and the Rich King	...	...	...	...	...	2	1	...	3	+	—	...	...	4	+	...	5	...	3	5
116. The Angel of Death and the King of the Children of Israel	...	...	...	...	...	2	1	3	3	+	2	...	...	...	+	...	5	...	3	5
117. Iskandar zu Al-Karnayn and a certain Tribe of Poor Folk	...	...	...	...	...	2	1	...	3	+	—	...	...	4	+	...	5	...	3	5
118. The Righteousness of King Anushirwan	...	...	...	...	...	2	1	...	3	+	—	...	...	4	+	...	5	...	3	5
119. The Jewish Kazi and his Pious Wife	...	...	...	...	...	2	1	...	3	+	—	...	...	4	+	...	5	...	3	5
120. The Shipwrecked Woman and her Child	...	...	...	...	...	2	1	...	3	+	—	...	...	4	+	...	5	...	3	5
121. The Pious Black Slave	...	...	...	...	...	2	1	...	3	+	—	...	...	4	+	...	5	...	3	5
122. The Devout Tray-maker and his Wife	...	...	...	...	...	2	1	...	3	+	2	...	...	4	+	...	5	...	3	5
123. Al-Hajjaj bin Yusuf and the Pious Man	...	...	...	...	...	2	1	...	3	+	—	...	...	...	+	...	5	...	3	5
124. The Blacksmith who could Handle Fire Without Hurt	...	...	...	...	...	2	1	...	3	+	—	...	...	4	+	...	5	...	3	5
125. The One to whom Allah gave a Cloud for Service and the Devout King	...	...	...	...	...	2	1	...	3	+	—	...	...	4	+	...	5	...	3	5
126. The Moslem Champion and the Christian Damsel	...	...	...	...	...	2	1	...	3	+	2	...	...	4	+	...	5	...	3	5
127. The Christian King's Daughter and the Moslem	...	...	...	...	...	2	1	...	3	+	—	...	...	...	+	...	5	...	3	5
128. The Prophet and the Justice of Providence	...	...	...	...	...	2	1	...	3	+	2	...	...	4	+	...	5	...	3	5
129. The Ferryman of the Nile and the Hermit	...	...	...	...	...	2	1	...	—	+	—	...	...	...	+	...	5	...	3	5
130. The Island King and the Pious Israelite	...	...	6	...	...	2	1	...	3	+	—	...	10	4	+	...	5	...	3	5
131. Abu Al-Hasan and Abu Ja'afar the Leper	...	...	...	...	...	2	1	...	3	+	—	...	...	...	+	...	5	...	3	5
132. The Queen of the Serpents	...	...	...	...	...	2	1	3	1	+	—	...	...	4	+	...	5	...	3	5
a. The Adventure of Bulukiya	...	...	...	...	...	2	1	3	1	+	—	...	...	4	+	...	5	...	3	5
b. The Story of Janshah	...	...	...	...	...	2	1	3	1	+	—	...	...	4	+	...	5	...	3	5
133. Sindbad the Seaman and Sindbad the Landsman	3	2	2	...	2	3	—	...	—	+	3	+	2	1	+	...	5	+	3	6
a The First Voyage of Sindbad the Seaman	3	2	2	...	2	3	—	...	—	+	3	+	2	1	+	...	5	+	3	6

b. The Second Voyage of Sindbad the Seaman	3	2	2	...	2	3	−	...	−	+	3	+	2	1	+	...	5	+	3	6
c. The Third Voyage of Sindbad the Seaman	3	2	2	...	2	3	−	...	−	+	3	+	2	1	+	...	5	+	3	6
d. The Fourth Voyage of Sindbad the Seaman	3	2	2	...	2	3	−	...	−	+	3	+	2	1	+	...	5	+	3	6
e. The Fifth Voyage of Sindbad the Seaman	3	2	2	...	2	3	−	...	−	+	3	+	3	1	+	..	5	+	3	6
f. The Sixth Voyage of Sindbad the Seaman	3	2	2	...	2	3	−	...	−	+	3	+	3	1	+	...	5	−	4	6
ff. The Sixth Voyage of Sindbad the Seaman	...	...	...	...	...	...	...	...	...	−	3	−	...	...	−	...	III	+	...	−
g. The Seventh Voyage of Sindbad the Seaman	3	2	2	...	2	3	−	...	−	+	3	+	3	1	+	...	5	−	4	6
gg. The Seventh Voyage of Sindbad the Seaman	−	...	...	...	−	−	−	...	−	−	3	−	...	−	−	...	III	+	4	6
134. The City of Brass	...	...	...	...	...	3	2	1	1	+	3	+	...	2	+	...	5	...	4	6
135. The Craft and Malice of Women	...	...	...	A	A	3	−	...	−	+	3	+	15	...	+	...	5	...	4	6
a. The King and his Wazir's Wife	...	...	...	A	A	...	−	...	−	+	3	+	15	...	+	...	5	...	4	6
b. The Confectioner, his Wife and the Parrot	...	...	...	A	A		−	.	−	+	−	+	...	..	+	.	5	...	4	6
c. The Fuller and his Son	...	...	...	A	A	(Would include subordinate tales.)	...	...	...	+	−	+	15	...	+	..	5	...	4	6
d. The Rake's Trick against the Chaste Wife	...	...	...	...	...		...	...	...	+	−	+	15	...	+	...	5	...	...	6
e. The Miser and the Loaves of Bread	...	...	...	...	...		...	...	...	+	−	+	15	...	+	...	5	...	4	6
f. The Lady and her two Viziers	...	...	...	A	A		...	...	...	+	3	+	15	...	+	...	5	...	4	6
g. The King's Son and the Goose	...	...	...	A	A		...	...	...	+	−	+	15	...	+	...	5	...	4	6
h. The Drop of Honey	...	...	...	A	A		...	...	...	+	3	+	15	...	+	...	5	...	4	6
i. The Woman who made her husband sift dust	...	...	...	A	...		...	...	...	+	3	+	15	...	+	...	5	...	4	6
j. The Enchanted Spring	...	...	...	A	A		...	...	...	+	3	+	15	...	+	...	5	...	4	6
k. The Wazir's Son and the Hammam-keeper's Wife	...	...	...	A	...	...	...	...	...	+	−	+	...	...	+	...	5	...	...	6
l. The Wife's Device to cheat her Husband	...	...	...	A		...	...	...	...	+	3	+	15	...	+	...	5	...	...	6
m. The Goldsmith and the Cashmere Singing-girl	...	...	1	A		...	...	...	...	+	3	+	1	1	+	...	5	...	4	6
n. The Man who never laughed during the rest of his days	...	...	...	A	A	...	...	...	...	+	3	+	15	...	+	...	5	...	4	6
o. The King's Son and the Merchant's Wife	...	...	...	A	A	...	...	...	...	+	−	+	15	...	+	...	5	...	4	6
p. The Page who feigned to know the Speech of Birds	...	...	...	...	...	...	...	...	...	+	−	...	...	...	+	...	5	...	4	6
q. The Lady and her five Suitors	...	...	...	A	A	...	...	...	...	+	−	...	...	...	+	...	5	...	4	6
r. The Three Wishes or the Man who longed to see the Night of Power	...	...	...	A	...	...	...	...	...	+	−	+	...	...	+	...	5	...	4	6
s. The Stolen Necklace	...	...	...	A	A	...	...	...	...	+	3	+	15	...	+	...	5	...	4	6
t. The Two Pigeons	...	...	...	...	...	...	...	...	...	+	3	...	...	...	+	...	5	...	4	6

	Galland.	Caussin de Perceval.	Gautier.	Scott's MS.	Scott.	Von Hammer's MS.	Zinserling.	Lamb.	Trébutien.	"Bul." Text.	Lane.	"Bres." Text.	Habicht.	Weil.	"Mac." Text.	Torrens.	Payne.	Calc.	Burton (Lady).	Burton (Sir R.F.)
u. Prince Behram and the Princess Al-Datma .	...	...	...	A	A	...	...	...	...	+	3	+	15	...	+	...	5	...	4	6
v. The House with the Belvedere	...	...	...	A	A	...	...	...	...	+	3	+	15	...	+	...	5	...	4	6
w. The King's Son and the Ifrit's Mistress .	...	...	...	...	...	...	...	...	...	+	—	...	...	...	+	...	5	...	4	6
x. The Sandal-wood Merchant and the Sharpers	...	...	...	...	...	...	...	...	...	+	3	+	15	...	+	...	5	...	4	6
y. The Debauchee and the Three-year-old Child	...	...	...	...	...	...	...	...	...	+	—	+	...	...	+	...	5	...	4	6
z. The Stolen Purse	...	...	...	...	...	...	...	...	...	+	3	+	15	...	+	...	5	...	4	6
aa. The Fox and the Folk	...	...	...	...	...	...	...	...	...	—	—	+	15	...	—	...	5	...	4	6
136 Judar and his Brethren	...	...	...	...	...	3	2	1	1	+	3	+	...	2	+	...	6	...	4	6
137. The History of Gharib and his Brother Ajib . .	...	...	...	...	...	3	2	...	1	+	—	+	...	...	+	...	6	...	4	6, 7
138. Otbah and Rayya	...	...	...	...	...	3	2	...	3	+	3	...	...	...	+	...	6	...	4	7
139. Hind, daughter of Al-Nu'man and Al-Hajjaj . .	...	...	...	...	...	3	2	...	3	+	—	...	...	...	+	...	6	...	4	7
140. Khuzaymah bin Bishr and Ekrimah al-Fayyaz . .	...	...	...	...	...	3	2	...	3	+	3	...	...	4	+	...	6	...	4	7
141. Yunus the Scribe and the Caliph Walid bin Sahl .	...	...	...	...	...	3	2	...	3	+	—	...	...	4	+	...	6	...	4	7
142. Harun Al-Rashid and the Arab Girl . . .	...	...	...	...	...	3	2	...	3	+	—	...	...	...	+	...	6	...	4	7
143. Al-Asma'i and the three girls of Bassorah . . .	...	...	...	...	...	3	—	...	—	+	—	...	...	...	+	...	6	...	...	7
144. Ibrahim of Mosul and the Devil	...	...	...	...	...	3	—	...	...	+	—	...	...	...	+	...	6	...	4	7
145. The Lovers of the Banu Uzrah	...	...	6	4	6	3	—	...	...	+	3	...	11	...	+	...	6	...	4	7
146. The Badawi and his Wife	...	...	...	...	...	3	2	...	3	+	—	...	...	...	+	...	6	...	4	7
147. The Lovers of Bassorah	...	...	...	...	...	3	2	...	3	+	—	...	...	...	+	...	6	...	4	7
148. Ishak of Mosul and his Mistress and the Devil . .	...	...	...	...	...	3	2	...	3	+	—	...	...	...	+	...	6	...	4	7
149. The Lovers of Al-Medinah	...	...	...	...	...	3	2	...	3	+	3	...	...	...	+	...	6	...	4	7
150. Al-Malik Al-Nasir and his Wazir	...	...	...	...	...	3	2	...	3	+	—	...	...	...	+	...	6	...	4	7
151. The Rogueries of Dalilah the Crafty and her Daughter Zaynab the Coney-Catcher	...	...	...	...	...	3	2	...	2	+	—	+	...	4	+	...	6	...	4	7
a. The Adventures of Mercury Ali of Cairo .	...	...	...	...	...	3	2	...	2	+	—	+	...	4	+	...	6	...	4	7
152. Ardashir and Hayat Al-Nufus	...	...	...	7	...	3	2	1	2	+	—	+	...	2	+	...	6	...	4	7

153. Julnar the Sea-born and her son King Badr Basim of Persia	7	4	3	...	3, 4	3	–	...	–	+	3	...	6	3	+	...	7	...	4	7
154. King Mohammed bin Sabaik and the Merchant Hasan	...	...	...	1	...	3	2	...	2	+	3	+	...	–	+	...	7	...	4	7
a. Story of Prince Sayf Al-Muluk and the Princess Badi'a Al-Jamal	...	...	...	1	...	3, 4	2	...	2	+	3	+	...	2	+	...	7	...	4. 5	7, 8
155. Hasan of Bassorah	...	...	...	3	...	4	3	2	2	+	3	+	...	2	+	...	7	...	5	8
156. Khalifah the Fisherman of Baghdad	...	...	...	...	...	4	3	...	2	+	3	–	...	2	+	...	7	...	5	8
a. The same from the Breslau Edition	...	...	...	...	...	...	...	...	...	...	–	+	...	...	...	...	7	...	5	8
157. Masrur and Zayn Al-Mawassif	...	...	...	...	...	4	3	2	2	+	–	+	...	...	+	...	8	...	5	8
158. Ali Nur al-Din and Miriam the Girdle-Girl	...	...	...	...	...	4	3	2	2	+	–	+	...	...	+	...	8	...	5	8,9
159. The Man of Upper Egypt and his Frankish Wife	...	...	...	...	...	4	3	–	3	+	–	+	...	...	+	...	8	...	5	9
160. The Ruined Man of Baghdad and his Slave-Girl	...	...	...	...	...	4	3	–	3	+	3	+	...	4	+	...	8	...	5	9
161. King Jali'ad of Hind and his Wazir Shimas, followed by the history of King Wird Khan, son of King Jali'ad, with his Women and Wazirs	...	...	...	...	...	4	3	3	3	+	–	+	...	4	+	...	8	...	5	9
a. The Mouse and the Cat	...	...	...	...	...	4	3	3	3	+	–	+	...	4	+	...	8	...	5	9
b. The Fakir and his Jar of Butter	...	...	...	...	...	4	3	3	3	+	–	+	...	4	+	...	8	...	5	9
c. The Fishes and the Crab	...	...	...	...	...	4	3	3	3	+	–	+	...	4	+	...	8	...	5	9
d. The Crow and the Serpent	...	...	...	...	...	4	3	3	3	+	–	+	...	4	+	...	8	...	5	9
e. The Wild Ass and the Jackal	...	...	...	...	...	4	3	3	3	+	–	+	...	4	+	...	8	...	5	9
f. The Unjust King and the Pilgrim Prince	...	...	...	...	...	4	3	3	3	+	–	+	...	4	+	...	8	...	5	9
g. The Crows and the Hawk	...	...	...	...	...	4	3	3	3	+	–	+	...	4	+	...	8	...	5	9
h. The Serpent-Charmer and his Wife	...	...	...	...	...	4	3	3	3	+	–	+	...	4	+	...	8	...	5	9
i. The Spider and the Wind	...	...	...	...	...	4	3	3	3	+	–	+	...	4	+	...	8	...	5	9
j. The Two Kings	...	...	...	...	...	4	3	3	3	+	–	+	...	4	+	...	8	...	5	9
k. The Blind Man and the Cripple	...	...	...	...	...	4	3	3	3	+	–	+	...	4	+	...	8	...	5	9
l. The Foolish Fisherman	...	...	...	...	...	4	3	3	3	+	–	+	...	4	+	...	8	...	5	9
m. The Boy and the Thieves	...	...	...	...	...	4	3	3	3	+	–	+	...	4	+	...	8	...	5	9
n. The Man and his Wife	...	...	...	...	...	4	3	3	3	+	–	+	...	4	+	...	8	...	5	9
o. The Merchant and the Robbers	...	...	...	...	...	4	3	3	3	+	–	+	...	4	+	...	8	...	5	9
p. The Jackals and the Wolf	...	...	...	...	...	4	3	3	3	+	–	+	...	4	+	...	8	...	5	9
q. The Shepherd and the Rogue	...	...	...	...	...	4	3	3	3	+	–	+	...	4	+	...	8	...	5	9
r. The Francolin and the Tortoises	...	...	...	...	...	4	3	3	3	+	–	+	...	4	+	...	8	...	5	9

	Galland.	Caussin de Perceval.	Gauttier.	Scott's MS.	Scott.	Von Hammer's MS.	Zinserling.	Lamb.	Trébutien.	"Bul." Text.	Lane.	"Bres." Text.	Habicht.	Weil.	"Mac." Text.	Torrens.	Payne.	Calc.	Burton (Lady).	Burton (Sir R.F.)
162. Abu Kir the Dyer and Abu Sir the Barber	...	...	...	...	...	4	3	1	3	+	3	+	...	4	+	...	8	...	5	9
163. Abdallah the Fisherman and Abdullah the Merman	...	...	...	...	...	4	3	1	3	+	3	+	...	...	+	...	8	...	5	9
164. Harun Al Rashid and Abu Hasan the Merchant of Oman	...	...	...	...	...	4	3	...	3	+	—	+	...	2	+	...	9	...	6	9
165. Ibrahim and Jamilah	...	...	...	...	...	4	3	1	3	+	3	...	...	...	+	...	9	...	6	9
166. Abu Al-Hasan of Khorasan	...	...	...	...	...	4	3	1	3	+	—	...	...	...	+	...	9	...	6	9
167. Kamar Al-Zaman and the Jeweller's Wife	...	...	...	...	...	4	3	1	3	+	—	...	...	4	+	...	9	...	6	9
168. Abdallah bin Fazil and his Brothers	...	...	...	...	...	4	3	...	3	+	—	...	...	...	+	...	9	...	6	9
169. Ma'aruf the Cobbler and his wife Fatimah	...	...	...	...	...	4	3	3	3	+	3	...	...	4	+	...	9	...	6	10
170 Sleep and Wake	9	5	4	...	4	...	...	...	...	...	2	+	7	1	...	...	I.	...	...	I.
a. Story of the Lackpenny and the Cook	...	...	...	...	...	...	...	...	...	...	—	+	...	...	...	...	I.	...	...	I.
171. The Caliph Omar ben Abdulaziz and the Poets	...	...	...	...	...	...	...	...	...	...	—	+	...	2	...	...	I.	...	...	I.
172. El Hajjaj and the Three Young Men	...	...	...	...	...	...	...	...	...	...	—	+	...	...	...	...	I.	...	...	I.
173. Haroun Er Reshid and the Woman of the Barmecides	...	...	...	...	...	...	...	...	...	...	—	+	...	...	...	...	I.	...	...	I.
174. The Ten Viziers, or the History of King Azadbekht and his Son	...	8	6	...	...	...	...	...	...	...	—	+	10	2	...	...	I.	...	...	I.
a. Of the uselessness of endeavour against persistent ill-fortune.	...	...	...	...	...	...	...	...	...	...	...	...	...	...	...	...	...	...	...	I.
aa. Story of the Unlucky Merchant.	...	8	6	...	...	...	...	...	...	...	—	+	10	2	...	...	I.	...	...	I.
b. Of looking to the issues of affairs	...	...	...	...	...	...	...	...	...	...	...	...	...	...	...	...	...	...	...	I.
bb. Story of the Merchant and his Sons	...	8	6	...	...	...	...	...	...	...	...	+	10	2	...	...	I.	...	...	I.
c. Of the advantages of Patience.	...	...	...	...	...	...	...	...	...	...	...	...	...	...	...	...	...	...	...	I.
cc. Story of Abu Sabir	...	8	6	...	...	...	...	...	...	...	...	+	10	2	...	...	I.	...	...	I.
d. Of the ill effects of Precipitation	...	...	...	...	...	...	...	...	...	...	...	...	...	...	...	...	...	...	...	I.
dd. Story of Prince Bihzad	...	8	6	...	...	...	...	...	...	...	...	+	10	2	...	...	I.	...	...	I.

e. Of the issues of good and evil actions	...	...	...	...	...	...	...	...	...	...	...	...	...	...	...	...	...	...	...	...
ee. Story of King Dabdin and his Viziers	...	8	6	...	...	...	...	...	...	...	...	+	10	2	...	...	I.	...	...	I.
f. Of Trust in God	...	...	...	...	...	...	...	...	...	...	...	...	...	...	...	...	...	...	...	...
ff. Story of King Bekhtzeman	...	8	...	...	...	...	...	...	...	...	...	+	...	2	...	...	I.	...	...	I.
g. Of Clemency	...	...	...	...	...	...	...	...	...	...	...	...	...	...	...	...	...	...	...	...
gg. Story of King Bihkerd	...	8	6	...	...	...	...	...	...	...	...	+	10	2	...	...	I.	...	...	I.
h. Of Envy and Malice	...	...	...	...	...	...	...	...	...	...	...	...	...	...	...	...	...	...	...	...
hh. Story of Ilan Shah and Abou Temam	...	8	6	...	...	...	...	...	...	...	...	+	10	2	...	...	I.	...	...	I.
i. Of Destiny, or that which is written on the Forehead	...	...	...	...	...	...	...	...	...	...	...	...	...	...	...	...	...	...	...	...
ii. Story of King Ibrahim and his Son	...	8	7	...	...	...	...	...	...	...	...	+	13	2	...	...	I.	...	...	I.
j. Of the appointed Term, which if it be advanced, may not be deferred, and if it be deferred, may not be advanced	...	...	...	...	...	...	...	...	...	...	...	...	...	...	...	...	...	...	...	...
jj. Story of King Suleiman Shah and his Sons	...	8	...	...	...	...	...	...	...	...	...	+	...	2	...	...	I.	...	...	I.
k. Of the speedy Relief of God	...	...	...	...	...	...	...	...	...	...	...	...	...	...	...	...	...	...	...	...
kk. Story of the Prisoner, and how God gave him relief	...	8	...	...	...	...	...	...	...	...	...	+	...	2	...	...	I.	...	...	I.
175. Jaafer Ben Zehya and Abdulmelik Ben Salih the Abbaside	...	...	...	...	...	...	...	...	...	...	...	+	...	2	...	...	I.	...	...	I.
176. Er Reshid and the Barmecides	...	...	...	...	...	...	...	...	...	...	...	+	...	2	...	...	I.	...	...	I.
177. Ibn Es-Semmak and Er-Reshid	...	...	...	...	...	...	...	...	...	...	...	+	...	...	...	...	I.	...	...	I.
178. El Mamoun and Zubeideh	...	...	...	...	...	...	...	...	...	...	...	+	...	...	...	...	I.	...	...	I.
179. En Numan and the Arab of the Benou Tai	...	...	...	...	...	...	...	...	...	...	...	+	...	...	...	...	I.	...	...	.
180. Firouz and his Wife	...	...	...	...	...	...	...	...	...	...	...	+	...	...	...	...	I.	...	...	I.
181. King Shah Bekht and his Vizier Er Rehwan	...	...	...	...	...	...	...	...	...	...	...	+	14	...	...	...	I.	...	...	I.
a. Story of the Man of Khorassan, his son and his governor	...	...	...	...	...	...	...	...	...	...	...	+	14	...	...	...	I.	...	...	I.
b. Story of the Singer and the Druggist	...	...	...	...	...	...	...	...	...	...	...	+	14	...	...	...	I.	...	...	I.
c. Story of the King who knew the quintessence of things	...	...	...	...	...	...	...	...	...	...	...	+	14	...	...	...	I.	...	...	I.
d. Story of the Rich Man who gave his fair Daughter in Marriage to the Poor Old Man	...	...	...	...	...	...	...	...	...	...	...	+	14	...	...	...	I.	...	...	I.
e. Story of the Rich Man and his Wasteful Son	...	...	...	...	...	...	...	...	...	...	...	+	14	...	...	...	I.	...	...	I.

	Galland.	Caussin de Perceval.	Gauttier.	Scott's MS.	Scott.	Von Hammer's MS.	Zinserling.	Lamb.	Trébutien.	"Bul." Text.	Lane.	"Bres." Text.	Habicht.	Weil.	"Mac." Text	Torrens.	Payne.	Calc.	Burton (Lady).	Burton (Sir R. F.)
f. The King's Son who fell in love with the Picture	...	...	...	...	...	...	...	...	...	...	...	+	14	...	...	...	I.	...	...	I.
g. Story of the Fuller and his Wife	...	...	...	...	...	...	...	...	...	...	...	+	14	...	...	...	I.	...	...	I.
h. Story of the Old Woman, the Merchant, and the King	...	...	...	...	...	...	...	...	...	...	...	+	14	...	...	...	I.	...	...	I.
i. Story of the credulous Husband	...	...	...	...	...	...	...	...	...	...	...	+	14	...	...	...	I.	...	...	I.
j. Story of the Unjust King and the Tither	...	...	...	...	...	...	...	...	...	...	...	+	14	...	...	...	I.	...	...	I.
jj. Story of David and Solomon	...	...	...	...	...	...	...	...	...	...	...	+	14	...	...	...	I.	...	...	I.
k. Story of the Thief and the Woman	...	...	...	...	...	...	...	...	...	...	...	+	14	...	...	...	I.	...	...	I.
l. Story of the Three Men and our Lord Jesus	...	...	...	...	...	...	...	...	...	...	...	+	14	...	...	...	I.	...	...	I.
ll. The Disciple's Story	...	...	...	...	...	...	...	...	...	...	...	+	14	...	...	...	I.	...	...	I.
m. Story of the Dethroned King whose kingdom and good were restored to him	...	...	...	...	...	...	...	...	...	...	...	+	14	...	...	...	I.	...	...	I.
n. Story of the Man whose caution was the cause of his Death	...	...	...	...	...	...	...	...	...	...	...	+	14	...	...	...	I.	...	...	I.
o. Story of the Man who was lavish of his house and his victual to one whom he knew not	...	...	...	...	...	...	...	...	...	...	...	+	14	...	...	...	I.	...	...	I.
p. Story of the Idiot and the Sharper	...	...	...	...	...	...	...	...	...	...	...	+	14	...	...	...	I.	...	...	I.
q. Story of Khelbes and his Wife and the Learned Man	...	...	...	...	...	...	...	...	...	...	...	+	14	...	...	...	I.	...	...	I.
r. Story of the Pious Woman accused of lewdness	...	...	...	...	...	...	...	...	...	...	...	+	...	...	...	...	II.	...	...	I.
s. Story of the Journeyman and the Girl	...	...	...	...	...	...	...	...	...	...	...	+	14	...	...	...	II.	...	...	I.
t. Story of the Weaver who became a Physician by his Wife's commandment	...	...	...	...	...	...	...	...	...	...	...	+	14	...	...	...	II.	...	...	I.
u. Story of the Two Sharpers who cheated each his fellow	...	...	...	...	...	...	...	...	...	...	...	+	14	...	...	...	II.	...	...	I.

v. Story of the Sharpers with the Money-changer and the Ass	...	...	...	...	...	...	...	...	...	...	...	+	14	...	...	...	II.	...	...	I.
w. Story of the Sharper and the Merchants	...	...	...	...	...	...	...	...	...	...	...	+	14	...	...	...	II.	...	...	I.
wa. Story of the Hawk and the Locust	...	...	...	...	...	...	...	...	...	...	...	+	14	...	...	...	II.	...	...	I.
x. Story of the King and his Chamberlain's Wife	...	...	...	...	...	...	...	...	...	...	...	+	14	...	...	...	II.	...	...	I.
xa. Story of the Old Man and the Draper's Wife	...	...	...	...	...	...	...	...	...	...	...	+	14	...	...	...	II.	...	...	I.
y. Story of the Foul-favoured Man and his Fair Wife	...	...	...	...	...	...	...	...	...	...	...	+	14	...	...	...	II.	...	...	I.
z. Story of the King who lost Kingdom and Wife and Wealth, and God Restored them to him.	...	...	...	...	...	...	...	...	...	...	...	+	14	...	...	...	II.	...	...	I.
aa. Story of Selim and Selma	...	...	...	...	...	...	...	...	...	...	...	+	14	...	...	...	II.	...	...	I.
bb. Story of the King of Hind and his Vizier	...	...	...	...	...	...	...	...	...	...	...	+	14	...	...	...	II.	...	...	I.
182. El Melik Ez Zahir Rukneddin Bibers El Bunducdari, and the Sixteen Officers of Police	...	...	...	...	...	...	...	...	...	...	...	+	14	...	...	...	II.	...	...	II.
a. The First Officer's Story	...	...	...	...	...	...	...	...	...	...	...	+	14	...	...	...	II.	...	...	II.
b. The Second Officer's Story	...	...	...	...	...	...	...	...	...	...	...	+	14	...	...	...	II.	...	...	II.
c. The Third Officer's Story	...	...	...	...	...	...	...	...	...	...	...	+	14	...	...	...	II.	...	...	II.
d. The Fourth Officer's Story	...	...	...	...	...	...	...	...	...	...	...	+	...	...	...	...	II.	...	...	II.
e. The Fifth Officer's Story	...	...	...	...	...	...	...	...	...	...	...	+	14	...	...	...	II.	...	...	II.
f. The Sixth Officer's Story	...	...	...	...	...	...	...	...	...	...	...	+	...	...	...	...	II.	...	...	II.
g. The Seventh Officer's Story	...	...	...	...	...	...	...	...	...	...	...	+	14	...	...	...	II.	...	...	II.
h. The Eighth Officer's Story	...	...	...	...	...	...	...	...	...	...	...	+	14	...	...	...	II.	...	...	II.
ha. The Thief's Story	...	...	...	...	...	...	...	...	...	...	...	+	14	...	...	...	II.	...	...	II.
i. The Ninth Officer's Story	...	...	...	...	...	...	...	...	...	...	...	+	14	...	...	...	II.	...	...	II.
j. The Tenth Officer's Story	...	...	...	...	...	...	...	...	...	...	...	+	14	...	...	...	II.	...	...	II.
k. The Eleventh Officer's Story	...	...	...	...	...	...	...	...	...	...	...	+	14	...	...	...	II.	...	...	II.
l. The Twelfth Officer's Story	...	...	...	...	...	...	...	...	...	...	...	+	14	...	...	...	II.	...	...	II.
m. The Thirteenth Officer's Story	...	...	...	...	...	...	...	...	...	...	...	+	14	...	...	...	II.	...	...	II.
n. The Fourteenth Officer's Story	...	...	...	...	...	...	...	...	...	...	...	+	14	...	...	...	II.	...	...	II.
na. A Merry Jest of a Thief	...	...	...	...	...	...	...	...	...	...	...	+	14	...	...	...	II.	...	...	II.
nb. Story of the Old Sharper	...	...	...	...	...	...	...	...	...	...	...	+	14	...	...	...	II.	...	...	II.
o. The Fifteenth Officer's Story	...	...	...	...	...	...	...	...	...	...	...	+	14	...	...	...	II.	...	...	II.
p. The Sixteenth Officer's Story	...	...	...	...	...	...	...	...	...	...	...	+	14	...	...	...	II.	...	...	II.

	Galland.	Caussin de Perceval.	Gauttier.	Scott's MS.	Scott.	Von Hammer's MS.	Zinserling.	Lamb.	Tré utien	"Bûl." Text.	Lane.	"Bres." Text.	Habicht.	Weil.	"Mac." Text.	Torrens.	Payne.	Calc.	Burton (Lady).	Burton (Sir R. F.)
183. Abdallah Ben Nafi, and the King's Son of Cashgbar	...	...	...	...	...	...	...	...	...	...	...	+	14	...	...	...	II.	...	...	II.
a. Story of the Damsel Tuhfet El Culoub and Khalif Haroun Er Reshid . . .	...	...	...	...	...	...	...	...	...	...	..	+	14	...	...	...	II.	...	...	II.
184. Women's Craft	...	...	2	3	6	...	...	...	...	...	...	...	14	...	...	...	II.	+	...	II.
185. Nureddin Ali of Damascus and the Damsel Sitt El Milah	...	...	...	...	...	...	...	...	...	...	...	+	15	...	...	...	III.	...	...	II.
186. El Abbas and the King's Daughter of Baghdad .	...	...	...	...	...	...	...	...	...	...	...	+	15	...	...	...	III.	...	...	II.
187. The Two Kings and the Vizier's Daughters . .	...	...	...	...	..	...	...	...	...	...	...	+	15	...	...	...	III.	...	...	II.
188. The Favourite and her Lover.	...	...	...	...	...	...	...	...	...	...	...	+	15	...	...	...	III.	...	...	II.
189. The Merchant of Cairo and the Favourite of the Khalif El Mamoun El Hakim bi Amrillah . .	...	...	...	...	...	...	...	...	...	...	...	+	15	...	...	...	III.	...	...	II.
190. Conclusion	...	...	...	...	...	4	3	...	3	+	3	+	15	...	+	}	9 & III.	...	6	10
*191. History of Prince Zeyn Alasnam	8	5	4	...	4	...	...	...	...	...	...	...	6	3	...	...	...	...	...	III.
*192. History of Codadad and his Brothers . . .	8	5	4	...	4	...	...	...	...	...	...	...	6	3	...	...	...	...	...	III.
*a. History of the Princess of Deryabar . .	8	5	4	...	4	...	...	...	...	...	...	...	6	3	...	...	...	...	...	III.
*193. Story of Aladdin, or the Wonderful Lamp . .	9,10	5,6	4	...	4,5	...	...	...	...	...	...	...	7,8	3	...	...	...	...	...	III.
*194. Adventures of the Caliph Harun Al-Rashid . .	10	6	5	...	5	...	...	...	...	...	...	...	8	3	...	...	...	...	...	III.
*a. Story of the Blind Man, Baba Abdallah .	10	6	5	...	5	...	...	...	...	...	...	...	8	3	...	...	...	..	...	III.
*b. Story of Sidi Numan	10	6	5	...	5	...	...	...	...	...	...	...	8	3	...	...	...	...	...	III.
*c. Story of Cogia Hassan Alhabbal . . .	10, 11	6	5	...	5	...	...	...	...	...	...	...	8	3	...	...	...	...	...	III.
*195. Story of Ali Baba and the Forty Thieves . .	11	6	5	...	5	...	...	...	...	...	..	...	9	3	...	...	...	...	...	III.
*196. Story of Ali Cogia, a Merchant of Baghdad . .	11	7	5	...	5	...	...	...	...	...	...	...	9	3	...	...	...	...	...	III.
*197. Story of Prince Ahmed and the Fairy Peri Banou .	12	7	5	...	5	...	...	...	...	...	...	...	9	3	...	...	...	...	...	III.

•198. Story of the Sisters who envied their younger sister	12	7	5	...	5	...	...	...	...	...	...	...	10	3	...	...	...	...	...	III.
199. (Anecdote of Jaafar the Barmecide, = No. 39)	...	...	...	...	...	...	...	...	...	...	...	...	...	2	...	...	...	...	...	...
200. The Adventures of Ali and Zaher of Damascus	...	...	...	...	...	...	...	...	...	...	...	...	...	4	...	...	...	...	...	...
201. The Adventures of the Fisherman, Judar of Cairo, and his meeting with the Moor Mahmood and the Sultan Beibars	...	...	...	...	...	...	...	...	...	...	...	...	...	4	...	...	...	...	...	...
202. The Physician and the young man of Mosul	...	...	...	I	...	...	...	...	...	...	...	...	...	...	...	...	...	...	...	...
203. Story of the Sultan of Yemen and his three sons	...	...	6	3	6	...	...	...	...	...	...	...	11	...	...	...	...	...	...	...
204. Story of the Three Sharpers and the Sultan	...	...	6	3	6	...	...	...	...	...	...	...	11	...	...	...	...	...	...	...
a. Adventures of the Abdicated Sultan	...	...	6	3	6	...	...	...	...	...	...	...	11	...	...	...	...	...	...	...
b. History of Mahummud, Sultan of Cairo	...	...	6	3	6	...	...	...	...	...	...	...	11	...	...	...	...	...	...	...
c. Story of the First Lunatic	...	8	6	3	6	...	...	...	...	...	...	...	11	...	...	...	...	...	...	...
d. (Story of the Second Lunatic = No. 184)	...	...	2	3	6	...	...	...	...	...	...	...	11	...	...	...	...	...	...	...
e. Story of the Sage and his Pupil	...	...	6	3	6	...	...	...	...	...	...	...	11	...	...	...	...	...	...	...
f. Night Adventure of the Sultan	...	...	6	3	6	...	...	...	...	...	...	...	11	...	...	...	...	...	...	...
g. Story of the first foolish man	...	...	...	3	...	...	...	...	...	...	...	...	...	...	...	...	...	...	...	...
h. Story of the broken-backed Schoolmaster	...	...	6	3	6	...	...	...	...	...	...	...	11	...	...	...	...	...	...	...
i. Story of the wry-mouthed Schoolmaster	...	...	6	3	6	...	...	...	...	...	...	...	11	...	...	...	...	...	...	...
j. The Sultan's second visit to the Sisters	...	...	6	3	6	...	...	...	...	...	...	...	11	...	...	...	...	...	...	...
k. Story of the Sisters and the Sultana, their mother	...	...	6	3	6	...	...	...	...	...	...	...	11	...	...	...	...	...	...	...
205. Story of the Avaricious Cauzee and his wife	...	...	6	3	6	...	...	...	...	...	...	...	11	...	...	...	...	...	...	...
206. Story of the Bang-Eater and the Cauzee	...	...	6	3	6	...	...	...	...	...	...	...	11	...	...	...	...	...	...	...
a. Story of the Bang-Eater and his wife	...	...	6	3	6	...	...	...	...	...	...	...	11	...	...	...	...	...	...	...
b. Continuation of the Fisherman, or Bang-Eater's Adventures	...	...	6	3	6	...	...	...	...	...	...	...	11	...	...	...	...	...	...	...
207. The Sultan and the Traveller Mhamood Al Hyjemmee	...	...	6	3	6	...	...	...	...	...	...	...	11	...	...	...	...	...	...	...
a. The Koord Robber (= No. 33)	...	...	...	3	6	...	...	...	...	...	...	...	...	...	...	...	...	...	...	...
b. Story of the Husbandman	...	...	...	3	6	...	...	...	...	...	...	...	...	...	...	...	...	...	...	...
c. Story of the Three Princes and Enchanting Bird	...	...	6	3	6	...	...	...	...	...	...	...	11	...	...	...	...	...	...	...
d. Story of a Sultan of Yemen and his three Sons	...	...	6	4	6	...	...	...	...	...	...	...	11	...	...	...	...	...	...	...

	Galland.	Caussin de Perceval.	Gautier.	Scott's MS.	Scott.	Von Hammer's MS.	Zinserling.	Lamb.	Trébutien.	"Bul." Text.	Lane.	"Bres." Text.	Habicht.	Weil.	"Mac." Text.	Torrens.	Payne.	Calc.	Burton (Lady).	Burton (Sir R. F.)
e. Story of the first Sharper in the Cave	...	...	...	4	6	...	...	...	...	...	...	...	...	...	...	...	...	...	...	...
f. Story of the [illegible]nd Sharper	...	...	...	4	—	...	...	...	...	...	...	...	...	...	...	...	...	...	...	...
g. Story of the third Sharper	...	...	...	4	—	...	...	...	...	...	...	...	...	...	...	...	...	...	...	...
h. History of the Sultan of Hind	...	...	5	4	6	...	...	...	...	...	...	...	10	...	...	...	...	...	...	...
208. Story of the [illegible]n's Son	...	...	...	4	6	...	...	...	...	...	...	...	...	...	...	...	...	...	...	...
209. Story of Abu Neeut and Abu Neeuteen	...	...	6	4	6	...	...	...	...	...	...	...	11	...	...	...	...	...	...	...
210. Story of the Prince of Sind, and Fatima, daughter of Amir bin [illegible]	...	...	6	4	6	...	...	...	...	...	...	...	11	...	...	...	...	...	...	...
211. Story of the Lovers of Syria, or the Heroine	...	...	6	4	6	...	...	...	...	...	...	...	11	...	...	...	...	...	...	...
212. Story of Hyjauje, the tyrannical Governor of [illegible]h, and the young Syed	...	...	...	4	6	...	...	...	...	...	...	...	...	...	...	...	...	...	...	...
213. Story [illegible] Haieshe	...	...	...	4	—	...	...	...	...	...	...	...	...	...	...	...	...	...	...	...
214. Story told by a [illegible]	...	...	...	4	—	...	...	...	...	...	...	...	...	...	...	...	...	...	...	...
215. The [illegible]es of Mazin of Khorassaun	...	...	6	4,5	6	...	...	...	...	...	...	...	...	10	...	...	...	...	...	...
216. [illegible] of Haroon Al Rusheed	...	...	6	5	6	...	...	...	...	...	...	...	...	11	...	...	...	...	...	...
a. Story of the [illegible] of Bussorah	...	...	...	5	—	...	...	...	...	...	...	...	...	...	...	...	...	...	...	...
b. Nocturnal adventures of Haroon Al Rusheed	...	...	...	5	6	...	...	...	...	...	...	...	...	...	...	...	...	...	...	...
c. Story related by Munjaub	...	...	...	5	6	...	...	...	...	...	...	...	...	...	...	...	...	...	...	...
d. Story of the [illegible], the Dirveshe and the Barber's Son	...	...	...	5	6	...	...	...	...	...	...	...	...	...	...	...	...	...	...	...
e. Story of the Bedouin's Wife	...	...	...	5	—	...	...	...	...	...	...	...	...	...	...	...	...	...	...	...
f. Story of the Wife and her two Gallants	...	...	...	5	—	...	...	...	...	...	...	...	...	...	...	...	...	...	...	...
217. Adventures of [illegible]efa, daughter of Mherejaun, Sultan of Hind, and [illegible], son of Sohul, [illegible] of Sind	...	...	6	5	6	...	...	...	...	...	...	...	...	11	...	...	...	...	...	...
218. Adventures of the [illegible] Princes, [illegible] of the Sultan of [illegible]	...	...	5	5	6	...	...	...	...	...	...	...	...	10	...	...	...	...	...	...

VIII.

219. Story of the Gallant [illegible]er	...	...	...	5	–	...	...	...	...	...	...	...	...	...	...	...	...	...	...	...
220. Story of [illegible]ther [illegible]er	...	...	...	5	–	...	...	...	...	...	...	...	...	...	...	...	...	...	...	...
221. Story of the Idiot [illegible]nd his Asses	...	...	...	5	–	...	...	...	...	...	...	...	...	...	...	...	...	...	...	...
222. Story of the Lady of Cairo [illegible]nd the [illegible]e Debauchees	...	...	...	5	–	...	...	...	...	...	...	...	...	...	...	...	...	...	...	...
223. S[illegible]y of the [illegible]d Vizier unjustly i[illegible]d	...	...	6	5	6	...	...	...	...	...	...	...	...	11	...	...	...	...	...	...
224. Story of the Prying Barber [illegible]d the young [illegible]n of [illegible]ro	...	...	...	5	–	...	...	...	...	...	...	...	...	...	...	...	...	...	...	...
225. Story of the Lady of [illegible] [illegible] her four Gallants	...	...	6	5	6	...	...	...	...	...	...	...	...	11	...	...	...	...	...	...
a. [illegible]e Cauzee's Story	...	...	...	5	6	...	...	...	...	...	...	...	...	...	...	...	...	...	...	...
b. [illegible]e Syrian	...	...	...	5,6	–	...	...	...	...	...	...	...	...	...	...	...	...	...	...	...
c. [illegible]e [illegible]m[illegible]'s Wife	...	...	...	6	–	...	...	...	...	...	...	...	...	...	...	...	...	...	...	...
d. Story told by the Fourth Gallant	...	...	...	6	–	...	...	...	...	...	...	...	...	...	...	...	...	...	...	...
226. Story of a [illegible]d Porter	...	...	...	6	–	...	...	...	...	...	...	...	...	...	...	...	...	...	...	...
227. [illegible]e [illegible]d Porter of Cairo [illegible]nd the Artful Female Thief	...	...	...	6	–	...	...	...	...	...	...	...	...	...	...	...	...	...	...	...
228. [illegible]n [illegible]d his tried friend Mousch	...	...	...	6	–	...	...	...	...	...	...	...	...	...	...	...	...	...	...	...
229. [illegible]d Julbee, [illegible]n to an [illegible]er of Cairo	...	...	...	6	–	...	...	...	...	...	...	...	...	...	...	...	...	...	...	...
230. The Farmer's Wife	...	...	...	6	–	...	...	...	...	...	...	...	...	...	...	...	...	...	...	...
231. [illegible]e Artful Wife	...	...	...	6	–	...	...	...	...	...	...	...	...	...	...	...	...	...	...	...
232. [illegible]e Cauzee's Wife	...	...	...	6	–	...	...	...	...	...	...	...	...	...	...	...	...	...	...	...
233. S[illegible]y of the Merchant, his Daugher, and the Prince of Eerauk	...	...	...	6	6	...	...	...	...	...	...	...	...	...	...	...	...	...	...	...
234. [illegible]e [illegible]o [illegible]s	...	...	...	6	–	...	...	...	...	...	...	...	...	...	...	...	...	...	...	...
235. Story of another Farmer's Wi[illegible]	...	...	...	6	–	...	...	...	...	...	...	...	...	...	...	...	...	...	...	...
237. [illegible]e two Wits of Cairo [illegible]d [illegible]ja	...	...	...	6	–	...	...	...	...	...	...	...	...	...	...	...	...	...	...	...
238. Ibrahim [illegible]d [illegible]h	...	...	...	6	–	...	...	...	...	...	...	...	...	...	...	...	...	...	...	...
239. [illegible]e Viziers [illegible]d [illegible]d Mahummud	...	...	...	6,7	–	...	...	...	...	...	...	...	...	...	...	...	...	...	...	...
240. [illegible]e Son addicted to [illegible]ft	...	...	...	7	–	...	...	...	...	...	...	...	...	...	...	...	...	...	...	...
241. Adventures of the [illegible]c, his Wife, &c.	...	...	6	7	6	...	...	...	...	...	...	...	...	11	...	...	...	...	...	...
a. [illegible]e Sultan's Story of Himself	...	...	6	7	6	...	...	...	...	...	...	...	...	11	...	...	...	...	...	...
242. Story of [illegible]h Nukheet the Fisherman, who became favourite to a [illegible]n	...	...	...	7	–	...	...	...	...	...	...	...	...	...	...	...	...	...	...	...
a [illegible]y of the King of Andalusia	...	...	...	7	–	...	...	...	...	...	...	...	...	...	...	...	...	...	...	...
243. Story of T[illegible]e, Sultan of Egypt	...	...	...	7	–	...	...	...	...	...	...	...	...	...	...	...	...	...	...	...

X

	Galland.	Caussin de Perceval.	Gauttier.	Scott's MS.	Scott.	Von Hammer's MS.	Zinserling.	Lamb.	Trébutien.	"Bul." Text.	Lane.	"Bres." Text.	Habicht.	Weil.	"Mac." Text.	Torrens.	Payne.	Calc.	Burton (Lady).	Burton (Sir R. F.)
244. Story of the [illegible] Man and his Servant	...	...	...	7	–	...	...	...	...	...	...	...	...	...	...	...	...	...	...	...
245. The [illegible] Daughter who married the Emperor of China	...	...	...	7	–	...	...	...	...	...	...	...	...	...	...	...	...	...	...	...
*246. New Adventures of the Caliph Harun Al-Rashid	...	8	7	...	...	...	...	...	...	...	...	...	12	...	...	...	...	...	...	...
247. The Physician and the young Purveyor of Bagdad	...	8	...	...	...	...	...	...	...	...	...	...	13	...	...	...	...	...	...	...
*248. The Wise Heycar	...	8	7	...	...	...	...	...	...	...	...	...	13	...	...	...	...	...	...	...
249. Attaf the [illegible]	...	9	7	...	...	...	...	...	...	...	...	...	13	...	...	...	...	...	...	...
*250. [illegible] and Dorrat-al-[illegible]	...	9	7	...	...	...	...	...	...	...	...	...	12	...	...	...	...	...	...	...
*251. The Forty Wazirs	...	...	1	...	...	...	...	...	...	...	...	...	1	...	...	...	...	...	...	...
a. Story of [illegible]	...	...	1	...	...	...	...	...	...	...	...	...	1	...	...	...	...	...	...	...
b. Story of the Gardener, his Son, and the Ass	...	...	1	...	...	...	...	...	...	...	...	...	1	...	...	...	...	...	...	...
c. The [illegible] Mahmoud and his Wazir	...	...	1	...	...	...	...	...	...	...	...	...	1	...	...	...	...	...	...	...
*d. Story of the [illegible] [illegible]manaba and the young Fyquai	...	...	1	...	...	...	...	...	...	...	...	...	1	...	...	...	...	...	...	...
e. Story of Sultan Akshid	...	...	1	...	...	...	...	...	...	...	...	...	1	...	...	...	...	...	...	...
*f. Story of the [illegible], the Lover and the Thief	...	...	1	...	...	...	...	...	...	...	...	...	1	...	...	...	...	...	...	...
*g. Story of the Prince of Carisme and the Princess of Georgia	...	...	1	...	...	...	...	...	...	...	...	...	1	...	...	...	...	...	...	...
*h. The [illegible] and the King's [illegible]	...	...	1	...	...	...	...	...	...	...	...	...	1	...	...	...	...	...	...	...
*i. The [illegible] and the [illegible]	...	...	1	...	...	...	...	...	...	...	...	...	1	...	...	...	...	...	...	...
*j. The Royal Parrot	...	...	1	...	...	...	...	...	...	...	...	...	1	...	...	...	...	...	...	...
*252. Story of the King and Queen of [illegible]ssinia	...	...	6	...	...	...	...	...	...	...	...	...	10	...	...	...	...	...	...	...
*253. Story of [illegible] Amina	...	...	7	...	...	...	...	...	...	...	...	...	12	...	...	...	...	...	...	...
a. Story of the [illegible] of Tartary	...	...	7	...	...	...	...	...	...	...	...	...	12	...	...	...	...	...	...	...
*b. Story told by the Old [illegible]'s Wife.	...	...	7	...	...	...	...	...	...	...	...	...	12	...	...	...	...	...	...	...

*254. Story of Ali J hard	...	...	7	...	...	...	...	...	...	...	...	...	12	...	...	...	–	...	..	...
*255. Story of the two Princes of Chin China . .	...	...	7	...	...	...	...	...	...	...	...	...	12	...	...	...	...	...	...	...
*256. Story of the two Husbands	...	...	7	...	...	...	...	...	...	...	...	...	12	...	...	...	...	...	...	...
*a. Story [illegible]	...	...	7	...	...	...	...	...	...	...	...	...	12	...	...	...	...	...	...	...
*b. Story of the Favourite	...	...	7	...	...	...	...	...	...	...	...	...	12	...	...	...	...	...	...	...
*257. Story of [illegible]uf and the [illegible] Merchant . . .	...	...	7	...	...	...	...	...	...	...	...	...	12	...	...	...	...	...	...	...
*258. Story of Prince Benazir	...	...	7	...	...	...	...	...	...	...	...	...	12	...	...	...	...	...	...	...
*259. Story of Selim, Sultan of Egypt	...	...	7	...	...	...	...	...	...	...	...	...	13	...	...	...	...	...	...	...
*a. Story of the Cobbler's Wife	...	...	7	...	...	...	...	...	...	...	...	...	13	...	...	...	...	...	...	...
*b. Story of Adileh	...	...	7	...	...	...	...	...	...	...	...	...	13	...	...	...	...	...	...	...
*c. Story of the scarred Kalender . . .	...	...	7	...	...	...	...	...	...	...	...	...	13	...	...	...	...	...	...	...
*d. Continuation of the story of S[illegible]dim. . .	...	...	7	...	...	...	...	...	...	...	...	...	13	...	...	...	...	...	...	...
*260. Story of Seif Sul Yesn	...	...	...	...	...	...	...	...	...	...	...	...	14	...	...	...	...	...	...	...
261. Story of the [illegible]er and the Chair . . .	...	...	...	A	A	...	...	...	...	...	...	...	...	...	...	...	...	...	...	...
262. Story of A[illegible]d the [illegible]n	...	...	...	A	A	...	...	...	...	...	...	...	...	...	...	...	...	...	...	...

N.B.—In using this Table, some allowance must be made for differences in the titles of many of the tales in different editions. For the contents of the printed text, I have followed the lists in Mr. Payne's "Tales from the Arabic," vol. iii.

W. F. KIRBY.

Appendix II.

INDEX I.—A.

TABLE OF CONTENTS OF THE UNFINISHED CALCUTTA (1814-18) EDITION (FIRST TWO HUNDRED NIGHTS ONLY) OF THE ARABIC TEXT OF THE BOOK OF THE THOUSAND NIGHTS AND ONE NIGHT.

Introduction—	Night
a. The Bull and the Ass.	
1. The Trader and the Jinni	i
a. The First Old Man's Story	ii
b. The Second Old Man's Story	iv
(The Third Old Man's Story is wanting.)	
2. The Fisherman and the Jinni	viii
a. The Physician Duban	xi
aa. The Merchant and the Parrot	xiv
ab. The Prince and the Ogress	xv
b. The Ensorcelled Youth	xxi
3. The Porter and the Three Ladies of Baghdad	xxviii
a. The First Kalandar's Tale	xxxix
b. The Second Kalandar's Tale	xlii
ba. The Envier and the Envied	xlvi
c. The Third Kalandar's Tale	liii
d. The Eldest Lady's Tale	lxiv
(The Story of the Portress is wanting.)	
4. The Three Apples	lxviii
5. Nur al-Din Ali and his Son Badr al-Din Hassan	lxxii
6. Isaac of Mosul's Story of Khadijah and the Caliph Al-Maamun	xciv
7. The Hunchback's Tale	ci
a. The Nazarene Broker's Story	cix
b. The Cook's Story	cxxi
(The Reeve or Comptroller's Tale in the Bresl., Mac. and Bul. Edits.)	
c. The Jewish Physician's Story	cxxix
d. Tale of the Tailor	cxxxvi
e. The Barber's Tale of himself	cxliii
ea. The Barber's Tale of his First Brother	cxlv
eb. The Barber's Tale of his Second Brother	cxlviii
ec. The Barber's Tale of his Third Brother	cli
ed. The Barber's Tale of his Fourth Brother	clii
ee. The Barber's Tale of his Fifth Brother	cliv
ef. Story of the Barber's Sixth Brother	clviii

8. Ali bin Bakkar and Shams Al-Nahar clxic
9. Nur al-Din Ali and the Damsel Anis al-Jalis clxxxi
10. Women's Craft . . . . cxcv-ci
11. Sindbad the Seaman and Hindbad the Hammal. . . .

(In Mac. and Bresl. Edit.; "Sindbad the Sailor and Sindbad the Hammal.")

- *a.* The First Voyage of Sindbad the Seaman.
- *b.* The Second Voyage of Sindbad the Seaman.
- *c.* The Third Voyage of Sindbad the Seaman.
- *d.* The Fourth Voyage of Sindbad the Seaman.
- *e.* The Fifth Voyage of Sindbad the Seaman.
- *f.* The Sixth Voyage of Sindbad the Seaman.
- *g.* The Seventh Voyage of Sindbad the Seaman.

INDEX I.—B.

TABLE OF CONTENTS OF THE BRESLAU (TUNIS) EDITION OF THE ARABIC TEXT OF THE BOOK OF THE THOUSAND NIGHTS AND ONE NIGHT, FROM MR. PAYNE'S VERSION.

	Night
INTRODUCTION.—Story of King Shehriyar and his Brother.	
a. Story of the Ox and the Ass	
1. The Merchant and the Genie	i
a. The First Old Man's Story	iv
b. The Second Old Man's Story	vi
c. The Third Old Man's Story	viii
2. The Fisherman and the Genie	,,
a. Story of the Physician Duban	xi
aa. Story of the Jealous Man and the Parrot[1] . .	xiv
ab. Story of the King's Son and the Ogress . .	xv
b. Story of the Enchanted Youth	xxi
3. The Porter and the Three Ladies of Baghdad	xxviii
a. The First Calender's Story	xxxvii
b. The Second Calender's Story	xl
ba. The Envier and the Envied	xlvi
c. The Third Calender's Story	liii
d. The Eldest Lady's Story	lxiii
e. Story of the Portress	lxvii
4. The Three Apples	lxix
5. Noureddin Ali of Cairo and his son Bedreddin Hassan . .	lxxii
6. Story of the Hunchback	cii
a. The Christian Broker's Story	cvii
b. The Controller's Story	cxix
c. The Jewish Physician's Story	cxxix
d. The Tailor's Story	cxxxvii
e. The Barber's Story	cxlix
ea. Story of the Barber's First Brother . . .	cl
eb. Story of the Barber's Second Brother . . .	cliv
ec. Story of the Barber's Third Brother . . .	clvii
ed. Story of the Barber's Fourth Brother . . .	clvii
ee. Story of the Barber's Fifth Brother . . .	clx
ef. Story of the Barber's Sixth Brother . . .	clxiv
7. Ali ben Bekkar and Shemsennehar	clxix
8. Noureddin Ali and the Damsel Enis el Jelis	cxcix
9. Kemerezzeman and Budour	ccxviii
10. The Enchanted Horse	ccxliv

1 Calcutta (1839-42) and Boulac 134b. "The Merchant's Wife and the Parrot."

11. The Voyages of Sindbad the Sailor ccl
a. The First Voyage of Sindbad the Sailor cclii
b. The Second Voyage of Sindbad the Sailor . . . ccliii
c. The Third Voyage of Sindbad the Sailor cclv
d. The Fourth Voyage of Sindbad the Sailor . . . cclix
e. The Fifth Voyage of Sindbad the Sailor cclxiii
f. The Sixth Voyage of Sindbad the Sailor cclxvi
g. The Seventh Voyage of Sindbad the Sailor . . . cclxix
12. Asleep and Awake cclxxi
a. The Lackpenny and the Cook cclxxiii
13. Seif el Mulouk and Bediya el-Jemal ccxci
14. Khelif the Fisherman[1] cccxxi
15. Ghanim ben Eyoub the Slave of Love cccxxxii
a. Story of the Eunuch Sewab[2] cccxxxiv
b. Story of the Eunuch Kafour . . . . ,,
16. Uns el Wujoud and the Vizier's Daughter Rose-in-bud . . cccxli
17. The Merchant of Oman cccliv
18. Ardeshir and Heyat en Nufous ccclxiv
19. Hassan of Bassora and the King's Daughter of the Jinn . . ccclxxxvi
20. Haroun er Rashid and the Three Poets ccccxxxii
21. Omar ben Abdulaziz and the Poets . . . . ,,
22. El Hejjaj and the Three Young Men ccccxxxiv
23. Er Reshid and the Woman of the Barmecides . . . . ,,
24. The Ten Viziers; or the History of King Azadbekht and his Son ccccxxxv
a. The Unlucky Merchant ccccxl
b. The Merchant and his Sons ccccxliv
c. Abu Sabir ccccxlviii
d. Prince Bihzad ccccliii
e. King Dadbin and his Viziers . . . . ccccl v
f. King Bekhtzeman . . . . ccccl xi
g. King Bihkerd . . . . ccccl xiv
h. Ilan Shah and Abou Temam . . . . ccccl xvi
i. King Ibrahim and his Son . . . . ccccl xxi
j. King Suleiman Shah and his Sons . . . . . . ccccl xxv
k. The Prisoner and how God gave him Relief . . ccccl xxxv
25. The City of Brass. . . . . ccccl xxxvii
26. Nimeh ben er Rebya and Num his Slave-girl . . . . di
27. Alaeddin Abou es Shamat . . . . dxx
28. Hatim Tai; his Generosity after Death . . . . . . dxxxi
29. Maan ben Zaïdeh and the three Girls . . . . dxxxii
30. Maan ben Zaïdeh and the Bedouin . . . . ,,
31. The City of Lebtait . . . . ,,
32. The Khalif Hisham and the Arab Youth . . . . . . dxxxiv
33. Ibrahim ben el Mehdi and the Barber-Surgeon . . . . ,,
34. The City of Iram . . . . dxxxviii
35. Isaac of Mosul's Story of Khedijeh and the Khalif Mamoun . dxl
36. The Mock Khalif . . . . dxliii

---

1 This will be found in my "Book of the Thousand Nights and One Night," vol. vii. p. 307, as an Appendix to the Calcutta (1839-42) and Boulac version of the story, from which it differs in detail.

2 Called "Bekhit" in Calcutta (1839-42) Boulac Editions.

37. The Imam Abou Yousuf with Er Reshid and Jaafar . . . dlv
38 The Lover who feigned himself a Thief to save his Mistress's Honour . . . . dlvii
39. Abou Mohammed the Lazy . . . . dlviii
40. Jaafar ben Yehya and Abdulmelik ben Salih . . . . . dlxv
41. Jaafar ben Yehya[1] and the man who forged a Letter in his Name dlxvi
42. Er Reshid and the Barmecides . . . . dlxvii
43. Ibn es Semmak and Er Reshid . . . . dlxviii
44. El Mamoun and Zubeideh . . . . ,,
45. Ali Shir[2] and Zummurrud . . . . dlxix
46. The Loves of Budour and Jubeir ben Umeir . . . . . dlxxxvii
47. The Man of Yemen and his Six Slave-girls . . . . . dxcv
48. Haroun Er Reshid with the Damsel and Abou Nuwas . . dc
49. The Man who stole the Dog's Dish of Gold . . . . . dcii
50. El Melik en Nasir and the Three Masters of Police . . . dciii
  a. Story of the Chief of the New Cairo Police . . dciv
  b. Story of the Chief of the Boulac Police . . . . . dcv
  c. Story of the Chief of the Old Cairo Police . . . . ,,
51. The Thief and the Money-changer . . . . ,,
52. Ibrahim ben el Mehdi and the Merchant's Sister . . . . dcvi
53 King Kelyaad[3] of Hind and his Vizier Shimas . . . . . dcix
  a. The Cat and the Mouse . . . . ,,
  b. The Fakir and his Pot of Butter . . . . . . dcx
  c. The Fishes and the Crab . . . . dcxi
  d. The Crow and the Serpent . . . . ,,
  e. The Fox and the Wild Ass . . . . ,,
  f. The Unjust King and the Pilgrim Prince . dcxii
  g. The Crows and the Hawk . . . . dcxiii
  h. The Serpent-Charmer and his Wife . . . . . . dcxiv
  i. The Spider and the Wind . . . . dcxv
  j. The Two Kings . . . . dcxvi
  k. The Blind Man and The Cripple . . . . . . ,,
  l. The Foolish Fisherman . . . . dcxxvi
  m. The Boy and the Thieves . . . . dcxxvii
  n. The Man and his Wilful Wife . . . . . . dcxxvii
  o. The Merchant and the Thieves . . . . . dcxxix
  p. The Foxes and the Wolf. . . . . dcxxx
  q. The Shepherd and the Thief . . . . dcxxxii
  r. The Heathcock and the Tortoises . . . . . . dcxxxiv
54. The Woman whose Hands were cut off for Almsgiving . . dcxli
55. The Poor Man and His Generous Friend . . . . . . dcxliii
56. The Ruined Man who became Rich again through a Dream . dcxliv
57. Abou Nuwas with the Three Boys and the Khalif Haroun er Reshid . . . . dcxlv
58. The Lovers of the Benou Udhreh[4] . . . . dcxlvi
59. El Mutelemmis and his Wife Umeimeh . . . . . . dcxlviii

---

1 Yehya ben Khalid (Calcutta) (1839-42) and Boulac).
2 "Shar" (Calcutta (1839-42) and Boulac).
3 "Jelyaad" (Calcutta (1839-42) and Boulac).
4 Calcutta (1839-1842) and Bonlac, No. 63. See my "Book of the Thousand Nights and One Night," vol. iv. p. 211.

60. Haroun er Reshid and Zubeideh in the Bath . . . dcxlviii
61. Musab ben ez Zubeir and Aaïsheh his Wife . . dcxlix
62. Aboulaswed and his Squinting Slave-girl . . . . . . dcli
63. Haroun er Reshid and the Two Girls . . . . . . ,,
64. Haroun er Reshid and the Three Girls . . . . . . ,,
65. The Simpleton and the Sharper . . . . dclii
66. The Imam Abou Yousuf with Er Reshid and Zubeideh . . ,,
67. The Khalif El Hakim and the Merchant . . . . . . dcliii
68. Kisra Anoushirwan and the Village Damsel . . . . ,,
69. The Water-Carrier and the Goldsmith's Wife . . . . . dcliv
70. Khusrau and Shirin and the Fisherman . . . . . . dclvi
71. Yehya ben Khalid and the Poor Man . . . . . . ,,
72. Mohammed el Amin and Jaafar ben el Hadi . . . . . dclvii
73. The Woman's Trick against her Husband. . . . . . dclviii
74. The Devout Woman and the Two Wicked Elders . . . . dclix
75. El Fezl ben Rebiya[1] and the Old Bedouin . . . . . dclx
76. En Numan and the Arab of the Benou Tai . . . . . ,,
77. The Draper and the Thief[2]. . . . . dclxi
78. Mesrour and Ibn el-Caribi. . . . . dclxii
79. The Devout Prince . . . . dclxiv
80. The Schoolmaster who fell in Love by Report . . . . . dclxv
81. The Foolish Schoolmaster. . . . . dclxvi
82. The Ignorant Man who set up for a Schoolmaster . . . dclxvii
83. Adi ben Zeid and the Princess Hind . . . . dclxviii
84. Dibil el Khuzaï with the Lady and Muslim ben el Welid . . dclxx
85. Isaac of Mosul and the Merchant . . . . ,,
86. The Three Unfortunate Lovers . . . . dclxxii
87. The Lovers of the Benou Tai . . . . dclxxiii
88. The Mad Lovers. . . . . dclxxiv
89. Firouz and his Wife . . . . dclxxv
90. The Apples of Paradise . . . . dclxxvi
91. The Loves of Abou Isa and Curret el Ain . . . . . . dclxxviii
92. El Amin and his Uncle Ibrahim ben el Mehdi . . . . . dclxxxii
93. El Feth ben Khacan and El Mutawekkil . . . . . . dclxxxiii
94. The Man's Dispute with the Learned Woman of the relative Excellence of the Sexes. . . . . ,,
95. Abou Suweid and the Handsome Old Woman . . . . . dclxxxvii
96. Ali ben Tahir and the Girl Mounis . . . . dclxxxviii
97. The Woman who had a Boy and the other who had a Man to Lover . . . . ,,
98. The Haunted House in Baghdad . . . . ,,
99. The History of Gherib and his brother Agib . . . . . dcxcviii
100. The Rogueries of Delileh the Crafty and her daughter Zeyneb the Trickstress . . . . dcclvi
101. The Adventures of Quicksilver Ali of Cairo . . . . . dcclxvi
102. Joudar and his Brothers . . . . dcclxxvi
103. Julnar of the Sea and her Son King Bedr Basim of Persia . dccxciv
104. Mesrour and Zein el Mewasif . . . . dccccxxi

---

1 Calcutta (1839-42) and Boulac, "Jaafar the Barmecide."
2 Calcutta (1839-42) and Boulac, "The Thief turned Merchant and the other Thief," No. 88.

105. Ali Noureddin and the Frank King's Daughter . . . . . dccccxxxi
106. The Man of Upper Egypt and his Frank Wife . . . . . dccclxii
107. The Ruined Man of Baghdad and his Slave-girl . . . . dccclxiv
108. Aboukir the Dyer and Abousir the Barber . . . . . dccclxvii
109. Abdallah the Fisherman and Abdallah the Merman . . . dccclxxvii
110. King Shah Bekht and his Vizier Er Rehwan . . . . . dccclxxxv
a. The Man of Khorassan, his Son and his Governor . . dccclxxxvi
b. The Singer and the Druggist . . . . dccclxxxviii
c. The King who knew the Quintessence of Things . . dccccxci
d. The Rich Man who gave his Fair Daughter in Marriage to the Poor Old Man . . . . dccccxcii
e. The Rich Man and his Wasteful Son . . . . . dccccxciii
f. The King's Son who fell in Love with the Picture . . dccccxciv
g. The Fuller and his Wife . . . . dccccxcvi
h. The Old Woman, the Merchant and the King . . . "
i. The Credulous Husband . . . . dccccxcviii
j. The Unjust King and the Tither . . . . . . dccccxcix
ja. Story of David and Solomon . . . . . "
k. The Thief and the Woman . . . . "
l. The Three Men and our Lord Jesus . . . . . . dcccci
la. The Disciple's Story . . . . "
m. The Dethroned King whose Kingdom and Good were Restored to Him . . . . "
n. The Man whose Caution was the Cause of his Death . dcccciii
o. The Man who was lavish of his House and his Victual to one whom he knew not . . . . dcccciv
p. The Idiot and the Sharper . . . . dccccv
q. Khelbes and his Wife and the Learned Man . . . . dccccvi
r. The Pious Woman accused of Lewdness . . . . . dccccvii
s. The Journeyman and the Girl . . . . dccccix
t. The Weaver who became a Physician by his Wife's Commandment . . . . "
u. The Two Sharpers who cheated each his Fellow . . dccccxi
v. The Sharpers with the Money-Changer and the Ass . dccccxiv
w. The Sharper and the Merchants . . . . . . dccccxv
wa. The Hawk and the Locust . . . . . . dccccxvi
x. The King and his Chamberlain's Wife . . . . . dccccxvii
xa. The Old Woman and the Draper's Wife . . "
y. The foul-favoured Man and his Fair Wife . . . . dccccxviii
z. The King who lost Kingdom and Wife and Wealth and God restored them to him . . . . dccccxix
za. Selim and Selma . . . . dccccxxii
zb. The King of Hind and his Vizier . . . . . dccccxxviii
111. El Melik er Zahir Rukneddin Bibers el Bunducdari and the Sixteen Officers of Police . . . . dccccxxx
a. The First Officer's Story . . . . "
b. The Second Officer's Story . . . . dccccxxxii
c. The Third Officer's Story . . . . "
d. The Fourth Officer's Story . . . . dccccxxxiv
e The Fifth Officer's Story . . . . "
f. The Sixth Officer's Story . . . . "
g. The Seventh Officer's Story . . . . "

h. The Eighth Officer's Story . . . . dcccccxxxv
ha. The Thief's Story. . . . . . . dcccccxxxviii
i. The Ninth Officer's Story. . . . . "
j. The Tenth Officer's Story . . . . "
k The Eleventh Officer's Story . . . . "
l. The Twelfth Officer's Story . . . . dcccccxxxix
m. The Thirteenth Officer's Story . . . . . . "
n. The Fourteenth Officer's Story . . . . . . "
na. A Merry Jest of a Thief . . . . . . dcccccxl
nb. Story of the Old Sharper . . . . . . "
o. The Fifteenth Officer's Story . . . . "
p. The Sixteenth Officer's Story . . . . "
112. Abdallah ben Nafi and the King's Son of Cashghar . . dcccccxli
a. Story of Tuhfet el Culoub and Haroun er Reshid . . dcccccxlii
113. Noureddin Ali and Sitt el Milah . . . . dcccclviii
114. El Abbas and the King's Daughter of Baghdad . . . dcccclxvi
115. The Malice of Women . . . . dcccclxxix
a. The King and his Vizier's Wife . . . . . . dcccclxxx
b. The Merchant's Wife and the Parrot . . . . . "
c. The Fuller and his Son . . . . "
d. The Lover's Trick against the Chaste Wife . . . . "
e. The Niggard and the Loaves of Bread . . . . . dcccclxxx
f. The Lady and her Two Lovers . . . . "
g. The King's Son and the Ogress . . . . . . dcccccxlxxv
h. The Drop of Honey . . . . dcccclxxxvi
i. The Woman who made her Husband Sift Dust . . "
j. The Enchanted Springs . . . . "
k. The Vizier's Son and the Bathkeeper's Wife . . dcccclxxxviii
l. The Wife's Device to Cheat her Husband . . . dcccclxxxix
m. The Goldsmith and the Cashmere Singing-Girl . . dcccccxc
n. The Man who never Laughed again . . . . . . dcccccxci
o. The King's Son and the Merchant's Wife . . . . dcccccxciii
p. The Man who saw the Night of Power . . . . . "
q. The Stolen Necklace . . . . dcccccxciv
r. Prince Behram of Persia and the Princess Ed Detma . "
s. The House with the Belvedere . . . . dcccccxcv
t. The Sandalwood Merchant and the Sharpers . . . dcccccxcviii
u. The Debauchee and the Three-year-old Child . . . "
v. The Stolen Purse . . . . dcccccxcix
w. The Fox and the Folk[1] . . . . m
116. The Two Kings and the Vizier's Daughters . . . . . mi
117. The Favourite and her Lover . . . . "
118. The Merchant of Cairo and the Favourite of the Khalif El Mamoum El Hakim bi Amrillah . . . . . .
Conclusion.

1 This story will be found translated in my "Book of the Thousand Nights and One Night," vol. v. p. 345.

INDEX I.—C.

TABLE OF CONTENTS OF THE MACNAGHTEN OR TURNER-MACAN TEXT (1839-42) AND BULAK EDITION (A.H. 1251 = A.D. 1835-36) OF THE ARABIC TEXT OF THE BOOK OF THE THOUSAND NIGHTS AND A NIGHT, AS TRANSLATED BY MR. JOHN PAYNE.

	Night
INTRODUCTION.—Story of King Shehriyar and his Brother	
a. Story of the Ox and the Ass	
1. The Merchant and the Genie	1
a. The First Old Man's Story	"
b. The Second Old Man's Story	ii
c. The Third Old Man's Story	"
2 The Fisherman and the Genie	iii
a. Story of the Physician Douban	iv
aa. Story of King Sindbad and his Falcon[1]	v
ab. Story of the King's Son and the Ogress	"
b. Story of the Enchanted Youth	vii
3. The Porter and the Three Ladies of Baghdad	ix
a. The First Calender's Story	xi
b. The Second Calender's Story	xii
ba. Story of the Envier and the Envied[2]	xiii
c. The Third Calender's Story	xiv
d. The Eldest Lady's Story	xvii
e. The Story of the Portress	xviii
4. The Three Apples	xix
5. Noureddin Ali of Cairo and his Son Bedreddin Hassan	xx
6. Story of the Hunchback	xxv
a. The Christian Broker's Story	"
b. The Controller's Story	xxvii
c. The Jewish Physician's Story	xxviii
d. The Tailor's Story	xxix
e. The Barber's Story	xxxi
ea. Story of the Barber's First Brother	"
eb. Story of the Barber's Second Brother	"
ec. Story of the Barber's Third Brother	xxxii
ed. Story of the Barber's Fourth Brother	"
ee. Story of the Barber's Fifth Brother	"
ef. Story of the Barber's Sixth Brother	xxxiii

---

1 After this I introduce the Tale of the Husband and the Parrot.
2 The Bulak Edition omits this story altogether.

7. Noureddin Ali and the Damsel Enis el Jelis xxxiv
8. Ghanim ben Eyoub the Slave of Love xxxix
a. Story of Eunuch Bekhit . . . . ,,
b. Story of the Eunuch Kafour . . . .
9. *The History of King Omar ben Ennuman and his Sons Sherkan and Zoulmekan* xlv
a. Story of Taj el Mulouk and the Princess Dunya cvii
aa. Story of Aziz and Azizeh cxii
b. Bakoun's Story of the Hashish-Eater cxliii
c. Hemmad the Bedouin's Story cxliv
10. *The Birds and Beasts and the Son of Adam* cxlvi
11. *The Hermits* cxlviii
12. *The Waterfowl and the Tortoise* . . . . ,,
13. *The Wolf and the Fox* . . . . ,,
a. The Hawk and the Partridge cxlix
14. *The Mouse and the Weasel* cl
15. *The Cat and the Crow* . . . . ,,
16. *The Fox and the Crow* . . . . ,,
a. The Mouse and the Flea cli
b. The Falcon and the Birds clii
c. The Sparrow and the Eagle . . . . ,,
17. *The Hedgehog and the Pigeons* . . . .
a. The Merchant and the Two Sharpers . . . . . .
18. *The Thief and his Monkey* . . . .
The Foolish Weaver . . . . ,,
19. *The Sparrow and the Peacock* . . . . ,,
20. Ali ben Bekkar and Shemsennehar cliii
21. Kemerezzeman and Budour. clxx
a. Nimeh ben er Rebya and Num his Slave-girl ccxxxvii
22. Alaeddin Abou esh Shamat ccl
23. Hatim et Taï; his Generosity after Death cclxx
24. Maan ben Zaïdeh and the three Girls. cclxxi
25. Maan ben Zaïdeh and the Bedouin . . . . ,,
26. The City of Lebtait cclxxii
27. The Khalif Hisham and the Arab Youth . . . . . . ,,
28. Ibrahim ben el Mehdi and the Barber-surgeon cclxxiii
29. The City of Irem cclxxvi
30. Isaac of Mosul's Story of Khedijeh and the Khalif Mamoun . cclxxix
31. *The Scavenger and the Noble Lady of Baghdad* cclxxxii
32. The Mock Khalif cclxxxvi
33. *Ali the Persian and the Kurd Sharper* ccxciv
34. The Imam Abou Yousuf with Haroun er Reshid and his Vizier Jaafer ccxcvi
35. The Lover who feigned himself a Thief to save his Mistress's Honour ccxcvii
36. *Jaafer the Barmecide and the Bean-Seller* ccxcix
37. Abou Mohammed the Lazy ccc
38. *Yehya ben Khalid and Mensour* cccv
39. Yehya ben Khalid and the Man who forged a Letter in his Name cccvi
40. *The Khalif El Mamoun and the Strange Doctor* cccvii
41. Ali Shar and Zumurrud cccviii
42. The Loves of Jubeir ben Umeir and the Lady Budour . . cccxxvii

43 The Man of Yemen and his six Slave-girls . . . . .
44. Haroun er Reshid with the Damsel and Abou Nuwas . .
45. The Man who stole the Dog's Dish of Gold . . . .
46. *The Sharper of Alexandria and the Master of Police* . . . .
47. El Melik en Nasir and the three Masters of Police . . .
    a. Story of the Chief of the New Cairo Police . . .
    b. Story of the Chief of the Boulac Police . . . .
    c. Story of the Chief of the Old Cairo Police . . .
48. The Thief and the Money-Changer . . . .
49 The Chief of the Cous Police and the Sharper . . . . .
50 Ibrahim ben el Mehdi and the Merchant's Sister . . .
51. The Woman whose Hands were cut off for Almsgiving . .
52. *The Devout Israelite* . . . .
53. *Abou Hassan es Ziyadi and the Man from Khorassan* . . .
54. The Poor Man and his Generous Friend . . . . . .
55 The Ruined Man who became Rich again through a Dream .
56. *El Mutawekkil and his Favourite Mehboubeh* . . . . . .
57. *Werdan the Butcher's Adventure with the Lady and the Bear* . .
58. *The King's Daughter and the Ape* . . . .
59. The Enchanted Horse . . . .
60. Uns el Wujoud and the Vizier's Daughter Rose-in-bud . .
61. Abou Nuwas with the three Boys and the Khalif Haroun er Reshid . . . .
62 *Abdallah ben Maamer with the Man of Bassora and his Slave-girl* .
63. The Lovers of the Benou Udhreh . . . .
64. *The Vizier of Yemen and his young Brother* . . . . . .
65. *The Loves of the Boy and Girl at School* . . . . . .
66. El Mutelemmis and his Wife Umeimeh . . . . . .
67. Haroun er Reshid and Zubeideh in the Bath . . . . .
68. Haroun er Reshid and the three Poets . . . . . .
69. Musab ben er Zubeir and Aaïsheh his Wife . . . . .
70 Aboulaswed and his squinting Slave-girl . . . . . .
71. Haroun er Reshid and the two Girls . . . . . .
72. Haroun er Reshid and the three Girls . . . . . .
73. *The Miller and his Wife* . . . .
74. The Simpleton and the Sharper . . . .
75. The Imam Abou Yousuf with Haroun er Reshid and Zubeideh .
76. The Khalif El Hakim and the Merchant . . . . . .
77. King Kisra Anoushirwan and the Village Damsel . . .
78 The Water-Carrier and the Goldsmith's Wife . . . . .
79 Khusrau and Shirin and the Fisherman . . . . . .
80. Yehya ben Khalid and the Poor Man . . . . . .
81. Mohammed el Amin and Jaafer ben el Hadi . . . . .
82. *Said ben Salim and the Barmecides* . . . .
83. The Woman's Trick against her Husband . . . . .
84. The Devout Woman and the Two Wicked Elders . .
85. Jaafer the Barmecide and the Old Bedouin . . . .
86. Omar ben el Khettab and the Young Bedouin . . . . .
87. *El Mamoun and the Pyramids of Egypt* . . . .
88. The Thief turned Merchant and the other Thief .
89. Mesrour and Ibn el Caribi . . . .
90. The Devout Prince . . . .

91. The Schoolmaster who fell in love by Report ccccii
92. The Foolish Schoolmaster cccciii
93. The Ignorant Man who set up for a Schoolmaster . . . ,,
94. *The King and the Virtuous Wife* ccccciv
95. *Abdurrehman the Moor's Story of the Roc* . . . ,,
96. Adi ben Zeid and the Princess Hind ccccv
97. Dibil el Khuzaï with the Lady and Muslim ben el Welid . . ccccvii
98. Isaac of Mosul and the Merchant . . . . ,,
99. The Three Unfortunate Lovers[1] ccccix
100. The Lovers of the Benou Tai ccccx
101. The Mad Lover ccccxi
102. The Apples of Paradise ccccxii
103. The Loves of Abou Isa and Curret el Ain ccccxiv
104. El Amin and his Uncle Ibrahim ben el Mehdi ccccxviii
105. El Feth ben Khacan and El Mutawekkil ccccxix
106. The Man's Dispute with the Learned Woman of the relative Excellence of the Sexes . . . . ,,
107. Abou Suweid and the Handsome Old Woman ccccxxiii
108. Ali ben Tahir and the Girl Mounis ccccxxiv
109. The Woman who had a Boy and the other who had a Man to Lover . . . . ,,
110. The Haunted House in Baghdad . . . . ,,
111. *The Pilgrim and the Old Woman who dwelt in the Desert.* . . ccccxxxiv
112. *Aboulhusn and his Slave-girl Taweddud* ccccxxxvi
113. *The Angel of Death with the Proud King and the Devout Man.* . cccclxii
114. *The Angel of Death and the Rich King* . . . . ,,
115. *The Angel of Death and the King of the Children of Israel* . . cccclxiii
116. *Iskender Dhoulkernein and a certain Tribe of Poor Folk* . . . cccclxiv
117. *The Righteousness of King Anoushirwan* . . . . . . ,,
118. *The Jewish Cadi and his Pious Wife* cccclxv
119. *The Shipwrecked Woman and her Child* cccclxvi
120. *The Pious Black Slave* cccclxvii
121. *The Devout Platter-maker and his Wife* cccclxviii
122. *El Hejjaj ben Yousuf and the Pious Man* cccclxx
123. *The Blacksmith who could Handle Fire without Hurt* . . . cccclxxi
124. *The Saint to whom God gave a Cloud to serve Him and the Devout King* cccclxxiii
125. *The Muslim Champion and the Christian Lady* cccclxxiv
126. *Ibrahim ben el Khawwas and the Christian King's Daughter* . . cccclxxvii
127. *The Justice of Providence* cccclxxviii
128. *The Ferryman of the Nile and the Hermit* cccclxxix
129. *The King of the Island* . . . . ,,
130. *Abulhusn ed Durraj and Abou Jaafer the Leper* cccclxxxi
131. *The Queen of the Serpents* cccclxxxii
    a. The Adventures of Beloukiya cccclxxxvi
    b. The Story of Janshah ccccxcix
132. Sindbad the Sailor and Sindbad the Porter . . . . . dxxxvi
    a. The First Voyage of Sindbad the Sailor . . . . . dxxxviii
    b. The Second Voyage of Sindbad the Sailor . . . . dxliii
    c. The Third Voyage of Sindbad the Sailor . . . . . dxlvi
    d. The Fourth Voyage of Sindbad the Sailor . . . . dl

1 After this I introduce How Abu Hasan brake wind.

e. The Fifth Voyage of Sindbad the Sailor . . . . . dlvi
f. The Sixth Voyage of Sindbad the Sailor . . . . . dlix
g. The Seventh Voyage of Sindbad the Sailor . . . dlxiii
133. The City of Brass . . . . dlxvi
134. The Malice of Women . . . . dlxxviii
a. The King and his Vizier's Wife . . . . . . ,,
b. The Merchant's Wife and the Parrot . . . . dlxxix
c. The Fuller and his Son . . . . ,,
d. The Lover's Trick against the Chaste Wife . . . dlxxx
e. The Niggard and the Loaves of Bread . . . . ,,
f. The Lady and her Two Lovers . . . . . . dlxxxi
g. The King's Son and the Ogress . . . . . . ,,
h. The Drop of Honey . . . . dlxxxii
i The Woman who made her Husband sift Dust . . ,,
j. The Enchanted Springs . . . . ,,
k. The Vizier's Son and the Bath-keeper's Wife . . . dlxxxiv
l. The Wife's Device to Cheat her Husband . . . ,,
m. The Goldsmith and the Cashmere Singing-girl . . . dlxxxvi
n. The Man who never Laughed again . . . . . dlxxxvii
o. The King's Son and the Merchant's Wife . . . dxci
p. *The Page who feigned to know the Speech of Birds* . . . dxcii
q. *The Lady and her five Suitors* . . . . dxciii
r. The Man who saw the Night of Power . . . . . dxcvi
s. The Stolen Necklace . . . . ,,
t. *The two Pigeons* . . . . dxcvii
u. Prince Behram of Persia and the Princess Ed Detma . ,,
v. The House with the Belvedere . . . . dxcviii
w. *The King's Son and the Afrit's Mistress* . . . . dcii
x. The Sandal-wood Merchant and the Sharpers . . dciii
y. The Debauchee and the Three-year-old Child . . dcv
z. The Stolen Purse . . . . ,,
135. Jouder and his Brothers . . . . dcvi
136. The History of Gherib and his Brother Agib . . . . . dcxxiv
137. *Otbeh and Reyya* . . . . dclxxx
138. *Hind Daughter of En Numan and El Hejjaj* . . . . . dclxxxi
139. *Khuzeimeh ben Bishr and Ikrimeh el Feyyaz* . . . . . dclxxxii
140. *Younus the Scribe and the Khalif Welid ben Sehl* . . . . dclxxxiv
141. *Haroun er Reshid and the Arab Girl* . . . . dclxxxv
142. *El Asmaï and the three Girls of Bassorah* . . . . . dclxxxvi
143. *Ibrahim of Mosul and the Devil* . . . . dclxxxvii
144. *The Lovers of the Benou Udhreh* . . . . dclxxxviii
145. *The Bedouin and his Wife* . . . . dcxci
146. *The Lovers of Bassora* . . . . dcxciii
147. *Isaac of Mosul and his Mistress and the Devil* . . . . dcxcv
148. *The Lovers of Medina* . . . . dcxcvi
149. *El Melik en Nasir and his Vizier* . . . . dcxcvii
150. The Rogueries of Delileh the Crafty and her Daughter Zeyneb the Trickstress . . . . dcxcviii
151. The Adventures of Quicksilver Ali of Cairo: a Sequel to the Rogueries of Delileh the Crafty . . . . dccviii
152. Ardeshir and Heyat en Nufous . . . . dccxix
153. Julnar of the Sea and her Son King Bedr Basim of Persia . dccxxxviii

154. King Mohammed ben Sebaïk and the Merchant Hassan . . dcclvi
a. Story of Prince Seif el Mulouk and the Princess Bediya el Jemal . . . . dcclviii
155. Hassan of Bassora and the King's Daughter of the Jinn . . dcclxxviii
156. Khelifeh the Fisherman of Baghdad . . . . dccccxxxii
157. Mesrour and Zein el Mewasif . . . . dccccxlv
158. Ali Noureddin and the Frank King's Daughter . . . . dccclxiii
159. The Man of Upper Egypt and his Frank Wife . . . . dccccxciv
160. The Ruined Man of Baghdad and his Slave-girl . . . dccccxcv
161. King Jelyaad of Hind and his Vizier Shimas: whereafter ensueth the History of King Wird Khan son of King Jelyaad and his Women and Viziers . . . . . . dccccxcix
a. The Cat and the Mouse . . . . dcccc
b. The Fakir and his Pot of Butter . . . . . . dccccii
c. The Fishes and the Crab . . . . dcccciii
d. The Crow and the Serpent . . . . ,,
e. The Fox and the Wild Ass . : . . . . . dcccciv
f. The Unjust King and the Pilgrim Prince . . . . dccccv
g. The Crows and the Hawk . . . . dccccvi
h. The Serpent-Charmer and his Wife . . . . . dccccvii
i. The Spider and the Wind . . . . dccccviii
j. The Two Kings . . . . dccccix
k. The Blind Man and the Cripple . . . . . . dccccx
l. The Foolish Fisherman . . . . dccccxviii
m. The Boy and the Thieves . . . . ,,
n. The Man and his Wilful Wife . . . . dccccxix
o. The Merchant and the Thieves. . . . . . . dccccxx
p. The Foxes and the Wolf . . . . dccccxxi
q. The Shepherd and the Thief . . . . ,,
r. The Heathcock and the Tortoises . . . . . . dccccxxiv
162. Aboukir the Dyer and Abousir the Barber. . . . . . dccccxxx
163. Abdallah the Fisherman and Abdallah the Merman . . . dccccxl
164. The Merchant of Oman . . . . dccccxlvi
165. *Ibrahim and Jemileh* . . . . dccccclii
166. *Aboulhusn of Khorassan* . . . . dccccclix
167. *Kemerezzeman and the Jeweller's Wife* . . . . dccccclxiii
168. *Abdallah ben Fazil and his Brothers* . . . . . .dccccclxxviii
169. *Marouf the Cobbler and his Wife Fatimeh* . . . . . dccccclxxxix-mi
Conclusion.

INDEX I.—D.

COMPARISON OF THE SAME WITH MR. LANE'S AND MY VERSION.

Introduction and

Nos. 1 to 9 of the preceding list form Volume I. of this Edition.		
(contd.)		
,, 9 ,, 20		II.
,, 21 to 59		III.
,, 60 to 132	,,	IV.
,, 133 to 151	,,	V.
,, 152 to 157	,,	VI.
,, 158 to 168	,,	VII.
,, 169 and conclusion		VIII.

For full details, see contents pages to each of the respective Volumes.

INDEX II.

INDEX TO THE TALES AND PROPER NAMES.

N.B.—*The Roman numerals denote the volume, the Arabic the page.*

Abdullah the Fisherman and Abdullah the Merman, vii. 237
  Do. bin Fazl and his brothers, vii. 364
  Do. bin Ma'amar with the Man of Bassorah and his slave-girl, iv. 35
Abd al-Rahman the Moor's Story of the Rukh, iv. 84
Abu Hasan al-Ziyadi and the Khorasan Man, iii. 397
Abu Hasan, how he brake Wind, iv. 95
Abu Isa and Kurrat al-Ayn, The Loves of, iv. 104
Abu Ja'afar the Leper, Abu al-Hasan al-Durraj and, iv. 242
Abu Kir the Dyer and Abu Sir the Barber, vii. 208
Abu al-Aswad and his squinting slave-girl, iv. 45
Abu al-Husn and his slave-girl Tawaddud, iv. 144
Abu al-Hasan al-Durraj and Abu Ja'afar the Leper, iv. 242
Abu al-Hasan of Khorasan, vii. 297
Abu Mohammed hight Lazybones, iii. 282
Abu Nowas, Harun al-Rashid with the damsel and, iii. 374
Abu Nowas and the Three Boys, iv. 31
Abu Sir the Barber, Abu Kir the Dyer and, vii. 208
Abu Suwayd and the handsome old woman, iv. 120
Abu Hasan with Harun al-Rashid and his Wazir Ja'afar, vii 258
Abu Yusuf with Al-Rashid and Zubaydah, The Imam, iii. 273
Adam, The Birds and Beasts and the Son of, ii. 337
Adi bin Zayd and the Princess Hind, iv. 85
Ajib, The History of Gharib and his brother, v. 162
Ala al-Din Abu al-Shamat, iii. 157
Alexandria (The Sharper of) and the Master of Police, iii. 381
Ali bin Bakkar and Shams al-Nahar, ii. 383
Ali of Cairo, The Adventures of Mercury, v 366
Ali Nur al-Din and Miriam the Girdle-Girl, vii 1
Ali the Persian and the Kurd Sharper, iii. 270
Ali Shar and Zumurrud, iii. 306
Ali bin Tahir and the girl Munnis, iv. 121
Al-Malik al-Nasir (Saladin) and the Three Chiefs of Police, iii. 383
Almsgiving, the Woman whose hands were cut off for, iii. 393
Amin (Al-) and his uncle Ibrahim bin al-Mahdi, iv. 111
Anushirwan, Kisra, and the village damsel, iv. 51
Anushirwan, The Righteousness of King, iv 205
Angel of Death and the King of the Children of Israel, The, iv. 201
  Do. with the Proud King and the Devout Man, The, iv. 197
  Do. and the Rich King, The, iv. 199

Anis al-Jalis, Nur al-Din Ali and the damsel, i. 329
Ape, The King's daughter and the, iii. 408
Apples, The Three, i. 171
Arab Girl, Harun al-Rashid and the, v. 306
Arab Youth, The Caliph Hisham and the, iii. 225
Ardashir and Hayat al-Nufus, vi. 1
Asma'i (AL) and the three girls of Bassorah, v. 308
Ass, The Ox and the, i. 14
Ass, The Wild, The Fox and, vii. 127
Ayishah, Musab bin al-Zubayr and his wife, iv. 44
Aziz and Azizah, Tale of, ii. 193
Azizah, Aziz and, ii. 193
Badawi, Ja'afar the Barmecide and the old, iv. 61
Do. Omar bin al-Khattab and the young, iv. 63
Do. and his Wife, The, v. 321
Badi'a, al-Jamal, Sayf al-Muluk and, vi. 100
Badr Basim of Persia, Julnar the Seaborn, and her Son King, vi 54
Badr al-Din Hasan, Nur al-Din Ali of Cairo and his son, i. 179
Baghdad, The Haunted House in, iv. 122
Do. Khalifah the Fisherman of, vi. 296
Do. The Porter and the Three Ladies of, i. 75
Do. (The ruined man of) and his slave-girl, vii. 104
Do. The Sweep and the noble Lady of, iii. 247
Bakun's Story of the Hashish-Eater, ii. 315
Banu Tayy, The Lovers of the, iv. 97
Banu Ozrah, The Lovers of the, iv. 36
Barber's Tale of himself, The, i. 292
Barber's First Brother, Story of the, i. 294
Barber's Second Brother, Story of the, i 299
Barber's Third Brother, Story of the, i. 303
Barber's Fourth Brother, Story of the, i. 306
Barber's Fifth Brother, Story of the, i. 309
Barber's Sixth Brother, Story of the, i 317
Barber, Abu Kir the Dyer and Abu Sir the, vii. 208
Barber-Surgeon, Ibrahim bin al-Mahdi and the, iii. 227
Barmecide, Ja'afar the, and the old Badawi, iv. 61
Bassorah (the man of) and his slave-girl, Abdullah bin Ma'amar with, iv. 35
Do. Al-Asma'i and the three girls of, v. 308
Do. (Hasan of) and the King's daughter of the Jinn, vi. 166
Do. The Lovers of, v. 326
Bath, Haroun al-Rashid and Zubaydah in the, iv. 41
Bathkeeper's Wife, The Wazir's Son and the, v. 63
Beanseller, Ja'afar the Barmecide and the, iii. 280
Bear, Wardan the Butcher's adventure with the Lady and the, iii 404
Beasts and the Son of Adam, The Birds and, ii. 337
Behram, Prince of Persia, and the Princess Al-Datma, v. 94
Belvedere, The House with the, v. 98
Birds and Beasts and the Carpenter, The, ii. 337
Birds, The Falcon and the, ii. 360
Birds (the Speech of), The Page who feigned to know, v. 81
Black Slave, The pious, iv. 212
Blacksmith who could handle fire without hurt, The, iv. 220

Blind Man and the Cripple, The, vii. 145
Boys, Abu Nowas and the Three, iv. 31
Boy and Girl at School, The Loves of the, iv. 39
Boy and the Thieves, The, vii. 171
Boy (The woman who had to lover a) and the other who had to over a man. iv. 121
Brass, The City of, v. 1
Broker's Story, The Christian, i. 241
Budur and Jubayr bin Umayr, The Loves of, iii. 344
Budur, Kamar al-Zaman and, iii. 1
Bukhayt, Story of the Eunuch, i. 372
Bulak Police, Story of the Chief of the, iii. 385
Bull and the Ass (Story of), i. 14
Bulukiya, Adventures of, iv. 251
Butcher's adventure with the Lady and the Bear, Warden, the, iii. 404
Butter, The Fakir and his pot of, vii. 119
Cairo (New) Police, Story of the Chief of the, iii. 384
Do. (Old) Police, Story of the Chief of the, iii. 387
Do., The Adventures of Mercury Ali of, v. 366
Caliph Al-Ma'amun and the Strange Doctor, iii. 304
Caliph, The Mock, iii. 152
Cashmere Singing-girl, The Goldsmith and the, v. 68
Cat and the Crow, The, ii. 370
Do. and the Mouse, The, vii. 115
Champion (The Moslem) and the Christian Lady, iv. 226
Chaste Wife, The Lover's Trick against the, v. 48
Christian Broker's Story, The, i. 241
City of Brass, The, v. 1
Cloud (The saint to whom Allah gave a) to serve him, iv. 223
Cobbler (Ma'aruf the) and his wife Fatimah, viii. 1
Confectioner, his Wife and the Parrot, The, v. 46
Crab, The Fishes and the, vii. 123
Craft and Malice of Women, The, v. 36
Cripple, The Blind Man and the, vii. 145
Crow, The Fox and the, ii. 372
Do. and the Serpent, The, vii. 125
Crow, The Cat and the, ii. 370
Crows and the Hawk, The, vii. 132
Dalilah the Crafty and her daughter Zaynab the Coney-catcher, The Rogueries of, v. 340
Datma (The Princess Al-), Prince Behram of Persia and, v. 94
Death (The Angel of) and the King of the Children of Israel, iv. 201
Do. do. with the Proud King and the Devout Man, iv. 197
Do. do. and the Rich King, iv. 199
Debauchee and the Three-year-old Child, The, v. 116
Desert (The old woman who dwelt in the) and the pilgrim, iv. 141
Device (The Wife's) to cheat her husband, v. 64
Devil, Ibrahim of Mosul and the, v. 311
Do. Ishak ,, and his mistress and the, v. 332
Devout Israelite, The, iii. 395
Do. Tray-maker and his wife, The, iv. 215
Do. Prince, The, iv. 73

Devout woman and the two wicked elders, The, iv. 60
Dibil al-Khuzai and Muslim bin al-Walid, iv. 88
Dish of Gold, The man who stole the Dog's, iii. 378
Doctor (The Strange) and the Caliph Al-Maamun, iii 304
Dog's Dish of Gold, The man who stole the, iii 378
Dream, The ruined man who became rich through a, iii. 401
Drop of Honey, The, v. 55
Duban, The Physician, i. 41
Dunya, Taj al-Muluk and the Princess, ii 179
Durraj (Abu al-Hasan al-) and Abu Ja'afar the Leper, iv. 242
Dust, The woman who made her husband sift, v. 56
Dyer, Abu Sir the Barber and Abu Kir the, vii. 208
Eagle, The Sparrow and the, ii. 376
Ebony Horse, The, iii. 415
Egypt (The man of Upper) and his Frank wife, vii. 99
Elders, The Devout woman and the two wicked, iv. 60
Eldest Lady's Story, The, i. 149
Enchanted Spring, The, v. 58
Do Youth, The, i. 64
Envied, The Envier and the, i. 113
Envier and the Envied, The, i. 113
Eunuch Bukhayt, Tale of the, i. 372
Do Kafur, Tale of the, i. 374
Fakir and his jar of butter, The, vii. 119
Falcon and the Partridge, The, ii 360
Falcon, King Sindibad and his, i 46
Fatimah, Ma'aruf the Cobbler and his wife, viii. 1
Fath bin Khakan (Al) and Al-Mutawakkil, iv. 112
Ferryman of the Nile and the Hermit, The, iv. 236
First Old Man's Story, i. 25
Fisherman, Abdullah the Merman and Abdullah the, vii. 237
Do of Baghdad, Khalifah the, vi. 296
Do. The Foolish, vii. 169
Do and the Jinni, The, i. 34
Do Khusrau and Shirin and the, iv. 54
Fishes and the Crab, The, vii. 123
Five Suitors, The Lady and her, v 83
Flea and the Mouse, The, ii. 373
Folk, The Fox and the, v. 120
Forger, Yahya bin Khalid and the, iii. 301
Fox and the Crow, The, ii. 372
Fox and the Folk, The, v. 120
Fox. The Wolf and the, ii. 354
Francolin and the Tortoises, The, vii. 187
Frank King's Daughter, Ali Nur al-Din and the, vii 1
Frank wife, The man of Upper Egypt, and his, vii. 99
Fuller and his son, The, v. 48
Generous Friend, The poor man and his, iii. 400
Ghanim bin Ayyub the Thrall o' Love, i. 369
Gharib and his brother Ajib, The History of, v. 162
Girl, Harun al-Rashid and the Arab, v. 306
Girl at School, The Loves of the Boy and, iv. 39

Girls of Bassorah, Al-Asma'i and the three, v. 308
Girls, Harun al-Rashid and the three, iv. 46
Do. Do. and the two, iv. 46
Goldsmith and the Cashmere Singing-Girl, The, v. 68
Goldsmith's wife, The water-carrier and the, iv. 52
Hajjaj (Al-) Hind daughter of Al-Nu'uman and, v. 295
Do. and the pious man, iv. 219
Hakim (The Caliph Al-) and the Merchant, v. 50
Hammad the Badawi, Tale of, ii. 327
Harun al-Rashid and the Arab girl, v. 306
Do. and the Slave-Girl and the Imam Abu Yusuf, iii 273
Do. with the Damsel and Abu Nowas, iii. 374
Do. and Abu Hasan the Merchant of Oman, vii. 258
Do. and the three girls, iv. 46
Do. and the two girls, iv. 46
Do. and the three poets, iv. 43
Do. and Zubaydah in the Bath, iv. 41
Hashish-Eater, Bakun's tale of the, ii. 315
Hasan of Bassorah and the King's daughter of the Jinn, vi. 166
Hasan, King Mohammed bin Sabaik and the Merchant, vi. 95
Hatim al-Tayyi: his generosity after death, iii. 219
Haunted House in Baghdad, The, iv. 122
Hawk, The Crows and the, vii. 132
Hayat al-Nufus, Ardashir and, vi. 1
Hedgehog and the Wood Pigeons, The, ii. 377
Hermit, the Ferryman of the Nile and the, iv. 236
Hermits, The, ii. 348
Hind, Adi bin Zayd and the Princess, iv. 85
Hind daughter of Al-Nu'uman and Al-Hajjaj, v. 295
Hind (King Jall'ad of) and his Wazir Shimas, vii. 112
Hisham and the Arab Youth, The Caliph, iii. 225
Honey, The Drop of, v. 55
Horse, The Ebony, iii. 415
House with the Belvedere, The, v. 98
Hunchback's Tale, The, i. 234
Husband and the Parrot, The, i. 48
Ibn al-Karibi; Masrur and, iv. 71
Ibrahim al-Khawwas and the Christian King's Daughter, iv. 231
Do. bin al-Khasib and Jamilah, vii. 276
Do. of Mosul and the Devil, v. 311
Do. bin al-Mahdi and Al-Amin, iv. 111
Do. bin al-Mahdi and the Barber-Surgeon, iii. 227
Do. Do. and the Merchant's Sister, iii. 390
Ifrit's Mistress and the King's Son, The, v. 103
Ignorant man who set up for a Schoolmaster, The, iv. 81
Ikrimah al-Fayyaz, Khuzaymah bin Bishr and, v. 297
Imam Abu Yusuf with Al-Rashid and Zubaydah, The, iii 273
Introduction. Story of King Shariyar and his brother, i. 1, 2
Iram, The City of, iii. 236
Isaac of Mosul's Story of Khadijah and the Caliph Maamun, iii 242
Isaac of Mosul and the Merchant, iv. 90
Ishak of Mosul and his Mistress and the Devil, v. 332

Iskander, Zu Al-Karnayn and a certain Tribe of poor folk, iv. 203
Island, The King of the, iv. 238
Israelite, The Devout, iii. 395
Ja'afar bin al-Hadi, Mohammed al-Amin, and, iv. 57
Ja'afar the Barmecide and the Beanseller, iii. 280
Do. Do. and the old Badawi, iv. 61
Jackals and the Wolf, The, vii. 178
Jamilah, Ibrahim bin al-Khasib, and, vii. 276
Jall'ad of Hind and his Wazir Shimas, King, vii. 112
Janshah, The Story of, iv. 274
Jeweller's Wife, Kamar al-Zaman and the, vii. 313
Jewish Kazi and his pious Wife, The, iv. 206
Jewish Doctor's Tale, The, i. 265
Jinni, The Fisherman and the, i. 34
Jinni, The Trader and the, i. 22
Jubayr bin Umayr and Budur, The Loves of, iii. 344
Judar and his brethren, v. 121
Julnar the Sea-born and her son King Badr Basim of Persia, vi. 54
Justice of Providence, The, iv. 234
Kafur, Story of the Eunuch, i. 374
Kalandar's Tale, The first, i. 96
Do., The second, i. 104
Do., The third, i. 128
Kamar al-Zaman and Budur, iii. 1
Do. and the Jeweller's Wife, vii. 313
Kazi, The Jewish, and his pious wife, iv. 206
Khadijah and the Caliph Maamun, Isaac of Mosul's Story of, iii. 242
Khalif the Fisherman of Baghdad (note from Bresl. Edit.), vi. 333
Khalifah the Fisherman of Baghdad, vi. 296
Khawwas (Ibrahim al-) and the Christian King's daughter, iv. 231
Khorasan, Abu Hasan al-Ziyadi and the man from, iii. 397
Do., Abu al-Hasan of, vii. 297
Khusrau and Shirin and the Fisherman, iv. 54
Khuzaymah bin Bishr and Ikrimah al-Fayyaz, v. 297
King Jall'ad, Shimas his Wazir and his son Wird Khan, vii. 112
King of the Island, The, iv. 238
Do. and the Pilgrim Prince, The Unjust, vii. 129
Do. and the virtuous wife, The, iv. 83
Do. and his Wazir's wife, The, v. 43
King's Daughter and the Ape, The, iii. 408
Do. son and the Ifrit's Mistress, The, v. 108
Do. Do. and the Merchant's Wife, The, v. 79
Do. Do and the Ghulah, The, v. 53
Kings, The Two, vii. 143
Kisra Anushirwan and the Village Damsel, iv. 51
Kurd Sharper, Ali the Persian and the, iii. 270
Kurrat al-Ayn and Abu Isa, iv. 104
Kus Police and the Sharper, Chief of the, iii. 389
Labtayt, the City of, iii. 223
Lady of Baghdad, The Sweep and the noble, iii. 247
Lady's Story, The Eldest, i. 149
Lady and her five suitors, The, v. 83
Do. and her two Lovers, The, v. 51

Ladies of Baghdad, The Porter and the Three, i. 75
Laughed again, The man who never, v. 72
Lazybones, Abu Mohammed hight, iii. 282
Leper, Abu al-Hasan al-Durraj and Abu Ja'afar the, iv. 242
Lover, The mad, iv. 98
Lover who feigned himself a thief (to save his mistress honour), The, iii. 276
Lover's trick against the chaste Wife, The, v. 48
Lovers of Bassorah, The, v. 326
Do. of the Banu Tayy, The, iv. 97
Do. of the Banu Ozrah, The, iv. 36
Do. The Lady and her two, v. 51
Do. of Al-Medinah, The, v. 335
Do. The Three unfortunate, iv. 94
Loves of the Boy and Girl at School, The, iv. 39
Loves of Abu Isa and Kurrat al-Ayn, The, iv. 104
Maamun, Isaac of Mosul's Story of Khadijah and the Caliph, iii. 242
Do. (Al-) and the Pyramids of Egypt, iv. 67
Do. and the strange Scholar, The Caliph, iii. 304
Ma'an bin Zaidah and the Badawi, iii. 222
Ma'an the son of Zaidah and the Three Girls, iii. 220
Mad Lover, The, iv. 98
Madinah (Al-), The Lovers of, v. 335
Magic Horse, The, iii. 415
Mahbubah, Al-Mutawakkil and his favourite, iii. 402
Malik al-Nasir (Al-) and the three Masters of Police, iii. 383
Do. and his Wazir, v. 338
Man and his Wife, The, vii. 173
Man who never laughed during the rest of his days, The, v. 72
Man, (The Woman who had to lover a) and the other who had to lover a boy, iv. 121
Man of Upper Egypt and his Frankish Wife, vii. 99
Man of Al-Yaman and his six Slave-girls, iii. 360
Man who stole the dog's dish of gold, iii. 378
Man who saw the Night of Power (Three Wishes), v. 91
Man's dispute with the learned Woman about boys and girls, iv. 113
Ma'aruf the Cobbler and his wife Fatimah, viii. 1
Mansur, Yahya bin Khalid and, iii. 298
Masrur and Ibn al-Karabi, iv. 71
Masrur and Zayn al-Mawasif, vi. 352
Merchant of Oman, The, vii. 258
Do. and the Robbers, The, vii. 175
Do. and the two Sharpers, The, ii. 379
Merchant's Sister, Ibrahim bin al-Mahdi and the, iii 390
Do. Wife, The King's son and the, v. 79
Do. Wife and the Parrot, The, i. 48
Mercury Ali of Cairo, The Adventures of, v. 366
Merman, and Abdullah the Fisherman, Abdullah the, vii. 237
Miller and his wife, The, iv. 47
Miriam, Ali Nur al-Din and, vii. 1
Miser and Loaves of Bread, The, v. 50
Mock Caliph, The, iii. 152
Mohammed al-Amin and Ja'afar bin al-Hadi, iv. 57

Mohammed bin Sabaik and the Merchant Hasan, King, vi. 95
Money-changer, The Thief and the, iii. 387
Monkey, The Thief and his, ii. 380
Moslem Champion and the Christian Lady, The, iv. 226
Mouse, The, and the Cat, vii. 115
Mouse and the Flea, The, ii. 373
Mouse and the Ichneumon, The, ii. 369
Munnis, Ali bin Tahir and the girl, iv. 121
Musab bin al-Zubayr and Ayishah his wife, iv. 44
Muslim bin al-Walid and Di'ibil al-Khuzai, iv. 88
Mutawakkil (Al-) and Al-Fath bin Khakan, iv. 112
Do. and his favourite Mahbubah, iii. 402
Mutalammis (Al-) and his wife Umaymah, iv. 40
Naomi, Ni'amah bin al-Rabi'a and his slave-girl, iii. 131
Nazarene Broker's Story, The, i. 241
Necklace, The Stolen, v. 92
Niggard and the Loaves of Bread, The, v. 50
Night of Power, The man who saw the, v. 91
Nile (The Ferryman of the) and the Hermit, iv. 236
Ni'amah bin al-Rabi'a and Naomi his Slave-girl, iii. 131
Nur al-Din Ali and the Damsel Anis al-Jalis, i. 329
Nur al-Din of Cairo and his son Badr al-Din Hasan, i. 179
Ogress, The King's Son and the, v. 53
Old Man's Story, The First, i. 25
Do. Do. The Second, i. 29
Do. Do. The Third, i. 33
Old Woman, Abu Suwayd and the handsome, iv. 120
Omar bin al-Nu'uman and his Sons Sharrkan and Zau al-Makan, The Tale of King, i. 398
Omar bin al-Khattab and the young Badawi, iv. 63
Oman, The Merchant of, vii. 258
Otbah and Rayya, v. 289
Page who feigned to know the speech of Birds, The, v. 81
Paradise, The Apples of, iv. 100
Parrot, The Merchant's wife and the, i. 48
Partridge, The Hawk and the, ii. 360
Peacock, The Sparrow and the, ii. 382
Persian and the Kurd Sharper, Ali the, iii. 270
Physician Duban, The, i. 41
Physician's Story, The Jewish, i. 265
Pilgrim and the old woman who dwelt in the desert, The, iv. 141
Pilgrim Prince, The Unjust King and the, vii. 129
Pious black slave, The, iv. 212
Pigeons, The Hedgehog and the, ii. 377
Pigeons, The Two, v. 94
Platter-maker and his wife, The devout, iv. 215
Poets, Harun al-Rashid and the three, iv. 43
Police of Bulak, Story of the Chief of the, iii. 385
Do. of Kus and the Sharper, the Chief of the, iii. 389
Do. of New Cairo, Story of the Chief of the, iii. 384
Do. of Old Cairo, Story of the Chief of the, iii. 387
Do. (The Three Masters of), Al-Malik, al-Nasir and, iii 383

Poor man and his friend in need, The, iii. 400
Porter and the Three Ladies of Baghdad, The, i. 75
Portress, The Tale of the, i 160
Prince Behram and the Princess Al-Datma, v. 94
Do. the Ensorcelled, i. 64
Do. and the Ghulah, The, i. 50
Do. The Devout, iv 73
Do (the Pilgrim), The Unjust King and, vii 129
Prior who became a Moslem, The, iv. 100
Providence, The justice of, iv. 234
Purse, The Stolen, v. 117
Pyramids of Egypt, Al-Maamun and the, iv. 67
Queen of the Serpents, The, iv. 245
Rake's trick against the Chaste Wife, The, v. 48
Rayya, Otbah and, v. 289
Reeve's Tale, The, i. 256
Rogueries of Dalilah the Crafty and her daughter Zaynab the Coney-catcher, The, v 340
Rose-in-Hood, Uns al-Wujud and the Wazir's Daughter, iv 1
Ruined Man of Baghdad and his Slave-girl, The, vii. 104
Do who became rich again through a dream, The, iii. 401
Rukh, Abd al-Rahman the Moor's Story of the, iv. 84
Sa'id bin Salim and the Barmecides, iv. 58
Saint to whom Allah gave a cloud to serve him, The, iv 223
Saker and the Birds, The, ii. 375
Sandal-wood Merchant and the Sharpers, The, v. 111
Sayf al-Muluk and Badi'a al-Jamal, vi. 100
School, The Loves of the Boy and the Girl at, iv. 39
Schoolmaster who fell in love by report, The, iv. 78
Do The Foolish, iv. 80
Do. The ignorant man who set up for a, iv. 81
Serpent, The Crow and the, vii. 125
Serpent-charmer and his Wife, vii. 135
Serpents, The Queen of the, iv. 245
Sexes, Relative excellence of the, iv. 113
Shahryar and his brother, King (Introduction), i. 1
Shahryar (King) and his brother, i. 2
Shams al-Nahar, Ali bin Bakkar and, ii. 383
Sharper of Alexandria and the Chief of Police, The, iii. 381
Sharper. Ali the Persian and the Kurd, iii. 270
Do The Chief of the Kus Police and the, iii. 389
Do The Simpleton and the, iv. 48
Sharpers, The Merchant and the Two, ii. 379
Do The Sandal-wood Merchant and the, v. 111
Sharrkan and Zau al-Makan; The History of King Omar bin Al-Nu'uman and his Sons, i. 398
Shaykh's Story (The First). i 25
Do. (The Second), i. 29
Do. (The Third), i. 33
Shepherd and the Thief, The, vii. 181
Shimas, King Jali'ad of Hind and his Wazir, vii 112
Shipwrecked Woman and her child, The, iv. 209

Shirin and the Fisherman, Khusrau and, iv. 54
Simpleton and the Sharper, The, iv. 48
Sindibad and his Falcon, King, i. 46
Sindbad the Seaman and Sindbad the Porter, iv. 343
Do. First Voyage of. iv. 346
Do. Second Voyage of, iv. 355
Do. Third Voyage of, iv. 363
Do. Fourth Voyage of, iv. 374
Do. Fifth Voyage of, iv. 387
Do. Sixth Voyage of, iv. 396
Do. Seventh Voyage of, iv. 407
Do. (note from Cal. Edit), iv. 416
Singing-girl, The Goldsmith and the Cashmere, v. 68
Six Slave-girls, The Man of Al-Yaman and his, iii 360
Slave, The pious black, iv. 212
Slave girl, The ruined man of Baghdad and his, vii 104
Slave-girls, The Man of Al-Yaman and his six, iii. 360
Sparrow and the Eagle, The, ii. 376
Do. and the Peacock, The, ii. 382
Spider and the Wind, The, vii. 137
Spring, The Enchanted, v. 58
Squinting slave-girl, Abu al-Aswad and his, iv. 45
Stolen Necklace The, v. 92
Do. Purse, The, v. 117
Suitors, The Lady and her five, v. 83
Sweep and Noble Lady of Baghdad, The, iii. 247
Tailor's Tale, The, i 276
Taj al-Muluk and the Princess Dunya, The Tale of, ii. 179
Tawaddud, Abu al-Hasan and his slave-girl, iv 144
Thief, The Lover who feigned himself a, iii. 276
Do. and the Shroff, The, iii 387
Do. and his Monkey, The, ii. 380
Do. The Shepherd and the, vii. 181
Do. turned Merchant and the other Thief, The, iv. 69
Thieves, The Boy and the, vii 171
Do. The Merchant and the, vii. 175
Do. The Two, iv. 69
Three-year-old-child, The Debauchee and the, v. 116
Three Apples, The, i. 171
Three unfortunate Lovers, iv. 94
Three Wishes, or the Man who longed to see the Night of Power, The, v. 91
Tortoise, The Waterfowl and the, ii 352
Tortoises, The Heathcock and the, vii. 187
Trader (the) and the Jinni, i. 22
Trick (the Lover's) against the chaste wife, v. 48
Do. (the Wife's) against her husband, v. 64
Two Kings, The, vii. 143
Two Pigeons, The, v. 94
Umaymah, Al-Mutalammis and his wife, iv. 40
Unfortunate Lovers, The Three, iv. 94
Unjust King and the Pilgrim Prince, The, vii. 129
Uns al-Wujud and the Wazir's Daughter Rose-in-Hood, iv. 1

Upper Egypt (The man of) and his Frank wife, vii 99
Walid bin Sahl, Yunus the Scribe and the Caliph, v. 302
Wardan, the Butcher, Adventure with the Lady and the Bear, iii. 404
Water-Carrier and the Goldsmith's Wife, The, iv. 52
Waterfowl and the Tortoise, The, ii. 352
Wazir and the Sage Duban, The, i. 41
Wazir, Al-Malik al-Nasir and his, v. 338
Do. of Al-Yaman and his young brother, The, iv. 38
Wazir's Son and the Hammam Keeper's Wife, The, v. 63
Do. Wife, The King and his, v. 43
Weasel, The Mouse and the, ii. 369
Weaver, The Foolish, ii. 381
Wife, The Badawi and his, v. 321
Do. (the Chaste) The Lover's Trick against, v. 48
Do. The King and his Wazir's, v. 43
Do. The Man and his Wilful, vii. 173
Do. (The Merchant's) and the Parrot, i 48
Do. (The Virtuous) and the King, iv. 83
Wife's Device to cheat her husband, The, v 64
Do. trick against her husband, The, iv 59
Wild Ass, The Jackal and the, vii 127
Wilful Wife, The Man and his, vii. 173
Wind, The Spider and the, vii. 137
Wird Khan (King) and his Women and Wazirs, vii 112
Wolf and the Fox, The, ii. 354
Wolf, The Foxes and the, vii. 178
Woman (The Shipwrecked) and her child, iv. 209
Woman's trick against her husband, iv. 59
Woman who made her husband sift dust, The, v. 56
Woman whose hands were cut off for Almsgiving, The, iii 393
Women, the Malice of, v. 36
Do. The Two, iv. 121
Yahya bin Khalid and the Forger, iii. 301
Do. and Mansur, iii. 298
Do. and the Poor Man, iv. 56
Yaman (The Man of Al-) and his six slave-girls, iii. 360
Do. (The Wazir of Al-) and his young brother, iv. 38
Yunus the Scribe and the Caliph Walid bin Sahl, v. 302
Zau al-Makan, The History of King Omar bin al-Nu'uman and his Sons Sharrkan and, i. 398
Zayn al-Mawasif, Masrur and, vi. 352
Zaynab the Coney-Catcher, The Rogueries of Dahlah the Wily, and her Daughter, v. 340
Zubaydah in the bath, Harun al-Rashid and, iv. 41
Zumurrud, Ali Shar and, iii. 306

INDEX III.

ALPHABETICAL TABLE OF THE NOTES (ANTHROPOLOGICAL, &c.).

A'AMASH (Al-), traditionist, iv. 46
A'amash (Al-) = one with watering eyes, v. 13
A'aráf (Al-) = partition-wall (chapter of the Koran), iv. 170
A'araj (AL) traditionist, iv. 46
Aaron's rod, ii. 140
—— (becomes with Moslems Moses' staff), iv. 189
Abá, Abáah = cloak of hair, ii. 36, vi. 199
Abá al-Khayr = my good sir, etc., vi. 133
Abad = eternity, without end, ii. 104
Abbás "hero eponymus" of the Abbasides, i. 173
—— (= the grim-faced), iii. 260
Abbasides (descendants of the Prophet's uncle), i. 383
—— (black banners and dress), i. 386, ii. 187
'Abd = servile, ii. 270
Abd al-Ahad = slave of the One (God), v. 128
Abd al-Aziz (Caliph), ii. 67
Abd al-Malik (Caliph), i. 398, ii. 68
Abd al-Kádir of Gilán (founder of the Kádiri order), iii. 169
Abd al-Malik ibn Marwán (Caliph), iii. 98, 137
Abd al-Rahím = slave of the Compassionate, v. 128
Abd al-Salám = slave of salvation, v. 128
Abd al-Samad = slave of the Eternal, v. 128
Abd al-Samad al-Samúdí (for Samanhúdí ?), v. 4
Abdallah (a neutral name), iv. 101
Abdallah bin Abbás, companion and traditioner, i. 280
Abdallah bin Abi Kilábah, iii. 236
Abdallah bin al-Zubayr, iii. 98
Abdallah bin Málik al-Khuzá'i, iii. 301
Abdallah bin Mas'úd (traditionist), iv. 46
Abdallah bin Sálim (traditionist), *ib.*
Abdallah ibn al-Mu'tazz (poet-prince), viii. 37
Abdún (convent of), viii. 37
Abhak = Allah bless him and keep (see Sal'am), i. 350
'Abir (a fragrant powder sprinkled on face, body and clothes), vi. 386
Abjad (Hebrew-Arabic alphabet), iv. 181
—— (logogriphs derived from it), vi. 248

Ablution (difference of fashion in performing it), iv. 75
—— (obligatory after copulation), vii. 39
Abraham (an Imám to mankind), ii. 103
—— (place of), ii. 168, iii. 269
—— (the Friend = mediæval St. Abraham), iv. 159, v. 174
Abtan (Al-) = the most profound (*see* Bátiní), v. 129
Abú al-Abbás al-Mubarrad (grammarian), iv. 98
Abú al-Abbás al-Rakáshi (poet), iv. 43
Abú al-Ayná, iv. 121
Abú al-Hamlát = father of assaults, burdens, pregnancies, v. 344
Abú al-Hasan (not Husn), ii. 383
Abú al-Husn = Father of Beauty (a fancy-name), iv. 144
Abú al-Hosayn (Father of the Fortlet) = fox, ii. 354, 358
Abú al-Lays (Pr. N.) = Father of the Lion, vii. 279
Abú al-Muzaffir = Father of the Conqueror, iii. 286
Abú al-Nowás (Pr. N.) = Father of the Sidelocks, iii. 181, 377
Abú al-Ruwaysh = Father of the Featherkin, vi. 232
Abú al-Sa'ádát = Father of Prosperities, vi. 299; viii. 27
Abú al-Sakhá = Father of Munificence, v. 330
Abú Ali, *see* Di'ibil al-Khuzá'i
Abú Ali al-Husayn the Wag, v. 326
Abu Ámir bin Marwán (Wazir to Saladin), v. 338
Abú Bakr (Caliph), ii 68, 97
Abú Bakr Mohammed al-Anbári (grammarian), iv. 100
Abú Dalaf al-Ijili (a soldier famed for liberality and culture), vii. 259
Abú Háris = Father of Spoils (lion), iv. 9
Abú Hanífah (Founder of the Senior School), ii 107
—— (scourged for refusing to take office), ii. 109
Abú Hassán al-Ziyadi, iii. 397
Abú Házim, ii. 105
Abú Horayrah (uncle of Mohammed), iv. 46
Abú Hosayn = Father of the Fortlet (fox), v. 120
Abú Ishak (Hárún's cup-companion), i. 355
Abú Karn = Father of the Horn (unicorn ?), iv. 362
Abú Kidr = Father of the Cooking-pot, i. 248
Abú Kir = Father of the Pitch (Abou Kir), vii. 208
Abú Kurrat = Father of the Coolness (Chamæleon), ii. 386
Abú Lahab and his Wife, vii. 27
Abú Lúlúah (murderer of Caliph Omar), ii. 64
Abú Maryam (a term of contempt), vii. 40
Abú Miján (song of), viii. 38
Abú Mohammed al-Battál (hero of an older tale), vii. 67
Abú Músá al-Ashári, ii. 64
Abú Riyáh = Father of Winds (a toy), i 413
Abú Shámah = Father of the Cheek-mole, i 247
Abú Shámmah = Father of a Smeller or nose, i 247
Abú Shawárib = Father of Mustachios, i. 247
Abú Shiháb, Father of the Shooting-star = evil spirit, i 204
Abú Sir (corruption of Pousiri = Busiris), vii. 208
Abú Sirhán = Father of (going out to prey by), Morning, ii. 368, vii. 179
Abú Tabak = Father of Whipping, viii. 5
Abú Tammám (poet), iv. 116

Abú Yakzán = awakener (ass, cock), i. 15, 16
Abú Yúsuf (the Lawyer), iii. 274
Abú Zanád (traditionist), iv. 46
Abú Zarr (companion of the Prophet), ii. 100, iv. 65
Abyssinians (hardly to be called blackamoors), iv. 402
Account asked from outgoing Governors, v. 300
Account of them will be presently given = "we leave them for the present," v. 351
Acids applied as counter-inebriants, v. 233
Acquit me of responsibility = pardon me, i. 397
——(formula of dismissing a servant), v. 149
Acquittance of all possible claims after business transactions (quoted on Judgment-Day), vii. 346
'Ád (tribe of the prehistoric Arabs), i. 60, iii. 78, vii. 245
'Ád bin Zayd (poet), iv. 85
Adab = anything between good education and good manners, i. 122, vii. 120
Adam's loins, iii 234
Adam's Peak (Ar. Jabal al-Ramun), iv. 403
Ádami = an Adamite (opposed to Jinn), vii. 241
Adan = our Aden, vi. 394
Address without vocative particle more emphatic, v. 322
Addressing by the name not courteous, v. 312
Adi (son of Hátim al-Táyyi), iii. 220
Ádil (Al-) = the just (Caliph Omar), iv. 66
'Ádiliyah (Mosque in Cairo), viii. 5
Adím = leather (Bulghár, Morocco), vi. 236
Adim al-Zauk = lack-tact, vii. 329
Adites (first and second), v. 174
Adl = just (ironically), iii. 384
Adm (Udm) = any relish, iii. 250
Admiral (fishing for the King's table), vii. 231
Adnán (Arab genealogy begins with), iv. 63
—— (land of Arabia), v. 11
Adolescent (Un, aime toutes les femmes), vi. 86
Adultery (none without an adulterer), iv. 54
—— (to be proved by four witnesses), iv. 61
—— (son of = base-born), vii. 389
—— (son of, to one's own child), iii. 8
Æolipyla, ii. 6
Æsop the fable-writer, viii 101
Af'à = ὄφις (a snake), vii. 116
Affirmative and negative particles, v. 386
Afridun (Furaydun) absurd name for a Greek king, i. 402
Africa (suggested derivation of the name), v. 260
Aftah (Al-) = Broad-o'-Brow, i. 15
Aghá = master, sir, gentleman (politely applied to a Eunuch), i. 216, 373
——(AL) for chief police officer, v. 351
Ahassa bi 'l-shurbah = "he smelt a rat," v. 339
Ahd (Al-) wa al-Misák = oath and covenant, vii 385
Ahdab = hunchback (opposed to Ak'as), i. 196
Áhirah = strumpet (*see* Fájirah), vi. 263
Abjár al-Kassárín = falling-stones, vii. 65
Ahl al-Bayt = the person of the house (euphemistic for wife), v. 108

Ahlan = as one of the household, vii. 5
Ahmad = the praised one, Mohammed, ii. 125
Ahmad al-Danaf (Pr. N.) = Calamity Ahmad, iii. 201
—— bin Abi Duwád (High Chancellor to the Abbasides), vii. 311
—— bin Hanbal (founder of the fourth Moslem School), ii. 104
Ahnaf (AL) bin Kays, ii. 62
Ahr (ihr) = fornication, in the sense of irreligion, ii. 155
Ahrám (Al-) = the Pyramids, iv. 67
Ahwáz (city and province of Khuzistan), v. 191
"Aidance from Allah and victory are near," vii. 375
'Áin = Smiter with the evil eye, i. 113
Air (I fear it for her when it bloweth), vi. 209
'Ajáib al-Hind = marvels of Ind, viii. 138
Ajal = appointed time of life, i. 69
—— = yes verily, v. 386
'AJam (AL) = region not Arab, Persia, i. 2
'Ajami = foreigner, esp. Persian, i. 110
AJib (Pr. N.) = wonderful, v. 163
Ajúz, for old woman, highly insulting, i. 160
'Ajwah = dates pressed into a solid mass and deified, v 216
Akabah (mountain pass near Meccah), iv. 243
Akákír = drugs, spices, v. 342
Akásirah (= Kisra-Kings), i. 69, vii. 382
—— (= sons of the royal Chosroës), iii. 423
Akh = brother (wide signification of the word), v. 149
Akh al-Jahálah = Brother of Ignorance, ii. 383
Akhawán shakíkán = (two) brothers german, vii. 71
Ákhir al-Zamán = the latter days, iv. 251
Akhlát (town in Armenia), v. 286
Akhzar = green, grey, fresh (applied to cheek-down), ii. 187
Akik (AL), two of the name, v. 336
'Akík = carnelian ("seal with seals of"), vi. 375
Akil (son of Abú Tálib), vi. 321
'Akká = Acre, vii. 100
Akkám = Cameleer, Caravan-manager, iii. 168
Akl al-hishmah = eating decorously, vii. 395
Akmán, pl. of Kumm = sleeve, petal, vii. 11
Akr Kayrawán = ball of silver dross, vii. 4
Akún fidá-ka = I may be thy ransom, vi. 194
Akyál, title of the Himyarite Kings, v. 260
Akrás = cakes, i. 77
Al (the Article with Proper Names), iii. 89
Alà júdi-k = to thy generosity, vii. 223
Alá al-Din (Aladdin) = Glory of the Faith, iii. 157, 161
Alá kulli hál = in any case, any how, vi. 61
Alà mahlak = at thy leisure, vii. 239
Alá raghm = in spite of, v. 319
A'láj = sturdy miscreants, viii. 36
Alak = clotted blood, ii. 252
Alam = way-mark, etc., iv. 146
—— (not Ilm) al-Din = flag of the faith, i 345
Aláma = alá-má = upon what? wherefore? iii 319

Alas for his chance of escaping = there is none, v. 376
Alast (day of), iii. 234
Albatross (supposed never to touch land), iv. 374
Alchemy (its practice has cost many a life), vi. 170
Alcinous (of the Arabian Odyssey), iv. 403
Alcove (corruption of Al-Kubbah), iii. 431
Ál Dáud (David's family), iii. 177
Aleppo (noted for debauchery), iv. 31
Alexander (of the Koran), not to be confounded with the Macedonian, ii. 99
Alexandria (praise of), vii 25
Alhambra = (Dár) al-Hamrá, the Red, v. 249
Alhamdolillah (pronounced to avert the evil eye), iii. 421
Ali bin Abi Tálib (Caliph), iv. 167, 178
—— (his deeds of prowess), ii. 12
—— (murder of), iii. 98
—— bin Mohammed bin Abdullah bin Táhir (Governor), iv 121
—— al-Mulúk = high of (among the Kings), vi. 138
—— al-Zaybak (Pr. N. = Mercury Ali), iii. 201, v. 366
Ali Shár (Pr. N.), iii. 306
Alif (stature like one), iii. 24, 363
——Há, Wáw as tests of caligraphy, v 309
All will not be save well = it will be the worse for him, vii. 354
Allah (will open thee) a formula of refusal, i. 29
—— (hath said), formula of quoting the Koran, i. 57
—— (names, by Edwin Arnold), i. 354
—— Wa'llahi tayyib (exclamation of the Egyptian Moslem), *ib.* 359
—— (His name pronounced against the evil eye), iii. 162
—— (is all-knowing, swearing by, forbidden), *ib.* 294, 295
—— (= I don't know), *ib.* 395
—— (give thee profit), ii. 244
—— (unto, we are returning), iii. 97
—— (requite you abundantly = "thank you"), iv. 127
—— (seeking refuge with), *ib.* 155
—— (names of), *ib.* 168
—— (be praised whatso be our case), iv. 345
—— (the "Manifest Truth") v. 10
—— (is omniscient), formula used when telling an improbable tale, *ib.* 119
—— (the Opener), *ib.* 124
—— (it is He who gives by our means), *ib.* 140
—— (sight comprehendeth Him not), *ib.* 186
—— (confound the far One, hard swearing), v. 350
—— (succour the Caliph against thee), v. 354
—— (is All-knowing, for our tale is no "Gospel truth"), v. 400
—— I take refuge with—from gainsaying thee = God forbid that I should oppose thee), vi. 210
—— (perpetuate his shadow), vi. 320
—— (we seek refuge with him from the error of the intelligent) vii. 59
—— (will make no way for the Infidels over the True Believers), vii. 97
—— (I seek refuge with), vii. 115
—— (He was jealous for Almighty), vii. 180
—— (I fear him in respect of = I am governed by Him in my dealings with), vii. 197

Allah (pardon thee, showing that the speaker does not believe in another's tale), vii. 227
—— (the Provider), vii. 238
—— (for the love of), vii. 24
—— (Karím = God is bountiful), vii. 239
—— (grant thee grace = pardon thee), vii. 344
—— (yasturak = will veil thee), vii. 369
—— (sole Scient of the hidden things, be extolled), vii. 370
—— (raised the heavens without columns, etc), vii. 382
—— (will make things easy = will send us aid), viii. 2
—— (give thee quittance of responsibility), viii. 10
—— (will send thee thy daily bread), viii. 12
Allah ! Allah ! = I conjure thee by God, i. 319
Alláh Karím = Allah is all beneficent, i. 29
Allaho a'alam = God is all knowing, i. 2, 46
Allaho akbar (as a war cry), i. 409; iv. 151; v. 210; vii 2
Allahumma = Yá Allah with emphasis, i. 36
Allusions (far-fetched, fanciful, and obscure), ii. 283, 389, 396; iii. 49
Almá = brown- (not "damask-") lipped, iv. 33
Almás = Gr. Adamas, vii. 383
Almenichiaka, v. 38
Almond-apricot, v. 181
Alms to reverend men to secure their prayers, i. 393
Alnaschar (Story of), viii. 132
Aloes, *see* Sabr.
—— (well appreciated in Eastern medicine), vii. 176
—— (the finest used for making Nadd), vii. 223
Alpinism (unknown), iii. 103
Al-Safar Zafar = voyaging is victory, i. 230
Alwán (pl. of Laun, colour) = viands, dishes, vi. 181
Amáira (pl. of Imamah) = turbands, iii. 224
'Amal = action, operation (applied to drugs, etc.), vii. 336
'Amala hilah for tricking, a Syro-Egyptian vulgarism, v. 244
Amalekites, v. 169, 170
Amám-ak = before thee, v. 292
Amán = quarter, mercy, i. 315
'Amáriyah (Pr. N. of a town), vi. 138
Amazon (a favourite in folk-lore), i. 415
Amazons (of Dahome), vi. 197
Ambar al-Khám = rude Ambergris, vi. 240
Ambiguity, iv. 13
Amend her case = bathe her, etc., vi. 51
Amid (Amidah) town in Mesopotamia, v. 22
Amin (AL) = the Trusted of Allah, iii. 374
—— son and successor of Hárún al-Rashid, i. 170; iv. 57, 111
Ámin (Amen) = So be it! vii. 204
Amír = military commander, i. 238
'Ámir = one who inhabiteth, haunter, viii. 6
Amir and Samúl = Jones, Brown and Robinson, iii. 230
Amir al-Muuminín = Prince of the Faithful, i. 103
Ammá ba'ad = but after (initiatory formula), i. 362
'Amm = uncle (polite address to a father-in-law), viii. 30

Ammá laka au 'alayka = either to thee (the gain) or upon thee (the loss), vii. 92
Amor discende non ascende, iii. 27
Amr (Al-) = command, matter, affair, vii. 145
Amrad = beardless and handsome, effeminate, i. 301
Amrú (pronounced Amr) or Zayd = Tom, Dick or Harry, iii. 132
—— bin Ma'adi Karib (poet), iv. 106
—— bin Masa'dah (Pr. N.), iv. 104
——Amsá = he passed the evening, etc., iii. 26
Amsár (pl. of Misr) = cities, i. 10
—— = settled provinces, vi. 155
Amshát (combs) perhaps = Kanáfah (vermicelli), i. 77
Amtár, pl. of Matr, *q.v.*, iii. 79
Amúd al-Sawári = the Pillar of Masts (Diocletian's column), vii 55
Amúríyah = the classical Amorium, iv. 100
"Ana" from night ccclxxxi. to ccccxxiv.), iv. 31
Ana a'amil = I will do it (Egypto-Syrian vulgarism), iv. 311
Ana fí jíratak = I crave thy intercession (useful phrase), iii. 208
Anagnorisis, admirably managed, vi. 258
Analphabetic Amirs, vii. 200
Anasa-kum = ye are honoured by knowing him, viii. 11
Anbár (pronounced Ambár), town on the Euphrates, iii. 273
Anbar (Ambar) = ambergris, iv. 399
Andalib = nightingale (masc. in Arab.), vii. 17
Andalusian = Spanish (*i.e.* of Vandal-land), v. 18
Andam = the gum called dragon's blood; brazil-wood, i. 162; vi. 372
Anemone on a tomb, ii. 217
Angels (taking precedence in the order of created beings), vii. 158
—— (appearing to Sodomites), iii. 84
—— (ride piebalds), v. 59
—— (shooting down the Jinn), vii. 27
Anis al-Jalís = the Cheerer of the Companion, i. 333
Animals (have no fear of man), vii. 251
Anista-ná = thy company gladdens us, vi. 378
Ansár = Medinite auxiliaries, v. 291; vi. 332
Ant (chapter ix. of the Koran), iv. 166
Antar (Romance quoted), iii. 168
—— (and the Chosroë) v. 189
—— (contest with Khosrewan), v. 191
Antiochus and Stratonice, iii. 139
Ants (a destructive power in tropic climates), vii. 125
Anúshírwán = Anúshín-rawán = Sweet of Soul, iv. 51
Anwá, pl. of Nau, *q.v.*, vii. 3
Anwár = lights, flowers, vii. 7, 18
Anyáb (pl. of Náb) = grinder teeth, vii. 214
Ape-names (expressing auspiciousness), ii. 380
Apes (isle of), iv. 364
—— (gathering fruits), iv. 394
—— (remnant of some ancient tribe), vi. 130
Apodosis omitted, v. 112, 146
Apple (wine), iii. 256
—— (many a goodly one rotten at the core), iii. 306
Apricots (various kinds), vii. 5
'Ár (AL) = shame, iv. 98

Arab al-Arbá = prehistoric tribes of the Arabs, i. 103; iv. 64
—— al-Musta'ajimah = barbarised Arabs, *ib.*
—— al-Musta'aribah = naturalised Arabs, *ib.*
—— al-Muta'arribah = Arabised Arabs, *ib.*
—— (exaggerates generosity), i. 361
—— (shouting under his ruler's palace), *ib.* 363
—— temperament, *ib.* 377; ii. 5, 82
—— cap (Tartúr), ii. 45
—— (Derivation of the name), *ib.* 43
—— (pathos), *ib.* 280
—— (the noble merciful), *ib.* 312
—— (shop), *ib.* 384
—— (style compared with Persian), v. 40
A'ráb = dwellers in the desert, vii. 354
Arab horses (breeds of), iv. 197
Arab-land and Ajam = all the world over, iv. 97
Arabian Night converted into an Arabian Note, vi. 100
Arabian Odyssey, vi. 166
Arabs (for plundering nomades), viii. 24
Arafat (Mount, where the victims are *not* slaughtered), iv. 243
—— (day of), ii. 70
Aráki (capparis shrub), i. 386
—— (tooth-stick of the wild caper-tree; Aráka = I see thee), iii. 61
Arakíyah = white scull-cap, i. 198
Ar'ar = Juniper-tree, "heath," iii. 40; v. 12
Ardabb (Irdabb) = five bushels, i. 242
Ardashir (Artaxerxes), three Persian Kings of the name, ii. 58; vi 1
Arianism and early Christianity, viii. 171
Arif (Al-) = monitor, i. 212
Arish (AL), frontier town between Egypt and Palestine, vii. 347
'Arishah = arbour, etc., vii. 287
Aristomenes and his fox, iv. 384
Arithmetic (not mastered by Moslems), iv. 188
Arithmology (cumbrous in Arabic for lack of the higher numerals), vii. 197
Arman = Armenia, ii. 169
Armaniyah (Armenia), iii. 301
Armenians (porters of Constantinople), iv. 343
Armpits (taking a dismounting person under the, a sign of respect), iii. 329
Arms and armour, viii. 80
Army (divided into six divisions), iii. 74
Arsh = the ninth Heaven, iv. 123
Artál, *see* Rotl.
Arúbah (AL) = Friday, v. 100
Arún (Heb) = in his shirt, i. 72
'Arús (AL) = the bride (tropical name for wine), vi. 351
As'ad = more (or most) fortunate, iii. 124
Asaf bin Barkhiyah (Solomon's Wazir), v. 16; vi. 104, 284
Asáfíri = Sparrow-olives, iii. 79
'Asákir = corner-terminals of a litter, viii. 30
Asal Kasab = cane-honey, viii. 3
Asal Katr = drip-honey, viii. 2
Asal Nahl = bee's honey, i. 249
Asár = traces, vii. 318

Ash'ab (proverbial for greed), viii. 14
Asháb = companions, v. 291; vi. 332
Asháb al-Ráy (epithet of the Hanafi school), v. 59
Asháb al-Suffah, iv. 65
Asháb al-Ziyá = Feudatories, vi. 113
Ashhab = grey-white, ii. 19
A-Sharif anta = art thou a noble, vii. 299
Ashirah = clan, v. 318
Ashjár = door-posts or wooden bolts, v. 101
Ashkánián, race of Persian Kings, i. 69
Asidah (custard, pap), iii. 165
'Ásim = defending, vi. 100
Askar Jarrár = drawing (*i.e.* conquering), army, v. 284
Aslah = head-kerchief, i 382
Aslán (Pr. N., probably for Arslan = lion), iii. 203
Asma'i (AL), author of Antar, iii. 279; v. 308
Asoka's wife and Kunála, v. 42
Ass (held ill-omened), i. 350
—— (-goad), ii. 339
—— (voice "most ungrateful"), *ib.* 340
—— (the wild, "handy" with his hoof), iii. 22
Asr (AL) = time or prayer of mid-afternoon, i. 221
Astár (pl. of Satr = chopper?), vi. 333
Astrolabe, father of our sextant, i. 280
Aswad = black (used for any dark colour), vii 5
'Atb = blame, reproach (for disgrace), vi. 265
Atbák = trays, iv. 215
Atheist (Ar. Zindik), vi. 185
Atmár = rags (for travelling clothes), v. 315
Atnáb = tent-ropes, vi. 386
Atr = any perfume, i. 309
Atsah (AL) = sneezing, vii. 288
'Attár = perfume-seller, druggist, viii. 8
Attraction of like to like, ii. 190
Auhashtani = thou hast made me desolate, i 57
'Aúj = Persian town, Kúch (?), vii., 404
Aun (of Jinns, etc), iii. 213
Aurat = shame, nakedness (woman, wife), iv. 370
—— (of man and woman), v. 33
Avanie (Ar. Gharámah), vi. 302
Avaunt = Ikhsa, be chased like a dog, v. 245
Awáh! Awáh! = Alas! Alas! ii. 213
Awák = ounces (pl. Ukiyah, *q.v.*), vi. 171, vii 284
'Awálim, pl. of 'Álimah dancing girls, i. 197
'Awáshik = hucklebones, cockles, vii. 330
Awwá (name of Satan's wife), iii. 17
Awwádah = lute-player, iii. 263
Áyat = Koranic verses, ii. 140; iii. 87, 264
Áyát al-Naját = Verses of Safety, v. 24
Áyishah bint Talhah (grand-daughter of Abú Bakr), iv. 44
Aylúlah = slumbering after morning prayers, ii. 79
Ayn = eye (for helper), iv. 27
Ayns (verset of the 140), iv. 170

Aysh (Egypt.) = Ayyu Shayyin for classical "Má" what, i. 73
'Aysh = that on which man lives (for bread), viii. 3
Ayshat al-durrah murrah = the sister-wife has a bitter life, iii. 88
Aywá (Ay wa'lláhi) = Ay, by Allah, i. 279; v. 387
Aywan = saloon with estrades, vi. 132
Ayyás (Issus of Cilicia), iii. 202
Ayyúb = Job, i. 369
Azal = eternity without beginning (opposed to Abad = infinity) ii. 104; iv. 333
Azán (call to prayer), ii. 199; iv. 156
Az'ar = having thin hair; tail-less, vii. 255
Azarbiján = Kohistán, v. 302
Azdashír, misprint for Ardashir, vi. 1
Azghán = camel litters, ii. 177
Azim = "deuced" or "mighty fine," i. 164; vii. 120
Aziz (fem. Azizah) = dear, excellent, highly prized, ii. 193
'Aziz (Al-) al-Misr = Magnifico of Misraim, vii. 193
Azrak = blue-eyed (so is the Falcon!) v. 358; vi. 164
Azrár (buttons), ii. 210

BA'ALBAK = Ba'al's city, iv. 19
Báb = gate, chapter, i. 125; v. 205
—— (sometimes for a sepulchral cave) vii. 348
Báb (AL) al-'Ali = Sublime Porte, viii. 5
Báb al-Bahr and Báb al-Barr, vi. 212; vii. 51
Báb al-Farádís = gate of the gardens at Damascus, i 220
Báb al-Lúk (of Fustat), iii. 372
Báb al-Nasr = Gate of Victory (at Cairo), v. 141; viii. 5
Báb al-Salám (of the Al-Medinah Mosque), iii. 400
Babel = Gate of God, i. 79
Babes of the eye = pupils, i. 92; iii. 361
Baboon (Kird), iii. 408
Bábúnaj = white camomile, ii. 283
Babylonian eyes = bewitching ones, vii. 14
Bachelor not admitted in Arab quarters, ii. 410
Back-parts compared to revolving heavens, ii 244
Bactrian camel, iv. 315
Badal = substitute, iv. 200
Badawi (not used in the Koran for Desert Arab), ii. 43
—— (bonnet), *ib.* 45
—— (a fool as well as a rogue), *ib.* 48
—— (cannot swim), ii. 294
—— (baser sort), *ib.* 294
—— (shifting camp in spring), *ib.* 304
—— (noble), *ib.* 312
—— (bluntness and plain-speaking of), iii. 226; iv. 62
Badawi's dying farewell, i. 69
Bádhanj = windshaft, ventilator, i. 237
Bád-i-Sabá = breeze o' the morn, ii. 81
Badinján = Solanum pomiferum or S. Melongena, iii. 417
Badlah Kunúzíyah = treasure-suit, vii. 390
Badmasti = le vin mauvais, i. 81
Bádrah = 10,000 dirhams, iii. 393

Badr Básim = full moon smiling, vi. 63
Bághdád = Garden of Justice, ii. 323
—— (House of Peace), vi. 208
—— (of Nullity, opposed to the Ubiquity of the World), vii. 94
Baghlah = she-mule, i. 119
Bahá al-Din ibn Shaddád (Judge Advocate-General under Saladin), vii. 103
Bahádur = the brave, iii. 114
Baháim (pl. of Bahímah = Behemoth) applied to cattle, iii. 181
Bahak = white leprosy, iv. 242
Bahímah, mostly = black cattle, vii. 149
Bahr = water cut or trenched in the earth, sea, large river, i. 41
Bahr (AL) al-azrak = Blue River, not "Blue Nile," vi. 164
Bahr al-Kunúz = Sea of Treasures, iv. 6
Bahr al-Muhít = circumambient ocean, i. 123
Bahrám (Varanes) = planet Mars, iii. 118
Bahramáni = Brahman, iii. 225
Bahríyah = crew, vi. 176
Bahrwán (Pr. N. for Bihrún?), iv. 274
Bakh! Bakh! = bravo! brava! ii. 53; iii 244
Bakhkharaní = he incensed me, vii. 305
Bakhshish naturalized as Anglo-Egyptian, ii. 271
—— (such as to make a bath-man's mouth water), vii. 224
Bakk = bug, iii. 107
Bakkát = greengrocer, vi. 83
Baklámah = almond pastry, ii. 204
Balábil pl. of bulbul (nightingale) and of balbalah (grief), iv 196
Balah = green date, ii. 207
Baldricks (Ar. Hamáil), iv. 117
Balíd = simpleton, i. 15
Ballán = body-servant, i. 286
Ballánah = tire-woman, i. *ib*
Baltiyah = Labrus Niloticus (fish), vii. 26
Bán = myrobolan, vi. 37; vii. 54
Banát = daughters, protégées, vi. 197
Banát al-Na'ash = the Great Bear, ii. 254; iii. 9
Bandaged eyes (before beheading), iii. 266
Bands of Bandits, ii. 324
Bandukáníyah (quarter of Cairo), v 160
Banj = Nibanj = Nepenthe, i. 65
Banner (bound to a spear sign of investiture), iii. 87; v. 299
Banni (Bunni) = Cyprinus Bynni, vi. 336
Banquets (royal), iii. 330
—— (daintily deviced), iii. 342
Banú Abbás (their colours black), v. 3
—— al-Asfar (people of the yellow faces), ii. 129
—— Israíl, iii. 395
—— Kahtán, v. 166
—— Nabhán, v. 167
—— Shaybán (tribe), iii. 349
—— Tamim (tribe), v. 322
—— Umayyah (their colours white), v. 3
—— 'Uzzah (tribe famous for love passion), ii. 198; iv. 36
Banyán = Ficus Indica, v. 418

Baradiyah=wide-mouthed Jug, i. 33
Baras=white leprosy, iv. 242; vi. 183
Barge (Ar. Bárijah), iv. 365
Bárid=cold (vain, foolish, insipid), i. 196; ii. 235
Baríd=Post, vi. 126
Bárijah (pl. bawáriJ)=Jarm, barge, iv. 365
Barley, food for horses, i. 319
Barmahát (seventh Coptic month), iv. 183
Barmarkis (history of the family), viii. 124
Barmecides (Ar. Barámikah), i. 173
Barmúdah (eighth Coptic month), iv. 184
Barr al-Manákhah in al-Madinah, ii. 42
Barsh=matting, i. 344
Barsh (Bars) commonest form of Bhang, iii. 159
Bartaut=Berthold, vii. 90
Barzakh=bar, partition, Hades, ii. 217
Basaltic statues in Hauranic ruins give rise to the idea of men transformed intc black stones, i. 156
Bashárah (al-)=gift of good tidings, guerdon, i. 27
Báshik (small sparrow-hawk), ii. 285
Basil=the Indian Tulsi, i. 17
Basil of the bridges=Ocymum basilicum, pennyroyal, i. 83
Basmalah=pronouncing the formula Bismillah, iv. 160; vii. 83
—— (commonly pronounced Bismillah), iv. 167
Bastardy (a sore offence amongst Moslems), vi. 268
Bastinado of women, i. 168
Batáyikh (Batálíkh)=water melons, v. 117
Batánah=lining, vi. 115
Batárikah (half ecclesiastic half military term) vi. 401; vii. 52, 56
Batárikh=roe, spawn, vii. 213
Bath (first, after sickness), iii. 52
—— (coming out of, shows that consummation has taken place), iii. 359
—— (and privy, favourite haunts of the Jinns), v. 54
—— (may it be a blessing to thee), vi. 348
—— (setting it a-working, turning on the water, hot and cold), vii. 222
Bathers pay on leaving the Hammám, ii. 223
Bathsheba and Uriah (congeners of), v. 43
Bátiní=gnostic; a reprobate, i. 355; v. 129
Batiyah=jar, flagon, vii. 55
Batrak (Batrik)=patriarch, i. 410
Batrík (Bitrík)=patricius, *ib.*
Batshat al-Kubrá=the great disaster (battle of Badr), v. 255
Battál (AL), Story of, viii. 69
Battásh al-Akrán=he who assaults his peers, v. 255
Battle-pieces, v. 261
Bawd (admirably portrayed), iii. 281
Bawwáb=door-keeper, v. 99
Bawwák=trumpeter (a discreditable character), vi. 341
Bayáz=Silurus Bajad (cat-fish), vi. 301
Bayáz=whiteness (lustre, honour), vii. 29
Bayáz al-Sultáni=the best kind of gypsum, i. 248
Baydah (AL)=pawn in chess, iv. 195
Bayt (Al-)=the house (for cage), iv. 219

Bayt al-Mukaddas = Jerusalem, ii. 35
Bayt Sha'r = house of hair; Bayt Shi'r = a couplet, vii. 15
Bayzatán = testicles, i. 378
Báz (vulg. for Tabl.) = kettledrum, vi. 177
Bazar (locked at night), viii. 13
Bazar of Damascus famous in the Middle Ages, i. 220
Bázi (Pers. Báz) = F. peregrinator, hawk, falcon, ii. 360
BE! and IT IS (the creative word), iv. 191, 234
Bead thrown into a cup (signal of delivery), vi. 110
Bean-eating in Egypt, iii. 281
Beard (long, and short wits), iii. 33
—— (forked, characteristic of a Persian), iii. 105
—— (combed by the fingers in the Wuzú) iv. 152, 162
Beast-stories (oldest matter in The Nights), ii. 337
Beauties of nature provoke hunger in Orientals, ii. 258
Beckoning (Eastern fashion the reverse of ours), v. 25
Before the face of Allah = for the love of God, i. 125
Beheading or sacking of a faithless wife unlawful but connived at, i. 167
Belle fourchette (greatly respected), vii. 287
Belle passion in the East, i. 385
Belt (Ar. Kamar), vi. 307
"Ben" of an Arab. shop as opposed to "but," iii. 218
Benches (in olden Europe more usual than chairs), iv. 367
Berbers from the Upper Nile (the "Paddies" of Egypt), v. 99
Betrothed (for "intended to be married with regal ceremony"), viii. 52
Better largesse than the mace, vi. 314
Bhang (its kinds and uses), ii. 27
—— (properties of the drug), *ib.* 315
—— (preparation of), iii. 159
—— (drugging with = tabannuj), *ib.* 197
Bida'ah = innovation, iv. 123
Bier (the bulging = hadbá), iii. 189
Bi-fardayn = "with two singles" (for with two baskets), vi. 312
Biká'a (= low-land), ii. 13
—— (= convents, pilgrimages to), iv. 86
Bilád al-Filfil = home of pepper (Malabar), iv 378
Bilád al-Rúm (applied to France), vii. 70
Bilád al-Súdán = Land of the Blacks (our Soudan), ii 300
Bilál (first Mu'ezzin), ii. 199, 330
"Bilking" (popular form of), vii. 218
Bilkis and her throne, ii. 1; vi. 237
Bi 'l-Salámah = in safety (to avert the evil eye), i 266
Bint 'arús = daughter of the bridegroom (Ichneumon), ii. 369
Bint Shumúkh (Pr. N.) = Daughter of Pride, iv 325
Bir (AL) al-Mu'utallal = the Ruined Well, vi. 131
Bird (created by Jesus), iv. 164
—— seen by Abú Bakr in the cave, iv. 187
Bird-girls, vi. 187
Birds (sing only in the pairing season), iv. 356
—— denote neighbourhood of a village, iii. 64
—— (huge ones discovered on the African coast), iv. 357
—— (left to watch over wives), v. 46
—— (pretended understanding of their language), v. 81

Birds (songs and cries of), iv. 17
Birkat = pool of standing water, iii. 383; iv. 396
Birkat al-Habash = Abyssinian pond, i. 268
Birth-stool (Ar. Kursi al-Wiládah), i. 401
Bishr (al-Háfi = Barefoot), ii. 103; vii. 101
Bisát (Al-) wa 'l-masnad = carpet and cushion, vi. 212
Bismillah = in the name of God, i. 37; iv. 160
—— (said before taking action), i. 73
—— (civil form of dismissal), i. 85
—— (= fall to), i. 243
—— (= enter in Allah's name), vi. 350
—— (parodied), ii. 122
—— (Bi 'Smi 'llah = in the name of God, etc.), ii. 402
Bismillah Námí = Now please go to sleep, vi. 327
Biting the finger ends (not nails), sign of confusion, etc., i 362
Black (colour of the Abbaside Banner), ii. 187; v. 3
Blackamoors preferred by debauched women, i. 5
Black-mail (paid to the Badawin of Ramlah), iii. 202
Blast (of the last trumpet), iv. 257
Blaze (Ar. Ghurrah, *q.v.*), ii. 340
Blessings at the head of letters, v. 330
Blind (The, notorious for insolence), i. 304
Blinding a common practice in the East, now done, i. 99
Blue and yellow turbands prescribed to Christians and Jews, i. 71
Blue-eyed (frequently = fierce-eyed), iii. 311
Blue-eyes = blind with cataract or staring, glittering, hungry, v. 358
Boasting of one's tribe, ii. 304
Boccaccio quoted, i. 10, *et seq.*
Body-guard (consists of two divisions), iii. 188
Boils and pimples supposed to be caused by broken hair-roots, i. 254
Books (black as her), viii. 1
Books (of the Judgment-day), vii. 29
Bostán (female Pr. N.) = flower-garden, iii. 124
Bostáni = gardener, family name from original occupation, i. 245
Bow, a cowardly weapon, v. 320
Box (Ar. 'Ulbah), vi. 227
Boycotting (Oriental forms of), vii. 36
Breaking wind loudly (for fear), ii 340
Brasier (Kánún, Minkal), iv. 222
Brass (Ar. Nuhás asfar), v. 1
Braying of the Ass, ii. 340
Bread and salt (bond of), vi. 171
Bread and salt (to be taken now "cum grano salis"), iii. 319
Breast broadening with delight, i. 44
—— straitened, the converse of the previous, i. 109
Breast-bone (Taráib), iv. 93
Breath (healing by the), iii. 442
—— (of crocodiles, serpents, etc.), iv. 370
Breeze (rude but efficacious refrigerator), iii. 309
Breslau Edition quoted, i. 13 *et seq.*
Brethren (for kinsfolk), vii. 107
—— (of trust and brethren of society = friends and acquaintances), vii. 153
Bridal couch (attitudinising thereon), iv. 41

Bride of the Hoards, v. 25, 343; viii. 30
Bride's throne, i. 198
Bridle (not to be committed to another), vi. 91
Brother (has a wide signification amongst Moslems), v. 149
—— (of Folly = a very fool), ii. 175
—— (of Purity), ii. 371
—— (of Ignorance = Ignoramus), ii. 383
—— ("of the Persians"), iii. 141
Brotherhood (forms of making), ii. 372
—— (sworn in Allah Almighty), iv. 12
—— of Futurity = lookers out for a better world, ii. 97
Brow (like the letter Nún), iii. 363
Búdíkak (Bútakah) = crucible, vi. 167
Budúr (Badoura) = full moons, iii. 15; iii. 355
Buffalo = bœuf á l'eau (?), vii. 251
Buhayrah = tank, cistern, vi. 188
Buka'ah = Cœlesyria, ii. 13
Buka'at al-dam = place of blood (where it stagnates), iii. 194
Bukhayt = little good luck, i. 371
Bukhti (dromedary), ii. 78, 292
Bukjah = bundle, v. 133
Bulád (Pers. Pulád) = steel, v. 30
Bulak Edition quoted, i. 10, *et seq.*
Bulbul (departed with Tommy Moor, Englished by "Nightingale"), iv. 16
Bull (followers preceding), ii. 3
Bull (of the Earth = Gáw-i-Zamin), iv. 270
Bullúr (Billaur) = crystal, etc., ii. 414
Búm = owl (introduced to rhyme with Kayyúm = the Eternal), vii. 22
Bun = kind of cake, vii. 243
Burckhardt quoted, i. 61, *et seq.*
—— (fable anent his death), iii. 203
Burdah = mantle or plaid of striped stuff, v. 293
—— (poem of the), iii. 238
Burká = nosebag, i. 375; v. 29, 102
Burning (a foretaste of Hell-fire), vii. 230
Bursting of the gall-bladder = our breaking of the heart, i. 214
Burying a rival, i. 379
Buttons (Ar. Azrár), ii. 210
Búzah = beer, i. 67
Bystanders forcing on a sale, vii. 44

CABBALA = Spiritual Sciences, ii. 53
Cæsarea, i. 398, 403
—— "of Armenia," ii. 169
Cairene (vulgarism), v. 182
—— (chaff), iii. 333
—— (slang), iv. 200
—— (jargon), viii. 7
—— (savoir faire), viii. 9
—— (bonhomie), viii. 26
—— (knows his fellow Cairene), viii. 33
Cairenes held exceedingly debauched, i 275

Cairo, *see* Misr.
—— (nothing without the Nile), i. 272
Caitiff = Captivus, ii. 13
Calamity (*i.e.*, to the enemy), viii. 31
Calcutta Edition quoted, i. 15, *et seq.*
Caliphate (defective title to), iv. 78
Caliphs 'Abd al-'Aziz, ii. 67
—— 'Abd al-Malik, i. 398; ii. 68; iii. 98, 137
—— Abú Bakr, ii. 68, 97
—— Ali, ii. 12; iii. 98
—— Amin (AL), i. 170; iv. 57, 111
—— Hakim (AL), bi-Amri 'lláh, iii. 407
—— Harún al-Rashid, vi. 311; vii. 98
—— Hishám bin 'Abd al-Malik, ii. 72; v. 302
—— Maamun (AL), i. 170; iii. 232
—— Mahdí (AL), v. 332
—— Mansúr (AL), ii. 45, 60, 109
—— Mu'áwiyah, ii. 62, 63; iii. 99
—— Musta'ín (AL) bi 'lláh, vii. 312
—— Mustansir (AL) bi 'lláh, i. 292
—— Mu'tasim (AL) bi 'llah, ii. 305; vii. 300
—— Mutawakkil (AL) 'alá 'lláh, iii. 402; vii. 299
—— Mu'tazid (AL), vii. 297
—— Mu'tazz (AL), vii. 309
—— 'Omar, ii. 60, 61, 63, 64, 65; iv. 66
—— 'Othmán, ii. 64
—— Sulaymán bin 'Abd al-Malik, ii. 68; v. 297
—— Tá'i (AL) li 'lláh, ii. 276; iii. 87
—— Walid (AL), ii. 68, 294; v. 304
—— Wásik (Al-), ii. 305
Calligraphy, iii. 314
Camel (how slaughtered), i. 320; iii. 220
Camel-load = 300 lbs., for long journeys 250 lbs., i. 369
—— (-men do not accept drafts on futurity), i. 391
—— (-colts roasted whole), iv. 95
—— (feeding on and vindictiveness), iv. 95
—— (Bactrian), iv. 315
—— (seen in a dream is an omen of death; why ?), v. 9
Camels (breeds of), ii. 292, 333
—— (names), *ib.* 333
—— (haltered; nose-ring used for dromedaries), iv. 342
—— (Mehari, Mehríyah), iii. 62
—— (red the best kind), vii. 37
Camphor (simile for a fair face), ii. 399
—— (primitive way of extracting it), iv. 361
Camphor-apricot, v. 181
Cannibal tribes in Central Africa, i. 371
Cannibals and Cannibalism, iv. 376
Canton (city of), vi. 119
Capo bianco, coda verde, iii. 164
Carat (= Kirát), iii. 26
—— ($=\frac{1}{24}$ of a dinar or miskal, something under 5d), iv. 226
Caravan (each one has to keep his place in a), ii 85

Carelessness of the Story-teller, vii. 86
Carmel = Karam-El (God's vineyard), vi. 351
Carnelion stone bit with pearls = lips bit with teeth in sign of anger, ii. 399
Carpet (let him come to the King's = before the King as referee), vii. 185
Carpet-room = throne-room, vii. 195
Carpet-beds, i. 271
Carob (Cassia fistularis), ii. 139
—— bean, emblem of constancy, ii. 208
Carrier-pigeons, ii. 144
Cat (puss, etc.), ii. 370
Cat-fish (Ar. Bayáz) vi. 301
Cask (for "home" of the maiden wine) viii. 36
Cask in Auerbach's Keller, vi. 283
Ceruse (Ar. Isfídáj), v. 40
Cervantes and Arab romance, ii. 291
Ceylon (Ar. Sarandib), iv. 403, 418
Chaff, i. 342; ii. 249; vi. 298, 303, 324, 338
—— or banter allowed even to modest women, i. 246
Chameleon (Father of Coolness), ii. 386
Champing, sign of good breeding, i. 318
Change (sudden, of disposition), vi. 360
Character-sketch (making amends for abuse of women), viii. 23
Chaste forbearance towards a woman frequently causes love, v 382
Chawáshiyah = Chamberlains, vi. 113
Cheating (not only venial but laudable under circumstances), vi. 364
Checkmate (Pers. Ar.) = the King is dead, vi. 364
Cheese a styptic, ii. 231
Chess and chessmen, ii. 8; iv. 194
Chess anecdote, i. 122
Chewing a document that none may see it after, i. 363
Child of the nurse, etc. = delicately reared, iii. 162
Children (carried astraddle upon hip or shoulder), i. 283
—— (one of its = a native of), viii. 8
China (kingdom), iii. 295
China-ware displayed on shelves, i. 375
Chinese shadows, iii. 312
Chin-veil donned (showing intention to act like a man), vi. 253
Cider (Ar. Sharáb al-tuffáh), iii. 256
Circumcision (how practised), iv. 163
—— (female), iv. 228
Citadel (contains the Palace), vii. 177
Cities (two-mosqued, for large and consequently vicious ones), iv. 33
City of Brass (Copper), iii. 295; v. 1
Claimant of blood-revenge, iii. 232
—— and Defendant, *ib.* 271
Claims of Virginity, i. 175
Clairvoyance of perfect affection, viii. 24
Clapping hands preliminary to a wrestling-bout, i. 411
Clapping of hands to summon servants, i. 163; ii. 393
Clerical error of Mac. Edition, ii. 17
Clever young ladies dangerous in the East, i. 14
Climate (water and air), i. 332

Clitoris (Ar. Zambúr) and its excision, iv. 228
Cloak (Ar. Abáah), vi. 199
Clogs=Kubkáb, ii. 316
Closet (the forbidden and the bird-girls), vi. 187
Cloth of frieze and cloth of gold, iii. 266
"Cloth" (*not* "board" for playing chess), vii. 278
Clothes (tattered, sign of grief), iii. 278
Clothing and decency, vii. 253
Clout (hung over the door of a bath shows that women are bathing), vii. 225
Cocoa-nut (Ar. Jauz al-Hindi), iv. 394
Coffee (see Kahwah), ii. 158
—— (first mention of), iv. 125; viii. 82
—— (anachronism), vii. 10
—— (mention of probably due to the scribe), vii. 214
—— (its mention shows a comparatively late date), vii. 318
Cohen (Káhin)=diviner priest, esp. Jewish, ii. 120
Cold-of-Countenance=a fool, ii. 235
Cold speech=a silly or abusive tirade, *ib.*
Colocasia (Ar. Kallakás), v. 346
Coloquintida (Ar. Hanzal), iii. 432
Colossochelys=colossal tortoise, iv. 373
Colours (of the Caliphs), v. 3
—— (names of), v. 27
Combat, reminding of that of Rustam and Sohráb, v. 287
"Come to my arms my slight acquaintance," vii. 248
Commander of the Faithful (title introduced by Omar), v 153
Commune (Ar. Jamá'ah), iv. 159
Comorin (derivation of the name), iv 395
"Compelleth" in the sense of "burdeneth," vi. 73
Compliment (model of a courtly one), vi. 315
Composed of seed by all men shed=superfetation of iniquity, vi. 174
Comrades of the Cave, ii. 351
Conciseness (verging on obscurity), vii. 242
Confession after concealment, a characteristic of the servile class, i 49
—— on the criminal's part required by Moslem law, i. 252
Confusion (of metaphors characteristic of The Nights), i. 79
—— (of religious mythologies by way of "chaff," vi. 303
—— (universal in the undeveloped mind of men), vii. 155
Conjugal affection (striking picture of), vi. 34
Conjunctiva in Africans seldom white, v. 377
Connection (tribal, seven degrees of), v. 318
Constipation (La) rend rigoureux, iii. 29
Consul (Sháh-bandar), iii. 158
—— (Kunsul), *ib.* 209
Contemplation of street-scenery, one of the pleasures of the Harem, i. 295
Continuation in dignities requested by office-holders from a new ruler, ii. 93
Contrast (artful between squalor and gorgeousness), vii. 242
Contrition for romancing, vi. 222
Converts, theoretically respected and practically despised, v. 243
Copa d'agua, apology for a splendid banquet, v. 362
Coptic convents, i. 407
—— visitations to, still customary, ii. 14

Copulation (praying before or after), ii. 63
Coquetries (requiring as much inventiveness as a cotillon), viii. 55
Coral (name of a slave-girl), ii. 4
Corpse pollutes the toucher, i. 272
Cousin (term of familiarity = our "coz"), i. 367
—— (first, affronts an Arab if she marries any save him without his leave), v. 58
—— (has a prior right to marry a cousin), vii. 293
Covered (The, chapter of the Koran), iv. 168
Cow (chapter ii. of the Koran), iv. 164
Cowardice equally divided, ii. 393
—— (proverb anent), vii. 65
—— (of the Fellah, how to be mended), vii. 87
Cowrie (shells, etc., for small change), iii. 202
Craft (many names for, connected with Arabic), vii. 212
Creases in the stomach insisted upon, v. 327
Created for a mighty matter (*i.e.* for worship and to prepare for futurity), v. 8
Creation (is it and its Empire not His?), iv. 219
—— (from nothing), vii. 154
Crenelles = Sharáríf, iii. 285
Crepitus ventris and ethnology, iv. 97
Crescent of the breakfast-féte, vii. 316
Crescent-like = emaciated, vii. 34
Crew (Ar. Bahriyah, Nawátíyah), vi. 176
Criss-cross row, iii. 24
Crocodiles (breath of), iv. 370
Cross-bows, v. 262
Crow (an ill-omened bird), v. 81
Crow-claw and camel-hoof, iii. 334
Cruelty (The mystery of, explained only by a law without law-giver), vii. 117
—— (of the "fair sex" in Egypt), viii. 42
Cubit (the Háshimi = 18 inches), iv. 315
Curs (set them on the cattle = show a miser money, etc.), viii. 17
Curtain (screening a reverend woman from the sight of men-invalids), vii. 405
Cutting (alluding to the scymitar), ii. 129
—— (bones before flesh = "sharp as a razor"), iii. 406
—— (off the right hand, Koranic punishment for theft), i. 254
—— (of the navel string preliminary to naming the babe), i. 212
—— the rope = breaking bounds, i. 322
Cynocephalus (kills men and rapes women), vi. 128

Dabbús = mace, v. 155
Dádat = nurse (Pers.), vi. 356
Dáhish (Al-) = the Amazed, v. 13
Dáirah = circle, inclosure, vii. 348
—— (for a basin surrounded by hills), vii. 376
Dajláh (Dijlah) = Tigris (Heb. Hid-dekel), vi. 301
Dajjál (Al-) = Moslem Anti-Christ, iv. 35
Dakhil-ak = under thy protection, i. 56
Dakiánús = Decianus, ii. 142
Dakkah = settle, v. 309; vi. 239
Dalak = foot-rasp, iii. 368
Dalhamah (Romance of), ii. 335

Dalil = guide ; f. Dalílah = *mis*guiding woman, bawd, ii. 221
Damascus women faméd for sanguinary jealousy, i. 271
Damon and Pythias, iv. 67
Damsel of the tribe = daughter of the chief, v 293
Danaf (Al-) = distressing sickness, iii. 201
Dandán (N.P.) = tooth, i. 404
Dandán (a monstrous fish), vii. 250
Dáni wa Gharíb = friend and foe, iv. 11
Dánik = sixth of drachma or dirham, ii. 103 ; iv. 74
Dár al-Na'ím = Dwelling of Delight, vi. 332
Dara' (dira') = habergeon, coat of ring-mail, etc , ii. 332
Darabukka = tom-tom, i. 286
Darakah = target, iv. 350
Darb al-Ahmar = Red Street (in Cairo), viii. 8
Darb al-Asfar = the Street called Yellow, iii. 218
Darbar = public audience, i. 26
Dárfíl = dolphin, vii. 403
Darr al-Káil = divinely he spoke who said, iii. 149
Darrij = Let them slide, iii. 337
Dastúr = leave, permission, i. 61
Datura Stramonium (the insane herb), iv. 376
Dáúd = David, ii. 181
Daughter of my uncle = my wife, i. 64
"Daughters of God" (the three), v. 186
—— (of Sa'adah = zebras), ii. 290
—— (of the bier = Ursa major), ii. 254 ; iii. 9
Daulat (Pr. N.) = fortune, empire, kingdom, vi. 132
Daurak = narrow-mouthed jug, i. 33
David (makes coats of mail), ii. 181 ; v. 28
Dawá' = medicine (for a depilatory), vii. 228
Dawát = wooden ink-case with reed-pens, vii. 195
Dawn-breeze, ii. 81
Day of Doom (mutual retaliation), ii. 350
—— (length of), iii. 83
—— (when wealth availeth not, etc.), vii. 96
—— (ye shall be saved from its misery), vii. 374
Daylam (AL), soldiers of = warlike as the Daylamites, vi. 237
Daylamites, i. 414
Dayyús = pimp, wittol, vii. 358
Dead (buried at once), iv. 145
Death (from love), iv. 94
—— (every soul shall taste of it), iv. 123
—— (of a good Moslem), iv. 124
—— (manners of, symbolised by colours), v. 156
—— (simply and pathetically sketched), viii. 44
"Death in a crowd as good as a feast" (Persian proverb), ii. 363
Death-prayer (usually a two-bow prayer), iv. 408
Debts (of dead parents sacred to the children), vii. 370
Deeds of prowess not exaggerated, ii. 12
Deity of the East despotic, iii. 240
Delicacy of the female skin, vii. 379
"Delight of the Intelligent" (fancy title of a book), iv. 417

Demesne (Ar. Himá), vi. 372
Democracy of despotism, vii. 170
Deposits are not lost with Him = He disappointeth not, etc., vi. 120
Despite his nose = against his will, i. 23
Despotism (tempered by assassination), v. 115
Destiny blindeth human sight, i. 62
Destructiveness of slaves, i. 378
Devil (was sick, etc.), ii. 161
—— (stoned at Mina), iv. 157, 166
—— (allowed to go about the world and seduce mankind), vii. 159
Devotees (address Allah as a lover would his beloved), iv. 214
Devotees (white woollen raiment of), vi. 6
Dhámí = the Trenchant (sword of Antar), v. 176
Diamond (its cutting of very ancient date), vii. 383
Diamonds (occurring in alluvial lands), iv. 309
Diaphoresis (a sign of the abatement of a disease), vii. 219
Dihliz = passage, v. 25
Di'ibil al-Khuzá'i (poet), iv. 88
Dijlah (Tigris), River and Valley of Peace, vi. 208
Dimágh = brain, meningx (for head), v. 372
Dimyat (vulg. Dumíyat) = Damietta, iv. 127
Din (AL) al-a'raj = the perverted Faith, vii. 92
Dinár = gold-piece, Daric, Miskál, i. 29
—— (description of one), vii. 355
Dinghy, (Kárib), iii. 288
Dirás = thrashing sled, ii. 12
Dirham = silver-piece, i. 30
Dirham-weight = 48 grains avoir., ii. 209
Dirhams (50,000 = about £1,250), v. 303
—— (thousand = £375), vii. 169
Disposition (sudden change of), vi. 360
Dissection (practised on simiads), iv. 173
Dist (Dast) = large copper cauldron, vi. 327
Diversion of an Eastern Potentate, vi. 321
Divining rod (dowsing rod), iii. 198
Divorce (triple), iii. 76
Diwán (fanciful origin of the word), vii. 182
Diwán al-Baríd = Post-office, vi. 126
Diyár-i-Bakr = maid-land, iv. 33
Do not to others what thou wouldest not they do unto thee, v. 40
"Dog" and "hog" popular terms of abuse, i. 173
Doggerel (royal), iv. 22
—— (phenomenal), iv. 236
—— (sad), iv. 244
—— (not worse than usual), vi. 372, 374
Dogs (clothed in hot-damp countries), iii. 379
—— (in Eastern cities), v. 394
Donánmá (rejoicings for the pregnancy of a Sultana), vi. 110
Donkey-boy, like our "post-boy," of any age, v. 355
Donning woman's attire in token of defeat, v. 381
Doomsday (horrors of, come upon a man), ii. 130
Door (behind it the door-keeper's seat), iv. 129

Door-hinges, ii. 113
Door-keepers (in Egypt mostly Berbers), v. 99
Doors (usually shut with a wooden bolt), ii. 417
—— (pulled up = raised from the lower hinge-pins), vi. 136
Double entendre, iii. 21; vi. 304, 396
Dove and turtle-dove female, i. 349
Down (of the cheek), ii. 137
Drama (in Turkey and Persia), viii. 150
Dramatic scene (told with charming naïveté), viii. 8
Draught of air (Zug) feared by Orientals, i. 336
Drawbridges in Coptic convents, i. 414
Dream (Speaker in a), iii. 401
Dreams (true at later night), iii. 44
—— (lovers meet in), iv. 15
—— (play an important part in the romances of chivalry), vi. 267
Dress (scarlet, of a King in anger), iii. 197
Drinking at dawn, ii. 247
—— their death-agony = suffering similar pain, iii. 95
—— (before or after dinner), v. 329
—— (in the dark disliked), i. 318
—— first to show the absence of poison, i. 81, 253
—— bouts (attended in bright dresses), v. 86
Dromedary (*see* Camel).
—— (guided by a nose-ring), ii. 342
"Drop" unknown to the Eastern gallows, i. 239
Drop (black, of the heart), iii. 365
Drowning (a martyr's death), vii. 230
"Drugging" not a Badawi sentiment, ii. 26
Drugs (is this an art of——?), v. 342
Drunk with the excess of his beauty, iii. 162; v. 356
Drunken habits of Central African races, vi. 142
Drunken son (excused by mother, rebuked by father), vii. 22
Dúbarah (Dubárá) = Dubrornik, Ragusa, ii. 118
Due demanded leads to imprisonment for arrears, vi. 320
Dukhán = smoke (meaning tobacco for the Chibouk), vii. 210
Dukhúl = going in to the bride, iii. 158
Duláb = water-wheel; buttery; cupboard; vii. 365
Dung (used as fuel, etc.), ii. 51
Dunyá (Pr. N.) = world, ii. 234; iii. 99; viii. 25
Dunyázad = world free (?), i. 13
Darbar of idols, vii. 384
Durká'ah = lower part of the floor (opposed to Liwán), iii. 197
Durrah (vulg. for Zarrah, *q.v.*)
Dust-storm in tropical lands, i. 102
Duwámah = whirlpool, vii. 169

"Early to bed," etc. (modern version of the same), vi. 8
East and West (confounded by a beauty-dazed monk), vii 15
Easterns sleep with covered heads, iii. 123
Eatables (their exchange must be equal), iv. 158
Eating (together makes friends), ii. 296

Eating (gives rights of guestship), iii. 331
—— (superstitious belief in its power), iii. 335
—— (how it should be done), iv. 160
Eating and drinking (before thinking of the lover), vi. 405
Eedgáh (*see* Idgáh), ii. 102
Effendi (Turkish title = our esquire), iii. 179
Eginhardt (belonged to the clerical profession), vii. 58
Egypt (derivation of the name), vii. 347
Egyptian (= archi-) polisonnerie, iii. 30
Egyptian vulgarism, iii. 231
—— characteristic, *ib.* 374
Elephant (derivation of the word), ii. 8
Elephant-faced, Vetála, v. 235
Elephant's roll = swaying and graceful gait, i 200
Elephants frightening horses, v. 260
Elevation (nothing strange in sudden), viii. 50
Eli-Fenioun = Polyphemus, vi. 146
Elliptical expression, v. 192
Elliptical style of the Eastern story-teller, vii. 232
Emancipation (the greater = pardon for sins or holy death), ii. 65
Embracing (like the Lám embraceth the Alif), iii. 358
Emerald (white?), iii. 284
—— (mace-head of), iv. 405
—— (-rods in lattice windows), v. 29
Emirs (of the wild Arabs) = "Phylarchs," vii. 382
Emma (hides her lover under her cloak), vii. 89
Empire (endureth with infidelity but not with tyranny), iv 142
Enemy (his offered hand to be kissed or cut off), ii. 45
"Enfants terribles" in Eastern guise, v. 119
Entertainments (names of), vi. 378
Envying another's wealth wrongs him, iv. 415
Ephesus (The Seven Sleepers of), ii. 351
Epistasis without prostasis, vii. 307
Ernest (Duke of Bavaria, Romance of), viii. 138
Erotic specialists among the Ancients, viii. 182
Eunuch best go-between, i. 260
—— employed as porter, i. 317
—— different kinds of, i. 122
—— (driving the people out of a lady's way), iii. 248
—— (avoid allusion to their misfortune), iv. 15
Eunuch-in-Chief a most important Jack-in-Office, i. 261
Euphemisms, i. 28, *et seq.*
Euphemy (announcing death), iii. 187
—— (thou shalt die), *ib.* 215
—— (all is well), *ib.* 259
—— (the far one is a Nazarene), *ib.* 332
Euphuistic speech, vi. 73; vii. 122
Euthanasia and anæsthetics, vii. 166
Evacuation (and constipation), iii. 29
Eve (Ar. Hawwá), iv. 99
Evil (befalling thee is from thyself), v. 51
Exaggeration part of humour, i. 11

Exaggeration characteristic of The Nights, iii. 385; iv. 253
Expiation of oaths, ii. 87
Eye (darkening from wine or passion), iii. 12
—— (orbits slit up and down the face of a hideous Jinn), iii. 22
—— (man of the=pupil), iii. 70
—— (white=blind), iii. 103
—— (the evil), on children, *ib.* 165
—— (babes of the), *ib.* 361
—— (likened to the letter Sád, the brow to Nún), iv. 2
—— (for helper), iv. 27
—— (Thou shalt be in mine=I will keep thee as though thou wert the apple of my eye), vi. 244
" Eye of the needle " (for wicket), vii. 379
Eyebrows joined a great beauty in Arabia, i. 209
Eyes (of me=my dears), i. 150
—— (hot=full of tears), ii. 3
—— (becoming white=blind), ii. 179
—— (bandaged before beheading), iii. 266
—— (blue ones), iii. 311
—— (one-eyed men), *ib.* 313
—— (plucking or tearing out of, a Persian practice), vi. 143
—— (" sunk " into the head for our " starting " from it), v. 237
—— (Babylonian=bewitching), vii. 14
—— (no male has ever filled mine=none hath pleased me), vii. 290

FABLES proper (oldest part of the Nights), ii. 337
Face-veil=" nose-bag," i. 76
Faces (on the Day of Judgment), iii. 364
Fadaises of a blue stocking, ii. 58
Faghfúr (Mosl. title for the Emperor of China), vi. 120
Fa-immá 'alayhá wa-immá bihá=whether (luck go) against it or (luck go) with it, vi. 307
Faintings and trances (common in romances of chivalry), vi. 271
Fairer to-day than fair of yesterday=ever increasing in beauty, iii. 110
Fájirah=harlot (often mere abuse without special meaning), vi. 263
Fakíh=divine, vi. 111
Fakír=religious mendicant generally, i. 87; iv. 7
—— (The, and his jar of butter; congeners of the tale), vii. 119
Fakru (AL) fakhrí=poverty is my pride (saying of Mohammed), iv. 218
Fál=omen, iv. 97
Falak (clearing)=breaking forth of light from darkness, ii. 248
Falastin, degraded to " Philister," v. 299
Falcon (*see* Hawk, Bázi)
Falcon (binding the quarry), i. 47
Falling on the back (a fair fall in wrestling), i. 412
—— (with laughter), iii. 86
Fals ahmar=a red cent, i. 296
Familiarity between the great and paupers, i. 357
—— of girls with black slave-boys, i. 373
Family (euphemistically for wife), iv. 413
Far off one (The, shall die), iii 215
Faráis (pl of farísah)=shoulder-muscles, vi. 10

Faráiz = orders expressly given in the Koran, i 155
Farajiyah = a long-sleeved robe, i. 193, 296
Faránik (Al-) = letter-carrier, vi. 126
Faranj (Al-) = European, i. 273
Faráshah, noun of unity of Farásh = butterfly-moth, vi. 93
Pard Kalmah = a single word (vulgarism), vi. 337
Farid = unique; union-pearl, viii. 51
Fáriki, adjective of Mayyáfárikin, v. 203
Fárikin for Mayyáfárikin (city in Diyarbakr), v. 22
Fáris = rider, knight, vi. 100
Farkh Akrab (vulgarism for Ukayrib) = a young scorpion, iii. 173
Farkh Samak = fish-chick (for young fish), vi. 300
Farrásh, a man of general utility, tent-pitcher, etc., v. 206
Fars = Persia, iii. 439
Farsakh = parasang, iii. 346
—— = three English miles, ii. 18
Farsalah = parcel, vi. 312
Farz = obligatory prayer, v. 103
—— (mentioned after Sunnat because jingling with Arz), vii. 96
Fás = city of Fez, v. 131
Fass = bezel of a ring, gem cut en cabochon, contenant for contenu, i. 152; ii. 2
Fast (and its break), iv. 155
—— (when forbidden), iv. 215
Faswán Salh al-Subyán (Pr. N) = Dung of children, vii. 92
Fat and Thin (dispute between), iii. 368
Fatà = a youth; generous man, etc., i. 62
Fatalism and Predestination, vii. 124
Fate (written in the Sutures of the skull), vi. 383
—— (and Free-will), vii. 157
Fath (Al-), bin Khákán (boon companion of Al-Mutawakkil), vii 312
Father of Bitterness = the Devil, v. 314
Fátihah (the opening chapter of the Koran), iii. 164
—— (position of the hands in reciting it), iv. 45
—— (recited seven times for greater solemnity), iv 139
—— (repeated to confirm an agreement), v. 125
—— (quoted), vi. 74
—— (pronouncd to make an agreement binding), vii. 211
Fátimah (Pr. N.) = the Weaner, v. 58
—— (daughter of Mohammed), vi. 396
Fatimite (Caliphs, their colours green), v. 3
Fátin = tempter, seducer, ii 306
Fátir = Creator, (chapter of the Koran), vi. 150
Fatis = carrion, corps crévé, v. 375
Fatúrát = light food for early breakfast, viii. 11
Fausta and Crispus, v. 42
Favours foresnadowing downfall, i. 45
—— (not lawful until sanctified by love), vi. 373
Fawn (for a graceful youth), vii. 61
Faylasúf = philosopher, iv. 186
Faylasúfiyah = philosopheress, v. 341
Faylúlah = slumbering after sunset, ii. 79
Fayyáz (AL) = the overflowing (with benefits), v. 297
Fazl = grace, exceeding goodness, vi. 12

Fealty of the Steep, iv. 243
Fearing for the lover first, vi. 46
Fee delicately offered, v. 357
Feet (lack the European development of sebaceous glands), vi. 200
—— (coldness of), a symptom of impotence, vii. 50
Fellah = peasant, husbandman, vii. 120
Fellah chaff, vii. 225
Female depravity going hand in hand with perversity of taste, i. 67
Female (Amazon) Island, vi. 217
Feminine mind prone to exaggeration, vi. 184
—— friend does not hesitate to prescribe fibs, vi. 195
—— persistency of purpose (confirmed by "consolations of religion"), vi. 253
Festival (Ar. Íd), vi. 293
Fi al-Khawáfik = among the flags, etc., iv. 28
Fi al-Kamar = in the moonshine (perhaps allusion to the Comorin Islands), vi. 58
Fiat *in*justitia ruat Cœlum, i. 232
Fidá = ransom, self-sacrifice, vi. 194
Fidáan = instead of, vi. 194
Fig and sycamore, vii. 6
Fights easily provoked at Funerals or wedding processions, v. 383
Fikh = theology, vi. 111
Fillet = the Greek "Stephane," vi 357
Fillets hung on trees to denote an honoured tomb, v. 294
Fine feathers make fine birds, vi. 349
Fingán (for Finján) = (coffee-) cup, vi. 348
Finger in mouth (sign of grief), ii. 197
—— (run round the inside of a vessel), vi 348
Finger-tips (making marks in the ground), vi. 228
Fingers (names of), vii. 232
Fingers and toes (separated to wash between them), iv. 152
Finján = egg-shell cup for coffee, vii. 330
Firásah = physiognomy, vii. 59
Firdaus = Paradise, vii. 282
Firdausi, the Persian Homer, quoted, ii. 307
Fire (and sickness cannot cohabit), ii. 284
—— (worshippers slandered), iii. 106
—— (of Hell, but not shame), iv. 98
—— (handled without injury, a common conjuring trick), iv. 220
—— (there is no blower of = utter desolation), iv. 356
—— (forbidden as punishment), iv. 366
—— (none might warm himself at their), v. 166
—— = Hell (home of suicides), vii. 106
Fire-arms mentioned, v. 262
Fire-sticks (Zand, Zandah), iv. 20
Firmán = Wazirial order, iii. 187
First at the feast and last at the fray, ii. 306
First personal pronoun placed first for respect, i. 217
Fí sabili 'llahi = on Allah's path (martyrdom), iii. 362
Fish (begins to stink at the head), ii. 69
—— (-island), iv. 347
—— (the ass-headed), iv. 373
—— (great = Hút, common = Samák), iv. 408

Fish (changed into apes, true Fellah "chaff"), vi. 298
—— (of Paradise, promising acceptance of prayer), vi. 313
Fishár=squeeze of the tomb, iv. 73
Fisherman (Arab contrasted with English), iv. 19
Fist (putting into fist=putting one's self at another's mercy), ii. 176
Fitnah=revolt, seduction, mischief, beautiful girl, aphrodisiac perfume, i. 201, 397
Fits of religious enthusiasm, ii. 35
Flatterers (the worst of foes), i. 338
Flattery (more telling because proceeding from the heart), vi. 258
Flea (still an Egyptian plague), v. 114
Flirtation impossible in the East, v. 375
Floor (sitting upon the, sign of deepest dejection), vi. 101
Flowers of speech, i. 408
Flying for delight, ii. 252
Food-tray of Sulayman, iv. 417
Folk follow their King's faith, ii. 59
Following one's face=at random, i. 320
Food (partaken gives rights of protection), iii. 331
—— (superstitious belief in its power), *ib.* 335
Foot (smallness of, sign of blood) iii. 15
—— (prehensile powers of the Eastern), v. 373
"Forbid not yourselves the good things which Allah hath allowed you," iv. 169
"Forcible eateth feeble," vii. 250
Fore-arm (for proficiency), vii. 365
Formality (a sign of good breeding) vii. 42
Formication (accompanying a paralytic stroke), iv. 202
Formula of praise pronounced to avert the evil eye, iii. 12
Fortalice of Fruits (Ar. Hisu al-Fakihah), v. 274
Fortune makes kneel her camel by some other one=encamps with a favourite, ii. 363
"Forty days"=our "honeymoon," vi. 204
Foster-brother (dearer than kith and kin), iii. 43
Fountain-bowl (ornamented with mosaic, etc.), ii. 203
Fourteen (expressed by seven and seven, or five and five plus four), vi. 226
Fox (Ar. Abú Hosayn, Salab), v. 120
—— (cunning man), ii. 354
—— and Jackal (confounded by the Arabic dialects), viii. 112
Frail (Ar. Farsalah) vi. 312
Frame (crescent-like by reason of its leanness), vii. 34
Freedom (granted to a slave for the sake of reward from Allah), vii. 310
Freeing slaves for the benefit of the souls of the departed, ii 430
Free-will (and the Korán), iii. 387
Friday night=our Thursday night, i. 247
Friday service described, i. 289
Friend (feminine, does not hesitate to prescribe a fib), vi. 195
Friends (weeping when they meet after long parting), iii. 154
—— ("damned ill-natured ones"), iii 259
Frolics of high-born ladies, i 303
Front-teeth wide apart (a beauty amongst the Egyptians, not the Arabs), vi. 298
Fruit of two kinds, v. 181
Fruits (fresh and dry), iv. 261

Fulán (fulano in Span. and Port.) = a certain person, ii. 411; iii 390
Fulk = boat, iv. 400
Full, Fill = Arabian jessamine, vii. 9
Fumigations to cite Jinnis, etc, vi. 147; vii 109
"Fun" = practical jokes of the largest, i. 204
"Fundamentals (Usúl) remembered" = the business is not forgotten, i. 341
Funduk = Fondaco, vi. 333
Funerals (meritorious to accompany), i. 370
Furát = Euphrates (derivation of the name), vii. 98
Furaydun, *see* Afridun, i. 402
Furkán = Korán, iii. 215
Fustát = Old Cairo, v. 4
Fútah = napkin, waistcloth, vi. 129
Futúr = breakfast, i. 276; vii. 367
Fuzayl bin 'Iyáz (Sufi ascetic), vii. 102

GALACTOPHAGI (use milk always in the soured form), v. 110; vi. 144
Gall-bladder and liver allusions, i. 202
Galland, Antoine (memoir of), viii. 87 *et seqq.*
"Gallery" (speaking to the), vi. 280
Garden (in the Prophet's tomb at Al-Medinah), v. 289
—— (the Perfumed of the Cheykh Nefzaoui), viii. 121.
Gardeners touchy on the point of mated visitors, i. 348
Gardens (with rivers flowing underneath, Koranic phrase), iv. 301
Gate (of war opened), vii. 91
Gates (two to port towns), iii. 66
—— (of Heaven are open), vii. 289
—— (shut during Friday devotions from fear of "Sicilian Vespers"), vii. 322
Gaw-i-Zamín = the Bull of the Earth, iv. 270
Gazelles' blood red (dark red dye), viii. 11
Gems and their mines, iv. 359
Genealogy (Arab. begins with Adnán), iv. 63
Generosity (an Arab's ideal because the reverse of his nature), i. 361
—— (peculiar style of), vi. 109
Geography in its bearings on morality, iii. 28
Geomantic process, iii. 55
German Translations of The Nights, viii 102 *et seqq.*
Ghábah = thicket, i 406; iii. 168
Ghadir = a place where water sinks, low land, i. 215
Ghadr = cheating, vi. 364
Gháliyah (Al-) = older English Algallia, vi. 367
Ghalyun = galleon, vii. 212
Ghamz = winking, signing with the eyes, i. 269
Ghandúr = a gallant, v 375
Gharám (Pr. N.) = eagerness, desire, love-longing, ii. 392
Gharámah = avanie, vi. 302
Gharíb = foreigner, i. 87
Ghashim = "Johnny Raw," ii. 222
Gháshiyah = étui, scabbard; sleeved cloak, iii 253
Ghatrafán (Pr. N) = proud, petulant, iv. 305

Ghaut = Sarídah, *q.v.*, iv. 175
Ghawási = singing-girls, i. 197
Ghaylúlah = slumbering in the morning, ii. 79
Ghayúr = jealous (applies to Time), vi. 223
Ghazá = Artemisia (a desert shrub), i. 350; iii. 9; v. 102; vii. 107
Ghazálah = gazelle (a slave-girl's name), vii 278
Ghazanfar ibn Kamkhil = Lion son of (?), iv. 307
Ghayb (AL) = secret purpose, future, vii. 374
Ghazbán (N P) = an angry, violent man, ii. 28
Ghází = fighter for the faith, ii. 138; vi 358
Ghazl al-banát (girls' spinning) = vermicelli, i. 77
Ghazwah = raid, foray, razzia, ii. 116
Ghilmán = Wuldán, the beautiful youths of Paradise, i. 194
—— (counterpart of the Houris), iv. 31
Ghimd (Ghamad) = scabbard, iv. 117
Ghost (phantom = Tayf), iii. 38
Ghúl = ogre, cannibal, iv. 376
Ghúlah = ogress, i 50
Ghulámíyah = girl dressed like a boy to act cup-bearer, viii. 37
Ghull = iron collar, vii. 391
Ghúls (whose bellies none may fill but Allah), vii. 225
Ghuráb al-Bayn = raven of parting, iii. 178; vi. 17
Ghuráb = galleon (grab), vii. 56
Ghurbah (AL) Kurbah = "Travel is Travail," vii. 320
Gurrah = blaze on a horse's forehead, ii. 340; viii. 37
Ghusl = complete ablution, iv. 153
Ghusl al-Sihhah = washing of health, iii. 52
Ghussah = calamity which chokes, wrath, ii. 50
Ghútah = thickly grown lowland, i. 106
"Gift (from me to," etc. = "I leave it to you, sir"), vi 80
—— (is for him who is present), vii. 293
Giraffe, exceedingly timid, v. 254
—— unfit for riding, v. 261
Girding the Sovereign (found in the hieroglyphs), vi. 114
Girl (of nine plus five = in her prime), iv. 147
Give a man luck and throw him into the sea, iii. 120
Glance compared with a Yamáni sword, ii. 30
Gloom = black hair of youth, vi. 65
Glooms gathering and full moons dawning, for hands and eyes, vi. 37
Gnostic absurdities, viii. 172
Goad (of the donkey-boy), ii. 339
Godiva (an Arabic Lady—of the wrong sort), vii 324
Gold (makes bold), i. 313
—— (different names of, required by Arabic rhetoric), iii. 221
—— (when he looked at it, his life seemed a light thing to him), vi. 30
—— (liquid = Vino d'Oro), viii. 38
Gold-pieces (stuck on the cheeks of singing-girls, etc.), vii. 12
Gong (Ar. Mudawwarah), iii. 257
Good news, Inshallah = is all right with thee? vii. 292
Gospel of Infancy, ii 127
Gossamer (names for), iii. 6
Gourd (Ar. Hanzal), vii. 236

Grammatical double entendres, vii. 334
Grandfather's name given familiarly, i. 342
Grapes (bunch of, weighing twenty pounds, no exaggeration), vi 142
Grave (levelling slave and sovereign), iii. 103
"Greatness belongeth to God alone" (used elliptically), v. 192
Green (colour of the Fatimite Caliphs), v. 3
Green garb (distinguishing mark of Al-Khisr), vii. 382
Greetings before the world, iv. 3
Grim joke (showing elation of spirits), vi. 110
Grimm's "Household Tales," quoted, v. 137
Groom (falling in love with), vii. 76
Ground (really kissed), vi 47
Ground-floor usually let for shops, i. 294
Guadalajara = Wady al-Khara (of dung), vii. 91
"Guebre" introduced by Lord Byron, vi. 167
Guest-rite, v. 318
Guest (must be fed before his errand is asked), vi. 105
Gull-fairs, vi. 245

Habáb (Habá) = motes, iii. 371
Habash = Abyssinia and something more, iv. 337
Habb = grain of the heart, i. 230
Habb al 'ubb (a woman's ornament), v. 396
Habbániyah = grain-sellers' quarter, i. 247
Habba-zá! = good this! iv. 19
Habib, euphemism for lover, i. 205
Habibi wa tabíbí = my love and leach, vii. 360
Habitations (names given to them by the Arabs), vi. 376
Habl = cord; cause, vi. 254
Habzalam (Pr. N. = seed of tyranny; "Absalom?"), iii. 192
Hadas = surmise, vi. 89
Hadbá (the bulging bier), iii. 189
Hádí (AL) Caliph, iv. 57
Hadíd = iron, ii. 209
Hadís = tradition of the Prophet, iii. 325; iv. 156
Hadís = saying of the Apostle, tradition, iv. 156
Háfiz (f Háfizah) = 1. Traditionist; 2. One who can recite the Koran by rote; v. 104
Háfiz quoted, vi. 272
Hafsah (Caliph Omar's daughter and wife of Mohammed), ii. 66
Hafsites (Dynasty in Mauritania), *ib.*
Hail (within sight of the Equator), vi. 122
Hair (should be allowed all to grow or be shaven off), i. 284
Hair-dyes (all vegetable matter), i. 301
—— (Mohammed on), iii. 312
Hair-strings (of black silk), iii. 91
—— (significance of), iii. 93
Hájah = a needful thing (for something, somewhat), vi. 134
Hajar-coinage, v. 293
Hajar Jahannam = hell-stone, lava, basalt, iv. 321

Hájib = groom, chamberlain, ii. 198; iii. 20
Hajin (tall camel), ii. 292
Hajj = Pilgrimage, iv. 157
Hájj (or Háji, not Hajji), iii. 333
Hajj al-Akbar and Hajj al-Asgar, ii. 70
Hajjáj (AL) bin Yúsuf, Governor of Al-HiJáz and Al-Irák, iii. 133; v. 295
Hajjám = barber-surgeon, cupper, bleeder, iii. 235
Hákim = ruler, not to be confounded with Hakim, doctor, etc., v. 230
Ha'kim (AL) bi-amri 'llah (Caliph), iii. 407
—— (not to be confounded with the Fatimite), iv. 50
Hakk (Al-) = the Truth (Allah), iv. 232
Hakk = right (Hakkí = mine), vii. 66
Halab = Aleppo, i 269
Halabi Shalabí = the Aleppine is a fellow fine, iv. 31
Haláwat = sweetmeat, iii. 186; v. 396
Haláwat al-Salámah = sweetmeat for the returning of a friend, vii. 57
Halfah-grass (Poa), i. 344
Halib = fresh milk, v. 110
Halimah = the mild, gentle (fem), vii. 327
Haling by the hair a reminiscence of "marriage by capture," vi. 198
Hallaling, Anglo-Indian term for the Moslem rite of killing animals for food, v 211
Halumma = bring! v. 315
Halummú = drew near (plur.), vii. 123
Halwá = sweetmeats, i. 370; ii. 111
Hamadán (town in Persian Mesopotamia), vii. 281
Hámah (soul of a murdered man in form of a bird sprung from his head), iii. 77
Hamáil = baldricks, iv. 117
Hamám = wood-pigeon, iv. 17
—— (al-Ayk) = culver of the copse, iv. 17
Hamath = Hightown, ii. 79
Hamid (fem Hamidah) = praiseworthy, satisfactory, vii. 153
Hammál al-Hatabi = one who carries fuel, v. 259
Hammám (going to the = convalescence), i. 266
—— (hired for private parties), iv. 30
Hammám-bath (a luxury as well as a necessity), ii. 245
Hamzah (uncle of the Prophet), vi. 321
Hanabát = "hanap," vi 350
Hanbal, *see* Ahmad bin Hanbal, ii. 104
Hand (left, how used), iii. 252
—— (white, symbol of generosity; black, of niggardness), *ib.* 304
—— (his for her), *ib.* 391
—— (cut off in penalty for theft), vi. 314
—— (cut off for striking a father), vii. 22
Handfuls (the two), iv. 161
Handkerchief of dismissal, viii. 45
Hands (behind the back, posture of submission), iii 7
—— (stained in stripes like ring-rows of a chain armour), ii. 396
—— (how held in reciting the Fátihah), iv. 45
—— (bitten in repentance), iv. 146
—— (their feel guides the physician), iv. 173
Hanien = pleasant to thee! after drinking, i. 333

Hanífah, *see* Abú Hanífah, ii. 107
Hanút = tavern, booth, etc., iv. 101
Hanzal = gourd, iii. 432 ; vii. 236
Harámí = one who lives on unlawful gains, vii. 220
Harbak = javelin, v. 245
Hard of heart and soft of sides, i. 332
Harf = letter, syllable, ii. 200
Harím = Harem, used for the inmates, i. 152
—— (double entendre = Harem and Honour), iii. 222
—— (= wife), *ib.* 248
—— (hot-bed of Sapphism and Tribadism), iv. 349
Hariri (Al-) = the silk-man (poet), iv. 116
—— (lines quoted from), viii. 42
Harisah, a favourite dish, i. 121
Harjáh = (a man of) any place, iii. 440
Hark, you shall see, vii. 95
Harrák (ship = Carrack ?), iii. 253
Harrákát = carracks (also used for cockboat), vi. 122
Hárún al-Rashid (described by Al-Siyúti), vi. 311
—— (as a poet), vii. 98
—— (said to have prayed every day a hundred bows), vii. 397
—— (and Charlemagne), viii. 123
Hárút and Márút (sorcerer angels), iii. 6
Harwalah = pas gymnastique, ii. 343
Hasá (Al-) = plain of pebbles, west of Damascus, i. 215
Hasab = quantity opposed to Nasab = birth, iii. 291
Hasab wa nasab = inherited degree and acquired dignity, iii. 291 ; vi 68
Hasan al-Basri (theologian), ii. 67
Hasan bin Sahl (Wazir of Al-Maamun), iii. 247
Hasanta yá Hasan = bene detto, Benedetto ! i. 231
Háshimí = descendant of Háshim (Mohammed's great-grandfather), vii 105
—— cubit = 18 inches, iv. 315
—— vein, i. 345
Hashish (intoxicant prepared of hemp), i. 207 ; ii. 315
—— (orgie in London), ii. 315
—— (said to him = his mind, under its influence, suggested to him), vi. 306
Hashsháshún = assassins, ii. 315
Hásib Karim al-Din (Pr. N.), iv. 246
Hásid = an envier, iii. 258
Hásil, Hásilah = cell, vi. 333, 334
Hassún (diminutive of Hasan), vi. 237
Haste ye to salvation, part of the Azán, i. 206
Hátif = mysterious voice, i. 131
Hatím = broken wall (at Meccah), vi. 10
Hátim (Pr. N)—black crow, vi. 135
Hátim al-Asamm (the Deaf), ii. 107
Hátim of Tayy (proverbial for liberality), iii. 219
Hattin (battle of), vii. 100
Haudaj (Hind. Howda) = camel-litter for women, vi. 381
Hauk ! Hauk ! = hee haw ! i. 203
"Haunted" = inhabited by Jinns, iv. 131
Haurání towns (weird aspect of), v. 19

Haurani towns (their survival accounted for by some protracted drought), v. 31
Hawá al-Uzri = platonic love, ii. 198
Hawar = intensity of black and white in the eyes, iii. 20
Háwi = juggler playing tricks with snakes, ii. 367; vii. 135
Háwiyah (name of a hell), vii. 77
Hawk, ii. 285, 360
Hawwá = Eve, iv. 99
Hayát al-Nufús = Life of Souls, iii. 68
Hayhát, onomatopoetic for lover, i. 70
Haykal = temple, chapel, iv. 147
Hazár = (the bird of) a thousand (songs), iv. 16
Hazár Afsáneh (tales from the), vii. 112; viii. 67, 85
Házir and Bádi = townsman and nomad, iii. 22
Hazramaut (Hazarmaveth), iii. 241; iv. 96
Hazrat = our mediæval "presentia vostra," vi. 399
Hazza-hu = he made it (the javelin) quiver, v. 245
"He" for "she" out of delicacy, ii. 80
Head (must always be kept covered), iii. 60
Head in the poke = into the noose, i. 165
Head-kerchief (déshabillé), ii. 220
Headsman delaying execution, ii. 267
"Hearer" not "reader" addressed, vii. 49
Heart (black drop in the), iii. 365
—— (from one full of wrath = in spite of himself), iv. 35
Heart-ache (for stomach-ache = mal au cœur), v. 104
Heaven (Ar. Na'ím), iii. 264
Heavens (names of the seven), vi. 264
Hell (Sa'ír), iii. 264
—— (cold as well as hot), iii. 367
Hells (names of the seven and their intended inhabitants), vi. 264
Hemistichs divided, ii. 386
Henna-flower (its spermatic odour), vi. 40
Herb (the insane), iv. 376
Heroes and heroines of love-tales are bonnes fourchettes, vi. 87
Heroine of Eastern romance eats well, ii. 388
Heroism of a doubtful character, vi. 185
Hesperides (apples of the, probably golden nuggets), vii. 8
Hibá = cords, garters, ii. 133
Hibál = ropes, iii. 312
High-bosomed damsel a favourite with Arab tale-tellers, i. 78
Hijáz (Al-) = Moslem Holy Land, ii. 200
Hijl = partridge, ii. 360
"Him" for "her," ii. 302
Himà = guarded side, demesne, vi. 256, 372
Himalayan brothers, ii. 111, 157
Hind (Al-) al-Aksà = Outer Hind or India, vii. 190
Hind bint Asmá and the poet Jarir, v. 295
Hindi = Indian Moslem opposed to Hindú, iii. 415
Hindibà = endive, iv. 178
Hinges (of ancient doors), ii. 266
Hippopotamus, iv. 373
Hirah (Christian city in Mesopotamia), iv. 85

Hirakl (monastery of), iv. 99
"His" for "her," vi 206
Hishám bin Abd al-Malik (Caliph), ii. 72, v 302
Hisham ibn Orwah (traditionist), iv. 46
Hisn al-Fákihah = Fortalice of Fruits, v. 274
Hiss = (sensual) perception, vi. 89
Hizám = girdle, vi. 310; viii. 33
Hizb = section of the Koran, iv. 170
Hobbling a camel (how done), v. 316
Hog, popular term of abuse, i. 173
Holiness supposed to act as talisman, ii 148
Honayn (scene of one of Mohammed's battles), iv 33
Honey (of bees as distinguished from cane honey), iv 248
—— (simile for the delights of the world), vii. 142
"Honeymoon" (lasts a week), iv. 29
Honour amongst thieves, ii. 61
Hoof (of the wild ass), iii. 22
Horoscopes, etc., i. 195
Horripilation = goose flesh, ii. 229
Horse (names of), ii. 297
Horse-stealing honourable, *ib*
Horseplay frequently ending in bastinado, i. 300
Horses, (not taught to leap), i. 409
—— (Arab breeds), iv. 197
Hosh = mean courts at Cairo, iv. 126
Hospitals hated, i. 392
Host (enters first as safeguard against guetapens), ii. 427
Hour (of Judgment), iv. 186
Houris, iii. 20
House (haunted = inhabited by Jinns), iv 131
—— (the Holy of Allah = Ka'abah), vii. 249
House of Peace = Baghdad, i. 128
"House of Sadness," vi. 220
House-breaking (four modes of), v. 153
Houses of Lamentation in Moslem burial-grounds, i 68
Housewife (looks to the main chance), vi. 296
Hubb al-Watan = patriotism, ii. 84
Hubkah = doubling of a woman's waistcloth, v 373
Hubúb (Pr. N.) = awaking; blowing hard, vi. 356
Húd (prophet = Heber?), iii. 241
Hudhud = hoopoe, ii. 351
Hudúd al-Haram = bounds of the Holy Places, iv 107
Hullah = dress, v. 373
Hulwán al-miftáh = dénier á Dieu, vii. 281
Humbly (expressed by "standing on their heads"), vii. 15
Humility of the love-lorn Princess artfully contrasted with her previous furiosity, vi. 50
Humming not a favourite practice with Moslems, i. 287
Humours (of Hippocrates), iv. 171
Hump-back (graphically described), vii. 31

Hunchback looked upon with fear and aversion, i. 237
Hunger (burns), ii. 46
Hungry judges, "hanging judges," ii. 98
Húr, pl. = Houris, iii. 20
Húr al-Ayn = with eyes of lively white and black, i. 83
Hurák = tinder, iii. 232
Hurr = gentleman, i. 233
—— = free, noble, independent, opp. to 'Abd = servile, ii. 270
Hurry is from Hell, i. 243
—— (in a newly married couple indecent), iii. 359
Hurúf al-mutabbakát = the flattened sounds, iii. 340
Hút = great fish, iv. 408
Huwayná (AL) = now drawing near now moving away, vii. 316
Hydropathic treatment of wounds held dangerous, iv. 154
Hymeneal blood resembles that of pigeon-poult, i. 373
Hypocrite (Ar. Munáfik), iv. 161
Hysterical Arab temperament, i. 377; ii. 5, 82

Ibáziyah sect, v. 322
Iblis (diabolus) = Despairer, i. 11; iii. 11; vii. 360
—— (Cherubim cherished by Allah), iv. 266
—— (cursed and expelled), iv. 266
Ibn Abbás (Companion), iv. 166
Ibn Abdún al-Andalúsi (poet), iii. 98
Ibn Abi Aufa, ii. 100
Ibn al-Kirnás = son of the chase (for Persian Kurnas = pimp, cuckold?), vi. 308
Ibn al-'Ukáb (Pr. N.) = Son of the Eagle, vi. 346
Ibn Hamdún (transmitter of poetry and history), vii. 297
Ibn Harám = son of adultery, abuse not necessarily reflecting on the parent, i. 213
Ibn 'Irs = weasel, vii. 189
Ibn Muljam (murderer of the Caliph Ali), iii. 99
Ibn Síná = Avicenna, ii. 260
Ibráhim bin Adham, ii. 103
Ibrahim bin al-Mahdi (Pretender to the Caliphate), iii. 227
Ibrahim al-Mausilí iii. 232
Ibrat = needle graver and 'Ibrat = warning, a favourite jingle, i 95
Ibrík = ewer, and Tisht = basin, used for washing the hands, i. 222; v. 341
Ibrísam = raw silk, floss, vi. 136
Ichneumon (mongoose), ii. 369
Ichthyological marvels, iv. 373
'Íd = festivals (the two of Al-Islám), vi. 293
Íd al-Kabír = the Great Festival, i 25
Ídán = festivals (the two of Al-Islam), vi. 293
Iddah = months of a woman's enforced celibacy after divorce, iii. 76
—— (of widowhood), v. 162; vi i. 41
Ídgáh (place of prayer), ii. 102
Ifrit divided into two races like mankind, i. 10
Ifrítah = she-Ifrit, i. 31
Ihdak = encompassing, as the white encloses the black of the eye, i. 45
Ihtiláj-námah = Book of palpitations, vi. 184
Ihtizáz = shaking with delight, i. 54

I'itikáf (Al-) = retreat, iv. 156
Ijtilá = displaying of the bride on her wedding night, v. 389
Ikálah (Al-) = cancelling, "resiliation," iv. 158
Ikh! Ikh! (cry to a camel to make it kneel down), ii. 42
Ikhlás (Al-) = Chapter of Unity, iii. 87
Ikhtiyán al-Khutan = Khaitan (?), viii. 9
Ikhwán al-Safá = Brethren of Purity, ii. 371
Iklil = diadem, now obsolete, i. 249
Iklím = the seven climates of Ptolemy, i. 214
Iksah = plait, etc., v. 345
Iksír (Al-) = dry drug (from ξηρον), iv. 261; vi. 168, 171
Ikyán = living gold, vii. 9, 12
Iláh = God, iv. 150
Iláh al-Arsh = the God of the Empyrean, ii 329
Iliad and Pentaur's Epic, vi. 146
Ill is thy abiding place, ii. 360
Ill-treatment (a plea for a lawful demand to be sold), vi. 211
Ilm al-Káf = K-science for Alchemy, iv 254
Ilm al-Rúhání = Spiritualism, i. 281
Images of living beings forbidden, iii. 417
—— (= statues), iv. 176
Imám = leader, antistes, ii 103
—— (the Seventh = Caliph al-Maamún), iii. 234
Imámah = turband, iii. 224
Imlik (great-grandson of Shem), v. 169
Improvising still common among the Badawin, i. 36
Impudence (intended to be that of a captive Princess), vii 30
Impurity (ceremonial different from dirtiness), iv. 162
Inadvertency of the tale-teller, vi. 293
In'ásh = raising from the bier (a "pick-me-up"), iv 34
Incest (lawful among ancient peoples), i. 102
—— (repugnant to Moslem taste), ii. 73
Inconsequence (of the Author of the Nights), iii. 276
—— (characteristic of the Eastern Saga), iv. 399
—— (of writer of The Nights), v. 114
Incuriousness of the Eastern story-teller, v 257
Index finger (Sháhid), ii. 194
Indian realm, vi. 122
Indraját = white magic, iv 254
Infidel should not be killed unless refusing to become a Moslem or a tributary, v. 265
Infirmity (and infirm letters), iii. 358
Inheritance, law of, settled by the Koran, i 160
Ink-case (descendant of the wooden palette with writing reeds), vi. 320
'Innín = impotence, vii. 50
Innovation (Ar. Bida'ah), iv. 123
Insane (treatment of the), iii. 42
Inscriptions (on trays, plates, etc.), iii 350
Inshád = conjuring by Allah, i. 10
—— = reciting, improvising, ii. 29
Inshallah (Allah willing) = D.V., iii. 398; vi. 258.
Inshallah bukrah = to-morrow D.V., ii. 216

Insolence and licence of palace-girls, i. 264
Insomnia (curious treatment of), iii. 344
Insula (for peninsula), iv. 395
Intellect of man stronger than a Jinni's, i. 40
Intention (of prayer, Niyat), iv. 120, 151
Intercession-doctrine disputed amongst Moslems, i. 365; iv. 194
Internally wounded=sick at heart, i. 5
Inverted speech (forms of), ii. 161; v. 167; vi. 328
Inwá=Jerking the date-stone, i. 22
Iradáh=Sultan's order, iii. 187
Irák=level country beside river banks, ii. 35
—— (etc., used always with the article), v. 193, 194
—— (for Al-Irák in verse), v. 222
Iram (the many-columned), iii. 236; viii. 27
Irán=hearse; Moses' ark, v. 398
Irdabb, *see* Ardabb.
Irishman (the typical, in Arab garb), vi. 340
Irk=root, also sprig, twig, vii. 317
Iron (conjures away friends), ii. 209
Iron padlock (instead of the usual wooden bolt), ii. 417
Irony, iii. 75, 384; vi. 163, 314
Isaak (Ishák) of Mosul, iii. 242; vii. 364
Isbánír=Ctesiphon (?), v. 183
Isengrim (wolf), ii. 368
Isfídáj=ceruse, v. 40
Ishá=the first watch of the night, i. 161
Ishárah=signing, beckoning, v. 25; vi. 379
Ishk 'uzri (in the sense of platonic love), v. 318; vii. 316
Ishmael (place of his sacrifice), iii. 201
Iskandar Zú al-Karnayn=Alexander Matagrobolised, iv. 203; viii. 54
Iskandaríyah=city of Alexander, vii. 25
Island for land, vii. 50
Ism al-A'azam=the Most Great Name of Allah, vi. 284
Ismid=Ithmid, stibium (eye-powder), iii. 87
Israfil (blows the last trumpet), iv. 257
Istikbál=coming forth to greet, ii. 182
Istikhárah=praying for direction by omens, etc., iv. 12
Istinshák=snuffing water through the nostrils, iv. 152
Istitá'ah (=ableness), vii. 157
—— (=free-will), vii. 160
Ithmid (stibium antimone)=Sp. Altimod, ii. 7
"I told you so" (even more common in East than West), iii. 194
Italian Translations of The Nights, viii. 104
Izár=sheet worn as veil, i. 150; iv. 390

J (how it came to take the place of Y in the English Bible), i. 369
Ja'afar contrasting strongly with his master, i. 94
—— (mode of his death), iii. 280
—— (his suspected heresy), viii. 128
—— (river or rivulet), iii. 404

Ja'afar bin Musá al-Hádi (Caliph), iv. 57
Jabábirah = tyrants, giants, conquerors, v. 283; vii. 184, 382
Jabal = mountain (for mountainous island), vii. 374
Jabal al-Ramun = Adam's Peak, iv. 403
Jabal al-Saklá (Thaklá) = mount of the woman bereft of children, iv. 6
Jabal al-Tárik = Gibraltar, iii. 224
Jabal Mukattam (sea-cliff upon which Cairo is built), iv. 326
Jabal Núr, iv. 168
Jábarsá, the city of Japhet, v. 241, 243
Jabarti = Moslem Abyssinian, i. 341
Jábir Atharát al-Kirám = Repairer of the slips of the generous, v. 298
Jábir bin Abdallah (disciple of Mohammed), iv. 168
Jackal's gall (used aphrodisiacally), viii. 112
Jacob's daughters, iii. 143
Jadíd = new (coin), copper, viii. 12
Jáh = high station, dignity, vii. 245
Jahábiz pl. of Jahbaz = acute, intelligent, vii. 141
Jahannam = Hell, iv. 253, 265
Jahárkas = Pers. Chehárkas, four persons, i. 244
Jaláal = small bells for falcons, vii. 7
Jalálah = saying "Jalla Jalalu-hu" = magnified be His Majesty, iv. 170
Jalálikah = Gallicians, vii. 229
Jalaud, not Julned, v. 217
Jalláb = slave dealer, iii. 119
Jallábiyah = gaberdine, iv. 216
Jamá'ah = community, iv. 159
Jamal (Gamal) = camel, ii. 333
Jámi' = cathedral mosque, iv. 212
Jámi'án = two cathedrals, iv. 33
Jamil ibn Ma'amar (poet), ii. 6; v. 314
Jamiz (Jummayz) = sycamore fig, iii. 85
Jamm = ocean, iv. 56
Jammár = palm-pith and cabbage, vii. 7
Janázah = bier with corpse, i. 370
Janázir for Zanájír = chains, vii. 369
Jannat al-Khuld = the Eternal Garden, vii. 282
Jannat al-Na'ím = The Garden of Delights, *i.e.* Heaven, i 90; ii. 245
Jánsháh (Pr. N.) = King of Life, iv. 274; v. 281
Japhet (Ar. Yáfis or Yáfat), v. 241
—— his sword, v. 241
Jar (ridden by witches), vi. 283
Jarir (poet), iv. 107
Jarm (Ar. Bárijah), iv. 365
Jarrah = jar, vi. 327
Jars for cooling water, i. 347
Jásalik (Al-) = Καθολικὸς, Primate, ii. 127
Jauharah (Pr. N. = Jewel), vi. 94
Jauz al-Hindi = cocoa-nut, iv. 394
Jauzá Gemini, viii. 36
Jauzar Bubalus (Ariel), iv. 91
Javelines, v. 168
Jawáb-club, v. 167

Jawámard for Jawanmard=un giovane, a brave, v. 218
Jawán (Pr. N.) Pers.=a youth, Juvenis, iii. 326
Jawári=slave-girls rhyming with dam'a jári=flowing tears, iv. 118
Jawarnah (Júrnah)=Zara, ii. 119
Jawáshiyah=guards, vii. 62
Jawásis, pl. of Jásús=spies (for secret police), vii. 94
Jáwish=apparitor, sergeant, royal messenger, i. 373
Jazírat=Peninsular, Arabia, i. 2; vi. 119
Jazirah (Al-)=Mesopotamia, v. 298
Jazirát al-Khalidát=Eternal Isles=Canaries, i. 130
Jazirat ibn Omar (island and town on the Tigris), viii. 37
Jesus (bird of), iv. 164
—— (crucificed in effigy), iv. 189
—— (compared with Adam), iv. 190
Jew (prefers dying on the floor, not in bed), iv. 199
—— (never your equal, either above or below you), vi. 304
—— (marrying a Moslemah deserves no pity), vi. 407
Jeweller (in Eastern tales generally a rascal), ii. 406
Jews (adepts in magic), ii. 132
Jihád=fighting for the Faith, ii. 265
Jilá=displaying the bride before the bridegroom, i. 160
Jílbáb=habergeon, buff jacket, gown, v. 256; vii. 351
Jink (Al-) effeminates, viii. 18
Jinn=the French génie, the Hindu Rakshasa or Yaksha, i. 9
Jinnis (names of), iii. 13
Job (a Syrian), iii. 338
Joining prayers, ii. 395
Jokh=broad-cloth, ii. 15
Jokh al-Saklát=rich brocade on broad-cloth, vi. 350
Joseph of the Koran very different from him of Genesis, i. 11
—— (and Potiphar's wife), v. 42
Judad (for Judud), pl. of Jadid=new coin, vi. 273
Júdar (classical Arab name), v. 121
—— (and his brethren, version of a Gotha MS.), v. 162
Júdariyah (quarter of Cairo), v. 160
Judgment (hour of), iv. 186
Judri=small-pox, i. 235
Jufún=eyebrows or eyelashes, iii. 373
Juggling with heaven, vi 308
Jugular vein (from — to —), iii. 216
Jujube-sherbet, ii. 210
Julnár=Pers. Gul-i-anár (pomegranate flower), vi. 57
Jum'ah=assembly (Friday), v. 35, 100
Jumblat (for Ján-pulád, Life o' Steel, Pr. N.), v. 30
Junayd al-Baghdádí (Sufi ascetic), vii. 101
Junún=madness, i. 9
Juráb mi'adat-hu (bag of his belly=scrotum), ii. 131
Justice (poetical, not done), iii. 157
—— (poetical in the Nights), v. 161
—— Juzám=(black) leprosy, iii. 178; iv. 242; vi. 183

Ka'ab al-Ahbár (of the Scribes, two of the name), iii. 238
Ka'abah (Pilgrims clinging to its curtain), iii. 248

Ká'ah=ground-floor hall, i. 78
—— =fine house, mansion, i. 269
—— (=messroom, barracks), v. 362
Ka'ak al 'I'd=buns (cake?), v. 387
Kaannahu huwa=as he (was) he, vi. 24
Ka'b=heel, ankle, metaph. for fortune, v. 371
Kabáb (mutton or lamb grilled in small squares), v. 132
Kabasa=he shampoo'd, vii. 281
Kabbát=saucers, vi. 171
Kadisíyah (Al-) city in Irák, iv. 242
Kádús pl. Kawádís=pot of a water wheel, vii. 286
Káf, popularly=Caucasus, i. 66, 123
Kaff Shurayk=a single "Bun," *q.v.*, vii. 243
Káfir=Infidel, Giaur, ii. 187
Kafr=village (in Egypt and Syria), viii. 26
Káfs (verset of the three-and-twenty), iv. 170
Kafúr (Pr. N.)=Camphor, i. 371
Kafrá=desert place, vii. 68
Kabánah (Al-)=the craft of a Káhin or soothsayer, i. 25
Kahbah=whore, i. 65
Kahíl=whose eyes are kohl'd by nature, iii. 124
Kahílat al-Taraf=having the eyelids lined with kohl, i. 58
Káhirah=City of Mars (Cairo), iii. 383
Kahkahah=horse-laughter, i. 323
Kahlá (fem)=nature-kohl'd, iii. 20
Kahramán (Pers.)=braves, heroes, iii. 238; v. 163
Kahramánah=nursery governess, i. 212; vii. 289
Kahtán (sons of), v. 166
Kahwah (Kihwah)=strong old wine, ii. 158
—— (AL), used for coffee house, vii. 319
Kahwajíyah=coffee makers, iv. 125
Káid=leader, i. 305
Ka'ka'at=jangling noise, v. 224
Kákilí=Sumatran (eagle wood), viii. 54
Kala (island), iv. 386
Kalak=raft, vi. 127
Kalam=reed-pen, i. 118
—— =leg-cut, ii. 11
Kalám al-Mubáh=the permitted say, i. 26
Kalám wáti=vulgarism, ii. 17
Kalam-dán=reed-box (ink-case), iv. 190; v. 79
Kalandar=mendicant monk, i. 86
Kalandars (order of), viii. 78
Kallá=prorsus non, iii. 370
Kalla-má=it is seldom, iv. 110
Kallim al-Sultán (formula of summoning), vii. 292
Kámah=fathom, i. 379
Kamán=Kamá (as)-anna (that, since, because), vi. 345
Kamar=belt, vi. 307
Kamar al-Zamán (Pr. N.)=Moon of the Age, iii. 2; vii. 313
Kamaráni (AL)=the two moons for sun and moon, iii. 83
Kamariyah=moon-like, v 103

Kámat Alfiyyah = straight figure, i 79; iii. 24
Kamin al-Bahrayn = lurking place of the two seas, vi. 138
Kamís = shift, etc., i. 270
Kammir (Imp.) = brown (the bread), viii 13
Kanát = subterranean water-course, ii. 363
Kanjifah = pack of cards, iv. 194
Kánmákán (Pr. N.) = " was that which was," ii. 175
Kantar, (quintal) = 98·99 lbs. avoir., ii 131
Kánún (dulcimer, " zither "), ii. 430
Kánún = brasier, iv. 222; vi. 347
Kanz = enchanted treasure, vii. 379
Kapoteshwara and Kapoteshí, ii. 348
Kaptán = Capitano, iii. 210; vii. 213
Kara Gyuz, *see* Khiyál
Kárah = budget, large bag, vii 284
KaraJ (town in Persian Irak), v 276
Karawán = Charadrius œdicnemus, iv 343
Karbús = saddle-bow, vi. 233
Kári = Koran-reader, iv. 169
Kárib (pl. Kawárib) = dinghy, iii. 288
Karím = generous (cream of men) i. 360
Kárizán (AL) = the two mimosa-gatherers, v. 291
Karkadán, etc. = rhinoceros, iv. 362
Karkar (Carcer?), Sea of AL, v 17
Karkh (AL), quarter of Baghdad, iv. 88; vii. 373
Karmút = Silurus Carmoth Niloticus, vi. 334
Karr'aynan = keep thine eye cool, vi. 21
Karrat azlá 'hu = bis ribs felt cold (from hearty eating), vi. 338
Kárún = Korah of the Bible, iv. 178
—— (lake), v. 125
Karúrah = bottle for urine, iii. 141
Kasa'ah = wooden bowl, porringer, iii. 397
Kasab (AL) = acquisitiveness, vii. 157
Kasabah = rod (measurement), ii. 220
Kasabát = canes; bugles, ii. 192
Kásid = Anglo-Indian Cossid, vi 126
Kasídah = ode, elegy, iii. 48
Kasıdahs (their conventionalism) vii. 316
Kasr (= palace, one's house) v. 146
—— (= upper room), vii 344
Kasr al-Nuzhat = palace of delights, i. 348
Kasr (Al-) al Mashíd = the high-built castle, vi. 131
Kasri (Al-) Governor of the two Iráks, iii. 276
Kashmir people (have a bad name in Eastern tales), v. 68
Kassara 'llah Khayrak = Allah increase thy weal, v. 140
Kat'a = bit of leather, i. 18
Katá = sand grouse, i. 120; iii. 234
Kataba (for tattooing) vi. 40
Kátala-k Allah = Allah strike thee dead (facetiously) iii. 276, 377, 378
Katf = pinioning, i. 98
Kathá-Sarit-Ságara, poetical version of the Vrihat-Kathá, i. 11; viii. 145, etc.
Kathír = much, "no end," viii 10

Katíl = the Irish "kilt," iii. 261
Katúl (AL) = the slayer, ii. 297
Kaukab al-Sabáh = Star of the Morning, vii. 361
Kaukab al-durrí = cluster of pearls, vii. 27
Kaum = razzia: tribe, v. 171
Kaun = being, existence, vii. 141
Kaus al-Banduk = pellet-bow, i. 98
Kausaj = man with a thin, short beard, cunning, tricksy, iii 33
Kausar, lieu commun of poets, i. 222; ii. 87; iii. 314
Kawáid (pl. of Káid = governor), iv. 105
Kawárib, *see* Kárib.
Kawwád = pimp, i. 292; v 296
Kawwás = archer, jannisary, v 148
Káyánián, race of Persian kings, i. 69
Kayf hálak = how de doo? vi. 121
Kaylúlah = siesta, i. 47; ii. 79; vi. 340
Kayrawán = the Greek Cyrene, vii. 50
Kaysariyah = superior kind of Bazar, i. 244
Kaysúm = yellow camomile, ii. 283
Kaywán (Persian for Saturn), i. 396
Kayy (AL) = cautery, the end of medicine-cure, ii. 284
Kayyim (professional wrestler, names of such), i. 413
Kayyimah = guardian (fem.), vii. 62
Káz (Al-) = shears, vi. 169
Kazá, Kismat, and "Providence," v. 331
Kazdír = Skr. Kastíra (tin), iii. 386; iv. 379
Kázi = Judge in religious matters, i. 19
Kázi al-Kuzát = Chief Justice, i. 411; vi. 391
Kázi of the Army (the great legal authority of a country), v 45
Kazíb al-Bán = Willow-wand, i. 388
Kazis (the four of the orthodox schools), i. 363
Kerchief (of mercy), i. 316
—— (of dismissal) iii. 188
"Key" = fee paid on the keys being handed to a lodger, vi. 4
Khadd = cheek, vi. 65
Khádim = servant, politely applied to a castrato, i. 216; vii. 304
Khadiv (*not* Kédivé), vii. 193
Kháfiyah = concealed; Kháinah, perfidy, vi. 106
Khafz al-Jináh = lowering the wing (demeaning one's self gently), vii. 113
Khal'a al-'izár = stripping of jaws or side-beard, vi. 38
Khalanj = a hard kind of wood, i. 142; vii. 8
Khalbús = buffoon, ii. 45; v. 387
Khalí'a = worn out; wit, i. 287; iii. 345; v. 326
Khálid bin al-Walid, ii. 103
—— bin Safwán, ii. 71
Khálidán (for Khalidát) = the Canaries, iii. 1
Khalífah = Vicar of Allah; successor of a Santon, i. 170
Khalílu 'llah (friend of Allah = Abraham), iv. 159
Khalíyah = bee-hive; empty (pun on), v. 153; vii. 352
Khalkínah = copper cauldron, vi. 327
Khammárah = wine-shop, tavern, "hotel," iii. 204
Khán = caravanserai, i. 85; ii. 241

Khán al-Masrúr, in Cairo, famous in the 15th century, i. 244
Khánakah = Darwaysh's convent, v. 370
Khanjar = hanger, i. 214; ii. 314
Khara = dung (lowest insult), i. 379
Khara al-Sús = weevil's dung, vii 91
Kharajú = they (masc.) went forth (vulgarism for Kharajna) (fem.), vi. 295
Khassat-hu, ii. 272
Khatmah = reading or reciting of the whole Koran, i. 255
Khatt Sharíf = royal hand letter, i. 363; vii. 368
Khattíyah = writer, etc., spear, from Khatt HaJar, i 329
Khátún (Turk. lady), iii. 192; v. 342
Khauf (Al-) maksúm = fear (cowardice) is equally apportioned, ii. 392
Khaukhah = tunnel, vii. 62
Khayál (Al-) = phantom ghost, iv. 293
Khayr = good news by euphemy, iii. 259
Khayr wa 'Áfiyah = well and in good case, vii. 170
Khaysamah (traditionist), iv. 46
Khayt hamayán = threads of vanity (gossamer), iii. 6
Khayzáran = rattan, i 388; iii. 369
Kháwi (skin of), iv. 404
Khawwás (Al-) = basket-maker, iv. 231
Khaznah (Khazinah) = 1,000 kis of £5 each, 1 405; iii. 63
Khazrá (al-) = the Green, palace of Mu'áwiyah, v. 321
Khiláf (Khaláf) = Salix Ægyptiaca, i 388
Khilál = toothpick (emblem of attenuation), iv. 12; vi. 403
Khinsir = little (or middle) finger, vii. 232
Khinzír = hog, i. 101
Khirad Shah = King of Intelligence, v. 272
Khishkhánah = cupboard, v 391
Khitáb = exordium of a letter, vii. 200
Khizáb (dye used by women), ii. 328
Khizánah (AL) = treasury, vii. 102
Khizr (the Green Prophet), iii. 294; iv. 327
Khiyál (Chinese shadows), iii. 312
Khubz = scones, i. 120
Khuff = walking shoes, i. 76; iii. 231
Khuld = fourth heaven (of yellow coral), vi. 204
Khumásíyah = five feet high, iii. 310
Khunsa, iv. 55
Khurj (Al-) = saddle-bag (las Alforjas), v. 132
Khusrau Parwiz and Shírin, iv. 54
—— (his wealth), *ib.*
Khusyatán = testicles, i 378
Khutnah = circumcision, iv. 163
Khutúb (Pr. N.) = affairs, misfortunes, vi. 356
Khwájah (Howajee) = schoolmaster, man of letters, etc., iv. 385
Khwárazm = land of the Chorasmioi, v. 28
Khyas! Khyas! onomatopoetic, used in a sea-spell, i. 209
Kiblah (turning towards it in mortal danger), iv. 8
—— (anything opposite) applied to the Ka'abah, iv. 151
Kiblatayn = the two Kiblahs (Meccah and Jerusalem), iv. 151
Kidrah = pot, kettle, lamp-globe, vii. 379

Kil wa Kál = it was said and he said (chit-chat), iii. 325
Killed = Hibernicè "kilt," iii. 418; v. 82
Killing (of an unfaithful wife commended by public opinion), vii. 358
Kímiyá = Alchemy (from χυμεία = wet drug), vi. 168
Kimkhab = (velvet of) "Kimcob," vi. 349; vii. 289
Kiná' = veil, v. 102
Kinchin lay (Arab form of), ii. 326
King (dressing in scarlet when wroth), iii 197
—— (the, and the Virtuous Wife), iv. 84
Kingfisher (Lucian's), iv 388
King's barber a man of rank, i. 324
Kintár = a hundredweight (quintal), v. 11
Kír = bellows, vi. 169
Kiráb = wooden sword-case, vii. 4
Kirám = nobles; Kurám = vines, vi. 351
Kirámat = prodigy, ii. 135; iii. 173
Kirát (bean of Abrus precatorius), vi. 77
—— (weight = 2-3 grains; length = one finger-breadth), iii 26
Kird = baboon, iii. 408
Kirsh al-Nukhál = guts of bran, vi. 319
Kisás (Al-) = lex talionis, v. 364
Kishk (Kashk) = porridge, iii. 331
Kisrà = the Chosroë, applied to Anushirwan, iv. 51
Kiss (without mustachio = bread without salt), iv. 122
"Kiss ground" not to be taken literally, vi. 2
Kissing (the eyes, a paternal salute), i. 115
—— (like a pigeon feeding its young), iii. 60
—— (names for), iii. 372
—— (en tout bien et en tout honneur), vi. 184
Kissis = ecclesiast, ii. 126
Kit (of the traveller in the East), iv. 130
Kitáb al-Kazá = book of law-cases, vii. 185
Kitáb al-Fihrist (and its author), viii. 66
Kitab al-Báh = Book of Lust, viii. 182
Kitf al-Jamal = camel shoulder-blade, v. 361
Kitfír (Itfír) = Potiphar, v. 83
Kiyakh (fourth Coptic month), iv. 183
Kizán Fukká'a = jars for Fukká'a (a kind of beer), v. 5
Knife, "bravest of arms," v. 320
Knight-errant of the East, i. 398
Knuckle-bone, ii. 207
Kohl = powdered antimony for the eyelids, i. 54
—— proverbially used, i. 256
—— (-powder keeps the eyes from inflammation), ii. 186
—— (applying of = takhil), ii. 282
—— (-eyed = Kahlá) f. iii. 20
—— (he would steal it off the eye-ball = he is a very expert thief), iii. 194
Kohl'd with Ghunj = languor Kohl'd, viii. 37
Kohls (many kinds of), vi. 169
Korah (Kárún), iv. 178
Koran quoted: (xx.) i. 2, *et. seq.*

Koran abrogating and abrogated passages), iv. 148
—— (most excellent chapter of), iv. 164
—— (eminent and curious verses of), iv. 164, 165
—— (first English translation owing to France), viii. 91
Koss ibn Sa'idah (Bishop of NaJrán), i. 362
Kubbád = shaddock, ii. 203; vii. 9
Kubbah (AL) = alcove, iii. 431
Kubkáb = bath-clogs, ii. 316
Kudrat = Omnipotence, v. 331
Kuds (Al-) *see* Bayt al-Mukaddas, ii. 35
Kúfah (Al-) founded by Omar, iii. 131
—— (revolutionary spirit of), *ib.* 133
Kúfiyah = coif, etc., ii. 128
Kufr = rejecting the True Religion, i. 156
Kuhaylat (breed of Arab horses), iii. 124
Kulayb allows no one to approach his camp-fire, i. 398; v 166
Kulkasá = colocasia roots, i. 250
Kullah = gugglet, i. 32
Kulzum (AL), old name of Suez-town, vi. 132
Kumasrá (Kummasrá) = pear, vi. 141
Kumayt (AL) = bay horse with black points, v 324
Kumkum (cucurbite, gourd-shaped vessel), i. 37; iii. 194, 298
Kumm = sleeve (used as a bag), iii. 231; vii. 3, 11
Kun = Be (the creative word), iii. 97
Kunáfah = vermicelli cake, viii. 1
Kundur = frankincense, vii. 88
Kunfuz = hedgehog, i. 408
Kunsul = Consul, iii. 209
Kunyat = patro- or matro-nymic, iii. 398
Kúr = furnace, vi. 169
Kurbáj = cravache, vi. 176
Kurbán = sacrifice, vi. 175
Kurds (Xenophon's and Strabo's Carduchi), ii. 324
Kurdús = body of horse, vii. 186
Kurrah = ball in the Polo game, ii. 221
Kurrat al-Ayn = coolness of the eye, i 66; iv. 104
Kurs (has taken the place of Iklíl), i. 249
Kursán (Al-) = "Corsaro," a runner, vii 56
Kursi (choir, throne) = desk or stool for the Koran, i. 153; vi. 98
Kursi al-wiládah = birth-stool, i. 401
Kús (town in Upper Egypt), iii, 389
Kus(s) = vulva, vi. 248
Kush'arírah = horripilation, symptom of great joy, i. 231
Kussá'a = curling cucumber, iii. 222
Kusúf = eclipse of the moon, vii. 27
Kút al-Kulúb, vi. 308
Kutá'ah = a bit cut off, etc., v 176
Kutayt = little tom-cat, i. 364
Kutb = axle, pole; hence prince, doyen in sainthood, iv. 327
Kuthayyir (poet), ii. 6
Kutr Misr = tract of Egypt, vii. 347
Kuzia Fakán (Pr. N.) = "it was decreed by Destiny, so it came to pass," ii. 76

LÁ ADAMNÁK = Heaven deprive us not of thee, i. 247
Lá Báas (bi-zálik = there is no harm in that), iii. 284
—— (in Marocco) = "I am pretty well," vii. 11
—— (= no harm is [yet] done), vii. 177
Lá haula, etc. = there is no Majesty, etc., i. 64
La iláha illá 'llláh = there is no God but *the* God (tahlíl), ii. 133
Lá kabbata hámíyah = no burning plague, viii. 13
Lá rajma ghaybin = without stone-throwing of secrecy, vii. 83
La rayba fí-hi, ii. 110
Lá tankati'i = sever not thyself from us, vii. 312
Lá tuwáhishná = do not make me desolate, i. 57
Lá tuwákhizná = do not chastise us = excuse us, i. 151
La'alla = haply, belike; forsure, certainly, vii. 120
La'ab = (sword-) play, v. 245
La'abat = a plaything, a puppet, a lay figure, i. 226
La'al = ruby, iv. 287
La'an = curse, iv. 201; v. 89
Láb (Old Pers. for Sun), vi. 84
Laban (= milk artificially soured), v. 110
—— (= sweet milk), vi. 144
—— halíb = fresh milk, v. 110
Labbayka (= Here am I, called Talbiyah), i. 208; ii. 125
—— (pronounced on sighting Meccah), iv. 157
Labbis al-Búsah tabkí 'Arúsah = clothe the reed and it will become a bride, vi. 349
Labtayt (Pr. N. = Toledo), iii. 223
Lactation (term of), iv. 247
—— (no cohabitation during), iv. 247
Ladies of the family (waiting upon the guests), v. 144
Láhik = the Overtaker, vii. 71
Lajlaj = rolling anything in the mouth; stammering, vii. 381
Lájuward, *see* Lázuward, ii. 259
Lake Kárún, v. 125
Lakít = fœtus, foundling, contemptible fellow, v. 341
Lámi (Al-) = the l-shaped, forked (os hyoïdes), iv. 172
Lámíyat = poem rhyming in L, ii. 365
Lane quoted: i. 2, *et seq.*
Language of signs, ii. 198
Languages (study of, should be assisted by ear and tongue), viii. 87
Largesse (better than the mace), vi. 314
Lasm (Lathm) = kissing the lower face, iii. 372
Lasting calamity = furious knight, v. 194
Latter night = hours between the last sleep and dawn, i. 22
Laughing in one's face not meant for an affront, i. 295
Laughter rare and sign of a troubled mind, i. 228
Lauh = tablet used as slate, iv. 39
Lauh al-Mahfúz = the Preserved Tablet (of Allah's decrees), iv. 268
Lauláka = but for thee, for thy sake, iv. 253
Laun = colour, hue (for dish), v. 378
Láwandiyah (Al-) = Levantines, vii. 337
Layálí = nights, future, fate, iii. 98

Layl (night) frequently = the interval between sunset and sunset, ii. 156
Laylá (female Pr. N.), ii. 357
—— wa Majnún (love poem), *ib.* 403
Laylat al-Kábilah = to-night, vii. 333
Laylat al-Kadr = Night of Power, v. 91
Laylat al-Wafá = the night of completion of the Nile-flood, i. 268
Laylat ams = yesternight, v. 379
Lazá (Hell for Jews), ii. 43; vii. 77
Lázuward = lapis lazuli, azure, ii. 259; vii. 260
Leaving one standing (pour se faire valoir), v. 158
Leg-cut (severs horse's leg), ii. 124
Legs (making mute the anklets), v. 327
Lentils (cheapest and poorest food in Egypt), viii. 29
Leprosy (white = bahak or baras, black = juzám), iv. 242
—— (thickens voice), iii. 177
—— (shows first at the wrist), iii. 178
Letter (reading *not* always understanding), ii. 15
—— (model specimen), iii. 183
—— (torn tears a kingdom), v. 204
Letters and letter-writing, ii. 250
Li-ajal = for the sake of, low Egyptian, ii. 17
Libdah (skull-cap of felt), sign of a religious mendicant, ii. 287
Liberality (men proverbial for their), iii. 220
—— (after poverty), vi. 331
Libraries (large ones known by the Arabs), vi. 234
—— (much appreciated by the Arabs), viii. 157
Lice bred by perspiration, i. 390
Lie (only degrading if told for fear of telling the truth), vii. 163
—— (simulating truth), vii. 291
Lieu d'aisance (in Eastern crafts), vii. 390
Líf = fibre of palm fronds, iv. 13, 390
Life (by the, of thy youth) oath of women, iii. 176
—— (cheap in hot countries), *ib.* 387
Life-breath in the nostrils = heart in the mouth, i. 38
Light (of salvation shining from the face of Prophets), vii. 382
Light-worshippers (are liars), iii. 366
Lijám shadíd = sharp bit, vii. 148
Like mother, like daughter, i. 275
Li 'lláhi darru-ka = the Lord has been copious to thee, iii. 149
Lion (beguiled by flattery), iv. 8
—— (as Sultan of the beasts Jealous of a man's power), viii 32
—— at home, lamb abroad, ii. 84
Lisám (mouth-band for men, chin-veil = Tasmak for women), i. 356; ii. 128; iii. 67
Lisán al-Hamal = lamb's tongue (plantain), vii. 9
Listening not held dishonourable, vi. 67
Litholatry of the old Arabs, v. 174
Liver = seat of passion, i. 24
—— (for heart), iii. 27
—— (and spleen held to be congealed blood), iv. 173
Living (the, who dieth not), iv. 406
Liwá = Arab Tempe, v. 313

Liwán = Al-Aywán, iii. 197; vi. 132
Liyyah = fat sheep (calves like tails of), vii. 26
Loathing of prohibition, vii. 340
Locks (Mohammed's), ii. 128
Logah = Arabic language, also a vocabulary, dictionary, i 231
Logogriphs, vi. 248
Lokman (three of the name), viii. 108
Loosening the hair an immodesty in women sanctioned only by a great calamity, i. 290
Lord for Lady = she, iv. 27
—— (of the East and West), iv. 180
Lost on Allah's way = martyr, ii. 222
Lot (this is ours = I have been lucky and will share with you), vii. 387
Lote-tree (beyond which there is no passing), iv. 336
Lots = games of chance, iv. 176
Love (pure, becomes prophetical), ii. 234
—— (the ear conceiveth it before the eye), ii. 237
—— (ten stages of), ii. 261
—— (martyrs of), *ib.* 431
—— (platonic), iii. 20
—— (ousting affection), iii. 27
—— (martyrs of), *ib.* 323
—— (clairvoyance), *ib.* 353
—— (excess of), *ib.*
—— (strange chances of), iv. 38
—— (deaths from), iv. 94
—— (made public disgraces), iv. 110
—— (called upon to torment the lover still more), vi. 231
—— (cruelty of), viii. 24
Love-children (exceedingly rare amongst Moslems), vi. 268
Love-liesse (never lacked between folk, *i.e.*, people of different conditions). vi. 359
Lovers in Lazá (hell) as well as in Na'ím (heaven), ii. 283
—— (parting of, a stock-topic in poetry, ii. 283
—— (buried together), iv. 37
—— (becoming Moslems secure the good will of the audience), vi. 371
Loving folk = something more than benevolence, i. 330
Lúk-Gate (proverb referring to), iii. 372
Lukmah = mouthful, i. 240; vi. 151
Lukmán (Æsop of the Arabs), ii. 99
Lukmán (three of the name), iii. 50; viii. 108
Lullilooing (Tahlil Zagrútah, Kil), i. 401
Lúlúah = union-pearl; wild cow, vii. 286
Lumá = dark hue of the inner lips, iii. 365
Lupin-flour used as soap, ii. 39
Luss = thief, robber, vii. 181
Lute (personification of), vii. 16
Lutf (servile name = elegance, delicacy), iii. 348
Lying (until one's self believes the lie to be truth), viii. 1?
Lymph (alluding to the "Neptunist" doctrine), vii. 154
Lynx (trained for hunting), ii. 188

Ma al-Khalif, *see* Khiláf, ii. 39
Má al-Maláhat = water (brilliancy) of beauty, vi. 204
Má Dáhiyatak = what is thy misfortune? (for "what ill business is this?"), vii. 210
Má kaharani ahadun = none vexeth (or has overcome) me, vii. 229
Ma'abid (singer and composer), iv. 106
Maamún (AL), son and successor of Hárún al-Rashid, i. 170; iii. 232
Ma'n bin Záidah, iii. 71, 220
Ma'áni-há (her meanings = her inner woman), iii. 267
Ma'arúf = kindness, favour, viii. 1
Mace (Ar. Dabbús), v. 155
—— (a dangerous weapon), v. 225
Madinat al-Nabi (Al-Madinah) = City of the Prophet, iii. 237
Madness (there is a pleasure in), iii. 322
Mafárik (AL) = partings of the hair, vi. 13
Magazine (as one wherein wheat is heaped up = unmarried), vi. 155
Magháribah (pl. of Maghribi = Western man, Moor, "Maurus"), v. 127
Maghdád (for Baghdád, as Makkah and Bakkah), vi. 208
Maghrib (al-Aksá) = the land of the setting sun, vii. 129
Magic studied by Jews, ii. 132
Magic Horse (history of the fable), iii. 416
Magnet Mountains, fable probably based on the currents, i. 129
Mahá = wild cattle, vi. 69
Mahall = (a man's) quarters, vi. 376
Mahall al-Zauk = seat of taste, sensorium, vii. 160
Mahallah = the English "Cook's 'ill" with a difference, viii. 49
Maháráj = great Rajah, iv. 349, 406
Mahayá = Má al-Hayát = aqua vitæ, v. 329
Mahdi (AL) Caliph, v. 332; vii. 392
Mahmil (mahmal) = litter, ii. 34
Mahr = marriage dowry, settlement, v. 323; vii. 112
Mahríyah (Mehari) = blood-dromedary, iii. 62
Maid and Magpie, v. 93
Mail-coat and habergeon, simile for a glittering stream, i. 269
Ma'in, Ma'ún = smitten with the evil eye, i. 113
Maintenance (of a divorced woman during Iddah), vii. 112
Majájat = saliva, vi. 68
Ma'janah (a place for making bricks), i. 344
Majnún = madman, i. 9; ii. 297
Majzúb = drawn, attracted (Sufi term for ecstatic), iv. 24
Maka'ad = sitting-room, iii. 204
Makhaddah = pillow, i. 392
Makkamah = Kazi's Court, i. 19
"Making men" (and women), viii. 176
Making water, i. 238
Mál = Badawi money, flocks, "fee," v. 172
Malak = level ground, vii. 21
Malak or Malik = Seraph or Sovran, i. 233
Malákay bayti 'l-ráhah = slabs of the jakes, viii. 48
Malakút (Al) = the world of spirits (Sufi term), vi 296
Male children (as much prized as riches), vii. 375
Malih Kawi = very handsome (Cairene vulgarism), v. 345

Malíhah (al-) = salt-girl; beautiful, i. 314
Malik (used as "king" in our story-books), i. 329
—— bin Dinár (theologian), ii 104
—— (taken as title), ii. 276
—— (traditionist), iv. 46
—— al-Khuzá'i (intendant of the palace), iv. 58
—— (Al-) al-Násir = the conquering King, iii. 383; v. 338; vii 100
Málik (door-keeper of hell), ii. 246
Malikhulíyà (AL) = melancholy, iv 174
Malocchio or Gettatura (evil), vii. 313
Mamlúk (white slave trained to arms), i. 75
Mamarr al-Tujjár = passing place of the traders, vi. 305
Mamrak = sky-window, etc., vi. 306
Man (extract of despicable water), ii. 243
—— (is fire, woman tinder), ii. 284
—— (shown to disadvantage in beast-stories), ii 338
—— (his destiny written on his skull), ii 346
—— (pre-eminence above women), iii. 111
—— (handsomer than woman), iii. 145
—— (his advantages above woman), iv 114
—— (one's evidence = two women's), iv 114
—— (one's portion = two women's), iv. 114
—— (created of congealed blood), iv. 166
—— (one worthier in Allah's sight than a thousand Jinn), vi. 164, 201
—— (created after God's likeness, rather a Jewish-Christian than a Moslem doctrine), vii. 157
—— (I am a man of them = never mind my name), vii 305
—— (of the people of Allah = a Religious), vii. 130
—— (his wrong is from the tongue), vii 368
Manár al-Saná = Place of Light, vi 258
Manáshif (pl. of Minshafah, *q v.*), vi 247
Manázil (stations of the Moon), iv 180
Mandíl = kerchief, ii. 195
Maniyat = death; muniyat = desire, iii. 76
Manjaníkát (Al-) = Mangonels, vi. 120
Mankind (creates its analogues in all the elements), v. 35
—— (superior to Jinn), vii 397
Mann = from two to six pounds, iv 417
Man's creation, i. 411
Mansúr (Pr. N.) = triumphant, vii. 370
Mansúr (AL) Caliph, ii. 45, 60, 109
—— bin Ammár, ii. 104
—— al-Nimrí (poet), iii. 298
Mansúr wa Munazzam = oratio soluta et ligata, vi. 373
Manumission of slaves, i. 378
Manzil (Makám) = (a lady's) lodgings, vi. 376
Maragha = he rubbed his face, i. 382
Marba' = summer quarters, ii. 304
Mardán-i-Ghayb (Himalayan brothers), ii. 111
Mares (impregnated by the wind), iv. 351
Marhúb = terrible, vi. 329
Marhúm (f. Marhúmah) = late lamented, ii. 32, 96

Márid = contumacious, i. 38
Máridúna = rebels (against Allah), v. 240
Ma'rifah = article, vii. 334
Máristán (from Pers. Bímáristán = place of sickness), i. 266
Marján = Coral-branch (slave name), ii. 390
Marjánah (Pr. N.) = Coral-branch, ii. 4
—— (Morgante, Urganda, Morgain), vii. 373
Markúb = shoe, v. 115
Marmar = marble, i. 272; v. 12
Marriage (not valid without receipt of settlement), i. 254
—— (if consummated demands Ghusl), iii 71
—— (by capture), vi. 198
—— (one of the institutions of the Apostles), vi. 288
Marriage-sheet inspected, i. 373
Married men profit nothing, ii. 230
—— never once (emphasises poverty), vi. 297
Marseille (probably alluded to), vii. 48
Marsín = myrtle, vi. 77
Martyrdom, iii. 362
—— (of the drowned), vii. 398
Martyrs (still alive), ii. 139
—— (of love), ii. 431; iii. 323
Marwah (ground-wave in Meccah), iv 157
Marwazí = of Marw (Margiana), iii. 11
Marwán bin al-Hakam (Governor of Al-Madinah), v. 322
Maryam (a Christian Name), vii. 40
Maryam al-Husn = place of the white doe (Rím) of beauty. vii. 54
Marz-bán = Warden of the Marches, Margrave, iii. 43
Masculine for feminine, v. 335
Má sháa 'llah (as Allah willeth) = well done, ii. 316
Mashhad = head and foot stone of a grave, viii. 50
Mashá'ili = cresset-bearer, for public crier, hangman, i. 239; iii. 187
Masíhí = follower of the Messiah, i. 238
Maskharah = buffoon, ii. 45; v. 387
Maskhút = transformed (mostly in something hideous), a statue, i 152
Maslamah bin Abd al-Malik, ii. 69
Massacre (the *grand moyen* of Eastern state-craft), vii. 185
Massage, i. 159
Mastabah = bench of masonry, iv. 367
Masúkah = stick used for driving cattle, vi 298
Matáf = place of Tawáf, *q.v.*, iv. 157
Matárik (pl of mitrak) = targes, vii. 293
Matmúrah = underground cell, i. 364
Matr (pl amtár) = large vessel of leather or wood, iii 70
Matta'aka 'llah = Allah permit thee to enjoy, vii. 199
Maukab (Al-) = Procession-day, iii 399
Maulid = nativity, vii. 350
Maund, *see* Mann, iv. 417
Maurid = desert well and road to such, ii. 259
Mausil *(Mosul)* alluding to the junction of Assyria and Babylonia, i. 76
Mausúl (AL) = the conjoined (for relative pronoun or particle), vii. 334

Maut=death, v. 342
Mauz=Musa (Banana), iii. 319
Mawwál (for Mawáliyah)=short poem, vi. 248, 302
"May thy life be prolonged," iii. 187
Mayázib (pl. of mizáb)=gargoyles, v. 332
Maydán=parade-ground, i. 43
Maydán al-Fil=race-course of the Elephant, vi. 112
Maymúnah (proverbial noun now forgotten), i. 53
Maysir=game of arrows, iv. 176
Maysúm (Badawi wife of Caliph Mu'áwiyah), ii. 62
Maysum's song, v. 295
Mayyáfárikín, ancient capital of Diyár Bakr, v. 203
Meat rarely coloured in modern days' i. 285
Medicine, iv. 173
Melancholy (chronic under the brightest skies), iii. 355
Meniver=menu vair (Mus lemmus), vii. 372
Merchant (worth a thousand), viii. 7
Merchants and shopkeepers carrying swords, i. 50
Mercury Ali (his story sequel to that of Dalilah), v. 366
Mercy (quality of the noble Arab), ii. 312
Mer-folk (refined with the Greeks, grotesques with other nations), vii. 241
Messiah (made a liar by the Miscreants), vii. 96
Metamorphosis (terms of), vi. 81
Metempsychosis and sharpers' tricks, iv. 49
Metrical portion of the Nights (threefold distribution of), viii. 63
Miao or Man=eat, i. 203
Mihráb and Minaret (symbols of Venus and Priapus?), i. 153
Mihráj=Maháráj, *q.v.*, iv. 406
Mihrgán=Sun-fête, degraded into Michaelmas, iii. 415
Mikashshah=broom, iii. 326
Mikra'ah=palm-rod, i. 91
Mikbas (pot of lighted charcoal), iii. 361
Mikhaddah=cheek-pillow, vii. 10
Mikmarah=cover for a brasier, extinguisher, iv. 82
Miknás=town Mequinez, v. 131
Miknasah=broom, v. 70
Mi'lakah=spoon, vii. 215
Milh=salt, i. 314
Milk (white as, opposed to black as mud), iii. 262
—— (soured), iv. 177
—— (Ar. Laban, Halib), v. 110
—— (by nomades always used in the soured form), v. 110
Milk-drinking races prefer the soured milk to the sweet, vi. 144
Million (no Arabic word for, expressed by a thousand thousand), v. 14
Mim-like mouth, iii. 363
Mims (verset of the sixteen), iv. 170
Mina (and the stoning of the Devil), iv. 157
Minaret (simile for a fair young girl), ii. 294
Mind (one by vinegar, another by wine=each goes its own way), iii. 198
"Mine" (various idioms for expressing it), vii. 66
Minínah=biscuit, iii. 211
Minshafah (pl. Manáshif)=drying towel, vi. 247

Miracle (minor, known to Spiritualism), iv. 104
Miracles (performed by Saints' tombs), i. 222
—— (disclaimed by Mohammed but generally believed in), iii. 124
—— (growing apace in the East), vii. 393
Mirage = Saráb, iii. 99
Mirhad (Al) market-place at Bassorah, v. 327
Mirzá 'Abdullah-i-Híchmakání = Master Abdullah of Nowhere, iii. 440
Mishammah = an old gunny bag, vii. 242
Miskál = 71-72 grains in gold, used for dinar, i. 116; vii. 324
Misr, Masr = Capital (applied to Memphis, Fostat and Cairo), v. 366
—— (for Egypt), vi. 155
Misra (twelfth Coptic month), iv. 184
Misrayn (Al) = Basrah and Kúfah, vi. 155
Mitrahinna (Minat-ro-hinnu) = port at mouth of canal, ii. 134
Mizr, Mizar = beer, i. 67
Mohammed (best of the first and last), i. 333
—— (Mustafa), i. 365
—— (his letter to the Mukaukis), i. 400
—— (Periclytus and Paracletus), ii. 125
—— (abhors the shaveling), ii. 145
—— (bearer of glad and bad tidings), ii. 154
—— (Congratulator and Commiserator), ii. 157
—— (Best of Mankind), ii. 160
—— ("born with Kohl'd eyes"), iii 20
—— (his uncles), iii. 151
—— (traditional saying of), *ib.* 163
—— (cleanses the Ka'abah of idols), *ib* 205
—— (on dyeing the hair, etc.), iii. 312
—— (on lovers), *ib.* 323
—— (on his being seen in sleep), *ib.* 399
—— (places the "black stone"), *ib.* 374
—— (mentioned in the Koran), iv. 164
—— (Allah's right hand), vi. 150
—— (sent with the guidance and True Faith), vii. 96
—— (before and after the Hijrah), viii 176
Mohammed al-Amin (Caliph), iv. 57
Mohammed bin Sulaymán al-Rabi'i (Governor of Bassorah), v. 327
Moharram = first month of the Moslem year, vi. 227
Mohr = signet, vi. 115
Mohtasib = inspector of weights and measures, etc., vii 23
Mole on cheek (black as Bilál), iii. 264
Moles compared with pearls, i. 163
Monasteries (best wine made in), iv. 32
—— (Ar. Biká'a), iv. 86
—— (places of confinement for madmen), iv. 99
Money (carried in the corner of a handkerchief), i 250
—— (large sums weighed), i. 259; ii. 47
—— (carried round the waist), vii. 23
—— (let lie with the folk = not dunned for), vii 371
Monkery (abhorred by Mohammed), ii. 145
—— (none in Al-Islam), vi. 288
Monoculars (unlucky to meet), i. 307

Monoculars (famed for mischief), iii. 313; vii. 50
Monsters (abounding in Persian literature), vi. 124
Months (of peace), iv. 21
—— (Coptic names of), iv. 183, 184
—— (Arabic names explained), iv. 184
Moon (blighting effect of its rays), i. 332
—— masculine in Semitic, i. 369
—— (masc., Sun fem.), ii. 254; iii. 374
—— (simile for female beauty), iii. 422
—— (shall be cloven in twain), iv. 170
—— (its stations), iv. 180
—— (taking in hand the star=girl handing round the cup), vii 261
Moon-faced (not absurd), iii. 310
Moons (for cup-bearers), vi. 374
Moore (Thomas, anticipated), iii. 86
Morality (geographical and chronological), iii. 28
—— (want of, excused by passion), iii. 54
Morning draught, ii. 247
"Morosa voluptas," v. 329
Mortal (one better in Allah's sight than a thousand Jinn), vi. 64, 201
Moses (derivation of the name), ii. 105
—— and Jethro, ii. *ib.*
—— and the next world, ii. 106
—— and Al-Khizr, ii. 187
—— describes his own death and burial, v 31
Moslem (external), i. 355
—— (familiarity between high and low), i. 357
—— (peasants kind-hearted), i. 391
—— (kind feeling shown to a namesake), iv. 355
—— (corpses should be burnt under certain circumstances), iv. 366
—— (commonplaces of condolence), iv. 380
—— (sales, formula of), iv. 412
—— (a free-born's sale is felony), v. 147
—— (can circumcise, marry and bury himself), vi. 181
—— (on a journey tries to bear with him a new suit of clothes for the festivals and Friday service), vii. 129
—— (bound to discharge the debts of his dead parents), vii. 370
—— (doctrine ignores the dictum "ex nihilo nihil fit"), vii. 142
—— (resignation, noble instance of), viii. 40
Moslems (their number preordained), vi. 305
—— (deal kindly with religious mendicants), vii. 130
—— (not ashamed of sensual appetite), vii. 161
—— (bound to abate scandals amongst neighbours), vii. 174
—— (husbands among them divided into three classes), vii. 325
Mosque al-Ahzáb=mosque of the troops, v. 291
Mosques serving as lodgings for poor travellers, i 390
Mosul (exempted from idolatrous worship), iv. 31
—— stuff=muslin, i. 211
Mother (waiting upon the adult sons), v. 144
—— (in Arab tales=ma mére), vi. 186
Mother's milk=nature, i. 368
Mounds=rubbish heaps outlying Eastern cities, i 66

Mountain (coming from the = being a clodhopper), iii. 103
—— (sit upon the = turn anchorite), iii. *ib.*
—— (the, at Cairo), iii. 405
Mountains (the pegs of the earth), iii. 294
Mourning (perfumes not used during), ii. 288
—— (normal term of forty days), vii. 370
Moustachio (salt to a kiss), iv. 122
Mouth compared to the ring of Sulayman, i. 78
Mrigatrishna = the thirst of the deer (mirage), v. 10
MS. copy of The Nights (price of one in Egypt), vi. 99
Muákhát = entering in a formal agreement for partnership, vi 379
Mu'allim = teacher, master (address to a Jew or Christian), vi. 301
Mu'arras = pimp, i. 312
Mu'attik al-Rikáb = Liberator of Necks, vi. 116
Mu'áwiyah (Caliph), ii. 62, 63
—— (his "mildness"), iii. 71
Muayyad (Sultan and calligrapher), i. 357
Mu'ezzin (who calls to prayer), ii. 199
Mubárak (f. mubárakah) = blessed (a favourite slave-name), vii. 137
Mubárakah = the blessed (fem.), vii. 389
Mudarris = professor, viii. 8
Mudawwarah (a gong ?), iii. 257
Mufti (Doctor of Law), v. 160
Muffawak = well-notched, iv. 2
Muhabbat (AL) al-ghariziyah = natural affection, vi. 263
Muháfiz = district-governor, i. 238
Muhájirún = companion in Mohammed's flight, v. 291
Muhakkah = "Court-hand," i. 119
Muhallil, *see* Mustahall
Muhammad, Ahmad and Mahmúd, v. 178
Muhammarah = fricandoed, i. 264
Muhárabah = doing battle, vii. 169
Muharramát (the three forbidden things), iii. 119; iv. 107
Mu'in al-Din = Aider of the Faith, vi. 138
Mujáhid (Al-) = fighter in Holy War, ii. 276
Mujáhidún, plur. of the previous, ii. 265
Mujauhar = damascened, v. 282
Mujáwirún = lower servants, sweepers, etc., iv. 81
Mujtabá = the Accepted, i. 71
Mukaddam (Anglo-Indicé Muccudum) = overseer, iii. 170
Mukarrabín = those near Allah, iv. 266
Mukhammas = cinquains, iii. 65
Mukri = Koranist, i. 104; iv. 169
Mulabbas = dragees, v. 396
Mulákát = going to meet an approaching guest, iv. 276
Mummery = "Mahommerie," viii. 161
Munádamah = table-talk, "conversation over the cup," vi. 95
Munáfik = hypocrite, iv. 161
Munakkishah = woman who applies the dye to a face, i. 249
Munawwarah (AL) = the Illumined (title of Al-Medinah), v. 293
Munázarah = dispute, vii. 310

Munázirah = like (fem.), vii. 310
Munkar and Nakir (the questioning angels), iv. 73; vii 235; viii. 44
Munkasir (broken) = languid, iii. 314
Munkati' = cut off, vi. 182
Muráhanah = game at forfeits, v. 113
Murder (to be punished by the family), iv. 66
—— (to save one's life approved of), iv. 384
Murjiyy (sect and tenets), iii. 120
Murtazà = the Elect, i. 71
Músà = Moses, ii. 105
Músá bin Nusayr (conqueror of Spain), v. 3
Mus'ab bin al-Zubayr, iv. 44
Musáfahah = joining palms for "shaking hand," v. 190, 252; vii. 399
Musáhikah = tribade, vi. 282
Musakhkham (AL) = the defiled Cross, ii. 119
Musallà = place of prayer, oratory, iv. 212
Musámarah = chatting at night, iii. 352; vi. 8
Music (forbidden by Mohammed), vii. 111
Musk (scent of heaven), ii. 194
—— (sherbet flavoured with), iv. 33
Mushayyad = lofty, high-builded, vi. 182
Muslim bin al-Walid (poet), iv. 89
Musquito caught between the toes, v. 373
Mustafá (the chosen) = Mohammed, i. 71, 365
Mustahakk = deserving, viii. 49
Mustahall (Mustahill) = one who marries a thrice divorced woman and divorces her to make her lawful for her first husband, iii. 175
Musta'in (Al-) bi'llah (Caliph), vii. 312
Mustansir bi 'llah (AL) = one seeking help in Allah, i. 292
Mutalammis (AL), the poet and his fatal letter, iv. 40
Mutanakkir = disguised, proud, reserved, v. 299
Mu'tasim (AL) bi 'llah (Caliph), vii. 300
Mutawakkil (AL) Caliph, iii. 402; iv. 112; vii. 299
Mutawallí = Prefect of Police, i. 238
Mutawwif = leader in the Tawáf, *q.v.*, iv. 167
Mu'tazid (AL) bi 'lláh (Caliph), vii. 297
Mu'tazz (AL) bi 'lláh (Caliph), vii. 309
Mu'ujizah = miracle of a prophet, ii. 135
Muunah = provisions, vi. 23; vii. 179
Muunis (Pr. N. = Companion), iv. 121
Muwallad = a slave born in a Moslem land, iii 402
Muwashshah (Stanza), iii. 181
Muzaní (AL), ii. 108
Muzayyin (Figaro of the East), i. 280
Myrtle-bush = young beard, iii. 264
Mystification explained by extraordinary likeness, vi. 197

NA'AL = sandal, shoe, horse-shoe, v. 115
Náb (pl. Anyáb) = canine tooth, tusk, vi. 124
Nabbút = quarter-staff, i. 215; vi. 335
Nabhán (sons of), v. 167
Nabí = prophet, vii. 249
Nábighah al-Zubvání (pre-Islamitic poet), v. 3

Nadd (a compound perfume), i. 286
Naddábah = mourning woman, i. 287
Nadím = cup-companion, i. 42
Nafahát = breathings, benefits, iii. 442
Nafakah = sum necessary for the expenses of the pilgrimage, vii. 249
Nafas = breath, i. 98
Náfilah = supererogatory Koran rĕcitation, iii. 10
Nafisah (great-grand-daughter of the Imám Hasan), iii 173
Nafisah (Pr. N.) = the Precious one, vii. 60
Nafs-í = my soul for "the flesh," v. 315
Nafs = soul, life, i. 98
Nafs Ammárah = "the Flesh," vi. 189
—— al-Nátikah = intellectual soul, vi. 189
—— al-Ghazabíyah = animal function, vi. 189
—— al-Shahwáníyah = vegetative property, vi. 189
Nága-kings (of Hinduism), iv. 250
Nahás (vulg. for Nubás, *q.v.*), ii. 219; iii. 298, 346
Náhi-ka = let it suffice thee, viii. 21
Nahnu málihín = we are on term of salt, i. 371
Nahr = slaughtering a camel by stabbing, iii. 220
Nahr = river, v. 75
Nahs = nasty, i. 277
Nái' (traditionist), iv. 158
Ná'l al-maut = messenger of death, vi. 17
Náihah = keener, hired mourner, i. 287
Na'ím = delight (name for Heaven), ii. 245; iii. 264
Na'íman = may it benefit thee! after bathing, etc., i 333
Naïveté (of the Horatian kind), vii. 283
Najásah = nastiness (anything unclean), v. 89
Najib (al-taraf = son of a common Moslemah by a Sayyid, *q v.*), iv 209
Najib (al-tarafayn = whose parents are both of Apostolic blood), iv. 209
Najis = ceremonially impure, vii. 395
Nájiyah = Salvadora, ii. 47
Najm al-Munkazzi = shooting star, vii. 61
Najm al-Sabáh (Pr. N.) = Star o' Morn, vi. 260
Najrán (in Syria), ii. 131
Naká = sand-hill, viii. 25
Nakat = to spot; to handsel, vii. 3
Naked = without veil or upper clothing, v. 346
Nakedness (Ar. Aurat), iv. 370
—— (paraphrased), i. 302
Nakfúr = Nicephorus, i. 398
Nakh = make a camel kneel down by the cry Ikh! Ikh! ii. 42
Nákhúzah Zulayt = skipper rapscallion, vi. 324
Nakíb, a caravan-leader, chief, syndic, i. 247
Nákisátu 'aklin wa dín = failing in wit and faith, vii. 358
Nakkár = Pecker (a fabulous fish), vii. 255
Nakl-i-safar (move preliminary to a journey), i. 405
Nákús = wooden gong (used as bell), iv. 386; vii. 60
Name of Allah introduced into an indecent tale essentially Egyptian, i. 10
Names (of God), iv. 168
—— (= magical formula), iv. 312
—— (frequently do not appear till near the end of a tale), v. 274; vi. 62

Names (approved by Allah), vii. 237
Naming of a child, ii. 75
Naming a girl by name offensive, vi. 74
Naml (ant) simile for a young beard, ii 283
Námúsiyah = mosquito curtains, vii 62
Napoleonic pose (attitude assumed by a slave), vii. 378
Nár (fire), ii. 65
—— (fem. like, the names of other elements), vi. 175
Narcissus (with negro eyes = yellowish white), i. 350
Narjis = Narcissus, i. 271
—— (name of a slave-girl), vi. 326
Nashshár (Al-) = the sawer, i. 309
Násik = a devotee, vii. 119
Naskh = copying hand, i. 118
Nasím = Zephyr (emendation for Nadim = cup-companion), vi. 219
Násir (Pr. N.) = triumphing, vii. 370
Nasráni = follower of Him of Nazareth, i. 238
Nat'a = leather used by way of table-cloth, i. 18
Nat'a al-dam = the leather of blood, i. 293, 366
Nation (its power consists in its numbers of fighting men), iv. 205
Nau (pl. Anwá) = setting of one star simultaneous with another's rising, vii.
Naurúz = new (year's) day, iii. 359
Navel, as to beauty and health, i. 78
—— (largeness of, much appreciated), vi. 191
Nawá = date-stone; Nawáyah = severance, ii. 208
Nawátíyah = crew (navigata, nauta), vi. 176
Nay = reed-pipe, iv. 18
Naysábúr (town in Khorasan), vii. 297
Názih = travelled far and wide, iv. 20
Názir = overseer, ii. 198; iii. 20
Nearness of seat a mark of honour, i. 230
Negro (Legend of his origin), iii. 365
Negroes preferred by debauched women, i. 5
—— (familiarity of boys with white girls), i. 373
—— (their skin assumes dust-colour in cold, etc.), ii. 30
Negrofied races like "walking tun-butts," iii. 369
Neighbour before the house, companion before the journey, ii. 106
Neighbours (frequently on the worst of terms), v 143
Nemo repente fuit turpissimus (not believed in by Easterns), vii 167
"New Arabian Nights," v. 162
New-moon of Ramazán watched for, i. 78
New moon of the Festival = Crescent of the breakfast, vii. 315, 316
News (what is behind thee of, O Asám), vi. 369
Ni'am = yes in answer to a negative, v. 386
Ni'amat = a blessing, iii. 131
Night (and day, not day and night, with the Arabs), ii 344
—— (-cap), iii. 11
—— ("this" = our "last"), iii. 36
—— (for day), iii. 98
—— (its promise spread with butter that melteth with day-rise), iv. 43
—— (its last the bitter parting), vi. 34
—— (consists of three watches), i. 161; vii. 61

Nil (AL) = flood season corresponding to summer, i. 267
Nilah = indigo, dye-stuff, vii. 217
Nile-water sweet and light, i. 267
Nímchahrah = half-face (Pers., a kind of demon), iv. 279
Nimr = leopard, vii. 141
Nimrod of the desert, ii. 186
Nimsá = Germans, ii. 118
Nimshah (Namshah?) = dagger of state, ii. 94
Nineteen the age of an oldish old maid in Egypt, i. 195
Nisáb (AL), smallest sum for stealing which the hand is mutilated, iii. 278
Niták, a woman's waistcloth, v. 373
Niyab (Al-) = ceremonial intention of prayer, iv. 120
Nizámi (Persian poet), ii. 403
Noachian dispensation (revived Al-Islam as revealed to Adam), iv. 315
Noisy merriment scandalous to Moslem "respectability," i. 88
Nostrils (his life-breath was in his = his heart was in his mouth), vi. 48
Nostrums for divining the sex of the unborn child, vi. 57
Nothing for nothing, a sexual point d'honneur, i. 81
Nuhás (vulg. Nahás) = copper, brass, i. 37; ii 219; iii. 298, 346; v. 2
Nukl = quatre mendiants, vii. 248
Numbering the streets, etc., a classical custom vi. 243
Nún (simile for the eye-brow). iv. 2
Nún-like brow, iii. 363
Nur al-Huda (Pr. N.) = Light of Salvation, ii 244; vi. 251
Núrayn = two lights (town in Turkestan), v. 286
Nusf = half-dirham, i. 362; v. 123; vii. 212
Nusk = piety, abstinence from women, vii 310
Nu'mán (AL) bin Munzir (tyrant of Hirah), iv 40
Nu'mán's flower = anemone, ii. 217
Nuzhat al-Zamán = delight of the age, i. 401

Oath (a serious thing amongst Moslems), i. 165
—— (inconsiderately taken), ii. 87
—— (kept to the letter), iii. 196
—— (retrieved by expiation), vi. 408
—— (of divorce), vii. 22, 44
Obayd Allah (Pr. N.), iv. 121
Obayd ibn Táhir (Under-Prefect of Baghdad), iii. 403
Object first seen in the morning determines the fortunes of the day, vi. 298
Obscene abuse meant as familiarity, not insult, i. 408
O Champhor (antiphrase = O snowball). ii. 266
Ocean (Jamm), iv. 56
—— (of darkness), iv. 255
"Off-with-his-head" style (not to be taken literally), vii. 368
Offering for naught = closing with the offer, i. 332
Offerings (pious = ex votos, etc), v. 345
Oftentimes the ear loveth before the eye, ii. 237
Ohod (battle of), ii. 66
Old age (graphically described), iii. 417
"Old maids" ignored in the East, vi. 74
"Old Man of the Sea" (a Márid or evil Jinn), v. 124

Old woman (polite equivalents for), iv. 120
Oldest matter in The Nights the beast-stories, ii. 337
Olemá (pl. of 'Álim) = the learned in the law, iv. 139
—— (Time-serving), viii. 41
Omán = Eastern Arabia, i. 76
—— (with capital Maskat = Omana Moscha), v. 225
Omar bin al-Khattáb (Caliph), ii. 60, 61, 63, 65; iv. 66
Omar-i-Khayyám (astronomer-poet), vii. 297
Omen (Fál), iv. 97
One-eyed men considered rascals, iii. 313
Opener (of the door of daily bread), v. 124
Opening doors without a key is the knavish trick of a petty thief, v. 375
Ophidia (of monstrous size), iv. 370
Orange (a growth of India), vii. 8
Oriental orgie different from European, i. 86
Othello (even he does not kill Emilia), vii. 360
Othmán (Caliph), ii. 64
—— (Kátib al-Kuran), iv. 169
Oubliettes (in old Eastern houses), iii. 106
Out of the sight of my friend is better and pleasanter, iii. 95
O whose thrall am I, etc. = To her (I drink), vi. 371

Palace (of the Caliph at Baghdad), v. 99
Palaces (avoided by the pious), v. 92
—— (in ruins for want of repair), viii. 58
Palgrave and Al-Islam, viii. 170
Palmerin of England, vi. 220
Palm-stick (a salutary rod), i. 348
Palsy (creeps over him), iv. 202
Panel-dodge fatally common, i. 298
Paper (his = the whiteness of his skin), iv. 119
Paradise (of the Moslem not wholly sensual), ii. 245; vii. 381
Parapets (on terrace-roofs made obligatory by Moses), iv. 38
Parasite (Ar. Tufayli), iv. 91
Parent (ticklish on the Pundonor), vii. 349
Parisian MSS. of the Nights, viii. 94
Parody on the testification of Allah's Unity, i. 163; iii 4
Parrot-story a world-wide folk-lore, i. 48
Particles of swearing, vii. 44
Partner in very deed, vi. 330
Partridge (Ar. Hijl), ii. 360
Partridges (story of the two), v. 94
Pashas' agents for bribery in Constantinople, iii. 301
Passengers in difficulties take command, i. 129
Pathos (touch of), ii. 280
Patience (cutting the cords of), ii. 398
Pausing as long as Allah pleased = musing a long time, v. 25
Pay-chest (of a Hammám bath), vii. 225
Payne quoted, i. 119, *et. seq.*
Peaches (Sultani and Andam), vii. 6
Pearl supposed to lose 1 per cent. per ann. of its lustre, i. 152

Pearl-fisheries, iv 398
Pearls (shaded by hair = teeth under mustachio), iv. 116
(fresh from water), vi. 30
—— (resting on the sand-bank), vii. 236
Pears (various kinds of), vii. 6
Peccadillo in good olden days (murder), iii. 387
Pehlevi version of the Panchatantra, viii. 110
Pen and Preserved Tablet, i. 389
Pencilling the eyes with Kohl, vi. 40
Pens (gilded = reeds washed with gold), vi. 310
People of His affection = those who deserve His love, vii. 159
Pepper (and the discovery of the Cape route), iv. 378
—— (-plantations shaded by bananas), *ib.* 395
Perfumes (not used during mourning), ii. 288
—— (natural), iii. 19
Periphrase containing a negative adds emphasis, i. 403
Persian ("I am a, but not lying now"), iii. 439
—— (poets mostly addressing youths), iv. 115
Persians always suspected, vi. 167
Persians (delighting in practical jokes), vii. 248
Person (Ar. Shakhs), iii. 222; vi. 310
Peshadians (race of Persian Kings), i. 69
Petrified folk, vii. 377
Phaedra and Hippolytus, v. 42
Pharaoh (signs to), iii. 364
"Philippi" and "Alexanders" in Sidon, i. 403
Philosophic (used in a bad sense), v. 163
Physical prognostication familiar to Mesmerists, i. 393
Physiognomy (Ar. Firásah Kiyáfah), vii. 59
Physiologists (practice on the simiads), iv. 173
Physis and Antiphysis, iv. 266
Picnics (on the Rauzah island), iv. 125
Pidar-sokhtah = (son of a) burnt father (Persian insult), iv. 366
Piéces de circonstance (mostly mere doggerel), ii. 157, vi. 216
Pigeon (language, etc.), ii. 348
Pilgrimage not perfected save by copulation with the camel, vi. 308
Pilgrims (offcast of the = broken down pilgrim left to die on the road), vii 351
Pillow (wisádah, makhaddah), taking to = taking to one's bed, i 392
Pistachio-nut (tight-fitting shell of), iii. 333
Pitching tents within dog-bark from Royalty disrespectful, ii 188
Plain (ground), synonyms for, i. 43
Plain-speaking (of the Badawi), iii. 226
Plates as armature, iii. 4
Play "near and far" = "fast and loose," viii. 21
Pleiads (the stars whereby men sail), vii. 38
Plunder sanctioned by custom, i. 390
Plur. masc. used by way of modesty by a girl addressing her lover, i 90
Plural of Majesty, ii. 242; iii. 258
Poetical justice (administered with vigour in The Nights), v. 161
Poetry of the Arabs requires knowledge of the Desert to be understood), i. 211
Poison (deadly only in contact with abraded skin), v. 111
Poisons in the East, vii. 176

Policeman (called in, a severe punishment in the East: why ?), vii. 210
Police-master legally answerable for losses, v. 356
Polissonnerie (Egyptian), iii. 30, 342
Polo ("Goff"), iv. 1
Poltroon (contrasted with a female tiger-lamb), vii. 292
Polygamy and Polyandry in relation to climate, iii 28
Polyphemus (in Arab garb), iv. 365
—— (no Mrs. P. accepted), *ib.* 368
Pomegranate fruit supposed to contain seed from Eden garden, i 124
—— (Hadis referring to), vii. 4
Porcelain (not made in Egypt or Syria), iii. 284
Potter (simile of the), vii. 155
Pouch (Ar. Surrah), vi. 227
Poverty (Holy), iv. 218
Powders (coloured in sign of holiday making), viii. 52
Power (whoso has it and spareth, for Allah's reward he prepareth), vii. 398
Prayer (for the dead lack the Sijdah), i. 337
—— (of Ramazán), ii. 102
—— (rules for joining in), ii. 395
—— (two-bow), iii. 2
—— (-niche = way-side chapel), iii. 104
—— (without intention, Ar. Niyat, is valueless), iv 120
—— (of a sick person as he best can), iv. 154
—— (intonation of the voice in), iv. 155
—— (call to, Azán), iv. 156
—— (is a collector of all folk), iv. *ib.*
Praying against (polite form for cursing), vii 353
Pre-Adamite doctrine, viii. 161
Preachments (to Eastern despots), iv. 205
Precautions (thwarted by Fate and Fortune), v. 79
Precedence (claims pre-eminence), vii. 21
Precedent (merit appertains to), iii. 49
Predestination (not Providence, a Moslem belief), v. 111
Pre-eminence (appertaineth to precedence), vii. 21
Preliminaries of a wrestling bout, i. 411
Presence (I am *in thy = thy slave to slay or pardon*), vii. 198
Preserved tablet, i. 389
Preventives (the two), iii. 10
Price (without abatement = without abstracting a large bakhshish), vii. 225
—— (shall remain), vii. 325
Pride of beauty intoxicates, iii. 162
Priest hidden within an image (may date from the days of Memnon), vii. 383
Prime Minister carrying fish to the cookmaid, i. 58
Prince (of a people is their servant), vii. 175
Prin'cess, English; Prince'ss, French, vi. 35
Prison (in the King's Palace), vii. 131
Prisons (Moslem), v. 150
Privy, a slab with a slit in front and a round hole behind, i. 204
—— and bath favourite haunts of the Jinns, v 54
Procès verbal (customary with Moslems), iii. 199
Prognostication frequently mentioned, i. 393
—— (from nervous movements), vi. 184

Prolixity (heightening the effect of a tale), viii. 47
Property (of the heirless lapses to the treasury), iii. 183
—— (left by will), v. 122
Prophets (have some manual trade), ii. 181
—— (named in the Koran), iv. 164
—— (and their agnomina), v. 174
Proportion of horse and foot in Arab and Turcoman armies, v. 203
Prostitution (never wholly abolished in Al-Islam), vi. 268
Prostration (must be made to Allah only), v. 50
Protestants (four great *Sommités*), v. 321
Prothesis without apodosis (a favourite style in Arabic), v. 112, 146
Proverbs true to nature, i. 283
Providence (and Justice), iv. 234
Province ("some" = Sancho Panza's "insular"), ii. 88
Puellæ Wakwakienses, vi. 244
Punctilios of the Desert, v. 169
Puns (wretched and otherwise), i. 386; ii. 80; iii. 372; v. 253; vi. 76, 94; vii. 61, 340, 348; viii. 11, 25
Purgation (Easterns most careful during), iv. 112
Purity of love attains a prophetic strain, ii. 234
Pyramids (Ar. Al-Ahrám), iv. 67
—— (containing unopened chambers?), iv. 68
—— (verses on the), viii 136

QANOON-E-ISLAM quoted on the subject of horoscopes, etc. i. 195
Quarter (son of the = neighbour), v. 143
Queen's mischief = the mischief which may (or will) come from the Queen, vi. 252
Question (expressing emphatic assertion), vii. 252
Questions (indiscreet, the rule throughout Arabia), ii. 328
Quibbling away (a truly diplomatic art), iv. 50

RA'AD AL-KÁSIF (Pr. N.) = the loud-pealing Thunder, v. 129
Ra'ad Sháh A. P. = thunder-king v. 255
Raas al-Mál = capital, vi. 394
Raat-hu = she saw him, vii. 33
Ra'áyá (pl. of Ra'íyat) = Ryot, iii. 4
Rabbatí = my she-Lord, applied to the fire, v 237
Rabelaisian humour of the richest, iii. 273
Rabite, classical term for a noble Arab horse, ii. 296
Racing a favourite pastime, ii. 169
Raff = shelf running round a room, vi. 275
Ráfisi = dernier, Shi'ah, iii. 171
Rafw = artistic style of darning, v. 107
Rag (burnt, used as styptic), iii. 232
Rághib (= expecter; Záhid = rejecter), vii. 48
Ráh = pure old wine, iii. 305
Rahan = pledge, vii. 370
Ráhatáni (Al-) = the two rests, vii. 73
Rahil (small dromedary), ii. 292
Rahim (Rihm) = womb for uterine relations v. 320

Rahmah (Pr. N.) = the puritanical "Mercy," v. 133
Raiment of devotees (white wool), vi. 6
Rais = captain, master (not owner) of a ship, i. 117; iv. 353
Raising the tail, sign of excitement in the Arab blood-horse, ii 309
Rajab = worshipping (seventh Arab month), iv. 21
Rajaz = the seventh Bahr of Arabic prosody, i. 231
RaJul ikhtiyár = a middle-aged man, i. 51
Rakham = aquiline vulture, vi. 179
Ráki (distilled from raisins), iv. 32
Rakb = fast-going caravan, iii. 368
Ramazán (moon of), vi. 191
Ramlah (half-way house between Jaffa and Jerusalem), v. 301
Rank (derived from Pers. rang = colour), ii. 92
—— (thine is with me such as thou couldst wish = I esteem thee as thou deservest), vii. 121
—— (conferred by the Sovereign's addressing a person by a title), vii. 193
Rape (rendered excusable by wilfulness), v. 97
Rás al-Killaut = Head of Killaut, a son of the sons of the Jinn, vii. 90
Rás al-Tín = Headland of Clay (not Figs), iv. 74
Rashaa = fawn beginning to walk, iv. 108
Rashád = garden-cresses or stones, vi. 342
Rashíd = the heaven-directed, vi. 342
Rashid (Pasha, etc.), iii. 320
Rashid = Rosetta, vii. 24
Rasif (Al-) river-quay, dyke, vi. 301
Rasm = usage (justifies a father killing his son), i. 331
Rasúl = one sent, "apostle," not prophet, iii. 396
Rasy = praising in a funeral sermon, iii. 75
Raushan = window, ii. 391
Raushaná (splendour) = Roxana, *ib.*
Rauzah (AL) = the gardens, i. 268
—— (at Cairo), iv. 125
Raven of the waste or the parting, iii. 178; vi. 382
Ráwi = story-teller (also used for Reciter of Traditions), viii 117
Ráy = rede ("private Judgment"), v. 59
Ráyah káimah = pennons flying (not "beast standing"), v. 316
Raydaniyah (camping ground near Cairo), i. 226
Rayhán = scented herb, vi. 336
Rayháni = a curved character, i. 118; ii. 195
Ráyi = rationalist, v. 59
Rayy (old city of Media), iii. 227
Ready to fly for delight, ii. 252
Ream (It. risma, Ar. rizmah), iv. 70
Red dress (sign of wrath), iii. 197; v. 156
Red Sea (cleaves in twelve places), iv. 188
Reed = pen (title of the Koranic chapt. lxviii), i 389
Reed-pipe (Nay), iv. 18
Refusal of a gift, greatest affront, i. 310
—— (of a demand in marriage a sore insult), v. 167
Relations between Badawi tribes, v. 171
Rending of garments as sign of sorrow or vexation, i. 284
"Renowning it" (boasting of one's tribe), ii. 304, 331

"Renowning it" (naïve style of), vi. 132
Repentance (a strong plead for granting aid with a Moslem), iii 389
—— (acquits the penitent), v. 271
Repetition, vi. 81, 88
—— (of an address in token of kindness), iv. 314
Resignation (noble instance of), viii. 40
Respect shown to parts of the body, exuviæ, etc., i. 254
Rest (in Eastern travel before eating and drinking), vi. 293
Retorts (of a sharp Fellah), v. 139
Return unto Allah, iii. 97
Return-Salám, vii. 43
Revenge (a sacred duty), vi. 184
Ribá = interest, usury, iv. 155; vi. 394
Ridding the sea of its rubbish, vii. 241
Riddle "surprise" (specimen of), iv. 191
Riders (names of such on various beasts), vi. 384
Riding on the ass an old Biblical practice, i 241
Riding on men as donkeys (facetious exaggeration of African practice), vi. 141
Rihl = wooden saddle, ii. 340
Rijál al-Ghayb (invisible controls), ii. 111; viii. 13
Rims cars, i. 121
Rind (rand) = willow, bay, and aloes-wood, ii 393
Ring (in memoriam), v. 109
—— (lost in the Hárim raises Jealous suspicion), v. 109
Rings in the East, iii. 153
Rising up and sitting down sign of agitation, ii. 16
Ritánah = a jargon, ii. 419
River (the = Tigris Euphrates), vii. 372
Rivers (underground), iv. 401
Rizm (pl. of rizmah) = bales, reams, vi 70
Rizwán (approbation) = key-keeper of Paradise, ii. 242, 246; iii. 314; vii. 2
Robbing (to keep life and body together, an acceptable plea), vii. 211
Robe (the hidden, story of), v. 98
Robing one's self in rags = becoming a Fakir, ii. 72
Robinson Crusoe (with a touch of Arabic prayerfulness), iv. 239
Rock (falling upon ship), vi. 82
Rod (divining or dowsing) iii. 198
Roman superficiality (notable instance of), viii. 106
Rosary, ii. 347
Rose (in Arab. masculine), vii 11
Rose-water (for "nobility and gentry," even in tea), iv. 302
Rotl (pl. Artál) = rotolo, pound weight, iii. 247
Roum = Græco-Roman Empire, iii. 224
Roumi (in Marocco = European), vii. 5
Royalty in the guise of merchants, ii. 239
Rozistán = day-station, i 26
Rub' al-Kharáb (probably for the Great Arabian Desert), v. 279; viii. 39
Rubb = syrup, "Rob," i. 331
Rubbamá = perhaps, sometimes (more emphatic than rubba), vi. 10
Rubber (shampooer), ii. 244
Rubbah (townlet on the frontier of Syria), ii. 277
Ruby (La'al, Yákút), iv. 287

Ruby (of exceptional size), *ib.* 405
Rudaynah and Rudaynian lances, i. 329
Rudaynian lance (like a), vi. 54
Rúh=spirit, breath of life, vii. 145
Ruh=be off, vii. 240
Ruh bihi Fuzúl=Begone and none of your impudence, vi. 313
Rukbán=monks, vi. 401
Ruká'i=correspondence hand, i. 118
Ruk'atayn=two-bow prayer, i. 131
Rukb=travellers on camels, return caravan, vi 384
Rukh (Roc and "Roc's" feathers) iv. 84
—— (the world-wide "Wundervogel") *ib.* 357, 389
—— (study of, by Prof. Bianconi), iv. 389
Rukhám=alabaster, i. 272
Rumourers (the two)=basin and ewer, v. 341
Rustak (Al-), City of Oman, v. 193
Rustam (not Rustum or Rustem), iii. 336
Rutub (applying to pearls=fresh from water), vi. 30
Ryot=liege, subject; Fellah, peasant, iii. 4

SÁ'A (measure of corn, etc.), v. 112
Sa'ad=auspiciousness, prosperity; derivatives, i 8
Sa'adah (female Pr. N.), ii. 290
Sa'ádah=worldly prosperity and future happiness, vii 385
Sa'alab=fox, ii. 354
Sa'alabah (name of a tribe), ii. 330
Sabá=Biblical Sheba, iii. 236; vi. 102
Sabab=rope (hence a cause), i. 341; vi. 254
Sabaj (not Sabah) a black shell, v. 327
Sabaka=he out-raced, vii. 185
Sabaka Kúrabá, vi. 204
Sabb=low abuse, iii. 92
Sabbágh=dyer, ii. 199
Sabbáh bin Rammáh bin Humám=the Comely, son of the Spearman, son of the Lion, ii. 292
Sabbahaka 'llah bi-'l-Khayr=Allah give thee good morning, v. 106
Sabbath (kept in silence), iv. 285
Sabbation (River), iv. 283
Sabihat al-'Urs=gift on the wedding morning, viii. 17
Sábik=forerunner, vii. 71
Sabikah=bar, lamina, ingot, vi. 169
Sabiyah=young lady, vii. 294
Sabr=patience and aloes, source of puns, i 127; vi. 193; vii. 340
Sabt=Sabbath, ii. 199
Sabúr=Sapor ii., v. 179
Sacrifice (Ar. Kurbán), vi 175
Sacy, Silvestre de (on the origin of The Nights), viii 71
Sád (Letter, simile for the eye), iv. 2
Sadaf=cowrie, i. 17
Sadakah=voluntary alms, opposed to Zakát, i. 313
Sadd=wall, dyke, i. 105; ii. 31

Sádir = returning from the water (*see* Wárid), ii. 281
Sadness (House of), vi. 220
Sady = Hámah, *q.v.*; iii. 77
Safá (ground-wave *in* Meccah), iv. 157
Safe-guard (I am in thy = I appeal to thy honour), v. 70
Saffron (aphrodisiac), ii. 132
Safinah = (Noah's) Ark, vii. 369
Safiyu 'llah (Adam) = pure of Allah, ii. 27
Safwán (Pr. N.) = clear, cold, vi. 100
Saghr (Thagr), the opening of the lips showing the teeth, i. 143
Sahákah = tribadism, ii. 132
Sáhib = companion, used as a Wazirial title, i. 218; iii. 261; iv. 38
Sáhib al-Shartah = chief of the watch (Prefect of Police), i. 238
Sáhib Nafas = master of breath, a minor saint healing by expiration, i. 98
Sahífah = page, book, vi. 229
Sahikah = Tribade, vi. 282
Sáhil (Al-) = the coast (Phœnicia), vii. 102
Sáhil Masr = the river side (at Cairo), i. 269
Sahim al-Layl (Pr. N.) = he who shooteth an arrow by night, v. 166
Sáhirah = place for the gathering of souls on Doom-day, iii. 103
Sahm mush'ab = forked (not barbed) arrow, vii. 127
Sahr (Al-) = magic, black art, i. 281
Sáibah = she-camel freed from labour, ii. 303
—— = a woman who lets herself go (a-whoring, etc.), vi. 302
Sa'id bin Jubayr, ii. 101
Sa'id bin Sálim (Governor of Khorasan), iv. 58
Sa'id bin Zayd (traditionist), iv. 46
Sa'idah = the auspicious (fem.), vii. 389
Sá'ik = the Striker (Pr. N.), v. 236
Sá'ikah = thunderbolt, v. 176
Sailor (Ar. equivalents for), v. 148
Sáim al-dahr = perennial faster, iv. 74
Saint, Santon (Walí), iv. 74
Saint and Sinner, iv. 77
Sa'ir = Hell, iii. 264
Sáis = groom, horsekeeper (Syce), iv. 350
Saj'a (= rhymed prose), i. 107
—— (instance of), iv. 118
—— (bald in translation), v. 204
—— (answerable for galimatias), v. 237
Sajah (false prophetess), iv. 106
Sajjádah = prayer-rug, v. 103
Sakatí = second-hand dealer, iii. 202
Sakhr al-Jinní alluded to, i. 38; iv. 262
Sákí = cup bearer, i. 354
Sákin = quiescent (applied to a closing wound), vii. 318
Sákiyah = the Persian water-wheel, i. 113; vii. 285
Sakká (Anglo-Indian Bihishti) = water-carrier, iii. 172; iv. 52
Sakr = hawk, ii. 188
Saksar (Pers. Sag-sar = dog's head), iv. 377
Sa'lab = fox, jackal, v. 120; vii. 127, 178
Salaf (Al-) = ancestry (referring to Mohammed), iv. 54

Saláhitah (AL) island, iv. 370
Sal'am = S(allà) Al(lah) 'A(layhi wa, salla), M, *see* Abbak, i. 3;;0
Salám (to be answered by a better salutation), ii. 48
—— (of prayers), ii. 140
—— (becomes Shalúm with the Jews), vi. 369
—— (not returned, a Moslem form of Boycotting), vii. 36
Salámát = Welcome! v. 139
Salát (blessing, prayer), iii. 186
Salát mamlúkíyah = praying without ablution, v. 343
Salátah (how composed), v. 329
Salb = crucifying, ii. 251
Sale (forced on by the bystanders), vii. 44
Sales (formula of), iv. 412
Sálifah = silken plait, vi. 370
Sálih = a pious man, vi. 100, 340
—— prophet sent to Thámúd, i. 156
—— (grandson of Shem?), iv. 164
—— (his she-camel), iv. 187
—— al-Mazani (theologian), v. 212
Sálihiyah = the Holy (name of a town), vii. 348
Salim (Pr. N. = the "Safe and Sound"), iii. 184
Sallah = basket of wickerwork, vii. 135
Salli 'alá 'l-Nabi = bless the prophet (imposing silence), iv 12
Salmá and Laylá = our "Mary and Martha," i. 244
Salsabil (fountain of Paradise), ii. 282; iii. 313
Salutation (the first), iv. 154
—— (Salám, unwillingly addressed to a Christian), iv. 233
—— (from a rider to a man who stands, and from the latter to one who sits), vii. 84
Sama'an wa Tá'atan to be translated variously, i. 88
Samak = common fish, iv. 408
Samandal (Al-) = Salamander, vi. 69
Samar = night-story, vi. 99
Samáwah (AL), visitation place in Babylonian Irak, v. 292
Samharí = lance of Sambar (place or maker), iii. 371
Samír = night-talker, vi. 8
Samm-hu = his Shaft, v. 16
Samn = melted butter, Ghi, i. 132; iii. 180; vii. 119
—— = clarified butter, vii. 119
Samsam (sword of the Tobba Amru bin Ma'ad Kurb), ii. 30
Samúm = poisonous wind (Simoon), v. 5
Samúr (applied to cats and dogs, also to Admiral Seymour), iii. 183
Sana'á (capital of Al-Yaman), iii. 429
—— (famed for leather and other work), v. 327
Sanájik = banners, ensigns, etc., vii. 351
Sand (knowing by the = geomancy), vii. 191
Sandal (Pr. N.) = Sandal-wood, vi. 318
—— (scented with), iv. 147
—— (Ar. Na'al), v. 115
Sandals (kissed and laid on the head in token of submission), vi. 154
Sandúk al-Nuzur = box of vowed oblations, vii. 61
Sapphic venery, ii. 132
Sapphism (practised in wealthy Harims), iii. 349

Sar'a (epilepsy, falling sickness, possession), iii. 213, 441
Sár = vendetta, i. 93, 106
Saráb = mirage, iii. 99; v. 10
Sarandib = Selan-dwípa (Ceylon), iv. 403
Saráwíl = bag or petticoat trousers, i. 205
—— (plural or singular?), vii. 293
Sardáb = underground room, souterrain, tunnel, i. 314; iv. 89
Sari al-Sakati (Sufi ascetic), vii. 101
Sarídah (Tharídah) = brewis, iv. 175
Sarír = bier (empty), i. 370
Sarmújah = leggings, sandals, slippers, vi. 154
Sarráf = Anglo-Indian "Shroff," i. 193; iii. 382
Sásá bin Shays, v. 178
Sassanides, i. 69
Satan (his malice weak in comparison with women's), v. 57
Satl = kettle, bucket (situla?), v. 376
Sátúr = chopper, vi. 313
Saub (Tobe) 'Atábi = tabby silk, vi. 349
Saudá = black bile, melancholia, iii. 366
Saudawí = of a melancholic temperament, vi. 29
Sauf (particle to express future), ii. 165, 191
Saulajan = bat in "bat and ball," ii. 221
Sawáb = reward in Heaven, i. 89
Sawád = blackness of the hair, viii. 56
Sawáhílí = shore-men, vii. 102
Sawálif = tresses, locks, iv. 117
Sawík = parched corn, vi. 90
Sawwáhún = wanderers, pilgrims, vii. 67
Sawwán = Syenite, iii. 103
Sayd wa Kanas = hunting and coursing, i. 8
Sayf (ξίφος) al-Mulúk = Sword of the Kings, vi. 111
Sayf Zu al-Yazan (hero of Persian romance), vi. 180
Sayhún and Jayhún = Jaxartes and Bactrus, i. 399; iv. 10
Sáyih = wanderer (not "pilgrim"), vii. 130
Sayl = torrent, v. 76
Sayr = broad girdle, vii. 57
Sayyib (Thayyib) = woman who leaves her husband after lying once with hi vii. 56
Sayyib-hu = let him go, vi. 302
Sayyid (descendant from Mohammed through Al-Hasan), iv 209
Scabbard (Ar. Ghimd), iv. 117
Scalding a stump in oil a common surgery practice, i. 273
Schoolmaster (derided in East and West), iv. 80
Schools (attached to mosques), viii. 157
Scorpions of the brow = accroche-cœurs, etc., i. 155; vi. 356
Scoundrels (described with superior gusto), vii. 209
Scrotum (curdling in fear), ii. 131
Sea of Al-Karkar, v. 17
Sea (striking out sparks), vii. 373
Sea-stallion (myth of the), iv. 351
Seal (and sealing-wax), ii. 408
—— (affixed to make an act binding), iv. 140

Sealing a covered dish (a necessary precaution against poison), i. 224
Seal-ring of Solomon (oath by), vi. 104
Seas (the two = the Mediterranean and the Indian Ocean), i 159
—— (fresh = lakes and river), iv. 272
Seclusion (royal, and its consequences), vii. 167
Secrets (instances and sayings with regard to their keeping), iv 48
Secrets (of workmanship, withheld from apprentices), vii. 325
Seditions in Kúfah caused by Caliph Othman's nepotism, ii. 64
Seeing sweetness of speech = finding it out in converse, vii. 95
Seeking refuge with Allah, iv. 155
Separation (spoken of as a defilement), iii. 329
Septentriones (four oxen and their wain), i. 331
Sepulchre, erroneously called a little Wali, i. 97
Serpent does not sting or bite, but strikes, ii. 381
—— (breaks the bones of its devoured prey by winding round a tree or rock), iv. 369
—— (breath of), *ib.* 370
—— (preserving from sickness), *ib.* 405
—— (in Ar. mostly feminine), *ib.* 414
Set-off for abuse of women, v. 326
Seven schools or editions of the Koran, i. 104
Seven sleepers, ii. 351
Sévigné of pearls, iii. 364
Sha'abán (moon of), iv. 146
Shább = youth between puberty and forty, i. 51
Shabistán = night station, i. 26
Shadow (may yours never be less), vi. 320
Sháfi'i (school of theology), ii. 53
Shahádatayn = the two Testimonies, i. 337; iii. 125
Shah-bandar = lord of the port (Consul), iii. 158
Shah (AL) mát = the King is dead (checkmate), vi. 364
Sháhid = index, pointer, ii. 194
Sháhmiyah (large tent), ii. 94
Sháh-púr = King's son, Σαβὼρ, Sapor, iii. 416
Shahrazád (various explanations of the name), i. 13, 329
Shahrimán *not* Shah Zemán, ii. 234; iii. 1
Shahryár = city friend, i. 2
Shahyál bin Shárukh (Pr. N.), vi. 117
Shah Zamán = King of the Age, i. 2
Sháib al-Ingház = grey beard shaking with disapproval, iii. 87
Sha'ilah = link (also lamp, wick, etc.), i. 239
Shakespeare and musical glasses, i. 331
Shakespearean "topothesia" out-Shakespeared, iii. 1
Shakhs = a person; a black spot, iii. 52; vi. 310
Shakhtúr = dinghy, vi. 146
Shaking and nodding the head, universal items of gesture language, i. 276
Shakiriyah = Kshatriya caste, iv. 352
Shákuriyah = chicoré, iv. 178
Shám (Syria) = land on the left, opposed to al-Yaman = land on the right, i. 76
Shámah = Khál, mole on the cheek, i. 154
Shamardal (AL) = the Tall One, v. 129
Shambar = Cassia fistularis, ii. 139

"Shame" alluded to in cursing parents of an abused person, i. 360
—— (extends from navel to knees), vi. 342
Shamlah = gaberdine, vi. 310
Shammara = he tucked up (sleeve or gown), v. 330
Shammir = up and ready! vi. 408
Shampooer (rubber) = Mukayyis or bag-man, ii. 244
Shampooing the feet, i. 108
Shams al-Daulah (imaginary king of Egypt), v. 148
Shams al-Nahár (Pr. N.) = Son of the Day, iii. 422
Shams al-Zubá (Pr. N.) = Son of Unduru, vi. 260
Shamtá = the grizzled (name for wine), viii. 36
Shanak = hanging, ii. 251
Shanfarà (poet), *ib.* 365
Shár, Sher and Shir, iii. 306
Sha'r = hair of the body, pile, vii. 229
Shara (Al-) mountain in Arabia, v. 225
Shar'a = holy law, v. 364
Sharáb al-Tuffáh = cider, iii. 256
Sharaf al-Banat (Pr. N.) = Honour of Maidenhood, vi. 260
Sharárif = trefoil-shaped crenelles, iii. 285
Sharíf = a descendant of Mohammed, iii. 290
Sharít = chopper, sword, v. 371
Sharmútah = rags, tatters; a strumpet; shreds of meat = Kadíd, i. 150
Sharrkán (Sharrun kána) = bane to the foe, i. 399
Shart = a single Talbiyah or cry Labbayka, i. 208
Shásh Abyaz = white turband (distinctive sign of the True Believer), vi. 167
Shatm = obscene abuse, i. 167
Shaukat = sting; pride, ii. 10
Shaving and depilation (process of), ii. 62; vii. 212
Sháyban (Arab tribe), iv. 63
Shaykh = an old man, elder, chief, i. 23, 51; ii. 47
—— (attended by a half-witted lunatic), v. 347
—— (after the type of Abú Nowás), vii. 316
—— (for syndic of a guild), vii. 323
—— (of the thieves one of the worthies of a Moslem capital), v. 113
—— al-Bahr = Chief of the Sea (-coast), iv. 390, 392; vi. 141
Shaykh al-Islám = Chief of the Olema, vii. 350
—— (his mention sign of modern composition), viii. 18
Shaykh Nasr (Pr. N. = Elder of Victory), iv. 289
Shaykhah Rájihah = the excellent Religious, vii. 405
Shaykhs (five, doubtful allusion), ii. 256
Shays = Ab Seth, v. 187
Shaytán (Satan), term of abuse, ii. 251
—— (his wife and nine sons), iii. 17
Shayyun li 'lláhi = per amor di Dio, i. 303
Shawáhi (from Shauh) = having fascinating eyes, ii. 165
Shawáhi Umm al-Dawáhi = the Fascinator, Mother of Calamities, vi. 242
Shazarwán = Pers. = Shadurwán, palace, cornice, etc., v. 251
Shedding tears no disgrace for a man, i. 63
Shem hamphorash = the hundredth name of God engraved on the seal-ring of Solomon, i. 159
Shibábah = reed-pipe, vi 316

Shiháb=shooting stars, i. 206
Shikk=split man (a kind of demon), iv. 279
Shinf=gunny-bag, iv. 14
Shiraj=sesame oil, vii. 254
Shirk (partnership=Polytheism, Dualism, Trinitarianism), i. 167; ii. 10[1]
—— (=syntheism) of love, iii. 422
—— of the Mushrik, iv. 102
Shoe (Ar. Markúb, Na'al), v. 115
Shop (front shelf of, a seat for visitors), vii. 324
Shops composed of a "but" and a "ben," i. 291; ii. 384
Shouting under a ruler's palace to attract attention, i. 363
Shovel-iron stirrup, ii. 342
Shower (how delightful in rainless lands), v. 336
Shroud (Joined in one=shrouded together?), iv. 37
Shrouds (carried by the pilgrims to Meccah), iv. 400.
Shu'ayb=Jethro, ii. 105; iv. 164
Shúbash=bravo! v. 387
Shudder preceding the magnetic trance, i. 40
Shuhadá=martyrs (extensive category), i. 158
Shuhúd=accessors of the Kazi's court, i. 19
Shujá al-Din (Pr. N.)=the brave of the Faith, vii. 99
Shukkah=piece of cloth, vii. 304
Shúm (a tough wood used for staves), vi. 138
Shuraih (a Kazi of Kufah in the seventh century), i. 232
Shúshah=top-knot of hair, i. 284
Shumán=pestilent fellow, iii. 201
Sibawayh (grammarian), vi. 24
Siddík=true friend, ii. 97
Siddíkah (AL)=the veridical (apparently undeserved title of Ayishah), vi. 303
Side-muscles (her, quiver)=she trembles in every nerve, vi 10
Sidi (from Sayyidí)=my lord, iv. 231
Sidi Ibrahim bin al-Khawwás (Pr. N.), iv. 231
Sidillah=seats, furniture, vii. 260
Sifr=whistling, iii. 324; iv. 279
Sight comprehendeth him not, etc., v. 186
Sign of the cross on the forehead, ii. 122
Signet-rings, iii. 153
Signing with the hand *not* our beckoning, vi. 234
Signs (of a Shaykh's tent), ii. 327
—— (lucky in a horse), ii. 340
—— (to Pharaoh), iii. 364
—— (of Allah=Koranic versets), v. 57
—— (by various parts of the body), vi. 379
—— (language of) vii. 332
Sijdah=prostration, i. 337
Sijn al-Ghazab=Prison of Wrath, viii. 42
Sikankúr=Σκίγκος, *see* Aphrodisiacs, iii. 160
Siláh-dár=armour-bearer, ii. 114
Simát=dinner table, i 164
Simiyá=white magic, i. 281, 306
Simoon (Ar. Sámúm=poisonous wind), v. 5
Símurgh (guardian of the Persian mysteries), viii. 118

Sin (permitted that men might repent), vii. 160
——(thy, shall be on thine own neck, vii. 280
Sin=China, i. 399
Sinai (convent famous for Ráki), iv. 32
Sindán, Sandán=anvil, vi. 168
Sindbád (not to be confounded with the eponym of the Sindibád-námah) iv. 346
Sindibád the Sage, v. 39
Sindibád-námah (Persian romance), v. 36
Singing (not harám=sinful, but makrúh=objectionable), vii. 312
Sinnaur=cat, prince, ii. 370
Sinning (for the pleasure of being pardoned), iii. 234
Sirah (small fish, fry, sprat), v. 124; vii. 237
Sirát (Al-), the bridge of Hell, iii. 340
Sisters (their abiding together after marriage frequently insisted upon, viii. 53
Sister (by adoption), vi. 183
Sisterhood=companions, suite, vi. 198
Sitt al-Masháikh=Lady of Shaykhs, iv. 113
Sitting on shins and knees, a trying posture, i 120
Siwák=tooth-stick; Siwá-ka=other than thou, iii 60
Sixth Abbaside Caliph, error for Fifth, vi. 213
Siyágosh, *see* Tufah.
Skin (free from exudation sounds louder under the clapping of the hand), vii. 222.
—— (extreme delicacy of the female), vii 379
"Slain were those who were slain"=many were slain, iv 308
Slander (poisoned=fatal), ii. 160
Slapping on the nape of the neck=boxing the ears, iii 312
Slate (Ar. Lauh), iv. 39
Slaughter (wholesale, for the delight of the gallery), vi. 400
Slaughtering (ritual for), iv. 333
—— (by cutting the animal's throat) vi. 201
Slave (holds himself superior to a menial freeman), vii 28
Slave-girl (Moslemah can compel an infidel master who has attempted her seduction to sell her), v. 395
—— (when newly bought frequently pretentious and coquettish), vi 55
—— (can only be sold with her consent), vii. 27
—— (free, not forward in her address), vii 331
—— (lewd and treacherous by birth), vii 342
—— (to be sent as a spy into the Harims), vii 353
Slaves (fancied by debauched women), i 176
—— (cannibals), i. 371
—— (familiarity) i. 373
—— (called "Camphor," like "Snowball"), i 371
—— (refuse to be set free), i. 378
—— (manumission of), *ib.*
—— (destructiveness), *ib.*
—— (girls' names), i. 380
—— (returning from a journey), i. 387
—— (Christian girls sent to Moslems), i 400
—— (girls examined as to virginity), ii. 49
—— (Behaving like one), ii. 166
—— (O Camphor), ii. 266

Slaves (set free for the benefit of the dead), ii. 430
—— (dealer in = Jalláb), iii. 119
—— (ambitious to have slaves of their own), iii. 425
—— (if ill-treated may demand to be sold), vi. 211
Sledge (thrashing = tribulum), i. 12
Sleeper and Waker (tale of the), iii. 221
Sleepers (the Seven, of Ephesus), ii. 351
Sleeping (and slumbering), ii. 79
—— (with covered head and face), iii. 123
—— (naked), iii. 422
—— (with head and body covered by a sheet), iii. 432
—— (with a sword between them), vi. 137
Sleeplessness (contrivance against), iii. 344
Slice of the moon = digit of the moon, i. 84
Smile (like Mim), iii. 363
—— (and laughter), iv. 147
Smoking out (a common practice), ii. 152
Smothering a rival (common in Harims), i. 380
Smuggling men into the Harim, i. 260
Snatching off the turband, a paying industry, i. 238
Sneezing (etiquette of), vii. 288
Sodomites (angels appear to), iii. 84
Soft-sided, attribute of beauty, i. 154
Soko (Maghribi form for Súk = bazar-street), vi. 377
Sold to thee for moneys received (formula of Moslem sales), iv. 412
Soldiers of Al-Daylam = warlike as the Daylamites, vi. 237
Sole of a valley often preferred to encamp in, i. 406
Solomon (his carpet), iii. 53
—— (his food-tray), iv. 417
—— (his seal ring), v. 1
—— (the Apostle of Allah), v. 15
—— (his Wazir Asaf), v. 16
—— (his trick upon Bilkis), v. 29
—— (oath by his seal-ring), vi. 104
—— and David (their burial place), iv. 257
—— and Al-Sakhr, ii. 1
Solomon's death fixing the date of a tale, i. 38
—— prison (the copper cucurbites in which he imprisoned the rebellious Jinns), vi. 308
"Son" used for "grandson" as more affectionate, i. 223
—— (the lamp of a dark house), ii. 176
—— (of a century = hundred years old), i. 116
—— (of Persian kings, not Prince but descendant), ii. 384
—— (of ten years dieth not in the ninth), vi. 226
Sons of Adam = men, i. 120
—— of Sásán = Sassannides, i. 2
—— (brought as servants unto Kings), vii. 122
—— of the road = wayfarers, i. 348
Sophia (Pr. N. and Mosque), i. 400
Sortes Virgilianæ, iv. 12
Soul (Thou knowest what is in mine, and I know not what is in thine), iv. 169
—— (you may have his, but leave me his body), vii. 20

Soul (for lover), vii. 105
Souls (doctrine of the three) iv. 171
Spartivento=mountain whereon the clouds split, vi. 178
Speaker puts himself first, i. 30
Speaking *en prince*, ii. 85
Speaking to the "gallery," vi. 280
Spears and Javelines, v. 168
Speech (this my=the words I am about to speak) vi 299
—— (inverted), vii. 51
Spells, (for prayers imprecating parting), vii. 77
Sperm (though it were a drop of marguerite), vi. 358
Spider-web, frailest of houses (Koranic), vii. 137
Spindle (thinner than a), iii. 46
Spiritual Sciences (Moslem form of Cabbala) ii. 53
Spittle dried up from fear, i. 263
Spoon (Ar. Mi'lakah), vii. 215
Spurring=kicking with the shovel-stirrup, i. 409
Squatting against a wall, iii. 242
Squeeze of the tomb (Fishás), iv. 73
Staff broken in the first bout=failure in the first attempt, i. 59
Stages (ten, of love-sickness), ii. 261
Stallion (I am not one to be struck on the nose), v. 167
Standards reversed in sign of defeat, ii. 156
Stations of the Moon (Ar. Manázil), iv. 80
Stature (Alif-like), iii. 363
Steel (Ar. Bulád), v. 30
Steward (pendant to the Parable of the UnJust), vii. 145
Stirrup (walking by the), v. 141
"Stone-bow" *not* "cross-bow," ii. 338
Stoning (of the devil at Mina), iv. 157
Stones (precious), iv. 287
—— (ditto, and their mines), iv. 359
—— (removed from the path by the pious), v. 100
Story-teller (picture of the), viii. 148
Strangers (treated with kindly care), iv. 127
"Strangers yet" (Lord Houghton quoted), iv. 232
Street (the, called Yellow), iii. 218
—— (-watering), *ib.* 231
Street-cries of Cairo, v. 366
Street-melodies changing with fashion, i. 287
Striking the right hand upon the left in sign of vexation, i. 275
Striking with the shoe, the pipe-stick, etc., highly insulting, i. 101
Stuff his mouth with jewels (reward for poetry), iii. 227
Stuff a dead man's mouth with cotton, iii. 311
Style (of a Cairene public scribe), v. 330
—— (intended to be worthy of a statesmen), vii 121
Su'adá=Beatrice, iii. 380
Subán=dragon, vii. 339
Subhána 'llah, pronounced to keep off the evil eye, iii. 12
Subhat-hu=in company with him, vi. 51
Subh-i-kázib=false dawn, i. 72
Subh-i-sádik=true dawn, i. 72

Submission (Ar. Khafz al-Jinah=lowering the wings), vii. 152
Sucking the dead mother's breast, touch of Arab pathos, ii. 31
Sucking the tongue=" kissing with the inner lips," i. 249
Súdán=our Soudan, ii. 300
Súdán-men=Negroes, vii. 2
Suez (Ar. Al-Suways), iv. 417
Súf (wool); Súfi (Gnostic), ii. 362
Sufiism (rise of), viii. 117
Súfis (stages of their Journey), iv. 214
—— (address Allah as a lover would his beloved), iv. 214, 237
Suffah=" sofa" (shelf), iii. 388
Sufrah (provision-bag and table-cloth), i. 164; iii. 421; vii 5, 215
Sufyán al-Thauri, ii. 102; iv. 46
Sugar-stick=German Zuckerpüppchen, i. 154
Sughr (Thughr), *see* Saghr.
Suha, star in the Great Bear, i. 154; ii. 254
Sujúd=prostration, iii. 363
Sukát (pl. of Sáki=cup-bearer), iv. 33
Sukita fi aydíhim=it repented them, iv 146
Sukúb (Pr. N.)=flowing, pouring, vi. 356
Suláf al-Khandarísi (a contradiction), vi. 351
Suláfat=ptisane of wine, must, iii. 371; iv. 117
Sulamí=belonging to the Banu Sulaym tribe, v. 292
Sulaymá, dim. of Salma=any beautiful woman, iii 49
Sulaymán and Sakhr al-Jinni, i. 38
Sulaymán bin Abd al-Malik (Caliph), ii. 68; v. 297
Sulaymáníyah=Afghánr, v. 365
Sullam=ladder; whipping-post, i. 305
Sultán (anachronistic use of the title). iv 52, 135
—— (fit for the service of=for the service of a temporal monarch), vii. 57
Suls=engrossing hand, i. 118
Sumbul al-'Anbari=spikenard, vii 9
Sumr=brown, black, iii 365
Sums of large amount weighed, i. 259
Sun (greeting Mohammed), i. 42
—— (likened to a bride displaying her charms to man), viii 36
Sun and Moon (luminaries for day and night), iv. 180
—— (do not outstrip each other), iv. 180
Sunan (used for Rasm)=usage. customs. vii 151
Sundus=brocade, iv. 25
Sunnat=practice of the Prophet, etc. iv. 6, 123
Sunni (versus Shi'ah) iii. 207
Suns (for fair-faced boys and women), vi. 388
Superiority of man above woman, iii 111
Supernaturalism (has a material basis), vi 189
Superstitious practices not confined to the lower orders, i 36
Suráhiyah (vulg. Suláhiyah)=glass-bottle, vi. 153
Surayyá=Stars of Wealth (lit moderately rich), vii. 37
Suritu=I was possessed of a Jinn, vii. 107
Surrah=purse, pouch, vi 227
Surriyah=concubine, i. 25
Susannah and the Elders in Moslem garb, iv. 60
Sutures of the skull, ii. 346

Su'ubán = dragon, cockatrice = Tammím, i. 158; vi. 108
Su'ud used as a counter-odour, i. 257
Suwán = syenite, i. 219; vii. 375
Suways (AL) = Suez, iv. 417; vii. 91
Swan-maidens, iv. 291; vi. 188
Swearing (on Blade and Book), ii. 224
—— (by Allah, forbidden), iii. 194
Sweet (the, slang for fire), ii. 65
Sweetmeat of Safety, iii. 186; vi. 259
Swevens (an they but prove true), vii. 345
Swimming (studied in Baghdad), v. 48
Sword (making invisible), iii. 296; v. 137
—— (between sleepers represents only the man's honour), vi. 137
Sycamore fig, iii. 85
Syene (town on the Nile), iii. 273
Syria (Shám) = left-hand land, ii. 123

Taakhír = acting with deliberation, vii. 385
Ta'álík = hanging lamps, vii. 379
Ta'ám = meat; millet, i. 389
Táb (game) = tip-cat, ii. 207
Tabannuj = drugging with Bhang, iii. 197
Tabban lahu = perdition on him! iii. 263
Tábik = coffer, vi. 135
Tabl = kettle-drum, vi. 177
Tablet (Ar. Lauh), iv. 39
—— (the Preserved), iv. 268
Tábút = bier, ark, etc., i. 370; v. 398; vi. 135
Tadmúrah (founds Tadmur or Palmyra), v. 31
Tafazzal = favorisca (have the kindness), ii. 7
Taggáa, i. 409
Taghaddá = he dined, v. 374
Taghum, a kind of onomatopoetic grunt, i. 209
Tághút (idol), iii. 6
Tahlíl = Refrain of Unity, ii. 133
Táif (Al-) town famous for scented leather, vii. 10
Táifi leather, vii. 37
Tail (wagging of, a sign of anger with felidæ), vii. 149
Tai'li 'llah (Caliph), ii. 276; iii. 87
Tailor made to cut out the cloth in owner's presence, i. 296
Táir al-bayn = parting-bird, vi. 17
Táj al-Mulúk Khárán = crown of the kings, of amorous blandishment, ii. 186
Táj Kisrawi = Chosroan crown, vii. 378
Tájir Alfi = a merchant worth a thousand (left indefinite), vii. 372
Takaddum and Takádum (difference between), iii. 291
Tákah = arched hollow in the wall, niche, vi. 145
Takhíl = adorning with Kohl, ii. 282
Takhmish = tearing the face in grief, vii. 260
Takht (sitting accommodation from a throne to a saddle, capital), iv. 280; v. 255
—— (more emphatical than Sarir), vi. 114
Takht-rawan = moving throne (mule-litter), ii. 81; iv. 131

Tákiyah = calotte worn under the Fez, skull-cap, i. 206; vi. 273
Taklíd = baldricking, not girding, a sword, v. 205
Takliyah = onion-sauce, vi. 108
Takrúrí = Moslem from Central and Western North Africa, i. 341
Taksím = distribution, analysis, vii. 154
Takwím = Tacuino (for almanac), vi. 84
Talák bi 'l-Salásah = triple divorce, iii. 76
Talbiyah = the cry Labbayka, i. 208; ii. 125
Talking birds (watching over wives), v. 46
Tamar al-Hindí (Tamarind) = the Indian date, iii. 81
Tamar Hanná = flower of privet, i. 76; vi. 326
Tam Múz = July, i. 49
Ta'mím = crowning with turband or tiara; covering, wetting, iv. 153
Tamsir (derived from Misr) = founding a military cantonment, vi. 155
Tanjah = Tangiers, v. 22
Tanwin al-Izáfah = the nunnation in construction, vii. 334
Tár = tambourine, i. 198
Taráib = breast-bone, iv. 93
Tarbúsh = Pers. Sar-púsh, head cover, i. 198
Target (Ar. Darakah), iv. 350
Tárhah = head-veil, i. 375
Tarík = clear the way, i. 61
Tárik (Jabal al-) = Gibraltar, iii. 224
Taríkah = musical mode, modulation, vii. 108
Taríkah = (mystic), path to knowledge, iv. 73
Ta'ris-ak = thy going between (pimping), v. 106
Tarjumán = truchman, i. 92
Tarn-Kappe (Siegfried's), vi. 273
Tars Daylamí = Median Targe, vii. 26
Tartúr (an Arab's bonnet), ii. 45
Tás (from Pers. Tásah) = tasse, vi. 370
Tasawwuf (rise of), viii. 117
Tasbíh = saying Subhán Allah; Rosary, i. 238; ii. 347
Tasmeh-pá = strap-legs, iv. 390
Tasnim (from sanam) = a fountain in Paradise, ii. 4; iv. 214
Tásúmah = sandal, slipper, v. 389
Taswíf = saying "Sauf," *q.v.*, ii. 191
Taub (Saub, Tobe) = loose garment, ii. 105
Tanbah (Bi'l-) = by means or on account of penitence, vii. 160
Taufik (Pr. N. = causing to be prosperous), iii. 131
Taur (Thaur, Saur), a venerable remnant of an un-split speech, i. 14
Taverns, vi. 110
Tawáf = circumambulation of the Ka'abah, v. 148
Tawáf = Ka'abah-circuit, iv. 157
Tawáshi, obnoxious name for a Eunuch, i. 216
Tawashshuh = shoulder-cut, ii. 11
Tawakkul 'alá 'llah = trust in Allah, iv. 162
Tawil (and Abt Vogler), vi. 248
Tawílan jiddan, now a Cairenism, v. 215
Tayammum = washing with sand, iv. 152
Tayf = ghost, phantom, iii. 38
Taylasán (turband worn by a preacher,) iii. 398

Tayr=any flying thing bird, vi. 19
Tayrab (Al-) a city, iii. 46
Taysh=vertigo, giddiness, viii. 9
Tayy (noble Arab tribe), iii. 219
Tazríb=quilting, vi. 115
Tears shed over past separations, i 261
—— (pouring blood like red wine), ii. 389
Teeth (their cleansing enjoined by Mohammed), iv. 12
"Tell the truth!" way of taking an Eastern liar, v 377
Ten stages of love-sickness, ii. 261
Tent (signs of a Shaykh's), ii. 327
Tent (how constructed), v. 307
Testicles (names for), i. 378
—— (curdling in fear), ii. 131
Testimonies (the two=Shahádatayn), i. 337
Thakilata-k Ummak=be thy mother bereaved of thee, iii. 276
Thamúd (pre-historic Arab tribe), iii. 78
Thank you (Eastern equivalent for), iii. 136, iv. 127
Theft (penalty of), vi. 314
"Them" for "her," vi. 192
"There is no Majesty," etc., as ejaculation of impatience, v 272
"They" for "she," iv. 9, 100; vii. 17
Thigh-bite allowed in wrestling, i. 413
Third=Tuesday, vi. 133
Thirst (affecting plea; why ?), iii. 317
Thongs (of the water skins cut, preparatory to departure), vii. 362
Thorn of lance=eye-lash, iii. 110
Thou fillest mine eyes=I find thy beauty all-sufficient, vi. 214
Thousand dinárs and five thousand dirhams=£500 and £125 respectively, i. 259
Thousand thousand=a million, v. 14
Three days, term of hospitality, i. 3
Three hundred and three score rooms=one for each day of the Moslem year, vii. 140
Three things (are better than other three) iv. 346
—— (not to be praised before death), vii. 119
Threshold (of marble in sign of honour), vii. 306
Throne-verse, iv. 164
Throwing one=bastinado on the back, i. 224
"Throwing the handkerchief," v. 189
Thrusting (applied to spear and lance), ii. 129
Thursday night (in Moslem parlance=Friday night), iv 270
Tibn=crushed straw, i. 25; vii. 181
Tigris (Ar. Dajlah, Dijlah), vi. 301
Timbák (Tumbák)=stronger variety of Tobacco, vii 210
Time (distribution of), vii. 149
Time-measurers (of very ancient date), viii 79
Timsah=crocodile, vi. 128
Tin (Kazdír), iii. 386; iv. 379
—— =clay puddled with chaff iv 74
Tinder (a styptic), iii. 232
Tingis=Tanjah (Tangiers), v. 22
Tip-cat stick, ii. 207

Tiryák = theriack, treacle (antidote), ii. 290
Title (used by a Sovereign in addressing a person confers the rank), vii. 193
Tob = Span. Adobe (unbaked brick), ii. 344
Tobacco (its mention inserted by some scribe), vii. 210
—— first mention of, viii. 83
Tobba (Himyaritic) = the Great or Chief, i. 199
Tohfah = rarity, present, vi. 211
Tongue (of the case = words suggested by circumstances), i 111
—— (made to utter (?) what is in the heart of man), iv. 171
—— (my, is under thy feet), vi. 29
Too much for him (to come by lawfully), vii. 245
Tooth-pick (Ar. Khilál), iv. 12
Topothesia (designedly made absurd), vii. 69
Tor (Mount Sinai), ii. 139
—— (its shaking), ii. 176
Torrens quoted. i. 53, *et seq.*
Torrents (Ar. Sayl), a dangerous feature in Arabia, v. 76
Tortoise (the colossal), iv. 373
Torture easier than giving up cash, vi. 338
Tossing upon coals of fire, ii. 286
Touch of nature (making all the world kin), viii. 23
Toujours perdrix, v. 44
Toutes putes, vii. 358
Traditionists:
Al-Zuhri, ii. 98
Ibn Abi Aufá, *ib.* 100
Sa'id bin Jubayr, *ib.* 101
Sufyán al-Thauri, *ib.* 102
Bishr al-Háfi, ii. 103
Mansúr bin Ammár, *ib.* 104
Trafalgar = Taraf al-Gharb (edge of the West), vii. 129
Trailing the skirts = humbly, ii. 67; vii. 35
Trances and faintings (common in romances of chivalry), vi. 271
Transformation (sudden of character frequent in Eastern stories), vi. 327
Translators (should be "bould"), vii. 292
Traveller (a modern one tells the truth when an untruth would not serve him), iv. 349
Travelling at night, ii. 182
Treasure (resembling one from which the talismans had been loosed), vii. 348
Treasures (enchanted in some one's name and nature), iii 407
Trébutien quoted, iii. 381, *et seq.*
Tree of Paradise (Ar. Túbà), vi. 189
Tribade (Ar. Sahíkah, Musáhikah), vi. 282
Tribadism, iii. 349
Tribe (one fortuneth another), vii. 400
Tribes (relations between), v. 171
Tribulum (thrashing sledge), ii. 12
Triregno (denoted by the Papal Tiara), ii. 134
Trouser-string, i. 382
Truth (most worthy to be followed), iv. 104
—— (is becoming manifest), iv. 117

Truth (told so as to be more deceptive than a lie), vii. 291
—— prevailing, falsehood failing, iii. 205
Túbá (tree of Paradise), iv. 189
Tubah (fifth Coptic month), iv. 183
Tufat = felis caracal, lynx, v. 165
Túfán (Typhoon, etc.), iii. 257
Túfán = Deluge of Noah, vii. 77
Tufayl (proverbial intruder), iii. 245
Tufayli = parasite, iv. 91
Tuff = Sordes unguinum (fiel), vi. 343
Tughrà = imperial cypher, iv. 140
Tughrái (AL), poet, ii. 365
Tughyán = Kufr, rejection of the True Religion, i. 156
Túmár = uncial letters, i. 119
Tuning (peculiar fashions of Arab musicians with regard to it), vii. 108
Turband (not put upon the ground out of respect), i. 205
—— (white, distinctive of Moslems), iii. 332
—— (substitute for a purse), vi. 339
—— (worn large by the learned), iv. 81
—— (inclining from the head-tops), vii. 289
" Turk " probably a late edition, i. 49
Turk (= Turkoman, nomade), ii. 117
—— (= plunderer, robber), ii. 198
—— (provoked to hunger by beauties of nature), ii. 258
—— (appears under the Abbasides), ii. 305
Turkey (Future of), vii. 170
Turks (fair boy-slaves abounding in Baghdád), iv. 33
—— (forming the body-guard of the Abbasides), vii. 312
Turning round in despair against an oppressor, i. 225
Tusks (of elephants, not teeth), iv. 419
Tuwuffiya = he was received (into the grace of God), vii. 132
Two sayings (double entendre), vi. 304
Tyrant (from, to tyrant = from official to official), v. 122

'Ubb = breast-pocket (poche au sein), v. 396
Ubi aves ibi angeli, iii. 64
Ubullah (canal leading from Bassorah to Ubullah-town), vii. 111
'Úd Jalakí = Damascus lute, ii. 4
Udah, properly Uta = private room of a concubine, i. 263
Udm = " kitchen " (see Adm), vii. 281
Uff 'alayka = fie upon thee (Uft = sordes aurium), vi. 343
Uhnúkh = Enoch (Idris ?), iv. 164
Ujb = arrogance (in the Spanish sense of gaiety, etc.), v 76
Ukáb = eagle, vulture, iii. 296
Ukáb al-Kásir = the breaker eagle, vii. 148
Ukayl (Akil ?), iii. 151
Ukhuwán = camomile, ii. 283
Ukiyyah (pl. Awák) = ounce, vii. 284
'Ulbah = box, vi. 227
Ultra-Shakespearean geography " Fars of Roum," i. 41
Ulysses (the Arabian), iv. 380

Umámah and 'Ásikah, tale of two women now forgotten, i. 56
Umm al-banát wa 'l-banín = mother of daughters and sons, vii. 246
Umm al-raas = crown of the head, viii. 42
Umm al Su'úd (Pr. N.) = Mother of Prosperities, vii. 245
Umm 'Ámir = mother of Amir, nickname for the hyena, i 40
Umm Amru (mother of Amr') and the ass, iv. 79
'Ummál (pl. of 'Ámil = governor), vii. 106
'Umrah = lesser Pilgrimage, ii. 70; iv. 157
"Unberufen," vii. 251
Underground rivers, iv. 401
Unguinum fulgor, iii. 366
Unhappy thou! v. 189
'Unnábí = between dark yellow and red (JuJube-colour), vii. 215
Union opposed to "Severance," v. 317
Uns al-Wujúd (Pr. N.) = Delight of existing things, iv. 2
Unveiling the face a sign of being a Christian, ii. 23
Upakoshá (Vararuchi's wife), v. 83
'Urb = Arabs of pure race, vii. 354
'Urbán = wild Arabs, i. 103
Urkúb = tendon Achilles, hough, vi. 334
'Urrah = dung, viii. 1
Urwah = handle, buttonhole, iv. 180
"Use this" (*i.e.* for thy daily expenses), vi. 85
Usfúr = safflower, i. 202
Ushári = camel travelling ten days, ii. 292
Usirát (AL), island, iv. 395
Usúl (= fundamentals), i. 341
—— (= forbears, ancestors), vii. 313
Usury (Ar. Ribá), iv. 155
—— (= verset of), iv. 168
Usus = os sacrum, iv. 172
'Utbí (AL), poet, iv. 94
Uzayr = Esdras, i. 236
Uzn al-Kuffah = ear (handle) of the basket, vi. 311
Uzrah = Azariyah, v. 353

VARIETIES of handwriting, i. 119
Veil, *see* Lisám, i. 356
Veiling her honour = saving her from being ravished, vii. 389
Vengeance (of a disappointed suitor apprehended), v. 190
Verses (purposely harsh), vii. 68
—— (afore-mentioned, distinguishing formula of "Hassan of Bassorah"), vi. 278
Versets (number of the Koranic), iv. 164
View (gorgeous description of), vi. 188
"Vigilance Committees" (for abating scandals), vii. 174
Vile water (Koranic term for semen), vi. 5
Violent temper (frequent amongst Eastern princesses), vi. 44
Virgil (a magician) iv. 12
Virginity of slave.girls (respected by the older slave-trader, rarely by the young), vi. 56
Visit (confers a blessing in polite parlance), vii. 255
Visits (in dreamland), iv. 15
—— (to the tombs), v. 321

Visits (should not be overfrequent), vii. 335
Visvakarma=anti-creator, iv. 266; viii. 119
Vivisepulture, iv. 381
Voice (thickened by leprosy), iii. 177

Wa=and (introducing a parenthetic speech), vii. 344
Wa'ar=rough ground unfit for riding, v. 53
Wa ba'ad (*see* Amma ba'ad)=and afterwards, ii. 401
Wada'a, *see* Cowrie, iii. 202
Wadd, Suwa'a and Yagús (idols), v. 186
Waddle of "Arab ladies," ii. 263
Wády=valley; slayer, i. 47, 406; iii. 21
Wády al-Naml=Valley of the Emmets, iv. 282
Wády al-Ward=Vale of Roses, v. 181
Wády Zahrán=Valley Flowery, iv. 304
Waggid (Hebr. speaker in a dream), iii. 401
Wahk, Wahak=Lasso, v. 261
Wahsh=wild beast and synonyms, i. 223
Wahtah (Al-)=quasi-epileptic fit, v. 324
Wailing over the past, iii. 355
Waist (slender, hips large), iii. 63
Wakálah, described in Pilgrimage (i. 60), i. 245
Wakíl=agent (*see* Pashas), iii. 301
Wakites (number their islands), vi. 243
Wakkád=stoker, i. 287; ii. 37
Wák Wák (Islands of), vi. 217
Walad=son (more ceremonious than "ibn") iv. 329
Walgh=lapping of a dog, iii. 99
Walhán (Al-)=the distracted, iii. 14; vi. 191; vii. 88
Wáli=(civil) Governor, i. 238
Wali=Saint, Santon, iv. 74
—— 'ahd=heir-presumptive, vii. 164
Walid (AL) bin Abd al-Malik, Caliph, iii. 224
—— bin Marwán (Caliph), ii. 68, 294
—— bin Sahl (Caliph), v. 304
Wálidati=my mother, speaking to one not of the family, ii. 428
Walímah=marriage feast, iv. 412; vi. 378
Walking afoot (not dignified), v. 134
Wa 'lláhi=I swear by Allah, vii. 44
—— tayyib=by Allah, good! i. 359
Wa 'l-Salám=and here ends the matter, i. 94
—— (used in a variety of senses), vi. 230
Wanderer in the mountains=a recluse avoiding society, v. 70
Wárahmatáh=Alas, the pity of it, iv. 11
Ward=rose; Wardah=a single rose, vii. 11
—— (AL) fi 'l-Akmám (Pr. N.)=Rose in Hood, iv. :
—— Shah=Rose King, v. 269
Wardán (a Fellah name, also of a village), iii. 404
Wárid=resorting to the water, ii. 281
Warid (Jugular vein), iii. 216
Warm one's self at a man's fire, i. 398
Wars (caused by trifles, frequent in Arab history), v. 55
—— (Al-)=carthamus tinctorius, v. 291

Wartah = precipice, quagmire, etc., vii. 158
Washing the dead *without doors* only in case of poverty, i. 337
Washings after evacuation, i. 203
Wasíf = servant; fem. Wasífah = concubine, ii. 392
Wásik (AL) Caliph, ii. 305
Wásit = Middle (town of Irák Arabi), vii. 106
Wasm = tribal sign, v. 75
Watad = tent-peg (also a prosodical term), vii. 15
Water (sight of running, makes a Persian long for strong drink), iii. 200
—— (had no taste in his mouth), iv. 8
—— (carrier = Sakká) iv. 52
Watering the streets, iii. 231
Water-melons (eaten with rice and meat), v. 117
Waters flowing in heaven, ii. 290
Way of Allah = common property, i. 84
Waybah = six to seven English gallons, iii 211
Wayha = Alas! iv. 209
Wayha-k, equivalent to Wayla-k, v. 324
Wayla-k = Woe to thee! ii. 307
Wazír = Minister, i, 2
—— (the sharp-witted in the tales), ii. 143
Weal (I see naught but), vii. 251
Weapons (carried under the thigh), v. 256
——magic, v. 258
——new forms of, v. 262
Web and pin (eye-disease of horses), vii. 72
Week-days (only two names for), iii. 36
—— (old names for), v. 100
Weeping (not for form and face alone), iii. 98
—— (over dead friends), vii. 258
Whale (still common off the East African coast), iv. 352
What calamity is upon thee = what a bother thou art, vi 327
What happened, happened = fortune so willed it, ii. 293
"What is it compared with," popular way of expressing great difference, i. 34
What manner of thing is Al-Rashíd? = What has he to do here? vi. 326
"Whatso thou wouldest do, that do," = Do what thou wilt, vi. 110
Where is—and where? = What a difference is there between, etc., iv. 32
"Where lies China-land?" = it is a far cry to Loch Awe, vi. 129
Whistling (Sifr), iii. 324
—— (held to be the devil's speech), iv. 279
—— (to call animals to water), vii. 14
White as milk (opposed to black as mud, etc.), iii. 262
—— hand (symbol of generosity, etc.), *ib.* 304
—— (turband, distinctive of Moslems), *ib.* 332
—— hand of Moses (sign to Pharaoh), *ib.* 364
—— and black faces on the Day of Judgment, *ib.*
—— (colour of the Ommiades), v. 3
—— robes (denote grace and mercy), v. 156
—— (mourning colour under the Abbasides), vi. 348
Whiteness (for lustre, honour), vii. 29
Whitening and blackening of the faces on Judgment-Day, ii. 205
"Who art thou?" etc. (meaning "you are nobodies"), vi. 74

"Whoso beguileth folk, him shall Allah beguile," vi. 294
"Whoso loveth me, let him bestow largesse upon this man," vi. 109
"Whoso praiseth and then blameth lieth twice," viii. 14
"Why don't (*can't*) you buy me?" vii. 34
Wicket (small doorway at the side of a gate), vii. 379
Wife (euphemistically spoken of in the masculine), i. 62
—— (Aurat), iv. 370
—— (called "Family"), *ib.* 413
—— (contrast between vicious servile and virtuous of noble birth), vii. 362
Will he not care? = he shall answer for this! v. 151
Window-gardening, old practice in the East, i. 278
Windows (looking out of, a favourite occupation in the East and South), v. 79
Wine (why strained) i. 250
—— (boiled) = vinum coctum, i. 121
—— -drinking vitiates the Pilgrimage-rite, i. 89
—— (flying to the head, effect of the cold after a heated room), i. 206
—— (kahwah), ii. 158
—— (table and service), ii. 26
—— (a sun, with cupbearer for East and the drinker's mouth for West), iii. 49
—— (its prohibition not held absolute), iv. 177
—— (breeds gladness, etc), vi. 350
—— (in cup, or cup in wine?), vii. 13
—— (Mohammed makes up his mind about it by slow degrees), v i. 13
Wird = the last twenty-five chapters of the Koran, iv. 140
—— (Pers.) = pupil, disciple, vii. 139
Wisádah = pillow, i. 392
Wisháh = belt, scarf, vi. 356
Wishes (tale of the three), v. 91
Wiswás—diabolical temptation or suggestion, i. 98
Witches (and their vehicles), v. 70
Witness (bear, against me, *i.e.* in case of my denial), v. 190; vi. 181
Witnesses (one man = two women), iv. 114
Wittol (pictured with driest Arab humour), vii. 331
Wives have their night in turns, i. 399
—— (why four, *see* Women), iii. 1
—— (and their suitors), v. 83
Wolf (wicked man); fox (cunning one), ii. 354
Woman, Women (debauched prefer Blackamoors), i. 5
—— (their depravity goes hand in hand with perversity of taste), i. 67
—— (old must not be called Ajúz but Shaybah), i. 160
—— (bastinadoed), i. 168
—— (chaff and banter allowed to), i. 246
—— (of Damascus famed for sanguinary jealousy), i. 271
—— (Cairene held exceedingly debauched), i. 275
—— mourning, i. 287
—— (high-born and their frolics), i. 303
—— (cries of), i. 334
—— weeping and wailing before cenotaphs, i. 390
—— maltreated under the Caliphate, i. 391
—— Women captives, i. 415
—— of the blue-stocking type ii. 58
—— created of a crooked rib ii. 62

Woman (consult them and do the contrary), ii. 61
—— (peculiar waddle of), ii. 263
—— (are tinder, men fire), ii. 284
—— (monkish horror of), ii. 349
—— (Laylah, name of), ii. 357
—— (Wálidatí=my mother), ii. 428
—— (four wives, and why), iii. 1
—— (compared to an inn), iii. 5
—— (large hips and thighs), iii. 14
—— (small fine foot), iii. 15
—— (names of), iii. 26, 49
—— (more passionate than men), iii. 28
—— (head must always be kept covered), iii. 60
—— (slender-waisted but full of hips, etc), iii 63
—— (all charges laid upon them), iii. 114
—— (old bawd), *ib.* 133
—— (names of), *ib.* 142
—— (less handsome than man), *ib.* 145
—— (walk and gait), *ib.*
—— (bride night), *ib.* 158
—— (oath of a), *ib.* 176
—— (insolence of princesses), *ib.* 266
—— (inner, her meanings), *ib.* 267
—— (answering question by counter-question), *ib.* 269
—— (slave-names), *ib.* 348
—— (intercourse between), *ib.* 349
—— (white-skinned supposed to be heating and unwholesome), *ib.* 367
—— (sleep naked in hot weather), *ib.* 422
—— (making the first advances), iv. 3
—— (and secrets), iv. 4, 48
—— (visiting their lovers in a dream), iv. 15
—— (thought to be Jinn or Ghúl), iv. 19
—— (called Zaurá, the crooked), iv. 33
—— (allowed to absent themselves from the house of father or husband), *ib.* 59
—— (old, polite equivalents for), iv. 120
—— Women (in their prime at fourteen to fifteen), iv. 147
—— (inferior to man), *ib.* 114
—— (unveiling to a man, if not slaves, insult him), *ib.* 149
—— (in Hindostani jargon=Aurat), *ib.* 370
—— (her shame extends from head to toes), v. 33
—— (their cunning and malice), v. 57
—— (corrupts woman more than men do), v. 64
—— (knowing enough without learning to read and write), v 79
—— (of Kashmir), v. 68
—— (her female visitors unknown to the husband except by hear-say), v. 108
—— (words used only by them, not by men), v. 142
—— (blue-eyed of good omen), v. 358
—— (stealing of their clothes), vi. 188
—— (her heart the only bond known by her), vi. 211
—— (always to be addressed Ummí=my mother), vi. 242
—— (often hide their names from the husband), vi. 254
—— (semi-maniacal rancour of a good one against an erring sister), vi. 271

Woman (when old the most vindictive of her kind), vi. 288
—— (who are neither thine nor another's), vi 355
—— (their bodies impregnated with scents), vii. 15
—— (to be respected by the King), vii 151
—— (great is their malice), vii. 193
—— (their marrying a second time reckoned disgraceful), vii. 313
—— (the sin lieth with them), vi. 357
—— (fail in wit and faith), vi. 358
—— (delicacy of their skin), vii. 379
—— (treated leniently in a Kázi's court), viii 4
Womankind (seven ages of), vii. 246
—— (their status in Al-Islam), viii. 173
Wonder (=cause) in every death, i. 323
Word (the creative "Kun"), vii. 155
Words (divided in a couplet), ii. 386
Worlds (the three=Triloka), ii. 134
Wreckers, ii. 15
Wrestling and Wrestlers, i 413
—— (amongst the Egyptian Fellah), vi 347
Writer of the Nights careless, iii. 276
Writing (styles of), iii. 314
Writing without fingers=being unable to answer for what is written, ii. 401
Wuldán=Ghilmán, the beautiful youths of Paradise, i. 194
Wuzu-ablution=lesser ablution, i 135
—— (necessary before joining in prayers), i. 370
—— (Koranic order for), iv 152
—— (angels and devils at the side of a man who prepares for it), iv. 153

Xisisthrus=Noah, i. 346, 350

Yá A'awar=O, one eye, vi 334
Yá Abati=O dear father mine, vii. 165
Yá Abú Libdah=O father of a felt-calotte, ii 287
Yá Abú Sumrah=O father of brownness, ii. 266
Yá Ahmak=O fool, vii. 334
Yá 'Ajúz=O old woman (now insulting), iv. 120
Yá Bunayyi=O dear (lit. little) my son, vii. 156
Yá Ba'íd=thou distant one, euphemism for gross abuse, i. 38
Yá Bárid=O fool, i. 288
Yá Dádatí=O my nurse, "ma mie," vi. 155
Yá Fulán=O certain person, ii. 411; vii. 392
Yá Fulánah=O certain person (fem), vii 332
Yá Hájj=O Pilgrim, i. 341
Yá házá=O this one, somewhat slightingly, i 221
Yá hú=O he! Swift's Yahoo? i 221
Yá Jáhil=O ignorant, vii. 130
Yá Kawwád=O pimp, iv. 90
Yá Khálatí=O mother's sister, in addressing the old, i. 279
Yá Khawand=O Master, vi. 101
Yá Khwájah=O Master, vi. 177
Yá Kisrawi=O subject of the Kisrá, iii. 439

Yá layta = would to heaven, vi 205
Yá Ma'ashar al-Muslimín = Ho Moslems! iii. 270
Yá Mashúm = O unlucky one, i. 203
Yá Mauláya = O, my lord, vii. 295
Yá Miskín = O poor devil, v. 127
Yá Mumátil = O Slow o' Pay, vi. 319
Yá Nasrání = O Nazarene, iii. 317
Yá Sáki 'al-Dakan = O frosty-beard, iv. 62
Yá Sáki 'al-Wajh = O false face, vi. 137
Yá Salám = O safety (a vulgar ejaculation), vi. 252
Yá Sátir = O veiler (of sins), ii. 266
Yá Sattár = O Thou who veilest the discreditable secrets of Thy creatures, i. 237
Yá Shátir = O clever one! (in a bad sense), iii 326
Yá Shukayr = O little Tulip, vi. 318
Yá Taljí = O snowy one, ii. 266
Yá Tayyib al-Khál = O thou nephew of a good uncle, i. 279
Yá Ustá (for Ustaz) = O my master, v 384
Yá Wadúd = O loving one, iii. 180
Yá Sín (heart of the Koran, chapt. xxxvi.), iii 177
Ya'arub (eponymus of an Oman tribe), v 166, 226
Yáfis, Yáfat = Japhet, v. 241
Yaftah Alláh = Allah will open, an offer being insufficient, ii. 51
Yahúdi for Jew, less polite than Banú Isráil, i. 194
Yaji miat khwánjah = near a hundred chargers, vi. 130
Yájúj and Májúj, iv. 265
Yakhní = stew, broth, v. 379
Yákút = ruby, garnet, etc., iv. 287
Yaman (AL) = right-hand region, ii. 80
—— (lightning on the hills of), ii. 80
Yásamín = Jessamine (name of a slave-girl), vi. 326
Yashmak (chin-veil for women), i. 357
Yasrib (ancient name of Al-Medinah), iii. 237
Yastaghibúni = they take advantage of my absence, vii. 291
Yaṇh (conversationally Yehh) expression of astonishment. ii 213
Yauh! Yauh! = Alas! v. 142
Yathrib (old name of Al-Medinah), *see* Yasrib, vii 248
Yaum al-Íd = the great festival, i. 292
Yaum al-Tanádí = Resurrection Day, ii. 299
Yaum-i-Alast = Day of "am-I-not" (your Lord)? i 411
Yaum mubárak = a blessed day, v. 123
Yellow girl (for light-coloured wine), viii 37
Yes, Yes! and No, No! trifles common amongst the Arabs, i. 382; vii 315
Yohanná = John, iii. 212
Yuhanná (Greek Physician), iv. 113
Yúnán Yúnániyah = Greece, ii. 402; iii. 224
Yúsuf bin Omar, ii. 71
Yúsuf (Grand Vizier, and his pelisse), vi 109

ZA'AR = a man with fair skin, red hair, and blue eyes (Marocco), vii. 32
Zabbah = lizard; bolt, v. 153, 375
Zabbál = dung-drawer, etc., i. 287; ii. 276
Zábit = Prefect of Police, i. 238

Zabiyah (Pr. N.) = roe, doe, iv. 107
Zaffú (in the sense of "they displayed her"), vii. 311
Zaghab = the chick's down, iv. 122
Zaghzaghán (Abú Massáh = Father of the Sweeper) = magpie, v. 93
Záhiri = plain honest Moslem, i. 355
Zahra = the flowery, v. 58
Zahr Sháh (Pr. N.), ii. 180
Zahrawiyah = lovely as the Venus-star, vi. 396
Zahwah = mid-time between sunrise and noon, iv. 375
Záka = he tasted, iii. 307
Zakar = that which betokens masculinity, ii. 231
Zakát = legal alms, i. 313
Zakhmah (Zukhmah) = strap, stirrup-leather, vi. 177
Zakkúm (AL) tree of Hell, iii. 372
Zakzúk = young of the Shál, vi. 334
Zalábiyah bi- 'Asal = honey-fritters, v. 359
Zalamah (Al-) = tyrants, oppressors (police and employés) i. 251; v. 122
Zalzál, son of Muzalzil = Earthquake, son of Ennosigaius, v. 278
Zamiyád = guardian angel of Bihisht, *see* Rizwán, ii. 246; iii. 20
Zanah Sirhán (wolf's tail) = early dawn, ii. 368
Zand and Zandah = fire-sticks, iv. 20
Zanj = negroes of Zanzibar, i. 332; v. 20
Zanzibar (cannibals, etc.), iii. 288
Zarábín = slaves' shoes, viii. 1
Zarbu 'l-Nawákísí = striking of gongs (pun on the word), vii. 61
Zardah = rice dressed with honey and saffron, ii. 207; v. 378
Zardakhánah = Zarad (Ar. for hauberk), Khanáh (Pers. for house), vi. 147
Zarká = the blue-eyed (Cassandra of Yamámah), ii. 8
Zarr wa 'urwah = button and button-hole, iv. 180
Zarráf = giraffe, v. 254
Zarrat (vulg. Durrah) = co-wife, sister-wife, iii. 88
Zát al-Dawáhí = Lady of Calamities, i. 408
Zau al-Makán = Light of the Place, i. 401
Zaurà = the crooked, for woman, iv. 33
Zaurá (Al-) = the bow (name of Baghdad), vii. 94
Záwiyah = oratory, v. 146; vi. 113
Zaybak (Al-) = the quicksilver, iii. 201
Zayn al-Abidín (grandson of Ali), ii. 102
Zayn al-Mawásif (Pr. N.) = Adornment of (good) qualities, vi. 352
Zaynab and Zayd (generic names for women and men), vii. 310
Zebra (daughter of Sa'adah), ii. 290
Zemzem (its water saltish), i. 262; ii. 168
Zi'bh = village, hamlet, farm, vii. 107
Zibl = dung, ii. 276
Zibl Khán = Le Roi Crotte, ii. 322
Zidd = opposite, contrary, iv. 160
Zikr = litanies, i. 114
—— (and Edwin Arnold's Pearls of Faith), i. 354
Zimbíl (Zambíl = limp basket of palm-leaves), iii. 242
Zimmi = a (Christian, Jewish or Majúsí) tributary, iii. 317
Zindah = fire-sticks, iv. 20
Zindík = Agnostic, atheist, iv. 182; vi. 185

Zirbájah = meat dressed with cumin-seed, etc., i. 256
Zirt = broken wind; derivatives, i. 409
Ziyád bin Abi Sufyán, ii. 64
Ziyárat = visit to a pious person or place, i. 115
—— = visiting the Prophet's tomb, vii. 248
Zobabah (Zauba'ah?) = sand-storm in the desert, i. 105
Zú al-Autád = the contriver of the stakes (Pharaoh), v. 31
Zú al-Kurá'a (Pr. N.) = Lord of cattle feet, iii. 219
Zubaydah (Pr. N.) = creamkin, iii. 175; vi. 213, 309
"Zug" (draught) feared by Orientals, i. 336
Zuhal = Saturn, i. 396
Zubri (AL), traditionist, ii 98; iv. 46
Zujáj bikr = unworked glass, vii. 72
Zukák al-Nakíb = Syndic street, ii. 218
Zukhruf = glitter, tinsel, vii. 163
Zulf = side-lock, i. 284
Zulm = injustice, tyranny; worst of a monarch's crimes, i. 175
Zunnár = ζωνάριον confounded with the "Janeo," ii. 114; vii. 39
Zur ghibban tazid hubban = call rarely that friendship last fairly, vii. 335
Zurayk (dim. of Azrak = blue-eyed), vi. 343
Zurk = blue-eyed, dim-sighted, purblind, v. 358
Zuwaylah gate, more correctly Báb Zawilah, i. 248

AND here I end this long volume with repeating in other words and other tongue what was said in "L'Envoi":—

ان تجد عيبا فسدّ الخللا * جلّ من لا عيب فيه و علا

Hide thou whatever here is found of fault;
And laud The Faultless and His might exalt!

After which I have only to make my bow and to say

والسلام